Southern Living®
ANNUAL RECIPES
MASTER INDEX

1979-1987

Oxmoor
House®

© 1987 by Oxmoor House, Inc.
Book Division of Southern Progress Corporation
P.O. Box 2463
Birmingham, Alabama 35201

Southern Living® is a federally registered
trademark of Southern Living, Inc.

Library of Congress Catalog Number: 79-88364
ISBN: 0-8487-0718-4
ISSN: 0272-2003

Manufactured in the United States of America
First Printing 1987

Annual Recipes Master Index 1979-1987

Southern Living® Foods Editor: Jean Wickstrom Liles
Editor: Olivia K. Wells
Copy Editor: Mary Ann Laurens
Editorial Assistant: Pam Bullock
Designer: Carol Middleton
Illustrator: Barbara Ball

To find out how you can receive *Southern Living*
magazine, write to *Southern Living*®, P.O. Box C-119,
Birmingham, AL 35283.

Introduction

Our nine volumes of *Southern Living Annual Recipes* bring together all of the recipes published in *Southern Living* since 1979. These books—a convenient collection of delicious recipes prepared by some of the South's best cooks—have become popular additions to many kitchen libraries.

In 1985 we responded to requests for a cumulative index of all recipes in our annual cookbooks by preparing the *Annual Recipes Master Index 1979-1985*. We have updated that index with this *Master Index 1979-1987*. Our index patterns itself after the General Recipe Index of the annual volumes, cross-referencing each recipe by type of dish and major ingredient. And, as in the annual indexes, the page numbers of all microwave recipes are labeled "M."

In addition to listing recipes under both recipe category and major ingredient, this comprehensive index contains categories from the *Southern Living* monthly columns, "Cooking Light" and "Microwave Cookery," as well as categories of wok cooking and food processor recipes.

This *Master Index* lists titles of all the *Southern Living* recipes appearing in the last nine years. Included are those recipes in the bonus articles that are featured in different state issues in different years. To ensure that you can find your favorite recipe, the cumulative index gives all of the page references to those recipes that appeared in more than one *Annual Recipes*.

With this index you have convenient access to a treasury of Southern recipes. It will save you an enormous amount of time. Use the alphabetized guide word at the bottom of each page to assist you in finding recipe categories. In a jiffy, you should have any recipe from our nine volumes at your fingertips.

Jean Wickstrom Liles

Master Index

All recipes are listed by their complete titles under a specific food category and ingredient. The volume is indicated in boldface followed by the page number. All Microwave recipe page numbers are preceded by an "M."

A

Almonds

Asparagus, Almond, **'83** 86
Balls, Coconut-Almond, **'84** 256
Balls, Toasted Almond Chip, **'84** 240
Bars, Almond-Chocolate, **'83** 304
Beans Amandine, Green, **'79** 276; **'82** M20
Beans with Almonds, Green, **'84** 253
Beans with Almonds, Italian Green, **'81** 207
Bread, Cocoa-Nut Swirl, **'80** 257
Broccoli with Almonds, Glazed, **'80** 12
Brussels Sprouts Amandine, **'79** 213
Butter, Asparagus with Almond, **'84** 85
Butter-Nut Strips, **'82** 167
Cabbage with Almonds, Creamed, **'79** 4
Cake, Almond-Blueberry Coffee, **'85** 152
Cake, Almond-Butter, **'86** 107
Cake, Almond-Butter Wedding, **'86** 106
Cake, Almond Legend, **'82** 8
Cake, Almond Whipping Cream, **'80** 295
Cake Squares, Almond, **'79** 111
Cake with Cherry Filling, Chocolate-Almond, **'84** 225
Candied Nuts, **'81** 261
Candy, Almond Brittle, **'80** 255
Catfish Amandine, Mandarin, **'84** 183
Celery Almondine, **'85** 116
Celery Amandine, Buttered, **'82** 98
Chicken and Vegetables, Almond, **'86** 21
Chocolate Almond Velvet, **'81** 148
Cinnamon Stars, Swiss, **'87** 293
Cobbler, Blackberry-Almond, **'81** 132
Coffee, Chocolate-Almond, **'84** 54
Coffee Delight, Almond-, **'84** 115
Coleslaw with Grapes and Almonds, **'83** 59
Combs, Almond, **'84** 136
Confections, Almond Cream, **'87** 198
Cookies, Almond, **'83** 22, 181
Cookies, Almond Butter, **'79** 52
Cookies, Almond Spritz, **'82** 306
Cookies, Light Almond, **'83** 151
Cookies, Swedish Almond, **'85** 312
Cream, Peach Almond, **'82** 108
Cream, Peaches 'n' Almond, **'86** 229
Cream with Fresh Strawberries, Almond, **'87** 93
Crêpes Gelée Amandine, **'83** 126
Crunch, Almond Butter, **'80** 301
Curried Almonds, **'82** 297
Curried Almonds, Cauliflower and Peas with, **'79** 221; **'80** 82
Danish, Almond, **'87** 301
Dessert, Chocolate-Almond, **'82** 306
Dessert, Mocha-Almond, **'80** 289; **'81** 62
Drops, Cherry-Almond, **'81** 20

Drops, Chocolate-Coconut Almond, **'87** 223
Eggplant with Almonds, **'79** 179
Filling, Almond, **'87** 301
Filling, Almond Cream, **'85** 320
Filling, Ground Almond, **'87** 14
Fish Amandine, **'85** 179
Fish Amandine, Fillet of, **'80** M54
Float, Nutmeg-Almond, **'84** 106
Frosting, Almond-Butter, **'86** 107
Frosting, Chocolate-Almond, **'83** 241
Fruit, Almond-Curried, **'83** 261
Glaze, Honey-Nut, **'87** 15
Ice Cream Balls, Almond, **'86** 315
Leaves, Almond Holly, **'86** 319
Liqueur, Almond-Flavored, **'81** 287
Meringue Fingers, Chocolate-Almond, **'84** 158
Muffins, Peachy-Almond, **'86** 301
Orange Lake Amandine, **'80** 99
Pastry, Almond, **'85** 177
Pears, Almond-Stuffed, **'83** 207
Phyllo Nests, Nutty, **'87** 277
Pie Amandine, Chocolate, **'83** 300
Pie, Creamy Chocolate-Almond, **'85** 102
Pie, Toasted Almond, **'86** 163
Pineapple-Almond Delight, **'85** 96
Pollo Almendrado, **'81** 193
Potatoes, Almond-Fried, **'82** 25
Potatoes, Broccoli-and-Almond-Topped, **'83** 3
Pudding, Chocolate-Almond, **'82** 142
Pudding, Mandarin-Almond, **'85** M12
Puffs, Chicken Nut, **'81** 260
Quiche, Almond-Topped Crab, **'79** 127
Rice, Almond, **'81** 195; **'85** M112
Rice, Almond Wild, **'86** 50
Rice with Almonds, Curried, **'83** M285
Roca, Almond, **'86** 49
Rolls, Cherry-Almond, **'84** M198
Salad Amandine, Chicken, **'81** 37
Salad, Cheesy Fruit-'n'-Nut, **'87** 56
Salad, Chicken-Almond, **'81** 133
Salad, Cucumber-Almond, **'86** 147
Salad Dressing, Almond, **'81** 37
Sandwiches, Chicken-Almond Pocket, **'81** 240; **'83** 69
Sauce, Cauliflower with Almond, **'82** 270
Sauce, Chicken in Orange-Almond, **'79** 219; **'80** 13
Sauce, Mandarin-Almond Cream, **'84** 183
Sauce, Shrimp-and-Almond, **'87** 282
Soup, Almond, **'79** 48
Spread, Almond Cheese, **'87** 292
Squares, Cream Cheese-Almond, **'85** 68
Stir-Fry, Almond-Vegetable, **'86** 222
Syrup, Almond, **'82** 47
Tarts, Almond Tea, **'85** 120
Tea, Almond, **'85** 43; **'86** 329
Tea, Almond-Lemonade, **'86** 229
Toast Amandine, Baked, **'82** 47

Topping, Almond, **'85** 152; **'86** 200
Tortoni, Coffee-Almond, **'81** 30
Truffles, Almond, **'83** 298

Ambrosia

Anytime Ambrosia, **'86** 182
Baked Ambrosia, **'83** 303
Bowl, Ambrosia, **'80** 138; **'84** 313
Brunch Ambrosia, **'83** 57
Cake, Ambrosia, **'79** 229
Carrot-Marshmallow Ambrosia, **'80** 5
Chicken Salad Ambrosia, **'85** 216
Citrus Ambrosia, **'82** 287
Cookies, Ambrosia, **'81** 301; **'82** 110; **'86** 313
Cups, Sherbet Ambrosia, **'82** 159
Custard Sauce Ambrosia, **'84** 256
Fruit Ambrosia, Mixed, **'83** 10
Honey Bee Ambrosia, **'83** 267
Mold, Ambrosia, **'79** 241
Mold, Ambrosia Cream Cheese, **'79** 249
Old-Fashioned Ambrosia, **'80** 5
Orange Ambrosia Supreme, **'79** 37
Peach Ambrosia, **'83** 53
Pie, Ambrosia, **'79** 284
Pie, Orange Ambrosia, **'80** 237
Salad, Ambrosia, **'83** 231
Salad, Carrot-Ambrosia, **'81** 252
Sherried Ambrosia, **'84** 324; **'86** 317
Tropical Ambrosia, **'79** 74

Anchovies

Appetizers, Zesty Anchovy, **'83** 93
Mayonnaise, Anchovy, **'86** 179

Appetizers

Almonds, Curried, **'82** 297
Anchovy Appetizers, Zesty, **'83** 93
Antipasto Relish, **'86** 327
Apple Quarters, Honey-Baked, **'86** 93
Artichoke Appetizer, Zesty, **'80** 146
Artichoke-Caviar Mold, **'87** 239
Artichoke-Parmesan Phyllo Bites, **'87** 54
Artichokes, Marinated, **'87** 250
Artichokes, Spring, **'86** 62
Asparagus Croquettes, **'85** 265
Asparagus Rolls, **'79** 296; **'80** 31
Asparagus Rollups, **'79** 63
Asparagus Roll-Ups, **'84** 270
Avocado-Crabmeat Cocktail, Sherried, **'87** 95

Bacon Appetizers, Hot, '80 248
Bacon-Chestnut Wraps, '84 M216
Bacon Rolls, '84 270
Bacon Rollups, '79 34
Bacon-Wrapped Pineapple Chunks, '84 25
Bacon-Wrapped Water Chestnuts, '79 63
Bagel Crisps, '86 278
Bean Appetizer, Black, '83 50
Beef on a Stick, Marinated, '85 234
Beefy Party Snacks, '80 249
Broccoli, Cocktail, '80 192
Broccoli Soup, Mock Cream of, '85 288
Burgers, Saucy Cocktail, '83 217
Burritos, Chinese, '87 181
Canapés, Cheesy Crab, '86 262
Canapés, Fruit-Topped, '85 80
Canapés, Green Onion, '84 M216
Canapés, Hot Crab, '86 70; '87 239
Canapés, Hot Swiss, '83 259
Canapés, Lemon-Cheese, '87 93
Canapés, Mushroom, '80 285
Canapés, Party, '86 128
Canapés, Shrimp, '84 116
Caponata, '87 166
Caramel Corn, Baked, '81 218
Caramel Good Stuff, Baked, '80 284
Caraway Wafers, '81 261
Carrots, Dilled Baby, '84 80
Carrots, Dill-Spiced, '87 200
Cauliflower, Crispy Fried, '80 220
Cauliflower, Dilled, '83 93
Cauliflower, French-Fried, '86 211
Cauliflower, Golden Fried, '82 78
Cauliflower with Cheese Sauce,
   Fried, '87 231
Caviar Crown, '83 78
Caviar Mousse, '83 258; '85 86
Caviar Pie, '79 154
Caviar Potatoes, '84 80
Caviar Potatoes, Appetizer, '86 223
Caviar, Texas, '86 218
Celery, Creamy Stuffed, '82 102
Celery, Jalapeño Stuffed, '79 70
Celery, Stuffed, '82 98
Celery Trunks, Stuffed, '85 115
Cereal Nibblers, Great, '82 297
Cereal Snack, Toasted, '85 215
Ceviche (Marinated Raw Fish), '80 194
Cheese
   Ball, Blue Cheese, '80 259; '84 221
   Ball, Blue Cheese-Olive, '82 248
   Ball, Bourbon Cheese, '81 57
   Ball, Brandied Blue Cheese, '85 283
   Ball, Carrot-Cheese, '86 325
   Ball, Cheese, '82 161
   Ball, Cheese and Chutney, '87 247
   Ball, Cheese 'n' Beef, '83 230
   Ball, Chicken-Curry Cheese, '85 118
   Ball, Cocktail Cheese, '83 174
   Ball, Curried Shrimp Cheese, '86 135
   Ball, Deviled Pecan, '80 258
   Ball, Festive Cheese, '79 44
   Ball, Holiday Cheese, '79 285
   Ball, Olive Cheese, '80 258
   Ball, Party Cheese, '84 258
   Ball, Party Pecan Cheese, '81 235
   Ball, Peanut Butter-Cheese, '86 136
   Ball, Pecan Cheese, '83 127
   Ball, Peppered Cheese, '79 100
   Ball, Pimiento Cheese, '80 258
   Ball, Pineapple Cheese, '81 160
   Ball, Pineapple-Cheese, '84 26
   Balls, Cheese and Mushroom, '79 63

Balls, Fried Ham-and-Cheese, '84 221
Ball, Shrimp-Cheese, '85 208
Ball, Smoky Salmon Cheese, '82 247
Balls, Olive-Cheese, '84 206
Ball, Tangy Cheese, '81 263, 287
Bars, Bacon-Cheese Toast, '79 36
Bars, Camembert, '86 58
Bear Claws, '81 161
Biscuits, Cheese, '79 296; '80 31
Biscuits, Cheesy Sausage, '80 78
Biscuits, Petite Ham and
   Cheese, '79 193
Biscuits, Tiny Cheese, '80 192
Bites, Benne Cheese, '80 121
Bites, Cheesy Pecan, '82 248
Bites, Curried Swiss, '85 220
Bites, Fried Cheese, '82 77
Bonbons, Cheese, '87 93
Cracker Nibbles, Cheese, '84 328
Crackers, Cheddar, '84 236
Crispies, Cheese-Bacon, '84 270
Crispies, Pecan-Cheese, '87 168
Cucumber Slices, Cheesy, '84 80
Cups, Cottage Cheese-Spinach,
   '87 190
Cutouts, Sesame-Cheese, '82 296
Feta Cheesecakes, Little, '86 277
Flaming Cheese, '84 187
Fondue, Cheese, '81 40
Fried Cheese, Italian-Style, '83 250
Herb Cheese, Pot-of-, '85 210
Little Bits, '79 196
Log, Cheesy Surprise, '82 247
Log, Garlic Cheese, '85 21
Log, Toasted Pecan
   Cheese, '86 M288
Meat-and-Cheese Appetizers, '87 7
Mexicali Appetizer, Cheesy, '82 108
Mold, Blue Cheese, '85 210
Mold, Cheese-and-Wine, '84 197
Mold, Garlic-Chive Cheese, '85 210
Mousse, Roquefort, '82 71
Nuggets, Cheesy Ham, '81 290
Olive Appetizers, Cheesy, '85 113
Olive Appetizers, Cheesy-, '87 246
Pasta Bites, Pesto-Cheese, '87 251
Pastries, Cream Cheese, '80 250
Pastries, Date-Filled Cheese, '83 259
Pastry, Brie Wrapped in, '80 241
Pastry, Sausage Balls in
   Cheese, '80 248
Patty, Lemon-Pepper Cheese, '84 117
Peppers, Cheesy Jalapeño, '80 195
Phyllo-Cheese Triangles, '87 246
Phyllo Triangles,
   Cheese-Filled, '83 259
Potato Skins, Cheesy, '82 78
Puffs, Bavarian Cheese, '80 191
Puffs, Cheese, '79 110
Puffs, Cheese-and-Spinach, '87 246
Puffs, Cream Cheese, '84 151
Puffs, Gouda-Shrimp, '79 234
Puffs, Ham-and-Cheese, '86 277
Puffs, Mexican Cheese, '87 8
Puffs, Surprise Cheese, '79 295;
   '80 31
Quiches, Miniature Bacon-
   Cheese, '83 93
Quiches, Miniature Cheese, '80 150
Ring, Cheese, '81 261
Ring, Strawberry-Cheese, '86 14
Roll, Chili-Cheese, '84 114
Roll, Ham-and-Cheese, '79 234

Rollups, Ham-and-Swiss, '85 113
Round, Brie Appetizer, '82 41
Round, Herbed Cheese, '84 300
Rounds, Cheese, '86 262
Rounds, Parmesan, '85 131
Rounds, Parmesan Party, '82 248
Sour Cream Appetizer,
   Cheesy, '84 51
Squares, Cream Cheese-
   Almond, '85 68
Squares, Green Chile-Cottage
   Cheese, '86 85
Squares, Jalapeño Cheese, '80 195
Squares, Quick Cheese, '84 191
Sticks, Parmesan, '82 297
Sticks, Parmesan Sesame, '81 39
Sticks, Peppery Cheese, '81 M289
Straws, Cheese, '80 150; '82 137
Tarts, Blue Cheese Appetizer,
   '85 300; '86 18
Three-Cheese Appetizer, '80 174
Toast Treats, Cheese, '83 100
Twists, Double Cheese, '85 131
Wafers, Cheese, '80 151
Wafers, Pecan-Cheese, '81 119
Wedges, Cheesy Party, '84 84
Wontons with Hot Sauce,
   Cheese, '83 74
Cherries, Stuffed, '85 81
Chicken Bites, Curried, '85 40
Chicken Bites, French-Fried, '85 160
Chicken, Deep-Fried Walnut, '87 175
Chicken Little Fingers, '80 249
Chicken Liver and Bacon
   Roll-Ups, '80 200; '81 57
Chicken Livers, Party, '83 242
Chicken Liver Turnovers, '79 141
Chicken Nuggets, Baked, '81 149
Chicken Nuggets, Lemon-, '87 283
Chicken Nuggets Supreme, '85 160
Chicken Nuggets with Pineapple
   Sauce, '84 236
Chicken Nut Puffs, '81 260
Chicken-Pecan Log, '81 290
Chicken Puffs, Appetizer, '85 72
Chicken Salad, Old-Fashioned, '83 79
Chicken Salad Tarts, '84 257
Chicken Tempura Delight, '85 66
Chicken Terrine, Vegetable-, '83 224
Chicken Wings, Broiled, '80 149
Chicken Wings, Teriyaki, '85 300; '86 18
Chile-Sausage Squares, '86 297
Chiles Rellenos, Bite-Size, '87 246
Chutney Roll, '83 259
Chutney with Cream Cheese,
   Cranberry-Amaretto, '87 244
Cinnamon Wafers, '84 324
Clam Crisps, '80 151
Clams Casino, '81 125
Clams Oreganata, '85 104
Confetti Appetizers, '84 191
Crab Crisps, '79 63
Crab, Devilish Deviled, '85 264
Crab Mold, '85 318
Crab Puffs, '80 20; '84 269
Crab Snacks, '83 93
Crab-Zucchini Bites, '84 M216
Cracker Bread, Sesame, '87 2
Crackers, Easy Bisque, '83 252
Crackers, Fennel-Rye, '87 2
Crackers, Florida, '86 179
Cracker Snackers, '86 229
Crackers, Oatmeal-Wheat Germ, '84 236

Appetizers (continued)

Crackers, Olive-Rye Snack, '84 191
Cucumber Delights, '84 117
Cucumber Fingers, Fried, '86 146
Dates, Apricot-Stuffed, '80 250
Dips
    Apricot Dip, '86 178
    Artichoke Dip, Deluxe, '80 87
    Artichoke Dip, Seasoned
      Mayonnaise, '80 87
    Artichoke-Seafood Dip, Hot, '80 241
    Artichoke Seafood Dip,
      Hot, '85 M212
    Avocado Dip, '80 285; '81 57, 306
    Avocado Dip, Zippy, '82 9; '83 69
    Bacon Dip, '82 197

Bacon-Guacamole Dip, '85 25
Basket, Dips and Dippers in a,
  '83 171
Bean Dip, Hotshot, '87 195
Bean Dip, Prairie Fire, '80 195
Beau Monde Dip in Rye Bread,
  Party, '83 127
Beef Dip, Hot Cheesy, '80 85
Blue Cheese Dip, '80 285; '83 169
Braunschweiger-and-Beer Dip, '85 69
Broccoli Dip, Cheesy, '83 92
Broccoli-Garlic Dip, '82 59
Cabbage, Dock Dip in, '86 179
Cheese-and-Chile Dip, '83 31
Cheese and Crab Dip, Hot, '81 261
Cheese-Bean Dip, '85 208
Cheese Dip, Meaty, '82 59
Cheese Dip, Seaside, '85 284
Cheese Dunk, Deviled, '80 265
Cheese-Garlic Dip, '80 192
Chicken Dip, Hot, '80 86
Chile-Beef Dip, Hot, '83 218
Chile-Cheese Dip, '87 173
Chile con Queso, '80 194; '81 195
Chile con Queso Supreme, '80 265
Chile Dip, Hot, '82 248
Chili con Queso Dip, '86 81
Chili Dip, '82 161
Chili Dip, Cheesy, '80 150
Clam Dip, '79 151; '80 265
Clam Dip, Hot, '82 59
Confetti Snack Dip, '79 107
Crab Dip, Creamy, '80 M135
Crab Dip, Oven-Baked, '82 59
Crab Dip, Tangy, '83 5
Cranberry-Horseradish Dip, '85 65
Cream Cheese-Onion Dip, '79 236

Crudité Dip, '86 105
Crudité Platter with Dip, '84 139
Curried Dip, '81 262
Curry Dip, '80 84; '81 9; '85 132;
  '86 184; '87 25
Curry Dip, Creamy, '84 206
Deviled Dip, '87 25
Dill Dip, '80 265
Dilled Garden Dip, '84 324
Egg Dip, Festive, '79 285
Fiesta Dip, '81 206
Fish Dip, Smoked, '84 46
Fruit Dip, Coconut-Honey, '84 171
Fruit Dip, Creamy, '84 51
Fruit Dip, Fresh, '80 265
Fruit Dip, Heavenly, '81 160
Fruit Dip, Marshmallow, '84 171
Grand Marnier Dip, '86 142
Green Goddess Dip, '84 159
Guacamole, '79 185; '80 74; '83 179
Guacamole, Creamy, '79 91;
  '83 174
Guacamole Dip, '86 4
Guacamole in Shells, '86 74
Herbal Dip, '86 14
Holiday Dip, '83 321; '84 289
Leek Dip, Creamy, '86 77
Mexican Appetizer, Chilled, '87 197
Mint Dip with Fresh Fruit, '87 146
Nacho Dip, '83 239
Nacho Dip, Layered, '81 261
Olive-Relish Dip, '84 205
Onion Dip, Cheesy, '83 145
Onion Dip, Chunky, '84 257
Orange Dip, Creamy, '84 117;
  '87 247
Orange Dip, Spicy, '85 230
Orange Sour Cream Dip, '79 208
Oyster Dip, Smoked, '79 233
Parsley-Dill Dip with Fresh
  Vegetables, '85 79
Peach Dip, Creole, '80 142
Pea Dip, Black-Eyed, '81 8
Peanut Butter Dip, '86 135
Peanut Butter-Honey Dip, '85 19
Pepper-Cheese Stacks, '87 80
Pineapple Dip, Cheesy, '80 249
Pineapple-Ginger Dip, '86 104
Salsa Cruda, '87 180
Salsa, Fresh Summer, '87 89
Salsa Picante, '84 108
Seafood Dip, '79 3
Seafood Dip, Hot Cheesy, '84 221
Shrimp Dip, '86 84
Shrimp Dip, Hot, '87 190
Shrimp Dip, Quick, '79 153
Shrimp Dip, Zesty, '80 150
Six-Layer Dip, '81 160
Sour Cream Dip, '86 278
South-of-the-Border Dip, '81 235
Spinach Dip, '80 86; '86 159;
  '87 25, 214
Spinach Dip, Cheesy, '82 59
Spinach Dip, Hot, '80 249
Spinach Dip in Cabbage, '82 155
Tarragon Dip, '83 78
Tofu Dip, '86 109
Tostada Dip, '84 206
Tuna-Curry Dip, '84 31
Tuna Dip, Low-Cal, '87 25
Vegetable Dip, '79 52; '82 161
Vegetable Dip, Creamy, '82 132;
  '83 99, 180

Vegetable Dip, Cucumber-
  Cheese, '83 128
Vegetable Dip, Fresh, '80 249
Vegetable Dip, Starburst, '82 248
Vegetable Dip, Tangy, '87 196
Vegetable Dip, Zippy, '84 256
Vegetable Garden Dip, '85 215
Water Chestnut Dip, '80 86; '86 183
Yogurt Dip, Fruited, '84 171
Yogurt Herring Dip, '80 232
Zesty Party Dip, '83 259
Eggplant Appetizer, '83 187
Eggplant, Fried Parmesan, '87 166
Egg Rolls, '86 81
Egg Rolls, Chiles Rellenos, '86 296
Eggrolls, Shrimp and Pork, '82 240;
  '83 18
Egg Rolls, Vegetarian, '86 148
Endive Boats, '84 80
Escargots Provençal, '82 238; '83 156
Fast Goodies, '84 206
Fondue, Fruitcake, '84 258
Frankfurter Appetizers, Bourbon, '85 207
Franks, Pickled Party, '83 174
Franks, Saucy Appetizer, '84 M12
Franks, Tipsy, '85 52
Frog Legs, Crispy, '80 99
Fruit and Cheese Tray, '83 171
Fruit Bowl, Sparkling Fresh, '80 146
Fruit Cascade, '86 104
Fruit Cup, Appetizer, '86 131
Fruit Kabobs, '86 181
Fruit Kabobs with Coconut
  Dressing, '87 251
Fruit with Dressing, Chilled, '85 222
Green Onion Teasers, '82 42
Guacamole Mold, '86 184
Ham-Filled Party Puffs, '84 116
Ham Rolls, '79 153
Ham Rolls, Party, '85 318
Ham Turnovers, Party, '82 39
Ham Twists, Deviled, '82 86
Hawaiian Dream Boats, '86 151
Hot Munch, Oriental, '87 8
June Bugs, '85 11

Meatballs
    Bacon-Wrapped Meatballs, '79 81
    Brandied Meatballs, '83 78
    Burgundy-Bacon Meatballs, '80 283
    Chafing Dish Meatballs, '81 260
    Chestnut Meatballs, '79 110
    Cocktail Meatballs, '79 63, 207
    Flavorful Meatballs, '84 206
    Ham Balls, '86 256
    Ham Balls, Appetizer, '82 39

Polynesian Meatballs, '80 207
Saucy Party Meatballs, '80 149
Sauerkraut Meatballs, '86 257
Spiced Meatballs, '79 284
Sweet-and-Sour Meatballs, '82 247
Sweet-and-Sour Party Meatballs,
   '79 233
Tamale Meatballs, '80 194
Venison Sausage Balls, '80 42
Zesty Meatballs, '80 250
Melon Balls, Minted, '87 162
Melon, Berry-Filled, '86 93
Mints, Party, '81 119
Mix, Granola Snack, '86 229
Mix, Mexicali Snack, '86 230
Mix, Party, '87 257
Mix, Quick Party, '83 92
Mix, Raisin-Nut Party, '83 60
Mix, Snack-Attack Party, '84 328
Mix, Spicy Party, '81 M138
Mousse, Caviar, '82 71; '83 258; '85 86
Mousse, Crab, '79 117
Mousse, Horseradish, '84 126
Mousse, Irresistible Salmon, '79 284
Mousse, Mustard, '84 127; '86 184
Mousse, Oyster, '81 245
Mousse, Salmon, '83 79
Mousse, Salmon Dill, '81 21
Mousse, Shrimp, '87 196, 251
Mousse, Smoked Oyster, '84 320
Mousse, Tuna, '80 275
Mushroom Caps, Crab-Stuffed, '84 160
Mushroom Caps, Marinated, '83 128
Mushroom Caps, Vegetable, '81 246
Mushroom Delight, Stuffed, '87 281
Mushroom Logs, '84 206
Mushroom Rollups, '85 318
Mushrooms, Black Olive-Stuffed, '86 258
Mushrooms, Cheese 'n' Bacon-Stuffed,
   '86 258
Mushrooms, Crab-Stuffed, '81 190
Mushrooms, Crawfish-Stuffed, '86 258
Mushrooms, Drunk, '83 174
Mushrooms, Easy Marinated, '86 217
Mushrooms, Elegant Cheese-Stuffed,
   '81 57
Mushrooms, Flavor-Stuffed, '85 288
Mushrooms, French-Fried, '82 78
Mushrooms, Italian Sausage-
   Stuffed, '83 127
Mushrooms, Marinated, '80 82, 270;
   '86 135
Mushrooms, Marinated Herb, '86 327
Mushrooms, Parmesan Stuffed, '83 115
Mushrooms, Pâté-Stuffed, '85 118
Mushrooms, Pecan-Stuffed, '84 261
Mushrooms, Pesto-Stuffed, '86 150
Mushrooms, Pistachio-Stuffed, '86 141
Mushrooms, Ricotta-Stuffed, '85 20
Mushrooms, Sausage-Stuffed, '80 248
Mushrooms, Seasoned Stuffed, '84 206
Mushrooms, Shrimp-Stuffed, '80 M135
Mushrooms, Spinach-Stuffed, '86 81
Mushrooms, Stuffed, '79 212; '81 239;
   '83 13, 66, 126, 136
Mushrooms Stuffed with Crab, '82 249
Mushrooms, Tipsy, '84 M216
Mushrooms with Stems, '86 258
Mushrooms with Tartar Sauce,
   French-Fried, '86 233
Mushroom Tarts, Hot Sherried, '83 78
Nachos, Best-Ever, '79 91
Nachos, Chicken, '84 244

Nachos, Easy, '84 30
Nachos, Make-Ahead, '80 M135
Nachos Supreme, '81 306
Nectarine Cocktail, '85 107
Nuts, Hot Chili, '81 254
Nuts, Sherry-Orange, '86 M289
Nuts, Spiced, '84 257
Nuts, Spicy, '82 161
Nuts, Spicy Curried, '82 250
Olive Quiche Appetizers, '86 159
Orange-Berry Appetizer, '85 81
Orange Halves, Broiled, '85 288
Oyster Nachos, Texas, '87 39
Oysters à la Casino, '80 296
Oysters, Barbecued, '82 247
Oysters Buccaneer, '87 40
Oysters in Patty Shells, '85 257
Pâtés
   Braunschweiger Pâté, '83 251
   Cheese Pâté, Layered, '86 105
   Chicken Liver Pâté, '79 153; '81 235;
     '83 108; '84 205
   Chutney-Cheese Pâté, '84 152
   Cognac, Pâté with, '86 159
   Country Pâté, '86 66
   Crab Pâté, '79 233
   Cream Cheese Pâté, '80 154
   Duck Liver Pâté, '79 227
   Duck Pâté, '79 226
   en Croûte, Pâté, '86 65
   Ham Pâté, '85 279
   Liver-Cheese Pâté, '85 276
   Maison, Pâté, '84 222
   Mock Pâté, '87 251
   Pastry, Pâté, '86 65
   Pork Pâté with Spinach and
     Cream, '83 224
   Shrimp Pâté with Dill Sauce, '85 39
   Spread, Quick Pâté, '84 117
   Vegetable-Chicken Pâté, '86 66
Pea Appetizers, Sugar Snap, '86 115
Peanuts, Sugared, '82 249
Pea Pinwheels, Black-Eyed, '85 300;
   '86 18
Pears, Pineapple-Honey, '86 94
Peas and Dip, Crunchy Snow, '86 62
Peas, Crab-Stuffed Snow, '85 288
Peas, Stuffed Snow, '84 80
Peas with Dip, Sugar, '86 170
Pecans, Barbecued, '83 222
Pecans, Hot Pepper, '85 4
Pecans, Orange, '87 292
Pecans, Pepper, '87 137
Pecans, Southern Salted, '80 285
Pecans, Spiced, '79 296; '80 31
Pecans, Sugar and Spice, '82 297
Pecans, Sugar-and-Spice, '86 121
Pecans, Toasted, '84 321; '86 229
Pecans, Toasted Chili, '85 154
Pepperoni Rolls, Ground-, '83 244
Pickles, French-Fried, '82 77
Pickles, Fried Dill, '84 206
Pineapple and Strawberries,
   Skewered, '84 251
Pineapple Delight, Fresh, '79 111
Pineapple Spritz, '86 94
Pizza-Burger Snacks, '84 30
Pizza Party Snacks, '86 262
Pizzas, Cocktail, '79 110
Pizza Slices, '84 269
Pizza Snacks, Tasty Little, '79 248
Pizza Squares, '87 168
Pizza Turnovers, Little, '85 327

Pizzettes, Party, '80 192
Popcorn and Peanuts, Candied, '82 295
Popcorn, Bacon-Cheese, '86 74
Popcorn, Caramel, '79 219; '86 M212
Popcorn, Crispy Caramel, '85 247
Popcorn Crunch, Cinnamon-, '86 136
Popcorn, Garlic, '83 M315
Popcorn, Harvest, '84 300
Popcorn Mix, Curried, '86 326
Popcorn, Nutty, '85 208
Popcorn, Orange, '86 230
Popcorn, Oriental, '86 74
Popcorn, Pizza-Flavored, '85 236
Popcorn, Pretzel, '84 30
Popcorn Scramble, '87 185
Popcorn, Sesame-Cheese, '79 220
Popcorn Snack, Spiced, '87 8
Potato Skins, Baked, '86 81
Pretzels, Chewy Soft, '87 159
Pretzels, Homemade, '84 159
Pretzels, Soft, '83 18
Puff Nibbles, '84 191
Quiche Squares, '84 222
Quiches, Tarragon Cocktail, '84 127
Relish Tree, Christmas, '84 257
Riblets, Sweet-and-Sour, '85 276
Rice Balls, '81 51
Rice Mix, Crunchy, '85 327
Rumaki, '80 136
Rye Appetizers, Party, '86 262
Salmon Ball, '80 149; '86 262
Salmon Log, '81 22
Salmon Party Roll, '83 127
Sandwiches, Asparagus Spear, '84 165
Sandwiches, Bread Basket of, '86 126
Sandwiches, Dainty Cucumber, '81 119

Sandwiches, Stacking, '86 127
Sandwich Wreath, Festive, '86 333
Sausage Pinwheels, '80 209
Sausages, Saucy Cocktail, '87 173
Sausages with Mustard Sauce,
   Smoked, '81 56
Scallop Appetizer, '86 155
Scallop Appetizers, Flaky, '86 327
Scallops, Bacon-Wrapped, '87 94
Seafood Mold, Chilled, '86 70
Seafood Tartlets, '87 247
Seviche Cocktail, '83 258
Shrimp Cocktail, '87 173
Shrimp, Coconut-Beer, '85 230
Shrimp Conga, Rock, '80 2
Shrimp Dippers, '84 324
Shrimp, Icy Marinated, '84 215
Shrimp-in-a-Pickle, '86 326
Shrimp Kabobs, '80 150
Shrimp Manale, '86 268
Shrimp Miniquiches, '87 146
Shrimp Mold, '87 94

Appetizers *(continued)*

Shrimp-Pineapple Appetizer, '85 80
Shrimp Rémoulade, '83 173
Shrimp, Spicy Boiled, '84 289
Shrimp Toast, '86 91
Shrimp Tree, '83 320; '84 288; '85 318
Shrimp with Cocktail Sauce,
  Boiled, '79 151
Shrimp with Herbed Jalapeño
  Cheese, '87 112
Shrimp, Zesty Marinated, '87 173
Soup, Appetizer Tomato, '86 258
Spinach-Filled Phyllo Triangles, '84 52
Spinach Madeleine in Chafing
  Dish, '85 319
Spinach Quichelets, '87 67
Spinach Quiche, Miniature, '82 38
Spinach Supreme, Layered, '82 38
Spinach Tarts, '82 249
Spinach Triangles, Phyllo-, '87 53
Spreads and Fillings
  Aloha Spread, '83 93
  Antipasto Spread, '81 25
  Apricot Brie Spread, '86 275
  Apricot-Cream Cheese
    Spread, '82 161; '87 158
  Artichoke-Crab Spread, Hot, '85 81
  Artichoke Hearts with Caviar,
    '79 142
  Artichoke Spread, Hot, '79 110
  Beef Spread, Hot, '83 50; '84 M216
  Beer Cheese Spread, '81 160
  Beer-Cheese Spread, '85 69
  Braunschweiger-Onion Spread, '79 82
  Caraway Spread, '85 276
  Caviar-Cream Cheese Spread, '84 256
  Cheese-Horseradish Spread, '84 222
  Cheese-Olive Spread, '79 82
  Cheese Spread, '86 135
  Cheese Spread, Confetti, '84 256
  Cheese Spread, Creamy Sweet,
    '79 264
  Cheese Spread, German, '79 82
  Cheese Spread, Hawaiian, '87 158
  Cheese Spread, Herbed, '87 247
  Cheese Spread, Tipsy, '80 150
  Cheese Spread, Zippy, '85 4
  Cheesy Beer Spread, '87 196
  Chicken Spread, Festive, '87 158
  Chicken Spread, Tasty, '84 193
  Corned Beef Spread, '87 196
  Crabmeat Spread, '79 81
  Crabmeat Spread, Layered, '83 127
  Crab Soufflé Spread, '85 4
  Crab Spread, Baked, '80 86
  Crab Spread, Superb, '81 235
  Cream Cheese Spread,
    Deviled, '81 235
  Cucumber Spread, '79 295; '80 31
  Edam-Sherry Spread, '84 257
  Egg Mound, Frosted, '79 33
  Egg, Sour Cream, and Caviar
    Spread, '85 279
  Fruit and Cheese Spread, '81 245
  Fruit-and-Cheese Spread,
    Nutty, '87 246
  Fruit Spread, '85 135
  Garden Spread, '86 135
  Garlic Spread, '85 111
  Gruyère-Apple Spread, '81 160
  Ham and Pimiento Spread, '80 285;
    '81 56

Ham Spread, Cold, '82 248
Ham Spread, Country, '87 8
Herb-Cream Cheese Spread, '83 24
Honey-Nut Spread, '87 157
Italian Spread, '85 135
Jalapeño-Cheese Spread, '82 248
Liver Spread, Sherried, '80 86
Mushroom Spread, Hot, '81 190
Olive Spread, Creamy, '81 290
Olive Spread, Tomatoes with, '85 114
Party Bread Spread, '82 161
Pea Spread, Black-Eyed, '86 77
Pimiento Cheese, Hot, '87 173
Radish Spread, Fresh, '84 166
Salmon-and-Horseradish
  Spread, '87 146

Salmon Spread, '81 149
Salmon Spread, Smoked, '84 324
Seafood Spread, '86 M58; '87 146
Shrimp Spread, '81 306; '85 135;
  '87 111
Shrimp Spread, Chunky, '85 300;
  '86 18
Shrimp Spread, Curried, '87 158
Shrimp Spread, Tempting, '79 57
Sombrero Spread, '87 111
Spinach Spread, Savory, '82 180
Sweet 'n' Sour Spread, '86 184
Tomato-Cheese Spread, '81 157
Tomato-Cheese Spread, Fiery,
  '87 196
Turkey Party Spread, '83 282
Vegetable Party Spread, '84 166
Vegetable Sandwich Spread,
  '85 135
Steak-and-Chestnut Appetizers,
  Marinated, '84 323
Steak, Marinated Flank, '83 258
Strawberries with Chocolate
  Cream, '85 81
Strawberries with Walnuts,
  Stuffed, '85 122
Taco Appetizer, Layered, '84 206
Tamales, Miniature, '85 154
Tomato Bites, '84 80
Tomatoes, Stuffed Cherry, '84 160
Tortilla Appetizers, Tex-Mex, '86 297
Tortilla Dippers, Rolled, '86 4
Tuna Mound, '80 276
Tuna-Pecan Ball, '87 94
Turnovers, Meat, '86 326
Vegetable Appetizer, Tarragon, '83 277
Vegetable Party Tray, Fresh, '82 122
Walnuts, Chinese Fried, '81 254
Wings, Hot Buffalo, '87 176
Wings, Satan's, '87 214
Wonton Nibbles, '85 287
Wontons, Tex-Mex, '87 196
Zucchini French Fries, '82 78
Zucchini Hors d'Oeuvres, '80 151
Zucchini with Cocktail Sauce,
  French Fried, '86 146

Apples

Aspic, Sunshine Apple, '81 73
Baked Alaska, Apple, '80 226
Baked Apple Quarters, Honey-, '86 93
Baked Apples, '79 276; '86 40
Baked Apples, Easy, '82 22, 238
Baked Apples, Honey-, '83 234; '84 244
Baked Apples, Imperial, '82 273
Baked Apples, Maple, '85 232
Baked Apples, Orange-Pecan, '85 45
Baked Apples with Orange Sauce, '84 314
Baked Ham and Apples, '82 M237
Baked Mincemeat-Filled Apples, '80 276
Bake, Squash and Apple, '79 210
Bake, Sweet Potato-Apple, '83 25;
  '86 282
Bars, Apple Butter, '84 153
Beets and Apples, '80 137
Betty, Apple Brown, '83 213
Betty, Pineapple-Apple, '85 46
Brandied Apples, '81 248
Brandied Apples and Cream, '82 M237
Bread, Apple, '79 205; '80 226
Bread, Apple Butter, '84 49; '86 69
Bread, Apple-Nut, '79 12; '85 281
Bread, Apple Pull-Apart, '86 330
Bread, Apple Swirl, '85 4
Bread, Banana-Apple, '85 250
Bread, Fresh Apple-Nut, '87 256
Bread, Zucchini-Apple, '87 255
Brownies, Frosted Apple, '86 216
Burgers, Apple, '86 137
Butter, Apple, '79 200; '81 217
Butter, Half-Hour Apple, '81 203
Cabbage and Apples, Red, '85 32
Cabbage with Apples and Franks, '87 42
Cake, Apple, '83 312; '84 262
Cake, Apple Cider Pound, '84 10
Cake, Apple Coconut, '80 226
Cake, Apple Coffee, '81 249
Cake, Apple-Nut, '87 76
Cake, Apple-Pecan Coffee, '84 242
Cake, Apple Pie, '82 226; '86 301
Cake, Apple Slice, '85 93
Cake, Dried-Apple, '79 13
Cake, Dried Apple Stack, '85 242
Cake, Fresh Apple-Date, '83 300
Cake, Golden Apple-Oatmeal, '86 301
Cake Squares, Apple-Date Dream, '85 10
Cake Squares, Apple-Orange, '84 150
Candied Red Apples, '81 217
Candy Apples, '84 243
Caramel Apples, '79 220
Caramel Apples, Old English, '85 231
Casserole, Apple-Cheese, '84 287
Casserole, Apple-Egg, '85 44
Casserole, Apple Ham, '79 213
Casserole, Cranberry-Apple, '83 311
Casserole, Squash and Apple, '79 209
Cheesecake, Dieter's Apple, '86 318
Chicken, Apple, '85 57
Chutney, Tomato-Apple, '84 180
Cider, Holiday, '82 264
Cider, Hot Mexican, '87 213
Cider, Hot Mulled, '79 205; '84 323
Cider, Hot Spiced Apple, '84 318
Cider Ice, '83 162
Cider Nog, Hot Apple, '84 42
Cider, Red Apple, '80 259
Cider Sauce, '87 224
Cinnamon Apples, Rosy, '87 M37
Cinnamon Apples with Brandied
  Date Conserve, '85 315

Cobbler, Apple-Pecan, '84 M198
Cobbler, Apple Walnut, '79 154
Cobbler, Apple-Walnut, '81 248
Cobbler, Cranberry-and-Apple, '84 306
Cobbler, Easy Apple, '83 174
Cobbler for Two, Apple, '85 261
Conserve, Apple-Cranberry, '82 308
Cookies, Apple Butter Spice, '79 291
Cookies, Apple-Nut, '80 228
Cookies, Apple-Oatmeal, '85 215
Cookies, Fresh Apple, '84 36
Crisp, Apple, '84 122
Crisp, Delicious Apple, '82 303
Crisp, Granola Apple, '85 78
Crisp, Orange-Apple, '80 295
Crunch, Apple-Cranberry, '86 300;
  '87 178
Crunch, Apple-Nut, '82 M238
Cupcakes, Apple-Nut, '82 279
Danish, Deep-Dish Apple, '86 161
Delight, Apple, '80 109
Dessert, Cranberry Apple, '80 253
Dumplings, Apple, '82 273
Dumplings, Old-Fashioned Apple, '84 226
Filling, Apple, '85 5
Filling, Apple-Date, '83 301
Filling, Dried Apple, '85 242; '87 229
Flan, Apple, '81 309
Foldovers, Apple, '84 136
Fritters, Apple, '81 105; '82 273; '85 14
Fritters, Apple Holiday, '86 314
Glazed Apples, Orange-, '82 51
Golden Apples, '82 254
Ice, Cranberry-Apple, '82 290
Jelly, Apple, '82 149
Jelly, Apple-Mint, '87 134
Jelly, Crabapple, '79 120; '81 217
Juice, Hot Apple, '86 270
Juice, Nectarines in Apple, '83 183
Julep, Apple, '86 103, 215
Kuchen, Apple, '79 24
Loaf, Fresh Apple, '82 206
Loaf, Spiced Apple, '79 215
Marmalade, Apple, '79 120
Muffins, Apple, '83 96; '84 193; '87 23
Muffins, Apple-Bran, '85 M89
Muffins, Fresh Apple, '84 264
Muffins, Spiced Apple, '79 60
Muffins, Spicy Apple-Oat, '86 45
Pancake, Apple-Filled, '86 96
Pancakes with Cider Sauce, Spicy
  Apple, '87 224
Pie, Apple-Cheese, '85 284
Pie, Apple Cider, '84 227
Pie, Apple-Cream Cheese, '81 247
Pie, Apple-Lemon Chess, '86 220
Pie, Apple-Mincemeat, '85 316
Pie, Apple-Pear, '83 249
Pie, Autumn Apple, '79 205
Pie, Blackberry-Apple, '87 130
Pie, Brandy-Apple, '86 301
Pie, Brandy Raisin-Apple, '83 192
Pie, Caramel-Pecan Apple, '85 247
Pie, Cornbread-Sausage-Apple, '87 171
Pie, Cranberry-Apple, '79 264
Pie, Cranberry-Apple Holiday, '81 M269
Pie, Dutch Apple, '81 105; '82 273
Pie, Easy-Crust Apple, '87 11
Pie, Fresh Apple, '84 178
Pie, Grandmother's Apple, '87 212
Pie, Grated Apple, '83 304
Pie, Holiday Apple, '87 260
Pie, Old-Fashioned Apple, '82 M299

Pie, Red Apple, '79 282
Pies, Delicious Fried, '83 84
Pies, Fried Apple, '81 217; '86 302
Pie, Tart Lemon-Apple, '80 100
Pinwheel, Quick Apple, '85 42
Poached Lemon Apples, Chilled, '86 182
Poppyseed Dressing, Apple Wedges
  with, '86 131
Pork Chops and Apples, Baked, '81 10
Pork Chops, Apple-Crumb
  Stuffed, '81 234; '82 26
Pork Chops, Apple-Glazed, '84 212;
  '87 35
Pork Chops, Apple-Kraut, '84 50
Pork Chops, Apple-Stuffed, '79 125
Pork Chops, Glazed Apple, '86 300
Pork Chops, Spicy Apple, '87 230
Pork Chops with Crabapple Peaches,
  Broiled, '81 83
Pork Tenderloin, Apple-Ginger, '86 75
Potatoes, Apple-Glazed Sweet, '82 303
Potatoes Stuffed with Apples,
  Sweet, '82 228
Pot Roast, Spicy Apple, '83 7
Pudding with Hot Rum Sauce,
  Apple-Nut, '79 86

Punch, Apple-Tea, '85 82
Punch, Hot Apple, '84 324
Punch, Hot Spiced, '80 250
Quiche, Crustless Sausage-Apple, '87 70
Relish, Cran-Apple, '84 300
Relish, Spicy Apple, '84 M323
Ribs, Apple Barbecued, '80 111
Rice, Apple-Cinnamon, '86 249
Rings, Apple, '85 232
Rings, Cinnamon Apple, '82 M237
Rings, Cinnamon-Apple, '85 107
Rings, Fried Apple, '81 209
Rings, Honey Apple, '80 243
Roll, Apple, '82 178
Salad, Apple, '87 233
Salad, Apple-Carrot, '85 22
Salad, Apple Cider, '83 123
Salad, Apple Crunch, '84 232; '86 331
Salad, Apple-Nut, '80 220
Salad, Apple Snow, '81 224
Salad, Blue Cheese-Pear-Apple, '81 224
Salad, Cheesy Apple, '86 301
Salad, Cherry-Apple, '86 31
Salad, Congealed Apple, '85 252
Salad, Congealed Waldorf, '82 80
Salad, Creamy Waldorf, '87 311
Salad, Crunchy Apple, '80 138
Salad, Curried Apple-Raisin, '80 24
Salad, Deluxe Waldorf, '83 81
Salad, Double Apple, '84 227
Salad, English Pea-and-Apple, '87 24
Salad, Fresh Apple, '81 207
Salad, Frozen Apple-Cream, '82 80
Salad, Frozen Waldorf, '79 126; '82 145

Salad, Lemony Apple-Bran, '86 223
Salad Mold, Apple Cider, '85 54
Salad, Old-Fashioned Waldorf, '81 295
Salad, Peanut-Apple, '80 5
Salad, Spicy Apple, '85 215
Salad, Summer Apple, '80 149
Salad, Swiss-Apple, '84 81
Salad with Blue Cheese Dressing,
  Apple, '87 103
Sandwiches, Apple, '79 164; '80 130
Sandwiches, Apple-Cinnamon
  Breakfast, '85 298
Sauce, Apple Dessert, '87 M165
Sauce, Apple-Horseradish, '82 229
Sauce, Spicy Apple Dessert, '82 177
Sausage Patties, Apples on, '82 120
Scalloped Apples, '84 70; '87 156
Shells, Sweet Potatoes in Apple,
  '85 206
Shrub, Shenandoah Apple Juice, '79 282
Slaw, Apple-Pineapple, '79 241
Slaw, Fresh Apple, '81 63
Slaw, Red Cabbage-and-Apple, '87 31
Spiced Apple Slices, '83 289
Spiced Apples, Skillet, '83 234; '84 244
Spread, Gruyère-Apple, '81 160
Squares, Sour Cream Apple, '82 262
Squash, Apple-Stuffed, '85 206
Squash, Apple-Stuffed Acorn, '83 296;
  '84 285
Squash, Apple-Stuffed Butternut,
  '81 232
Strudel, Apple, '85 259
Stuffed Apples, Peanutty, '85 25
Stuffing, Apple-Crumb, '81 234; '82 26;
  '83 39
Sundaes, Spicy Apple Ice Cream,
  '86 M195
Syrup, Spiced Apple, '79 114
Tart, Apple Cream, '84 207
Tart, Deluxe Apple, '84 227
Tarte aux Pommes, La, '80 125
Tarts, Apple-Pecan, '80 282
Tea, Hot Apple-Cinnamon, '87 57
Tea, Johnny Appleseed, '85 23
Toast, Apple, '81 278
Topping, Spicy Apple, '87 125
Turnovers, Delicious Apple, '86 25
Turnovers, Fried Apple, '81 161
Turnovers, Puffy Apple, '87 276
Veal Chops, Apple, '87 220

Applesauce
Bread, Applesauce-Honey Nut, '87 300
Bread, Applesauce Nut, '81 305
Bread, Bran-Applesauce, '84 229
Butter, Half-Hour Apple, '81 203
Cake, Applesauce, '80 270
Cake, Applesauce Carrot, '81 202
Cake, Applesauce-Spice, '83 42
Cake, My Favorite Applesauce, '87 263
Cake Squares, Applesauce, '86 8
Doughnuts, Applesauce, '81 203
Dressing, Apple, '83 181
Fruitcake, Applesauce, '83 258
Loaf, Brandy Applesauce, '81 263
Muffins, Applesauce, '84 284
Muffins, Bite-Size Applesauce, '82 104
Pancakes, Applesauce, '79 114
Pudding, Applesauce-Graham
  Cracker, '81 34
Ribs, Apple Barbecued, '80 111
Spicy Applesauce, '82 296
Squares, Applesauce-Spice, '86 248

Apricots

Baked Apricots, Delicious, '82 10
Bake, Sweet Potato-Apricot, '85 206
Balls, Apricot, '79 274
Bars, Apricot, '81 247
Bars, Apricot-Oatmeal, '86 216
Bars, Apricot-Raisin, '87 32
Bread, Apricot-Nut, '79 24
Bread, Pineapple-Apricot, '84 7
Bread, Tangy Apricot, '81 249
Breakfast Dish, Sausage-Apricot, '82 10
Butter, Apricot, '82 308
Cake, Apricot Brandy Pound, '83 267
Carrots, Apricot, '84 6

Carrots, Apricot Glazed, '80 89
Cobble Up, Apricot, '82 138
Cookie Rolls, Apricot, '80 282
Cookies, Frosted Apricot, '81 192
Cooler, Apricot, '81 100
Cornish Hens, Apricot-Glazed, '80 84; '87 306
Cornish Hens, Apricot-Stuffed, '84 6
Cream, Peachy-Apricot, '86 163
Dates, Apricot-Stuffed, '80 250
Delight, Apricot, '81 42
Dip, Apricot, '86 178
Divinity, Apricot, '83 297
Dressing, Honeydew Salad with Apricot Cream, '84 191
Filling, Apricot, '83 84; '86 107
Freeze, Apricot, '82 10
Frosting, Apricot, '81 192
Frozen Apricot Fluff, '86 242
Glaze, Apricot, '80 280; '82 8; '86 197
Glaze, Apricot-Kirsch, '87 14
Glaze for Ham, Apricot, '85 256
Glaze, Sweet Apricot, '82 304
Ham, Apricot Baked, '84 160
Ice, Apricot Yogurt, '81 177
Jam, Golden Apricot, '80 31
Kolaches, Apricot, '83 84
Loaf, Apricot-Cranberry, '79 235
Loaf, Apricot-Nut, '81 8
Loaf, Tasty Apricot-Nut, '82 10
Mousse, Apricot, '82 72
Nectar, Hot Apricot, '81 265
Nectar, Mulled Apricot, '86 229
Pastries, Apricot, '83 297
Pie, Dried Fruit, '83 249
Pies, Apricot Fried, '86 269
Pie, Yogurt-Apricot, '85 132
Pinwheels, Apricot, '87 276
Pork Chops, Apricot-Sauced, '85 22
Pork Chops, Apricot-Stuffed, '86 76
Potatoes, Apricot-Glazed Sweet, '81 295
Potatoes, Apricot Sweet, '82 228
Pudding, Apricot Bread, '85 24
Punch, Apricot Spiced, '80 269

Salad, Apricot, '81 251; '83 123
Salad, Apricot Fruit, '82 132
Salad, Apricot Nectar, '83 218; '87 236
Salad, Creamy Apricot, '85 263
Salad, Frosted Apricot, '80 248
Sauce, Apricot, '82 212; '87 172
Sauce, Fresh Cranberry-Apricot, '87 243
Shake, Apricot, '84 115
Sherbet, Apricot, '81 177
Spread, Apricot Brie, '86 275
Spread, Apricot-Cream Cheese, '82 161; '87 158
Syrup, Apricot Fruit, '82 10
Tarts, Apricot, '79 282
Turnovers, Fried Apricot, '86 24
Wassail, Pineapple-Apricot, '83 275

Artichokes

Antipasto Spread, '81 25
Appetizer, Zesty Artichoke, '80 146
Aspic, Tomato-Artichoke, '84 320; '86 92
Avocado Acapulco, '83 2
Baked Chicken and Artichoke Hearts, '82 260
Bake, Tomato-and-Artichoke Heart, '85 81
Beef with Artichokes, Creamed Dried, '85 81
Casserole, Asparagus-Artichoke, '86 279
Casserole, Italian Green Bean-and-Artichoke, '85 81
Casserole, Mushroom-Artichoke, '87 241
Casserole, Spinach and Artichoke, '81 103
Caviar, Artichoke Hearts with, '79 142
Chicken, Artichoke, '81 97
Chicken with Artichokes, Sherried, '87 143
Chilled Artichokes with Lemon-Pepper Dressing, '87 55
Dip, Deluxe Artichoke, '80 87
Dip, Hot Artichoke-Seafood, '80 241
Dip, Hot Artichoke Seafood, '85 M212
Dip, Seasoned Mayonnaise Artichoke, '80 87
Dressing, Artichoke, '84 126
Herb-Mayonnaise Dip, Artichokes with, '84 67
Marinated Artichokes, '87 250
Marinated Cucumbers and Artichokes, '82 111
Mold, Artichoke-Caviar, '87 239
Pasta with Artichoke Hearts, '86 209
Phyllo Bites, Artichoke-Parmesan, '87 54
Pie, Artichoke, '79 25
Pizza with Artichoke and Prosciutto, '87 182
Salad, Artichoke, '86 333
Salad, Artichoke-Rice, '80 178; '81 41; '85 81
Salad, Artichoke-Stuffed Tomato, '82 101
Salad, Artichoke-Tomato, '82 239
Salad, Asparagus-Artichoke, '85 162
Salad, Italian, '87 145
Salad, Marinated Artichoke, '83 241
Salad with Artichoke Hearts, Rice, '80 232
Salad with Artichokes, Chicken, '86 186
Soup, Cream of Artichoke, '82 232
Spread, Hot Artichoke, '79 110
Spread, Hot Artichoke-Crab, '85 81
Spring Artichokes, '86 62
Steamed Artichokes, '81 59
Stuffed Artichokes, '79 76; '82 92

Stuffed Artichokes, Shrimp-, '84 67; '87 55
Stuffed with Shrimp and Scallops, Artichokes, '84 174
Veal with Artichoke Hearts, Lemon, '87 219

Asparagus

Almond Asparagus, '83 86
Almond Butter, Asparagus with, '84 85
Basil Butter, Asparagus with, '85 40
Basil Sauce, Asparagus with, '86 33
Cashew Butter, Asparagus with, '87 56
Casserole, Asparagus-and-English Pea, '86 324
Casserole, Asparagus and Peas, '80 152
Casserole, Asparagus-Artichoke, '86 279
Casserole, Asparagus-Spaghetti, '80 77
Casserole, Cheesy Asparagus, '82 281; '83 32
Casserole, Chicken-Asparagus, '83 76; '84 71
Casserole, Creamy Asparagus, '80 76
Casserole, Easy Asparagus, '83 255
Casserole, Turkey-Asparagus, '86 284
Company Asparagus, '85 82
Croquettes, Asparagus, '85 265
Cutlets, Asparagus, '80 147
Delight, Asparagus, '82 269
Delight, Ham-Asparagus, '86 48
Dinner, Ham-Asparagus, '80 M10
Eggs à la Asparagus, Creamed, '81 201
en Papillote, Shrimp with Asparagus, '86 145
Fish-Asparagus Divan, '87 128
Fried Asparagus, French-, '79 66; '83 46
Goldenrod, Asparagus, '79 66
Holiday Asparagus, '85 260
Jeweled Asparagus, '80 42
Lemon Butter, Asparagus in, '80 M123
Lemon Butter, Asparagus with, '87 M151
Lemon Sauce, Asparagus with, '86 62
Loaf, Asparagus-Pimiento, '84 86
Marinated Asparagus, '81 108; '83 46; '84 67, 86; '86 92; '87 74
Marinated Asparagus, Easy, '81 148
Mayonnaise, Asparagus with Hot Wine, '81 83
Mold, Asparagus, '80 104
Mold, Asparagus-Cucumber, '85 252
Mushrooms, Asparagus and, '85 108
Orange Butter Sauce, Asparagus with, '85 43
Orange Sauce, Asparagus with, '83 46
Pickled Asparagus, '83 46
Pork Arlo, '87 229
Quiche, Springtime, '83 122
Rarebit, Uptown Welsh, '87 279
Rolls, Asparagus, '79 296; '80 31
Rolls, Chicken-Asparagus, '86 M211
Rolls, Ham-Asparagus, '79 41
Rollups, Asparagus, '79 63
Roll-Ups, Asparagus, '84 270
Roulade, Asparagus, '86 102
Salad, Asparagus-and-Egg, '86 305
Salad, Asparagus-and-New Potato, '86 69
Salad, Asparagus-Artichoke, '85 162
Salad, Asparagus-Horseradish, '87 80
Salad, Asparagus Mousse, '86 252
Salad, Congealed Asparagus, '83 260
Salad Cups, Asparagus, '83 47
Salad, Marinated Asparagus, '79 20
Salad, Peas-and-Asparagus, '83 141
Salad, Tart Asparagus, '81 203

Salad with Asparagus, Curried
Chicken, '81 36
Salad with Crabmeat-and-Asparagus,
Congealed, '84 86
Sandwiches, Asparagus Grill, '79 164;
'80 130
Sandwiches, Asparagus Spear, '84 165
Sauce, Asparagus White, '80 147
Sautéed Asparagus, '79 66
Soufflé, Asparagus, '79 66; '83 265
Soup, Asparagus, '84 67
Soup, Asparagus-Potato, '85 23
Soup, Cream of Asparagus, '84 111
Sour Cream, Asparagus with, '83 46
Squares, Asparagus, '79 161
Squash Rings, Asparagus in, '87 68
Stir-Fried Asparagus, '87 52
Supreme, Asparagus, '80 77
Supreme, Cauliflower and
Asparagus, '79 287; '80 35
Tangy Asparagus, '84 86
Tarragon Marinade, Asparagus
with, '83 47

Tomato Sauce, Asparagus with, '83 46
Vinaigrette, Asparagus, '80 77
Vinaigrette, Light Asparagus, '82 50
Yogurt Dressing, Asparagus with, '79 66

Aspic
Apple Aspic, Sunshine, '81 73
Basic Aspic for Garnishing, '84 189
Coating, White Aspic, '85 151
Fish Aspic, '84 190
Fish 'n Aspic, '84 190
Grapefruit Aspic, '80 297; '82 112;
'83 153
Madeira Aspic, '86 65
Orange-and-Carrot Aspic, '86 199
Shrimp-Coleslaw Aspic, '79 88
Shrimp-Cucumber Aspic, '83 108
Sunshine Aspic, '80 103
Sunshine Artichoke Aspic, '84 170;
'86 92
Tomato Aspic, Bloody Mary-, '81 77
Tomato Aspic, Chicken in, '84 190
Tomato Aspic, Chili Sauce, '85 252
Tomato Aspic, Herbed, '81 73
Tomato Aspic, Light, '85 83
Tomato Aspic, Ranch, '83 218
Tomato Aspic, Spicy, '81 40
Tomato Aspic, Tangy, '83 124
Tomato Aspic with Shrimp, '79 241
Tomato-Crab Aspic, '85 287
Two, Aspic for, '83 209
Vegetable Aspic, Cheesy, '81 73
Vegetable Aspic with Horseradish
Dressing, Crisp, '87 152

Avocados
Acapulco, Avocado, '83 2
Baked Avocado-and-Crabmeat, '84 119
Broiled Crab and Avocado, '79 116
Chicken, Orange-Avocado, '80 38
Cocktail, Sherried Avocado-Crabmeat,
'87 95
Crabmeat, Avocado with, '86 119
Dip, Avocado, '80 285; '81 57, 306
Dip, Six-Layer, '81 160
Dip, Zippy Avocado, '82 9; '83 69
Dressing, Avocado, '80 15
Dressing, Avocado Fruit Salad, '82 93
Filled Avocados, Shrimp-, '83 2
Guacamole, '79 185; '80 74; '83 179
Guacamole, Creamy, '79 91; '83 174
Guacamole Dip, '86 4
Guacamole Dip, Bacon-, '85 25
Guacamole in Shells, '86 74
Guacamole Mexican Coleslaw, '82 302
Guacamole Mold, '86 184
Guacamole Salad, '80 14
Guacamole Sandwiches, '82 9; '83 68
Guacamole Subs, '84 293
Guacamole-Tomato Salad, '81 302
Ice, Avocado, '83 179
Kabobs, Chicken-Avocado, '82 9; '83 68
Omelet, Yogurt-Avocado, '81 33
Pie, Chili-Tamale, '83 68
Pie, Mexican Cheese, '83 69
Potatoes, Avocado-Topped, '83 3
Relish, Avocado, '87 120
Salad, Avocado, '81 195; '82 9; '83 69
Salad, Avocado-Chicken, '87 107
Salad, Avocado Fruit, '87 41
Salad, Avocado-Garbanzo, '81 33
Salad, Avocado-Grapefruit, '85 26
Salad, Avocado-Melon, '82 164
Salad, Chicken-Avocado, '80 139
Salad, Citrus-Avocado, '82 265
Salad, Congealed Avocado, '84 266
Salad, Congealed Avocado Crunch, '85 26
Salad, Crab-Avocado, '81 114
Salad, Creamy Avocado and
Zucchini, '79 208
Salad, Dude Ranch, '80 15
Salad, Fruited Chicken-Avocado, '82 101
Salad, Grapefruit-Avocado, '83 316;
'84 16
Salad, Green Spinach, '79 142
Salad, Guacamole, '87 181
Salad in Avocados, Chicken, '85 216
Salad in Avocados, Fruited
Chicken, '87 41
Salad on the Half Shell, Shrimp, '86 73
Salad Platter, Chicken-Avocado, '83 2
Salads, Congealed Avocado, '87 42
Salad, Shrimp and Avocado, '80 266
Salad, Spanish Avocado, '87 41
Salad Supper, Mexican, '82 9; '83 68
Salad, Tangy Romaine, '80 155
Salad, Tomato-Avocado, '86 74
Salad, Tossed Chicken-Avocado, '80 4
Sandwiches, Avocado, Bacon, and
Cheese, '87 279
Sandwiches, Avocado-Crabmeat, '83 2
Sauce, Avocado, '80 198; '83 200
Shells, Ceviche in Avocado, '81 33
Sherbet, Avocado, '83 162
Sherbet, Mexican, '79 155
Soup, Avocado-Banana-Yogurt, '80 78
Soup, Chilled Avocado, '81 34; '87 37
Soup, Creamy Avocado, '79 107

Soup, Creamy Avocado-Mushroom, '85 25
Soup, Sherried Avocado, '84 181
Stuffed Avocados, Crab-, '86 73
Stuffed Avocados, Salmon-, '86 74
Stuffed with Shrimp Salad,
Avocado, '82 207
Tomatoes, Avocado-Stuffed, '82 101
Tostadas, Crispy, '83 2
Whip, Avocado, '79 107

B

Bacon
Appetizers, Hot Bacon, '80 248
Bake, Lima-Bacon, '86 9
Bars, Bacon-Cheese Toast, '79 36
Beans, Bacon-Topped Green, '80 M123
Bread, Bacon-and-Cheese, '83 255
Breakfast Bake, '85 45
Breakfast Eye-Openers, '82 231
Breakfast, Farmer's, '81 44
Bundles, Bean, '80 246
Burgers, Cheesy Bacon, '81 29
Butternut and Bacon, Skillet, '85 9
Canadian Bacon, Lima Beans
with, '83 219; '84 245
Canadian-Style Bacon, Glazed, '82 197
Carrots with Bacon and Onion,
Glazed, '87 200
Casserole, Bacon and Egg, '81 225
Casserole, Egg-and-Bacon, '85 248
Champignons au Vin, '79 47
Cheesy BLT's, '85 92
Chestnuts, Bacon-Wrapped Water, '79 63
Chestnut Wraps, Bacon-, '84 M216
Chicken Bundles with Bacon
Ribbons, '87 68
Coleslaw, Bacon, '83 58
Cookies, Take-Along Breakfast, '84 59
Cornbread, Cowboy, '81 188
Crispies, Cheese-Bacon, '84 270
Delight, Bacon-and-Egg, '85 143
Dip, Bacon, '82 197
Dip, Bacon-Guacamole, '85 25
Dressing, Green Beans with Bacon,
'85 147
Dressing, Hot Bacon, '84 12
Eggs, and Hominy, Bacon, '85 143
Eggs, Bacon Deviled, '86 136
Eggs Benedict, Bacon-and-
Tomato, '87 195
Franks, Bacon-Wrapped, '81 202
Kabobs, Scallop-Bacon, '81 111
Linguine Carbonara, '87 108
Meatballs, Bacon-Wrapped, '79 81
Meatballs, Burgundy Bacon, '80 283
Mushrooms, Cheese 'n' Bacon-
Stuffed, '86 258
Mushrooms with Bacon,
Stir-Fried, '80 123
Oysters, Bacon-Baked, '86 132
Oysters in Bacon, '83 211
Poor Boys, Oyster-and-Bacon, '87 40
Pineapple Chunks, Bacon-
Wrapped, '84 25
Popcorn, Bacon-Cheese, '86 74
Potatoes, Bacon-Stuffed, '86 193
Potatoes, Bacon-Stuffed Sweet, '86 224
Potatoes, Bacon-Topped Blue
Cheese, '79 46
Potatoes, Cheesy Bacon-Stuffed, '81 M61

Bacon *(continued)*

Quiche, Bacon, '85 60
Quiche Lorraine, '80 M108
Quiche Lorraine, Classic, '81 131
Quiche Lorraine, Mushroom-, '86 242
Quiche Lorraine, Peppery, '81 228
Quiches, Miniature Bacon-Cheese, '83 93
Rice, Bacon-Chive, '83 129
Rice, Bacon Fried, '80 115
Rolls, Bacon, '84 270
Rollups, Bacon, '79 34
Roll-Ups, Chicken Liver and
    Bacon, '80 200; '81 57
Rumaki, '80 M136
Rutabaga with Bacon, '83 243
Salad, Bacon-Topped Potato, '85 59
Salad, BLT Chicken, '87 144
Salad, Escarole-and-Bacon, '84 85
Salad, Hot Bacon and Black-Eyed, '85 7
Salad, Spinach and Bacon, '81 143
Salad, Wilted Bacon-and-Lettuce, '85 69
Salad with Bacon, Rice, '79 52
Sandwiches, Avocado, Bacon, and
    Cheese, '87 279
Sandwiches, Bacon, Cheese, and
    Tomato, '84 14
Sandwiches, Breakfast, '82 M123
Sandwiches, Grilled
    Bacon-Cheese, '83 242
Sandwiches, Open-Faced Cheesy
    Bacon, '80 78
Scallops, Bacon-Wrapped, '87 94
Scramble, Bacon-and-Eggs, '80 M267
Soup, Bacon-Beer Cheese, '87 M7
Soup, Bacon-Topped Cheese, '80 M224
Soup, Bean and Bacon, '83 26
Soup, Potato-Bacon, '84 M38
Spaghetti, Bacon, '86 213; '87 82
Spoonbread, Corn and Bacon, '81 129
Spread, Bacon-Cheese, '83 241
Squash, Bacon-Flavored, '82 158
Steak, Bacon-Wrapped Flank, '85 59
Supper Supreme, Sunday, '79 76
Tomatoes, Bacon-and-Egg-Stuffed, '80 162
Tomatoes with Bacon, Saucy
    Fried, '81 210
Vegetable-Bacon Bowl,
    Marinated, '79 191

Bananas

Alaskas, Banana Split, '87 10
Baked Bananas, '79 103
Baked Bananas, Honey-, '81 268
Baked Bananas with Orange
    Sauce, '79 115
Bars, Banana Breakfast, '79 124
Boats, Banana, '82 50
Bread, Banana, '87 72
Bread, Banana-Apple, '85 250
Bread, Banana-Blueberry, '81 163
Bread, Banana Butterscotch, '79 116
Bread, Banana-Jam, '84 73
Bread, Banana-Nut, '86 8, 70
Bread, Banana-Nut-Raisin, '81 59
Bread, Banana Wheat, '81 14
Bread, Banana-Zucchini, '85 326
Bread, Cranberry-Banana, '80 281
Bread, Hawaiian Banana Nut, '79 235
Bread, Sour Cream-Banana, '79 190
Bread, Whole Wheat Banana, '80 88
Bread, Whole Wheat-Banana Nut, '84 50
Broiled Bananas with Honey, '84 175
Brownies, Chocolate-Banana, '80 160

Cake, Banana, '84 151
Cake, Banana-Blueberry, '86 247
Cake, Banana Coffee, '81 288
Cake, Banana Cream Coffee, '85 46
Cake, Banana-Sour Cream Coffee,
    '80 186
Cake, Banana Waldorf, '85 118
Cake, Chocolate-Banana, '86 138
Cake, Deluxe Light Banana, '84 314
Cake, Marvelous Banana, '79 115
Cake, Peanut Butter-Banana, '80 87
Candied Bananas, '83 179
Casserole, Sweet Potato-Banana, '86 276
Cookies, Banana Oatmeal, '79 217
Crêpes Flambé, Banana, '84 262
Crush, Banana, '80 88; '83 142
Cupcakes, Banana-Cocoa, '80 130
Curried Bananas, Fillets with Horseradish
    Sauce and, '85 230
Dessert, Banana Cream, '81 180
Doughnuts, Banana, '86 137
Flambé, Banana-Peach, '85 316
Flip, Banana, '83 303
Flip, Orange-Banana, '82 48
Float, Strawberry-Banana, '87 160

Foster, Bananas, '79 18; '83 M114;
    '86 139
Foster, Elegant Bananas, '81 59
Foster for Two, Bananas, '80 115
Foster, Tropical Bananas, '79 231
Fritters, Banana, '79 213
Frost, Banana-Strawberry, '87 199
Frosting, Banana-Nut, '79 115
Ice Cream, Banana Split, '80 176
Ice Cream, Straw-Ba-Nut, '80 177
Jam, Banana, '82 296
Jam, Rosy Peach-Banana, '80 142
Kabana, Banana, '86 316
Loaf, Banana-Oat Tea, '87 256
Loaf, Chocolate Chip-Banana, '85 115
Loaf, Hawaiian, '80 225
Milkshake, Banana, '85 47
Milk Shake, Banana-Pineapple, '84 59
Muffins, Banana, '80 88; '84 75
Muffins, Banana Bran, '83 48
Muffins, Banana-Oat, '87 188
Muffins, Banana-Oatmeal, '84 20
Muffins, Banana-Orange, '84 148
Muffins, Banana Surprise, '82 105
Nog, Banana, '82 290
Nutty Bananas, '79 251
Pancakes, Island, '87 225
Pancakes, Wheat Germ-Banana, '79 114
Pie, Banana Cream, '84 48; '87 207
Pie, Caramel-Banana, '86 M165
Pie, Layered Banana Split, '83 189
Pie, Luscious Caramel Banana, '79 115
Pie, Strawberry-Banana Glazed, '81 181
Pops, Banana, '83 60; '84 44
Pops, Orange-Banana, '82 129
Praline Bananas, '84 313
Pudding, Banana, '82 53; '84 94; '85 255
Pudding, Banana-Mallow, '86 139
Pudding, Basic Banana, '81 59

Pudding, Delicious Banana, '80 9
Pudding, Surprise Banana, '86 7
Regal Bananas, '85 46
Roll, Banana-Nut, '85 112
Salad, Banana, '87 80
Salad, Banana-Mixed Fruit, '79 270
Salad, Frozen Banana, '82 80, 132
Sauce, Banana-Pineapple, '83 48
Sauce, Banana Sundae, '84 275
Sauce, Strawberry-Banana, '81 41
Shake, Pineapple-Banana, '85 215
Sherbet, Banana-Orange, '83 162
Slaw, Banana-Nut, '86 250
Slush, Banana, '83 56
Slush, Banana-Orange, '80 48; '81 155
Smoothie, Banana, '87 160
Smoothie, Strawberry-Banana, '81 59
Smoothie, Tropical, '81 50
Soufflé, Banana Daiquiri, '84 317
Soup, Avocado-Banana-Yogurt, '80 78
Soup, Strawberry-Banana, '86 181
Splits, Cottage Cheese-Banana, '87 56
Supreme, Banana-Berry, '81 205
Supreme, Bananas, '84 256
Topping, Strawberry-Banana, '87 125
Waffles, Banana-Ginger, '86 96

Barbecue

Backbones, Smoked Country-Style,
    '82 162
Beans, Barbecued Lima, '82 2
Beans, Barbecued Pork and, '79 100
Beef, Barbecued, '81 18
Beef Brisket, Barbecued, '83 11
Beef Brisket, Denton, Texas,
    Barbecued, '81 55
Beef Brisket with Sauce,
    Barbecued, '86 153
Beef Eye of Round, Grilled, '82 91
Beef Roast Barbecue, '79 159
Beef Roast, Barbecued, '82 96; '83 103
Beef Sandwiches, Barbecued, '81 25;
    '82 31; '83 34
Beef, Saucy Barbecued, '82 156
Beef Short Ribs, Barbecued, '83 178
Beef Shortribs Supreme, '79 14
Brisket, Barbecued, '86 154
Burgers, Barbecued, '82 168
Burgers, Sausage, '83 212
Cabrito, Barbecued, '86 153
Catfish, Barbecued, '80 157
Catfish, Smoked, '84 47
Chicken Bake, Barbecued, '81 97
Chicken, Barbecue, '86 122
Chicken, Barbecued, '82 97, 106; '83 103;
    '85 144; '86 153
Chicken, Barbecued Cranberry, '83 178
Chicken Breasts, Grilled, '84 172
Chicken, Golden Barbecued, '83 136
Chicken, Grilled Barbecued, '81 154
Chicken, Grilled Yogurt-Lemon, '81 111
Chicken, Lemonade, '82 163
Chicken, Marinated Barbecued, '79 90
Chicken, Old South Barbecued, '82 97;
    '83 103
Chicken, Saucy Barbecued, '83 11
Chicken, Smoky Grilled, '85 160
Chicken, Tangy Barbecued, '86 186
Chicken, Zesty Barbecued, '80 M76
Chicken, Zippy Barbecued, '83 213
Corned Beef Sandwiches, Barbecued,
    '83 130
Cornish Hens, Smoked, '86 142, 154
Corn on the Cob, Barbecued, '81 128

Cups, Barbecue, '79 129
Dressing, Barbecue Salad, '80 74
Fish Fillets, Barbecued, '86 182
Flounder Fillets, Grilled, '83 213
Frank Barbecue, Tangy, '79 63
Frankfurters, Barbecued, '83 144
Frankfurters, Oven-Barbecued, '83 11
Franks, Barbecued, '85 192
Franks, Grilled Stuffed, '82 163
Grouper, Grilled, '86 185
Hamburgers, Flavorful Grilled, '81 110
Ham Slices, Barbecued, '81 110
Ham, Smoked, '86 92
Kabobs, Barbecued Steak, '79 89
Kabobs, Grilled Scallop, '83 101
Kabobs, Marinated Sirloin, '82 162
Kabobs, Pineapple-Beef, '83 212
Kabobs, Sea Scallop, '82 162
Lamb, Barbecued, '79 58
Lamb Chops, Barbecued, '79 89
Liver, Barbecued, '85 219
Mackerel, Smoked Salmon or, '84 46
Meatballs, Oven Barbecued, '82 233
Meat Loaf, Barbecued, '80 60; '81 275;
    '87 216
Mullet, Smoked, '84 47
Outdoor Cooking, '82 109

Oysters, Barbecued, '82 247
Pork, Barbecued, '80 72
Pork Chops, Barbecued, '81 10
Pork Chops, Marinated Barbecued, '79 90
Pork Chops, Marinated Grilled, '81 110
Pork Chops, Oven-Barbecued, '81 234;
    '82 26; '83 40
Pork Roast Barbecue, '82 97; '83 104
Pork Roast, Berry Barbecued, '80 288
Pork Shoulder, Barbecued, '81 111;
    '82 11
Pork Shoulder, Smoked, '82 225
Pork, Spicy Barbecued, '84 296
Pot Roast, Barbecued, '79 17; '83 319
Rabbit, Hickory Barbecued, '82 216
Ribs, Apple Barbecued, '80 111
Ribs, Barbecued, '80 111; '85 159
Ribs, Country-Style Barbecued, '79 42
Ribs, Herbed Barbecued, '86 185
Ribs, Saucy-Sweet, '81 166
Ribs, Smoky, '84 172
Ribs, Smoky Barbecued, '80 111
Ribs, Smoky Oven, '81 166
Ribs, Tangy Barbecued, '83 160
Roast, Barbecued Rib, '86 152
Roast, Grilled Pepper, '81 111
Salad, Barbecue Macaroni, '82 276
Salmon, Barbecued, '81 181
Salmon or Mackerel, Smoked, '84 46

Sauces
    Barbecue Sauce, '84 172; '86 153
    Barbecue Sauce, Baked Fish
        with, '84 92
    Beef Marinade, Tangy, '86 113
    Beer Barbecue Sauce, '84 173
    Bourbon Barbecue Sauce, '85 90
    Brisket with Barbecue Sauce,
        Smoked, '85 144
    Dressed-Up Barbecue Sauce, '84 173
    Easy Barbecue Sauce, '79 90; '82 178
    Mustard Barbecue Sauce, '84 173
    Orange Barbecue Sauce, Spareribs
        with, '83 11
    Oven Barbecue Sauce, '82 233
    Paprika Barbecue Sauce, '79 90
    Peanut Butter Barbecue
        Sauce, '81 233
    Piquant Barbecue Sauce, '79 159
    Savory Barbecue Sauce, '86 153
    Special Barbecue Sauce, '82 177
    Sweet-and-Sour Marinade, '86 113
    Teriyaki Marinade, '86 114
    Tomato Barbecue Sauce,
        Fresh, '84 172
Sausage, Barbecued, '86 153
Sausage, Smoked, '86 154
Shrimp, Barbecued, '82 74; '84 93
Shrimp, Cajun Barbecued, '87 95
Shrimp, Grilled, '85 103
Spareribs, Barbecued, '81 112; '82 12;
    '86 232
Spareribs, Barbecued
    Country-Style, '80 73
Spareribs, Easy Barbecued, '82 97;
    '83 104
Spareribs, Honey-Glazed, '82 163
Spareribs, Orange-Glazed, '84 296
Spareribs, Saucy Barbecued, '79 14
Spareribs, Southern Barbecued, '79 90
Spareribs, Spicy Barbecued, '84 93
Spareribs, Tangy Barbecued, '82 106
Steak, Barbecued Flank, '79 89
Steak, Grilled Black Pepper, '86 184
Steak, Grilled Flank, '80 152
Steak, Marinated Barbecued
    Chuck, '80 156
Steak, Marinated Flank, '82 162
Steak, Saucy Oven-Barbecued, '83 10
Steaks with Green Chiles, Grilled, '85 144
Steak Teriyaki, Flank, '81 110
Steak with Mushroom Sauce, '83 212
Trout, Smoked, '84 47
Trout with Ginger and Soy Sauce,
    Grilled, '85 228
Tuna, Barbecued, '80 275
Turkey, Smoked, '79 293; '84 160
Venison Steaks, Grilled, '82 215
Barley
    Casserole, Barley, '84 281
    Rolls, Wine-Sauced
        Beef-and-Barley, '87 269
Beans
    Bake, Cheesy Beef-and-Bean, '82 89
    Baked
        Barbecued Pork and Beans, '79 100
        Beefy Baked Beans, '80 136; '84 149;
            '85 142
        Chuckwagon Beans, '81 188
        Crowd-Pleasing Baked Beans, '82 127
        Easy Baked Beans, '85 141
        Favorite Baked Beans, '86 210
        Franks, Beans and, '85 142

Franks, Beany Kraut and, '79 64
Franks, Hawaiian Baked Beans
    and, '80 136
Genuine Baked Beans, '83 26
Ham, Baked Beans with, '80 136
Hawaiian-Style Baked Beans, '86 210
Meat Baked Beans, Three-, '86 210
Medley, Baked Bean, '80 100
Mixed Baked Beans, '87 92
Molasses Baked Beans, '82 139;
    '84 327; '86 20
Old-Fashioned Baked Beans, '84 25
Picnic Baked Beans, '83 143; '85 142
Polynesian Beans-and-Franks,
    '84 M11
Quick Baked Beans, '80 136
Rum-Laced Bean Bake, '82 283;
    '83 72
Smoked Baked Beans, '79 150
Spiced Baked Beans, '85 142
Three-Bean Bake, '81 155

Beef-and-Bean Supper, '82 2
Beefy Beans, '82 59
Black Bean Appetizer, '83 50
Black Beans and Cilantro, Southwestern
    Scallop Broth with, '87 123
Black Beans and Rice, '80 222
Black Beans and Salsa, Poached Chicken
    with, '87 217
Black Beans, Spanish, '84 327
Black Beans with Yellow Rice, '82 2
Black Bean Terrine with Goat
    Cheese, '87 120
Black Bean-Tomatillo Relish, '87 121
Burritos, Meat-and-Bean, '81 194
Casserole, Spicy Mexican Bean, '84 114
Chili and Beans, Ranch, '79 270; '80 11
Chili Bean Roast, '87 268
Chili Surprise, '82 229
Chili with Beans, Meaty, '85 250
Chimichangas (Fried Burritos), '81 196
Chowder, Sausage-Bean, '83 20
Creole Beans and Rice, '80 223
Dip, Cheese-Bean, '85 208
Dip, Hotshot Bean, '87 195
Dip, Layered Nacho, '81 261
Dip, Prairie Fire Bean, '80 195
Dip, South-of-the-Border, '81 235
Frijoles con Cerveza (Beans with
    Beer), '81 66
Garbanzo Dinner, Beef-and-, '84 31
Green
    Almonds, Green Beans with, '84 253
    Amandine, Green Beans, '79 276;
        '82 M20; '85 156
    Appalachian Green Beans, '81 215
    au Gratin, Green Beans, '80 116
    Bacon Dressing, Green Beans
        with, '85 147

Beans, Green (continued)

Bacon-Topped Green Beans, '80 M123
Barbecued Green Beans, '86 252
Basil Beans and Tomatoes, '83 172
Basil, Green Beans with, '82 96
Beans, Green, '80 126; '87 M151
Bundles, Bean, '80 246; '83 67
Bundles, Green Bean, '83 180; '87 118
Casserole, Chicken-Green Bean, '85 296
Casserole, Easy Green Bean, '87 284
Casserole, Green Bean, '79 106; '84 145
Casserole, Italian Green Bean-and-Artichoke, '85 81
Celery, Green Beans and Braised, '84 254
Cheese-Topped Green Beans, '79 100
Cheesy Green Beans, '80 157
Cumin Green Beans, '82 90
Dilled Green Beans, '82 106; '86 157
Dilly Green Beans, '80 116
French Quarter Green Beans, '80 298; '81 26
Fresh Green Beans, '79 122
Goldenrod Beans, '83 111
Herbed Green Beans, '83 M147, 177
Herbs, Green Beans with, '82 90
Italian Green Beans, '85 147
Italian, Green Beans, '87 10
Italian Green Beans with Almonds, '81 207
Italiano, Green Beans, '86 144
Lemony Green Beans, '85 190
Marinated Green Beans, '83 145
Marinated Italian Beans, '86 M226
Marinated Vegetables, '81 239
Mediterranean-Style Green Beans, '79 100
Medley, Green Bean, '85 108
Minted Green Beans, '84 104
Mushrooms, Green Beans with, '82 21
Mustard, Green Beans and Tomatoes with, '87 83
Pepper Strips, Green Beans and, '86 170
Pickled Beans, Dressed-Up, '86 251
Pole Beans, Old-Fashioned, '80 100
Potatoes, Down-Home Beans and, '85 254
Potatoes, Green Beans with New, '87 164
Provençal, Green Beans, '81 182
Salads. See Beans/Salads.
Saucy Green Beans, '83 206
Sesame Italian Green Beans, '82 174
Snap Beans, '86 218
Snap Beans, Simple, '85 148
Snap, or Wax Beans, Green, '85 105
Sour Cream, Green Beans in, '80 116
Sour Cream, Green Beans with, '82 90
Southern-Style Green Beans, '79 283
Spanish Green Beans, '80 116
Spanish-Style Green Beans, '84 128
Squash, Beans, and Tomatoes, '83 148

Stir-Fried Green Beans, '85 148; '86 305
Surprise, Green Bean, '86 9
Sweet-and-Sour Beans, '87 197
Sweet-and-Sour Green Beans, '79 184; '81 158; '82 90
Sweet-and-Sour Green Beans and Carrots, '83 6
Tangy Green Beans, '85 M142
Tomatoes, Bean-Stuffed, '84 34
Tomatoes, Green Beans with, '85 137
Tomatoes, Green Beans with Cherry, '86 177
Vegetable-Herb Trio, '83 172
Zucchini, Green Beans with, '84 128
Hot Dogs, Beany, '82 190
Lentil-and-Rice Supper, '84 202
Lentil-Rice Stew, '82 232
Lentils with Cheese, Baked, '84 113
Lima
Bake, Lima-Bacon, '86 9
Barbecued Lima Beans, '82 2
Beans, Lima, '80 127
Beef-and-Lima Bean Dinner, '84 292
Canadian Bacon, Lima Beans with, '83 219; '84 245
Casserole, Ham and Lima, '79 192
Casserole, Lima Bean, '79 189; '83 313; '86 225; '87 284
Casserole, Lima Bean Garden, '83 218; '84 246
Casserole, Spicy Lima Bean, '79 189
Casserole, Swiss Lima Bean, '80 191
Cheese and Limas in Onion Shells, '81 86
Cheese Limas, Spanish, '86 225
Chilly Lima Beans, '81 206
Combo, Hot Lima and Tomato, '83 219
Creole, Lima Beans, '80 191; '85 137
Deluxe, Lima Beans, '79 289; '80 26
Fresh Lima Beans and Scallions, '82 133
Hominy-Sausage Skillet, '81 29
Marinated Limas, '86 225
Medley, Carrot-Lima-Squash, '80 123
Rancho Lima Beans, '80 191
Savory Lima Beans, '83 219; '84 246
Savory Sauce, Lima Beans and Carrots with, '84 196
Sour Cream, Lima Beans in, '79 189
Spanish-Style Lima Beans, '83 25
Succotash, Easy, '80 165
Super Lima Beans, '79 189
Supper, Sausage-Bean, '86 52
Nachos, Best-Ever, '79 91
Nachos, Easy, '84 30
Nachos, Make-Ahead, '80 M135
Pinto
Beef and Bean Supper, '82 2
Chalupa, Bean, '80 223
Chalupas, Bean, '83 313
Chalupas, Pork, '83 160
Chili, Tex-Mex, '83 26
Pie, Pinto Bean, '80 40
Pinto Beans, '87 303
Ranch Beans, Laredo, '81 75
Razorback Beans, '84 328
Sandwiches, Bean Salad, '81 243
Spicy Hot Pintos, '83 26
Sweet-Hot Pinto Beans, '86 114
Trailride Pinto Beans, '85 154

Red Beans and Rice, '80 58; '83 89; '84 37; '87 45
Red Beans and Rice, Cajun, '83 26
Refried Beans, '79 185
Rice, South Texas Beans and, '85 252
Salads
Cannellini Bean Salad, Tuna-and-, '86 143
Chilled Bean Salad, '80 178
Cucumber-Bean Salad, '83 81
Five-Bean Salad, Hot, '81 149
Four-Bean Salad, '79 20; '84 82
Full o' Beans Salad, '81 38
Garbanzo Salad, '82 2
Garbanzo Salad, Avocado-, '81 33
Garden Medley Salad, '80 122
Green Bean-and-Tomato Salad, '86 180
Green Bean-Peanut Salad, '86 117
Green Bean-Potato Salad, '83 80
Green Bean Salad, '87 90
Green Bean Salad, Cold, '84 106
Green Bean Salad, Crispy, '82 239
Green Bean Salad, Hot, '86 298; '87 176
Green Bean Salad, Lettuce and, '80 79
Green Bean Salad, Molded, '85 252
Green Bean Salad, Paprika-, '86 191
Green Bean Salad, Pickled, '82 239
Green Bean Salad, Speedy, '84 283
Green Beans Vinaigrette, '83 25
Kidney Bean-Salami Pasta Toss, '85 165
Layered Salad, '86 35
Lima Bean-Tomato Salad, '85 137
Marinated Bean-and-Rice Salad, '87 152
Marinated Bean Salad, '85 137, 296
Marinated Bean Salad, Crunchy, '84 197
Marinated Combo Salad, '82 267
Marinated Corn-Bean Salad, '87 9
Mexican Tossed Salad, '81 280
Mixed Bean Salad, '83 217
Niçoise, Salad, '86 35
Overnight Fiesta Salad, '83 80
Pinto Salad, '86 169
Pole Bean-Potato Salad, Hot, '79 74
Pork-'n'-Bean Salad, '87 83
Potato-Bean Salad, '82 301
Red Bean Slaw, '79 247
Rice-and-Bean Salad, '85 22
Saucy Bean Salad, '84 18
Six-Bean Salad, Colorful, '87 82
Southwest Salad, '81 113
Sprout Salad, Bean, '82 113
Sweet-and-Sour Bean Salad, '85 198; '86 147
Sweet-and-Sour Beans with Sprouts, '86 32
Sweet-and-Sour Vegetable Salad, '81 25
Sauce, Pork-and-Onions with Bean, '85 76
Sausage, Beans, and Rice, Texas, '84 296
Shuck Beans, '81 216
Soup, Bean, '80 25
Soup, Bean and Bacon, '83 26
Soup, Beefy Lentil, '87 282
Soup, Capitol Hill Bean, '80 222
Soup, Chill-Chaser, '87 282
Soup, Chunky Navy Bean, '83 291
Soup, Cream of Green Bean, '84 111

Soup, Drunken Bean, '87 283
Soup, Ham-and-Bean, '84 4
Soup, Hearty Bean-and-Barley, '86 304
Soup, Leafy Bean, '86 223
Soup, Lentil, '83 292; '86 304
Soup, Navy Bean, '84 280
Soup, Sausage-Bean, '85 88
Soup, Savory Navy Bean, '87 282
Soup, Spicy Sausage-Bean, '83 229
Soup, Vegetable-Bean, '83 317
Soup, White Bean, '83 229
White Bean Pot, '86 194

Beef
Appetizers, Meat-and-Cheese, '87 7
Ball, Cheese 'n' Beef, '83 230
Barbecued Beef, Saucy, '82 156
Bouilli, '80 58
Bourguignon, Beef, '79 104; '82 288
Bourguignon, Royal Beef, '80 106
Brisket, Barbecued, '86 154
Brisket, Barbecued Beef, '83 11
Brisket, Denton, Texas, Barbecued
  Beef, '81 55
Brisket, Home-Style, '87 303
Brisket, Marinated, '86 129
Brisket with Barbecue Sauce,
  Smoked, '85 144
Brisket with Sauce, Barbecued
  Beef, '86 153
Burgoo, Five-Meat, '87 3
Burgoo, Old-Fashioned, '87 3
Burgundy, Beef, '82 259; '83 125, 281
Burgundy with Pearl Onions,
  Beef, '81 108
Burritos, Cheesy Beef, '85 193
Burritos, Meat-and-Bean, '81 194
Chalupa, Bean, '80 223
Chili, Chuck Wagon, '81 282; '82 57
Chili, Chunky, '82 M282; '86 3
Chili con Carne, '82 310; '83 30; '86 2
Chili, Cowboy, '86 2
Chili, North Texas Red, '87 303
Chili, South-of-the-Border, '83 283
Chili, Texas Championship, '81 54
Chili, Zippy, '87 110
Chimichangas (Fried Burritos), '85 244;
  '86 114
Chinese-Style Beef, '87 50
Chipped Beef and Toast, Creamy, '79 180
Corned Beef
  Brunch Bake, Corned Beef, '82 44
  Cabbage au Gratin, Corned Beef
    and, '83 16
  Cabbage, Corned Beef and, '83 104
  Cabbage, Corned Beef Squares
    and, '82 86
  Cabbage, Quick Corned Beef
    and, '79 54
  Dijon Glaze, Corned Beef with,
    '87 54
  Dinner, Corned Beef, '87 54
  Hash, Red Flannel, '79 191
  Reuben Meat Pie, '80 189
  Reuben Sandwiches, '80 M201
  Reuben Sandwiches, Broiled, '81 240
  Reuben Sandwiches, Crispy, '85 299
  Reuben Sandwiches, Grilled, '81 206
  Roll, Corned Beef, '85 66
  Salad, Corned Beef, '80 104
  Salad, Corned Beef-
    Cauliflower, '83 16
  Salad, Corned Beef-Potato, '85 213
  Salad, Molded Corned Beef, '82 86

Salad, Potato-Corned Beef, '81 36
Salad, Vegetable-Corned Beef,
  '80 148
Sandwich, Corned Beef and
  Cheese, '79 214
Sandwiches, Barbecued Corned
  Beef, '83 130
Sandwiches, Corned Beef, '83 291;
  '85 242
Sandwiches, Grilled Corned
  Beef, '87 54
Sandwiches, Meal-in-One, '80 218
Soup, Corned Beef, '83 16
Soup, French Onion-Beef, '87 54
Spread, Corned Beef, '87 196
Creamed Beef and Chicken-Topped
  Potatoes, '83 210
Creamed Dried Beef with
  Artichokes, '85 81
Cubes in Wine Sauce, Beef, '79 264
Curried Beef Dinner, '83 4
Dip, Hot Cheesy Beef, '80 85
Élégante, Beef, '80 125
en Daube, Beef, '79 163
Eye of Round, Grilled Beef, '82 91
Fajitas, Favorite, '86 114
Goulash, Beef, '83 231
Goulash, Hungarian, '81 227
Gumbo, Texas Ranch-Style, '82 226
Jerky, Beef, '80 269; '81 26
Kabobs, Barbecued Steak, '79 89
Kabobs, Beef, '85 110
Kabobs Deluxe, Beef, '82 182
Kabobs, Marinated Beef, '82 105; '85 159
Kabobs, Marinated Sirloin, '82 162

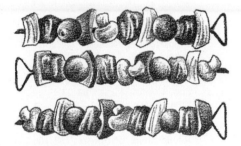

Kabobs, Marinated Steak, '80 184
Kabobs, Pineapple-Beef, '83 212
Kabobs, Saucy Beef, '83 109
Kabobs, Spirited Beef, '87 142
Kabobs, Steak, '82 4
Kabobs, Steak-and-Shrimp, '80 184
Kabobs, Teriyaki Beef, '80 207
Kabobs with Rice, Marinated Beef, '84 32
Liver
  Creamy Liver and Noodle
    Dinner, '80 11
  Creole Sauce, Liver in, '87 33
  French-Style Liver, '80 10
  Gravy, Liver and, '80 10
  Herbs, Liver with, '81 277
  Kabobs, Liver, '80 185
  Patties, Beef Liver, '81 277
  Saucy Liver, '81 277
  Sauté, Liver, '81 277
  Spanish-Style Liver, '80 11
  Stroganoff, Liver, '79 54
  Sweet-and-Sour Liver, '81 277
  Tasty Liver, '83 29

Meatballs, Quick Processor, '87 111
Medallions, Italian Beef, '87 305
Medallions of Beef with Ancho Chile
  Sauce, '87 122
Mongolian Beef, '85 2, 75
Oriental, Beef and Cauliflower, '80 220
Oriental Beef and Snow Peas, '79 105
Oriental Beef with Pea Pods, '86 M328
Pastichio, '85 194
Peppers, Beef and Green, '79 104
Pies, Carry-Along Beef, '80 224; '81 56
Ribs
  Barbecued Beef Short Ribs, '83 178
  Hearty Beef Shortribs, '79 14
  Supreme, Beef Shortribs, '79 14
Roasts
  Barbecue, Beef Roast, '79 159
  Barbecued Beef Roast, '82 96;
    '83 103
  Beer-and-Onion Sauce, Roast
    in, '80 124
  Brisket Roast, Peppery, '83 319
  Burgundy Roast, Beef, '85 291
  Chili Bean Roast, '87 268
  Chuck Roast, Marinated, '80 59
  Chuck Roast, Orange Marinated,
    '85 179
  Cola Roast, '81 298
  Diablo, Beef, '79 17
  Grilled Pepper Roast, '81 110
  Java Roast, '83 319
  Marengo, Beef, '82 284; '83 14
  Marinated Roast, '85 3
  Patio Steak, '87 141
  Pot Roast, All-Seasons, '86 89
  Pot Roast, Autumn Gold, '83 7
  Pot Roast, Barbecued, '79 17;
    '83 319
  Pot Roast, Basic, '81 M208
  Pot Roast, Bavarian-Style, '79 17
  Pot Roast, Bloody Mary, '86 47
  Pot Roast, Cardamom, '79 12
  Pot Roast, Company, '79 162
  Pot Roast, Country, '87 216
  Pot Roast, Dillicious, '81 187
  Pot Roast, Easy Oven, '86 52
  Pot Roast, Hawaiian, '81 298
  Pot Roast, Indian, '87 215
  Pot Roast in Red Sauce, '87 215
  Pot Roast in White Wine
    Gravy, '81 299
  Pot Roast, Italian, '81 299; '87 95
  Pot Roast, Marinated, '85 21
  Pot Roast Medley, Vegetable-,
    '83 319
  Pot Roast, Mushroom, '79 17
  Pot Roast, Peppered, '87 215
  Pot Roast, Perfect, '83 7
  Pot Roast, Polynesian, '80 59
  Pot Roast, Regal, '79 17
  Pot Roast, Spicy Apple, '83 7
  Pot Roast, Swedish, '80 59
  Pot Roast, Sweet-and-Sour, '83 8
  Pot Roast with Gravy, '81 298
  Pot Roast with Sour Cream
    Gravy, '79 17
  Pot Roast with Spaghetti, '80 59
  Pot Roast with Vegetables, '80 59;
    '81 M208
  Pot Roast, Zesty, '81 206
  Rib-Eye Beef, Spicy, '84 259
  Rib Roast, Barbecued, '86 152
  Rib Roast, Standing, '80 246; '84 187

Beef, Roasts *(continued)*

Rib Roast with Yorkshire Pudding, Standing, '80 252
Sauerbraten, Quick, '80 139
Simple Roast, '81 298
Supreme, Roast Beef, '83 8
Wellington, Beef, '83 319
Rolls, Stuffed Sherried Beef, '79 105
Rolls, Wine-Sauced Beef-and-Barley, '87 269
Rollups with Rice, Royal Beef, '79 105
Roulades, Beef, '83 47
Salad, Beef-and-Broccoli, '87 187
Salad, Roast Beef, '80 223; '81 56
Salad, Tangy Beef, '87 M218
Salad, Zesty Beef, '79 56
Sandwiches, Beef and Pork Tenderloin, '80 175
Sandwiches, Beef Salad Pocket, '83 267
Sandwiches, Dried Beef Pita, '86 160
Sandwiches, Wake-Up, '84 58
Sandwich, Saucy Beef Pocket, '80 92
Shredded Beef over Rice Noodles, '85 74
Soup, Beefy Lentil, '87 282
Soup, Hearty Vegetable-Beef, '84 102
Spaghetti, Meaty, '82 19
Spread, Hot Beef, '83 50; '84 M216
Steaks
Appetizers, Marinated Steak-and-Chestnut, '84 323
Barbecued Beef, '81 18
Barbecued Steak, Saucy Oven-, '83 10
Bean Sprouts, Beef and, '82 281; '83 42
Benedict for Two, Steaks, '85 295
Blue Cheese Steaks, '84 171
Braised Steaks, Beer-, '87 96
Broiled Oriental Steaks, '83 110
Carpetbagger Steak, '84 87
Chuck Steak, Marinated Barbecued, '80 156
Continental, Steak, '83 178
Country-Fried Steak and Cream Gravy, '84 8
Country-Fried Steak, Mock, '87 163
Cutlets, Lemon-Flavored, '79 105
de Burgo, Steak, '84 117
Diane Flambé, Steak, '79 103

Diane, Steak, '82 275
Dianne, Steak, '83 47
Fajitas, '84 233
Filet Mignon, Marinated, '84 171
Fillets au Vin, Beef, '79 137
Fillets with Horseradish Sauce and Curried Bananas, '85 230
Fingers, Golden Steak, '85 110
Flank Steak and Mushrooms, '87 61

Flank Steak, Bacon-Wrapped, '85 59
Flank Steak, Barbecued, '79 89
Flank Steak, Beer-Marinated, '87 35
Flank Steak, Grilled, '80 152
Flank Steak, Herb-Marinated, '85 275
Flank Steak, Marinated, '82 162; '83 35, 258; '85 86
Flank Steak, Oriental, '83 178
Flank Steak Pinwheels, '87 141
Flank Steaks, Delicious Marinated, '83 110
Flank Steak, Tangy, '86 184
Flank Steak, Tenderized, '82 105
Flank Steak Teriyaki, '81 110
Flank Steak, Texas, '86 185
French Quarter Steak, '81 17
Garlic Steak, '84 8
Greek Pocket Steaks, '81 262
Grilled Black Pepper Steak, '86 184
Grilled Steaks, Mesquite-, '85 154
Grilled Steaks with Green Chiles, '85 144
Grill, Steak Brunch, '82 44
Ham-and-Mushroom Sauce, Steak with, '83 109
Kabobs, Hot-and-Spicy, '87 193
Lemon-Butter Steak with Brandy Sauce, '85 78
London Broil, Marinated, '87 32
Marinated Beef on a Stick, '85 234
Mexican Steak, '84 76
Mushroom Sauce, Steak with, '83 212
Mush, Steak and Gravy with, '81 215
Oriental Beef, '85 20
Parmigiana, Beef, '84 8; '85 234
Pepper-Beef Steak, '85 21
Pepper Steak, '81 273; '85 57
Pepper Steak and Rice, '81 17
Pepper Steak, Chinese, '82 236
Pepper Steak, Cracked, '83 109
Pepper Steak Salad Cups, '86 206
Pepper Stir-Fry Steak, '81 240
Pies, Cornish Meat, '84 23
Pirate Steak, '79 89
Roulades, Beef, '85 234
Round Steak, Braised, '87 35
Round Steak, Parmesan, '80 106
Round Steak, Savory Stuffed, '81 18
Round Steak, Skillet, '83 29
Round Steak, Tangy, '82 284; '83 14
Round Steak, Tender Grilled, '85 3
Saltillo, Beef (Beef with Tomatillos), '82 219
Sirloin Steak, Secret, '81 110
Sirloin Supreme, Shrimp and, '81 131
Skewered Steak with Vegetables, '81 124
Skillet Steak in Red Wine Sauce, '85 21
Skillet Steak 'n Potatoes, '81 18
Smothered Beef and Onions, '85 293
Smothered Steak, '79 212
Smothered Steak, Onion-, '87 M189
Stick, Steak on a, '83 109
Stir-Fried Beef, '84 26
Stir-Fried Steak, Fast-and-Easy, '87 50
Stir-Fry, Beef-and-Vegetable, '87 22
Stir-Fry Beef-and-Vegetables, '84 141
Stir-Fry, Steak-and-Vegetable, '84 8
Stuffed Steak Rolls, '82 135
Stuffed Steaks, Cheese-, '81 17

Sweet-and-Sour Marinated Steaks, '83 110
Swiss Steak Cheese Skillet, '80 106
Swiss Steak, Deviled, '80 107
Swiss Steak, Oven, '85 234
Swiss Steak Surprise, '81 17
Swiss Steak with Vegetables, '81 273
Tartare, Steak, '83 78
Teriyaki, Marinated Steak, '84 50
Tournedos Mouton, '83 262
Vegetables, Beef with Chinese, '81 211
Vegetables, Beef with Oriental, '84 140
Wellingtons, Individual Beef, '82 259
Stew, Bama Brunswick, '87 4
Stew, Beef, '86 51
Stew, Beef-and-Onion, '87 18
Stew, Brown, '85 239
Stew, Company Beef, '83 85
Stew, Mexican, '82 231
Stew Olé, Mexican, '86 296
Stew, Oven Beef, '79 222; '80 64
Stew, Spicy Beef, '86 228
Stew, Sweet-and-Sour Beef and Vegetable, '85 87
Stew, White Wine, '82 228
Stew with Drop Dumplings, Burgundy, '83 125
Stew with Dumplings, Beef, '84 3
Stew with Noodles, Hungarian, '80 263
Stew with Parsley Dumplings, Beef, '81 76; '82 13; '85 M246
Stir-Fry Beef and Broccoli, '79 47
Stir-Fry Beef and Pea Pods, '86 19
Stir-Fry, Beef and Snow Pea, '82 98
Stir-Fry Beef and Snow Peas, '83 22
Stir-Fry, Beef-and-Vegetable, '81 211
Stir-Fry Broccoli and Beef, '83 110
Stir-Fry, Chinese Beef, '83 151
Stir-Fry, Teriyaki, '83 110
Stroganoff, Beef, '79 163; '81 179
Stroganoff, Beef Burgundy, '85 31
Stroganoff, Light Beef, '86 36
Stroganoff, Liver, '79 54
Stroganoff Sandwiches, Steak, '85 110
Stroganoff, Sirloin, '81 297
Stroganoff with Parslied Noodles, Steak, '85 31
Tacos al Carbón, '86 19
Tacos al Carbon, Tailgate, '79 185
Tamales, '80 195
Tempting Twosome, '81 240
Tenderloin Deluxe, Beef, '85 109
Tenderloin, Herb Marinated, '83 109
Tenderloin, Lobster-Stuffed Beef, '87 248
Tenderloin, Marinated, '80 146
Tenderloin, Marinated Beef, '81 246; '85 302
Tenderloin, Spicy Marinated Beef, '83 262
Tenderloin, Stuffed, '86 323
Tenderloin with Mushrooms, Beef, '87 115
Tenderloin with Mushroom-Sherry Sauce, Beef, '87 306
Tips and Noodles, Beef, '86 293
Tips on Rice, Beef, '85 87
Tournedos Diables, '87 60
Vegetables in a Noodle Ring, Beef and, '85 285
Vegetables, Savory Beef and, '79 163

Beef, Ground
- Appetizer, Cheesy Mexicali, '82 108
- Barbecue Cups, '79 129
- Bean Bake, Cheesy Beef-and-, '82 89
- Bean Medley, Baked, '80 100
- Beans, Beefy, '82 59
- Beans, Beefy Baked, '80 136; '84 149; '85 142
- Beans, Rancho Lima, '80 191
- Beans, Three-Meat Baked, '86 210
- Burgoo, Harry Young's, '87 3
- Burritos, Chinese, '87 181
- Burritos, Fiesta, '86 114
- Cabbage, Italian Stuffed, '84 294
- Cabbage Rolls, '83 104
- Cabbage Rolls, Beef Stuffed, '81 87; '82 7

- Cabbage Rolls, Spicy, '84 2
- Cabbage Rolls, Stuffed, '84 217
- Cabbage Rollups, Beef-and-, '80 63
- Cabbage, Stuffed, '84 282
- Casseroles
    - Biscuit Casserole, Beef-and-, '83 75
    - Cabbage Beef Bake, Zesty, '80 300
    - Cheesy Ground Beef Casserole, '79 44
    - Cheesy Mexican Casserole, '82 224
    - Chili-Rice Casserole, '79 54
    - Cornbread Casserole, '81 91
    - Cornbread Skillet Casserole, '83 243; '84 101
    - County Fair Casserole, '79 130
    - Creamy Ground Beef Casserole, '81 142
    - Crusty Beef Casserole, '82 88
    - Easy Beef Casserole, '86 M58
    - El Dorado Casserole, '81 140
    - Enchilada Casserole, '87 287
    - Enchilada Casserole, Firecracker, '80 260
    - Enchilada Casserole, Sour Cream, '82 113
    - Five-Layer Meal, '81 140
    - Italian Cabbage Casserole, '87 42
    - Italian Casserole, '80 81
    - Layered Beef Casserole, '82 M203
    - Layered Grecian Bake, '82 119
    - Macaroni Combo, Beef-, '79 194
    - Matador Mania, '86 19
    - Mexi Casserole, '83 M87
    - Moussaka Casserole, '79 179
    - Noodle Bake, Hamburger-, '81 140
    - Noodles Casserole, Beef-and-, '84 72
    - Pizza Casserole, Quick, '83 266
    - Sausage Casserole, Ground Beef and, '80 260
    - Seashell-Provolone Casserole, '80 189
    - Sour Cream-Noodle Bake, '79 55
    - Spaghetti and Beef Casserole, '79 129
    - Spinach and Beef Casserole, '79 192
    - Spinach-Beef-Macaroni Casserole, '83 313
    - Taco Beef-Noodle Bake, '81 141
    - Taco Casserole, '80 33
    - Vegetable Casserole, Beefy, '79 248
    - Vegetable Chow Mein Casserole, Beef-and-, '83 313
    - Zucchini-Beef Bake, '86 146
- Chiles Rellenos Egg Rolls, '86 296
- Chili
    - Basic Chili, '82 M11
    - Cheese-Topped Chili, '82 M11
    - Cheesy Chili, '82 310
    - Chili, '87 17
    - Company Chili, '82 311; '83 30
    - con Carne, Beef and Sausage Chili, '83 284
    - con Carne, Chili, '84 72
    - con Carne, Favorite Chili, '86 293
    - con Carne, Quick-and-Easy Chili, '86 2
    - Double-Meat Chili, '79 269; '80 12
    - Easy Chili, '82 310; '83 30
    - Friday Night Chili, '86 228
    - Hominy Bake, Chili, '81 282; '82 58
    - Hot Texas Chili, '80 222; '81 77
    - Lunchtime Chili, '81 230
    - Meaty Chili, '81 282; '82 58
    - Meaty Chili with Beans, '85 250
    - Noodles, Chili with, '81 282; '82 57
    - Potato Chili, Savory, '83 284
    - Potatoes, Chili-Topped, '83 3
    - Quick and Simple Chili, '81 282; '82 58
    - Quick Chili, '83 283
    - Ranch Chili and Beans, '79 270; '80 11
    - Rice, Chili with, '82 M11
    - Roundup Chili, '79 269; '80 12
    - Sauce, Chili Meat, '83 4
    - Sausage-Beef Chili, '86 232
    - Sausage Chili, Beefy, '82 M11
    - Simple Chili, '79 269; '80 11
    - Spiced Chili, Hot, '83 214
    - Spicy Chili, Old-Fashioned, '79 269; '80 11
    - Texas-Style Chili, '82 311; '83 30
    - Tex-Mex Chili, '83 26
    - Tree-Hunt Chili, '87 292
- Cornbread, Beefy Jalapeño, '82 142
- Cornbread, Cheesy Beef, '81 242
- Cornbread Tamale Bake, '79 163
- Crêpes, Sherried Beef, '85 M29
- Dinner, Beef-and-Garbanzo, '84 31
- Dinner, Beef-and-Lima Bean, '84 292
- Dinner, Beef-Cabbage, '81 179
- Dinner, Beefy Sausage, '80 M9
- Dinner, Black-Eyed Pea Skillet, '86 6
- Dinner, Fiesta, '85 110
- Dinner, Ground Beef Skillet, '82 60
- Dip, Hot Chile-Beef, '83 218
- Dip, Meaty Cheese, '82 59
- Dip, Tostada, '84 206
- Eggplant, Baked Stuffed, '81 133
- Eggplant, Beefy Stuffed, '81 204
- Eggplant, Cheesy Stuffed, '79 188
- Enchiladas, American, '81 170
- Enchiladas, Hot and Saucy, '81 141; '82 6
- Enchiladas, Skillet, '82 89
- Enchiladas, Sour Cream, '87 37
- Fiesta, '87 180
- Filet Mignon, Mock, '80 81
- Filet Mignon Patties, Mock, '82 M68
- Fillets, Poor Boy, '82 106
- Filling, Beef, '80 81
- Flips, Pea, '80 7
- Gumbo, Ground Beef, '87 283
- Hamburgers
    - Apple Burgers, '86 137
    - au Poivre Blanc, Burgers, '87 186
    - Bacon Burgers, Cheesy, '81 29
    - Barbecued Burgers, '82 168
    - Beefburger on Buns, '84 71
    - Beerburgers, '79 129
    - Burgundy Burgers, '80 156
    - Cheeseburger Biscuits, '79 194
    - Cheeseburger Loaves, '86 19
    - Cheesy Beef Burgers, '83 217
    - Chili Burgers, Open-Face, '81 24; '82 31; '83 33
    - Cocktail Burgers, Saucy, '83 217
    - Deluxe, Burgers, '84 125
    - Glorified Hamburgers, '81 73
    - Grilled Hamburgers, Flavorful, '81 110
    - Hawaiian, Beefburgers, '86 137
    - Mexicali Beef Patties, '86 137
    - Nutty Burgers, '87 185
    - Old-Fashioned Hamburgers, '79 149
    - Oven Burgers, '83 130
    - Party Burgers, '83 164; '84 39
    - Patties, Deviled-Beef, '87 22
    - Patties, Hamburger, '82 M172
    - Pineapple Burgers, '82 169
    - Pizza Burger, '87 185
    - Pizza Burgers, '80 M201; '81 73
    - Pizza Burgers, Easy, '82 190
    - Pizza, Quick Hamburger, '85 243
    - Sauce, Hamburgers with Tomato, '81 73
    - Saucy Burgers, '80 93
    - Saucy Hamburgers, Quick, '82 60
    - Sausage Burgers, '83 212
    - Seasoned Burgers, '85 158
    - Seasoned Hamburgers, '84 230
    - Seasoned Stuffed Burgers, '86 136
    - Sour Cream Burgers, Grilled, '87 287
    - Steak-House Burgers, '87 186
    - Steaks, Company Hamburger, '82 169
    - Steaks with Mustard Sauce, Hamburger, '84 230
    - Stuffed Burgers, '85 159
    - Superburgers, '79 89
    - Super Hamburgers, '79 129
    - Super Supper Burgers, '82 110
    - Surprise Burgers, '82 169
    - Tahiti Burgers, '85 170
    - Teriyaki Burgers, '81 72
    - Vegetable Burgers, Beef-and-, '84 125
    - Venison Burgers, '87 304
- Kheema, Indian, '81 226
- Lasagna, '82 119; '83 M6
- Lasagna, Beefy, '80 81
- Lasagna, Cheesy, '82 224
- Lasagna, Cheesy Spinach, '83 204
- Lasagna for Two, '81 91
- Lasagna, Quick, '84 220
- Lasagna, Quick 'n Easy, '80 M10
- Lasagna, Simple, '81 188
- Lasagna, South-of-the-Border, '84 31
- Lasagna, Vintage, '79 194
- Log, Stuffed Beef, '79 71

Beef, Ground (continued)

Macaroni, Ground Beef and, '85 218
Macaroni, Skillet Beef and, '82 130
Madras, Beef, '87 284
Manicotti, Quick, '79 6
Manicotti, Saucy Stuffed, '83 288
Meatballs
    Bacon-Wrapped Meatballs, '79 81
    Barbecued Meatballs, Oven, '82 233
    Brandied Meatballs, '83 78
    Burgundy-Bacon Meatballs, '80 283
    Chafing Dish Meatballs, '81 260
    Chestnut Meatballs, '79 110
    Chinese Meatballs, '83 116; '87 194
    Cocktail Meatballs, '79 63, 207
    Creole, Meatball-Okra, '83 156
    Creole, Meatballs, '82 233
    Español, Meatballs, '82 110
    Flavorful Meatballs, '84 206
    Golden Nugget Meatballs, '82 233
    Gravy, Meatballs in, '79 136
    Hawaiian Meatballs, '85 86
    Hawaiian Meatballs, Tangy, '79 129
    Heidelberg, Beef Balls, '83 164;
      '84 39
    Paprikash with Rice, Meatballs,
      '85 31
    Pizza Meatballs, '85 86
    Polynesian Meatballs, '80 207
    Red Delicious Meatballs, '85 85
    Royal Meatballs, '87 268
    Saucy Meatballs, '85 68
    Saucy Party Meatballs, '80 149
    Sauerbraten Meatballs, '85 85
    Spaghetti-and-Herb Meatballs, '84 75
    Spaghetti with Meatballs, '81 38
    Spiced Meatballs, '79 284
    Spicy Meatballs and Sausage, '79 163
    Stew, Meatball, '79 198
    Stroganoff, Meatball, '81 297
    Stroganoff, Mushroom-Meatball,
      '85 85
    Swedish Meatballs, '80 80; '86 256
    Sweet-and-Sour Meatballs, '82 233;
      '86 240
    Sweet-and-Sour Party
      Meatballs, '79 233
    Tamale Meatballs, '80 194
    Zesty Meatballs, '80 250
Meat Loaf
    Barbecued Meat Loaf, '80 60;
      '81 275; '84 50; '87 216
    Cheeseburger Loaf, '81 236, 276
    Cheesy Meat Roll, '82 136
    Chili Meat Loaf, '81 275
    Corny Meat Loaf, '86 68
    Crunchy Meat Loaf Oriental, '79 212
    Curried Meat Loaf, '86 43
    German Meat Loaf, '87 216
    Glazed Beef Loaf, '86 19
    Hurry-Up Meat Loaf, '82 21
    Individual Meat Loaves, '81 279;
      '82 24; '83 154
    Italian Meat Loaf, '79 187
    Meat Loaf, '81 170
    Mexicali Meat Loaf, '81 275
    Mexican Meat Loaf, '87 217
    Miniature Meat Loaves, '85 24
    Mozzarella-Layered Meat Loaf,
      '79 71
    Oriental Meat Loaf, '81 M122;
      '83 M194

Parsleyed Meat Loaf, '83 35
Parsley Meat Loaf, '87 22
Pineapple Loaves, Individual,
  '81 M121
Pizza Meat Loaf, Cheesy, '81 M121
Roll, Meat Loaf, '79 129
Saucy Meat Loaves, '79 186
Savory Meat Loaf, '87 216
Spicy Meat Loaf, '79 71
Sprout Meat Loaf, '85 51
Stuffed Beef Log, '79 71
Stuffed Meat Loaf, '79 187
Stuffed Meat Loaf, Rolled, '80 80
Swedish Meat Loaf, '81 M121
Tasty Meat Loaf, '83 213
Triple Meat Loaf, '79 186
Vegetable Loaf, Beef-, '79 164
Vegetable Meat Loaf, '85 M29
Wellington, Meat Loaf, '79 186;
  '87 284
Mix, Ground Beef, '84 71
Moussaka, '87 166
Moussaka, Corn, '87 190
Mushrooms, Stuffed, '83 13
Noodle Dinner, Beefy, '81 179
Noodles, Easy Beef and, '83 288
Omelet, Beefy Vegetable, '83 188
Omelet con Carne, Tex-Mex, '81 209
Pastitsio, '87 12
Patties, Foo Yong, '80 223

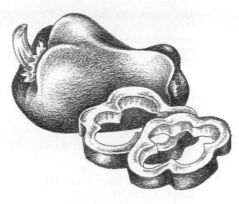

Peppers, Beefed-Up, '82 186
Peppers, Beef-Stuffed, '84 154; '85 146
Peppers, Beefy Stuffed Green, '81 86
Peppers for Two, Stuffed, '80 84
Peppers, Mexican Green, '80 65
Peppers, Stuffed, '81 239; '83 66
Peppers Stuffed with Beef, '84 72
Picadillo (Spicy Beef over Rice), '80 193;
  '84 118; '85 57
Pie, Broccoli-Beef, '83 196
Pie, Cheese-Beef, '85 33
Pie, Corn Burger, '83 156
Pie, Country, '83 155
Pie, Crescent Taco, '80 80
Pie, Enchilada, '83 155
Pie, Hamburger, '81 92; '84 13
Pie, Meat-and-Potato, '84 23
Pie, Mexicali Meat, '81 194
Pie, Mexican Burrito, '87 287
Pie, Old-Fashioned Meat, '82 110
Pie, Shepherd, '83 116
Pies, Individual Taco, '82 M282
Pies, Natchitoches Meat, '84 21
Pie, Sombrero, '81 140
Pie, Spaghetti, '81 32

Pies, Vegetable-Beef, '80 286
Pitas, Curried Beef, '85 220
Pizza, Best Ever Homemade, '80 233
Pizza-Burger Snacks, '84 30
Pizza Cups, '81 215
Pizza, Double Cheesy
  Beef-and-Sausage, '86 77
Pizza, Quick Hamburger, '85 243
Pizza Supreme, '81 214
Pizza, Tostada, '81 16; '82 13
Quiche, Green Chile, '83 31
Ravioli, Homemade, '87 230
Rice, Spanish, '81 51
Rice, Spiced Beef and, '84 285
Rice, Spicy Beef and, '83 231
Rolls, Italian Meat, '86 137
Rolls, Spicy Beef, '85 110
Roulades, Beef, '80 80
Salad Cups, Taco, '85 M29
Salad, Dude Ranch, '80 15
Salad in a Shell, Mexican, '86 4
Salad, Mexican, '81 36
Salad, Mexican Chef, '85 84
Salad, Mexican Olive, '85 84
Salad, Mexi-Pea, '81 7
Salad, Spicy Chili, '86 71
Salad, Spicy Taco, '87 287
Salad Supper, Mexican, '82 9; '83 68
Salad, Taco, '79 56; '83 145; '84 221;
  '85 84
Salisbury Steak Deluxe, '81 170
Sandwiches, Barbecued Beef, '81 25;
  '82 31; '83 34
Sandwiches, Bavarian Pita, '83 31
Sandwiches, Beef-Eater, '86 72
Sandwiches, Hearty Pocket, '80 93
Sandwiches, Hot Pita, '83 217; '87 M6
Sandwiches, Open-Face Pizza, '82 3
Sauce, Beer Spaghetti, '85 13
Sauce, Herbed Spaghetti, '85 13
Sauce, Italian Meat, '83 193
Shells, Cheesy Beef-Stuffed, '83 217
Skillet, Vegetable-Beef, '86 172
Slice, French Beef, '79 125
Sloppy Joe Dogs, '85 192
Sloppy Joe Pocket Sandwiches, '81 200
Sloppy Joes, '81 279; '82 24; '83 153
Sloppy Joes, Easy, '82 31, 278; '83 34
Sloppy Joes, Pocket, '85 M328
Sloppy Joes, Simple, '82 130
Sloppy Joes, Super, '83 130
Snacks, Beefy Party, '80 249
Soup, Beefy Black-Eyed, '85 6
Soup, Beefy Vegetable, '79 113; '84 M38
Soup, Hamburger, '80 263
Soup, Quick Beefy Vegetable, '80 25
Soup, Vegetable-Burger, '82 6
Spaghetti, Black-Eyed Pea, '81 7
Spaghetti, Easy, '83 M317; '84 72
Spaghetti, Meaty, '82 19
Spaghetti, Real Italian, '81 233
Spaghetti Sauce, Thick, '84 118
Spaghetti, Thick-and-Spicy, '83 287
Spaghetti with Mushrooms, Spicy, '85 2
Spaghetti with Pizzazz, '80 85
Spaghetti, Zucchini, '83 160
Squash, Beef-Stuffed, '83 134
Squash, Stuffed Acorn, '83 15
Steak, Spanish, '80 80
Stew, Hamburger Oven, '84 4
Stew, Mixed Vegetable, '84 13
Stew, Quick Beef, '86 302
Stroganoff, Easy Hamburger, '79 208

Stroganoff, Ground Beef, '84 71
Stroganoff, Hamburger, '82 108, 110
Stroganoff, Quickie, '81 200
Stromboli, '87 283
Supper, Beef-and-Bean, '82 2
Supper, Beef-and-Eggplant, '84 291
Supper, Oriental Beef, '79 192
Supper, Quick Skillet, '84 69
Supreme, Beef, '83 196
Tacos, '80 196
Tacos, Basic, '83 199
Tacos, Corn Chip, '81 67
Tacos, Jiffy, '83 M318
Texas Straw Hat, '85 293
Tostada Compuestas, '81 194
Tostadas, Crispy, '83 2
Tostadas, Super, '83 199
Turnovers, Meat, '86 326
Wontons, Tex-Mex, '87 196
Zucchini, Beef-Stuffed, '86 M139

Beets
Apples, Beets and, '80 137
Borscht, Ruby Red, '83 176
Cake, Chocolate Beet, '80 40
Cake with Almond Topping,
  Beet, '86 200
Chilled Beets and Cauliflower, '80 137
Creamy Beets, '80 136
Deviled Beets, '84 217; '86 252
Glazed Beets, Orange-, '81 167;
  '85 289; '86 187
Glazed Beets, Strawberry-, '83 234
Glazed Fresh Beets, '81 167
Harvard Beets, '83 M195
Ivy League Beets, '84 122
Orange-Ginger Beets, '80 137
Pickled Beets, '79 276; '81 216; '87 163
Pickled Beets, Easy, '80 137
Pickles, Beet, '81 210
Pineapple, Beets with, '79 249; '82 204
Relish, Beet, '84 179
Relish, Colorful Beet, '85 136
Rice Ring with Beets, '79 225
Salad, Beet-Nut, '79 74
Salad, Marinated Beet, '83 216
Salad Mold, Beet, '82 267
Salad, Pickled Beet, '83 234
Salad, Tangy Beet, '86 199
Spiced Beets, '79 22
Stuffed Beets, Potato-, '83 234
Sweet-and-Sour Beets, '81 167; '82 22

Beverages
Alcoholic
  Almond-Flavored Liqueur, '81 287
  Amaretto Breeze, '83 172
  Banana Flip, '83 303
  Banana Kabana, '86 316
  Bloody Mary, '80 221
  Bloody Mary, Easy, '84 115
  Bloody Marys, '79 33, 38; '80 51
  Bloody Marys, Eye-Opener, '82 48
  Bloody Marys, Overnight, '81 270
  Bloody Marys, Pitcher, '81 198
  Bloody Marys, Spicy, '87 173
  Bourbon Slush, '84 58
  Bourbon Slush, Summertime, '81 101
  Brandy Cream, '84 312
  Burgundy Bowl, Sparkling, '83 276
  Café Colombian Royal, '80 M290
  Café Cream, '82 312
  Café Diablo, '80 259
  Café Mocha Cream, '84 54
  Café Royal, '80 259

Cappuccino, Flaming, '79 293
Champagne Delight, '83 304
Chocolate, Flaming Brandied,
  '80 M290
Cider, Hot Mexican, '87 213
Cider, Hot Mulled, '84 323
Cider, Red Apple, '80 259
Coconut Frost, Pink, '79 174; '80 128
Coconut Nog, '83 275
Coconut-Pineapple Drink, '83 172
Coffee, After-Dinner, '81 262
Coffee, Brandied, '81 244
Coffee, Chocolate, '82 43
Coffee Cream, Icy Rum, '83 172
Coffee, Creamy Irish, '79 232
Coffee Delight, Almond-, '84 115
Coffee, Flaming Irish, '79 293
Coffee-Flavored Liqueur, '86 266
Coffee, Mexican, '83 175
Coffee Nog, Brandied, '86 329
Coffee Nog, Irish, '84 258
Coffee, Praline-Flavored, '87 69
Coffee Refresher, Velvet, '79 149
Cranberry Cooler, '86 229
Cranberry-Rum Slush, '84 259
Cranberry Wine Cup, '85 23
Daiquiris, Cranberry, '81 245
Daiquiris, Freezer Lime, '79 141
Daiquiri, Strawberry, '81 156
Daiquiritas, '82 160
Dessert, After Dinner-Drink, '82 100
Dessert Drink, Creamy, '86 131
Dessert Drink, Simply Super, '83 303
Eggnog, Christmas, '87 242
Eggnog, Creamy, '80 259; '83 303
Eggnog Deluxe, Holiday, '79 232
Eggnog, Edenton, '84 251
Eggnog, Thick and Creamy, '80 261
Frosty Sours, '81 156
Fuzz Buzz, '82 160
Ginger Beer, '84 159
Golden Dream, '82 100
Holiday Brew, '81 265
Irish Cream Nog, '82 312
Kahlúa Smoothie, '87 242
Kahlúa Velvet Frosty, '82 244
King Alfonso, '80 259
Lemon Cooler, '82 48
Lime Fizz, '81 172
Magnolia Blossoms, '87 72
Magnolias, '82 196
Margaritas, Frosted, '84 115
Margaritas, Frosty, '83 172
Margaritas, Pitcher, '83 175
Margaritas Supreme, Frozen, '80 160
Margaritas, Tart, '85 153
Melon Ball Cooler, '86 131
Mimosa Hawaiian, '85 44
Mimosas, '86 91
Minted Delight, '87 107
Mint Juleps, '81 155; '82 41; '85 40
Mocha Deluxe Hot Drink, '82 289
Oklahoma Sunrise, '87 67
Old-Fashioneds, '86 270
Orange Blossom Flips, '80 51
Orange-Champagne Cocktail, '79 39
Orange Liqueur, '81 287
Orange Milk Shake, '84 166
Peach Frosty, '81 156
Peppermint Flip, Hot, '86 329
Piña Coladas, Frosty, '83 176
Piña Coladas, Luscious, '81 134
Plum Slush, '84 139

Punch, Anytime Wine, '79 232
Punch, Bourbon-Tea, '87 57
Punch, Brandy Milk, '85 44
Punch, Brandy Slush, '87 72
Punch, Champagne, '85 153, 257;
  '86 101
Punch, Champagne Blossom, '81 50
Punch, Chatham Artillery, '80 121
Punch, Coffee-Eggnog, '86 281
Punch, Cranapple-Vodka, '87 72
Punch, Cranberry, '85 90
Punch, Fruit, '83 52
Punch, Gin, '80 160
Punch, Golden Gin, '79 233
Punch, Golden Spiked, '79 285
Punch, Health-Kick, '80 174
Punch, Hot Cranberry, '84 41
Punch, Hot Molasses-Milk, '86 329
Punch, Hot Pineapple, '82 264
Punch, Hot Wine, '85 265
Punch, Jefferson County, '86 267
Punch, Lime, '84 58
Punch, Milk, '79 38
Punch, New Orleans Milk, '81 50
Punch, Orange-Lime, '82 160
Punch, Party, '81 265
Punch, Perky Rum, '85 116
Punch, Pineapple, '79 174; '80 128
Punch, Raspberry-Rosé, '87 242
Punch, Refreshing Champagne,
  '84 259
Punch, Rum, '85 265
Punch, Sparkling Champagne, '84 58
Punch, Sparkling Holiday, '81 290
Punch, Spiked Tea, '86 101

Punch, Spirited Fruit, '81 100
Punch, Tropical Fruit, '83 176
Punch, Vodka, '85 265
Punch, Wedding, '86 107
Raspberry Kir, '86 183
Red Roosters, '87 147
Rum, Hot Buttered, '80 259; '82 244
Rum Slush, Easy, '79 174; '80 129
Sangría, '79 186; '81 67, 196;
  '82 121; '86 214
Sangría, Easy Citrus, '80 218
Sangría, Orange, '81 237
Sangría, Punchy, '80 160
Sangría, Quick, '81 156
Sangría, Spanish, '83 81
Sangría, Teaberry, '87 147
Sangría, White, '83 180
Screwdrivers, '79 33
Sherry Sour, '87 74

Beverages, Alcoholic *(continued)*

    Sipper, Sunshine, '86 179
    Slush, Mexican, '83 176
    Spritzers, Spiced, '86 229
    Strawberry-Banana Smoothie, '81 59
    Syllabub, '81 265; '84 319
    Tart Caribbean Cooler, '81 134
    Tequila Slush, '83 176
    Tequila Sunrise, '83 175
    Tomato-Orange Juice Cocktail, '83 169
    Wassail, '83 311
    Wassail, Bourbon, '86 270
    Whisky Sour Slush, '86 183
    Whispers, '86 317

    Wine Cooler, '82 41
    Wine Cooler, Fruited, '86 176
    Wine, Hot Mulled, '83 251
    Wine, Hot Spiced, '84 41
    Wine Mix, Hot, '81 287
    Wine Spice Mix, Mulled, '85 266
    Wine Spritzers, '81 94
    Wine Welcomer, '81 100
Apple Juice, Hot, '86 270
Apple Juice Shrub, Shenandoah, '79 282
Apple Julep, '86 103, 215
Apricot Cooler, '81 100
Apricot Nectar, Hot, '81 265
Apricot Nectar, Mulled, '86 229
Banana Crush, '80 88; '83 142
Banana Nog, '82 290
Banana-Orange Slush, '80 48; '81 155
Banana Slush, '83 56
Banana Smoothie, '87 160
Banana-Strawberry Frost, '87 199
Bloodless Mary, '80 146
Breakfast Eye-Opener, '87 199
Brew, Quilter's, '85 43
Bullshots, '86 91
Café Cappuccino, '82 253
Café Viennese, '82 254
Cappuccino, Chocolate Castle, '84 53
Chocolate, Creole Hot, '80 M290
Chocolate, Favorite Hot, '83 55
Chocolate, French Hot, '86 328
Chocolate Malt, '86 183
Chocolate, Mexican-Style, '81 187
Chocolate Milk, French, '79 38
Chocolate-Mint Smoothie, '84 166
Chocolate Mix, Deluxe Hot, '80 M290
Chocolate Mix, Spicy-Hot, '85 278
Chocolate, Old-Fashioned Hot, '85 23
Chocolate, Special Hot, '82 5
Chocolate, Spiced Hot, '80 50

Chocolate, Spicy Hot, '85 278
Cider, Holiday, '82 264
Cider, Hot Mulled, '79 205
Cider, Hot Spiced, '82 290
Cider, Hot Spiced Apple, '84 318
Cider, Hot Spicy, '84 265
Cider Mix, Beetle, '82 308
Cider Mix, Hot Spiced, '84 42
Cider Nog, Hot Apple, '84 42
Cider, Spiced Apple, '85 256
Cider, Spiced Cranberry, '84 261
Citrus Cooler, '82 160
Cocoa Mix, Hot, '81 287
Cocoa Mix, Hot Mocha-, '82 296
Cocoa Mix, Instant, '86 332
Cocoa, Mocha, '83 318
Cocoa, Quick Hot, '82 5
Coffee, Chocolate-Almond, '84 54
Coffee, Cocoa-, '83 55
Coffee, Creamy, '81 244
Coffee, Frosted, '81 244
Coffee, Mexican, '83 275
Coffee Mix, Fireside, '87 241
Coffee, Mocha, '85 M329
Coffee, Special Spiced, '84 284
Coffee, Viennese Orange, '84 54
Cooler, Spring, '86 214
Cranberry Frappé, '82 263
Cranberry-Orange Soda, '79 148
Cranberry Smoothie, '86 183
Eggnog, '83 318
Eggnog, Sparkling, '79 232
Float, Nutmeg-Almond, '84 106
Float, Pineapple Sherbet, '79 148
Floats, Maple-Coffee, '86 195
Float, Sparkling Cranberry, '86 195
Fruit Beverage, Blender, '83 318
Fruit Cooler, Four-, '86 101
Fruit Drink, Three-, '79 38; '80 50; '87 199
Fruit Drink, Tropical, '85 43
Fruit Float, Frosty, '87 159
Fruit Juicy, Breakfast, '86 176
Fruit Refresher, Four-, '79 174; '80 129
Fruit Slush, Refreshing, '82 35
Fruit Slushy, '80 146
Grapefruit-Orange Refresher, '82 174
Ice Bowl, '83 152
Ice Cream Ginger Fizz, '83 303
Kona Luscious, '84 54
Lemonade, Fresh Squeezed, '81 172
Lemonade Slush, Pink, '80 151
Lemonade, Strawberry, '80 160
Lemonade with Frozen Tea Cubes, '85 161
Lime Cooler, '87 160
Malt Special, '85 198
Mango Frappé, '86 216
Mango-Orange Smoothie, '86 216
Melon Julep, Rainbow, '80 183
Milkshake, Banana, '85 47
Milkshake, Fresh Strawberry, '82 113
Milkshake, Pineapple, '87 199
Milkshakes, Peanut Butter, '85 198
Mocha Espresso, Italian, '82 254
Mocha, Hot, '84 60
Mocha, Quick Viennese, '79 232
Mocha, Swiss-Style, '82 253
Nog, Speedy Breakfast, '82 47
Orange-Banana Flip, '82 48
Orange Blush, '80 51
Orange Frosty, '86 101
Orange-Lemon Mist, '79 288; '80 35

Orange Pick-Me-Up, '80 232
Orange Slush, '82 49
Orange Spiced Nog, '82 48
Peach Cooler, '85 198
Peaches 'n' Almond Cream, '86 229
Peach Frosty, '83 318
Peach Refresher, '86 103
Peanut Butter Cooler, '84 115
Pineapple Sherbet Float, '79 148
Punch. *See also* Beverages/Alcoholic.
    Apple Punch, Hot, '84 324
    Apple-Tea Punch, '85 82
    Apricot Spiced Punch, '80 269
    Bubbling Jade Punch, '79 174; '80 129
    Cantaloupe Punch, '81 147
    Children's Punch, '85 322
    Christmas Eve Punch, '86 314
    Christmas Punch, '84 259
    Cider Punch, Spiced, '84 258
    Citrus Party Punch, '83 141
    Citrus Punch, '85 319
    Citrus Punch, Budget, '82 121
    Citrus Punch, Fresh, '85 154
    Citrus Punch, Party, '84 117
    Coffee-and-Cream Punch, '85 116
    Coffee Punch, '80 50; '83 275
    Coffee Punch, Creamy, '81 50
    Coffee Punch, Rich-and-Creamy, '82 121
    Cranapple Punch, '83 142
    Cranberry-Cinnamon Punch, '86 270
    Cranberry Punch, '83 275
    Cranberry Punch, Holiday, '85 265
    Cranberry Punch, Hot, '80 288; '84 319; '85 265
    Cranberry Punch, Sparkling, '85 277
    Cranberry Punch, Tart, '83 318
    Eggnog Punch, Holiday, '86 281
    False-Kick Punch, '82 121
    Frozen Punch Ring, '83 152
    Fruit Punch, Golden, '80 299; '83 56

    Fruit Punch, Holiday, '79 232
    Fruit Punch, Hot, '83 33
    Fruit Punch, Party, '82 137
    Fruit Punch, Summertime, '80 160
    Fruit Punch, Tropical, '80 51
    Golden Punch, '85 207
    Grape Punch, Sparkling, '82 48
    Holiday Punch, '87 252
    Lemon Balm Punch, '80 42
    Lime-Pineapple Punch, '83 142
    Lime Punch, Foamy, '82 264

Merry Christmas Punch, '79 285
Mocha Punch, '84 58, 166; '86 270
Orange Blossom Punch, '83 142
Orange-Mint Punch, '82 121
Orange Punch, Refreshing, '81 39
Orange Sherbet Party Punch, '83 142
Orange Soda Punch, '87 214
Parsonage Punch, '79 148
Party Punch, Special, '81 119
Percolator Punch, Hot, '81 288
Pineapple-Orange Punch, '85 236
Pineapple Punch, '79 174
Pineapple Punch, Spiced, '83 33
Pink Lady Punch, '81 100
Ponche de Piña, '84 58
Raspberry Sparkle Punch, '84 57
Rum Punch, Spiced, '86 179
Sherbet Punch, Double, '79 232
Spiced Punch, Hot, '80 250
Strawberry-Lemonade Punch, '85 116
Strawberry Punch, Creamy, '86 195
Tangy Punch, '83 142
Tea Party Punch, '87 147
Tea Punch, Citrus-, '85 116
Traders' Punch, '87 94
Shake, Amazin' Raisin, '86 195
Shake, Apricot, '84 115
Shake, Banana-Pineapple Milk, '84 59
Shake, Cranberry, '83 171
Shake, Frosty Fruit, '87 23
Shake, Peach-Coffee Milk, '84 284
Shake, Peachy Orange, '81 156
Shake, Peanut Butter, '82 48
Shake, Pep, '79 38
Shake, Pineapple-Banana, '85 215
Shake, Strawberry-Orange
  Breakfast, '87 186
Shake, Strawberry-Pineapple, '84 166
Shake, Strawberry-Yogurt, '87 199
Shake, Summer, '82 161
Shake, Sunshine, '79 53
Shake, Tropical, '87 200
Spices, Barclay House Mulling, '86 289
Strawberry-Banana Float, '87 160
Strawberry Cooler, '83 56; '84 51
Strawberry-Mint Cooler, '84 57
Strawberry-Orange Slush, '83 172
Strawberry Slurp, '81 96
Strawberry Smoothie, '86 183
Strawberry Soda, '84 115
Strawberry Soda, Old-Fashioned, '79 49
Syllabub, Plantation, '79 233
Tahitian Flower, '87 159
Tea, Almond, '85 43; '86 329
Tea, Almond-Lemonade, '86 229
Tea, Bubbly Iced, '81 168
Tea, Christmas Fruit, '83 275
Tca Cooler, Spiced, '83 55
Tea, Frosted Mint, '84 161
Tea, Ginger, '81 100
Tea, Hawaiian, '87 57
Tea, Honey, '81 105
Tea, Hot Apple-Cinnamon, '87 57
Tea, Hot Citrus, '83 275
Tea, Hot Spiced, '83 244
Tea, Hot Spiced Fruit, '87 242
Tea, Iced Citrus, '85 162
Tea, Iced Mint, '83 170
Tea, Johnny Appleseed, '85 23
Tea, Lemon, '82 156
Tea, Lemon-Mint, '85 162
Tea, Mint, '87 107
Tea, Minted, '86 101

Tea Mix, Friendship, '83 283
Tea Mix, Spiced, '86 32
Tea, Southern Sun, '81 168
Tea, Spiced Grape, '79 174
Tea, Summer, '85 162
Tea, Summertime, '81 167
Tea, White Grape Juice, '87 57
Tea, Yaupon, '79 31
Toddy, Jolly, '86 229
Tomato Bouillon, '83 8
Tomato-Clam Cocktail, '87 252
Tomato Cocktail, '83 M203
Tomato Juice Cocktail, '79 212; '83 230
Tomato Juice Cocktail, Zesty, '83 289
Tomato Juice, Homemade, '81 50
Tomato Juice, Spicy, '85 189
Tomato Refresher, '83 318
Tomato Sipper, Spicy, '86 229
Tropical Cooler, '84 120
Tropical Ice, '79 174; '80 129
Tropical Refresher, '85 198
Tropical Smoothie, '81 50
Vanilla Frosty, French, '79 148
Vegetable Cocktail, Fresh, '82 165
Vegetable Juice Delight, '84 58
Wassail, '84 259, 318
Wassail, Pineapple-Apricot, '83 275

Biscuits
Angel Biscuits, '80 49
Angel Biscuits, Ham-Filled, '80 159
Baking Powder Biscuits, '82 195
Beaten Biscuits, '86 54
Benne Seed Biscuits, '79 38
Bran Biscuits, '83 228
Bread, Biscuit, '84 284
Buttermilk Biscuits, '83 208; '85 255, 321
Buttermilk Biscuits, Deluxe, '82 130
Buttermilk Biscuits, Favorite, '81 191
Buttermilk Biscuits, Fluffy, '84 102
Buttermilk Biscuits, Old-Fashioned, '80 77
Buttermilk Biscuits, Quick, '83 311
Casserole, Beef-and-Biscuit, '83 75
Casserole, Biscuit-Topped Tuna, '79 113
Cheese Biscuits, '79 296; '80 31; '81 288;
  '83 253; '85 32; '87 78
Cheese Biscuits, Easy, '81 99
Cheese Biscuits, Tiny, '80 192
Cheeseburger Biscuits, '79 194
Cheese Dips, Butter, '80 46
Cheesy Biscuits, Hot, '80 186
Chicken in a Biscuit, '79 263
Cloud Biscuits, '87 15
Cornmeal Biscuits, '85 228
Dressing, Cornbread-Biscuit, '79 296
Feather Biscuits, '80 78
Feather Light Biscuits, '80 246
Flaky Biscuits, '84 228
Grapefruit Juice Biscuits, '83 10
Ham and Cheese Biscuits, Petite, '79 193
Heart Biscuits, Country Ham in, '86 105
Heart Biscuits with Sausage, Angel,
  '87 156
Hearty Biscuits, '83 121
Herbed Biscuits, '85 228
Hot Biscuits, '86 269
Marmalade Biscuits, Carolina, '85 42
Marmalade Biscuit Squares, '79 193
Mile-High Biscuits, '85 41
Nannie's Biscuits, '82 156
One-Step Biscuits, '82 173
Orange Puffs, Upside-Down, '83 57
Parker House-Style Biscuits, '79 162
Pepperoni Biscuits, '84 95

Processor Biscuits, Easy, '84 218
Pudding, Biscuit, '79 86
Raised Biscuits, Southern, '82 94
Roquefort Biscuits, Herbed, '84 95
Rye Biscuits, '84 96
Sausage and Biscuits, Southern, '82 43
Sausage Biscuit Bites, '84 95
Sausage Biscuits, Cheesy, '80 78
Scones, Currant, '84 117
Sour Cream Biscuits, '79 128
Sour Cream Biscuits,
  Soft-as-a-Cloud, '86 138
Sourdough Biscuits, '82 201
Sweetened Biscuits, '80 42
Sweet Little Biscuits, '85 305
Sweet Potato Biscuits, '80 287; '84 140
Tomato Biscuits, '86 72
Topping, Biscuit, '86 157, 265
Wheat Bran Biscuits, '81 49
Wheat Germ Biscuits, '86 261
Wheat Quick Biscuits, '85 278
Whipping Cream Biscuits, '80 77
Whole Wheat Biscuits, '83 18;
  '84 60, 268; '85 227
Yeast Biscuits, '87 71, 301
Yeast Biscuits, Refrigerator, '85 48

Blackberries
Bars, Blackberry, '87 130
Bars, Blackberry-Filled, '79 124
Bars, Blackberry Jam, '82 M185
Cake, Fresh Blackberry, '81 132
Cobbler, Blackberry, '82 139; '83 175
Cobbler, Blackberry-Almond, '81 132
Cobbler, Deep-Dish Blackberry, '80 186
Cobbler, Deluxe Blackberry, '81 132
Cobbler, New-Fashioned Blackberry,
  '87 164
Cobbler, Southern Blackberry, '81 132
Dumplings, Blackberries and, '86 196
Flan, Blackberry, '79 182
Jam, Blackberry, '82 149
Jam, Freezer Blackberry, '84 M181
Jelly, Blackberry, '82 149
Parfait, Blackberries-and-Cream, '87 129
Pie, Blackberry, '84 141; '86 152
Pie, Blackberry-Apple, '87 130
Pie, Blackberry Cream, '81 132
Roll, Blackberry, '82 178
Sauce, Blackberry, '86 152
Sauce, Ducklings with Blackberry,
  '82 251
Tart, Cherry and Blackberry, '83 225
Blueberries
Appetizer, Orange-Berry, '85 81
Basket, Summer Berry, '84 158
Bread, Banana-Blueberry, '81 163

Blueberries (continued)

Bread, Blueberry-Lemon, **'85** 190
Bread, Blueberry-Oatmeal, **'83** 139
Bread, Blueberry-Orange, **'87** 140
Bread, Blueberry-Orange Nut, **'84** 141
Bread, Hot Blueberry, **'81** 164
Buckle, Blueberry, **'85** 30
Buns, Deluxe Blueberry, **'81** 164
Cake, Almond-Blueberry Coffee, **'85** 152
Cake, Banana-Blueberry, **'86** 247
Cake, Blueberry Brunch, **'83** 183
Cake, Blueberry Coffee, **'82** 206;
    '85 326
Cake, Fresh Blueberry Coffee, **'81** 164
Cheesecake, Blueberries 'n' Cream,
    '87 140
Cheesecake, Blueberry Chiffon, **'87** 76
Cobbler, Blueberry, **'83** 175
Cobbler, Blueberry Pinwheel, **'87** 140
Cobbler, Easy Blueberry, **'83** 183
Cobbler, Fresh Blueberry, **'80** 144
Cobbler, No-Dough Blueberry-
    Peach, **'86** 177
Cobbler, Peachy Blueberry, **'80** 143
Cointreau, Blueberries and, **'82** 100
Compote, Berry-Peach, **'82** 133
Conserve, Blueberry, **'82** 149
Crisp, Blueberry, **'84** 177
Crumble, Blueberry, **'81** 84
Crunch, Fresh Blueberry, **'82** 143
Dessert Squares, Chocolate-
    Blueberry, **'87** 299
Fritters, Blueberry, **'85** 152
Glaze, Blueberry, **'83** 143
Huckle-Buckle Blueberry, **'86** 151
Jam, Blueberry, **'79** 120; **'85** 130
Kuchen, Blueberry, **'80** 143
Muffins, Blueberry, **'80** 143
Muffins, Blueberry Buttermilk, **'80** 16
Muffins, Blueberry-Cream Cheese, **'86** 14
Muffins, Blueberry Ice Cream, **'82** 143
Muffins, Blueberry-Lemon, **'79** 7
Muffins, Blueberry-Oatmeal, **'87** 24
Muffins, Blueberry Streusel, **'80** 46
Muffins, Easy Blueberry, **'81** 197
Muffins, Golden Blueberry, **'79** 235
Muffins, Old-Fashioned Blueberry, **'86** 161
Pancakes, Blueberry, **'85** 152
Pancakes, Blueberry Buttermilk, **'79** 114
Pancakes, Sour Cream Blueberry, **'81** 164
Pie, Blueberry Cream, **'84** 142
Pie, Blueberry-Sour Cream, **'83** 183
Pie, Fresh Blueberry, **'83** 183; **'85** 152
Pie, Fresh Blueberry Cream, **'80** 144
Pinwheels, Blueberry, **'82** 205
Salad, Layered Berry, **'79** 173
Sauce, Blueberry, **'80** 144; **'86** 248
Sauce, Cinnamon-Blueberry, **'86** 11
Sauce, Melon Wedges with Berry, **'86** 178
Sauce, Peach-Berry, **'87** M165
Sauce, Peach-Blueberry, **'81** 170
Sauce, Peach-Blueberry Pancake, **'82** 177
Snow, Berries on, **'82** 227
Sorbet, Blueberry-Kirsch, **'83** 120
Squares, Blueberry-Amaretto, **'83** 220
Topping, Blueberry, **'87** 125

Bok Choy
Stir-Fry, Bok Choy-Broccoli, **'84** 2

Boysenberries
Cobbler, Boysenberry, **'82** 133
Compote, Berry-Peach, **'82** 133
Cream Mold, Peachy Berry, **'83** 130

Cream Supreme, Boysenberries
    and, **'82** 133
Crisp, Berry, **'83** 130
Pie, Boysenberry, **'82** 133

Bran
Biscuits, Bran, **'85** 228
Biscuits, Wheat Bran, **'81** 49
Bread, Bran-Applesauce, **'84** 229
Bread, Whole Wheat Bran, **'79** 58
Crêpes, Bran, **'83** 70; **'86** 44
Cupcakes, Carrot-Bran, **'82** 16
Eggplant, Ratatouille-Bran Stuffed, **'86** 44
Muffins, Apple-Bran, **'85** M89
Muffins, Banana Bran, **'83** 48
Muffins, Bran, **'84** 53
Muffins, Bran-Buttermilk, **'85** 7
Muffins, Easy Bran, **'83** 55
Muffins, Ever-Ready Bran, **'81** 106
Muffins for Two, Bran, **'84** 211
Muffins, High-Fiber, **'85** 250
Muffins Made of Bran, **'86** 103
Muffins, Oatmeal Bran, **'81** 236
Muffins, Quick Bran, **'86** 85
Muffins, Refrigerator Bran, **'79** 6
Muffins, Sour Cream-Bran, **'87** 98
Muffins, Spiced Bran, **'84** 229
Rolls, Bran, **'85** 145
Rolls, Bran Yeast, **'87** 116
Salad, Lemony Apple-Bran, **'86** 223

Breads. *See also* specific types.
Apple Bread, **'79** 205; **'80** 226
Apple Butter Bread, **'84** 49; **'86** 69
Apple Loaf, Fresh, **'82** 206
Apple Loaf, Spiced, **'79** 215
Apple-Nut Bread, **'79** 12; **'85** 281
Apple-Nut Bread, Fresh, **'87** 256
Applesauce-Honey Nut Bread, **'87** 300
Applesauce Loaf, Brandy, **'81** 263
Applesauce Nut Bread, **'81** 305
Apricot Bread, Tangy, **'81** 249
Apricot-Cranberry Loaf, **'79** 235
Apricot-Nut Bread, **'79** 24
Apricot-Nut Loaf, **'81** 8
Apricot-Nut Loaf, Tasty, **'82** 10
Asparagus Squares, **'79** 161
Bacon-and-Cheese Bread, **'83** 255
Banana-Apple Bread, **'85** 250
Banana-Blueberry Bread, **'81** 163
Banana Bread, **'87** 72
Banana Bread, Sour Cream-, **'79** 190
Banana Bread, Whole Wheat, **'80** 88
Banana Butterscotch Bread, **'79** 116
Banana-Jam Bread, **'84** 73
Banana-Nut Bread, **'86** 8, 70

Banana Nut Bread, Hawaiian, **'79** 235
Banana Nut Bread, Whole Wheat-, **'84** 50
Banana-Nut-Raisin Bread, **'81** 59
Banana-Nut Roll, **'85** 112
Banana-Oat Tea Loaf, **'87** 256
Banana Wheat Bread, **'81** 14
Banana-Zucchini Bread, **'85** 326
Batter Bread, Soft, **'84** 253
Beer Bread, Easy, **'79** 213; **'84** 160
Biscuit Bread, **'84** 284
Blueberry Bread, Hot, **'81** 164
Blueberry-Lemon Bread, **'85** 190
Blueberry-Oatmeal Bread, **'83** 139
Blueberry-Orange Bread, **'87** 140
Blueberry-Orange Nut Bread, **'84** 141
Bran-Applesauce Bread, **'84** 229
Breakfast Bread, Easy, **'83** 289
Brie Bread, **'87** 143
Brie Cheese Bake, **'87** 117
Brown Bread, **'84** 242
Brown Bread, Eighteenth-Century, **'79** 72
Brown Bread, Steamed
    Buttermilk, **'86** 261
Butternut-Raisin Bread, **'79** 25
Carrot Bread, Tasty, **'84** 328
Carrot-Nut Loaf, **'83** 117
Carrot-Pineapple Bread, **'82** 210
Carrot Puffs, **'87** 200
Cheddar-Nut Bread, **'85** 41
Cheese Bread, **'82** 174
Cheese Bread, Dilly, **'83** 5
Cheese Bread, Easy, **'82** 74; **'86** 17
Cheese Bread, Quick, **'83** 9
Cheese-Herb Bread, **'85** 283
Cheese Loaf, **'87** 92
Cheese Loaves, Little, **'86** 213
Cheese-Olive Bread, Spicy, **'84** 150
Cheese Puffs, Bavarian, **'80** 191
Cheesy Twists, **'84** 284
Cherry Nut Bread, **'81** 306; **'82** 36
Cherry Nut Bread, Maraschino, **'79** 234
Cherry-Nut Bread, Quick, **'85** 55
Chocolate Date-Nut Bread, **'81** 284
Cinnamon Puffs, **'81** 209
Citrus-Nut Bread, **'83** 294
Coconut Bread, **'83** 140
Cranberry-Banana Bread, **'80** 281
Cranberry Bread, **'79** 242
Cranberry Fruit-Nut Bread, **'79** 275
Cranberry-Orange Bread, **'87** 244
Cranberry-Orange Nut Bread, **'80** 288
Croutons, **'86** M288
Croutons, Celery, **'79** 16
Croutons, Crispy Italian, **'84** 126
Croutons, Garlic-Flavored, **'86** 47
Croutons, Herb, **'81** 150
Croutons, Microwave, **'86** M227
Croutons, Vegetable-Flavored, **'84** 148
Date-Nut Bread, **'85** 306
Date-Nut Loaf, **'85** 10
Date-Walnut Loaf, Blue Ribbon, **'80** 15
Easy Bread, **'87** 168
Eggnog Bread, **'83** 294
Flatbread, Mexican, **'80** 197
French Bread, Herbed, **'82** 174
French Bread, Herb-Seasoned, **'83** 198
French Bread, Hot Garlic, **'81** 83
French Loaf, Herbed, **'87** 243
Fruit-Nut Bread, Kahlúa, **'79** 235
Fruit-Nut Twists, **'82** 253
Fry Bread, **'84** 140; **'85** 155
Fry Bread, Indian, **'81** 56
Garlic Bread, **'82** 19

Garlic Bread, Cheesy, '84 150
Garlic Breadsticks, '79 70
Gingerbread Loaf, '82 14
Gingerbread, Mocha, '81 207; '82 14
Gingerbread, Old English, '79 265
Gingerbread, Old-Fashioned, '81 157, 207;
  '82 14
Gingerbread, Refrigerator, '80 52
Gingerbread, Spicy, '84 263
Gingerbread Squares, '84 16
Gingerbread, Very Moist, '86 261
Ham-and-Cheese Bread, '86 213
Hawaiian Loaf, '80 225
Herb-and-Cheese Pull Aparts, '87 143
Herb Bread, '86 17
Herb Loaf, Toasted, '84 150
Herb Sticks, '83 252
Hobo Bread, '86 86
Lemon Bread, '79 275; '87 256
Lemon-Cream Tea Loaf, '84 50
Lemon-Nut Bread, '79 24
Lemon-Pecan Bread, '83 54
Mix, Quick Bread, '81 90; '86 8
Molasses-Nut Bread, '84 24
Monkey Bread, Quick, '81 306; '82 36
Mustard-Rye Ovals, '84 149
Oatmeal Bread, '81 236, 300
Oatmeal Raisin Bread, '81 14
Onion Bread, Easy, '81 162
Onion-Cheese Bread, '79 180; '81 8
Onion-Cheese Supper Bread, '83 112
Onion-Herb Bread, Toasted, '83 266
Onion-Parmesan Bread, '84 284
Orange, Baba au, '86 138
Orange-Cranberry Bread, '85 266
Orange-Cream Cheese Bread, '82 210
Orange-Nut Bread, '82 75
Orange Nut Loaf, '80 226

Orange-Pecan Bread, '79 148
Orange-Pecan Bread, Glazed, '81 250
Orange-Pecan Loaves, '79 215
Orange Puffs, Upside-Down, '83 57
Orange-Pumpkin Bread, '87 300
Orange Tea Bread, '79 234
Parmesan Herb Bread, '82 235;
  '83 41
Parmesan Rounds, '79 170
Parmesan Sesame Sticks, '81 39
Parmesan Twists, '83 239
Peach Bread, '82 170
Peach Bread, Georgia, '79 161
Peanut Bread, '87 184
Pear Bread, '80 218
Pepper Bread, '85 156

Persimmon Bread, '80 228
Persimmon Date-Nut Bread, '82 218
Pineapple-Apricot Bread, '84 7
Pineapple Bread, '83 139
Pineapple-Carrot Bread, '79 106
Pineapple-Nut Bread, '79 215
Pineapple-Pecan Loaf Bread, '87 256
Popover Puffs, Cheese, '85 6
Popover Ring, Cheesy, '80 45
Popovers, Cheddar Cheese, '85 41
Popovers for Two, '81 304
Popovers, Giant Pecan, '83 208
Popovers, Good Old Southern, '79 138
Popovers, Jumbo, '83 225
Popovers, Muffin Tin, '79 138
Popovers, Perfect Blender, '79 53
Popovers, Pimiento, '79 138
Popovers, Seasoned, '86 86
Poppy Seed Bread, '83 140
Poppy Seed Loaf, Quick, '82 75
Prune-Nut Bread, '87 255
Puddings
    Amish Bread Pudding, '80 8
    Apricot Bread Pudding, '85 24
    Cheesy Bread Pudding, '83 68
    Chocolate Bread Pudding, '80 8
    French Bread Pudding, '85 231
    Old-Fashioned Bread
      Pudding, '83 213
    Whiskey Sauce, Bread Pudding
      with, '80 58
Pumpkin Bread, '81 8
Pumpkin Bread, Moist, '80 245
Pumpkin Bread with Cream Cheese and
  Preserves, '84 264
Pumpkin-Coconut Bread, '87 255
Pumpkin Loaf, Harvest, '85 232
Pumpkin-Nut Bread, '83 294
Pumpkin-Oatmeal Loaf, '81 49
Pumpkin-Pecan Bread, '87 221
Raisin-Cranberry Bread, '81 305; '82 36
Saffron Tea Bread, '85 26
Sally Lunn, Quick, '87 16
Salt-Rising Bread, '79 145
Sausage-Onion Squares, '83 112
Scones, Currant, '84 117
Scones, Lemon-Raisin, '87 69
Seasoned Breadsticks, '81 84
Sesame Bread Twists, '84 283
Sesame-Cheddar Sticks, '81 150
Sesame Sticks, '83 9
Sesame Wheat Crisps, '81 106
Shortbread, '85 266
Spinach Bread, '83 121; '87 144
Spoonbreads
    Cheddar Spoonbread, '82 196
    Cheese Spoonbread, '86 261
    Corn and Bacon Spoonbread, '81 129
    Garlic Spoonbread, '79 269; '80 14
    Golden Spoonbread, '83 286; '84 17
    Grits Spoonbread, '79 38
    Old Virginia Spoonbread, '84 102
    Spoonbread, '80 43; '81 138
Squash Bread, '79 210
Squash Bread, Spicy, '83 121
Squash Bread, Yellow, '84 140
Stollen, '86 291
Strawberry Bread, '81 250; '83 140;
  '84 49
Strawberry Jam Bread, '79 216
Strawberry-Nut Bread, '79 24
Tacos, Navajo, '84 246
Three-C Bread, '81 284

Toast
    Apple Toast, '81 278
    Bacon-Cheese Toast Bars, '79 36
    Cheese Delights, Toasted, '79 37
    Cinnamon Toast, Buttery
      Skillet, '79 36
    Orange Praline Toast, '79 36
    Shrimp Toast, '86 91
Tortillas, Flour, '81 303
Tortillas, Never-Fail Flour, '80 198
Vegetable Bread, Breakaway, '82 74
Wampus Bread, '81 305
Whole Wheat Cardamom Bread, '86 223
Whole Wheat Coffee Can Bread,
  Molasses-, '85 111
Whole Wheat Orange Bread, '85 5
Whole Wheat Quick Bread, '82 65
Wine-Date Nut Bread, '82 253
Yeast
    Almond Danish, '87 301
    Anise-Orange Bread, '83 295
    Apple Pull-Apart Bread, '86 330
    Apple Swirl Bread, '85 4
    Austrian Sweet Bread, '83 294
    Austrian Twists, '80 45
    Bagels, Whole Wheat, '84 20
    Baguettes, '85 70
    Beer Bread, Best-Ever, '82 129
    Beer Bread, Hearty, '87 226
    Beignets, '84 56
    Binning Bread, '80 68
    Braided Loaf, '82 17
    Braids, Cream Cheese, '82 243
    Braids, Festive, '87 297
    Braids, Holiday, '83 295
    Break-Away Bread, '86 56
    Brioche, '81 122
    Brioche Loaves, Vienna, '87 300
    Brown Bread, Light-, '84 268
    Bubble Bread, '81 107
    Butter-Egg Bread, '85 269
    Butterhorns, '84 267
    Cake Bread, Golden, '84 269
    Caramel Bread, '82 75
    Caramel-Orange Coffee Ring, '80 45
    Caraway Puffs, '82 174
    Caraway Seed Bread, Dark, '80 256
    Cheese Bread, '83 208; '87 11
    Cheese Bread, Cheddar, '84 268
    Cheese Bread, Crusty, '86 233
    Cheese Bread, Pimiento-, '85 223;
      '86 166
    Cheese Bread, Sour Cream-, '85 33
    Cheese Bread, Swiss, '79 60
    Cheese-Caraway Batter Bread, '85 33
    Cheese Crescents, '82 18
    Cheese-Dill Bread, Cottage, '83 154
    Cheese-Herb Bread, '84 M144
    Cheese Loaf, Jalapeño-, '84 76
    Cheese Loaves, Processor
      Cream, '85 48
    Cheese-Wine Bread, '87 254
    Chocolate Pinwheel Loaf, '80 256
    Christmas Bread, '87 296
    Christmas Bread, Norwegian, '79 234
    Christmas Wreath, '80 280
    Cinnamon Loaf, '82 18; '85 55
    Cinnamon-Nut Bubble Bread, '80 22
    Cinnamon Raisin Bread, '80 22
    Cinnamon Swirl Loaf, '79 23
    Cinnamon Twists, '83 53
    Cocoa-Nut Swirl Bread, '80 257
    Coffee Ring, Filled, '82 18

Breads, Yeast *(continued)*

Coffee Ring, Sugarplum, '83 M37
Cracker Bread, Sesame, '87 2
Crescents, Festive, '80 281
Croissants, '83 54; '84 188
Croissants, Flaky Butter, '85 42
Crust Bread, Country, '80 225
Easter Egg Bread, '84 94
Easy Yeast Bread, '79 147
Egg Bread, County Fair, '87 68
Elephant Ears, '84 18
English Muffin Loaf, '82 96
English Muffin Loaves, '85 42
Figure-8 Bread, '79 171
Flat Bread, Italian-Style, '82 235;
 '83 41
French Bread, '79 158; '87 227
French Bread, Herbed, '85 222;
 '86 166
French Bread, New Orleans, '80 212
French Loaves, Crusty, '85 37
Fruit-and-Cheese Braid, '86 214
Ham Bread with Herb Butter,
 Country, '86 255
Herb Bread, '84 268
Herb Bread, No-Knead, '81 217
Herb-Cheese Bread, '85 70
Herb Loaf, Butterflake, '86 261
Herb-Sour Cream Bread, '85 268
Herman Food, '82 200
Holiday Wreath, '81 284
Honey-Granola Bread, '86 56
Honey Loaves, Hint o', '81 104
Honey Twist, '79 80
Honey-Walnut Swirl, '80 21
Honey Wheat Bread, '85 18, 268
Italian Bread, '82 297
Kolecz (Polish Bread), '80 29
Lightbread, Coffee Can, '79 59
Light Yeast Bread, '81 299
Loaf Bread, Hospitality, '86 299
Marble Loaf, '80 230
Monkey Bread, '82 243
Multi-Grain Bread, '86 236
Oat Bread, Caraway-Raisin, '86 44
Oatmeal Bread, '81 300
Oatmeal Bread, Honey, '80 60
Oatmeal Bread, Round, '84 20
Oatmeal-Raisin Bread, '83 59
Oat-Molasses Bread, '82 139
Old-Fashioned Yeast Bread, '79 284
Onion-Dill Bread, Easy, '85 5
Onion Twist Loaves, '84 300
Party Bread, '86 218
Peanut Butter Bread, '86 171
Pizza Batter Bread, '85 56
Pocket Bread, '79 58
Poppy Seed Loaf, '83 254
Portuguese Round Bread, '83 295
Potato Bread, '85 56
Potato Bread, Old-Fashioned, '86 57
Potato Lightbread, '80 225
Potato Loaves, '86 162
Pretzels, Chewy Soft, '87 159
Pretzels, Homemade, '84 159
Pretzels, Soft, '83 18
Raisin Batter Bread, Salt-Free, '86 33
Raisin Bread, Curried Chicken Salad
 on, '85 96
Raisin Bread, Homemade, '87 300
Refrigerator Bread,
 No-Knead, '83 155

Rounds, Individual Bread, '83 159
Rye Bread, '84 21
Rye Bread, Swedish Orange-, '85 111
Rye Sandwich Bread, '82 65
Sally Lunn, '81 157
Sandwiches, Stacking, '86 127
Savarin, Holiday, '80 280
Soft Breadsticks, '83 115
Sopaipillas, '80 197
Sour Cream Bread, '79 59
Sourdough Bread, '82 201
Sourdough Starter, Herman, '82 200
Squares, Yeast Bread, '83 155
Sugar Plum Bread, '80 256
Sweet Christmas Loaf, '84 278
Techniques of Breadmaking, '82 17
Trinity Feast Bread, '82 92; '83 83
Wheat Bread, Buttermilk, '86 236
Wheat Bread, Pull-Apart
 Maple, '85 222; '86 166
White Bread, '79 275
White Bread, Cardamom, '82 236;
 '83 41
White Bread, Old-Fashioned, '81 285
White Bread, Special, '86 57
Whole Wheat Bran Bread, '79 58
Whole Wheat Bread, '83 17
Whole Wheat Bread and Rolls,
 Hearty, '79 92
Whole Wheat Breadsticks, '84 228
Whole Wheat Honey Bread, '82 65;
 '83 106
Whole Wheat-Oatmeal Bread, '87 85
Whole Wheat-Rye Bread, '83 M37
Whole Wheat-White Bread, '82 130
Zucchini-Apple Bread, '87 255
Zucchini Bread, '85 111; '86 93
Zucchini Bread, Spiced, '79 161; '86 162
Zucchini Bread, Spicy, '81 305; '82 36
Zucchini-Carrot Bread, '83 190

Broccoli
au Gratin, Broccoli, '82 M20
au Gratin, Broccoli-and-Eggs, '85 289
Bake, Broccoli, '81 246
Bake, Cheesy Broccoli, '83 255
Bake, Cheesy Italian Broccoli, '83 5
Bake, Company Broccoli, '83 279
Bake, Potato-Broccoli-Cheese, '80 114
Burritos, Broccoli, '83 200
Carnival Broccoli, '81 2
Casserole, Broccoli, '87 284
Casserole, Broccoli-and-Egg, '86 324
Casserole, Broccoli-Blue Cheese, '85 260
Casserole, Broccoli-Cheese, '82 269; '84 9
Casserole, Broccoli-Chicken, '82 33
Casserole, Broccoli-Corn, '83 313
Casserole, Broccoli-Rice, '81 101
Casserole, Broccoli-Swiss Cheese, '83 322;
 '85 M211
Casserole, Cheesy Broccoli, '84 293
Casserole, Chicken-Broccoli, '79 48
Casserole, Chicken Divan, '82 M203
Casserole, Crabmeat-Broccoli, '84 232
Casserole, Ham and Broccoli, '81 133
Casserole, Italian Broccoli, '82 6, 280;
 '83 32
Casserole, Quick Ham-Broccoli, '82 40
Casserole, Sausage and Broccoli, '80 33
Casserole, Tangy Tuna-Broccoli, '83 75
Casserole, Turkey-and-Broccoli, '86 332
Cheese Sauce, Broccoli with, '82 107
Chinese Broccoli, '85 M12
Chowder, Broccoli, '79 16

Chowder, Swiss-Broccoli, '80 73
Cocktail Broccoli, '80 192
Crêpes, Royal Brunch, '81 44
Deluxe, Broccoli-Onion, '81 75
Dip, Broccoli-Garlic, '82 59
Dip, Cheesy Broccoli, '83 92
Divan, Chicken, '80 10; '87 M218
Divan, Curried Chicken, '80 83
Divan, Gourmet Chicken, '82 83
Divan, Overnight Chicken, '83 198
Divan, Sherried Chicken, '80 38
Divan, Turkey, '82 268
Eggs, Broccoli and Creamed, '83 84

Elegant, Broccoli, '81 267
Filling, Broccoli, '81 44
French Sauce, Broccoli with, '81 295
Frittata, Broccoli-Cheese, '81 243
Fritters, Cheesy Broccoli, '79 53
Garden Surprise, '83 112
Glazed Broccoli with Almonds, '80 12
Hollandaise Sauce, Broccoli with,
 '79 244, 276
Hollandaise Sauce, Broccoli with
 Mock, '82 272
Horseradish Sauce, Broccoli with, '81 2;
 '83 206; '84 33
Italienne, Broccoli, '82 300
Jade-Green Broccoli, '80 12
Lemon-Broccoli Goldenrod, '84 M89
Lemon Sauce and Pecans, Broccoli
 with, '86 71
Marinated Broccoli, '80 79; '81 40;
 '85 207; '86 157
Marinated Broccoli, Tangy, '80 284
Marinated Fresh Broccoli, '81 M139
Medley, Broccoli, '81 206
Medley, Cauliflower-Broccoli, '81 69
Olive-Butter Sauce, Broccoli with, '83 118
Omelet, Broccoli-Mushroom, '85 45
Onions, Broccoli-Stuffed, '84 154
Orange Broccoli, Easy, '85 267
Orange Sauce, Broccoli with, '80 243
Pasta, Broccoli, '84 176
Pasta, Chicken-and-Broccoli, '87 286
Pasta with Broccoli and Sausage, '87 109
Pickled Broccoli, '81 308
Pie, Broccoli-Beef, '83 196
Pie, Broccoli-Cheese, '84 235
Pimiento Broccoli, '86 268
Polonaise, Broccoli, '86 55
Potatoes, Broccoli-and-Almond-
 Topped, '83 3
Potatoes, Broccoli-Topped Baked, '86 17
Puff, Broccoli, '81 94; '82 95
Quiche, Broccoli-Rice, '81 228
Quiche, Easy Broccoli, '82 34

Quiche, Italian Broccoli, '85 45
Quick-and-Easy Broccoli, '86 55
Rice, Holiday Broccoli with, '87 252
Rolls, Ham-and-Broccoli, '86 212; '87 82
Salad, Beef-and-Broccoli, '87 187
Salad, Broccoli, '82 24; '85 249
Salad, Broccoli and Cauliflower, '81 280
Salad, Broccoli and Red Pepper, '83 224
Salad, Broccoli-Corn, '87 24
Salad, Cauliflower-Broccoli, '79 20
Salad, Congealed Broccoli, '84 124
Salad, Creamy Broccoli, '79 143
Salad, Creamy Broccoli and
Cauliflower, '81 23
Salad, Crunchy Broccoli, '83 39
Salad, Curried Broccoli, '86 225
Salad, Fresh Broccoli, '82 34; '87 103
Salad, Hot Broccoli-Potato, '85 23
Salad, Marinated Broccoli, '83 240
Salad, Pepperoni-and-Broccoli, '83 216
Salad Supreme, Broccoli, '83 260
Sautéed Broccoli, '79 246
Savory Broccoli, '79 268; '80 14
Sesame Broccoli, '84 69; '85 8
Sesame, Broccoli with, '80 13
Sesame Seeds, Broccoli with, '82 34
Shrimp Sauce, Broccoli and Cauliflower
with, '84 248
Soufflé, Broccoli, '81 24
Soufflé, Golden Broccoli, '84 283
Soup, Broccoli, '86 161, M194; '87 288
Soup, Broccoli-Swiss, '86 6
Soup, Cheesy-Broccoli, '86 258
Soup, Creamed Broccoli, '85 24
Soup, Cream of Broccoli, '79 130;
'80 188, M225; '82 314; '83 66; '86 259
Soup, Creamy Broccoli, '81 75; '82 13;
'83 99
Soup, Easy Broccoli, '81 307
Soup, Hot Broccoli, '81 235; '83 44
Soup, Mock Cream of Broccoli, '85 288
Sour Cream Sauce, Broccoli with, '87 127
Spears, Saucy Broccoli, '84 35
Spears, Zesty Broccoli, '79 152
Stack-Ups, Jiffy Tomato, '80 161
Steamed Broccoli, '80 122
Steamed Broccoli with Tangy Chive
Sauce, '83 101
Stir-Fried Broccoli, '83 227
Stir-Fry Beef and Broccoli, '79 47
Stir-Fry, Bok Choy-Broccoli, '84 2
Stir-Fry Broccoli, '80 19
Stir-Fry Broccoli and Beef, '83 110
Stir-Fry, Chicken-Broccoli, '82 33
Strata, Ham and Broccoli, '80 261
Sunshine Sauce, Broccoli with, '84 248
Supreme, Broccoli, '82 34; '85 68
Supreme, Creamy Broccoli, '82 287
Tomatoes, Broccoli-Stuffed, '83 136
Toss, Broccoli, '86 294
Toss, Cauliflower-Broccoli, '82 54
Toss, Crunchy Broccoli and
Cauliflower, '83 25
Vinaigrette, Potato-Broccoli, '85 84
Wine, Broccoli with White, '80 12
Wine Sauce, Broccoli with, '84 187
Brussels Sprouts
Amandine, Brussels Sprouts, '79 213
Beer, Brussels Sprouts in, '85 69
Carrots and Brussels Sprouts, '82 300
Cashews, Brussels Sprouts with, '81 2
Casserole of Brussels Sprouts, '86 294
Celery, Brussels Sprouts and, '79 21

Cheese Sauce, Brussels Sprouts
with, '79 246
Citrus Brussels Sprouts, Calico, '85 303
Creamed Brussels Sprouts and
Celery, '83 322
Creamy Brussels Sprouts, '79 212
Deviled Brussels Sprouts, '84 248
Fried Brussels Sprouts, '81 308
Glorified Brussels Sprouts, '86 282
Lemon Sauce, Brussels Sprouts
in, '82 269
Lemon Sprouts, '85 288
Lemony Brussels Sprouts with
Celery, '85 25
Medley, Brussels Sprouts, '79 212;
'85 267
Mustard Sauce, Brussels Sprouts
in, '87 253
Onion Sauce, Brussels Sprouts in, '81 308
Orange Brussels Sprouts, '84 34
Orange Sauce, Brussels Sprouts in, '86 55
Pierre, Brussels Sprouts, '84 248
Polonaise, Brussels Sprouts, '85 79
Rice, Brussels Sprouts and, '79 288;
'80 26
Salad, Brussels Sprouts, '87 233
Salad, Cauliflower-Brussels
Sprouts, '83 240
Sesame Brussels Sprouts, '86 55
Shallots and Mustard, Brussels Sprouts
with, '85 258
Stir-Fry, Brussels Sprouts, '81 308
Tarragon Brussels Sprouts, '83 291
Wine Butter, Brussels Sprouts in, '86 327
Burritos
Breakfast Burritos, '84 57
Broccoli Burritos, '83 200
Burritos, '80 196
Cheesy Beef Burritos, '85 193
Chimichangas (Fried Burritos), '81 196;
'85 244
Chinese Burritos, '87 181
Fiesta Burritos, '86 114
Meat-and-Bean Burritos, '81 194
Monterey Burritos, '84 292
Pie, Mexican Burrito, '87 287
Vegetable Burritos, '80 197
Vegetable Burritos with Avocado
Sauce, '83 200
Butter
Apple Butter, '79 200; '81 217
Apple Butter, Half-Hour, '81 203
Apricot Butter, '82 308
Balls, Butter, '82 189
Basil Butter, '87 171
Basil Butter, Asparagus with, '85 40
Cashew Butter, Asparagus with, '87 56
Cheese Butter, '84 114
Chervil Butter, '83 129
Chili Butter, '82 219
Clarified Butter, '81 59
Clarifying Butter, '82 189
Curls, Butter, '82 51, 189
Garlic Butter, '83 193; '84 108
Herb Butter, '86 128, 255, 261, 306
Herb Butter, Cauliflower with, '81 2
Herb Butter, Corn-on-the-Cob
with, '84 160
Herbed Unsalted Butter, '82 67
Honey-Orange Butter, '79 36; '85 19
Horseradish-Chive Butter, '86 277
Lemon Butter, Asparagus with, '87 M151
Lime Butter, Chicken with, '84 68

Maple-Flavored Butter, Whipped, '79 36
Nectarine Butter, '79 175
Onion Butter, '86 253
Orange Butter, '81 8, 42
Orange-Pecan Butter, '84 75
Peach Butter, '82 308
Pear Butter, '85 130
Pear Butter, Spiced, '80 218
Raisin Butter, '81 272
Strawberry Butter, '79 36; '81 286
Tomato Butter, '86 128

Butterscotch
Bars, Butterscotch, '82 209; '83 297
Bars, Chocolate-Butterscotch, '81 197
Bread, Banana Butterscotch, '79 116
Brownies, Butterscotch, '85 248
Cheesecake, Butterscotch, '86 188
Cookies, Butterscotch, '87 58
Cookies, Butterscotch-Pecan, '84 36
Fantastic, Butterscotch, '83 76
Fudge Scotch Ring, '79 273
Pie, Butterscotch Cream, '84 48; '87 207
Pie, Butterscotch Meringue, '83 158
Pralines, Butterscotch, '81 253
Sauce, Butterscotch-Pecan, '82 212

C

Cabbage. *See also* Sauerkraut.
Apples and Franks, Cabbage with, '87 42
au Gratin, Cabbage, '83 279
Bake, Zesty Cabbage Beef, '80 300
Beef-Cabbage Dinner, '81 179
Bubbling Cabbage, '84 2
Caraway Cabbage, '85 32, 289
Casserole, Cheesy Cabbage, '79 4
Casserole, Creamy Cabbage, '80 63
Casserole, Italian Cabbage, '87 42
Casserole, Savory Cabbage, '82 168
Chop Suey, Cabbage, '81 101
Chow-Chow, '82 196
Chowchow, '87 150
Chowder, Hearty Cabbage, '80 25
Corned Beef and Cabbage, '83 104
Corned Beef and Cabbage au
Gratin, '83 16
Corned Beef and Cabbage, Quick, '79 54
Corned Beef Squares and
Cabbage, '82 86
Country-Style Cabbage, '81 271
Creamed Cabbage with Almonds, '79 4
Creole Cabbage, '87 189
Frankfurter-Cabbage Skillet, '80 166
Hot Cabbage Creole, '87 42
Kielbasa and Cabbage, '85 67
Kielbasa, Cabbage, '87 42

Cabbage (continued)

Medley, Cabbage, '80 64; '83 104
Piccalilli, Kentucky, '81 216
Red Cabbage and Apples, '85 32
Red Cabbage, German-Style, '84 2
Red Cabbage, Pickled, '81 271
Red Cabbage, Sweet-Sour, '79 5
Relish, Cabbage, '83 260
Rolls, Cabbage, '83 104
Rolls, Crunchy Cabbage-Rice, '85 32
Rolls, Hot-and-Spicy Cabbage, '84 249
Rolls, Spicy Cabbage, '84 2
Rollups, Beef-and-Cabbage, '80 63
Salad, Cabbage, '87 120, 233
Salad, Cabbage and Fruit, '79 286
Salad, Chinese Cabbage, '81 271
Salad, Garden Cabbage, '81 210
Salad, Nutty Cabbage, '87 42
Salad, Overnight Cabbage, '79 83
Sausage, Cabbage with Polish, '83 104
Sausage-Sauced Cabbage, '81 271
Sausage Surprise, '83 245; '84 42
Scalloped Cabbage, '82 269
Scalloped Cabbage, Cheese, '81 87; '82 7
Skillet, Cabbage-and-Tomato, '86 110
Slaws
    Apple-Pineapple Slaw, '79 241
    Apple Slaw, Fresh, '81 63
    Aspic, Shrimp-Coleslaw, '79 88
    Bacon Coleslaw, '83 58
    Banana-Nut Slaw, '86 250
    Chicken Coleslaw, '84 2
    Chili Coleslaw, '80 178
    Coleslaw, '79 152; '82 135
    Corn and Cabbage Slaw, '79 135
    Cottage Coleslaw, '80 64
    Country-Style Coleslaw, '83 59
    Creamy Coleslaw, '83 170
    Crunchy Coleslaw, '86 295
    Curried Coleslaw, '85 139
    Freezer Slaw, '81 279; '82 24;
      '83 154
    Fresh Cabbage Slaw, '85 139
    Frozen Coleslaw, '82 102
    Fruit Coleslaw, Three-, '86 250
    Fruited Coleslaw, '83 209; '85 139
    Grape-Poppy Seed Slaw, '86 225
    Grapes and Almonds, Coleslaw
      with, '83 59
    Guacamole Mexican
      Coleslaw, '82 302
    Ham Coleslaw, '84 195
    Hot-and-Creamy Dutch Slaw, '87 127
    Hot-and-Sour Chinese Slaw, '85 139
    Kentucky Coleslaw, '81 216
    Layered Coleslaw, '86 180
    Make-Ahead Coleslaw, '81 155
    Marinated Coleslaw, '79 135
    Mexicali Coleslaw, '84 18
    Old-Fashioned Coleslaw, '80 120;
      '82 225
    Old-Fashioned Slaw, '84 149
    Orange Slaw, Cabbage-, '79 135
    Overnight Cabbage Slaw, '81 88;
      '82 7
    Overnight Coleslaw, '79 135
    Overnight Slaw, '79 5
    Peach Slaw, Party, '86 250
    Peanut Slaw, '85 139
    Pear Slaw, Peanutty-, '86 250
    Pineapple Slaw, Colorful, '86 250
    Polka Dot Slaw, '83 59

    Red Bean Slaw, '79 247
    Red Cabbage-and-Apple Slaw, '87 31
    Seafood Slaw, '79 56
    Sour Cream Slaw, '87 10
    Swedish Slaw, '79 135
    Sweet and Crunchy Slaw, '79 104
    Sweet-and-Sour Slaw, '81 237
    Sweet Cabbage Slaw, '79 76
    Tangy Cabbage Salad, '82 55
    Tangy Coleslaw, '83 59
    Tomatoes, Coleslaw with, '80 34
    Vegetable Slaw, '81 280
    Zesty Slaw, '82 127
Soup, Cabbage, '83 291
Spinach Dip in Cabbage, '82 155
Stir-Fried Cabbage, '81 75, 271; '85 109
Stuffed Cabbage, '84 282
Stuffed Cabbage, Italian, '84 294
Stuffed Cabbage Rolls, '84 217
Stuffed Cabbage Rolls, Beef, '81 87;
  '82 7
Supreme, Cabbage, '79 4; '83 206
Sweet-and-Sour Cabbage, '86 295; '87 189
Tex-Mex Cabbage, '80 63
Tomatoes, Cabbage and, '83 104
Tomatoes, Tasty Cabbage and, '86 72
Wedges, Saucy Cabbage, '83 86
Wedges, Smothered Cabbage, '81 87;
  '82 7
Wilted Cabbage, '80 64

Cakes. *See also* Breads, Cookies.
Almond-Butter Cake, '86 107
Almond-Butter Wedding Cake, '86 106
Almond Legend Cake, '82 8
Almond Whipping Cream Cake, '80 295
Amaretto Cake, Easy, '85 79
Ambrosia Cake, '79 229
Angel Food
    Chocolate Angel Food Cake, '87 21
    Coconut Angel Cake, Spiked, '85 279
    Deluxe Angel Food Cake, '86 121
    Ice Cream Angel Cake, '83 23
    Lemon Angel Cake, '80 147
    Pineapple-Orange Sauce, Angel Cake
      with, '84 14
Apple Cake, '83 312; '84 262
Apple Cake, Dried-, '79 13
Apple-Date Cake, Fresh, '83 300
Apple-Nut Cake, '87 76
Apple-Oatmeal Cake, Golden, '86 301
Apple Pie Cake, '86 301
Applesauce Cake, '80 270
Applesauce Cake, My Favorite, '87 263
Applesauce-Spice Cake, '83 42
Apple Slice Cake, '85 93
Apple Stack Cake, Dried, '85 242
Banana-Blueberry Cake, '86 247

Banana Cake, '84 151
Banana Cake, Deluxe Light, '84 314
Banana Cake, Marvelous, '79 115
Banana Waldorf Cake, '85 118
Bars and Squares
    Almond Cake Squares, '79 111
    Apple-Date Dream Cake
      Squares, '85 10
    Apple-Orange Cake Squares, '84 150
    Applesauce Cake Squares, '86 8
    Applesauce-Spice Squares, '86 248
    Carrot-Lemon Squares,
      Golden, '80 40
    Carrot Squares, '79 256
    Cinnamon Cake Squares, '87 222
    Cream Cheese Cake Squares, '84 321
    Crumb Cake, Calico, '87 261
    Gingerbread Squares, '84 16
    Ginger Cake, '87 222
    Honey-Oatmeal Cake, '87 222
    Jam Squares, '81 M289
    Orange Cake Squares, '81 34
    Orange-Pumpkin Cake
      Squares, '83 242
    Pecan Squares, Easy, '81 230
    Pumpkin Cake Bars, '80 245
    Strawberry Shortcake
      Squares, '85 122; '86 124
Beet Cake with Almond Topping,
  '86 200
Blackberry Cake, Fresh, '81 132
Blackberry Flan, '79 182
Boston Cream Pie, '83 220
Bourbon-Pecan Cake, '84 25
Brown Mountain Cake, '84 39
Brown Sugar Meringue Cake, '81 70
Bûche de Noël, '84 304; '87 241
Bûche de Noël Cake, '82 262
Butter Brickle Cake, '85 118
Buttermilk White Cake, '86 235
Butter Pecan Cake, '80 229
Cajun Cake, '87 138
Caramel Layer Cake, Creamy, '81 71
Carrot Cake, '79 45; '82 137; '84 315
Carrot Cake, Applesauce, '81 202
Carrot Cake, Blue Ribbon, '81 70
Carrot Cake, Coconut-Pecan, '84 322
Carrot Cake, Easy, '83 215
Carrot Cake, Fresh Coconut-, '80 299
Carrot Cake, Old-Fashioned, '83 M232
Carrot Cake, Old-South, '80 120
Carrot Cake, Quick-and-Easy, '84 150
Carrot Cake, Spiced, '87 296
Carrot Cake, Spicy Fruited, '85 117
Carrot Pudding Cake, '83 24
Carrot Snack Cake, Easy, '82 235
Chart, Cake Failure, '81 72
Cheesecakes
    Amaretto Cheesecake, '81 150
    Apple Cheesecake, Dieter's, '86 318
    Black Forest Cheesecake, '84 74
    Blueberries 'n' Cream
      Cheesecake, '87 140
    Blueberry Chiffon Cheesecake,
      '87 76
    Brownies, Cheesecake, '85 249
    Butterscotch Cheesecake, '86 188
    Candy Bar Cheesecake, '85 298;
      '86 120
    Cherry Cheesecake, '79 50
    Cherry-Topped Cheesecake, '80 23
    Chocolate-Amaretto
      Cheesecake, '85 M294

Chocolate Cheesecake, '81 16;
'82 305
Chocolate Cheesecake,
German, '87 265
Chocolate Cheesecake, Rich, '84 74;
'85 38
Chocolate Cheesecake, White, '87 44
Chocolate Chip Cheesecake, '85 114
Chocolate Swirl Cheesecake, '84 295;
'85 26
Cottage Cheese Cheesecake, '80 24
Cream Cheesecake, Rich, '83 270
Crème de Menthe
Cheesecake, '82 263
Deluxe Cheesecake, '80 23
Feta Cheesecakes, Little, '86 277
Frozen Cheesecake with Raspberry
Sauce, '84 73
Fruit-Glazed Cheesecake, '80 24
Glazed Cheesecake, '83 142
Grasshopper Cheesecake, '80 191
Individual Cheesecakes, So
Easy, '85 30
Kahlúa Cheesecake, Heavenly, '83 48
Lemon Cheesecake, '86 194
Lemon Cheesecake with Orange-
Pineapple Glaze, '81 60
Make-Ahead Cheesecake Pie, '81 233
Marbled Cheesecake, '87 261
Marble Mint Cheesecake, '84 152
Mile-High Cheesecake, '86 334
Miniature Cheesecakes, '82 305

Mocha Swirl Cheesecake, '87 262
Orange Cheesecake, '81 84; '85 38
Pear-Berry Cheesecake, '82 M141
Pear-Glazed Cheesecake, '79 67
Pecan Cheesecake, '85 38
Pecan Cheesecake, Butter, '86 61
Petite Cheesecakes, Holiday, '86 321
Phyllo Cheesecakes, Little, '87 275
Pineapple Cheesecake, '81 32
Pineapple Cheesecake,
Ultimate, '85 38
Praline Cheesecake, '83 270
Pumpkin Cheesecake, '80 254;
'85 280
Raspberry Sauce, Cheesecake
with, '87 116
Sour Cream Cheesecake, '86 320
Squares, Cheesecake, '84 151
Strawberry Cheesecake,
Almost, '86 32
Sweet Potato Cheesecake, '80 287
Tarts, Cream Cheese, '84 74
Triple Layer Cheesecake,
Chocolate-Glazed, '86 315
Yam Cheesecake, '81 224

Cherry Bourbon Cake, '82 287
Cherry Cake, '79 165
Cherry Cake, Quick, '81 238
Cherry Upside-Down Cake, '82 56
Chocolate
Almond Cake with Cherry Filling,
Chocolate-, '84 225
Banana Cake, Chocolate-, '86 138
Banana Loaf, Chocolate
Chip-, '85 115
Beet Cake, Chocolate, '80 40
Black Forest Cake, '81 126
Black Forest Cake, Six-Layer, '85 125
Black Forest Cherry Cake, '83 302
Black Forest Dump Cake, '85 13
Brownie Baked Alaska, '80 66
Brownie Delight, Chocolate, '87 224
Buttermilk Chocolate Cake, '79 13
Candy Cake, Chocolate, '81 238
Caramel-Nut Cake,
Chocolate-, '83 23
Cherry Cake, Chocolate-, '84 200;
'86 239
Coconut Cake, Chocolate-, '83 23
Decadent Chocolate Cake, '86 142
Easy Chocolate Cake, '80 140
Frosting, Chocolate Cake with
Double, '86 314
Fudge Cake, Best, '83 301
Fudge Cake, Brown Sugar, '86 316
Fudge Cake, Chocolate, '80 279
Fudge Cake for Two, '81 205
German Chocolate Cake, '81 296;
'83 M233
German Chocolate Chip
Cake, '86 247
Kahlúa Chocolate Cake, '81 303
Marbled Cake, Cocoa, '82 265
Marshmallow Cake, No-Egg
Chocolate, '87 M97
Mayonnaise Cake, Chocolate, '83 99
Mocha Cake, Belgian, '84 316
Mocha Cake, Double, '84 311
Mocha-Chocolate Cake,
Dark, '84 311
Mousse Cake, Chocolate, '87 264
Nut Cake, Rich Chocolate-, '86 8
Peanut Butter Cake,
Chocolate-, '84 240
Peanut Butter Cake, Fudgy, '85 91
Peanut Cluster Cake,
Chocolate-, '87 184
Perfect Chocolate Cake, '82 244
Pound Cake. See Cakes/Pound.
Pudding, Chocolate Cake, '81 99
Rocky Road Cake, '81 178
Roll, Chocolate Cream, '85 317
Roll, Chocolate-Frosted Ice
Cream, '84 200
Roll, Chocolate-Mocha
Cream, '84 304
Roll, Chocolate Mousse, '83 290
Roll, Chocolate-Orange, '87 21
Royal, Chocolate Cake, '86 239
Rum Cake, Chocolate, '79 67
Sachertorte, '84 253
Sour Cream Cake,
Chocolate-, '87 222
Sour Cream Cake, Chocolate
Chip-, '85 115
Sour Cream Chocolate Cake, '79 282
Swiss Chocolate Chip Cake, '87 85
Torte, Chocolate Praline, '84 165

Torte, Chocolate-Strawberry Ice
Cream, '79 7
Torte, Chocolate Velvet, '86 316
Torte, Double-Chocolate, '79 67
Torte, Mocha Brownie, '85 102
Torte Royale, Chocolate, '82 263
Triangle Cake, Chocolate, '85 126
Yule Log, '79 281; '82 289
Zucchini Cake, Chocolate, '85 156
Cinnamon Crumb Cake, '85 290
Cinnamon Streusel Cake, '84 151
Coconut
Apple Coconut Cake, '80 226
Chocolate-Coconut Cake, '83 23
Chocolate-Coconut Cake,
White, '87 263
Christmas Coconut Cake, '82 262
Cream Cake, Coconut, '81 179
Creamy Coconut Cake, '84 43
Fresh Coconut Cake, '80 289; '82 52;
'85 281
Layer Cake, Coconut-
Pineapple, '80 140
Layer Cake, Stately Coconut, '81 70
Lemon-Coconut Cream Cake, '81 179
Lemon-Coconut Sheet Cake, '85 117
Pineapple Cake Roll,
Coconut-, '84 304
Pound Cake. See Cakes/Pound.

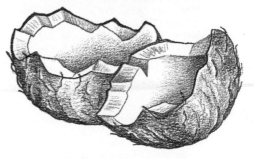

Regal Coconut Cake, '83 299
Spice Cake, Coconut-, '84 255;
'87 296
Toasted Coconut Cake, '86 60
Coffee Cakes
Almond-Blueberry Coffee
Cake, '85 152
Apple Coffee Cake, '81 249
Apple Loaf, Spiced, '79 215
Apple-Pecan Coffee Cake, '84 242
Banana Coffee Cake, '81 288
Banana Cream Coffee Cake, '85 46
Banana-Sour Cream Coffee
Cake, '80 186
Blueberry Brunch Cake, '83 183
Blueberry Coffee Cake, '82 206;
'85 326
Blueberry Coffee Cake,
Fresh, '81 164
Braid Coffee Cake, Daisy, '82 197
Breakfast Pullapart, '81 278
Butterflake Coffee Ring, '79 216
Buttermilk Crumb Cake, '79 72
Caramel Bread, '82 75
Caramel Breakfast Rolls, '79 193
Caramel-Orange Coffee Ring, '80 45
Caramel Ring, Easy, '85 M89
Cardamom Coffee Cake, '83 246;
'84 17
Cherry Blossom Coffee Cake, '80 21

Cakes, Coffee Cakes *(continued)*

Chocolate-Chip Coffee Cake, '79 249
Chocolate Chip Coffee Cake, '83 231
Christmas-Tree Coffee Cakes, '87 298
Christmas Wreath, '80 280
Cinnamon-Buttermilk Coffee Cake, '80 45
Cinnamon Coffee Cake, '83 M203
Cinnamon Crisps, '81 113
Cinnamon-Nut Bubble Bread, '80 22
Cinnamon-Pecan Coffee Cake, '87 69
Cinnamon Twist Coffee Cake, '84 322
Cinnamon Upside-Down Coffee Cake, '85 256
Cranberry Coffee Cake, '81 14
Cranberry-Nut Coffee Cake, '81 250
Cranberry-Orange Coffee Cake, '82 283
Cream Cheese Coffee Cake, '86 290
Crescent Coffee Cake, '81 229
Danish Coffee Ring, '80 20
Fig Coffee Cake, Easy, '80 116
Holiday Coffee Cake, '84 284
Holiday Wreath, '81 284
Honey Twist, '79 80
Lemon Coffee Cake, Lightly, '81 14
Macadamia Ring Coffee Cake, '85 326
Maple-Nut Coffee Twist, '86 290
Marbled Coffee Cake, '86 9
Muffins, Coffee Cake, '79 7
Oatmeal-Coconut Coffee Cake, '83 312
Orange Breakfast Ring, '81 229
Orange Coffee Cake, '85 M88
Orange Marmalade Swirl Coffee Cake, '81 107
Orange-Pecan Coffee Cake, '86 86
Overnight Coffee Cake, '80 52
Peach Flip, '79 217
Pecan-Topped Coffee Cake, '81 41
Raspberry Coffee Cake, '83 112
Ring, Coffee Cake, '85 M89
Savarin, Holiday, '80 280
Snack Cake, Coffee, '86 247
Sour Cream Coffee Cake, '81 270
Sour Cream-Walnut Coffee Cake, '79 209
Strawberry Coffee Cake, '85 46
Sugar Cake, Moravian, '87 228
Sugarplum Coffee Ring, '79 235; '83 M37
Sweet Roll Dough, '79 80
Tropical Coffee Cake, '80 232
Whole Wheat Coffee Cake, Crunchy-Topped, '79 93
Cola Cake, '81 238
Cranberry Upside-Down Cake, '87 8
Cream Cheese Cake, Regal, '80 140
Cream Cheese Loaf Cake, '84 151
Crème de Menthe Cake, '81 178
Cupcakes
Apple-Nut Cupcakes, '82 279
Banana-Cocoa Cupcakes, '80 130
Black Bottom Cups, '82 279
Brownie Cupcakes, '82 280
Carrot-Bran Cupcakes, '82 16
Chocolate Chip Cupcakes, Marble, '81 239

Chocolate Surprise Cupcakes, '85 91
Cinnamon-Chocolate Cupcakes, '81 M139
Cream Cheese Party Cupcakes, '82 279
Date Cupcakes, '84 7
Happy Day Cupcakes, '80 129
Lemon Moist Cupcakes, '82 112; '83 153
Mocha Cupcakes, '85 250
Pumpkin Cupcakes, '85 121
Self-Filled Cupcakes, '80 129
Vanilla Cupcakes, Golden, '85 121
Yellow Cupcakes, Easy, '83 241
Daffodil Cake, '84 161
Date Nut Cake, '79 176; '80 5
Decorating Techniques, Cake, '83 72, 240; '84 224
Fig Cake, '79 32
Fig Preserve Cake, '79 140; '84 316
Friendship Cake, '82 250
Fruit-and-Nut Cake, Stately, '84 226
Fruitcakes
Applesauce Fruitcake, '83 258
Aronowitz Fruitcake, '86 285
Bourbon Fruitcake, '85 315
Brandy Fruitcake, '82 261
Burgundy Fruitcake, '85 292
Fondue, Fruitcake, '84 258
Japanese Fruitcake, '83 268
Kentucky Fruitcake, '86 266
Layered Fruitcake, '87 265
Lemon Fruitcake, '83 258
Mom's Fruitcake, '85 321
Old-South Fruitcake, '79 289
Regal Fruitcake, '83 257
Sherry-Nut Fruitcake, '84 266
Spice Cake, Fruit and, '87 M97
White Fruitcake, '80 280; '85 316
Funnel Cakes, '83 250
Gingerbread, Old English, '79 265
Gingerbread, Refrigerator, '80 52
Gingerbread, Spicy, '84 263
Graham Cracker Cake, '79 13
Holiday Cake, Favorite, '81 264
Hummingbird Cake, '82 244
Ice Cream Cake, '86 321
Ice Cream Cake, Fruity, '87 110
Ice Cream Yule Log, '83 253
Jellyroll, Easy, '82 176
Jellyroll Layer Cake, '85 125
Jellyroll, Spiced, '82 176
Lane Cake, '80 121; '83 269
Lemon Cake, Easy, '83 24
Lemon Cake, Glazed, '86 70
Lemon Cake Roll, Elegant, '80 70
Lemon Gold Cake, '83 301
Lemon Layer Cake, Luscious, '86 61
Lemon Layer Cake, Old-Fashioned, '85 191
Lemon-Pineapple Cake, '86 60, 239
Lemon Pudding Cake, '83 106
Lemon Roll, Snow-Capped, '79 68
Lemon Sponge Cups, '83 10
Lime Layer Loaf, '85 96
Mandarin-Rum Cake, '84 150
Mango Cake, '83 150
Maraschino Nut Cake, '83 268
Mincemeat Spice Cake, '79 246
Molasses Snack Cake, '86 20
Nutmeg Feather Cake, '81 238
Oatmeal Cake, Dutch, '83 95
Orange Cake, '86 61

Orange Cake, Fresh, '83 300
Orange Cake, Mandarin, '83 24
Orange Cake, Williamsburg, '81 120; '82 23
Orange-Cranberry Cake, '85 314
Orange Liqueur Cake, '87 84
Orange Marmalade Cake, '85 53
Orange Meringue Cake, '86 336; '87 84
Orange-Nut Butter Cake, '80 254
Orange Nut Cake, '80 70
Orange-Pecan Crunch Cake, '83 10
Orange Rum Cake, '79 2
Orange Shortcake, Fresh, '80 100
Orange-Slice Cake, '81 264
Peach Cake, Fresh, '85 178
Peaches and Cream Cake, '80 142
Peach Upside-Down Cake, '87 8
Peachy Picnic Cake, '79 178
Peanut Butter-and-Jelly Cake, '85 34
Peanut Butter-Banana Cake, '80 87
Peanut Butter Cake, '79 51; '83 M233
Peanut Butter Swirl Cake, '86 109
Peanutty Layer Cake, Super, '83 222
Pear Cake with Caramel Drizzle, '86 247
Pear Preserve Cake, '85 52
Pecan Cake, Kentucky, '84 263
Pecan Cake with Praline Glaze, '82 196
Pecan Roulade, '87 183
Persimmon Cake, '79 205
Petits Fours, '79 117
Petits Fours, Teatime, '85 119
Pineapple Cake, Heavenly, '83 303
Pineapple-Pecan Upside-Down Cake, '84 25
Pineapple Upside-Down Cake, '80 102
Pineapple Upside-Down Cake, Skillet, '85 242
Pineapple Upside-Down Cake, Stacked, '86 239
Popcorn-Gumdrop Cake, '87 262
Poppy Seed Cake, Plantation, '79 13
Poppy Seed Loaf Cake, '81 63
Poppy Seed Loaf, Quick, '82 75
Pound
Apple Cider Pound Cake, '84 10
Apricot Brandy Pound Cake, '83 267

Brown Sugar Pound Cake, '82 135
Buttermilk Pound Cake, '79 285; '85 255
Buttermilk Pound Cake, Old-Fashioned, '82 52
Buttermilk Pound Cake, Spiced, '84 73
Butter-Nut Pound Cake, '86 235

Caramel Frosting, Pound Cake with, '87 39
Carrot Pound Cake, '87 41
Chocolate Chip Pound Cake, '86 178
Chocolate Pound Cake, '82 88; '84 10
Chocolate Pound Cake with Fudge Frosting, '87 296
Chocolate-Sour Cream Pound Cake, '83 239
Coconut-Cream Cheese Pound Cake, '85 297
Coconut Cream Pound Cake, '84 10
Coconut Pound Cake, '82 87
Cream Cheese Pound Cake, '81 290; '86 287
Favorite Pound Cake, '81 132
Five-Flavor Pound Cake, '87 264
Fruited Pound Cake, '81 265
I Remember Pound Cake, '86 180
Lemon Pound Cake, '82 88
Lemon-Sour Cream Pound Cake, '87 38
Loaf, Pound Cake, '85 306
Mini Pound Cakes, '86 148
Old-Fashioned Pound Cake, '80 279; '82 88
Orange Pound Cake, '87 84, 221
Pineapple Pound Cake, '79 148
Praline Pound Cake, '82 88
Problems to Avoid Chart, '84 319
Rose-Geranium Pound Cake, Mrs. Willoughby's, '84 318
Rum Pound Cake, Buttered, '83 220
Sour Cream Pound Cake, Cinnamon-Topped, '82 43
Sour Cream Pound Cake, Elegant, '83 79
Sweet Potato Pound Cake, '83 85
Yogurt Pound Cake, '84 10
Praline Cake, '81 162
Praline Ice Cream Cake, '80 84
Prune Cake, '85 223
Prune Cake and Sauce, '85 118
Prune Cake, Spicy, '79 136
Pumpkin Cake, '81 272
Pumpkin Date Cake, '79 251
Pumpkin Kahlúa Cake, '86 292
Pumpkin Layer Cake, '80 245
Pumpkin Roll, '79 206
Queen Bee Cake, '81 237
Raisin Layer Cake, Spicy, '79 230
Savarin, '79 171
Sorghum Cake, '85 239
Sorghum Tea Cakes, '85 239
Spice Cake, '81 162
Spice Cake, Buttermilk, '81 211
Spice Cake, Dark, '82 314; '83 43
Spice Cake, Old South, '84 263
Spice Cake, Sugar 'n, '84 226
Spice Cake with Caramel Frosting, '82 314; '83 42
Spice Cake, Yule Log, '85 314
Sponge
    Chocolaty Sponge Cake, '86 60
    Coffee Sponge Cake, '83 229
    Coffee Sponge Cake, Two-Day, '86 75
    Daffodil Sponge Cake, '79 175; '80 6; '84 315
    Strawberries 'n Cream Sponge Cake Roll, '81 95
    Yellow Sponge Cake, '80 250

Squash Cake, '86 200
Stack Cake, Favorite, '87 228
Stack Cake, Old-Fashioned, '81 216
Strawberry Cake Roll, '79 49; '83 129; '84 305; '85 172
Strawberry Cream Cake, '86 61
Strawberry Crunch Cake, '79 288; '80 35
Strawberry Delight Cake, '85 30
Strawberry Ice Cream Roll, '84 105
Strawberry Meringue Cake, '86 240
Strawberry Roll, '82 120
Strawberry Roll, Heavenly, '82 176
Strawberry Shortcake, '81 96; '83 122
Sweet Potato Cake, '79 207
Sweet Potato Loaf Cake, '81 224
Sweet Potato Log Roll, '82 227
Sweet Potato Surprise Cake, '80 287
Tea Cake, Lemon, '82 169
Tea Cakes, Mexican, '81 196
Teacakes, Old-Fashioned, '84 43
Tipsy Squire, '85 41
Torte, Amaretto, '82 303
Torte, Carob-Pecan, '85 218
Torte, Heavenly Pecan, '81 266
Torte, Mocha-Pecan, '86 26
Torte, Sugar Cookie, '79 68
Torte, Toffee Meringue, '87 118
Upside-Down Sunburst Cake, '87 9
Vanilla Chiffon Cake, '79 266
Walnut Cake, Black, '80 253; '84 316
Walnut Cream Roll, '84 192
White Cake with Strawberries and Chocolate Glaze, '87 76
Zucchini Cake, '79 24
Zuppa Inglese, '85 229

Candies

Almond Brittle Candy, '80 255
Almond Butter Crunch, '80 301
Almond Roca, '86 49
Apples, Candied Red, '81 217
Apples, Candy, '84 243
Apricot Balls, '79 274
Balls, No-Cook Candy, '85 14
Bourbon Balls, '81 254; '83 315
Bourbon Balls, Chocolate, '84 298
Brandy Balls, '86 319
Brittle with Crushed Peanuts, '87 184
Buckeyes, '85 321
Butter Creams, '80 302
Buttermilk Candy, '80 302
Caramel Corn Candy, '84 243
Caramel Good Stuff, Baked, '80 284
Caramel-Peanut Squares, '85 247
Chocolate Brittle, '83 315
Chocolate Brittle, Quick, '82 114
Chocolate-Coconut Almond Drops, '87 223
Chocolate-Covered Cherries, '81 286; '84 298

Chocolate-Covered Pecan Fritters, '79 205
Chocolate-Covered Pretzels, '82 295
Chocolate Drops, '84 111
Chocolate Greeting Card, '83 40
Chocolate-Nut Log Candy, '86 335
Chocolate-Peanut Butter Balls, '80 87
Chocolate-Peanut Clusters, '81 16
Chocolate Rum Balls, '80 302
Chocolates, Liqueur Cream-Filled, '87 258
Chocolate Spiders, '85 236
Chocolates, Spirited, '86 278
Chocolate Truffles, '85 114
Chocolate Velvets, '84 298
Coconut-Almond Balls, '84 256
Coconut-Black Walnut Bonbons, '82 307
Coconut Candy, '79 272; '80 250
Corn Brittle, Crunchy, '85 208
Crème de Cacao Balls, '86 266
Crystal Candy, '84 299
Date Loaf Candy, '80 302
Date Logs, '79 274
Divinity, Apricot, '83 297
Divinity, Christmas, '81 286
Divinity, Peanut, '85 233; '87 M278
Divinity, Pink, '86 49
Frosting, Chocolate Candy, '81 238
Fruit Balls, '82 296; '84 299
Fudge
    Cherry Nut Fudge, '83 315
    Chocolate Fudge, '82 20
    Chocolate-Peanut Butter Fudge, '87 257
    Coffee-Chip Fudge, '86 74
    Cream Cheese Fudge, '84 111
    Creamy Dark Fudge, '82 295
    Creamy Fudge, '81 218
    Double-Good Fudge, '79 M263
    Double Good Fudge, '87 M278
    Fast Fudge, '79 274
    Fudge, '86 266
    Mocha Fudge, Holiday, '84 298
    Nut Fudge, Quick, '83 316
    Nutty White Fudge, '81 253
    Peanut Butter Fudge, '80 302
    Peanut Fudge, Double, '85 91
    Pecan Fudge, Creamy, '84 321
    Penuche, '79 272
    Pistachio Fudge, '83 298
    Scotch Ring, Fudge, '79 273
    Tiger Butter, '86 48
Kentucky Colonels, '79 273
Lollipops, Colorful Molded, '81 218
Marzipan, '83 306
Millionaires, '79 M262
Mints, Easy Holiday, '84 299
Mints, Party, '79 273; '81 119
Mint Twists, '86 106
Molded Candies, '84 40
Nut Clusters, '81 254
Nuts, Candied, '81 261
Orange Peel, Candied, '81 286
Peanut Brittle, '79 M263; '80 87; '84 298
Peanut Brittle, Golden, '83 223
Peanut Brittle, Never-Fail, '79 273
Peanut Brittle, Orange, '80 302
Peanut Butter-Chocolate Balls, '80 269
Peanut Butter-Chocolate Candy Squares, '82 56
Peanut Butter Creams, '79 273
Peanut Butter Easter Eggs, '87 86
Peanut Butter Temptations, '84 29
Peanut Butter Yummies, '83 223

Candies *(continued)*

Peanut Clusters, **'87** 184
Peanutty Clusters, **'83** 143
Pecan Clusters, **'81** 266
Pecan Clusters, Roasted, **'85** 233
Pecan-Coconut Clusters, **'86** M251
Pecan Pralines, Original, **'81** 11
Pecan Rolls, **'79** 285
Pecans, Brown Sugar, **'81** 266
Pecans, Glazed, **'81** 254
Pecans, Honeycomb, **'84** 300
Pecans, Orange, **'84** 299
Pecans, Spiced, **'79** 296; **'81** 286
Pecans, Spicy, **'81** 289
Pecans, Sugar-and-Honey, **'86** 319
Peppermint Patties, **'86** 278
Potato Candy, **'79** 273
Praline Clusters, Dark, **'86** 313
Praline Delights, Spicy, **'84** 299
Pralines, **'79** 272; **'86** M288
Pralines, Butterscotch, **'81** 253
Pralines, Creamy, **'80** 198
Pralines, Dark, **'83** 52
Pralines, Maple-Pecan, **'83** 222
Pralines, New Orleans-Style, **'86** 335
Pralines, Plantation Coffee, **'86** 241
Pralines, Southern, **'79** M263
Pralines, Texas-Size, **'79** 186
Quemada (Burnt-Sugar Candy), **'87** 38
Raisin Candy, Mixed, **'84** 111
Rocky Road, **'84** 298
Taffy, Old-Fashioned, **'80** 302
Toffee, English, **'79** 273
Toffee, Nutty, **'79** M263
Truffles, Almond, **'83** 298
Truffles, Amaretto Dessert, **'86** 319
Truffles, White Chocolate, **'87** 45

Canning. *See also* Pickles and Relishes.

Apple Rings, Cinnamon, **'85** 107
Asparagus, Pickled, **'83** 46
Bean Salad, Pickled Green, **'82** 239
Beans, Appalachian Green, **'81** 215
Beans, Green, **'80** 126
Beans, Green, Snap, or Wax, **'85** 105
Beans, Lima, **'80** 127
Beets, Pickled, **'81** 216
Berries (except Strawberries), **'80** 128
Catsup, Homemade, **'85** 188
Chili Sauce, **'81** 175
Chili Sauce, Chunky, **'85** 188
Chow-Chow, **'82** 196
Corn, Cold-Pack, **'81** 216
Corn, Cream-Style, **'80** 127; **'85** 106
Corn, Whole Kernel, **'85** 106
Cranberry Conserve, **'83** 279
Fruit Juices, **'85** 107
Fruit, Unsweetened Mixed, **'83** 182
Nectarines in Apple Juice, **'83** 183
Okra, **'80** 127
Peaches, **'80** 128
Peaches and Pears, **'85** 106
Peaches, Honey-Sweet, **'85** 107
Peas, Black-Eyed, Field, and
   Crowder, **'80** 126
Piccalilli, Kentucky, **'81** 216
Sauerkraut, Homemade, **'81** 216
Squash, Summer, **'80** 127; **'85** 105
Succotash, **'85** 106
Tomato Catsup, Spicy, **'83** 182
Tomatoes, **'80** 128; **'85** 106
Tomatoes, Stewed, **'83** 182
Tomatoes with Okra, **'85** 106

Tomato Juice, Spicy, **'85** 189
Tomato Puree, Seasoned, **'83** 182
Vegetable Soup, **'80** 128; **'85** 106

Cantaloupe. *See* Melons.

Caramel

Apples, Caramel, **'79** 220
Apples, Old English Caramel, **'85** 231
Baked Caramel Good Stuff, **'80** 284
Bars, Oatmeal-Caramel, **'85** 247
Bread, Caramel, **'82** 75
Cake, Chocolate-Caramel-Nut, **'83** 23
Cake, Creamy Caramel Layer, **'81** 71
Candy, Caramel Corn, **'84** 243
Cobbler, Peach-Caramel, **'86** 300; **'87** 178
Corn, Baked Caramel, **'81** 218
Crème d'Ange, **'83** 91
Drizzle, Caramel, **'86** 247
Frosting, Caramel, **'81** 278, M289;
   '82 314; **'83** 43; **'84** 39, 263;
   '86 239; **'87** 265
Frosting, Creamy Caramel, **'81** 71
Frosting, Easy Caramel, **'87** 39
Frosting, Favorite Caramel, **'83** 106
Helado, Caramel-Vanilla (Caramel-Vanilla
   Ice Cream), **'81** 67
Millionaires, **'79** M262
Pie, Burnt Caramel, **'82** 53
Pie, Caramel-Banana, **'86** M165
Pie, Caramel Ice Cream, **'82** 181
Pie, Caramel-Peanut, **'86** 259
Pie, Caramel-Pecan Apple, **'85** 247
Pie, Luscious Caramel Banana, **'79** 115
Pies, Coconut-Caramel, **'87** 260
Popcorn, Caramel, **'79** 219; **'86** M212
Popcorn, Crispy Caramel, **'85** 247
Ring, Caramel-Orange Coffee, **'80** 45
Ring, Easy Caramel, **'85** M89
Rolls, Caramel Breakfast, **'79** 193
Rolls, Caramel-Nut, **'86** 312
Sauce, Caramel, **'79** 79
Sauce, Easy Caramel, **'87** 38
Squares, Caramel-Peanut, **'85** 247
Squares, Chocolate-Caramel Layer, **'79** 83
Syrup, Caramel, **'82** 43
Tarts, Caramel, **'82** 43

Carrots

Aloha Carrots, **'85** 261
Ambrosia, Carrot-Marshmallow, **'80** 5
Apricot Carrots, **'84** 6
Aspic, Orange-and-Carrot, **'86** 199
Bake, Creamy Carrot, **'85** 67
Ball, Carrot-Cheese, **'86** 325
Balls, Carrot-, **'79** 178
Bourbonnaise, Baby Carrots, **'85** 89
Braised Carrots and Celery, **'86** 327
Brandied Carrots, **'87** 253
Brandy Sauce, Carrots in, **'83** 86

Bread, Carrot-Pineapple, **'82** 210
Bread, Pineapple-Carrot, **'79** 106
Bread, Tasty Carrot, **'84** 328
Bread, Three-C, **'81** 284

Bread, Zucchini-Carrot, **'83** 190
Brussels Sprouts, Carrots and, **'82** 300
Cake, Applesauce Carrot, **'81** 202
Cake, Blue Ribbon Carrot, **'81** 70
Cake, Carrot, **'79** 45; **'82** 137; **'84** 315
Cake, Carrot Pound, **'87** 41
Cake, Carrot Pudding, **'83** 24
Cake, Coconut-Pecan Carrot, **'84** 322
Cake, Easy Carrot, **'83** 215
Cake, Easy Carrot Snack, **'82** 235
Cake, Fresh Coconut-Carrot, **'80** 299
Cake, Old-Fashioned Carrot, **'83** M232
Cake, Old-South Carrot, **'80** 120
Cake, Quick-and-Easy Carrot, **'84** 150
Cake, Spiced Carrot, **'87** 296
Cake, Spicy Fruited Carrot, **'85** 117
Candied Carrots, **'82** 269; **'83** 225
Caprice, Carrots, **'84** 6
Casserole, Carrot, **'86** 279; **'87** 285
Casserole, Carrot and Zucchini, **'83** 256
Casserole, Cauliflower-and-Carrot, **'83** 280
Casserole, Scrumptious Carrot, **'84** 328
Casserole, Squash-Carrot, **'81** 157
Combo, Carrot, **'79** 45
Cookies, Carrot, **'82** 137
Cookies, Carrot-Orange, **'83** 149
Cookies, Frosted Carrot, **'81** 7
Cornbread, Carrot, **'80** 89; **'81** 163
Cupcakes, Carrot-Bran, **'82** 16
Deviled Carrots, **'83** 322
Dilled Baby Carrots, **'84** 80
Dilled Carrots, **'85** 24
Dill-Spiced Carrots, **'87** 200
Dilly Carrots, **'85** 85
Fried Carrot Balls, **'82** 16
Garden Surprise, **'83** 112
Ginger Carrots, **'83** 9; **'85** 139
Gingered Carrots, **'85** 95
Glazed Carrots, **'81** 304; **'83** 117; **'85** 258
Glazed Carrots and Onions, **'83** 25;
   '87 128
Glazed Carrots, Apricot, **'80** 89
Glazed Carrots, Ginger-, **'87** 68
Glazed Carrots, Honey-, **'80** 115; **'84** 121;
   '85 18
Glazed Carrots, Lemon-, **'84** 16
Glazed Carrots, Orange-, **'79** 12;
   '81 M165
Glazed Carrots, Spice-, **'83** M58
Glazed Carrots with Bacon and
   Onion, **'87** 200
Glazed Carrots with Grapes, **'82** 287
Golden Carrots, **'85** 267
Harvard Carrots, **'83** 117
Herbed Carrots and Onions, **'87** 31
Honey-Kissed Carrots, **'84** 122
Horseradish Glaze, Carrots with, **'85** 66
Julienne Carrots, How to
   Prepare, **'84** 120
Julienne Carrots, Sautéed, **'82** 91
Julienne Carrots with Walnuts, **'84** 188
Julienne, Tarragon Carrots, **'84** 329
Julienne, Turnips and Carrots, **'86** 295
Lemon Carrots, **'82** 300; **'83** 111
Loaf, Carrot-Nut, **'83** 117
Madeira, Carrots, **'80** 125; **'83** 281
Marinated Carrots, **'86** 108, 111
Marinated Carrots, Creamy, **'87** 200
Marinated Carrots, Crispy, **'81** 7
Marmalade, Carrot-Citrus, **'81** 148
Marsala, Carrots, **'83** 56
Medley, Carrot-Lima-Squash, **'80** 123
Minted Carrots, **'81** 101

Minted Carrots, Saucy, '82 252
Muffins, Carrot-and-Raisin, '87 24
Muffins, Carrot-Date-Nut, '86 262
Muffins, Carrot-Pineapple, '81 6
Orange-Raisin Carrots, '80 24
Orange Sauce, Carrots in, '82 107
Parsleyed Turnips and Carrots, '79 253
Patties, Carrot, '80 89
Pecans, Carrots and Celery with, '84 254
Pie, Carrot, '83 117
Pie, Carrot Custard, '79 45
Pie, Carrot Ice Cream, '86 200
Pie, Cauliflower-Carrot, '82 191
Pineapple Carrots, '83 198
Polynesian, Carrots, '79 45
Puff, Carrot, '84 328
Puffs, Carrot, '87 200
Ring, Festive Carrot, '82 16
Ring, Rice-Carrot, '79 246
Salad, Apple-Carrot, '85 22
Salad, Carrot, '82 137
Salad, Carrot-Ambrosia, '81 252
Salad, Carrot-and-Zucchini, '83 240
Salad, Carrot-Raisin, '83 117; '84 174;
  '87 10
Salad, Carrot-Tangerine, '83 316; '84 16
Salad, Creamy Carrot-Nut, '86 331
Salad, Favorite Carrot, '80 33
Salad, Fruity Carrot-and-Seed, '86 223
Salad, Orange-Carrot, '80 89; '84 325
Salad, Shredded Carrot, '80 178
Salad, Simple Carrot, '82 101; '84 152
Salad, Sunshine Carrot, '82 132
Salad, Turkey-Carrot, '86 283
Saucy Carrots, '87 41
Savory Sauce, Lima Beans and Carrots
  with, '84 196
Scalloped Carrots, '81 6
Scalloped Carrots-and-Celery, '84 M112
Soufflé, Carrot, '79 73
Soufflé, Carrots, '83 265
Soup, Carrot, '80 88
Soup, Carrot-Leek, '86 34
Soup, Carrot-Orange, '79 172
Soup, Cheesy Carrot, '81 262
Soup, Cream of Carrot, '81 307
Soup, Curried Carrot, '82 157
Soup, Savory Carrot, '84 107
Special Carrots, '81 108; '84 6
Squares, Carrot, '79 256
Squares, Golden Carrot-Lemon, '80 40
Stuffed Carrots, '86 324; '87 40
Sunshine Carrots, '82 16; '83 25
Sweet-and-Sour Carrots, '82 137
Sweet-and-Sour Green Beans and
  Carrots, '83 6
Tarragon Carrots, '83 173
Tipsy Carrots, '87 40
Toss, Carrot-Fruit, '82 235
Tropical Carrots, '84 34
Veal and Carrots, Company, '85 22
Veal and Carrots in Wine
  Sauce, '86 M139
Wine, Carrots in White, '81 109
Wine Sauce, Carrots in, '80 88
Wine Sauce, Veal and Carrots in, '81 31
Zesty Carrots, '84 5
Zucchini and Carrots, Buttered, '83 252
Zucchini, Carrots and, '84 262

Casseroles
Apple-Cheese Casserole, '84 287
Apple-Egg Casserole, '85 44
Barley Casserole, '84 281

Bean
  Baked Bean Medley, '80 100
  Baked Beans, Hawaiian-Style, '86 210
  Baked Beans, Three-Meat, '86 210
  Baked Beans with Ham, '80 136
  Beef-and-Bean Bake, Cheesy, '82 89
  Green Bean and Artichoke Casserole,
    Italian, '85 81
  Green Bean Casserole, '79 106;
    '84 145
  Green Bean Casserole, Easy, '87 284
  Green Bean Salad, Hot, '86 298
  Green Beans au Gratin, '80 116
  Green Beans, French
    Quarter, '80 298; '81 26
  Green Beans in Sour Cream, '80 116
  Green Beans, Italian, '85 147
  Green Beans Italian, '87 10
  Green Bean Surprise, '86 9
  Green Beans with Sour
    Cream, '82 90

  Lentils with Cheese, Baked, '84 113
  Lima-Bacon Bake, '86 9
  Lima Bean Casserole, '79 189;
    '83 313; '86 225; '87 284
  Lima Bean Casserole, Spicy, '79 189
  Lima Bean Casserole, Swiss, '80 191
  Lima Bean Garden Casserole,
    '83 218; '84 246
  Lima Beans Deluxe, '79 289; '80 26
  Lima Beans, Savory, '83 219; '84 246
  Lima Beans, Super, '79 189
  Lima Beans with Canadian
    Bacon, '84 245
  Lima Casserole, Ham and, '79 192
  Limas, Spanish Cheese, '86 225
  Mexican Bean Casserole,
    Spicy, '84 114
  Three-Bean Bake, '81 155
Cheese Bake, Continental, '81 89
Cheese Casserole, Feather-Light, '79 84
Cheesy Breakfast Casserole, '85 247
Chile-Cheese Casserole, '82 90
Chile-Hominy Casserole, '81 29
Chiles Rellenos Casserole, '79 84
Chili-Rice Casserole, '79 54
Chili-Tamale Pie, '83 68
Cornmeal Puff, '82 42
Cranberry-Apple Casserole, '83 311
Egg-and-Cheese Casserole, '84 293
Egg-and-Cheese Puff, '85 45
Egg and Rice Bake, '83 119
Egg Casserole, '83 311
Egg Casserole, Brunch, '86 329
Egg Casserole, Cheesy, '81 244; '86 15
Egg Casserole, Scrambled, '80 51; '86 241

Egg-Mushroom Casserole, '83 49
Eggs, Bruncheon, '83 83
Eggs, Creole, '82 42
Egg Soufflé Casserole, '83 55
Enchilada Casserole, '87 287
Enchilada Casserole, Green, '79 76
Fruit Bake, Hot, '81 270
Fruit Casserole, Sherried, '80 284
Fruit, Gingered Baked, '81 232
Grits, Baked Cheese-and-Garlic, '83 292
Grits Casserole, Cheesy, '81 270
Grits Casserole, Garlic, '81 47
Grits, Garlic-Cheese, '86 180
Grits, Orange, '81 47
Hominy Casserole, Cheesy, '83 170
Hominy-Chili Casserole, '86 255
Hominy, Gold Coast, '83 52
Hominy, Hot Cheese, '84 77
Hominy, Jalapeño, '82 51
Hominy with Chiles and Cheese, '86 78
Huevos Rancheros, '82 197
Kale, Scalloped, '86 224
Macaroni and Cheese, Thick-and-
  Rich, '84 329
Macaroni Casserole, '84 220; '87 154
Macaroni, Glorious, '84 76
Macaroni-Mushroom Bake,
  Cheesy, '81 243
Meat
  Beef-and-Bean Bake, Cheesy, '82 89
  Beef-and-Biscuit Casserole, '83 75
  Beef-and-Noodles Casserole, '84 72
  Beef-and-Vegetable Chow Mein
    Casserole, '83 313
  Beef Bake, Zesty Cabbage, '80 300
  Beef Bake, Zucchini, '86 146
  Beef Casserole, Crusty, '82 88
  Beef Casserole, Spinach and, '79 192
  Beef-Macaroni Combo, '79 194
  Beef-Noodle Bake, Taco, '81 141
  Beef Supreme, '83 196
  Beefy Vegetable Casserole, '79 248
  Cheesy Mexican Casserole, '82 224
  Chiles Rellenos Casserole, '84 31, 234
  Chili Hominy Bake, '81 282; '82 58
  Cornbread Casserole, '81 91
  Cornbread Skillet Casserole, '83 243;
    '84 101
  Cornbread Tamale Bake, '79 163
  Corned Beef and Cabbage au
    Gratin, '83 16
  Corned Beef Brunch Bake, '82 44
  County Fair Casserole, '79 130
  El Dorado Casserole, '81 140
  Enchilada Casserole,
    Firecracker, '80 260
  Enchilada Casserole, Sour
    Cream, '82 113
  Five-Layer Meal, '81 140
  Ground Beef and Sausage
    Casserole, '80 260
  Ground Beef Casserole,
    Cheesy, '79 44
  Ground Beef Casserole,
    Creamy, '81 142
  Hamburger-Noodle Bake, '81 140
  Hamburger Pie, '81 92
  Italian Casserole, '80 81
  Layered Grecian Bake, '82 119
  Matador Mania, '86 19
  Moussaka, '87 166
  Moussaka Casserole, '79 179
  Moussaka, Corn, '87 190

Casseroles, Meat *(continued)*

Pastichio, '85 194
Pastitsio, '87 12
Pizza Casserole, Quick, '83 266
Sour Cream-Noodle Bake, '79 55
Spaghetti and Beef Casserole, '79 129
Spaghetti Casserole, '84 241
Spinach and Beef Casserole, '79 192
Spinach-Beef-Macaroni
    Casserole, '83 313
Taco Casserole, '80 33
Veal and Wild Rice
    Casserole, '79 180
Veal Cutlet Casserole, '79 109
Venison-Vegetable Bake, '87 304
Microwave
    Bacon-and-Eggs Scramble, '80 M267
    Beans-and-Franks,
        Polynesian, '84 M11
    Beans, Herbed Green, '83 M147
    Beef Casserole, Easy, '86 M58
    Beef Casserole, Layered, '82 M203
    Beefy Sausage Dinner, '80 M9
    Carrots-and-Celery,
        Scalloped, '84 M112
    Chicken Divan, '80 M10
    Chicken Divan Casserole, '82 M203
    Chicken Tetrazzini, Cheesy, '83 M87
    Ham-and-Potato Casserole, '83 M87
    Ham-Asparagus Dinner, '80 M10

    Macaroni-Ham Casserole, '81 M177
    Mexi Casserole, '83 M87
    Okra and Tomatoes, Fresh, '81 M165
    Onion-Potato Bake, '83 M195
    Pineapple, Scalloped, '84 M323
    Pork Casserole, Cheesy, '81 M74
    Potato Casserole, Creamy, '84 M113
    Sausage and Rice Casserole,
        Oriental, '82 M123
    Sausage Casserole, Easy, '87 M189
    Sausage-Egg Casserole, '86 M12
    Sausage Jambalaya
        Casserole, '82 M203
    Spinach Delight, '84 M144
    Squash Bake, Cheddar-, '84 M113
    Squash Casserole, Cheesy, '82 M21
    Squash Medley, Fresh, '81 M165
    Tuna Casserole, Easy, '82 M203
    Zucchini-Egg Casserole, '84 M113
    Zucchini, Italian, '83 M147
Pineapple Bake, '79 251
Pineapple, Baked, '84 287
Pineapple, Scalloped, '79 106
Pork
    Bacon and Egg Casserole, '81 225
    Bacon Casserole, Egg-and-, '85 248
    Brunch Casserole, '82 124
    Casserole, Pork, '83 116

Chop Casserole, Peppered
    Pork, '81 235; '82 25; '83 39
Chops and Potato Scallop,
    Pork, '82 114
Chops Italiano, Pork, '80 72
Fiesta Pork Bake, '79 265
Frankfurter Casserole,
    Layered, '79 64
Franks, Family-Style, '79 54
Ham and Broccoli Casserole, '81 133
Ham and Broccoli Strata, '80 261
Ham-and-Cheese Casserole, '87 78
Ham and Egg Casserole,
    Breakfast, '79 253
Ham and Lima Casserole, '79 192
Ham and Noodle Casserole, '80 300
Ham-and-Potato Casserole,
    Cheesy, '84 326
Ham-and-Rice Casserole, '84 75
Ham and Turkey Bake,
    Layered, '79 252
Ham Bake, Harvest, '79 210
Ham-Broccoli Casserole,
    Quick, '82 40
Ham Casserole, Apple, '79 213
Ham Casserole, Golden, '82 119
Ham Casserole, Macaroni-, '83 283
Ham Casserole, Vegetable-
    and-, '84 91
Ham Medley, Creamy, '84 90
Ham Pie, Golden, '87 78
Ham-Rice-Tomato Bake, '87 78
Ham Strata, Baked, '83 283
Ham Tetrazzini, '84 241
Salami-Corn Casserole, '80 209
Sausage and Broccoli
    Casserole, '80 33
Sausage and Noodle
    Casserole, '82 123
Sausage and Wild Rice
    Casserole, '83 196
Sausage Bake, Eggplant, '85 221
Sausage-Bean Supper, '86 52
Sausage Breakfast Casserole, '81 270
Sausage Casserole, '81 112; '82 12
Sausage Casserole, Cheesy, '82 124
Sausage Casserole, Country, '79 192
Sausage Casserole, Crunchy, '81 288
Sausage Casserole, Eggplant-,
    '84 215
Sausage Casserole, Grits-, '84 75;
    '86 241
Sausage Casserole, Ground Beef
    and, '80 260
Sausage Casserole, Hawaiian, '85 42
Sausage Casserole, Swiss, '80 209
Sausage, Country Grits and, '83 54
Sausage Egg Bake, '81 225
Sausage-Egg Bake, Smoked, '85 248
Sausage Grits, '86 92
Sausage-Lasagna Rollups, '80 236
Sausage-Mushroom Breakfast
    Casserole, '86 95
Sausage-Noodle Bake, '81 92
Sausage-Potato Casserole, '86 217
Sausage-Rice Casserole, '82 50;
    '83 75
Sausages, Baked Zucchini
    and, '80 300
Sausage Strata, '83 243
Sausage, Wild Rice and, '86 268
Sausage-Wild Rice Casserole, '84 250
Spaghetti Bake, Pork, '81 11

Supper Supreme, Sunday, '79 76
Vegetable-Pork Combo, '85 113
Poultry
    Chicken-and-Dressing
        Casserole, '81 263
    Chicken and Green Noodle
        Casserole, '80 32
    Chicken and Rice Casserole,
        '80 260
    Chicken-Asparagus Casserole, '83 76;
        '84 71
    Chicken Bake, Company, '80 301
    Chicken Bake, Spicy, '85 251
    Chicken-Broccoli Casserole, '79 48
    Chicken Casserole, Broccoli-, '82 33
    Chicken Casserole, Cheesy, '85 34
    Chicken Casserole, Macaroni
        and, '80 260
    Chicken Casserole,
        Make-Ahead, '84 241
    Chicken Casserole, Mexican, '82 143
    Chicken Casserole, Quick, '81 91
    Chicken Casserole, Rice-and-,
        '87 154
    Chicken Casserole, Sunday, '83 290
    Chicken Divan, Gourmet, '82 83
    Chicken Divan, Overnight, '83 198
    Chicken-Eggplant Parmigiana, '82 212
    Chicken Enchiladas, '80 301
    Chicken Enchiladas, Easy, '82 89
    Chicken, French Herbed, '86 89
    Chicken-Green Bean
        Casserole, '85 296
    Chicken-Macaroni Casserole, '85 219
    Chicken-Rice Casserole, '86 52
    Chicken Salad, Baked, '86 297
    Chicken, Scarborough, '80 38
    Chicken-Spaghetti Casserole, '84 15
    Chicken, Spicy Mexican, '82 89
    Chicken Supreme Casserole, '84 219
    Chicken Supreme, Hot, '81 76
    Chicken Tetrazzini, '79 268
    Chicken Tortilla Bake, '82 89
    Chicken Tortilla Casserole, '81 166
    Chicken-Wild Rice
        Casserole, '84 241; '85 65
    Crêpes Divan, Elegant, '81 91
    Duck and Wild Rice
        Casserole, '79 224
    Pollo, Chilaquiles con, '81 66
    Rice Casserole, Mexican, '83 31
    Turkey-and-Broccoli
        Casserole, '86 332

    Turkey-Asparagus Casserole, '86 284
    Turkey Bake, Layered Ham
        and, '79 252
    Turkey Casserole, '84 327
    Turkey Casserole, Golden, '80 271
    Turkey-Olive Casserole, '87 268
    Turkey Parmigiana, '87 193
    Turkey Salad Bake, '79 253
    Turkey Salad, Hot, '86 297
    Turkey-Spinach Casserole, '84 71
    Turkey-Swiss Casserole, '86 283
    Turkey Tetrazzini, Herbed, '86 47

Provolone Casserole, Seashell-, '80 189
Rice and Green Chiles, '83 152
Rice au Gratin Supreme, '86 78
Rice Bake, Green, '79 43
Rice Cassserole, '87 45
Rice Casserole, Brown, '87 118
Rice Casserole, Chili-, '79 54
Rice Casserole, Colorful, '82 199
Rice Casserole, Jalapeño, '81 66
Rice Casserole, Spanish, '79 192
Rice Casserole, Wild, '82 199
Rice Chantilly, '86 82
Rice, Fiesta, '84 76
Rice Mélange, '87 240
Rice, Mexican, '85 147
Rice Pilaf, '86 82
Rice, Spanish, '81 51
Rice, Spicy, '85 256
Rotini Romano, '87 193
Seafood
    Crab-and-Shrimp Casserole, '84 71
    Crab and Spinach Casserole,
        Creamy, '80 3
    Crab Bake, Quick, '87 192
    Crab Casserole, '79 228
    Crab, Dressed, '82 276
    Crab-Egg Casserole, '80 260
    Crab Imperial, '79 82, 116
    Crab Imperial, Elegant, '83 245
    Crabmeat-Broccoli Casserole, '84 232
    Crabmeat Imperial, '82 311
    Crab Puff, '79 116
    Fish and Potato Bake,
        Herbed, '79 287; '80 34
    Fish Casserole, Green
        Chile-and-, '84 32
    Oyster-and-Corn Bake, '83 34;
        '84 44
    Oyster-and-Spinach Casserole, '83 34;
        '84 44
    Oyster-and-Wild Rice
        Casserole, '83 34; '84 44
    Oyster Casserole, '79 228
    Oyster Casserole, Wild Rice-, '86 256
    Oysters Johnny Reb, '82 42
    Oysters, Scalloped, '79 225; '84 213;
        '86 132
    Salmon Casserole, '81 22
    Salmon Florentine, '83 43
    Scallop Casserole, '79 228
    Seafood Casserole, '87 109
    Shrimp and Rice Casserole, '79 228
    Shrimp au Gratin, '85 79
    Shrimp Casserole, '85 240
    Shrimp Casserole, Chayotes
        and, '80 230
    Shrimp-Crab Puff, '79 57
    Shrimp Delight, '79 192
    Tuna and Peas in Wine Sauce,
        Baked, '83 196
    Tuna-Broccoli Casserole,
        Tangy, '83 75
    Tuna Casserole, '82 119
    Tuna Casserole, Biscuit-
        Topped, '79 113
    Tuna Casserole, Nippy, '84 241
    Tuna-Macaroni Treat, '82 131
    Tuna Vegetable Casserole, '81 135
Vegetable. See also Casseroles/Bean.
    Asparagus-and-English Pea
        Casserole, '86 324
    Asparagus and Peas
        Casserole, '80 152

Asparagus-Artichoke
    Casserole, '86 279
Asparagus Casserole,
    Cheesy, '82 281; '83 32
Asparagus Casserole, Creamy, '80 76
Asparagus Casserole, Easy, '83 255
Asparagus Delight, '82 269
Asparagus, Holiday, '85 260
Asparagus-Pimiento Loaf, '84 86
Asparagus-Spaghetti Casserole, '80 77
Broccoli-and-Egg Casserole, '86 324
Broccoli-and-Eggs au Gratin, '85 289
Broccoli Bake, '81 246
Broccoli Bake, Cheesy, '83 255
Broccoli Bake, Cheesy Italian, '83 5
Broccoli Bake, Company, '83 279
Broccoli-Blue Cheese
    Casserole, '85 260
Broccoli Casserole, '87 284
Broccoli Casserole, Cheesy, '84 293
Broccoli Casserole, Italian, '82 6,
    280; '83 32
Broccoli-Cheese Casserole, '82 269;
    '84 9
Broccoli-Corn Casserole, '83 313
Broccoli Elegant, '81 267
Broccoli-Onion Deluxe, '81 75
Broccoli Puff, '82 95
Broccoli-Rice Casserole, '81 101
Broccoli Supreme, '82 34; '85 68
Broccoli-Swiss Cheese Casserole,
    '83 322; '85 M211
Broccoli with Rice, Holiday, '87 252
Brussels Sprouts, Casserole
    of, '86 294
Butternut Casserole, '83 280
Butternut Casserole, Sweet, '83 256
Cabbage au Gratin, '83 279
Cabbage, Caraway, '85 32, 289
Cabbage Casserole, Cheesy, '79 4
Cabbage Casserole, Creamy, '80 63
Cabbage Casserole, Italian, '87 42
Cabbage Casserole, Savory, '82 168
Cabbage, Cheese Scalloped, '81 87;
    '82 7
Cabbage, Scalloped, '82 269
Cabbage Wedges, Smothered, '81 87;
    '82 7
Cabbage with Apples and
    Franks, '87 42
Calabaza Mexicano (Mexican
    Squash), '81 196
Carrot and Zucchini
    Casserole, '83 256
Carrot Bake, Creamy, '85 67
Carrot Casserole, '86 279; '87 285
Carrot Casserole,
    Scrumptious, '84 328
Carrot Puff, '84 328
Carrots, Scalloped, '81 6
Carrots, Zesty, '84 5
Cauliflower and Asparagus
    Supreme, '79 287; '80 35
Cauliflower-and-Carrot
    Casserole, '83 280
Cauliflower and Peas with Curried
    Almonds, '80 82
Cauliflower Casserole, '86 10, 279
Cauliflower Casserole, Easy, '82 204
Cauliflower Casserole,
    Festive, '87 232
Cauliflower Casserole,
    Herbed, '79 221

Cauliflower Italiano, Cheesy, '82 300
Cauliflower, Main-Dish, '79 221;
    '80 83
Cauliflower Medley, '80 220
Cauliflower 'n' Chiles
    Casserole, '87 285
Cauliflower-Pea Casserole, '85 260
Cauliflower, Spanish-Style, '79 21
Celery and Cheese Casserole, '79 178
Celery au Gratin, '83 38
Celery, Baked, '82 98
Celery Casserole, '80 246
Celery Casserole, Creamy, '82 98;
    '83 255
Celery, Creamed, '79 247
Celery, Exotic, '83 280
Celery Oriental, '83 206; '85 116
Celery, Saucy, '83 39
Chayote-Cheese Bake, '80 230
Cheesy Vegetable Casserole, '81 103
Chilaquiles, '82 220

Corn and Cheese Casserole, '81 128
Corn and Tomato Casserole,
    '81 127
Corn-and-Tomato Casserole, '84 145
Corn, Baked Scalloped, '85 290
Corn Casserole, '79 247
Corn Casserole, Fresh, '80 165
Corn Casserole, Jalapeño-, '83 256
Corn, Elegant Scalloped, '86 268
Corn Pudding, '86 192
Corn, Scalloped, '80 164; '81 128;
    '86 111
Corn with Sour Cream,
    Baked, '86 170
Corn-Zucchini Bake, '79 178
Eggplant and Noodle
    Casserole, '82 230
Eggplant and Squash, '83 187
Eggplant-and-Tomato
    Casserole, '83 187
Eggplant and Zucchini,
    Italian-Style, '79 289; '80 26
Eggplant Bake, '80 82
Eggplant Casserole, '81 205; '84 217
Eggplant Casserole, Easy, '80 202
Eggplant Casserole, Elegant, '82 168
Eggplant Casserole, Flavorful, '79 92
Eggplant Casserole, Super, '80 202
Eggplant Creole, '86 110
Eggplant, Italian, '84 216
Eggplant, Lebanese, '81 24
Eggplant, Mexican, '83 187
Eggplant Parmesan, '83 186; '84 215
Eggplant Parmigiana, '81 19
Eggplant, Rolled Stuffed, '80 63

Casseroles, Vegetable *(continued)*

Eggplant Supreme, **'79** 188; **'86** 170
Fresh Vegetable Casserole, **'82** 225
Garden Casserole, **'82** 168
Garden Surprise, **'83** 112
Green-and-Gold Scallop, **'81** 159
Greens Dinner Bake,
 Grits 'n, **'84** 281
Green Vegetable Medley, **'79** 287;
 '80 34
Hash Brown Cheese Bake, **'82** 50
Medley, Baked Vegetable, **'81** 75
Medley Bake, Vegetable, **'81** 268
Mixed Vegetable Casserole, **'83** 208,
 256; **'86** 327
Mixed-Vegetable Casserole, **'87** 154
Mixed Vegetables, Scalloped, **'83** 5
Mushroom-Artichoke
 Casserole, **'87** 241
Mushroom-Cheese Casserole, **'83** 216
Mushrooms Supreme, **'84** 214
Okra Casserole, **'79** 160
Okra-Tomato Bake, **'80** 298; **'81** 26
Onion Casserole, Cheesy, **'79** 101
Pea Casserole, Cheesy
 English, **'83** 216
Pea Casserole, Curry, **'87** 154
Pea Casserole, Quick Fresh
 English, **'84** 145
Pea Casserole, Reunion, **'87** 11
Pea Casserole Supreme, **'82** 281;
 '83 32
Pea-Pimiento Casserole,
 English, **'83** 207
Peas, Chinese-Style Baked, **'86** 305
Peas, Party, **'79** 102
Peas with Rice, Black-Eyed, **'83** 12
Potato-Apple Bake, Sweet, **'83** 25
Potato-Apricot Bake, Sweet, **'85** 206
Potato Bake, **'83** 209
Potato Bake, Creamy, **'82** 201
Potato Bake, Sweet, **'80** 287
Potato-Banana Casserole,
 Sweet, **'86** 276
Potato Breakfast Casserole, **'80** 52
Potato-Broccoli-Cheese Bake, **'80** 114
Potato Casserole, **'87** 190
Potato Casserole, Cheesy, **'80** 244;
 '83 53
Potato Casserole, Easy, **'80** 114
Potato Casserole, Fluffy, **'80** 268
Potato Casserole, Hash
 Brown, **'81** 40
Potato Casserole, Irish, **'81** 263
Potato Casserole, Mashed, **'85** 296
Potato Casserole, Mushroom-, **'84** 5
Potato Casserole, Pear-Sweet, **'86** 280
Potato Casserole, Processor, **'86** 159
Potato Casserole, Saucy, **'81** 276
Potato Casserole, Sweet, **'79** 289;
 '80 26; **'85** 256
Potato-Cheese Casserole, **'79** 101
Potato Delight, Sweet, **'86** 335
Potato-Egg Casserole, Cheesy, **'84** 5
Potato-Eggplant Casserole, **'87** 166
Potatoes-and-Berries Casserole,
 Sweet, **'84** 231
Potatoes and Eggs au Gratin, **'79** 107
Potatoes and Turnips,
 Scalloped, **'85** 235
Potatoes-and-Zucchini au
 Gratin, **'84** 5

Potatoes, Bourbon Sweet, **'86** 324;
 '87 280
Potatoes, Candied Sweet, **'86** 111
Potatoes, Cheesy New, **'85** 156
Potatoes, Cheesy Scalloped, **'83** 82

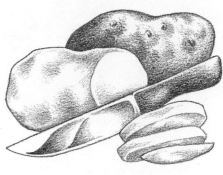

Potatoes, Double-Cheese, **'86** 6
Potatoes, Easy Oven-Baked, **'82** 202
Potatoes, Fluffy, **'84** 296; **'85** 196
Potatoes for Company,
 Saucy, **'82** 202
Potatoes, Garlic, **'84** 296; **'85** 196
Potatoes Gourmet, **'80** 114
Potatoes, Gruyère, **'83** 193
Potatoes, Hot Deviled, **'84** 296;
 '85 196
Potatoes, Jalapeño, **'84** 39
Potatoes, Jazzy Mashed, **'87** 192
Potatoes, Lemon and Nutmeg, **'80** 36
Potatoes Lorraine, **'87** 190
Potatoes, Missy, **'85** 259
Potatoes, Mushroom
 Scalloped, **'87** 191
Potatoes, Olive, **'80** 114
Potatoes, Parmesan, **'82** 270
Potatoes, Party Scalloped, **'87** 191
Potatoes, Scalloped, **'82** 300; **'83** 211
Potatoes, Sour Cream, **'84** 39
Potatoes, Two-Cheese, **'80** 114
Potatoes, Wayside Scalloped, **'79** 283
Potatoes with Feta Cheese, **'84** 295;
 '85 196
Potatoes with Ham Bits,
 Creamy, **'87** 191
Potatoes with Sherry and Walnuts,
 Sweet, **'86** 286
Potato-Rum Casserole, Sweet, **'84** 231
Potato Surprise, Sweet, **'81** 267
Potato-Tomato Bake, **'86** 17
Potato-Tomato Casserole,
 Saucy, **'79** 46
Potato Tuna Bake,
 Shoestring, **'82** 211
Pumpkin, Baked, **'82** 217
Spinach and Artichoke
 Casserole, **'81** 103
Spinach-and-Celery Casserole, **'84** 294
Spinach and Egg Casserole, **'82** 270
Spinach Casserole, **'79** 265
Spinach Casserole, Cheesy, **'81** 263
Spinach Casserole, Cottage
 Cheese-and-, **'84** 77
Spinach Casserole, Creamy, **'86** 111
Spinach-Cheese Casserole, **'83** 216
Spinach-Cheese Puff, **'84** 96
Spinach, Cheesy Topped, **'84** 85
Spinach, Creamy Lemon, **'82** 302

Spinach, Gourmet Baked, **'82** 180
Spinach-Parmesan Casserole, **'82** 281;
 '83 32
Spinach Rice, **'85** 146
Spinach Supreme, **'84** 77
Spinach Surprise, **'82** 42
Spinach with Cheese, Scalloped, **'79** 8
Squash and Apple Casserole, **'79** 209
Squash and Egg Casserole, **'80** 146
Squash, Bacon-Flavored, **'82** 158
Squash Bake, **'82** 107
Squash Bake, Cheddar-, **'84** 128
Squash Bake, Cheesy, **'80** 183
Squash-Carrot Casserole, **'81** 157
Squash Casserole, **'87** 163
Squash Casserole, Baked, **'83** 149
Squash Casserole, Blender, **'81** 212
Squash Casserole, Butternut, **'79** 210
Squash Casserole, Cheesy, **'79** 123
Squash Casserole, Company, **'81** 183
Squash Casserole, Crunchy, **'84** 293
Squash Casserole, Fresh, **'82** 204
Squash Casserole, Jiffy, **'81** M144
Squash Casserole, Summer,
 '81 102, 184
Squash Casserole, Two-, **'79** 101
Squash Casserole, Yellow, **'79** 179;
 '85 135
Squash Casserole, Zippy, **'80** 183
Squash, Mexican, **'83** 31
Squash, Posh, **'81** 159
Squash Puff, Butternut, **'85** 205
Squash, Tart Hubbard, **'80** 214
Tomato-and-Artichoke Heart
 Bake, **'85** 81
Tomatoes, Herbed, **'81** 102
Tomatoes, Italian-Sauced
 Green, **'85** 214
Tomatoes, Scalloped, **'84** 142
Turnip Casserole, **'83** 242; **'84** 229
Turnip Casserole, Baked, **'82** 274
Turnips au Gratin, **'84** 229
Turnips, Scalloped, **'79** 254
Zucchini and Tomato Bake, **'82** 158
Zucchini, Baked, **'83** 209
Zucchini Casserole, **'79** 157; **'87** 154
Zucchini Casserole,
 Cheese-Egg-, **'84** 114
Zucchini Casserole, Cheesy, **'82** 168;
 '84 145
Zucchini Casserole, Italian, **'85** 59
Zucchini-Jack Casserole, **'85** 296

Cauliflower
Almond Sauce, Cauliflower with, **'82** 270
au Gratin, Cauliflower, **'82** 204
Baked Swiss Cauliflower, **'79** 100
Beef and Cauliflower Oriental, **'80** 220
Beets and Cauliflower, Chilled, **'80** 137
Casserole, Cauliflower, **'86** 10, 279
Casserole, Cauliflower-and-Carrot, **'83** 280
Casserole, Cauliflower 'n' Chiles, **'87** 285
Casserole, Cauliflower-Pea, **'85** 260
Casserole, Easy Cauliflower, **'82** 204
Casserole, Festive Cauliflower, **'87** 232
Casserole, Herbed Cauliflower, **'79** 221
Cheese-Frosted Cauliflower, **'85** 68
Cheese Sauce, Cauliflower with, **'81** 101
Cheesy Cauliflower Italiano, **'82** 300
Dilled Cauliflower, **'83** 93
Festive Cauliflower, **'84** 34
Fried Cauliflower, **'83** 5; **'84** 248
Fried Cauliflower au Gratin,
 French-, **'79** 221; **'80** 82

Fried Cauliflower, Crispy, '80 220
Fried Cauliflower, French-, '86 211
Fried Cauliflower, Golden, '82 78
Fried Cauliflower with Cheese
  Sauce, '87 231
Garden Surprise, '83 112
Goldenrod, Cauliflower, '79 21
Herb Butter, Cauliflower with, '81 2
Lemon Cauliflower, Easy, '83 322
Main-Dish Cauliflower, '79 221; '80 83
Medley, Cauliflower, '80 220
Medley, Cauliflower-Broccoli, '81 69
Medley, Cauliflower-Snow Pea, '87 305
Oriental Cauliflower, '81 75
Peas and Cauliflower, '82 288
Peas with Curried Almonds, Cauliflower
  and, '79 221; '80 82
Pie, Cauliflower-Carrot, '82 191
Pimiento Sauce, Cauliflower with, '87 232
Quiche, Cauliflower, '83 86
Salad, Broccoli and Cauliflower, '81 280
Salad, Cauliflower, '79 221; '80 83;
  '81 225; '84 291; '85 240, 279
Salad, Cauliflower-Broccoli, '79 20
Salad, Cauliflower-Brussels
  Sprouts, '83 240

Salad, Cauliflower-Lemon, '81 23
Salad, Cauliflower-Pea, '87 231
Salad, Cauliflower-Vegetable, '85 158
Salad, Celery-and-Cauliflower, '83 39
Salad, Corned Beef-Cauliflower, '83 16
Salad, Creamy Broccoli and
  Cauliflower, '81 23
Salad, Creamy Cauliflower, '82 102
Salad, Crunchy Cauliflower, '80 4; '82 75
Salad, Layered Cauliflower, '83 240
Salad, Marinated Cauliflower, '82 303;
  '84 232
Salad, Orange-Cauliflower, '82 266
Salad, Savory Cauliflower and
  Pea, '81 280
Salad, Sweet-and-Sour Cauliflower, '81 2
Shrimp Sauce, Broccoli and Cauliflower
  with, '84 248
Soufflé, Cauliflower, '82 76
Soup, Cauliflower and Caraway, '82 264
Soup, Cream of Cauliflower, '87 M7
Soup, Cream of Cauliflower and
  Watercress, '83 126
Soup, Creamy Cauliflower, '82 76
Soup, Fresh Cauliflower, '84 279
Spanish-Style Cauliflower, '79 21
Supreme, Cauliflower and
  Asparagus, '79 287; '80 35

Toss, Cauliflower, '85 289
Toss, Cauliflower-Broccoli, '82 54
Toss, Cauliflower-Olive, '85 198;
  '86 147
Toss, Crunchy Broccoli and
  Cauliflower, '83 25

Caviar
Artichoke Hearts with Caviar, '79 142
Crown, Caviar, '83 78
Mold, Artichoke-Caviar, '87 239
Mousse, Caviar, '82 71; '83 258; '85 86
Pie, Caviar, '79 154
Potatoes, Appetizer Caviar, '86 223
Potatoes, Caviar, '84 80
Spread, Caviar-Cream Cheese, '84 256
Spread, Egg, Sour Cream, and
  Caviar, '85 279
Texas Caviar, '86 218

Celery
Almondine, Celery, '85 116
Amandine, Buttered Celery, '82 98
au Gratin, Celery, '83 38
Baked Celery, '82 98
Braised Carrots and Celery, '86 327
Braised Celery, Green Beans and,
  '84 254
Brussels Sprouts and Celery, '79 21
Brussels Sprouts with Celery,
  Lemony, '85 25
Carrots and Celery with Pecans, '84 254
Casserole, Celery, '80 246
Casserole, Celery and Cheese, '79 178
Casserole, Creamy Celery, '82 98;
  '83 255
Casserole, Spinach-and-Celery, '84 294
Creamed Brussels Sprouts and
  Celery, '83 322
Creamed Celery, '79 247
Croutons, Celery, '79 16
Curried Corn and Celery, '86 192
Dressing, Celery-Honey, '80 42
Dressing, Watermelon Salad with
  Celery-Nut, '80 182
Exotic Celery, '83 280
Orange Sauce, Celery in, '79 70
Oriental, Celery, '83 206; '85 116
Peas and Celery, Deluxe, '81 267
Peas with Celery, Skillet Snow, '84 123
Salad, Celery, '79 70
Salad, Celery-and-Cauliflower, '83 39
Salad, Chicken-Celery, '81 187
Salad, Overnight Alfalfa-Celery, '82 97
Salad, Pear-and-Celery, '87 56
Salad, Pineapple-Celery, '85 95
Sauce, Baked Fillets in
  Lemon-Celery, '84 91
Saucy Celery, '83 39
Scalloped Carrots-and-Celery, '84 M112
Soup, Burnet-Celery, '84 107
Soup, Celery-and-Potato, '84 279
Soup, Cream of Celery, '79 71
Soup, Light Cream-of-Celery, '82 279
Soup, Tomato-Celery, '83 M58
Stuffed Celery, '82 98; '86 324
Stuffed Celery, Creamy, '82 102
Stuffed Celery, Jalapeño, '79 70
Stuffed Celery Trunks, '85 115
Toss, Celery-Parmesan, '84 34

Chayotes
Bake, Chayote-Cheese, '80 230
Casserole, Chayotes and Shrimp,
  '80 230
Fried Chayotes, '80 230

Cheese. *See also* Appetizers/Cheese.
Aspic, Cheesy Vegetable, '81 73
Bake, Brie Cheese, '87 117
Bake, Chicken, Ham, and
  Cheese, '87 217
Bake, Pineapple-Cheese, '79 106
Banana Splits, Cottage Cheese-, '87 56
Beef Parmigiana, '85 234
Blintzes, Cheese, '82 146; '83 71
BLT's, Cheesy, '85 92
Breads
  Bacon-and-Cheese Bread, '83 255
  Batter Bread, Cheese-
    Caraway, '85 33
  Biscuits, Cheese, '81 288; '83 253;
    '85 32; '87 78
  Biscuits, Cheeseburger, '79 194
  Biscuits, Easy Cheese, '81 99
  Biscuits, Herbed Roquefort, '84 95
  Biscuits, Hot Cheesy, '80 186
  Biscuits, Petite Ham and
    Cheese, '79 193
  Biscuits, Tiny Cheese, '80 192
  Brie Bread, '87 143
  Buns, Cheesy Onion, '85 5
  Buns, Hurry-Up Cheese, '81 300
  Butter Cheese Dips, '80 46
  Cheddar Cheese Bread, '84 268
  Cheddar-Nut Bread, '85 41
  Cheese Bread, '82 174; '83 208;
    '87 11
  Cornbread, Cheddar, '83 285; '84 17
  Cornbread, Cheddar-Jalapeño, '85 3
  Cornbread, Cheesy Beef, '81 242
  Cornbread, Chile-Cheese, '87 171
  Cornbread, Cottage Cheese, '80 90
  Cornbread, Swiss Cheese, '79 60
  Cottage Cheese-Dill Bread, '83 154
  Cream Cheese Braids, '82 243
  Cream Cheese Bread,
    Orange-, '82 210
  Cream Cheese Loaves,
    Processor, '85 48
  Crescents, Cheese, '82 18
  Crusty Cheese Bread, '86 233
  Delights, Toasted Cheese, '79 37
  Dilly Cheese Bread, '83 5
  Easy Cheese Bread, '82 74; '86 17
  Fruit-and-Cheese Braid, '86 214
  Garlic Bread, Cheesy, '84 150
  Ham-and-Cheese Bread, '86 213
  Herb-and-Cheese Pull Aparts,
    '87 143
  Herb Bread, Cheese-, '84 M144;
    '85 283
  Herb Bread, Parmesan, '82 235;
    '83 41
  Herb-Cheese Bread, '85 70
  Jalapeño-Cheese Loaf, '84 76
  Lemon-Cream Tea Loaf, '84 50
  Little Cheese Loaves, '86 213
  Muffins, Blueberry-Cream
    Cheese, '86 14
  Muffins, Cheese-and-Pepper, '84 139
  Muffins, Marvelous Cheese, '83 96
  Muffins, Sausage-Cheese, '86 213
  Muffins, Sesame-Cheese, '86 16
  Olive Bread, Spicy Cheese-, '84 150
  Onion-Cheese Bread, '79 180; '81 8
  Onion-Cheese Supper Bread, '83 112
  Onion-Parmesan Bread, '84 284
  Parmesan Sesame Sticks, '81 39
  Parmesan Twists, '83 239

Cheese, Breads *(continued)*

Pimiento-Cheese Bread, '85 223;
  '86 166
Popover Puffs, Cheese, '85 6
Popover Ring, Cheesy, '80 45
Popovers, Cheddar Cheese, '85 41
Quick Cheese Bread, '83 9
Rolls, Cheese, '80 286
Rolls, Cottage Cheese, '81 78
Rolls, Ham-and-Cheese, '82 3
Rolls, Parmesan, '79 181
Rolls, Romano Sesame, '87 144
Sesame-Cheddar Sticks, '81 150
Sour Cream-Cheese Bread, '85 33
Spinach Bread, '87 144
Spoonbread, Cheddar, '82 196
Spoonbread, Cheese, '86 261
Swiss Cheese Bread, '79 60
Toast Bars, Bacon-Cheese, '79 36
Toast, Cottage-Topped French, '85 49
Twists, Cheesy, '84 284
Wine Bread, Cheese-, '87 254
Brownies, Cream Cheese Swirl, '79 51
Brownies, German Cream
  Cheese, '80 269
Brownies, Walnut-Cream Cheese, '84 240
Buns, Snack, '87 279
Burgers, Cheesy Bacon, '81 29
Burgers, Cheesy Beef, '83 217
Burritos, Cheesy Beef, '85 193
Butter, Cheese, '84 114
Cake, Coconut-Cream Cheese
  Pound, '85 297
Cake, Cream Cheese Coffee, '86 290
Cake, Cream Cheese Loaf, '84 151
Cake, Cream Cheese Pound, '81 290;
  '86 287
Cake, Regal Cream Cheese, '80 140
Cake Squares, Cream Cheese, '84 321

Casseroles
Apple-Cheese Casserole, '84 287
Asparagus Casserole,
  Cheesy, '82 281; '83 32
Bean Casserole, Swiss Lima, '80 191
Beef-and-Bean Bake, Cheesy, '82 89
Beef Casserole, Cheesy
  Ground, '79 44
Breakfast Casserole, Cheesy, '85 247
Broccoli Bake, Cheesy, '83 255
Broccoli-Blue Cheese Casserole,
  '85 260
Broccoli Casserole, Cheesy, '84 293
Broccoli-Cheese Casserole, '82 269;
  '84 9
Broccoli-Swiss Cheese Casserole,
  '83 322; '85 M211
Brunch Casserole, '82 124
Cabbage au Gratin, '83 279
Cabbage Casserole, Cheesy, '79 4

Celery and Cheese Casserole, '79 178
Celery au Gratin, '83 38
Chayote-Cheese Bake, '80 230
Chicken Casserole, Cheesy, '85 34
Chicken Tetrazzini, Cheesy, '83 M87
Chilaquiles, '82 220
Chile-Cheese Casserole, '82 90
Chiles Rellenos Casserole, '79 84;
  '84 31, 234
Continental Cheese Bake, '81 89
Corn and Cheese Casserole, '81 128
Corned Beef and Cabbage au
  Gratin, '83 16
Egg-and-Cheese Casserole, '84 293
Egg Casserole, Cheesy, '81 244;
  '86 15
Eggplant Parmesan, '83 186; '84 215;
  '86 53
Eggplant Parmigiana, '81 19
Feather-Light Cheese
  Casserole, '79 84
Grits, Baked Cheese, '80 49, 99;
  '83 311; '85 41
Grits, Baked Cheese-and-
  Garlic, '83 292; '84 78
Grits Casserole, Cheesy, '81 270
Grits, Cheese, '86 242
Grits, Garlic-Cheese, '80 47; '81 197;
  '86 180
Ham-and-Cheese Casserole, '87 78
Hominy Casserole, Cheesy, '83 170
Hominy with Chiles and
  Cheese, '86 78
Lentils with Cheese, Baked, '84 113
Limas, Spanish Cheese, '86 225
Macaroni-Mushroom Bake,
  Cheesy, '81 243
Mexican Casserole, Cheesy, '82 224
Mushroom-Cheese Casserole,
  '83 216
Mushrooms au Gratin, '81 108
Onion Casserole, Cheesy, '79 101
Pea Casserole, Cheesy
  English, '83 216
Pineapple-Cheese Bake, '79 106
Pork Casserole, Cheesy, '81 M74
Potato Casserole, Cheesy, '80 244;
  '83 53
Potato-Cheese Casserole, '79 101
Potato-Egg Casserole, Cheesy, '84 5
Potatoes and Eggs au Gratin,
  '79 107
Potatoes, Cheesy Scalloped, '83 82
Potatoes, Double-Cheese, '86 6
Potatoes Gourmet, '80 114
Potatoes, Gruyère, '83 193
Potatoes, Mushroom
  Scalloped, '87 191
Potatoes, Scalloped, '83 211
Provolone Casserole,
  Seashell-, '80 189
Rice au Gratin, '83 129
Rice au Gratin Supreme, '86 78
Rice Strata, Cheese-, '81 176
Sausage Casserole, Cheesy, '82 124
Spinach Casserole, Cheesy, '81 263
Spinach Casserole, Cottage
  Cheese-and-, '84 77
Spinach-Cheese Casserole, '83 216
Spinach-Parmesan Casserole, '82 281;
  '83 32
Squash Bake, Cheddar-,
  '84 M113, 128

Squash Casserole, Cheesy, '79 123;
  '82 M21
Swiss Sausage Casserole, '80 209
Tomato-Cheese Strata, '81 209
Turkey Parmigiana, '87 193
Turkey-Swiss Casserole, '86 283
Vegetable Casserole, Cheesy, '81 103

Zucchini Casserole,
  Cheese-Egg-, '84 114
Zucchini Casserole, Cheesy, '82 168;
  '84 145
Zucchini-Jack Casserole, '85 296
Catfish Parmesan, '79 184; '86 210
Cheesecake. *See* Cakes/Cheesecakes.
Chicken, Baked Parmesan, '83 320
Chicken Breasts Gruyère, '80 189
Chicken Breasts Romano, '79 218
Chicken Cordon Bleu, '81 304; '82 83;
  '86 37
Chicken, Crispy Parmesan, '80 M76
Chicken Monterey, '82 275
Chicken, Oven-Fried Parmesan, '81 97;
  '82 148
Chicken Parmesan, '83 184
Chicken Parmesan, Baked, '83 137
Chicken Rollups, Cheesy, '82 44
Chicken Skillet, Cheesy, '80 115
Chili-Cheese Dogs, '81 M176
Chili, Cheese-Topped, '82 M11
Chili, Cheesy, '82 310
Chunky Cream Cheese, '85 306
Coleslaw, Cottage, '80 64
Cookies, Cream Cheese, '80 282
Crab Bake, Quick, '87 192
Crabmeat au Gratin, '86 154
Cream Cheese, Cranberry-Amaretto
  Chutney with, '87 244
Cream Cheese Pinches, '87 85
Cream Puffs with Chicken Salad,
  Cheesy, '86 260
Cream-Style Cheese, '85 209
Crêpes, Cheese and Mushroom, '81 88
Crêpes, Cheesy Sausage, '82 240; '83 71
Crêpes, Mushroom-Cheese, '87 289
Crêpes, Spinach-Ricotta, '81 52
Crispies, Pecan-Cheese, '87 168
Crust, Cheese, '80 286; '86 264
Crust, Chicken Pot Pie with
  Cheese, '86 264
Cupcakes, Cream Cheese Party, '82 279
Delight, Strawberry Cheese, '79 50
Dessert Cheese, Nutty Date, '87 299

Dessert, Creamy Cottage Cheese, '87 191
Dessert, Lemon-Cream Cheese, '84 95
Dessert, Strawberry-Cream
  Cheese, '83 123
Dressing, Blue Cheese, '79 69; '82 166;
  '86 233
Dressing, Blue Cheese Salad, '82 94
Dressing, Creamy Blue Cheese, '81 150
Dressing, Creamy Blue Cheese
  Salad, '86 123
Dressing, Creamy Roquefort, '84 12
Dressing, Garden Salad with
  Tomato-Cream Cheese, '79 173
Dressing, Parmesan, '86 192
Dressing, Romano, '80 174
Dressing, Roquefort, '79 85; '80 74
Dressing, Special Blue Cheese, '80 74
Dressing, Tangy Blue Cheese, '87 81
Dressing, Zesty Blue Cheese, '79 104
Egg Medley, Cheddary, '81 M176
Eggs, Cottage, '85 44
Eggs, Cottage Cheese Scrambled, '81 142
Eggs, Cottage-Scrambled, '80 49
Eggs, Cream Cheese Scrambled, '81 287
Enchiladas, Cheese, '81 194; '85 154
Enchiladas, Cheesy Sour Cream, '79 25
Enchiladas, Saucy Cheese, '84 220
Fillets, Parmesan, '86 M112
Flounder au Fromage, Baked, '86 234
Flounder, Cheesy Broiled, '84 69
Fowl, Fancy, '81 76
Fried Brie, Walnut-, '86 244
Frills, Cream Cheese, '79 291
Frittata, Broccoli-Cheese, '81 243
Frosting, Coconut Cream Cheese, '86 60
Frosting, Cream Cheese, '79 45; '80 140,
  253, 299; '82 135, 244; '83 105, 215,
  M233; '84 201, 255, 315, 316; '85 118,
  121; '86 217, 337; '87 58
Frosting, Deluxe Cream Cheese, '80 120
Frosting, Fluffy Cream Cheese, '80 245
Frosting, Lemon-Cream Cheese, '81 157
Frosting, Nutty Cream Cheese, '85 117
Frosting, Orange Cream, '82 14
Frosting, Orange-Cream Cheese, '81 70;
  '82 16
Fruited Cream Cheese, '85 306
Fruit with Cheese, Luscious
  Fresh, '79 153
Fudge, Cream Cheese, '84 111
Glaze, Cream Cheese, '84 150
Grits, Good Morning, '87 156
Grits, Gruyère Cheese, '81 47
Grits, Jalapeño Cheese, '85 43
Grits, Quick Cheese, '83 M203
Grits, Sliced Cheese, '84 75
Ham and Swiss in the Pocket, '83 31
Ham and Turkey Specials, Cheesy, '84 14
Ham-Cheese Chips, '82 34
Ham Dinner, Cheesy, '84 90
Ham Towers, Cheesy, '82 M77
Hominy, Hot Cheese, '84 77
Kabobs, Swiss-Ham, '81 124
Kuchen, Cheese, '86 84
Lasagna, Cheesy, '82 224
Lasagna, Cheesy Spinach, '80 32; '83 204
Lasagna, Cheesy Vegetable, '79 84
Lettuce, Cheesy Stuffed, '79 175
Little Bits, '79 196
Loaf, Cheese, '87 92
Loaf, Cheeseburger, '81 236, 276
Loaf, Pepperoni and Cheese, '82 32
Macaroni and Cheese, '83 M7

Macaroni and Cheese, Baked, '82 199
Macaroni-and-Cheese Deluxe, '79 84
Macaroni and Cheese Deluxe, '80 236
Macaroni and Cheese Puff, '79 5
Macaroni-and-Cheese-Stuffed
  Peppers, '80 65
Macaroni and Cheese, Tasty, '83 288
Macaroni and Cheese,
  Thick-and-Rich, '84 329
Macaroni-and-Cheese with Wine, '86 78
Macaroni, Double Cheese, '82 224
Manicotti, Cheesy, '83 216
Manicotti, Stuffed, '83 M6
Mayonnaise, Parmesan, '86 79
Meatballs, Golden Nugget, '82 233
Meatballs, Mock, '81 243
Meat Loaf, Mozzarella-Layered, '79 71
Mold, Ambrosia Cream Cheese, '79 249
Mold, Cheesy Lemon, '79 241
Mold, Creamy Tuna-Cheese, '81 135
Molds, Heavenly Dessert Cheese, '85 209
Molds, Snowcap Cheese, '79 242
Noodles and Mushrooms, Cheesy, '79 84
Noodles, Cheesy Parmesan, '83 M7
Noodles, Ham and Swiss on, '87 108
Noodles, Parmesan, '83 118
Omelet, Cheddar-Vegetable, '83 205
Omelet, Cheesy Picante, '86 95
Omelet, Cheesy Vegetable, '85 49
Omelet, Ham and Cheese, '79 262;
  '80 123
Omelets, George's, '80 68
Omelet, Shrimp-and-Cheddar, '84 57
Omelet, Spinach-Cheese, '83 119
Omelet, Swiss Oven, '80 189
Omelet, Zippy Cheese, '87 287
Pancakes, Cottage Cheese, '79 115
Pastries, Cream Cheese, '80 250
Pastries, Date-Filled Cheese, '83 259
Pastries, German, '86 78
Pastry, Cheddar, '86 206
Pastry, Cheddar Cheese, '80 219; '82 194
Pastry, Cream Cheese, '82 39; '86 78
Pastry Shell, Cheese, '85 284
Pastry Shells, Cream Cheese, '86 13
Pastry Shells, Miniature Cream
  Cheese, '87 190
Pastry Tart Shells, Cheese, '85 216
Pâté, Cream Cheese, '80 154
Pâté, Liver-Cheese, '85 276
Patty Shells, Cream Cheese, '81 266;
  '82 249
Pears, Cheese-Filled, '81 268
Pears Stuffed with Cheese, '82 290
Pie, Apple-Cheese, '85 284
Pie, Apple-Cream Cheese, '81 247
Pie, Breakfast, '86 242
Pie, Broccoli-Cheese, '84 235
Pie, Cheese-Beef, '85 33
Pie, Cheesy Mexican Chicken, '82 142
Pie, Chocolate-Cream Cheese, '80 69
Pie, Cottage Cheese, '82 85
Pie, Green Chile-Cheese, '84 234
Pie, Lemon Cheese, '81 136; '82 146
Pie, Lemon-Cottage Cheese, '79 44
Pie, Lemon Cottage Cheese, '81 143
Pie, Mexican Cheese, '82 9; '83 69
Pie, Mincemeat-Cheese, '80 253
Pie, Quick and Cheesy Corn, '82 191
Pie, Tortilla, '85 M211
Pie, Yogurt-Cheese, '82 121
Pie, Zucchini-Ham-Cheese, '80 272
Pizza, Cheese-and-Mushroom, '83 226

Pizza, Double Cheesy Beef-and-
  Sausage, '86 77
Pizza, Gruyère-Chicken, '87 182
Popcorn, Bacon-Cheese, '86 74
Popcorn, Sesame-Cheese, '79 220
Pork Chops, Cheese-Stuffed, '84 81
Pork Tenderloin with Blue Cheese, '86 76
Preserves, Cream Cheese and
  Peach, '84 264
Pudding, Baked Cheese, '86 78
Pudding, Cheesy Bread, '83 68
Pudding, Corn-Cheese, '80 244
Puff, Egg-and-Cheese, '85 45
Puffs, Bavarian Cheese, '80 191
Puffs, Turkey-Cheese, '87 301
Quiches
  Bacon-Cheese Quiches,
    Miniature, '83 93
  Benedict Quiche, '80 M107
  Blue Cheese Quiche, '84 52
  Eggless Quiche, '87 220
  Green Onion Quiche, Cheesy,
    '83 194; '84 42
  Ham-Cheese Quiche, '79 26
  Jalapeño Quiche, Cheesy, '84 31
  Lorraine, Perfect Quiche, '79 127
  Lorraine, Quiche, '79 40; '80 M108
  Miniature Cheese Quiches, '80 150
  Sausage-Cheddar Quiche, '79 26
  Sausage Quiche, Spicy, '80 M108
  Spinach Quiche, Cheesy, '81 228
  Squares, Cheesy Hot Quiche, '79 124
  Swiss-Zucchini Quiche, '82 49
  Tasty Quiche, '82 264
  Vegetable Quiche, Cheese-, '81 228
  Zucchini Quiche, Cheesy, '83 312
Ramekins, Three-Cheese, '79 26
Rarebit, Cheese, '86 78
Rarebit, Uptown Welsh, '87 279
Rice, Chili-Cheesy, '79 43
Roll, Cheesy Meat, '82 136
Rollups, Date-Cream Cheese, '83 298
Rounds, Parmesan, '79 170
Rounds, Turkey-Mozzarella, '82 3
Salad, Blue Cheese-Pear-Apple, '81 224
Salad, Blue Cheese Tossed, '84 195
Salad, Cheddar-Pea, '84 82

Salad, Cheesy Apple, '86 301
Salad, Cheesy Fruit-'n'-Nut, '87 56
Salad, Cheesy Layered, '81 37
Salad, Cheesy-Vegetable
  Congealed, '86 199
Salad, Cottage Cheese-and-Fruit, '86 16
Salad, Cottage Cheese-
  Potato, '79 147, 285

Cheese (continued)

Salad, Cottage-Tomato, '85 163
Salad, Cranberry-Cheese Ribbon, '79 241
Salad, Creamy Roquefort, '79 73
Salad, Different Cottage Cheese, '85 328;
  '86 22
Salad, Dilled Macaroni-Cheese, '86 208
Salad, Frosted Lime-Cheese, '79 286
Salad, Hot Parmesan Potato, '79 78
Salad in Tomatoes, Cottage
  Cheese, '86 208
Salad, Lemon-Cheese, '85 240
Salad, Mexican, '81 36
Salad, Orange-Cottage Cheese, '79 44
Salad, Out-of-This-World Cottage
  Cheese, '79 44
Salad, Party Freeze, '82 145
Salad, Spinach-Blue Cheese, '82 166
Salad, Swiss-Apple, '84 81
Salad, Swiss Tuna, '86 186
Salad, Tomato-Feta, '81 246
Salad, Ziti-Cheddar, '85 165
Sandwich, Corned Beef and
  Cheese, '79 214
Sandwiches, Avocado, Bacon, and
  Cheese, '87 279
Sandwiches, Bacon, Cheese, and
  Tomato, '84 14
Sandwiches, Breakfast, '80 52
Sandwiches, Brown Bread-Cream
  Cheese, '87 M6
Sandwiches, Cheesy Chicken, '82 190
Sandwiches, Creamy Blue
  Cheese-Ham, '87 279
Sandwiches, Gingered Tea, '84 116
Sandwiches, Grilled Bacon-
  Cheese, '83 242
Sandwiches, Grilled Cheese, '82 M172
Sandwiches, Ham-and-Cheese
  Pita, '87 202
Sandwiches, Hot Crab-and-
  Cheese, '87 279
Sandwiches, Hot French Cheese, '82 3
Sandwiches, Hot Ham-and-
  Cheese, '85 299
Sandwiches, Open-Faced Cheesy
  Bacon, '80 78
Sandwiches, Open-Faced Cheesy
  Egg, '86 67
Sandwiches, Pimiento Cheese, '82 278
Sandwiches, Shrimp-Cheese, '85 242
Sandwiches, Tangy Ham-and-
  Swiss, '85 164
Sandwiches, Tasty Grilled, '84 30
Sandwiches, Toasted Chicken-and-
  Cheese, '85 242
Sandwiches, Yummy, '81 229
Sandwich, Tex-Mex Ham-and-
  Cheese, '86 4
Sauces
  Broccoli with Cheese Sauce, '82 107
  Brussels Sprouts with Cheese
    Sauce, '79 246
  Cauliflower with Cheese
    Sauce, '81 101
  Cheese Sauce, '79 M156; '81 43, 44,
    225; '82 M123; '83 49, 138, 188;
    '84 57; '85 92; '86 241
  Cottage Cheese Sauce, '87 232
  Cream Sauce, Cheesy, '82 79
  Devonshire Sauce, Processor, '86 337
  Easy Cheese Sauce, '79 22

Garlic-Cheese Sauce, '84 M70
Ham and Eggs on Toast with Cheese
  Sauce, '81 43
Lemony Cheese Sauce, '84 183
Monterey Jack Sauce, '84 293
Mornay Sauce, '80 120; '81 90
Mushroom-Cheese Sauce, '83 190;
  '86 48
Parmesan Cheese Sauce, '79 165;
  '80 162; '85 143
Potatoes with Cheese Sauce,
  Baked, '83 239
Potatoes with Cheese Sauce,
  Stuffed, '87 192
Rich Cheese Sauce, '81 89
Swiss Cheese Sauce, '79 35; '87 289
Swiss Sauce, '83 M195
Swiss Sauce, Creamy, '80 M53
Topper, Vegetable-Cheese
  Potato, '86 6
Tuna Salad, Cheese-Sauced, '87 M124

Turnips in Cheese Sauce, '84 229
Vegetable-Cheese Sauce,
  '85 M152
Scallops, Chip and Cheese, '80 301
Scallops Mornay, '80 164
Schnitzel, Swiss, '80 189
Shell, Rice-Cheese, '82 49
Shells, Cheesy Beef-Stuffed, '83 217
Shells, Cream Cheese, '79 2
Shrimp au Gratin, '85 79
Shrimp, Parmesan-Stuffed, '85 103
Soufflé, Cheese, '79 72, 261
Soufflé, Cheesy Spinach, '81 53
Soufflé Cups, Hot, '85 284
Soufflé for Two, Cheese, '81 226
Soufflé, Rice-Cheese, '79 270
Soufflés, Individual, '80 190
Soufflés, Individual Frozen, '80 52
Soufflé, Three-Egg Cheese, '87 234
Soups
  Anytime Soup, Cheesy, '81 307;
    '82 314; '83 66
  Bacon-Beer Cheese Soup, '87 M7
  Bacon-Topped Cheese
    Soup, '80 M224
  Beer-Cheese Soup, '84 246
  Broccoli Soup, Cheesy-, '86 258
  Broccoli-Swiss Soup, '86 6
  Carrot Soup, Cheesy, '81 262
  Cheddar Chowder, Hearty, '79 16
  Corn and Cheese Chowder, '80 228
  Cream of Cheese Soup, '83 99
  Golden Cheese Chowder, '80 73
  Ham 'n Cheese Chowder, '79 199
  Hearty Cheese Soup, '84 4

Monterey Jack Cheese Soup, '81 112;
  '85 M211
Onion-Cheese Soup, '87 81
Onion Soup, Double-Cheese, '85 227
Onion Soup, Double Cheese-
  Topped, '79 49
Oyster-Cheese Soup, '84 213
Roquefort Vichyssoise,
  Velvety, '83 223
Swiss-Broccoli Chowder, '80 73
Tomato Soup with Parmesan Cheese,
  Cream of, '86 161
Vegetable-Cheese Soup,
  Creamy, '81 244
Vegetable Cheese Soup,
  Creamy, '83 230
Vegetable Chowder, Cheesy, '80 25;
  '83 20
Vegetable Soup, Cheesy, '80 73
Velvet Soup, Cheese, '80 74
Spaghetti, Three-Cheese, '83 105
Spanakópita, '86 58
Spinach Ring au Fromage, '79 8
Spreads and Fillings
  Almond Cheese Spread, '87 292
  Aloha Spread, '83 93
  Apricot Brie Spread, '86 275
  Apricot-Cream Cheese
    Spread, '82 161; '87 158
  Bacon-Cheese Spread, '83 241
  Beer Cheese Spread, '81 160; '85 69
  Beer Spread, Cheesy, '87 196
  Caviar-Cream Cheese Spread, '84 256
  Chile-Cheese Spread, '86 297
  Chocolate Cheese Spread, '87 292
  Confetti Cheese Spread, '84 256
  Cottage Cheese Spread, '87 107
  Cottage-Egg Salad Spread, '82 146
  Crabmeat Spread, Layered, '83 127
  Crab Spread, Superb, '81 235
  Cream Cheese-Olive Spread, '82 35
  Cream Cheese Spread,
    Deviled, '81 235
  Cucumber and Cream Cheese
    Spread, '82 140
  Date Spread, Breakfast, '84 7
  Edam-Sherry Spread, '84 257
  Fruit and Cheese Spread, '81 245
  Fruit-and-Cheese Spread,
    Nutty, '87 246
  Garlic Pimiento Cheese
    Spread, '79 58
  German Cheese Spread, '79 82
  Gruyère-Apple Spread, '81 160
  Ham and Pimiento Spread, '80 285
  Hawaiian Cheese Spread, '87 158
  Herb-Cream Cheese Spread, '83 24
  Herbed Cheese Spread, '87 247
  Horseradish Spread, Cheese-, '84 222
  Jalapeño-Cheese Spread, '82 248
  Lemon-Cheese Filling, '79 68
  Olive Spread, Cheese-, '79 82
  Orange Cheese Spread, '87 292
  Pimiento and Three Cheeses,
    '86 296
  Pimiento Cheese, Chunky, '86 295
  Pimiento Cheese, Creamy, '86 296
  Pimiento Cheese Spread, '82 35;
    '83 93; '86 127
  Pimiento Cheese Spread,
    Low-Calorie, '85 215
  Pimiento Cheese, West Texas, '84 9
  Pineapple-Cheese Spread, '86 126

Pineapple-Cream Cheese
   Spread, '82 35
Ricotta Filling, '80 58
Sandwich Spread,
   Benedictine, '80 299
Spinach-Ricotta Filling, '81 53
Tomato-Cheese Spread, '81 157
Tomato-Cheese Spread,
   Fiery, '87 196
Tuna Spread, '83 174
Vegetable Sandwich Spread, '83 174
Zesty Cheese Spread, '82 140
Zippy Cheese Spread, '85 4
Squares, Lemony Cream Cheese, '82 159
Steak Cheese Skillet, Swiss, '80 106
Steak, Parmesan Round, '80 106
Steaks, Blue Cheese, '84 171
Steaks, Cheese-Stuffed, '81 17
Supper Supreme, Sunday, '79 76
Tart, Herb-Cheese, '87 98
Tart Milan, '87 70
Tarts, Cranberry-Cream Cheese, '80 154
Tarts, Cream Cheese, '84 74
Tarts, Lemon-Cheese, '79 2
Terrine with Goat Cheese, Black
   Bean, '87 120
Topping, Cheese, '86 233
Tortillas, Cheesy, '81 62
Tortilla Stack, Cheesy Chicken-, '86 3
Toss, Ham and Cheese, '79 55
Trout Florentine, Cheesy, '85 53
Tuna Cheesies, '82 191
Turkey Parmesan, '82 268
Veal Parmigiana, '81 227
Vegetables
   Beans au Gratin, Green, '80 116
   Beans, Cheese-Topped
      Green, '79 100
   Beans, Cheesy Green, '80 157
   Broccoli-and-Eggs au Gratin, '85 289
   Broccoli au Gratin, '82 M20
   Broccoli Fritters, Cheesy, '79 53
   Cabbage, Cheese Scalloped, '81 87;
      '82 7
   Cauliflower au Gratin, '82 204
   Cauliflower au Gratin,
      French-Fried, '79 221; '80 82
   Cauliflower, Baked Swiss, '79 100
   Cauliflower, Cheese-Frosted, '85 68
   Cauliflower Italiano, Cheesy, '82 300
   Chiles Rellenos (Stuffed
      Chiles), '82 220; '83 150
   Corn, Grilled Parmesan, '82 127
   Eggplant, Cheesy Stuffed, '79 188;
      '82 208
   Eggplant, Fried Parmesan, '87 166
   Eggplant Parmesan, '82 230
   Eggplant, Parmesan Fried, '79 189
   Hash Brown Cheese Bake, '82 50
   Limas in Onion Shells, Cheese
      and, '81 86
   Loaf, Pureed Vegetable-
      Cheese, '85 297
   Mushrooms, Parmesan
      Stuffed, '83 115
   Mushrooms, Ricotta-Stuffed, '85 20
   Okra with Cheese, '80 185
   Onion Bake, Cheese, '82 32
   Onions, Sherried Cheese, '82 32
   Potato-Broccoli-Cheese Bake, '80 114
   Potato Croquettes, Parmesan, '84 210
   Potatoes-and-Zucchini au
      Gratin, '84 5

Potatoes, Bacon-Topped Blue
   Cheese, '79 46
Potatoes, Blue Cheese
   Stuffed, '81 276
Potatoes, Cheesy, '82 211
Potatoes, Cheesy
   Bacon-Stuffed, '81 61
Potatoes, Cheesy Caraway, '86 17
Potatoes, Cheesy Chive, '79 46
Potatoes, Cheesy Crab-Stuffed, '86 17
Potatoes, Cheesy
   Frank-Topped, '83 3
Potatoes, Cheesy New, '85 156
Potatoes, Chicken-Cheese
   Stuffed, '86 55
Potatoes, Parmesan, '82 270
Potatoes Roquefort, '79 211
Potatoes, Two-Cheese, '80 114
Potatoes with Feta Cheese, '84 295;
   '85 196
Potato Skins, Cheese, '84 M239
Rutabaga au Gratin, '79 254
Spinach-Cheese Puff, '84 96
Spinach, Cheesy Topped, '84 85
Spinach, Savory Parmesan, '85 68
Spinach with Cheese, Scalloped, '79 8
Spinach with Feta, Lemon, '85 190
Squash Bake, Cheesy, '80 183
Squash Boats, Parmesan-
   Stuffed, '79 156
Squash, Cheesy Stuffed, '82 134
Squash Soufflé, Cheesy, '82 146
Squash with Cheese Sauce, Stuffed
   Yellow, '80 162
Tomato Cheese Puffs, '81 48
Tomatoes, Baked Cheddar, '85 43
Tomatoes, Cheese
   Herbed-Topped, '86 108
Tomatoes, Cheese-Topped, '81 160
Tomatoes, Cheesy Cherry, '83 135
Tomatoes, Cheesy Grilled, '79 150
Tomatoes, Cheesy Puff-Top, '86 187
Tomatoes, Cheesy Stuffed, '80 161
Tomatoes, Parmesan, '80 161
Tomatoes, Romano Broiled, '80 42
Turnip au Gratin, '79 289
Zucchini and Tomato au
   Gratin, '82 208
Zucchini, Ham and Cheese
   Stuffed, '79 157
Zucchini Parmesan, '81 108; '82 103
Zucchini, Parmesan, '81 234
Zucchini Pie, Cheesy, '82 103
Vermicelli, Shrimp and Feta Cheese
   on, '87 108
Wafers, Italian, '87 36
Cheesecakes. *See* Cakes/Cheesecakes.
Cherries
Bars, Delightful Cherry, '86 217
Bread, Cherry Nut, '81 306; '82 36
Bread, Maraschino Cherry Nut, '79 234
Bread, Quick Cherry-Nut, '85 55
Cake, Black Forest Cherry, '83 302
Cake, Cherry, '79 165
Cake, Cherry Blossom Coffee, '80 21
Cake, Cherry Bourbon, '82 287
Cake, Cherry Upside-Down, '82 56
Cake, Chocolate-Cherry, '84 200; '86 239
Cake, Maraschino Nut, '83 268
Cake, Quick Cherry, '81 238
Cake, Upside-Down Sunburst, '87 9
Cheesecake, Cherry, '79 50
Cheesecake, Cherry-Topped, '80 23

Chocolate-Covered Cherries, '81 286;
   '84 298
Cloud, Cherry-Berry on a, '79 94
Cobbler, Berry-Cherry, '83 270
Cobbler, Cherry, '82 91, 139
Cobbler, Fresh Cherry, '84 178
Compote, Cherry, '83 139
Cookies, Cherry Pecan, '82 136
Cookies, Chocolate-Cherry, '85 324
Cookies, Coconut-Cherry, '79 292
Cream, Maraschino Russian, '79 231
Crêpes Flambé, Cherry, '79 18
Dessert, Cherry Cordial, '84 312
Dessert, Holiday Cherry, '80 255
Drops, Cherry-Almond, '81 20
Filling, Cherry, '83 302; '84 225
Frosting, Cherry, '86 217
Fudge, Cherry Nut, '83 315
Glaze, Cherry, '83 143
Ice Cream, Cherry, '84 184
Ice Cream, Cherry-Nut, '86 129
Jubilee, Cherries, '79 18; '83 139
Jubilee, Quick Cherries, '82 M100
Jubilite, Cherries, '86 317
Muffins, Cherry, '82 105
Nuggets, Cherry Nut, '81 286
Pie, Easy Cherry, '82 M299
Pie, Prize-Winning Cherry, '82 57
Pie, Red Cherry, '83 192
Pie, Scrumptious Cherry, '83 250
Pie, Tart Cranberry-Cherry, '87 299
Rolls, Cherry-Almond, '84 M198
Salad, Best Cherry, '82 302
Salad, Cherry-Apple, '86 31
Salad, Cherry Cola, '80 104
Salad, Cherry Fruit, '87 236
Salad, Cherry-Orange, '79 74; '82 56
Salad, Delicious Frozen Cherry, '81 252
Salad, Elegant Cherry-Wine, '82 56
Salad, Festive Cherry, '84 265
Salad, Fresh Cherry, '83 120
Salad, Frozen Cherry, '79 126
Salad, Port Wine-Cherry, '86 11
Salad with Honey-Lime Dressing,
   Cherry, '83 139
Salad with Sherry Dressing,
   Cherry, '79 165
Sauce, Cherry, '79 91; '83 276; '84 91
Sauce, Chocolate-Cherry, '85 189
Sauce, Chocolate Cherry, '87 M165
Sauce, Elegant Cherry, '79 M156
Sauce, Ham Balls with Spiced
   Cherry, '81 112; '82 12
Sauce, Roast Ducklings with
   Cherry, '86 312
Sauce, Royal Cherry, '85 224; '86 83
Sauce, Spicy Cherry, '83 244
Slump, Cherry, '83 139
Snow, Berries on, '82 227
Squares, Surprise Cherry, '82 57
Stuffed Cherries, '85 81
Syrup, Cherry-Lemonade, '86 214
Tart, Cherry and Blackberry, '83 225
Tarts, Cheery Cherry, '80 238
Topping, Cherry-Pineapple, '87 126
Chicken
Acapulco, Chicken, '84 32
à la King, Chicken, '79 218; '83 137;
   '87 197
Almond Chicken and Vegetables,
   '86 21
à l'Orange, Chicken, '84 277
Andalusia, Chicken, '87 103

Chicken *(continued)*

Apple Chicken, **'85** 57
Ariosto, Shrimp and Chicken, **'79** 31
Artichoke Chicken, **'81** 97
Bag, Chicken in a, **'86** M57; **'87** 23
Bake, Chicken, Ham, and
  Cheese, **'87** 217
Bake, Chicken-Tomato, **'83** 35
Bake, Chicken Tortilla, **'82** 89
Bake, Company Chicken, **'80** 301
Bake, Crispy Chicken, **'83** 115
Baked Chicken and Artichoke
  Hearts, **'82** 260
Baked Chicken and Dressing, **'79** 296
Baked Chicken, Breaded, **'81** 76
Baked Chicken Breasts, Creamy, **'83** 24
Baked Chicken Breasts, Sherried, **'79** 83
Baked Chicken Breasts, Wine-, **'83** 177
Baked Chicken, Citrus Herb, **'85** 303
Baked Chicken, Fancy, **'79** 85
Baked Chicken, Herb-, **'82** 229
Baked Chicken in Wine, **'81** 109
Baked Chicken, Italian, **'82** 84
Baked Chicken Parmesan, **'83** 137
Baked Chicken, Tomato-, **'81** 281; **'82** 30
Baked Chicken with Wine-Soaked
  Vegetables, **'84** 277
Baked Italian Chicken, **'83** 184
Baked Lemon Chicken, **'85** 190
Baked Mustard Chicken, **'87** 10
Baked Parmesan Chicken, **'83** 320
Bake, Herb Chicken, **'82** 186
Bake, Pineapple Chicken, **'82** 120
Bake, Saucy Chicken, **'84** 220
Bake, Spicy Chicken, **'85** 251
Ball, Chicken-Curry Cheese, **'85** 118
Barbecued
    Bake, Barbecued Chicken, **'81** 97
    Breasts, Grilled Chicken, **'84** 172
    Bundles, Chicken-Mushroom, **'80** 157
    Charcoal Broiled Chicken, **'79** 90
    Chicken, Barbecue, **'86** 122
    Chicken, Barbecued, **'82** 97, 106;
      '83 103; **'85** 144; **'86** 153
    Cranberry Chicken,
      Barbecued, **'83** 178
    Cumin Chicken, Grilled, **'87** 142
    Garlic-Grilled Chicken, **'87** 180
    Golden Barbecued Chicken, **'83** 136
    Grilled Barbecued Chicken, **'81** 154
    Lemonade Chicken, **'82** 163
    Marinated Barbecued Chicken, **'79** 90
    Old South Barbecued Chicken,
      '82 97; **'83** 103
    Saucy Barbecued Chicken, **'83** 11
    Smoky Grilled Chicken, **'85** 160
    Tangy Barbecued Chicken, **'86** 186
    Yogurt-Lemon Chicken, Grilled,
      '81 111
    Zesty Barbecued Chicken, **'80** M76
    Zippy Barbecued Chicken, **'83** 213
Basil Chicken, **'87** 171
Bengalese Chicken, **'79** 12
Birds of Paradise, **'82** 224
Biscuit, Chicken in a, **'79** 263; **'80** 30
Bites, Curried Chicken, **'85** 40
Braised Bourbon Chicken, **'86** 51
Brandado, Chicken, **'84** 195
Breast of Chicken, Herbed, **'79** 100
Breasts, Island Chicken, **'84** 68
Breasts Lombardy, Chicken, **'82** 242
Breasts, Saucy Chicken, **'83** 184; **'87** 167

Broiled Chicken, Island, **'84** 288
Bundles, Cheesy Chicken-and-
  Ham, **'84** 261
Bundles, San Antonio-Style
  Chicken, **'85** 251
Bundles with Bacon Ribbons,
  Chicken, **'87** 68
Burgoo, Five-Meat, **'87** 3
Burgoo, Harry Young's, **'87** 3
Burgoo, Old-Fashioned, **'87** 3
Cacciatore, Chicken, **'80** 39; **'83** 118;
  '84 9; **'86** 42
Cajun Chicken over Rice, **'87** 268
Cashew Chicken, **'79** 255; **'80** 8; **'83** 21
Cashews, Chicken with, **'79** 207
Casserole, Broccoli-Chicken, **'82** 33
Casserole, Cheesy Chicken, **'85** 34
Casserole, Chicken-and-Dressing, **'81** 263
Casserole, Chicken and Green
  Noodle, **'80** 32
Casserole, Chicken and Rice, **'80** 260
Casserole, Chicken-Asparagus, **'83** 76;
  '84 71
Casserole, Chicken-Broccoli, **'79** 48
Casserole, Chicken-Green Bean, **'85** 296
Casserole, Chicken-Macaroni, **'85** 219
Casserole, Chicken-Rice, **'86** 52
Casserole, Chicken-Spaghetti, **'84** 15
Casserole, Chicken Supreme, **'84** 219
Casserole, Chicken Tortilla, **'81** 166
Casserole, Chicken-Wild Rice, **'84** 241;
  '85 65
Casserole, Macaroni and Chicken,
  '80 260
Casserole, Make-Ahead Chicken, **'84** 241
Casserole, Mexican Chicken, **'82** 143
Casserole, Quick Chicken, **'81** 91
Casserole, Rice-and-Chicken, **'87** 154
Casserole, Sunday Chicken, **'83** 290
Chafing Dish Chicken, **'82** 284
Chalupas, Chicken, **'79** 185
Chalupas, Chicken-Olive, **'81** 227
Champagne Chicken, **'85** 251
Champagne Sauce, Chicken Breasts
  with, **'86** 49
Charlemagne, Chicken, **'86** 293
Chilaquiles con Pollo (Tortillas with
  Chicken), **'81** 66
Chinese Chicken and Vegetables, **'81** 212
Chinese Chicken, Lazy Day, **'81** 3
Chinese-Style Dinner, **'84** 26
Chop Suey, Chicken, **'81** 227
Chowder, Chicken, **'83** 20
Chutney Chicken, **'86** 249
Company Chicken, **'80** 39; **'83** 125
Continental, Chicken, **'82** 274
Cordon Bleu, Chicken, **'81** 304; **'82** 83;
  '86 37
Cordon Bleu, Company Chicken, **'82** 274
Cordon Bleu in Mushroom Sauce,
  Chicken, **'86** 198
Country Poulet, **'86** 292
Crabmeat Stuffing, Chicken Breasts
  with, **'85** 302
Creamed Chicken, **'82** 49, 284; **'83** 14
Creamed Chicken, Company, **'82** 84
Creamed Chicken in a Shell, **'79** 138
Creamed Chicken in Patty Shells, **'86** 123
Creamed Chicken over Confetti Rice
  Squares, **'81** 282; **'82** 31
Creamed Chicken over
  Cornbread, **'86** 231
Creamed Ham and Chicken, **'81** M74

Creole, Chicken, **'86** 231
Crêpes, Chicken, **'80** 39
Crêpes, Chicken-Vegetable, **'83** 70
Crêpes, Creamy Chicken, **'81** 200
Crêpes Divan, Elegant, **'81** 91
Crispy Chicken, **'84** 152
Croquettes, Chicken, **'81** 133
Curried Chicken, **'86** 43
Curried Chicken, Regal, **'84** 110
Curry, Chicken, **'84** 110; **'85** 220; **'86** 21
Cutlets with Lemon, Chicken, **'85** 8
Dijon Chicken, **'81** 156
Dilled Chicken Paprika, **'86** 41
Dinner, Chicken-Mushroom, **'81** 3
Dinner, Chicken Peach, **'79** 77
Dinner, Healthful Chicken, **'83** 232
Dip, Hot Chicken, **'80** 86
Divan Casserole, Chicken, **'82** M203
Divan, Chicken, **'80** M10; **'87** M218
Divan, Curried Chicken, **'80** 83
Divan, Gourmet Chicken, **'82** 83
Divan, Overnight Chicken, **'83** 198
Divan, Sherried Chicken, **'80** 38
Dixie Manor, Chicken à la, **'85** 3
Dressing, Chicken and Rice, **'79** 288
Drumsticks, Cajun-Style, **'87** 159
Dumplings, Country Chicken and, **'85** 254
Dumplings, Easy Chicken and, **'86** 21
Dumplings, Old-Fashioned Chicken
  and, **'79** 55; **'83** 228
Dumplings with Vegetables, Chicken
  and, **'85** M56
Enchiladas, Chicken, **'80** 301; **'86** 296
Enchiladas, Easy Chicken, **'82** 89; **'86** 231
Enchiladas Terrificas, **'84** 32
Enchiladas with Spicy Sauce,
  Chicken, **'84** 76
English Muffin Delight, **'82** 45
en Papillote, Chicken and
  Vegetables, **'86** 145
Fancy Fowl, **'81** 76; **'82** 13
Fettuccine, Chicken-Pecan, **'86** 52
Fiesta Chicken, Spicy, **'84** 234
Filling, Chicken, **'81** 200
Filling, Chicken Divan, **'81** 91
Filling, Chicken-Olive, **'81** 227
Filling Luau, Chicken, **'79** 81
Fingers, Chicken Little, **'80** 249
Fingers, Herb-Baked Chicken, **'86** 249
Flautas, **'83** 199
Florentine with Mushroom Sauce,
  Chicken, **'87** 250

Fried
    Bites, French-Fried Chicken, **'85** 160
    Buttermilk Fried Chicken,
      Company, **'86** 177
    Cream Gravy, Fried Chicken
      with, **'85** 241
    Crispy Fried Chicken Breasts, **'80** 155
    Curried Fried Chicken, **'85** 160
    Delicious Fried Chicken, **'86** 156
    Drumsticks, Buttermilk, **'87** 175

Garlic-Flavored Fried
   Chicken, '79 147
Garlic Fried Chicken, '82 148
Golden Chicken Nuggets, '80 159
Herbed Fried Chicken, '87 91
Herb-Seasoned Fried Chicken, '80 8
Honey-Butter Sauce, Oven-Fried
   Chicken with, '85 18
Lemon-Fried Chicken, '79 77
Lemon Fried Chicken, '82 275
Mandarin Chicken, Crispy, '86 119
Mexican Fried Chicken, '81 166;
   '87 176
Nuggets, Lemon-Chicken, '87 283
Oven-Fried Chicken, '84 118
Oven-Fried Chicken, Crunchy,
   '87 163
Oven-Fried Chicken, Crusty, '79 77
Oven-Fried Chicken, Golden-
   Brown, '86 21
Oven-Fried Chicken, Nutty, '85 160
Oven-Fried Chicken, Southern, '86 37
Oven-Fried Parmesan Chicken,
   '81 97; '82 148
Oven-Fried Pecan Chicken, '84 288
Oven-Fried Sesame Chicken, '79 77
Sesame Chicken, '82 148
Spicy Country-Fried Chicken, '82 148
Spicy Fried Chicken, '83 5
Super Fried Chicken, '82 148
Traditional Fried Chicken, '82 148

Walnut Chicken, Deep-Fried, '87 175
Wings, Hot Buffalo, '87 176
Fruited Chicken en Crème, '83 264
Garden, Chicken-in-a-, '80 18
Ginger Chicken and Cashews, '85 M11
Glazed Chicken, Fruit-, '80 211
Gruyère, Chicken Breasts, '80 189
Gumbo, Chicken, '79 199
Gumbo, Chicken and Oyster, '81 198
Gumbo, Chicken-Ham-Seafood, '81 6
Gumbo, Combo, '81 198
Gumbo, Easy Chicken, '83 156
Gumbo with Smoked Sausage,
   Chicken, '81 199
Gumbo Ya Ya, '87 210
Hawaiian Chicken, '82 274
Hawaiian, Chicken, '81 80
Herbed Chicken, French, '86 89
Herbed Chicken, Sunny, '86 156
Herbed Chicken, Tangy, '87 M302
Honey Chicken, '82 55
Honey-Curry Chicken, '87 36
Honolulu Chicken, '85 52
Imperial Chicken, '81 238
Italian Chicken, '86 122
Kabobs, Chicken, '87 141
Kabobs, Chicken-Avocado, '82 9; '83 68
Kabobs, Good-and-Easy Chicken, '85 87
Kabobs, Hawaiian, '85 157
Kabobs, Marinated Chicken, '84 M144
Kabobs, Pineapple-Chicken, '86 M328
Kabobs, Sesame Chicken, '82 165

Kabobs, Soy-Chicken, '86 156
Kabobs Supreme, Chicken, '81 124
Kiev, Chicken, '80 39
Kiev, Cranberry Chicken, '87 250
Kiev, Oven-Baked Chicken, '86 37
Kiev, Oven Chicken, '82 83
la France, Chicken, '86 248
Lasagna, Chicken, '87 M302
Lemon and Wine, Chicken in, '83 281
Lemon Chicken, '81 M138; '86 173
Lemon Chicken, Sweet, '79 218
Lemon-Chicken, Sweet, '84 69
Lemon-Herb Chicken, '85 127
Lime Butter, Chicken with, '84 68
Livers
   Bits and Livers, Chicken, '84 222
   en Brochette, Chicken Livers,
      '84 222
   Italian Sauce, Chicken Livers
      in, '83 117
   Kabobs, Rumaki, '82 182
   Mushrooms, Chicken Livers
      with, '81 133
   Omelet, Chicken Liver, '82 44
   Orange Sauce, Chicken Livers
      in, '82 218
   Party Chicken Livers, '83 242
   Pâté, Chicken Liver, '79 153;
      '81 235; '83 108; '84 205
   Pâté Maison, '84 222
   Potatoes, Chicken Livers and, '82 218
   Rice, Chicken Livers with, '80 200;
      '81 58; '84 292
   Rice Dish, Chicken Livers
      and, '82 218
   Risotto, Chicken Livers, '82 218
   Roll-Ups, Chicken Liver and
      Bacon, '80 200; '81 57
   Rumaki, '80 M136
   Sautéed Chicken Livers, '80 200;
      '81 57
   Scrumptious Chicken Livers, '84 230
   Spread, Sherried Liver, '80 86
   Stroganoff, Chicken Livers, '80 200;
      '81 57
   Supreme, Chicken Livers, '81 298
   Turnovers, Chicken Liver, '79 141
   Wine Sauce, Chicken Livers
      in, '81 104
   Wine Sauce, Chicken Livers with
      Marsala, '81 76
Log, Chicken-Pecan, '81 290
Luzianne, Poulet, '86 197
Manicotti, Creamy Chicken, '85 60
Marinara, Chicken, '86 77
Marinated Breast of Chicken, '87 123
Marinated Chicken, '87 61
Marsala, Chicken, '83 137
Mexican Chicken, '80 124
Mexican Chicken, Spicy, '82 89
Milano, Chicken, '84 220
Minted Chicken, '81 102
Mole, Chicken, '81 193
Monterey, Chicken, '82 275
Mornay Sauce, Chicken Breasts
   in, '81 273
Mushrooms, Chicken-Stuffed, '80 162
Mustard Chicken, '80 222; '86 293
Nachos, Chicken, '84 244
Nuggets, Baked Chicken, '81 149
Nuggets, Golden Chicken, '80 159;
   '81 237
Nuggets, Lemon-Chicken, '86 337

Nuggets Supreme, Chicken, '85 160
Nuggets with Pineapple Sauce,
   Chicken, '84 236
Orange-Almond Sauce, Chicken
   in, '79 219; '80 13
Orange-Avocado Chicken, '80 38
Orange Chicken, '83 278; '86 M140
Orange Chicken Breasts with Parslied
   Rice, '87 242
Orange Sauce, Chicken Breasts
   with, '79 77
Orange Sauce, Chicken in, '83 8
Oriental Chicken, '80 40, 208; '82 131
Oriental Chicken with Peanuts, '82 236
Oriental Chicken with Pineapple, '86 42
Oriental Stuffed Pockets, '79 14
Paella, Chicken-Pork-Shrimp, '82 245
Paella, Spanish, '85 26
Paella Valenciana, '82 246
Parmesan, Chicken, '83 184
Parmesan Chicken, Crispy, '80 M76
Parmigiana, Chicken, '80 190
Parmigiana, Chicken-Eggplant, '82 212
Pasquale, Chicken, '83 67

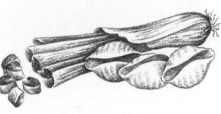

Pasta and Garden Vegetables, '87 192
Pasta, Chicken-and-Broccoli, '87 286
Pastry, Chicken in, '86 122
Pâté, Vegetable-Chicken, '86 66
Peanut Butter-Marmalade
   Chicken, '81 282; '82 30
Peas, Chicken with Snow, '83 137
Pecan-Rice Dressing, Chicken
   with, '85 M57
Peppers, Curried Chicken-Stuffed, '87 19
Peppers, Devilish Chicken, '80 65
Phyllo, Chicken in, '87 286
Piccata, Chicken, '83 35; '84 230
Pie, Biscuit-Topped Chicken,
   '86 157, 264
Pie, Cheesy Mexican Chicken, '82 142
Pie, Chicken, '81 281; '82 31
Pie, Chicken Pot, '81 210; '82 114; '84 21
Pie, Chicken-Vegetable Pot, '81 281;
   '82 30
Pie, Double-Crust Chicken, '87 111
Pie, Easy Chicken Pot, '83 156
Pie, Egg-Stra Special Chicken, '86 264
Pie, Montezuma Tortilla, '83 199
Pie, Thick 'n' Crusty Chicken
   Pot, '87 267
Pie with Cheese Crust, Chicken
   Pot, '86 264
Pilaf, Chicken, '82 246
Piña Colada Chicken, '86 21
Pineapple Chicken, '83 M194; '85 3
Pineapple, Chicken and, '81 281; '82 30
Pineapple Chicken, Oriental, '84 288
Piquant Chicken, '86 76
Pizza, Gruyère-Chicken, '87 182
Plum Sauce, Chicken with, '82 236
Poached Chicken Breasts, Wine-, '85 58
Poached Chicken with Black Beans and
   Salsa, '87 217

Chicken *(continued)*

Pollo Almendrado (Chicken in Almond Sauce), '81 193
Pollo con Calabacita (Mexican Chicken with Zucchini), '82 219
Pollo en Mole de Cacahuate (Chicken with Peanut Mole Sauce), '80 194
Potatoes, Chicken-Cheese Stuffed, '86 55
Potatoes, Creamed Beef and Chicken-Topped, '83 210
Potatoes, Sweet-and-Sour-Topped, '83 4
Pot, Chicken in a, '81 3
Princess Chicken, '86 122
Puffs, Appetizer Chicken, '85 72
Puffs, Chicken Nut, '81 260
Quiche Noël, '82 310
Roast Chicken and Brown Rice, '83 268
Roast Chicken and Vegetables, '81 3
Roasted Chicken, Herb-, '87 155
Rockefeller Chicken, '79 219
Rolls, Chicken-Asparagus, '86 M211
Rolls, Crispy Chicken, '84 288
Rolls Élégante, Chicken, '80 210
Rolls, Hearty Salad, '81 206
Rolls Jubilee, Chicken, '87 118
Rollups, Cheesy Chicken, '82 44
Rollups, Chicken, '85 179
Rollups, Chicken and Spinach, '80 90; '82 M68
Rollups, Imperial Chicken, '80 217
Rollups in Gravy, Chicken, '83 184
Rollups, Sunshine Chicken, '85 251
Romano, Chicken alla, '83 M58
Romano, Chicken Breasts, '79 218
Romanoff, Chicken, '84 292
Rotelle, Chicken and Tomato with, '87 108

Salads

Almond Salad, Chicken-, '81 133
Aloha Chicken Salad, '80 297
Amandine, Chicken Salad, '81 37
Ambrosia, Chicken Salad, '85 216
Artichokes, Chicken Salad with, '86 186
Avocado-Chicken Salad, '87 107
Avocado Salad, Chicken-, '80 139
Avocado Salad, Fruited Chicken-, '82 101
Avocado Salad Platter, Chicken-, '83 2
Avocado Salad, Tossed Chicken-, '80 4
Avocados, Chicken Salad in, '85 216
Baked Chicken Salad, '86 297; '87 176
BLT Chicken Salad, '87 144
Celery Salad, Chicken-, '81 187

Chicken Salad, '86 232, 261
Chop Suey Salad, '81 37
Chutney-Chicken Salad, '87 74
Chutney Salad, Chicken, '82 108
Coleslaw, Chicken, '84 2
Cream Puff Bowl, Chicken Salad in, '86 232
Crunchy Chicken Salad, '86 157, 207
Curried Chicken-and-Orange Salad, '87 144
Curried Chicken Salad, '79 219; '84 66; '85 96; '86 131
Curried Chicken Salad with Asparagus, '81 36
Exotic Luncheon Salad, '83 210
Fancy Chicken Salad, '79 55
Filling, Chicken Salad, '87 106
Fruit, Chicken Salad with, '82 171
Fruited Chicken Salad, '84 25, 290
Fruited Chicken Salad in Avocados, '87 41
Fruit Salad, Chicken-, '82 79
Fruity Chicken Salad, '83 157
Grapes, Chicken Salad with, '86 117
Green Salad with Chicken, Mixed, '80 54
Hot Chicken Salad, '81 201; '83 196
Hot Chicken Salad, Country Club-Style, '86 10
Hot Chicken Salad, Crunchy, '80 138
Hot Chicken Salad Pinwheel, '80 139
Macadamia Chicken Salad, '80 138
Macaroni-Chicken Salad, '85 296; '86 302
Mandarin Chicken, Carousel, '79 88
Mango, Chicken Salad with, '86 215
Marinated Chicken-Grape Salad, '85 74
Mexican Chicken Salad, '85 84
Mold, Chicken-Cucumber, '80 175
Mold, Chicken Salad, '83 80; '84 163
Nectarine Chicken Salad, '79 175
Old-Fashioned Chicken Salad, '83 79
Oriental Chicken Salad, '85 216
Pasta-Chicken Salad, Tarragon, '87 155
Pea Salad, Chicken-, '83 218
Persian Chicken Salad, '81 12
Pineapple-Chicken Salad Pie, '80 138
Pineapple-Nut Chicken Salad, '83 80
Poulet Rémoulade, '87 144
Rice Salad, Chicken-, '81 203
Rice Salad, Hot Chicken-and-, '83 22
Rice Salad, Nutty Chicken-, '83 157
Ring Salad, Chicken Jewel, '83 282
Sandwiches, Chicken-Salad Finger, '85 119
Special Chicken Salad, '85 82; '87 183
Spinach Tossed Salad, Chicken-and-, '83 157
Stack-Up Salad, Chicken, '83 80
Summer Chicken Salad, '83 145
Super Chicken Salad, '82 174
Supreme, Chicken Salad, '79 107, 152
Tahitian Chicken Salad, '84 120
Tarts, Chicken Salad, '84 257
Tortellini Salad, Chicken, '87 288
Tropical Chicken Boats for Two, '82 186
Tropical Chicken Salad, '85 216
Twist, Chicken Salad with a, '84 221

Vegetable-Chicken Vinaigrette Salad, '86 135
Wild Rice-Chicken Salad, '83 146
Saltimbocca alla Romana, Chicken, '80 212
San Antonio-Style Chicken, '81 166
Sandwich, Crispy Chicken, '81 114
Sandwiches, Baked Chicken, '79 164; '80 130; '84 165
Sandwiches, Cheesy Chicken, '82 190
Sandwiches, Chicken-Almond Pocket, '81 240; '83 69
Sandwiches, Chicken Club, '86 160
Sandwiches, Hot Brown, '80 202
Sandwiches, Hot Chicken, '83 291
Sandwiches, Marinated Chicken, '86 M45
Sandwiches, Puffed Chicken, '82 35
Sandwiches, Toasted Chicken-and-Cheese, '85 242
Sandwich, Marinated Chicken in a, '86 185
Sauce, Creamy Chicken, '81 91
Saucy Chick-Wiches, '81 25; '82 31; '83 34
Sautéed Chicken Breasts, '87 36
Sauté, Sherry-Chicken, '87 218
Scallopini with Lemon Sauce, Chicken, '86 156
Scaloppine with Peppers, Chicken, '85 78
Scarborough Chicken, '80 38
Seasoned Browned Chicken, '85 25
Seasoned Chicken, Crunchy, '87 217
Sesame Chicken, '85 252; '86 122
Sesame Chicken, Hawaiian, '81 106
Sherried Chicken, '79 214
Sherried Chicken with Artichokes, '87 143
Sherry Chicken with Rice, '81 97
Skillet, Cheesy Chicken, '80 115
Skillet Chicken, '81 180
Skillet Chicken Dinner, '86 249
Skillet Company Chicken, '82 60
Soufflé, Chicken-Chestnut, '79 107
Soups
Chicken Soup, '81 98
Chowder Sauterne, Chicken, '84 235
Cream of Chicken Soup, '85 243
Curried Chicken Soup, '86 34
Enchilada Soup, Chicken, '86 22
Ham, and Oyster Soup, Chicken, '79 198
Homemade Chicken Soup, '82 34
Mexican Chicken Soup, '84 234
Noodle Soup, Chicken, '80 264
Quick Chicken Soup, '86 M72
Sopa de Lima, '79 211
Soy and Wine, Chicken in, '84 26
Spaghetti, Chicken, '83 105; '87 221
Spiced Chicken, Crunchy, '85 M57
Spiced Fruited Chicken with Almond Rice, '81 195
Spicy Chicken Dish, '87 267
Spinach Noodles, Chicken and, '82 19
Spread, Festive Chicken, '87 158
Spread, Low-Fat Chicken, '82 290
Spread, Tasty Chicken, '84 193
Steamed Dinner, Easy, '83 M314
Stew and Dumplings, Chicken, '84 4
Stew, Bama Brunswick, '87 4
Stew, Brunswick, '80 264
Stew, Brunswick Chicken, '87 4
Stew, Sonny Frye's Brunswick, '87 4
Stir-Fried Chicken Curry, '87 51
Stir-Fried Chicken, Zesty, '83 82

Stir-Fry Chicken à l'Orange, **'83** 82
Stir-Fry, Chicken and Vegetable, **'82** 237
Stir-Fry Chicken-and-Vegetables, **'86** 68
Stir-Fry Chicken and Vegetables, **'86** 249
Stir-Fry, Chicken-Broccoli, **'82** 33
Stir-Fry, Chicken-Vegetable, **'83** 151;
   '84 13, 141
Stir-Fry, Chicken-Zucchini, **'84** 50
Stir-Fry, Kyoto Orange-Chicken, **'87** 96
Stir-Fry, Orange-Chicken, **'84** 68
Stir-Fry Vegetables with Chicken, **'84** 195
Strips, Zippy Chicken, **'84** 205
Stuffed Chicken Breasts, **'85** 291; **'87** 36
Stuffed Chicken Breasts, Peach-, **'79** 177
Stuffed Chicken Breasts Sardou, **'87** 269
Stuffed Chicken Breasts, Walnut-, **'85** 293
Stuffed Chicken Breasts with White
   Grape Sauce, **'80** 38
Stuffed Chicken, Crab-, **'84** 101
Stuffed Chicken, Rice-, **'81** 4
Stuffed Chicken Rolls, Spinach-, **'86** 248
Stuffed Chicken Thighs, **'82** 84
Stuffed Chicken, Wild Rice-, **'79** 219
Sunshiny Chicken, **'81** 309
Supreme, Hot Chicken, **'81** 76
Suprêmes de Volaille à Blanc (Chicken
   Breasts in Cream Sauce), **'82** 83
Sweet-and-Sour Chicken, **'79** 106;
   '83 184; **'84** 218; **'86** 217, 240
Sweet-and-Sour Lemon Chicken, **'84** 93
Sweet-and-Sour Shrimp and
   Chicken, **'87** 267
Szechwan Chicken, **'83** 85
Szechwan Chicken with Cashews, **'81** 212
Tahitian Chicken, **'84** 68
Tangy Chicken, **'85** 251; **'86** 292; **'87** 35
Tarragon Chicken, **'86** 231
Tempura Delight, Chicken, **'85** 66
Teriyaki, Chicken, **'80** M76
Teriyaki Chicken Wings, **'85** 300; **'86** 18
Terrine, Chicken-Vegetable, **'84** 131
Terrine Ring, Chicken, **'84** 132
Terrine, Vegetable-Chicken, **'83** 224
Tetrazzini, Cheesy Chicken, **'83** M87
Tetrazzini, Chicken, **'79** 268; **'80** M75;
   '83 288
Tomato Aspic, Chicken in, **'84** 190
Tortilla Stack, Cheesy Chicken-, **'86** 3
Toss, Quick Chicken, **'87** M124
Valencia, Chicken-and-Rice, **'85** 113
Vermouth, Chicken and
   Vegetables, **'87** M37
Véronique, Chicken, **'84** 260; **'85** 302
Waffles, Southern Chicken-Pecan,
   '82 231
Walnut Chicken, **'85** 126
Walnut Chicken and Vegetables, **'85** 194
Wellington, Chicken Breasts, **'84** 22
Wild Rice, Chicken and, **'79** 248
Wild Rice, Elegant Chicken
   with, **'80** M76
Wild Rice Supreme, Chicken-, **'79** 77
Wine, Chicken in White, **'81** 97
Wine Sauce, Chicken and Mushrooms
   in, **'81** 109
Wine Sauce, Chicken in, **'80** 8
Wings, Broiled Chicken, **'80** 149
Wings, Satan's, **'87** 214

Chili
Bake, Chili Hominy, **'81** 282; **'82** 58
Basic Chili, **'82** M11
Burgers, Open-Face Chili, **'82** 31; **'83** 33
Casserole, Chili-Rice, **'79** 54

Casserole, Hominy-Chili, **'86** 255
Cheese-Topped Chili, **'82** M11
Cheesy Chili, **'82** 310
Chili, **'87** 17
Chuck Wagon Chili, **'81** 282; **'82** 57
Chunky Chili, **'82** M282; **'86** 3
Company Chili, **'82** 311; **'83** 30
con Carne, Beef and Sausage
   Chili, **'83** 284
con Carne, Chili, **'82** 310; **'83** 30;
   '84 72; **'86** 2
con Carne, Favorite Chili, **'86** 293
con Carne, Quick-and-Easy Chili, **'86** 2
Cowboy Chili, **'86** 2
Dip, Cheesy Chili, **'80** 150
Dip, Chili, **'82** 161
Dogs, Chili-Cheese, **'81** M176
Double-Meat Chili, **'79** 269; **'80** 12
Easy Chili, **'82** 310; **'83** 30
Eggplant Chili, **'85** 88
Friday Night Chili, **'86** 228
Hot Spiced Chili, **'83** 214
Lunchtime Chili, **'81** 230
Meat Loaf, Chili, **'81** 275
Meaty Chili, **'81** 282; **'82** 58
Meaty Chili with Beans, **'85** 250
Noodles, Chili with, **'81** 282; **'82** 57
Pie, Chili-Tamale, **'82** 9; **'83** 68
Potato Chili, Savory, **'83** 284
Potatoes, Chili-Topped, **'83** 3
Potatoes, South-of-the-Border
   Stuffed, **'86** 54
Quick and Simple Chili, **'81** 282; **'82** 58
Quick Chili, **'83** 283
Ranch Chili and Beans, **'79** 270; **'80** 11
Red Chili, North Texas, **'87** 303
Rice, Chili with, **'82** M11
Roundup Chili, **'79** 269; **'80** 12
Salad, Spicy Chili, **'86** 71
Sauce, Chili, **'81** 175
Sauce, Chili Meat, **'83** 4
Sauce, Chunky Chili, **'85** 188
Sauce, Spicy Chili, **'87** 127
Sausage-Beef Chili, **'86** 232
Sausage Chili, Beefy, **'82** M11
Simple Chili, **'79** 269; **'80** 11
South-of-the-Border Chili, **'83** 283
Spaghetti, Herbed Chili-, **'84** 222
Spicy Chili, Old-Fashioned, **'79** 269;
   '80 11
Surprise, Chili, **'82** 229
Texas Championship Chili, **'81** 54
Texas Chili, Hot, **'80** 222; **'81** 77
Texas-Style Chili, **'82** 311; **'83** 30
Tex-Mex Chili, **'83** 26
Topping, Chili, **'84** 246
Tree-Hunt Chili, **'87** 292
Vegetarian Chili, **'84** 280, 327
Venison Chili, **'82** 216; **'86** 3; **'87** 304
Zippy Chili, **'87** 110

Chocolate
Banana Pops, **'84** 44
Bars and Cookies
   Almond Chip Balls, Toasted, **'84** 240
   Almond-Chocolate Bars, **'83** 304
   Almond Cream Confections, **'87** 198
   Blond Nut Squares, **'82** 156
   Brazil Squares, **'82** 306
   Brownie Alaskas, **'83** 299
   Brownie Bars, Cinnamon, **'81** 230
   Brownie-Mint Dessert, **'82** 227
   Brownie Mix, **'82** 6
   Brownies, Amaretto, **'86** 246

Brownies, Buttermilk Cake, **'87** 198
Brownies, Chewy
   Marshmallow, **'83** 306
Brownies, Chocolate-Banana, **'80** 160
Brownies, Chocolate Chip, **'81** 162
Brownies, Chocolate Chip-Peanut
   Butter, **'84** 73
Brownies, Chocolate-Mint, **'85** M294
Brownies, Chocolate-Nut, **'81** 129
Brownies, Chocolate-Pecan, **'81** 64
Brownies, Chocolate Tea, **'83** 79
Brownies, Choco-Mallow, **'87** 198
Brownies, Cream Cheese
   Swirl, **'79** 51
Brownies, Crème de Menthe, **'83** 244
Brownies, Crunch-Crust, **'87** 198
Brownies, Easy, **'83** 245
Brownies, Favorite, **'86** 158
Brownies, German Cream
   Cheese, **'80** 269
Brownies, Heavenly Hash, **'83** 245
Brownies, Heavenly Honey, **'79** 83
Brownies, Mocha, **'87** 93
Brownies, Nutty Blonde, **'81** 64
Brownies, Nutty Cocoa, **'81** 64
Brownies, Nutty Fudge, **'80** M171
Brownies, Peanut Butter, **'87** 199
Brownies, Quick, **'87** M302
Brownies, Quick and Easy, **'82** 6
Brownies, Rocky Road, **'86** 320
Brownies, Walnut-Cream
   Cheese, **'84** 240
Brownie Waffle Cookies, **'86** 245
Butter Cookies,
   Chocolate-Tipped, **'84** 258
Butterscotch Bars,
   Chocolate-, **'81** 197
By-Cracky Bars, **'84** 212
Caramel Layer Squares,
   Chocolate-, **'79** 83
Cherry Cookies, Chocolate-, **'85** 324
Chewy Chocolate Cookies, **'80** 208
Chip Bars, Chocolate, **'81** 130
Chip Cookies, **'84** 120

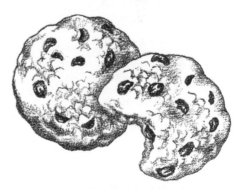

Chip Cookies, Chocolate, **'86** 245
Chip Cookies, Chocolate-
   Chocolate, **'82** 35
Chips Cookies, Loaded-with-, **'87** 223
Chip Squares, Chocolate, **'83** 170
Cinnamon Bars, Chocolate, **'82** 209
Cocoa Drop Cookies, **'80** 217
Cocoa Kiss Cookies, **'85** 171
Crème de Menthe Bars,
   Chocolate-, **'86** 245
Crispy Cookies, Chocolate, **'85** 115
Crumble Bars, Choco-, **'79** 292

Chocolate, Bars and Cookies (continued)

Deluxe Chocolate Chip
Cookies, '79 216
Devil Doggies, '84 37
Different Chocolate Chip
Cookies, '83 114
Double Chip Cookies, '81 301
Double Chocolate Chip
Cookies, '79 217
Doubly-Good Chocolate
Cookies, '82 M185
Dream Bars, Chocolate, '79 256;
'82 298
Drop Cookies, Chocolate, '84 36
Forget 'em Cookies, Chocolate, '83 256
Fudge Bars, '86 93
Fudge Bars, Yummy, '87 158
Giant Chocolate Chip
Cookies, '84 119
Jumbo Chocolate Chip
Cookies, '82 110
Light Chocolate Chip Cookies, '86 46

Log Cookies, Chocolate-
Tipped, '87 294
Macaroons, Chocolate, '83 300;
'87 57
Meltaways, Chocolate, '81 302
Melt-Aways, Chocolate Chip, '84 118
Meringue-Chocolate Chip
Bars, '84 118
Meringue Kiss Cookies, '86 121
Mint Chip Cookies,
Chocolate-, '86 245
Mint Snaps, Chocolate-, '83 103;
'84 96
Monster Cookies, '84 36
Nugget Cookies, '79 291
Nut Chews, Chocolate-, '81 92
Nutty Choco Snacks, '83 305
Nutty Oatmeal-Chocolate Chip
Cookies, '82 M185
Oatmeal Bars,
Chocolate-Topped, '86 110
Oatmeal Cookies, Chocolate-, '80 105
Oatmeal Cookies, Chocolate
Chip-, '84 119
Orange-Chocolate Cookies, '83 113
Peanut Butter-and-Fudge
Bars, '80 M172
Peanut Butter Bars, '84 243
Peanut Butter-Chocolate Chip
Cookies, Freezer, '86 230
Peanut Butter-Chocolate Kiss
Cookies, '86 49
Peanut Butter Cones,
Chocolate-, '85 14
Peanut Butter Cookies,
Chocolate-, '85 90
Peanut Butter Cups,
Chocolate-, '85 14

Peanut Butter Fingers, '79 256
Peanut Butter Squares, Chocolate
Chip-, '84 118
Peanut Cookies, Chocolate-, '83 223
Peppermint Squares,
Chocolate-, '81 119
Pinwheel Cookies, Chocolate, '86 245
Sandwich Cookies, Chocolate, '81 192
Sandwich Cookies,
Choco-Nut, '84 200
Sandwiches, Chocolate Cookie Ice
Cream, '87 147
Snappers, Jumbo Chocolate, '81 218
Snowball Cookies, Chocolate, '82 295
Surprise Cookies, Choco, '80 60
Teasers, Chocolate, '87 44
Whoopie Pies, '86 246
Beverages
Brandied Chocolate,
Flaming, '80 M290
Café Colombian Royal, '80 M290
Cappuccino, Chocolate Castle, '84 53
Cocoa Mix, Instant, '86 332
Coffee, Chocolate, '82 43
Coffee, Chocolate-Almond, '84 54
Coffee, Cocoa-, '83 55
Coffee, Mexican, '83 175, 275
Hot Chocolate, Creole, '80 M290
Hot Chocolate, Favorite, '83 55
Hot Chocolate, French, '86 328
Hot Chocolate Mix,
Deluxe, '80 M290
Hot Chocolate Mix, Spicy, '85 278
Hot Chocolate, Old-Fashioned, '85 23
Hot Chocolate, Special, '82 5
Hot Chocolate, Spiced, '80 50
Hot Chocolate, Spicy, '85 278
Hot Cocoa Mix, '81 287
Hot Cocoa, Quick, '82 5
Malt, Chocolate, '86 183
Mexican-Style Chocolate, '81 187
Milk, French Chocolate, '79 38
Mocha Cocoa, '83 318
Mocha-Cocoa Mix, Hot, '82 296
Mocha Coffee, '85 M329
Mocha Cream, Café, '84 54
Mocha Deluxe Hot Drink, '82 289
Mocha Espresso, Italian, '82 254
Mocha, Hot, '84 60
Mocha Punch, '84 58, 166
Mocha, Quick Viennese, '79 232
Smoothie, Chocolate-Mint, '84 166
Bread, Chocolate Date-Nut, '81 284
Bread, Cocoa-Nut Swirl, '80 257
Buns, Chocolate-Cinnamon, '85 5
Buns, Chocolate Sticky, '81 300; '82 124
Cakes and Tortes
Almond Cake with Cherry Filling,
Chocolate-, '84 225
Angel Food Cake, Chocolate, '87 21
Banana Cake, Chocolate-, '86 138
Banana-Cocoa Cupcakes, '80 130
Banana Loaf, Chocolate
Chip-, '85 115
Beet Cake, Chocolate, '80 40
Black Bottom Cups, '82 279
Black Forest Cake, '81 126
Brownie Cupcakes, '82 280
Brownie Delight, Chocolate, '87 224
Brown Mountain Cake, '84 39
Bûche de Noël, '84 304; '87 241
Bûche de Noël Cake, '82 262
Buttermilk Chocolate Cake, '79 13

Candy Cake, Chocolate, '81 238
Caramel-Nut Cake,
Chocolate-, '83 23
Cheesecake, Black Forest, '84 74
Cheesecake, Candy Bar, '86 120
Cheesecake, Chocolate, '81 16;
'82 305
Cheesecake, Chocolate-
Amaretto, '85 M294
Cheesecake, Chocolate Chip, '85 114
Cheesecake, Chocolate-Glazed Triple
Layer, '86 315
Cheesecake, Chocolate Swirl, '84 295;
'85 26
Cheesecake, German
Chocolate, '87 265
Cheesecake, Marbled, '87 261
Cheesecake, Marble Mint, '84 152
Cheesecake, Mocha Swirl, '87 262
Cheesecake, Rich Chocolate, '84 74;
'85 38
Cheesecake, White Chocolate, '87 44
Cherry Cake, Chocolate-, '84 200;
'86 239
Cinnamon-Chocolate
Cupcakes, '81 M139
Coconut Cake, Chocolate-, '83 23
Coconut Cake, White
Chocolate-, '87 263
Coffee Cake, Chocolate-Chip, '79 249
Coffee Cake, Chocolate Chip, '83 231
Crumb Cake, Calico, '87 261
Decadent Chocolate Cake, '86 142
Double-Chocolate Torte, '79 67
Easy Chocolate Cake, '80 140
Frosting, Chocolate Cake with
Double, '86 314
Fudge Cake, Best, '83 301
Fudge Cake, Brown Sugar, '86 316
Fudge Cake, Chocolate, '80 279
Fudge Cake for Two, '81 205

German Chocolate Cake, '81 296;
'83 M233
German Chocolate Chip
Cake, '86 247
Kahlúa Chocolate Cake, '81 303
Marble Chocolate Chip
Cupcakes, '81 239
Marbled Cake, Cocoa, '82 265
Marshmallow Cake, No-Egg
Chocolate, '87 M97
Mayonnaise Cake, Chocolate, '83 99
Mocha Brownie Torte, '85 102
Mocha Cake, Belgian, '84 316
Mocha Cake, Double, '84 311
Mocha-Chocolate Cake,
Dark, '84 311
Mocha Cream Roll,
Chocolate-, '84 304
Mocha Cupcakes, '85 250
Mocha-Pecan Torte, '86 26

Mousse Cake, Chocolate, '87 264
Nut Cake, Rich Chocolate-, '86 8
Peanut Butter Cake,
    Chocolate-, '84 240
Peanut Butter Cake, Fudgy, '85 91
Peanut Cluster Cake,
    Chocolate-, '87 184
Perfect Chocolate Cake, '82 244
Pound Cake, Chocolate, '82 88;
    '84 10
Pound Cake, Chocolate Chip, '86 178
Pound Cake, Chocolate-Sour
    Cream, '83 239
Pound Cake with Fudge Frosting,
    Chocolate, '87 296
Praline Torte, Chocolate, '84 165
Pudding, Chocolate Cake, '81 99
Rocky Road Cake, '81 178
Roll, Chocolate Cream, '85 317
Roll, Chocolate-Frosted Ice
    Cream, '84 200
Roll, Chocolate Mousse, '83 290
Roll, Chocolate-Orange, '87 21
Royal, Chocolate Cake, '86 239
Royale, Chocolate Torte, '82 263
Rum Cake, Chocolate, '79 67
Sachertorte, '84 253
Self-Filled Cupcakes, '80 129
Sour Cream Cake,
    Chocolate-, '87 222
Sour Cream Cake, Chocolate
    Chip-, '85 115
Sour Cream Chocolate Cake, '79 282
Sponge Cake, Chocolaty, '86 60
Strawberry Ice Cream Torte,
    Chocolate-, '79 7
Sugar Cookie Torte, '79 68
Surprise Cupcakes, Chocolate, '85 91
Swiss Chocolate Chip Cake, '87 85
Triangle Cake, Chocolate, '85 126
Velvet Torte, Chocolate, '86 316
Yule Log, '79 281; '82 289
Zucchini Cake, Chocolate-, '85 156
Candies
Almond Roca, '86 49
Bourbon Balls, '83 315
Bourbon Balls, Chocolate, '84 298
Brittle, Chocolate, '83 315
Brittle, Quick Chocolate, '82 114
Butter Creams, '80 302
Cherries, Chocolate-Covered, '81 286;
    '84 298
Coconut Almond Drops,
    Chocolate-, '87 223
Cream-Filled Chocolates,
    Liqueur, '87 258
Crème de Cacao Balls, '86 266
Drops, Chocolate, '84 111
Fudge, '86 266
Fudge, Cherry Nut, '83 315
Fudge, Chocolate, '82 20
Fudge, Chocolate-Peanut
    Butter, '87 257
Fudge, Coffee-Chip, '86 74
Fudge, Cream Cheese, '84 111
Fudge, Creamy, '81 218
Fudge, Creamy Dark, '82 295
Fudge, Creamy Pecan, '84 321
Fudge, Double-Good, '79 M263
Fudge, Double Good, '87 M278
Fudge, Double Peanut, '85 91
Fudge, Fast, '79 274
Fudge, Holiday Mocha, '84 298

Fudge, Pistachio, '83 298
Fudge, Quick Nut, '83 316
Fudge Scotch Ring, '79 273
Greeting Card, Chocolate, '83 40
Kentucky Colonels, '79 273
Millionaires, '79 M262
Molded Candies, '84 40
Nut Clusters, '81 254
Nut Log Candy, Chocolate-, '86 335
Peanut Butter Balls,
    Chocolate-, '80 87
Peanut Butter-Chocolate
    Balls, '80 269
Peanut Butter-Chocolate Candy
    Squares, '82 56
Peanut Butter Creams, '79 273
Peanut Clusters, Chocolate-, '81 16
Peanutty Clusters, '83 143
Pecan Fritters,
    Chocolate-Covered, '79 205
Pretzels, Chocolate-Covered, '82 295
Rocky Road, '84 298
Rum Balls, Chocolate, '80 302
Spiders, Chocolate, '85 236
Spirited Chocolates, '86 278
Tiger Butter, '86 48
Toffee, English, '79 273
Toffee, Nutty, '79 M263
Truffles, Almond, '83 298
Truffles, Amaretto Dessert, '86 319
Truffles, Chocolate, '85 114
Truffles, White Chocolate, '87 45
Velvets, Chocolate, '84 298
Cannoli, '80 58
Charlotte Russe, Chocolate, '87 74
Cocoa to Chocolate Equivalents, '84 200
Combo, Strawberry-Chocolate, '85 96
Cream, Strawberries with
    Chocolate, '85 81
Crêpes, Chocolate, '86 164
Crêpes, Chocolate Chantilly, '82 183
Crêpes, Chocolate Dessert, '84 84;
    '85 262
Crêpes, Chocolate Dream, '86 164
Crêpes, Chocolate-Orange, '85 263
Crust, Chocolate, '87 264
Crust, Chocolate-Coconut, '87 261
Crust, Chocolate Crumb, '87 261
Cups, Chocolate, '80 207
Cups, Chocolate Lace, '87 133
Cups, Chocolate-Mint, '80 71
Cups, Chocolate-Walnut, '85 213

Cups, Miniature Chocolate, '87 132
Custard, Chocolate-Topped
    Amaretto, '87 M37
Dessert, Chilled Chocolate, '83 177
Dessert, Chocolate-Almond, '82 306
Dessert, Chocolate-Coffee Frozen, '85 172
Dessert, Chocolate Dream, '83 198
Dessert, Chocolate Ladyfinger, '86 162
Dessert, Chocolate-Rum, '81 247

Dessert, Choco-Maple Frozen, '86 300;
    '87 178
Dessert, Cool Chocolate-Mint, '80 109
Dessert, Easy Chocolate, '79 75
Dessert, Frozen Chocolate, '83 76
Dessert, Layered Ice Cream, '83 189
Dessert, Peanut-Chocolate, '80 86
Dessert Squares, Chocolate-
    Blueberry, '87 299
Doughnuts, Chocolate, '83 95
Doughnuts, Chocolate-Covered, '84 55
Doughnuts, Chocolate-Glazed
    Potato, '85 6
Frostings, Fillings, and Toppings
    Almond Frosting, Chocolate-, '83 241
    Buttercream, Chocolate, '84 156
    Candy Frosting, Chocolate, '81 238
    Chocolate Frosting, '80 M171;
        '81 265; '82 262; '83 79, 99,
        M233, 253; '84 200; '85 323;
        '86 8, 93, 138, 239, 314;
        '87 M97, 198, 199, 293
    Cocoa Frosting, '86 60
    Coconut Chocolate Frosting, '79 13
    Coffee Frosting, Chocolate-, '84 36
    Creamy Chocolate Frosting, '85 314;
        '86 316; '87 241
    Creamy Chocolate Glaze, '82 88
    Fluffy Chocolate Frosting, '86 336;
        '87 58
    Fudge Frosting, '81 303; '87 296
    Fudge Frosting, Chocolate, '83 105
    Fudge Frosting, Quick, '81 278
    Glaze, Chocolate, '81 119; '83 220;
        '84 10, 55, 253; '85 6; '86 315, 316
    Glaze, White Cake with Strawberries
        and Chocolate, '87 76
    Honey Chocolate Frosting, '79 83
    Honey Glaze, Chocolate-, '82 306
    Marshmallow Frosting,
        Chocolate-, '83 245
    Mocha Butter Cream
        Frosting, '79 281
    Mocha-Buttercream Frosting, '86 26
    Mocha Cream Filling, '84 305
    Mocha Frosting, '83 301; '84 316;
        '87 224
    Mocha Frosting, Creamy, '82 289;
        '84 311
    Nut Frosting, Chocolate, '80 140
    Peanut Butter Frosting,
        Chocolate-, '84 240; '87 222
    Peanut Butter-Fudge Frosting, '87 184
    Peanut Topping, Chocolate-, '79 222
    Rich Chocolate Filling, '79 68
    Rich Chocolate Frosting, '84 304
    Rum Frosting, Chocolate, '79 67
    Satiny Chocolate Frosting, '86 136
    Truffle Filling, Chocolate, '87 69
Garnishes, Chocolate, '85 16
Gâteau Panache, '83 269
Granola with Chocolate Morsels, '86 69
Ice Cream Balls, Easy, '84 106
Ice Cream, Chocolate, '80 176; '86 129
Ice Cream, Chocolate Chunk-Peanut
    Butter, '85 297; '86 120
Kahlúa Delight, '83 67
Loaf, Chocolate Pinwheel, '80 256
Meringue Fingers,
    Chocolate-Almond, '84 158
Mexican Fiesta Confection, '82 223
Mint Dessert, Chocolate-, '82 100
Mocha Alaska Dessert, '84 191

Chocolate *(continued)*

Mocha Chiffon, **'86** 75
Mocha Dessert, Frozen, **'84** 311
Mocha Freeze, Royal, **'84** 53
Mocha-Mallow Parfaits, **'80** 219
Mocha Squares, Frozen, **'81** 187
Mousse, Amaretto-Chocolate, **'86** 50
Mousse Baked Alaska, Chocolate, **'85** 195
Mousse, Blender Chocolate, **'82** 71
Mousse, Blender-Quick
  Chocolate, **'80** 269
Mousse, Brandy-Chocolate, **'85** 102
Mousse, Chocolate-Orange, **'81** 16, 205
Mousse, Chocolate Rum, **'86** 189
Mousse, Creamy Chocolate, **'87** 133
Mousse, Elegant Amaretto-
  Chocolate, **'86** 337
Mousse, Honeyed Chocolate, **'87** 223
Mousse, Quick Chocolate, **'85** 87
Parfaits, Chocolate-Crème de
  Menthe, **'85** 161
Parfaits, Speedy, **'83** 76
Pies and Tarts
  Almond Pie, Creamy
    Chocolate-, **'85** 102
  Amandine, Chocolate Pie, **'83** 300
  Amaretto Mousse Pie,
    Chocolate-, **'80** 180; **'81** 30
  Berry Pie, Heavenly
    Chocolate-, **'85** 102
  Black Bottom Pie, **'82** 53
  Brownie Pie, Crustless, **'82** 33
  Chess Pie, Chocolate, **'81** 161;
    '86 220
  Chip Pie, Chocolate, **'85** 114
  Cream Cheese Pie, Chocolate-, **'80** 69
  Cream Pie, Chocolate, **'83** 192;
    '84 49;
  Creamy Chocolate Pie, **'85** 298;
    '86 119
  Double Chocolate Pie, **'82** M282
  Easy Chocolate Pie, **'83** 158
  French Silk Pie, **'80** 247
  French Silk Tarts, **'79** 236
  Frozen Chocolate Pie, **'80** 154
  Fudge Pie, **'87** 168
  Fudge Pie, Sweetheart, **'86** 316
  Heavenly Chocolate Pie, **'87** 260
  Ice Cream Pie, Chocolate-, **'87** 224
  Kahlúa Pie, **'83** 191
  Kentucky Derby Tarts, **'79** 102
  Meringue Pie, Chocolate, **'80** 238;
    '82 206; **'83** 158
  Meringue Pie, Chocolate-
    Filled, **'86** 121
  Mint Ice Cream Pie,
    Chocolate-, **'81** 144
  Mocha Crunch Pie, Chocolate-,
    '81 136
  Mocha Meringue Pie, **'80** 242
  Mousse Pie, Chocolate, **'81** 136
  Mud Pie, Tipsy, **'80** 255
  Peanut Butter Pie, Chocolate-, **'85** 91
  Peanut Butter Swirl Pie,
    Chocolate-, **'87** 262
  Pecan Pie, Choco-, **'82** 86
  Pecan Pie, Chocolate, **'80** 237; **'83** 12
  Praline Pie, Chocolate-, **'86** 259
  Tin Roof Pie, **'85** 91
  Whipped Cream Pie,
    Chocolate, **'79** 124
Pots de Chocolat, Petits, **'82** 272

Pots de Crème, **'81** 15; **'84** M145
Pots de Crème, Rum-Flavored, **'85** 102
Pudding, Brownie, **'79** 265; **'80** 295
Pudding, Chocolate-Almond, **'82** 142
Pudding, Chocolate Bread, **'80** 8
Pudding, Creamy Chocolate, **'83** 106
Pudding, Hot Fudge, **'81** 208
Roulage, Chocolate-Mocha, **'80** 216
Sauces
  Cherry Sauce, Chocolate-, **'85** 189
  Cherry Sauce, Chocolate, **'87** M165
  Chocolate Sauce, **'83** 189; **'84** 208,
    313; **'86** 322
  Cinnamon-Fudge Sauce, **'85** 141
  Classic Chocolate Sauce, **'85** 207
  Double Chocolate Sauce, **'83** 79
  Heavenly Chocolate Sauce, **'79** 79;
    '82 167
  Hot Fudge Sauce, **'82** 181, 295;
    '84 143
  Hot Fudge Sauce, Easy, **'84** 69
  Hot Fudge Sauce, Quick, **'82** 212
  Kahlúa Chocolate Sauce, **'85** 155

  Mint Sauce, Quick
    Chocolate, **'86** M58
  Orange Sauce, Chocolate-, **'86** 165
  Peanut Butter Sauce,
    Chocolate-, **'79** 91, M156
  Praline Sauce, Chocolate-, **'85** M295
  Supreme, Chocolate Sauce, **'85** 189
Shavings, Chocolate Hearts and, **'86** 26
Shell, Chocolate-Coconut
  Pie, **'82** 210; **'83** 100
Shell, Chocolate Pastry, **'87** 262
Soufflé, Chocolate, **'84** 317
Soufflé, Chocolate Mint, **'81** 16
Soufflé, Light Chocolate, **'83** 278
Spread, Chocolate Cheese, **'87** 292
Sundae Dessert, Hot Fudge, **'84** 313;
  '86 322
Sundaes, Cocoa-Kahlúa, **'83** M58
Supreme, Chocolate, **'84** 94
Velvet, Chocolate Almond, **'81** 148

Chop Suey
Cabbage Chop Suey, **'81** 101
Chicken Chop Suey, **'81** 227
Salad, Chop Suey, **'81** 37

Chowders
Bluefish Chowder, **'84** 282
Broccoli Chowder, **'79** 16
Cabbage Chowder, Hearty, **'80** 25
Cheddar Chowder, Hearty, **'79** 16
Cheese Chowder, Golden, **'80** 73
Chicken Chowder, **'83** 20
Chicken Chowder Sauterne, **'84** 235
Clam Chowder, **'79** 182; **'81** 32; **'85** 9;
  '86 36
Clam Chowder, New England, **'86** M72
Clam Chowder, Ocracoke, **'79** 31
Clam Chowder, Tomato-, **'84** 251

Corn and Cheese Chowder, **'80** 228
Corn Chowder, **'81** 128; **'83** 20;
  '84 M38; **'85** 10
Corn Chowder, Delicious, **'82** 279
Fish Chowder, **'79** 152; **'84** M38
Fish Chowder, Basque, **'86** 36
Fish Chowder, Creamy, **'79** 16
Fish Chowder, Tasty, **'80** 188
Ham and Corn Chowder, **'79** 16
Ham-and-Corn Chowder, **'82** 40
Ham 'n Cheese Chowder, **'79** 199
Harvest Chowder, **'83** 317
Mushroom Chowder, **'79** 16
Okra Chowder, Quick, **'80** 185
Oyster Chowder, **'83** 229
Oyster-Corn Chowder, **'83** 211
Sausage-Bean Chowder, **'83** 20
Seafood Chowder, **'85** 9
Seafood Chowder, Southern, **'83** 20
Shrimp and Corn Chowder, **'79** 199
Snapper Chowder, Red, **'85** 217
Swiss-Broccoli Chowder, **'80** 73
Turkey Chowder, **'85** 10
Turkey-Corn Chowder, **'81** 98
Vegetable Chowder, Cheesy, **'80** 25;
  '83 20

Chow Mein
Beef-and-Vegetable Chow Mein
  Casserole, **'83** 313
Noodles, Chow Mein over Crispy,
  '85 286
Pork Chow Mein, **'80** 208
Shrimp Chow Mein, **'82** 30

Christmas. *See also* Cookies/Christmas.
Bread, Christmas, **'87** 296
Bread, Norwegian Christmas, **'79** 234
Cake, Christmas Coconut, **'82** 262
Cinnamon Ornaments, **'85** 284
Cœur à la Crème, Christmas, **'86** 278
Coffee Cakes, Christmas-Tree, **'87** 298
Cookie Advent Calendar, **'85** 325
Cookie Cards, Christmas, **'84** 302
Cookie, Rudolph, **'80** 279, 303
Cookie, Santa Claus, **'80** 278, 303
Cookies, Eggnog Christmas, **'79** 255
Cookie, Sleigh, **'80** 279, 303
Cookies, Painted, **'86** 322
Cookies, Spiced Christmas, **'87** 294
Cookies, Swedish Christmas, **'79** 290
Dessert, White Christmas, **'82** 261
Divinity, Christmas, **'81** 286
Jam, Christmas Brunch, **'81** 286
Jelly, Christmas Freezer, **'86** M288
Lizzies, Christmas, **'87** 257
Loaf, Sweet Christmas, **'84** 278
Punch, Christmas, **'84** 259
Punch, Christmas Eve, **'86** 314
Punch, Merry Christmas, **'79** 285
Relish Tree, Christmas, **'84** 257
Salad, Christmas Snow, **'82** 266
Salad, Cranberry Christmas, **'79** 243
Salad, Eggnog Christmas, **'86** 281
Sandwich Wreath, Festive, **'86** 333
Santa's Whiskers, **'85** 323
Scent, Christmas, **'84** 325
Spices, Barclay House Mulling, **'86** 289
Strawberries, Christmas, **'87** 293
Tea, Christmas Fruit, **'83** 275
Wreath, Christmas, **'80** 280
Wreath, Della Robbia Fruit, **'87** 294

Clams
Backyard Clambake, **'81** 92
Bisque, Clam, **'86** 228

Casino, Clams, '81 125
Chase, Clams, '79 85
Chowder, Clam, '79 182; '81 32; '85 9; '86 36
Chowder, New England Clam, '86 M72
Chowder, Ocracoke Clam, '79 31
Chowder, Southern Seafood, '83 20
Chowder, Tomato-Clam, '84 251
Cocktail, Tomato-Clam, '87 252
Crisps, Clam, '80 151
Dip, Clam, '79 151; '80 265
Dip, Hot Clam, '82 59
Fritters, Clam, '79 151; '86 71
Oreganata, Clams, '85 104
Pizza, Baby Clam, '87 182
Quiche, Clam, '83 215
Sauce, Linguine in Clam, '81 83
Sauce, Linguine with Clam, '84 124
Sauce, Pasta with Clam, '84 291
Sauce, Vermicelli and Sprouts with Red Clam, '86 143
Sauce, Vermicelli with Clam, '85 295
Sauce with Linguine, Clam, '84 9
Shells, Baked Clam, '87 94
Soup, Clam Florentine, '85 23

Coconut
Ambrosia, Anytime, '86 182
Ambrosia, Baked, '83 303
Ambrosia Bowl, '80 138; '84 313
Ambrosia, Brunch, '83 57
Ambrosia Cake, '79 229
Ambrosia Cookies, '86 313
Ambrosia Cream Cheese Mold, '79 249
Ambrosia, Custard Sauce, '84 256
Ambrosia, Honey Bee, '83 267
Ambrosia, Mixed Fruit, '83 10
Ambrosia Mold, '79 241
Ambrosia, Old-Fashioned, '80 5
Ambrosia, Peach, '83 53
Ambrosia Pie, '79 284
Ambrosia Salad, '83 231
Ambrosia, Sherried, '84 324; '86 317
Ambrosia Supreme, Orange, '79 37
Ambrosia, Tropical, '79 74
Balls, Coconut-Almond, '84 256
Bars, Coconut Granola, '85 202
Bars, Golden, '84 255
Bars, Hawaiian, '84 153
Bonbons, Coconut-Black Walnut, '82 307
Bread, Coconut, '83 140
Bread, Pumpkin-Coconut, '87 255
Cake, Apple Coconut, '80 226
Cake, Chocolate-Coconut, '83 23
Cake, Christmas Coconut, '82 262
Cake, Coconut Cream, '81 179
Cake, Coconut-Cream Cheese Pound, '85 297
Cake, Coconut-Pineapple Layer, '80 140
Cake, Coconut Pound, '82 87
Cake, Coconut-Spice, '84 255; '87 296
Cake, Creamy Coconut, '84 43
Cake, Fresh Coconut, '80 289; '82 52; '85 281
Cake, Fresh Coconut-Carrot, '80 299
Cake, Lemon-Coconut Cream, '81 179
Cake, Lemon-Coconut Sheet, '85 117
Cake, Oatmeal-Coconut Coffee, '83 312
Cake, Regal Coconut, '83 299
Cake Roll, Coconut-Pineapple, '84 304
Cake, Spiked Coconut Angel, '85 279
Cake, Stately Coconut Layer, '81 70
Cake, Toasted Coconut, '86 60

Cake, White Chocolate-Coconut, '87 263
Candy, Coconut, '79 272; '80 250
Cloud, Coconut, '80 70
Clusters, Pecan-Coconut, '86 M251
Cookies, Coconut-Cherry, '79 292
Cookies, Crinkle Sunflower, '83 149
Cookies, Oatmeal-Coconut, '80 218
Cookies, Peanut Butter-Coconut, '83 113
Cream, Orange-Coconut, '84 24
Crust, Chocolate-Coconut, '87 261
Custard, Coconut, '86 109
Dessert, Chilled Coconut, '83 116
Dessert, Macaroon-Sherbet Frozen, '79 212
Dip, Coconut-Honey Fruit, '84 171
Dressing, Coconut, '87 251
Dressing, Orange-Coconut, '80 158
Dressing, Tangy Coconut-Fruit, '84 171
Drink, Coconut-Pineapple, '83 172
Drops, Chocolate-Coconut Almond, '87 223
English Cherubs, '83 257
Filling, Coconut, '81 265
Filling, Coconut Cream, '84 200
Frosting, Coconut, '82 262
Frosting, Coconut Chocolate, '79 13
Frosting, Coconut Cream Cheese, '86 60
Frosting, Coconut-Pecan, '81 296; '83 M233; '84 43, 322
Frosting, Creamy Coconut, '80 287
Frosting, Nutty Coconut, '86 8
Frost, Pink Coconut, '79 174; '80 128
Fruit Bowl, Coconut, '83 111
Ice Cream, Coconut Fried, '85 141
Ice Cream, Fresh Coconut, '79 166
Macaroon Charlotte, '81 296
Macaroons, Chocolate, '83 300
Macaroons, Coconut, '79 52
Macaroon-Stuffed Peaches, '79 178
Muffins, Coconut-Molasses, '82 210
Nog, Coconut, '83 275
Pears, Spicy Coconut, '83 207
Pie, Blender Coconut, '84 236
Pie, Coconut Chess, '86 220
Pie, Coconut Cream, '80 238; '81 136; '82 85; '84 49; '87 207
Pie, Coconut Custard, '82 33
Pie, Coconut Pecan, '81 161
Pie, Coconut-Pecan Chess, '81 248
Pie, Coconut-Pineapple, '84 256
Pie, Fresh Coconut Cream, '80 289
Pie, Magic Coconut, '79 53
Pie, Mock Coconut, '86 200
Pie, Quick Coconut, '83 115
Pies, Coconut-Caramel, '87 260
Pie Shell, Chocolate-Coconut, '82 210; '83 100
Potatoes, Coconut-Broiled Sweet, '84 231
Potatoes, Coconut-Orange Sweet, '84 252
Potatoes, Coconut-Stuffed Sweet, '82 204
Puffs, Coconut, '87 277
Salad, Chunky Fruit-and-Coconut, '84 24
Sauce, Coconut-Orange, '85 189
Sauce, Creamy Light Coconut, '82 177
Shrimp, Coconut-Beer, '85 230
Soufflé, Coconut, '79 73; '85 212
Tropical Snow, '86 34

Coffee
After-Dinner Coffee, '81 262
Almond-Coffee Delight, '84 115
Brandied Coffee, '81 244
Cake, Coffee Sponge, '83 229
Cake, Two-Day Coffee Sponge, '86 75

Cappuccino, Café, '82 253
Cappuccino, Chocolate Castle, '84 53
Cappuccino, Flaming, '79 293
Chocolate-Almond Coffee, '84 54
Chocolate Coffee, '82 43
Cocoa-Coffee, '83 55
Colombian Royal, Café, '80 M290
Cream, Café, '82 312
Cream, Icy Rum Coffee, '83 172
Cream Puffs, Java, '81 187
Creamy Coffee, '81 244
Crêpes, Coffee Ice Cream, '84 85
Dessert, Chocolate-Coffee Frozen, '85 172
Diablo, Café, '80 259
Floats, Maple-Coffee, '86 195
Frosted Coffee, '81 244
Frosting, Chocolate-Coffee, '84 36
Fudge, Coffee-Chip, '86 74
Ice Cream Crunch, Coffee, '82 182

Irish Coffee, Creamy, '79 232
Irish Coffee, Flaming, '79 293
Irish Coffee Nog, '84 258
Kahlúa Delight, Make-Ahead, '84 M89
Kona Luscious, '84 54
Liqueur, Coffee-Flavored, '86 266
Mallow, Coffee, '80 109
Mexican Coffee, '83 175, 275
Mix, Fireside Coffee, '87 241
Mocha Alaska Dessert, '84 191
Mocha-Almond Dessert, '80 289; '81 62
Mocha Brownies, '87 93
Mocha Brownie Torte, '85 102
Mocha Butter Cream Frosting, '79 281
Mocha-Buttercream Frosting, '86 26
Mocha Cake, Belgian, '84 316
Mocha Cake, Double, '84 311
Mocha Chiffon, '86 75
Mocha-Chocolate Cake, Dark, '84 311
Mocha Cocoa, '83 318
Mocha-Cocoa Mix, Hot, '82 296
Mocha Coffee, '85 M329
Mocha Cream, Café, '84 54
Mocha Cream Filling, '81 187; '84 305
Mocha Cream Roll, Chocolate, '84 304
Mocha Crunch Pie, Chocolate-, '81 136
Mocha Cupcakes, '85 250
Mocha Deluxe Hot Drink, '82 289
Mocha Dessert, Frozen, '84 311
Mocha Espresso, Italian, '82 254
Mocha Filling, '80 55; '82 262
Mocha Freeze, Royal, '84 53
Mocha Frosting, '83 301; '84 316; '87 224
Mocha Frosting, Creamy, '82 289; '84 311

Coffee *(continued)*

Mocha Gingerbread, '81 207; '82 14
Mocha, Hot, '84 60
Mocha-Mallow Parfaits, '80 219
Mocha Meringue Pie, '80 242
Mocha Punch, '84 58, 166; '86 270
Mocha, Quick Viennese, '79 232
Mocha Roulage, Chocolate-, '80 216
Mocha Squares, Frozen, '81 187
Mocha Swirl Cheesecake, '87 262
Mocha, Swiss-Style, '82 253
Mousse, Coffee, '84 126
Mousse, Coffee-Nut, '86 319
Mousse, Quick-as-a-Wink, '84 311
Nog, Brandied Coffee, '86 329
Orange Coffee, Viennese, '84 54
Parfaits, Coffee Crunch, '82 159
Pie, Coffee Ice Cream, '79 231
Pie, Coffee Pecan, '82 74
Praline-Flavored Coffee, '87 69
Pralines, Plantation Coffee, '86 241
Punch, Coffee, '80 50; '83 275
Punch, Coffee-and-Cream, '85 116
Punch, Coffee-Eggnog, '86 281
Punch, Creamy Coffee, '81 50
Punch, Rich-and-Creamy Coffee, '82 121
Refresher, Velvet Coffee, '79 149
Royal, Café, '80 259
Spiced Coffee, Special, '84 284
Tortoni, Coffee-Almond, '81 30
Viennese, Café, '82 254

Coleslaw. *See* Cabbage or Salads.

Cookies

Almond Butter Cookies, '79 52
Almond Chip Balls, Toasted, '84 240
Almond Cookies, '83 22, 181
Almond Cookies, Light, '83 151
Almond Cookies, Swedish, '85 312
Almond Spritz Cookies, '82 306
Bars and Squares
    Almond Cake Squares, '79 111
    Almond-Chocolate Bars, '83 304
    Almond Cream Confections, '87 198
    Apple Butter Bars, '84 153
    Apple Kuchen, '79 24
    Apricot Bars, '81 247
    Apricot-Oatmeal Bars, '86 216
    Apricot-Raisin Bars, '87 32
    Banana Breakfast Bars, '79 124
    Blackberry Bars, '87 130
    Blackberry-Filled Bars, '79 124
    Blackberry Jam Bars, '82 M185
    Blondie Swirls, '85 248
    Blond Nut Squares, '82 156
    Brazil Squares, '82 306
    Brownie Alaskas, '83 299
    Brownie Bars, Cinnamon, '81 230
    Brownie-Mint Dessert, '82 227
    Brownie Mix, '82 6
    Brownies, Amaretto, '86 246
    Brownies, Buttermilk, '85 249
    Brownies, Buttermilk Cake, '87 198
    Brownies, Butterscotch, '85 248
    Brownies, Cheesecake, '85 249
    Brownies, Chewy
      Marshmallow, '83 306
    Brownies, Chocolate-Banana, '80 160
    Brownies, Chocolate Chip, '81 162
    Brownies, Chocolate Chip-Peanut
      Butter, '84 73
    Brownies, Chocolate-Mint, '85 M294
    Brownies, Chocolate-Nut, '81 129

Brownies, Chocolate-Pecan, '81 64
Brownies, Chocolate Tea, '83 79
Brownies, Choco-Mallow, '87 198
Brownies, Cream Cheese
  Swirl, '79 51
Brownies, Crème de Menthe, '83 244
Brownies, Crunch-Crust, '87 198
Brownies, Easy, '83 245
Brownies, Favorite, '86 158
Brownies, Frosted Apple, '86 216
Brownies, German Cream
  Cheese, '80 269
Brownies, Heavenly Hash, '83 245
Brownies, Heavenly Honey, '79 83
Brownies, Mocha, '87 93
Brownies, Nutty Blonde, '81 64
Brownies, Nutty Cocoa, '81 64
Brownies, Nutty Fudge, '80 M171
Brownies, Oatmeal, '87 199
Brownies, Peanut Butter, '87 199
Brownies, Quick, '87 M302
Brownies, Quick and Easy, '82 6
Brownies, Rocky Road, '86 320
Brownies, Saucepan Pretzel, '85 171
Brownies, Walnut-Cream
  Cheese, '84 240
Butter Pecan Pie Squares, '81 262
Butterscotch Bars, '82 209; '83 297
By-Cracky Bars, '84 212
Carrot-Lemon Squares,
  Golden, '80 40
Carrot Squares, '79 256
Cherry Bars, Delightful, '86 217
Cherry Squares, Surprise, '82 57
Choco-Crumble Bars, '79 292
Chocolate-Butterscotch Bars, '81 197
Chocolate-Caramel Layer
  Squares, '79 83
Chocolate Chip Bars, '81 130
Chocolate Chip-Peanut Butter
  Squares, '84 118
Chocolate Chip Squares, '83 170
Chocolate Cinnamon Bars, '82 209
Chocolate-Crème de Menthe
  Bars, '86 245
Chocolate Dream Bars, '79 256;
  '82 298
Chocolate-Peppermint
  Squares, '81 119
Cinnamon Chews, '84 110
Coconut Granola Bars, '85 202
Coffee Bars, Frosted, '79 256
Date Bars, '84 313
Date Bars, No-Bake, '79 256
Date Bars, Nutty, '84 153
Date-Nut Bars, '80 166
Date-Oat Bars, '80 M172
English Cherubs, '83 257
Fudge Bars, '86 93
Fudge Bars, Yummy, '87 158
Golden Bars, '84 255
Granola Bars, '83 305
Granola Bars, Fruit and Nut, '81 49
Hawaiian Bars, '84 153
Jam-It Bars, '87 159
Jam Squares, '81 M289
Janhagel Cookies, '86 195
Lemon Bars Deluxe, '79 35
Lemon Bars, Tangy, '86 217
Lemon Squares, '81 197
Lemon Yogurt Wheat Bars, '79 93
Lime Squares, '79 2
Marmalade Biscuit Squares, '79 193

Meringue-Chocolate Chip
  Bars, '84 118
Nutmeg Logs, Frosted, '85 324
Nutty Choco Snacks, '83 305
Oatmeal Bars, Chocolate-
  Topped, '86 110
Oatmeal-Caramel Bars, '85 247
Oatmeal-Date Bars, Layered, '85 10
Peanut Bars, Chewy, '80 M172
Peanut Butter-and-Fudge
  Bars, '80 M172
Peanut Butter Bars, '84 243
Peanut Butter Fingers, '79 256
Peanut Butter Frosts, '84 153
Peanut Butter Logs,
  No-Bake, '84 211
Peanut Butter 'n' Jelly Bars, '83 305
Peanut Butter Squares, '83 116
Pecan Bars, '82 209
Pecan Squares, '79 205
Pecan Squares, Easy, '81 230
Pecan Squares, Twice-Baked, '79 291
Pumpkin Bars, '80 40
Pumpkin Nut Bars, '82 217
Raspberry Bars, '82 209; '84 212
Rhubarb Squares, Rosy, '79 111
Strawberry Bars, '81 301
Tropical Bars, '80 284
Wheat Germ Squares, Spicy, '80 44
Zucchini Bars, '85 77
Bourbon Balls, '81 254
Bourbon Dunkers, Crunchy, '85 90
Butter Cookies, '85 322
Butter Cookies, Melt-Away, '81 20
Butter-Nut Strips, '82 167
Butter Pecan Cookies, '82 139
Cheesecake Cookies, Chewy, '82 109
Cherry Nut Nuggets, '81 286
Chocolate Chip Cookies, Giant, '84 119
Chocolate Chip Melt-Aways, '84 118
Chocolate-Mint Snaps, '83 103; '84 96
Chocolate-Peanut Butter Cones, '85 14
Chocolate-Peanut Butter Cookies, '85 90
Chocolate-Peanut Butter Cups, '85 14
Chocolate Snappers, Jumbo, '81 218
Chocolate-Tipped Butter Cookies, '84 258
Chocolate-Tipped Log Cookies, '87 294
Choco-Nut Sandwich Cookies, '84 200

Christmas

Calendar, Cookie Advent, '85 325
Cards, Christmas Cookie, '84 302
Eggnog Christmas Cookies, '79 255
Elf Cookie, '80 279, 303
Gingerbread Cookies, '80 278
Lizzies, Christmas, '87 257

Mrs. Claus Cookie, '80 279, 303
Painted Cookies, '86 322
Rudolph Cookie, '80 279, 303
Santa Claus Cookie, '80 278, 303
Santa's Whiskers, '85 323
Sleigh Cookie, '80 279, 303
Spiced Christmas Cookies, '87 294
Strawberries, Christmas, '87 293
Swedish Christmas Cookies, '79 290
Cinnamon Balls, '79 23
Cinnamon Wafers, '81 192
Cocoa Kiss Cookies, '85 171
Curled Cookies, French, '87 16
Drop
Ambrosia Cookies, 81 301; '82 110;
'86 313
Apple Butter Spice Cookies, '79 291
Apple Cookies, Fresh, '84 36
Apple-Nut Cookies, '80 228
Apple Oatmeal Cookies, '85 215
Apricot Cookies, Frosted, '81 192
Banana Oatmeal Cookies, '79 217
Benne Seed Cookies, '84 318
Breakfast Cookies, Take-
Along, '84 59
Butterscotch Cookies, '87 58
Butterscotch-Pecan Cookies, '84 36
Candy Bit Cookies, '81 192
Carrot Cookies, '82 137
Carrot Cookies, Frosted, '81 7
Carrot-Orange Cookies, '83 149
Cherry-Almond Drops, '81 20
Chip Cookies, Double, '81 301
Chips Cookies, Loaded-with-, '87 223
Chocolate Chip Cookies, '84 120;
'86 245
Chocolate Chip Cookies,
Deluxe, '79 216
Chocolate Chip Cookies,
Different, '83 114
Chocolate Chip Cookies,
Double, '79 217
Chocolate Chip Cookies,
Jumbo, '82 110
Chocolate Chip Cookies,
Light, '86 46
Chocolate Chip Cookies, Nutty
Oatmeal-, '82 M185
Chocolate Chip-Oatmeal
Cookies, '84 119
Chocolate-Chocolate Chip
Cookies, '82 35
Chocolate Cookies,
Doubly-Good, '82 M185
Chocolate Crispy Cookies, '85 115
Chocolate Drop Cookies, '84 36
Chocolate Macaroons, '87 57
Chocolate-Mint Chip Cookies, '86 245
Chocolate-Nut Chews, '81 92
Chocolate-Oatmeal Cookies, '80 105
Chocolate-Peanut Cookies, '83 223
Chocolate Sandwich Cookies, '81 192
Cocoa Drop Cookies, '80 217
Coconut-Cherry Cookies, '79 292
Coconut Macaroons, '79 52
Cream Cheese Cookies, '80 282
Devil Doggies, '84 37
Forget 'em Cookies, '83 256
Fruitcake Cookies, '79 291; '86 320
Fruitcake Cookies, Holiday, '81 301
Fruit Cookies, Bourbon, '86 334
Fruit Cookies, Spicy Holiday, '83 298
Gumdrop Cookies, '79 292

Jack-O'-Lantern Cookies, '87 214
Lace Cookies, '86 8
Lemonade Cookies, '79 51
Lemon Yummies, '81 301
Macaroons, Chocolate, '83 300
Melting Moments, '85 191
Meringue Kiss Cookies, '86 121
Meringue Surprise Cookies, '86 320
Mincemeat Drop Cookies, '79 246
Molasses Cookies, Chewy, '87 257
Monster Cookies, '84 36
Nugget Cookies, '79 291
Nutmeg Sugar Cookies, '79 136
Oatmeal Cookies, Cinnamon, '84 72
Oatmeal Cookies, Crunchy, '85 202
Oatmeal Cookies, Easy, '80 105
Oatmeal Cookies, Nutty, '81 130
Oatmeal Cookies, Old-Fashioned,
'80 106; '85 250
Oatmeal Cookies, Orange-Glazed,
'80 60
Oatmeal Cookies, Peanutty, '80 106;
'83 95

Oatmeal Cookies, Spicy, '81 197
Oatmeal-Date Cookies, '82 109
Oatmeal Krispies, '85 115
Oatmeal-Peanut Butter
Cookies, '85 171
Oatmeal-Raisin Cookies, '87 221
Oatmeal-Raisin Cookies,
Frosted, '79 290
Oatmeal-Spice Cookies,
Giant, '80 105
Orange-Chocolate Cookies, '83 113
Orange Cookies, Frosted, '83 114
Peanut Butter-Oatmeal
Cookies, '81 218
Peanut Cookies, Salted, '87 92
Persimmon-Raisin Cookies, '85 232
Pineapple Cookies, '79 216
Potato Chip Cookies, '86 93
Pumpkin Drop Cookies, '79 206
Pumpkin-Walnut Cookies,
Frosted, '82 217
Raisin Cookies, Alltime
Favorite, '80 24
Sour Cream Cookies,
Southern, '83 113
Sour Cream-Nutmeg Cookies, '85 171
Sunflower Cookies, Crinkle, '83 149
Ginger Cookies, '85 306
Ginger Crinkles, '83 149
Gingersnaps, '79 146
Gingersnaps, Best-Ever, '79 208

Hazelnut Cookies, '84 111
Hazelnut-Lemon Logs, '84 117
Heavenly Delights, '85 324
Lemon Cookies, Sunshine, '86 69
Lemon Crinkle Cookies, '81 287
Lemon Zephers, '81 172
Madeleines, Snow-Capped, '85 120
Mailing Cookies, Tips on, '83 305
Miracle Cookies, '83 149
Oatmeal Cookies, Special, '81 236
Orange Fingers, '87 57
Peanut Butter-Chocolate Kiss
Cookies, '86 49
Peanut Butter-Cinnamon Cookies, '84 30
Peanut Butter Cookies, '82 56
Peanut Butter Cookies, Quick, '86 109
Peanut Butter-Oatmeal Cookies, '84 72
Peanut Butter Temptations, '84 29
Peanut-Date Balls, '81 92
Pecan-Butter Cookies, '83 113
Pecan Crescent Cookies, '85 324
Peppermint Wreaths, Melt-Away, '85 324
Pizzelles, '83 298
Refrigerator
Apricot Kolaches, '83 84
Butter Cookies, Valentine, '81 20
Cardamom Cookies, '79 12
Cherry Pecan Cookies, '82 136
Chocolate-Cherry Cookies, '85 324
Chocolate Meltaways, '81 302
Chocolate Pinwheel Cookies, '86 245
Chocolate Snowball Cookies, '82 295
Chocolate Teasers, '87 44
Crème de Menthe Cookies, '86 230
Crescents, '85 321
Date-Cream Cheese Rollups, '83 298
Date Nut Roll, '79 249
Gingerbread Men, '84 299
Gingerbread Men, Miniature, '84 318
Gingersnaps, Raisin, '85 324
Grandmother's Sandwich
Cookies, '82 306
Holiday Garland Cookies, '83 299
Holiday Riches, '83 257
Molasses Cookies, '86 20
Oatmeal-Date Sandwich
Cookies, '83 257
Orange Crispies, '84 205
Orange Refrigerator Cookies, '86 230
Peanut Butter-Chocolate Chip
Cookies, Freezer, '86 230
Peanut Butter-Coconut
Cookies, '83 113
Peanut Butter Cookies, '87 58
Peanut Butter Crisps, '79 50
Peanut Butter Slice-and-
Bakes, '82 M185
Peanut Butter Snaps, '81 237
Pecan-Cheese Wafers, '81 119
Pecan Crisps, Sugar, '86 230
Raspberry Sandwich Cookies, '82 306
Ribbon Cookies, '87 293
Sesame-Cheese Cutouts, '82 296
Shortbread Cookie Crumbs, '83 298
Shortbread Cookies, '87 58
Shortbread Cookies, Crispy, '83 113
Sour Cream Cookies, Dutch, '83 149
Spice Cookies, Slice-of-, '79 290
Springerle, '81 251
Sugar Cookies, Crisp, '84 243
Sugar Cookies, Molasses, '80 270
Sugar Cookies, Red-, '81 21
Sugar Cookies, Valentine, '82 20

Cookies, Refrigerator *(continued)*

Sugar 'n Spice Cookies, **'81** 21
Swedish Cookies, **'82** 306
Tea Cookies, **'83** 170
Vanilla Crescents, **'82** 307
Vanilla Slice-and-Bake
   Cookies, **'85** 171
Wafers, Italian, **'87** 36
Walnut Cookies, **'81** 301
Rolled
Almond Holly Leaves, **'86** 319
Apricot Cookie Rolls, **'80** 282
Cheese Straws, **'82** 137
Chocolate Cookies, Chewy, **'80** 208
Choco Surprise Cookies, **'80** 60
Cinnamon Stars, Swiss, **'87** 293
Cream Cheese Frills, **'79** 291
Crème de Menthe Cookies, **'80** 282
Currant Teacakes, **'80** 88
Frosted Cutout Cookies, **'85** 236
Fruit Cookies, Rolled, **'80** 15
Fruit-Nut Twists, **'82** 253
Gingerbread Animal Cookies, **'86** 70
Gingerbread Cookies, **'80** 278

Gingerbread Men, **'85** 259
Gingerbread Men Cookies, **'85** 319
Ginger Cookies, Swedish, **'85** 323
Grandmother's Cookies, **'85** 319
Ice Box Filled Cookies, **'79** 112
Lemon Pecan Dainties, **'80** 208
Lemony Cutout Cookies, **'85** 323
Maple Sandwich Cookies, **'85** 322
Mincemeat Cookies, **'79** 51
Mincemeat Sweetheart
   Cookies, **'87** 293
Oat Crispies, **'83** 96
Oatmeal-Coconut Cookies, **'80** 218
Oatmeal Cookies,
   Date-Filled, **'86** 314
Oatmeal Cookies,
   Slice-and-Bake, **'80** 105
Oatmeal Nut Crispies, **'80** 208
Peanut Butter Cookies,
   Double, **'80** 209
Pear Mincemeat Cookies, **'84** 264
Pecan Cookies, Easy, **'80** 208
Scones, Currant, **'84** 117
Sherry Snaps, **'87** 94
Shortbread Cookies, Butter
   Pecan, **'80** 282
Shortbread, Easy Roll-Out, **'81** 21
Shortbread Sugarplums,
   Pecan-, **'83** 298
Sorghum Tea Cakes, **'85** 239
Sugar Cookies, Crescent, **'87** 294

Sugar Cookies, Moravian, **'85** 321
Sugar Cookies, Old-
   Fashioned, **'86** 313
Sugar Cookies, Rolled, **'79** 291
Teacakes, Old-Fashioned, **'84** 43
Sandwich Cookies, Viennese, **'87** 293
Sesame Cookies, Italian, **'85** 311
Snappin' Turtle Cookies, **'85** 323
Spice Cookies, **'87** M278
Sugar Cookies, Cinnamon, **'84** 73
Sugar Cookies, Molasses, **'82** 140
Sugar Cookies, Sour Cream, **'79** 51
Swedish Heirloom Cookies, **'81** 129
Tea Cakes, Mexican, **'81** 196
Thumbprint Cookies, Childhood, **'85** 323
Waffle Cookies, Brownie, **'86** 245
Wedding Cookies, **'82** M185
Whoopie Pies, **'86** 246

Cooking Light
Appetizers
Ambrosia, Sherried, **'84** 324
Artichokes, Marinated, **'87** 250
Artichokes with Herb-Mayonnaise
   Dip, **'84** 67
Carrot-Cheese Ball, **'86** 325
Crudité Platter with Dip, **'84** 139
Dip, Curry, **'87** 25
Dip, Deviled, **'87** 25
Dip, Dilled Garden, **'84** 324
Dip, Low-Cal Tuna, **'87** 25
Dip, Spinach, **'87** 25
Dip, Tofu, **'86** 109
Dip, Vegetable Garden, **'85** 215
Fruit Kabobs with Coconut
   Dressing, **'87** 251
Fruit with Lemon Sauce,
   Fresh, **'82** 290
Mousse, Shrimp, **'87** 251
Nectarine Cocktail, **'85** 107
Orange Halves, Broiled, **'85** 288
Pasta Bites, Pesto-Cheese, **'87** 251
Pâté, Mock, **'87** 251
Pears Stuffed with Cheese, **'82** 290
Peas, Crab-Stuffed Snow, **'85** 288
Popcorn Mix, Curried, **'86** 326
Scallop Appetizer, **'86** 155
Shrimp Dippers, **'84** 324
Spread, Low-Fat Chicken, **'82** 290
Spread, Smoked Salmon, **'84** 324
Steak-and-Chestnut Appetizers,
   Marinated, **'84** 323
Tomatoes, Crab-Stuffed
   Cherry, **'82** 289
Vegetable Appetizer,
   Tarragon, **'83** 277
Apples, Baked, **'86** 40
Apples with Orange Sauce,
   Baked, **'84** 314
Beverages
Apple Julep, **'86** 103
Banana Nog, **'82** 290
Cider, Hot Spiced, **'82** 290
Cocoa, Mocha, **'83** 318
Eggnog, **'83** 318
Fruit Beverage, Blender, **'83** 318
Fruit Shake, Frosty, **'87** 23
Mocha, Hot, **'84** 60
Orange Slush, **'82** 49
Peach Cooler, **'86** 6
Peach Frosty, **'83** 318
Peach Refresher, **'86** 103
Punch, Apple-Tea, **'85** 82
Punch, Holiday, **'87** 252

Punch, Hot Apple, **'84** 324
Punch, Tart Cranberry, **'83** 318
Shake, Strawberry-Orange
   Breakfast, **'87** 186
Strawberry Cooler, **'83** 56
Tea Mix, Spiced, **'86** 32
Tomato-Clam Cocktail, **'87** 252
Tomato Refresher, **'83** 318
Vegetable Cocktail, Fresh, **'82** 165
Breads
Banana Bread, **'87** 72
Biscuits, Whole Wheat, **'84** 60
Biscuits, Yeast, **'87** 71
Cornbread, Dieter's, **'87** 164
Garlic Bread, **'82** 19
Muffins, Apple, **'84** 193
Muffins, Banana-Oat, **'87** 188
Muffins, Bran-Buttermilk, **'85** 7
Muffins Made of Bran, **'86** 103
Muffins, Spicy Apple-Oat, **'86** 45
Oat Bread, Caraway-Raisin, **'86** 44
Pumpkin-Pecan Bread, **'87** 221
Rolls, Honey Wheat, **'83** 278
Rolls, Vegetable Salad, **'82** 278
Toast, Cottage-Topped French, **'85** 49
Toast, Slender French, **'86** 103
Whole Wheat Cardamom
   Bread, **'86** 223
Crêpes, Basic, **'86** 38
Crêpes, Bran, **'83** 70; **'86** 44
Crêpes, Ham-and-Egg, **'83** 204
Crêpes, Light, **'86** 143
Crêpes, Low-Calorie, **'87** 77
Crêpes, Plain, **'83** 70
Crêpes Suzettes, Light, **'83** 71
Crêpes, Whole Wheat, **'83** 70
Desserts
Alaska, Orange, **'83** 177
Ambrosia, Baked, **'83** 303
Bananas with Honey,
   Broiled, **'84** 175
Bars, Apricot-Raisin, **'87** 32
Bars, Pineapple-Orange, **'82** 129
Bavarian Dessert, Light, **'86** 6
Blackberries and Dumplings, **'86** 196
Blintzes, Cheese, **'83** 71
Blueberry Crisp, **'84** 177
Cake, Apple-Nut, **'87** 76
Cake, Chocolate Angel Food, **'87** 21
Cake, Deluxe Light Banana, **'84** 314
Cake, Heavenly Pineapple, **'83** 303
Cake, Orange Pound, **'87** 221
Cake with Pineapple-Orange Sauce,
   Angel, **'84** 14
Cake with Strawberries and Chocolate
   Glaze, White, **'87** 76
Cheesecake, Almost
   Strawberry, **'86** 32
Cheesecake, Blueberry
   Chiffon, **'87** 76
Cheesecake, Dieter's Apple, **'86** 318
Cherries Jubilite, **'86** 317
Chocolate Cream Roll, **'85** 317
Chocolat, Petits Pots de, **'82** 272
Cobbler, Fresh Cherry, **'84** 178
Cobbler, New-Fashioned
   Blackberry, **'87** 164
Cobbler, Peach, **'84** 178
Compote, Baked Fruit, **'84** 314
Compote, Fresh Fruit, **'82** 272;
   '84 82
Compote, Melon Ball, **'85** 157
Cookies, Apple-Oatmeal, **'85** 215

Cookies, Light Almond, '83 151
Cookies, Light Chocolate
  Chip, '86 46
Cookies, Oatmeal-Raisin, '87 221
Cream Puffs,
  Strawberry-Lemon, '87 75
Crêpes, Tropical Fruit, '87 77
Crust, Graham Cracker, '86 32
Custard, Baked Vanilla, '82 129
Custard, Coconut, '86 109
Custard over Fruit, Stirred, '84 83
Custard, Range-Top Amaretto, '87 77
Flambé, Banana-Peach, '85 316
Fruit Dessert, Caribbean, '84 314
Fruit Dessert, Flaming, '83 302
Fruit Dessert Orange, '84 314
Fruit Dessert, Rainbow, '85 108

Fruit Dessert, Spiced, '82 50
Fruit, Gingered, '83 151
Fruit, Glazed, '85 83
Fruit Medley, Fancy, '84 82
Honeydew-Berry Dessert, '83 120
Ice, Cranberry-Apple, '82 290
Ice, Kiwi, '84 315
Ice, Peach-Yogurt, '84 83
Ice, Strawberry, '84 175; '85 108
Ice, Strawberry-Orange, '86 196
Ice, Tangy Cranberry, '87 305
Ice, Tart Cranberry-Orange, '86 317
Kiwi Jubilee, '83 120
Melon Mélange, '84 139
Melon-Mint Julep, '86 196
Meringue Shells, Fruited, '87 32
Meringues, Peach Melba, '87 76
Mousse, Coffee-Nut, '86 319
Mousse, Peach, '85 54
Mousse, Strawberry-Lemon, '82 128
Orange Molded Dessert, '83 302
Oranges and Pineapple,
  Glazed, '86 318
Parfait, Peach, '82 166
Parfait, Pineapple, '84 83
Peach Dessert, Spiced, '83 9
Peaches with Honey-Lime
  Whip, '85 108
Peaches with Nutty Dumplings,
  Spiced, '87 164
Peaches with Strawberry Sauce, '85 8
Peach Halves, Stuffed, '86 196
Pears in Orange Sauce,
  Poached, '82 19
Pears Poached in Red Wine, '83 302
Pears with Berry Sauce,
  Wine-Poached, '86 144
Pie, Eggnog, '83 205
Pie, Fresh Apple, '84 178
Pineapple, Meringue-Topped, '84 178
Plum Slush, '84 139
Pops, Orange-Banana, '82 129

Prune Bavarian, '86 223
Pudding, Layered Lemon, '82 128
Pudding, Light Plum, '86 318
Pudding, Raisin-Pumpkin, '84 315
Pumpkin Chiffon, '86 283
Rice Cream with Mandarin
  Oranges, '85 317
Roll, Chocolate-Orange, '87 21
Sauce, Melba, '87 77
Sherbet, Instant Fruit, '85 158
Sherbet, Pineapple, '84 83
Sorbet, Blueberry-Kirsch, '83 120
Sorbet, Mango, '86 196
Soufflé, Light Chocolate, '83 278
Soufflé, Orange Dessert, '83 206
Soufflé, Raspberry-Topped, '85 317
Soufflé, Tart Lemon, '85 82
Strawberries Juliet, '84 82
Strawberry Dessert, Glazed, '84 33
Strawberry Puff, '82 5
Tapioca Fluff, Orange, '87 31
Tart, Fancy Fruit, '82 128
Tart, Fresh Fruit, '84 178
Tart, Green Grape, '87 77
Tart Shell, '87 77
Topping, Blueberry, '87 125
Topping, Cherry-Pineapple, '87 126
Topping, Chunky Piña
  Colada, '87 125
Topping, Raspberry, '85 317
Topping, Raspberry-Peach, '87 126
Topping, Reduced-Calorie
  Whipped, '85 55
Topping, Spicy Apple, '87 125
Topping, Strawberry, '86 32
Topping, Strawberry-Banana, '87 125
Wafers, Cinnamon, '84 324
Watermelon Frost, '86 196
Yogurt, Lemon-Chiffon
  Frozen, '85 54
Yogurt, Vanilla Frozen, '87 125
Eggs and Omelets
  Benedict, Eggs, '85 49
  Cheddar-Vegetable Omelet, '83 205
  Florentine, Eggs, '83 56
  Primavera, Omelet, '87 71
  Scrambled Eggs, Mexican-
    Style, '85 50
  Scrambled Eggs, Spanish, '84 60
  Vegetable Omelet, Cheesy, '85 49
Filling, Chicken Salad, '87 106
Filling, Shrimp Salad, '87 106
Fruit Medley, Chilled, '84 60
Fruit Nuggets, Dried, '86 326
Fruit, Warm Spiced, '86 39
Grapefruit, Broiled, '85 7
Low Sodium
  Applesauce, Spicy, '82 296
  Asparagus with Basil Sauce, '86 33
  Beans, Minted Green, '84 104
  Beef and Rice, Spicy, '83 231
  Beef Burgundy, '83 281
  Beef Goulash, '83 231
  Biscuits, Flaky, '84 228
  Bread, Bran-Applesauce, '84 229
  Bread, Salt-Free Raisin Batter, '86 33
  Breadsticks, Whole Wheat, '84 228
  Brussels Sprouts, Calico
    Citrus, '85 303
  Butter, Herbed Unsalted, '82 67
  Carrots Madeira, '83 281
  Catsup, Spicy Tomato, '83 182
  Cereal Snack, Toasted, '85 215

Chicken à l'Orange, '84 277
Chicken-and-Vegetables,
  Stir-Fry, '86 68
Chicken, Citrus-Herb Baked, '85 303
Chicken Dinner, Healthful, '83 232
Chicken, Herb-Baked, '82 229
Chicken in Lemon and Wine, '83 281
Chicken Piccata, '83 35
Chicken-Tomato Bake, '83 35
Chicken with Wine-Soaked
  Vegetables, Baked, '84 277
Chili Surprise, '82 229
Cookies, Sunshine Lemon, '86 69
Cornish Hens in Vermouth, '86 33
Cornish Hens, Roasted Rock, '82 66
Dressing, Lemon-Herb Salad, '82 67
Dressing, Orange-Yogurt, '85 304
Fish, Curried Baked, '87 5
Flounder Rolls, Vegetable-
  Stuffed, '87 6
Fruit Delight, Hot, '83 281
Fruit Delight, Spiced, '82 229
Fruit, Unsweetened Mixed, '83 182
Ice, Pink Grapefruit, '85 304
Jam, Banana, '82 296
Jam, Freezer Peach, '83 182
Lamb Chops, Dijon, '84 277
Lamb Chops, Orange, '83 35
Linguine with Seafood Sauce, '83 232
Meat Loaf, Corny, '86 68
Meat Loaf, Parsleyed, '83 35
Mocha-Cocoa Mix, Hot, '82 296
Mousse, Orange, '86 69
Muffins, Honey-Oatmeal, '84 229
Muffins, Spiced Bran, '84 229
Mustard, Lower Sodium
  Horseradish, '86 325
Nectarines in Apple Juice, '83 183
Onions, Glazed, '84 104
Orange Scampi, '85 303
Pastry Shell, Sesame, '82 67
Peppers, Corn Stuffed, '84 104
Pie, Nutty Pumpkin, '82 67
Pork, Roast Loin of, '84 276
Potato Bake, Chive-, '82 229
Pretzels with Lower Sodium
  Horseradish Mustard, Herb, '86 325
Pudding, Lemon Fluff, '85 304
Ratatouille, '84 105

Rice and Shrimp, Curried, '83 231
Rice, Calico Brown, '86 33
Rolls, Low-Sodium
  Refrigerator, '82 67
Rolls, Low-Sodium Yeast, '84 228
Salad, Asparagus-and-New
  Potato, '86 69
Salad, Citrus Green, '85 304
Salad, Dilled Cucumber, '82 229
Salad Mold, Golden Citrus, '85 303
Salad, Mushroom-and-Pepper, '86 68
Salad, Sesame-Citrus Green, '86 33
Salmon, Poached, '83 35

Cooking Light, Low Sodium *(continued)*

Salmon Steaks, Marinated, '87 6
Sauce, Apple-Horseradish, '82 229
Sauce, Green Herb, '83 36
Sauce, Seafood, '83 36
Scallops, Sherried, '83 281
Scamp, Tangy Broiled, '87 5
Seasoning Blend, '82 296
Shake, Pineapple-Banana, '85 215
Shrimp Kabobs, Marinated, '84 276
Shrimp, Special Boiled, '83 36
Snapper, Caribbean, '87 5
Spaghetti, Veal, '84 276
Squash Sauté, '82 67
Squash, Vegetable-Stuffed, '84 104
Steak, Marinated Flank, '83 35
Stew, White Wine, '82 228
Stuffing, Low-Sodium, '82 66
Swordfish, Foil-Baked, '87 5
Tomatoes, Stewed, '83 182
Tomato Puree, Seasoned, '83 182
Tropical Snow, '86 34
Veal, Savory, '83 281
Vegetable Stir-Fry, '84 104
Waffles, Whole Wheat, '84 228
Zucchini, Herbed, '84 104
Macaroni and Cheese, Baked, '82 199
Main Dishes
Asparagus Roulade, '86 102
Beef-and-Barley Rolls,
Wine-Sauced, '87 269
Beef-and-Vegetable Stir-Fry, '87 22
Beef, Chinese-Style, '87 50
Beef Kabobs, Spirited, '87 142
Beef Kabobs with Rice,
Marinated, '84 32
Beef Medallions, Italian, '87 305
Beef Patties, Deviled-, '87 22
Beef Stir-Fry, Chinese, '83 151
Beef Stroganoff, Light, '86 36
Burgers, Seasoned, '85 158
Burritos, Cheesy Beef, '85 193
Catfish, Southern Oven-Fried, '87 163
Chicken and Spinach Noodles, '82 19
Chicken and Vegetables,
Stir-Fry, '86 249
Chicken and Vegetables,
Walnut, '85 194
Chicken Breasts Sardou,
Stuffed, '87 269
Chicken Breasts,
Wine-Baked, '83 177
Chicken Cacciatore, '86 42
Chicken, Chutney, '86 249
Chicken Cordon Bleu, '86 37
Chicken, Creamed, '82 49
Chicken, Crunchy
Oven-Fried, '87 163
Chicken, Curried, '86 43
Chicken Curry, Stir-Fried, '87 51
Chicken Cutlets with Lemon, '85 8
Chicken Dinner, Skillet, '86 249
Chicken Fingers,
Herb-Baked, '86 249
Chicken in a Bag, '87 23
Chicken in Orange Sauce, '83 8
Chicken Kabobs, Sesame, '82 165
Chicken Kiev, Oven-Baked, '86 37
Chicken la France, '86 248
Chicken, Orange, '83 278
Chicken Paprika, Dilled, '86 41
Chicken, Pineapple, '83 M194

Chicken Rolls, Spinach-
Stuffed, '86 248
Chicken, Southern Oven-Fried, '86 37
Chicken Spaghetti, '87 221
Chicken-Vegetable Stir-Fry, '83 151;
'84 13
Chicken with Artichokes,
Sherried, '87 143
Chicken with Pineapple,
Oriental, '86 42
Cornish Hens, Herbed, '82 271
Cornish Hens, Orange-Glazed
Grilled, '86 250
Crabmeat au Gratin, '86 154
Crawfish Étouffée, '86 156
Crêpes, Cannelloni, '86 143
Crêpes, Chicken-Vegetable, '83 70
Fish Florentine, '86 35
Fish Florentine in Parchment, '87 22
Flounder, Creole-Style, '85 180
Flounder Rolls with Citrus Sauce,
Stuffed, '85 180
Grits-and-Ham Pie, Crustless, '86 103
Halibut with Swiss Sauce, '83 M195
Hamburger Pie, '84 13
Kabobs, Hawaiian, '85 157
Lamb Chops, Broiled, '85 22

Lasagna, Cheesy Spinach, '83 204
Lasagna, Lean, '86 37
Lasagna, Vegetable, '84 201
Lasagna, Zucchini, '85 194
Lentil-and-Rice Supper, '84 202
Liver, Creole, '86 108
Liver in Creole Sauce, '87 33
Lobster Tails with Spiced Orange
Sauce, '86 155
London Broil, Marinated, '87 32
Manicotti, Spinach, '82 199
Meat Loaf, Curried, '86 43
Meat Loaf, Oriental, '83 M194
Meat Loaf, Parsley, '87 22
Pasta Primavera, Almost, '86 38
Pasta Salad, Main-Dish, '82 199
Pasta Verde, '84 201
Pastichio, '85 194
Pear Breakfast Treat, '87 72
Peas and Red Pepper, Sesame
Snow, '84 175
Pizza, Whole Wheat, '84 33
Pork Chops, Apricot-Sauced, '85 22
Pork, Stir-Fried, '87 51
Pork, Sweet-and-Sour, '85 34, 194
Pork Tenderloin, Marinated, '84 175
Pork Tenderloins, Fruit-
Stuffed, '87 270
Pot Roast, Marinated, '85 21

Quiche, Eggless, '87 220
Quiches, Individual Spinach, '86 38
Quiche, Swiss-Zucchini, '82 49
Salmon Loaf with Cucumber-Dill
Sauce, '86 5
Sausage, Dieters' Spicy, '85 49
Scallop Kabobs, Grilled, '83 101
Shrimp, Beer-Broiled, '87 142
Shrimp Skillet, Quick, '87 50
Shrimp, Sweet-and-Sour, '83 278
Snapper à l'Orange, Baked, '85 181
Snapper, Honey-Curried, '85 181
Snapper, Poached, '83 101
Snapper Rolls, Cucumber-Stuffed
Red, '83 176
Sole Divan, '87 21
Sole Véronique, '85 181
Spaghetti, Meaty, '82 19
Steak, Fast-and-Easy
Stir-Fried, '87 50
Steak in Red Wine Sauce,
Skillet, '85 21
Steak Kabobs, '82 4
Steak, Mock Country-Fried, '87 163
Steak, Pepper-Beef, '85 21
Tofu, Stroganoff, '84 202
Tuna Croquettes with Parsley
Sauce, '86 108
Turkey Breast, Stuffed, '87 270
Turkey Breast with Special Gravy,
Roast, '86 282
Veal and Carrots, Company, '85 22
Veal Picante, '87 31
Veal Picatta with Capers, '87 142
Veal Scallopini, '83 8
Vegetarian Supper, '86 222
Vermicelli and Sprouts with Red
Clam Sauce, '86 143
Vermicelli, Scallop-Vegetable, '87 143
Zucchini Frittata, '86 103
Pancakes, Shredded Wheat, '84 59
Pasta-Basil Toss, '87 33
Pasta, Garden, '82 199
Peaches, Spicy Baked, '86 39
Relish, Cranberry, '86 283
Rice and Mushrooms, Wild, '83 278
Rice, Apple-Cinnamon, '86 249
Rice Casserole, Colorful, '82 199
Rice-Cheese Shell, '82 49
Rice, Lime-Flavored, '84 175
Rice Mix, Fruited Curry-, '86 326
Rice, Orange, '82 200
Rice, Peppered, '82 4
Rice Pilaf, Browned, '87 305
Rice, Seasoned Onion, '82 166
Salad Dressings
Blue Cheese Dressing, '82 166
Coconut Dressing, '87 251
Cucumber-Mint Dressing, '87 153
Cucumber Salad Dressing,
Creamy, '82 79
Curry Dressing, '82 78
French Dressing, Miracle, '82 79
Fruit, Salad Dressing for, '86 40
Herb Salad Dressing, '86 40
Horseradish Dressing, '87 152
Lime Dressing, '83 120
Orange-Poppy Seed Dressing, '87 187
Pineapple-Poppy Seed
Dressing, '85 55
Raspberry Dressing, '87 153
Soy-Sesame Dressing, '87 153
Spring Garden Dressing, '85 157

Stay Trim Dressing, '86 40
Sweet-and-Sour Dressing, '87 305
Tangy Dressing, '83 9
Thousand Island Dressing,
  Special, '82 79
Yogurt Dressing, '85 59, 215
Yogurt Dressing, Sweet-Hot, '86 40
Yogurt-Honey Poppy Seed
  Dressing, '83 177

Salads
  Ambrosia, Brunch, '83 57
  Apple-Bran Salad, Lemony, '86 223
  Apple Cider Salad Mold, '85 54
  Apple Salad, Spicy, '85 215
  Asparagus, Marinated, '84 67
  Asparagus Vinaigrette, Light, '82 50
  Aspic, Light Tomato, '85 83
  Aspic, Tomato-Crab, '85 287
  Aspic with Horseradish Dressing,
    Crisp Vegetable, '87 152
  Bean-and-Rice Salad,
    Marinated, '87 152
  Bean Salad, Marinated, '85 137, 296
  Beans with Sprouts,
    Sweet-and-Sour, '86 32
  Bean-Tomato Salad, Lima, '85 137
  Beef-and-Broccoli Salad, '87 187
  Broccoli-Corn Salad, '87 24
  Cantaloupe, Fruit-Filled, '83 120
  Carrot-and-Seed Salad,
    Fruity, '86 223
  Carrot-Raisin Salad, '84 174
  Cauliflower-Vegetable Salad, '85 158
  Cheesy Italian Salad, '84 33
  Cherry-Apple Salad, '86 31
  Cherry Salad, Fresh, '83 120
  Chicken-Fruit Salad, '82 79
  Chicken Salad, Crunchy, '86 207
  Chicken Salad, Special, '85 82
  Coleslaw, Crunchy, '86 295
  Corn Salad, '85 236
  Cottage Cheese Salad in
    Tomatoes, '86 208
  Crab-Wild Rice Salad, '86 207
  Cucumber-Yogurt Salad, '87 33
  Fruit, Dressed-Up, '82 5
  Fruit Salad, Chef's, '86 35
  Fruit Salad, Curried, '85 107
  Garden-Patch Salad Molds, '86 283
  Garden Salad, Summer, '87 153

  Grape Salad Mold, '83 120
  Greens, Crimson, '87 153
  Layered Salad, '86 35
  Lettuce, Confetti-Stuffed, '87 24
  Macaroni-Cheese Salad,
    Dilled, '86 208
  Macaroni-Tuna Salad, Whole
    Wheat, '84 193
  Mandarin Salad Molds, '85 54
  Meal-in-One Salad, '86 43
  Melon Ball Bowl with Cucumber-Mint
    Dressing, '87 153
  Mushroom-Zucchini Salad, '85 8
  Niçoise, Salad, '86 35
  Oriental Salad Bowl, '87 153
  Paella Salad, '86 207
  Pasta Salad, '84 139
  Pasta Salad, Garden, '86 188
  Pea-and-Apple Salad, English, '87 24
  Peaches in a Garden Nest, '87 154
  Potato Salad, New, '84 139
  Rice-and-Vegetable Salad, '86 42
  Rice-and-Vegetable Salad,
    Brown, '84 202
  Shrimp Salad, Fruited, '86 156
  Shrimp Salad, Marinated, '85 82
  Spinach-Blue Cheese Salad, '82 166
  Spinach-Kiwifruit Salad, '87 305
  Spinach Salad with Orange
    Dressing, '87 187
  Steak Salad Cups, Pepper, '86 206
  Tuna-and-Cannellini Bean
    Salad, '86 143
  Tuna Chef Salad, '82 78
  Tuna-Mac in Tomatoes, '87 188
  Tuna Salad, Curried, '86 208
  Turnip Salad, '85 235
  Vegetable Salad, Crispy
    Marinated, '84 193
  Vegetable Salad, Italian, '82 19
  Vegetable Salad, Marinated, '84 13
  Vegetable Salad, Tarragon-, '85 288
  Vegetable Salad, Winter, '86 42
  Vegetables, Zesty Marinated, '82 272
Sandwiches
  Chicken Sandwiches,
    Marinated, '86 M45
  Crab Sandwiches,
    Open-Faced, '87 106
  Garden Sandwiches,
    Open-Faced, '87 105
  Ham Sandwiches, Open-Face, '85 8
  Lamb Pockets with Dilled Cucumber
    Topping, '87 104
  Open-Face Sandwiches, '84 13
  Pimiento Cheese Sandwiches, '82 278
  Pita Sandwiches, '84 139
  Pizza Sandwiches, Open-Face, '85 22
  Spread, Low-Calorie Pimiento
    Cheese, '85 215
  Tofu-Veggie Sandwiches,
    Open-Face, '86 5
  Vegetable Pockets, '85 215
  Vegetarian Melt,
    Open-Faced, '87 106
  Vegetarian Pita Sandwiches, '84 193
Sauces and Gravies
  Apple Dessert Sauce, Spicy, '82 177
  Barbecue Sauce, Easy, '82 178
  Barbecue Sauce, Special, '82 177
  Coconut Sauce, Creamy
    Light, '82 177
  Cucumber-Dill Sauce, '86 5

  Hard Sauce, Special, '86 318
  Hollandaise Sauce, Mock, '85 49
  Honey-Orange Sauce, '85 108
  Lemon-Chive Sauce, '86 249
  Lemon Sauce, '82 290
  Mandarin Sauce, '84 60
  Mango Sauce, '83 120
  Marinade, Tangy Light, '82 178
  Marinara Sauce, '82 178
  Mushroom Sauce, '83 205
  Mustard-Hollandaise Sauce,
    Mock, '87 269
  Mustard Sauce, '87 22
  Mustard Sauce, Light, '82 178
  Parsley Sauce, '86 108
  Pineapple-Orange Sauce, '84 14
  Pizza Sauce, '84 33
  Swiss Sauce, '83 M195
  Tarragon Sauce, '83 56
  Tomato Sauce, '85 193, 244
  Vegetable-Cheese Potato
    Topper, '86 6
  White Sauce, Low-Calorie
    Medium, '87 26
  Zippy Sauce, '86 44
Soups and Stews
  Asparagus Soup, '84 67
  Bean Soup, Leafy, '86 223
  Bean Soup, Navy, '84 280
  Bisque, Squash, '84 280
  Borscht, Ruby Red, '83 176
  Bouillon, Tomato, '83 8
  Broccoli Soup, Mock Cream
    of, '85 288
  Broccoli-Swiss Soup, '86 6
  Cantaloupe Soup, '83 120
  Carrot-Leek Soup, '86 34
  Chicken Soup, Curried, '86 34
  Chili, Vegetarian, '84 280
  Chowder, Basque Fish, '86 36
  Chowder, Clam, '86 36
  Cucumber Soup, Cold Minted,
    '86 34
  Cucumber-Yogurt Soup, '83 205
  Fish-and-Vegetable Stew, '87 220
  Gazpacho, Chilled, '84 138
  Gumbo, Light Seafood-Okra, '86 155
  Minestrone Soup, '86 144
  Peach Soup, '83 120
  Plum Soup, '85 107
  Seafood Stew, '84 280
  Spinach Soup, Oriental, '83 151
  Tomato Soup, Easy, '84 14
  Vegetable Soup, '86 187
  Vegetable Soup, Light, '84 280
  Vegetable Stew, Mixed, '84 13
Sour Cream, Mock, '83 71, 205
Spread, Cottage Cheese, '87 107
Spread, Hawaiian Ham, '87 106
Spread, Light Strawberry, '85 55
Spread, Peachy-Raisin, '86 326
Spread, Sugarless Fruit, '84 60
Spread, Tasty Chicken, '84 193
Spread, Vegetable-Egg, '87 106
Vegetables
  Artichokes, Shrimp-Stuffed, '84 67
  Artichokes Stuffed with Shrimp and
    Scallops, '84 174
  Asparagus, Company, '85 82
  Asparagus, Stir-Fried, '87 52
  Beans Creole, Lima, '85 137
  Beans, Herbed Green, '83 177
  Beans Italiano, Green, '86 144

Cooking Light, Vegetables *(continued)*

Beans with New Potatoes,
  Green, '87 164
Beans with Tomatoes, Green, '85 137
Beets, Harvard, '83 M195
Beets, Orange-Glazed, '86 187
Beets, Pickled, '87 163
Broccoli, Easy Orange, '85 267
Broccoli, Sesame, '85 8
Broccoli Toss, '86 294
Broccoli with Horseradish
  Sauce, '84 33
Broccoli with Tangy Chive Sauce,
  Steamed, '83 101
Brussels Sprouts, Casserole
  of, '86 294
Brussels Sprouts, Glorified, '86 282
Brussels Sprouts Medley, '85 267
Butternut-Orange Bake, '86 295
Cabbage-and-Apple Slaw, Red, '87 31
Cabbage, Sweet-and-Sour, '86 295
Carrots and Onions, Herbed, '87 31
Carrots, Ginger, '83 9
Carrots, Golden, '85 267
Carrots, Marinated, '86 108
Carrots Marsala, '83 56
Carrots, Tropical, '84 34
Cauliflower-Snow Pea
  Medley, '87 305
Celery-Parmesan Toss, '84 34
Crêpes, Vegetable-Filled Bran, '86 44
Eggplant, Ratatouille-Bran
  Stuffed, '86 44
Kabobs, Marinated
  Vegetable, '83 M195
Medley, Chinese Vegetable, '84 33
Medley, Sautéed Vegetable, '83 101
Mixed Vegetables, '83 M195
Mushrooms, Flavor-Stuffed, '85 288
Mushrooms, Savory Fresh, '85 268
Onion-Potato Bake, '83 M195
Onions and Wine, Stuffed, '85 268
Onions Stuffed with Peas, '84 68
Pea Medley, English, '85 236
Peas-and-Corn Medley, '85 138
Peas and Ham, Southern, '85 138
Peas and Peppers, Stir-Fried, '87 51
Peas, Deluxe English, '84 68
Peas, Seasoned Black-Eyed, '85 138
Peppers, Stuffed, '84 202
Potato-Apple Bake, Sweet, '86 282

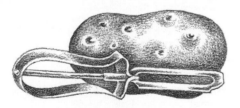

Potatoes and Turnips,
  Scalloped, '85 235
Potatoes, Double-Cheese, '86 6
Potatoes, Herbed New, '83 9
Potatoes, Mushroom-Dill-
  Topped, '86 41
Potatoes, Vegetable-Topped
  Stuffed, '85 235
Potato Puff, Sweet, '85 235
Rutabagas, Mashed, '86 295

Spinach Quiche, '85 49
Spinach Soufflé, '86 108
Squash Casserole, '87 163
Squash, Fruited Acorn, '85 235
Squash with Nutmeg, Acorn, '85 267
Stir-Fried Vegetables with
  Curry, '87 51
Stir-Fry, Almond-Vegetable, '86 222
Tomatoes and Okra, '87 164
Tomatoes, Bean-Stuffed, '84 34
Tomatoes, Cheese
  Herbed-Topped, '86 108
Tomatoes, Cheesy Puff-Top, '86 187
Tomatoes, Grilled, '85 158
Turnips and Carrots Julienne, '86 295
Zucchini-Basil Delight, '85 267
Zucchini-Basil Scramble, '87 34
Zucchini Dressing, '86 282
Zucchini, Stuffed, '86 187
Zucchini with Pecans, '87 31

Corn
Bake, Corn-Zucchini, '79 178
Baked Corn with Sour Cream, '86 170
Bake, Oyster-and-Corn, '83 34; '84 44
Balls, Zesty Corn Dressing, '82 307
Bisque, Crab-and-Corn, '87 137
Casserole, Broccoli-Corn, '83 313
Casserole, Corn, '79 247
Casserole, Corn and Cheese, '81 128
Casserole, Corn and Tomato, '81 127
Casserole, Corn-and-Tomato, '84 145
Casserole, Fresh Corn, '80 165
Casserole, Jalapeño-Corn, '83 256
Casserole, Salami-Corn, '80 209
Chowder, Corn, '81 128; '83 20;
  '84 M38; '85 10
Chowder, Corn and Cheese, '80 228
Chowder, Delicious Corn, '82 279
Chowder, Ham and Corn, '79 16
Chowder, Ham-and-Corn, '82 40
Chowder, Oyster-Corn, '83 211
Chowder, Shrimp and Corn, '79 199
Chowder, Turkey-Corn, '81 98
Cob, Barbecued Corn on the, '81 128
Cob, Corn on the, '79 122
Cob, Foil-Baked Corn on the, '81 128
Cob, Foiled Corn on the, '80 165
Cob, Microwaved Corn on the, '80 M122
Cob, Seasoned Baked Corn on
  the, '82 134
Cob, Spicy Corn-on-the-, '84 149
Cob, Spicy Corn on the, '87 M151
Cob with Herb Butter,
  Corn-on-the-, '84 160
Cold-Pack Corn, '81 216
Combo, Zucchini-Corn, '86 218
Creamed Corn, Southern-Style, '81 M165
Creamed Fresh Corn, '82 158
Cream-Style Corn, '80 127; '85 106
Creamy Corn, '79 213
Creole Corn, '81 128
Creole, Okra-Corn, '83 157
Curried Corn and Celery, '86 192
Deviled Corn, '86 192
Dinner, Corn-and-Ham Skillet, '83 190
Escalloped Corn, '79 251
Fresh Corn, Seasoned, '83 M147
Fried Corn, Skillet, '83 190
Frittata, Skillet Corn, '87 90
Fritters, Corn, '86 192
Fritters, Golden Corn, '80 165; '81 128
Fritters, Skillet-Fried Corn, '85 14
Grilled Parmesan Corn, '82 127

Herb Butter Sauce, Corn with, '79 150
Hush Puppies with Corn, '83 286; '84 17
Meat Loaf, Corny, '86 68
Medley, Okra-Corn-Tomato, '81 159
Medley, Peas-and-Corn, '85 138
Medley, Skillet Corn, '86 192
Medley, Summer Garden, '84 158
Medley, Zucchini-and-Corn, '80 298;
  '81 25
Mexican Corn, '80 157, 165
Mexi-Corn, '82 M21
Moussaka, Corn, '87 190
Okra and Corn in Cream, '79 160
Okra, Corn, and Peppers, '87 M151
Peppers, Corn-Stuffed, '84 104
Peppers, Ham-and-Corn Stuffed, '81 87
Pie, Quick and Cheesy Corn, '82 191
Pudding, Baked Corn '83 314
Pudding, Corn, '79 276; '81 128; '86 192
Pudding, Corn-Cheese, '80 244
Pudding, Creamy Corn, '81 267

Pudding, Easy Corn, '83 280
Pudding, Fresh Corn, '80 157, 165
Quiche, Jalapeño-Corn, '85 122
Quick Corn Fix-Up, '81 M4
Relish, Corn, '81 129, 175; '83 189;
  '84 107; '85 136; '87 120, 245
Relish Dogs, Corn, '85 192
Relish, Easy Corn, '83 260
Relish, Virginia Corn, '79 283
Salad, Broccoli-Corn, '87 24
Salad, Chilled Corn, '79 20
Salad, Corn, '80 247; '81 139; '85 236
Salad, Garden Medley, '80 122
Salad, Marinated Corn-Bean, '87 9
Salad, Shoepeg Corn, '81 23
Salad, Tasty Corn, '84 289
Sauté, Corn, '80 165
Sautéed Corn and Okra, '84 158
Scalloped Corn, '80 164; '81 128; '86 111
Scalloped Corn, Baked, '85 290
Scalloped Corn, Elegant, '86 268
Scalloped Corn for Two, '82 208
Slaw, Corn and Cabbage, '79 135
Smoked Corn, Hickory-, '85 145
Soufflé, Zucchini-and-Corn, '83 265
Soup, Corn, '80 56; '85 243; '87 156
Soup, Favorite Corn, '85 155
Soup, Grilled Corn, '87 121
Soup, Shrimp-and-Corn, '84 88
Spoonbread, Corn and Bacon, '81 129
Succotash, Easy, '80 165
Tomatoes-and-Corn, Creole-Style, '84 142
Tomatoes, Corn-Stuffed, '82 270
Tomatoes with Corn, Baked, '80 161
Whole Kernel Corn, '85 106
Zucchini and Corn, '86 177

Zucchini and Corn, Dilled, '83 173
Zucchini, Corn and, '83 190
Cornbreads
  Bake, Cornbread Tamale, '79 163
  Beef Cornbread, Cheesy, '81 242
  Bites, Corn Dog, '85 245
  Buttermilk Cornbread, '79 34; '82 70
  Carrot Cornbread, '80 89; '81 163
  Casserole, Cornbread, '81 91
  Casserole, Cornbread Skillet, '83 243;
    '84 101
  Cheddar Cornbread, '83 285; '84 17
  Cheddar-Jalapeño Cornbread, '85 3
  Cheese Cornbread, Swiss, '79 60
  Chicken over Cornbread,
    Creamed, '86 231
  Chile-Cheese Cornbread, '87 171
  Chile Cornbread, '86 254
  Chile Cornbread, Green, '82 134
  Cornbread, '80 272; '86 231; '87 197
  Cottage Cheese Cornbread, '80 90
  Cowboy Cornbread, '81 188
  Cracklin' Cornbread, Southern, '80 119
  Crackling Cornbread, '85 200
  Crackling Cowboy Cornbread, '82 114
  Crusty Cornbread, '85 255
  Dieter's Cornbread, '87 164
  Dressing, Cornbread, '86 286
  Dressing, Cornbread-and-Sausage, '83 213
  Dressing, Cornbread-Biscuit, '79 296
  Dressing, Cornbread-Sage, '80 262
  Dressing, Cornbread-Sausage, '82 307;
    '85 280
  Dressing, Fruited Cornbread, '80 262
  Dressing, Herb-Seasoned
    Cornbread, '83 315
  Dressing, Kentucky Cornbread, '86 281
  Dressing, Old-Fashioned
    Cornbread, '84 321
  Dressing, Sage-Cornbread, '84 283
  Dressing, Texas Cornbread, '82 243
  Dressing, Turkey with
    Sausage-Cornbread, '83 287
  Fresh Cornbread, '80 165
  Hoecake, Hot Water, '81 56
  Honey Cornbread, '83 286; '84 17
  Hush Puppies, '84 102; '87 15
  Hush Puppies, Aunt Jenny's, '84 88
  Hush Puppies, Cracker, '80 99
  Hush Puppies, Easy, '81 191; '85 14
  Hush Puppies, Fiery Beer, '86 233
  Hush Puppies, Golden, '82 135
  Hush Puppies, Onion, '85 14
  Hush Puppies, Peppery, '80 221
  Hush Puppies, Topsail Island, '79 152
  Hush Puppies with Corn, '83 286; '84 17
  Jalapeño Cornbread, '85 200
  Jalapeño Cornbread, Beefy, '82 142
  Jalapeño Pepper Bread, '83 121
  Lacy Corncakes, '81 242
  Lightbread, Corn, '81 137
  Light Cornbread, Old Southern, '81 242
  Loaf, Cornbread, '85 200
  Menfolks' Cornbread, '82 156
  Mexican Cornbread, '80 198; '81 137;
    '84 140, 242
  Mexican Cornbread, Hot, '83 286; '84 17
  Mexican Cornbread, Quick, '81 242
  Mexican Flatbread, '80 197
  Muffins, Corn, '82 M282; '84 16
  Muffins, Cornmeal, '80 90
  Muffins, Four-Grain, '80 46
  Muffins, Sage-Corn, '83 207

Muffins, Southern Cornbread, '85 201
Muffins, Tomato Corn, '81 137
Mush, '81 215
Old-Fashioned Cornbread, '81 242
Onion-Topped Cornbread, '84 153
Oysters Casino on Cornbread, '79 34
Pastry, Cornmeal, '81 140
Pie, Cornbread-Sausage-Apple, '87 171
Puff, Cornmeal, '82 42
Quick-and-Easy Cornbread, '83 9
Quick Cornsticks, '81 192
Salad, Cornbread, '87 172
Skillet Cornbread, '81 31; '84 102;
  '85 200
Sour Cream Cornbread, '81 137
Southern Cornbread, '79 123; '81 56;
  '83 12
Spoonbread, '81 138
Spoonbread, Cheddar, '82 196
Spoonbread, Golden, '83 286; '84 17
Spoonbread, Old Virginia, '84 102
Spoonbread, Ozark, '85 202
Sticks, Angel Corn, '84 20
Sticks, Blue Ribbon Corn, '84 102
Sticks, Buttermilk Corn, '80 120
Sticks, Corn, '79 275
Sticks, Corn, '87 15
Sticks, Favorite Corn, '85 202
Sticks, Firecracker Corn, '85 241
Sticks, Southern Corn, '81 242
Toasted Cornbread, '82 174
Ultimate Cornbread, '80 90

Waffles, Cornbread, '79 265
Waffles, Cornmeal, '85 201
Wampus Bread, '81 305; '82 36
Cornish Hens
  Brandied Cornish Hens, '81 259
  Brown Rice, Cornish Hens with, '82 275
  Buttered Cornish Hens, Brandy-, '79 292;
    '80 32
  Company Cornish Hens, '83 263
  Cranberry Cornish Hens, '86 303
  Cranberry-Orange Sauce, Cornish Hens
    with, '86 119
  Cranberry Sauce, Cornish Hens
    with, '79 180
  Elegant Cornish Hens, '80 227; '81 52
  Flambé, Cornish Hens, '80 227; '81 52
  Glazed Cornish Hens, Apricot-, '80 84;
    '87 306
  Glazed Cornish Hens, Orange-, '83 267
  Glazed Stuffed Cornish Hens,
    Orange-, '84 M89
  Grilled Cornish Hens,
    Orange-Glazed, '86 250

Herbed Cornish Hens, '82 271
Orange Glaze, Cornish Hens
  with, '79 244
Port and Sour Cream, Cornish Hens
  in, '86 323
Roast Cornish Hens, '86 89
Roasted Cornish Hens, Lemon, '82 260
Roasted Rock Cornish Hens, '82 66
Smoked Cornish Hens, '86 142, 154
Stuffed Cornish Hens, '85 261
Stuffed Cornish Hens, Apricot-, '84 6
Stuffed Cornish Hens, Rice-, '82 302
Tarragon, Cornish Hens with, '83 143
Teriyaki Cornish Hens, '86 198
Texas-Style Game Hens, '87 61
Vermouth, Cornish Hens in, '86 33
Wild Rice Stuffing, Cornish Hens
  with, '79 222; '80 64; '82 136
Crab
  au Gratin, Crabmeat, '86 154
  Avocados, Crab-Stuffed, '86 73
  Avocado with Crabmeat, '86 119
  Baked Avocado-and-Crabmeat, '84 119
  Bake, Quick Crab, '87 192
  Bisque, Crab-and-Corn, '87 137
  Bites, Crab-Zucchini, '84 M216
  Blue Crabs, Festive, '85 103
  Broiled Crab and Avocado, '79 116
  Cakes, Crab, '81 125
  Cakes, Crispy Fried Crab, '80 119
  Cakes, Down-East Crab, '79 151
  Canapés, Cheesy Crab, '86 262
  Canapés, Hot Crab, '86 70; '87 239
  Casserole, Crab, '79 228
  Casserole, Crab-and-Shrimp, '84 71
  Casserole, Crab-Egg, '80 260
  Casserole, Crabmeat-Broccoli, '84 232
  Casserole, Creamy Crab and
    Spinach, '80 3
  Chicken, Crab-Stuffed, '84 101
  Cocktail, Sherried
    Avocado-Crabmeat, '87 95
  Cornbread, Crab with Chile, '86 254
  Crêpes, Crab, '79 165
  Crêpes, Sautéed Crab, '84 84
  Crisps, Crab, '79 63
  Delight, Crab-and-Egg, '84 261
  Deviled Crab, '85 104
  Deviled Crab, Devilish, '85 264
  Dip, Creamy Crab, '80 M135
  Dip, Hot Cheese and Crab, '81 261
  Dip, Oven-Baked Crab, '82 59
  Dip, Tangy Crab, '83 5
  Dressed Crab, '82 276
  Eggs New Orleans, Crabmeat and, '82 45
  Eggs, Shrimp and Crab
    Scrambled, '79 261
  Flounder, Crab-Stuffed, '80 120
  Fresh Crab, Preparing, '82 127
  Gumbo, Crab and Shrimp, '81 200
  Gumbo, Seafood, '83 90
  Gumbo with Whole Crabs, Seafood,
    '85 2
  Imperial, Crab, '79 82, 116
  Imperial, Crabmeat, '82 311; '83 72
  Imperial, Elegant Crab, '83 245
  Imperial, Pineapple-Crab, '84 M286
  Imperials, Individual Seafood, '84 162
  Meunière, Soft-Shell Crab, '80 57
  Mold, Crab, '85 318
  Mousse, Crab, '79 117
  Mushroom Caps, Crab-Stuffed, '84 160
  Mushrooms, Crab-Stuffed, '81 190

Crab *(continued)*

Mushrooms on Toast Points, Crabmeat
  and, '82 M91
Mushrooms Stuffed with Crab, '82 249
Oysters and Crabmeat, Creamy, '83 211
Pâté, Crab, '79 233
Peas, Crab-Stuffed Snow, '85 288
Pie, Hot Seafood, '80 32
Potatoes, Cheesy Crab-Stuffed, '86 17
Potatoes, Crabmeat-Topped, '83 3
Puff, Crab, '79 116
Puffs, Crab, '80 20; '84 269
Puff, Shrimp-Crab, '79 57
Quiche, Almond-Topped Crab, '79 127
Quiche, Crab, '82 M122, 243
Quiche, Quick Crab, '84 96
Quiche, Sherried Crab, '83 180
Quiche, Simple Crab, '85 207
Ravigote, Crabmeat, '82 250
Salad, Crab and Wild Rice, '79 116
Salad, Crab-Avocado, '81 114
Salad, Crabmeat Luncheon, '82 207
Salad, Crabmeat-Shrimp Pasta, '86 208
Salad, Crab-Stuffed Tomato, '80 148
Salad, Crab-Wild Rice, '86 207
Salad, Delightful Crab, '87 145
Salad, Macaroni-Crabmeat, '81 153
Salad, Super Shrimp, '81 37
Salad with Crabmeat-and-Asparagus,
  Congealed, '84 86
Sandwiches, Avocado-Crabmeat, '83 2
Sandwiches, Crabmeat, '84 285
Sandwiches, Deluxe Crabmeat, '81 M74
Sandwiches, Hot Crab-and-
  Cheese, '87 279
Sandwiches, Open-Face Crab
  Tomato, '81 29
Sandwiches, Open-Faced Crab, '87 106
Sandwiches, Puffy Crab, '83 291
Sauce Piquante, Crab and Shrimp,
  '83 92
Sauce, Quick Crab Marinara, '85 M151
Sauce, Stone Crab Mustard, '80 3
Sauce, Tangy Stone Crab, '80 3
Sautéed Crabmeat, Roussos, '84 88
Sautéed Seafood Platter, '83 89
Seafood Boil, Low Country, '80 119
Shrimp Bundles, Crab-Stuffed, '81 176
Shrimp, Crab-Stuffed, '84 259
Snacks, Crab, '83 93
Sole in Papillote, '82 22
Soup, Crabmeat, '84 123
Soup, Creamy Crab, '80 M224
Soup, Elegant Crab, '80 188
Soup, Quick Crab, '84 279
Soup, Steamboat's Cream of
  Crab, '81 127
Soup with Marigold, She-Crab, '79 32
Spread, Baked Crab, '80 86
Spread, Crabmeat, '79 81
Spread, Crab Soufflé, '85 4
Spread, Hot Artichoke-Crab, '85 81
Spread, Layered Crabmeat, '83 127
Spread, Superb Crab, '81 235
Steamed Blue Crabs, Spicy, '84 162
Stroganoff, Crab, '79 116
Stuffed Soft-Shell Crabs, '83 91
Stuffed Soft-Shell Crabs,
  Steamboat's, '81 127
Stuffing, Chicken Breasts with
  Crabmeat, '85 302
Supreme, Crab, '79 181

Tomatoes, Crab-Stuffed Cherry, '82 289
Veal with Crabmeat, New Orleans, '86 94

Crackers
Bread, Sesame Cracker, '87 2
Cheddar Crackers, '84 236
Cheese Cracker Nibbles, '84 328
Dessert Crackers, '87 3
Fennel-Rye Crackers, '87 2
Florida Crackers, '86 179
Hush Puppies, Cracker, '80 99
Oatmeal-Wheat Germ Crackers, '84 236
Olive-Rye Snack Crackers, '84 191
Pie, Cracker, '79 113
Snackers, Cracker, '86 229

Cranberries
Brandied Cranberries, '86 269
Bread, Cranberry, '79 242
Bread, Cranberry-Banana, '80 281
Bread, Cranberry Fruit-Nut, '79 275
Bread, Cranberry-Orange, '87 244
Bread, Cranberry-Orange Nut, '80 288
Bread, Orange-Cranberry, '85 266
Bread, Raisin-Cranberry, '81 305; '82 36
Cake, Cranberry Coffee, '81 14
Cake, Cranberry-Nut Coffee, '81 250
Cake, Cranberry-Orange Coffee, '82 283
Cake, Cranberry Upside-Down, '87 8
Cake, Orange-Cranberry, '85 314
Casserole, Cranberry-Apple, '83 311
Casserole, Sweet Potatoes-and-
  Berries, '84 231
Chicken, Barbecued Cranberry, '83 178
Chicken Kiev, Cranberry, '87 250
Chutney, Cranberry, '80 243; '83 260;
  '84 265
Chutney, Cranberry-Orange, '79 292
Chutney, Orange-Cranberry, '86 266
Chutney with Cream Cheese,
  Cranberry-Amaretto, '87 244
Cider, Spiced Cranberry, '84 261
Cobbler, Cranberry, '81 275
Cobbler, Cranberry-and-Apple, '84 306
Cobbler, Easy Cranberry, '86 260
Cobbler Roll, Cranberry, '80 288; '81 248
Compote, Berry, '81 275
Conserve, Apple-Cranberry, '82 308
Conserve, Cranberry, '79 243; '83 279;
  '85 266
Cooler, Cranberry, '86 229
Cornish Hens, Cranberry, '86 303
Crêpes, Cranberry, '85 262
Crisp, Cranberry-Pear, '83 207
Crunch, Apple-Cranberry, '86 300;
  '87 178
Cup, Berry Grapefruit, '79 242
Daiquiris, Cranberry, '81 245
Dessert, Cranberry Apple, '80 253
Dessert, Cranberry Surprise, '79 242
Dip, Cranberry-Horseradish, '85 65
Float, Sparkling Cranberry, '86 195
Frappé, Cranberry, '82 263
Frosted Cranberries, '82 280
Glaze, Cranberry, '84 306; '86 171
Ham, Cranberry Glazed, '81 274
Ham, Cranberry-Orange Glazed, '81 295
Ice, Cranberry-Apple, '82 290
Ice, Tangy Cranberry, '87 305
Ice, Tart Cranberry-Orange, '86 317
Jam, Christmas Brunch, '81 286
Jelly, Cranberry-Wine, '81 290
Jubilee, Cranberries, '85 312
Jubilee, Tasty Cranberry, '84 305; '85 189
Lemonade, Spiced Cranberry, '87 292

Loaf, Apricot-Cranberry, '79 235
Loaf, Cranberry-Ham, '82 M77
Mold, Cranberry, '79 250
Muffins, Cranberry, '81 249
Muffins, Cranberry-Pecan, '84 269
Oriental, Cranberry, '79 126
Pie, Autumn Apple, '79 205
Pie, Cranberry-Apple, '79 264
Pie, Cranberry-Apple Holiday, '81 M269
Pie, Cranberry-Raisin, '80 283; '85 316
Pie, Cran-Raspberry, '87 244
Pie, Festive Cranberry Freezer, '84 306
Pie, Frosty Cranberry, '79 249
Pie, Nutty Cranberry, '82 M298
Pie, Peach-Cranberry, '83 249
Pie, Tart Cranberry-Cherry, '87 299
Pie, Walnut-Cranberry, '87 259
Pork Chops, Cranberry, '80 288
Pork Chops, Orange-Cranberry, '86 335;
  '87 84
Pork Roast, Berry Barbecued, '80 288
Pudding, Cranberry, '84 306
Punch, Cranberry, '83 275; '85 90
Punch, Cranberry-Cinnamon, '86 270
Punch, Holiday Cranberry, '85 265
Punch, Hot Cranberry, '80 288; '84 41,
  319; '85 265
Punch, Hot Spiced, '80 250
Punch, Pink Lady, '81 100
Punch, Sparkling Cranberry, '85 277
Punch, Tart Cranberry, '83 318
Red Roosters, '87 147
Relish, Cran-Apple, '84 300
Relish, Cranberry, '81 275; '83 144;
  '85 258, 264; '86 283; '87 245
Relish, Cranberry-Nut, '86 275
Relish, Cranberry-Orange, '81 M289
Relish, Cranberry-Pear, '85 232
Relish, Lemony Cranberry, '79 243
Relish, Old-Fashioned Cranberry,
  '82 297
Ring, Spicy Peach-Cranberry, '85 264
Rolls, Cranberry-Pineapple, '86 275
Salad, Cranberry-Cheese Ribbon,
  '79 241
Salad, Cranberry Christmas, '79 243
Salad, Cranberry-Topped Green, '87 311
Salad, Cranberry-Whipped Cream,
  '83 261
Salad, Festive Cranberry, '81 264, 296
Salad, Holiday Cranberry, '82 266, 288
Salad, Holiday Jewel, '81 252
Salad, Jellied Cranberry, '83 279;
  '85 281
Salad, Layered Cranberry, '84 322;
  '86 325
Salad, Lemon-Cranberry
  Congealed, '87 311
Salad Ring, Cranberry, '80 247
Salad, Tart Cranberry, '79 286
Sauce, Cornish Hens with
  Cranberry-Orange, '86 119
Sauce, Cranberry, '86 278
Sauce, Cranberry Juice, '85 224; '86 83
Sauce, Cranberry Wine, '83 276
Sauce, Fresh Cranberry, '79 283; '84 275
Sauce, Fresh Cranberry-Apricot, '87 243
Sauce, Tart Cranberry, '83 261
Shake, Cranberry, '83 171
Slush, Cranberry-Rum, '84 259
Smoothie, Cranberry, '86 183
Soda, Cranberry-Orange, '79 148
Sorbet, Cranberry, '82 251

Sorbet, Cranberry Juice, '85 259
Soufflé, Cranberry-Topped
  Holiday, '84 306
Spiced Cranberries, '82 254, 287
Squash, Cranberry-Filled Acorn, '81 M231
Supreme, Cranberry, '85 280
Tart, Cranberry-Nut, '84 305
Tartlets, Fresh Cranberry, '87 244
Tarts, Cranberry-Cream Cheese, '80 154
Tarts, Cranberry Holiday, '83 279
Turkey Loaf, Cranberry-Glazed, '86 171
Wild Rice, Cranberry-Pear, '83 279
Wine Cup, Cranberry, '85 23

Crawfish
Étouffée, Crawfish, '83 91; '86 156
Mushrooms, Crawfish-Stuffed, '86 258
Salad, Dilled Crawfish, '83 126
Spaghetti, Crawfish, '85 104

Crème Fraîche
Fraîche, Crème, '85 39
Sauce, Crème Fraîche, '79 281

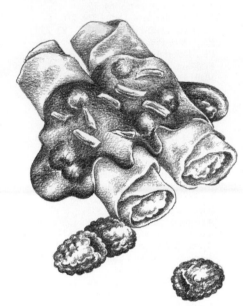

Crêpes
Amandine, Crêpes Gelée, '83 126
Amaretto-and-Orange Crêpes, '86 260
Banana Crêpes Flambé, '84 262
Basic Crêpes, '84 83; '86 38
Beef Crêpes, Sherried, '85 M29
Beef Roulades, '80 80
Bran Crêpes, '83 70; '86 44
Breakfast Crêpes, Country-Style, '79 22
Brunch Crêpes, Nutritious, '80 44
Brunch Crêpes, Royal, '81 44
Cannelloni Crêpes, '86 143
Cheese and Mushroom Crêpes, '81 88
Cheese Blintzes, '82 146; '83 71
Cheesy Party Wedges, '84 84
Cherry Crêpes Flambé, '79 18
Chicken Crêpes, '80 39
Chicken Crêpes, Creamy, '81 200
Chicken-Vegetable Crêpes, '83 70
Chocolate Chantilly Crêpes, '82 183
Chocolate Crêpes, '86 164
Chocolate Dessert Crêpes, '84 84; '85 262
Chocolate Dream Crêpes, '86 164
Chocolate-Orange Crêpes, '85 263
Coffee Ice Cream Crêpes, '84 85
Coquilles St. Jacques Crêpes, '83 13

Crab Crêpes, '79 165
Crab Crêpes, Sautéed, '84 84
Cranberry Crêpes, '85 262
Crêpes, '82 38, 46, 146, 240; '83 13, 71,
  122, 127, 205, 282; '84 186; '86 216;
  '87 126
Dessert Crêpes, '84 84; '86 260; '87 290
Dessert Crêpes, Basic, '82 183; '85 262;
  '86 275
Dessert Crêpes, Dixie, '79 222
Dessert Crêpes, Spicy, '84 262
Divan, Elegant Crêpes, '81 91
Entrée Crêpes, '79 264
Florentine Crêpe Pie, '79 34
Florentine, Crêpes, '80 190
Fruit Crêpes, Tropical, '87 77
Fruit Filling, Crêpes with, '81 96
Ham-and-Egg Crêpes, '83 204
Ham-and-Egg Crêpes with Mushroom
  Sauce, '82 46
Lemon Crêpes with Fruit Filling, '82 46
Light Crêpes, '86 143
Low-Calorie Crêpes, '87 77
Mango-Pineapple Crêpes, '86 216
Mushroom-Cheese Crêpes, '87 289
Orange Dream Crêpes, '82 183
Peach Crêpes, '82 184
Peach Crêpes, Fresh, '84 186
Plain Crêpes, '83 70
Processor Crêpes, Basic, '87 289
Raspberry Crêpes, '87 126
Sausage Crêpes, Cheesy, '82 240; '83 71
Sausage-Filled Crêpes, '79 39
Spinach-Ricotta Crêpes, '81 52
Strawberry Dessert Crêpes, '83 122
Strawberry Ice Cream Crêpes, '87 290
Suzette, Raspberry Crêpes, '84 84
Suzettes, Light Crêpes, '83 71
Tropical Crêpes, '86 275
Turkey Crêpes, Elegant, '83 282
Virginia Crêpes, '79 264
Whole Wheat Crêpes, '80 44; '83 70
Zucchini Crêpes, '79 157

Croutons
Celery Croutons, '79 16
Crispy Italian Croutons, '84 126
Croutons, '86 M288
Garlic-Flavored Croutons, '86 47
Herb Croutons, '81 150
Microwave Croutons, '86 M227
Vegetable-Flavored Croutons, '84 148

Cucumbers
Aspic, Shrimp-Cucumber, '83 108
Bisque, Shrimp-Cucumber, '79 172
Chips, Cucumber, '85 176
Cool Cucumbers, '84 152
Cooler, Simple Cucumber, '86 147
Delights, Cucumber, '84 117
Dilled Cucumber on Tomatoes, '84 142
Dills, Lazy Wife, '87 149
Dip, Cucumber-Cheese Vegetable, '83 128
Dressing, Creamy Cucumber Salad, '82 79
Dressing, Cucumber, '80 74
Dressing, Cucumber-Mint, '87 153
Dressing, Tomato, Onion, and Cucumber
  in Italian, '81 83
Fried Cucumber Fingers, '86 146
Marinated Cucumbers and
  Artichokes, '82 111
Marinated Cucumbers and
  Squash, '86 146
Mold, Asparagus-Cucumber, '85 252
Mold, Chicken-Cucumber, '80 175

Mold, Creamy Cucumber, '84 164
Mold, Lemon-Cucumber, '87 90
Mousse, Cucumber, '79 11
Pickles, Cucumber Sandwich, '81 174
Pickles, Dill, '81 174
Pickles, Mixed, '81 174
Pickles, Quick Sweet, '87 149
Pickles, Sour Cucumber, '85 176
Pickles, Sweet Icicle, '85 176
Relish, Cucumber, '85 176
Salad, Creamy Cucumber, '86 147
Salad, Cucumber-Almond, '86 147
Salad, Cucumber-Bean, '83 81
Salad, Cucumber-Pineapple, '84 124
Salad, Cucumber-Yogurt, '87 33
Salad, Dilled Cucumber, '82 229
Salad, Dilled Cucumber and
  Tomato, '81 153
Salad, Grapefruit-Cucumber, '80 100
Salad, Marinated Cucumber, '82 111
Salad Mold, Cucumber, '82 111;
  '83 81, 253
Salad, Pineapple-Cucumber
  Congealed, '83 118
Salad, Tomato-Cucumber, '86 218
Salad, Tomato-Cucumber-Onion, '81 239
Salad, Yogurt-Cucumber, '82 122
Sandwiches, Cucumber Pinwheel, '85 120
Sandwiches, Dainty Cucumber, '81 119
Sauce, Cucumber, '82 111; '84 M286
Sauce, Cucumber-Dill, '86 5
Sesame Cucumbers, '85 85
Slices, Cheesy Cucumber, '84 80
Slices, Fresh Cucumber, '86 177
Snapper Rolls, Cucumber-Stuffed
  Red, '83 176
Soup, Chilled Cucumber, '79 144
Soup, Cold Cucumber, '79 130; '81 130
Soup, Cold Minted Cucumber, '86 34
Soup, Cream of Cucumber, '81 98
Soup, Creamy Cucumber, '80 171
Soup, Cucumber-Yogurt, '82 157; '83 205
Sour Cream, Cucumber and Onion
  in, '81 69
Sour Cream, Cucumbers in, '79 52;
  '80 178
Spread, Cucumber, '79 295; '80 31
Spread, Cucumber and Cream
  Cheese, '82 140
Spread, Shrimp-Cucumber, '79 81
Stuffed Cucumbers, '81 237
Topping, Lamb Pockets with Dilled
  Cucumber, '87 104
Tuna Boats, Cucumber, '83 136
Vinaigrette Oriental, Cucumber-, '85 198;
  '86 147

Currants. *See* Raisins.

Curry
Almonds, Cauliflower and Peas with
  Curried, '79 221
Almonds, Curried, '82 297
Bananas, Fillets with Horseradish Sauce
  and Curried, '85 230
Beef Dinner, Curried, '83 4
Beef Pitas, Curried, '85 220
Bites, Curried Swiss, '85 220
Casserole, Curry Pea, '87 154
Cheese Ball, Chicken-Curry, '85 118
Cheese Ball, Curried Shrimp, '86 135
Chicken Bites, Curried, '85 40
Chicken, Curried, '86 43
Chicken, Curried Fried, '85 160
Chicken Curry, '84 110; '85 220; '86 21

Curry (continued)

Chicken Curry, Stir-Fried, '87 51
Chicken Divan, Curried, '80 83
Chicken, Honey-Curry, '87 36
Chicken, Regal Curried, '84 110
Chicken-Stuffed Peppers, Curried, '87 19
Chops, Pineapple-Curry Glazed, '82 106
Coleslaw, Curried, '85 139
Corn and Celery, Curried, '86 192
Dip, Curried, '81 262
Dip, Curry, '80 84; '81 9; '85 132;
  '86 184; '87 25
Dip, Tuna-Curry, '84 31
Dressing, Curried, '84 115
Dressing, Curry, '80 242; '82 78
Eggs, Saucy Shrimp-Curried, '84 143
Fish, Curried Baked, '87 5
Fruit, Almond-Curried, '83 261
Fruit Bake, Curried, '87 241

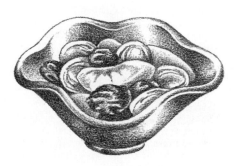

Fruit, Hot Curried, '79 225; '81 264;
  '84 287
Ham and Peaches, Curried, '82 60
Ham Steak, Curried, '82 120
Ham with Rice, Curried, '80 111
Hurry Curry, '79 103
Kheema, Indian, '81 226
Lamb Curry with Rice, '80 83; '81 10
Lamb with Rice Mold, Curried, '85 36
Meat Loaf, Curried, '86 43
Mushrooms, Curried, '84 214
Mushroom Soup, Curried, '84 M89
Nuts, Spicy Curried, '82 250
Pie, Crumb-Crust Curried Turkey, '86 265
Popcorn Mix, Curried, '86 326
Pork Tenderloin, Curried, '86 76
Rice and Shrimp, Curried, '83 231
Rice, Curry-Spiced, '86 M226
Rice Mix, Fruited Curry-, '86 326
Rice Mold, Curried, '85 36
Rice, Quick Curried, '86 81
Rice with Almonds, Curried, '83 M285
Rice with Curry, Raisin, '85 83
Rice with Pineapple, Curried, '79 142
Salad, Curried Apple-Raisin, '80 24
Salad, Curried Broccoli, '86 225
Salad, Curried Chicken, '79 219; '84 66;
  '85 96; '86 131
Salad, Curried Chicken-
  and-Orange, '87 144
Salad, Curried Rice, '80 84; '85 147, 220
Salad, Curried Tuna, '86 208
Salad, Curry Spinach, '80 242
Salad, Hot Indian Curry, '83 23
Salad with Asparagus, Curried
  Chicken, '81 36

Salad with Grapes, Curried Tuna, '87 201
Sauce, Curry, '79 156; '83 138; '84 M71
Sauce, Halibut with Orange-Curry, '87 91
Sauce, Pineapple-Curry, '79 252
Shrimp, Curried, '84 110
Shrimp Curry, Sour Cream, '80 83
Shrimp Curry, Sour Cream and, '81 10
Shrimp Malai Curry, '84 110
Shrimp, Quick Curried, '84 M198
Snapper, Honey-Curried, '85 181
Soup, Curried, '81 130
Soup, Curried Carrot, '82 157
Soup, Curried Chicken, '86 34
Soup, Curried Turkey, '86 332
Spread, Curried Shrimp, '87 158
Vegetables with Curry, Stir-Fried, '87 51

Custards

Amaretto Custard, Chocolate-
  Topped, '87 M37
Amaretto Custard, Range-Top, '87 77
Amaretto Custard with
  Raspberries, '86 152
Ambrosia, Custard Sauce, '84 256
Baked Custard, '80 219
Baked Custard, Creamy, '86 7
Baked Custard, Easy, '85 52
Baked Vanilla Custard, '82 129
Boiled Custard, Favorite, '81 181
Boiled Custard, Perfect, '81 34
Coconut Custard, '86 109
Crema, '80 175
Crème Pâtissière, '84 207
Filling, Creamy Custard, '81 180
Filling, Custard, '82 52, 298; '85 281
Filling, Egg Custard, '87 14
Flan Almendra, '80 199
Flan, Flaming, '85 313
Flan, Orange, '84 95
Flan, Pumpkin, '82 217
Flans, Individual, '85 52
Flan, Spanish, '85 51, 311
Lemon Custard in Meringue
  Cups, '80 295; '81 172
Napoleon Cream, '84 138
Peach Custard Dessert, Fresh, '86 162
Pie, Carrot Custard, '79 45
Pie, Coconut Custard, '82 33
Pie, Custard Pecan, '87 184
Pie, Old-Fashioned Egg Custard, '82 261
Pie, Perfect Custard, '82 92
Sauce, Custard, '85 41
Squash, Custard-Filled Acorn, '86 334
Stirred Custard, Old-Fashioned, '85 52
Stirred Custard over Fruit, '84 83

D

Dates

Balls, Date-Nut, '85 10
Balls, Peanut-Date, '81 92
Bars, Date, '84 313
Bars, Date-Nut, '80 166
Bars, Date-Oat, '80 M172
Bars, Layered Oatmeal-Date, '85 10
Bars, No-Bake Date, '79 256
Bars, Nutty Date, '84 153
Bread, Chocolate Date-Nut, '81 284
Bread, Date-Nut, '85 306
Bread, Persimmon Date-Nut, '82 218
Bread, Wine-Date Nut, '82 253
Cake, Date Nut, '79 176; '80 5

Cake, Fresh Apple-Date, '83 300
Cake, Pumpkin Date, '79 251
Cake, Queen Bee, '81 237
Cake Squares, Apple-Date Dream, '85 10
Candy, Date Loaf, '80 302
Cheese, Nutty Date Dessert, '87 299
Conserve, Brandied Date, '85 315
Cookies, Oatmeal-Date, '82 109
Cookies, Oatmeal-Date Sandwich, '83 257
Cookies, Rolled Fruit, '80 15
Cupcakes, Date, '84 7
Dressing, Date, '87 57
Filling, Apple-Date, '83 301
Filling, Date, '80 15; '83 257; '86 314
Filling, Date Cream, '81 303
June Bugs, '85 11
Loaf, Blue Ribbon Date-Walnut, '80 15
Loaf, Date-Nut, '85 10
Logs, Date, '79 274
Muffins, Carrot-Date-Nut, '86 262
Muffins, Date, '79 142
Muffins, Date-Nut, '84 75
Muffins, Surprise Date, '79 216
Pastries, Date-Filled Cheese, '83 259
Pie, Date-Pecan, '80 15
Pie, Dried Fruit, '83 249
Pudding, Steamed Date, '79 86
Roll, Date Nut, '79 249
Rollups, Date-Cream Cheese, '83 298
Salad, Festive Fruit, '80 16
Sauce, Date-Nut Sundae, '82 167
Spread, Breakfast Date, '84 7
Spread, Date-Walnut, '87 292
Stuffed Dates, Apricot-, '80 250

Desserts. See also specific types.

After Dinner-Drink Dessert, '82 100
Alaskas, Brownie, '83 299
Amaretto Cream Tortoni, '85 161
Ambrosia, Baked, '83 303
Ambrosia, Brunch, '83 57
Ambrosia, Honey Bee, '83 267
Apple Brown Betty, '83 213
Apple-Cranberry Crunch, '86 300; '87 178
Apple Crisp, Delicious, '82 303
Apple Crisp, Granola, '85 78
Apple Delight, '80 109
Apple Dumplings, '82 273
Apple Flan, '81 309
Apple Fritters, '82 273
Apple Kuchen, '79 24
Apple-Nut Crunch, '82 M238
Apple Rings, '85 232
Apple Rings, Cinnamon, '82 M237
Apples and Cream, Brandied, '82 M237
Apples, Baked Mincemeat-Filled, '80 276
Apples, Brandied, '81 248
Apples, Chilled Poached Lemon, '86 182
Apples, Golden, '82 254
Apples, Imperial Baked, '82 273
Apples, Old English Caramel, '85 231
Apples, Orange-Pecan Baked, '85 45
Apple Squares, Sour Cream, '82 262
Apples with Brandied Date Conserve,
  Cinnamon, '85 315
Apples with Orange Sauce,
  Baked, '84 314
Apricot Cream, Peachy-, '86 163
Avocado Whip, '79 107
Banana-Berry Supreme, '81 205
Banana Cream Dessert, '81 180
Banana Flip, '83 303
Banana-Peach Flambé, '85 316
Bananas, Candied, '83 179

Bananas Foster, '79 18; '83 M114; '86 139
Bananas Foster, Elegant, '81 59
Bananas Foster for Two, '80 115
Bananas Foster, Tropical, '79 231
Bananas, Praline, '84 313
Bananas, Regal, '85 46
Bananas Supreme, '84 256
Bananas with Orange Sauce, Baked, '79 115
Bavarian Dessert, Light, '86 6
Berries on Snow, '82 227
Berry Basket, Summer, '84 158
Berry Compote, '81 275
Berry Grapefruit Cup, '79 242
Berry-Peach Compote, '82 133
Biscuits, Sweet Little, '85 305
Blackberries and Dumplings, '86 196
Blackberry Flan, '79 182
Blueberries and Cointreau, '82 100
Blueberry-Amaretto Squares, '83 220
Blueberry Crumble, '81 84
Blueberry Crunch, Fresh, '82 143
Boysenberries and Cream Supreme, '82 133
Brandy Float, Blazing, '85 314
Bread, Fry, '85 155
Buñuelos, '80 199
Buñuelos, King-Size, '86 5
Butter-Nut Strips, '82 167
Butterscotch Fantastic, '83 76
Cakes, Funnel, '83 250
Cakes, Spanish Wind, '84 157
Cannoli, '80 58

Cantaloupe Compote, '81 147
Cantaloupe Cream Delight, '82 179
Champagne Delight, '83 304
Charlotte, Macaroon, '81 296
Charlotte, Peach, '79 68
Charlotte Russe, '80 71; '82 M142
Charlotte Russe, Fresh Lemon, '80 13
Charlotte Russe, Lemon, '84 192
Charlotte Russe, Wine Jelly and, '82 305
Cheese Blintzes, '82 146; '83 71
Cheese, Chunky Cream, '85 306
Cheese Dessert, Creamy Cottage, '87 191
Cheese, Fruited Cream, '85 306
Cheese Kuchen, '86 84
Cheese Molds, Heavenly Dessert, '85 209
Cheese, Nutty Date Dessert, '87 299
Cheese Squares, Lemony Cream, '82 159
Cherries Jubilee, '79 18; '83 139
Cherries Jubilee, Quick, '82 M100
Cherries Jubilite, '86 317
Cherry-Berry on a Cloud, '79 94
Cherry Compote, '83 139
Cherry Dessert, Holiday, '80 255
Chocolate
    Almond Dessert, Chocolate-, '82 306
    Almond Meringue Fingers, Chocolate-, '84 158

Almond Velvet, Chocolate, '81 148
Brownie-Mint Dessert, '82 227
Buttercream, Chocolate, '84 156
Charlotte Russe, Chocolate, '87 74
Chilled Chocolate Dessert, '83 177
Coffee Mallow, '80 109
Crêpes, Chocolate Dream, '86 164
Cups, Chocolate, '80 207
Cups, Chocolate Lace, '87 133
Cups, Chocolate-Mint, '80 71
Cups, Chocolate-Walnut, '85 213
Cups, Miniature Chocolate, '87 132
Dream Dessert, Chocolate, '83 198
Easy Chocolate Dessert, '79 75
Ladyfinger Dessert, Chocolate, '86 162
Mint Dessert, Chocolate-, '82 100
Mint Dessert, Cool Chocolate-, '80 109
Peanut-Chocolate Dessert, '80 86
Pots de Chocolat, Petits, '82 272
Pots de Crème, '81 15; '84 M145
Pots de Crème, Rum-Flavored, '85 102
Roll, Chocolate Cream, '85 317
Roll, Chocolate Mousse, '83 290
Roulage, Chocolate-Mocha, '80 216
Rum Dessert, Chocolate-, '81 247
Squares, Chocolate-Blueberry Dessert, '87 299
Strawberry-Chocolate Combo, '85 96
Sundae Dessert, Hot Fudge, '84 313
Supreme, Chocolate, '84 94
Coconut Cloud, '80 70
Coconut Dessert, Chilled, '83 116
Cœur à la Crème, Christmas, '86 278
Coffee-Almond Tortoni, '81 30
Crackers, Dessert, '87 3
Cranberries, Brandied, '86 269
Cranberries Jubilee, '85 312
Cranberry Apple Dessert, '80 253
Cranberry Jubilee, Tasty, '84 305
Cranberry Supreme, '85 280
Cranberry Surprise Dessert, '79 242
Cream, Bavarian, '86 M165
Cream, Molded French, '85 311
Cream Puffs, Captivating, '81 180
Cream Puffs, Java, '81 187
Cream Puffs, Strawberry, '81 95
Cream Puffs, Tutti-Frutti, '79 231
Crème d'Ange, '83 91
Crème Patissière, '84 207
Crêpes, Basic Dessert, '82 157; '86 275
Crêpes, Dessert, '86 260; '87 290
Crêpes, Dixie Dessert, '79 222
Crêpes Flambé, Cherry, '79 18
Crêpes, Strawberry Dessert, '83 122
Crêpes Suzettes, Light, '83 71
Custard Dessert, Fresh Peach, '86 162
Date-Nut Balls, '85 10
Doughnuts, Orange Spiced, '79 136
Drink, Creamy Dessert, '86 131
Drink, Simply Super Dessert, '83 303
Éclairs with Pecan Sauce, '83 219
Frappé, Hawaiian, '81 178
Frozen
    Amaretto Freeze, '82 182
    Amber Bombe, '80 255
    Apricot Fluff, Frozen, '86 242
    Apricot Freeze, '82 10
    Baked Alaska, '84 105; '85 295
    Baked Alaska, Apple, '80 226
    Baked Alaska, Brownie, '80 66

Baked Alaska, Chocolate Mousse, '85 195
Banana Pops, '83 60; '84 44
Banana Split Alaskas, '87 10
Banana Split Pie, Layered, '83 189
Cantaloupe Cream, Frozen, '82 159
Cherry Cordial Dessert, '84 312
Chocolate-Coffee Frozen Dessert, '85 172
Chocolate Dessert, Frozen, '83 76
Choco-Maple Frozen Dessert, '86 300; '87 178
Citrus Cup, Snowball, '79 2
Coffee Ice Cream Crunch, '82 182
Cranberry Sorbet, '82 251
Elegant Ending, '86 145
Fruit Cream Freeze, '82 144
Fruit Pops, '87 168
Grand Marnier Cream, '84 312
Grasshopper Freeze, Creamy, '81 180
Honeydew Granita, '87 162
Ice Cream Bombe, '82 305

Ice Cream Delight, '80 69
Ice Cream Dessert, Layered, '83 189; '84 94, 105; '86 163
Ice Cream Pie, Kona, '83 189
Ice Cream Sandwiches, Chocolate Cookie, '87 147
Ice Cream Treats, Crunchy, '86 300; '87 178
Lemon-Chiffon Frozen Yogurt, '85 54
Lemon Cream, Frozen, '83 118
Lime-Mint Refresher, '82 144
Little Bits, '79 196
Macaroon-Sherbet Frozen Dessert, '79 212
Mint Patty Alaska, '80 219
Mocha Alaska Dessert, '84 191
Mocha Dessert, Frozen, '84 311
Mocha Freeze, Royal, '84 53
Mocha Squares, Frozen, '81 187
Orange Alaska, '83 177
Orange-Banana Pops, '82 129
Peach Freeze, Creamy, '82 144
Pineapple Delight, Fresh, '79 111
Pineapple-Orange Bars, '82 129
Rainbow Delight, Frozen, '84 105
Raspberry Dessert, Frozen, '84 192
Sherbet Ambrosia Cups, '82 159
Sherbet Dessert, Layered, '87 109
Strawberry Delight, Frozen, '82 112, 174
Strawberry Frost, '82 24; '83 154
Strawberry Popsicles, Smoothie, '82 112
Strawberry Puff, '82 5
Toffee Ice Cream Dessert, '87 110
Vanilla Frozen Yogurt, '87 125

Desserts, Frozen *(continued)*

Vanilla Soufflé, Frozen, '79 230; '82 173
Watermelon Frost, '86 196

Fruit

Bake, Nutty Fruit, '83 127
Caribbean Fruit Dessert, '84 314
Cheese, Luscious Fresh Fruit with, '79 153
Chilled Fruit with Dressing, '85 222
Combo, Fresh Fruit, '86 178
Compote, Baked Fruit, '80 276; '84 314
Compote, Baked Mustard Fruit, '85 47
Compote, Champagne Fruit, '81 309; '82 124
Compote, Chilled Fruit, '83 123
Compote, Fresh Fruit, '79 162; '82 197, 272; '84 82
Compote, Fruit, '86 330
Compote, Hot Fruit, '81 203; '83 53
Compote, Warm Praline Fruit, '85 260
Compote, Wine Fruit, '81 272
Cup, Fruit, '81 141
Cup with Rum, Fruit, '83 55
Flame, Sherried Fruit, '85 313
Flaming Fruit Dessert, '83 302
Fondue, Fruitcake, '84 258
Fresh Fruit with Cheese, Luscious, '79 153
Gingered Fruit, '83 151
Glazed Fruit, '85 83
Hot Fruit Delight, '83 281
Kabobs with Mint Marinade, '82 157
Medley, Chinese Fruit, '83 22
Medley, Fancy Fruit, '84 82
Medley, Fresh Fruit, '81 141
Medley, Frosty Fruit, '82 226
Medley of Fruit, Tropical, '86 53
Meringue Shells, Fruited, '87 32
Orange, Fruit Dessert, '84 314
Rainbow Fruit Dessert, '85 108
Soup Dessert, Fruit, '79 172
Spiced Fruit Delight, '82 229
Spiced Fruit Dessert, '82 50
Tequila, Fruit in, '82 223
Turnovers, Fruit, '79 150

Gâteau Panache, '83 269
Golden Dream, '82 100
Grape Juice-Fruit Refresher, '86 182
Honeydew-Berry Dessert, '83 120
Ice Cream Ginger Fizz, '83 303
Kahlúa Cream, '87 134
Kahlúa Delight, '83 67
Kahlúa Delight, Make-Ahead, '84 M89
Kahlúa Velvet Dessert, '85 M294
Kiwi and Cream in Meringue Cups, '81 279
Kiwi-Berry Pizza, '86 198
Kiwi Jubilee, '83 120
Lemon-Cream Cheese Dessert, '84 95
Lemon Cups, Baked, '87 128
Lemon Delight, '82 227
Little Nothings, '79 135
Mango Pan Dowdy, '83 150
Maple Nut Dessert, '81 84
Maraschino Russian Cream, '79 231
Melon Ball Compote, '85 157
Melon Balls in Watermelon Sauce, '79 177

Melon-Mint Julep, '86 196
Melons in Mint Sauce, '85 164
Melon Wedges with Berry Sauce, '86 178
Meringue Cream Cups, Lemon, '84 23
Meringue Flowers, '84 156
Meringue, Piping, '84 156
Meringues, Baked Pear, '85 232
Meringues, Strawberry, '84 188
Mocha-Almond Dessert, '80 289; '81 62
Mocha Chiffon, '86 75
Nectarines Royale, '85 132
Orange-Apple Crisp, '80 295
Orange Baskets, '81 308
Orange Chantilly Cream, '84 156
Orange-Coconut Cream, '84 24
Orange Cream, '81 12
Orange Cream Dessert, '80 254; '84 165
Orange Dip, Creamy, '84 117
Orange Elegance, Baked, '80 13
Orange Flambé, Dessert, '85 313
Orange Flan, '84 95
Orange Molded Dessert, '83 302
Oranges, Frosted, '83 270
Oranges, Wine-Poached, '84 M323
Orange-Tapioca Crème, '82 M283
Orange Tapioca Fluff, '87 31

Parfaits

Blackberries-and-Cream Parfait, '87 129
Chocolate-Crème de Menthe Parfaits, '85 161
Coffee Crunch Parfaits, '82 159
Eggnog Bavarian Parfait, '79 255
Kiwi Parfait, '86 199; '87 55
Lime Parfaits, '80 153
Mocha-Mallow Parfaits, '80 219
Orange Parfaits, Chilled, '80 219
Peach Parfait, '82 166
Peanut Butter Parfaits, Crunchy, '79 176; '80 6
Pineapple Parfait, '84 83
Speedy Parfaits, '83 76
Strawberry-Lemon Parfaits, '84 198
Strawberry Parfait, '79 99
Strawberry Parfaits, Frosty, '85 213
Strawberry Parfait, Surprise, '86 151
Strawberry-Yogurt Parfait, Crunchy, '79 124

Peach Almond Cream, '82 108
Peach Cream, Bavarian, '82 171
Peach Dessert, Quick, '85 178
Peach Dessert, Spiced, '83 9
Peach Dumplings, '85 177
Peaches, Brandy, '85 275
Peaches Champagne, '79 146
Peaches Foster, '86 240
Peaches, Gingersnap, '85 M329
Peaches in Wine Sauce, '79 184
Peaches, Macaroon-Stuffed, '79 178
Peaches with Ginger, Oven-Baked, '82 170
Peaches with Nutty Dumplings, Spiced, '87 164
Peaches with Rum, Ginger, '84 M323
Peach Halves, Stuffed, '86 196
Peach Melba, '81 83; '83 M114
Peach Split, '85 277
Peachy Melt-Away Dessert, '87 298
Pears, Almond-Stuffed, '83 207
Pears Belle Helene, '86 164
Pears Flambé, Orange-Poached, '85 313
Pears, Flaming, '84 313
Pears in Red Wine, '82 254

Pears in Wine, Poached, '82 194
Pears, Lemon Poached, '82 74
Pears, Maple-Sugared, '81 232
Pears Poached in Red Wine, '83 302
Pears, Spicy Coconut, '83 207
Pears with Berry Sauce, Wine-Poached, '86 144
Pears with Raspberry Sauce, Poached, '84 213; '87 69
Pecans, Sugared, '82 167
Peppermint Bavarian, '80 153
Peppermint Wafer Dessert, '79 176; '80 7
Pineapple-Almond Delight, '85 96
Pineapple Dessert Chimichangas, '86 4
Pineapple, Meringue-Topped, '84 178
Pineapple, Scalloped, '79 106; '82 254
Pineapple with Natillas Sauce, Baked, '83 179
Pizzelles, '83 298
Plum Crunch, Layered, '86 174
Port Wine Jelly with Whipped Cream, '84 254
Profiteroles, '84 208
Prune Bavarian, '86 223
Pumpkin Chiffon, '82 216; '86 283
Pumpkin Flan, '82 217
Pumpkin Mold, '82 311
Pumpkin-Orange Delight, '86 321
Raspberry Dream, '83 108
Raspberry-Jellyroll Dessert, '85 95
Raspberry Prunes, '82 124
Rhubarb-Strawberry Bavarian, '86 140
Rhubarb Whip, '79 112
Rice Cream with Mandarin Oranges, '85 317

Sauces

Amaretto-Strawberry Sauce, '87 M165
Apple Dessert Sauce, '87 M165
Apple Dessert Sauce, Spicy, '82 177
Apple Topping, Spicy, '87 125
Apricot Sauce, '82 212
Banana-Pineapple Sauce, '83 48
Banana Sundae Sauce, '84 275
Berry Sauce, '87 290
Blackberry Sauce, '86 152
Blueberry Topping, '87 125
Bourbon Praline Sauce, '81 170
Brandied Hard Sauce, '80 264; '83 250; '85 313
Brandy-Butter Sauce, '79 230
Brandy-Macadamia Sauce, '82 311
Buttered Rum Sauce, '83 249
Butterscotch-Pecan Sauce, '82 212
Caramel Sauce, '79 79
Caramel Sauce, Easy, '87 38
Cherry-Pineapple Topping, '87 126
Cherry Sauce, '79 91
Cherry Sauce, Elegant, '79 M156
Chocolate-Cherry Sauce, '85 189
Chocolate Cherry Sauce, '87 M165
Chocolate Mint Sauce, Quick, '86 M58

Chocolate-Orange Sauce, '86 165
Chocolate-Peanut Butter
    Sauce, '79 91, M156
Chocolate-Praline Sauce, '85 M295
Chocolate Sauce, '83 189; '84 208,
    313; '86 322
Chocolate Sauce, Classic, '85 207
Chocolate Sauce, Double, '83 79
Chocolate Sauce, Heavenly, '79 79;
    '82 167
Chocolate Sauce Supreme, '85 189
Cinnamon-Blueberry Sauce, '86 11
Cinnamon-Fudge Sauce, '85 141
Coconut-Orange Sauce, '85 189
Coconut Sauce, Creamy
    Light, '82 177
Cranberry Jubilee, Tasty, '85 189
Cranberry Sauce, '86 278
Crème Fraîche Sauce, '79 281
Custard Sauce, '85 41
Date-Nut Sundae Sauce, '82 167
Fig Sauce, '79 140
Fruit Dessert Sauce, Hot, '87 299
Fruit Sauce, Quick, '82 212
Fudge Sauce, Easy Hot, '84 69
Fudge Sauce, Hot, '82 181, 295;
    '84 143
Fudge Sauce, Quick Hot, '82 212
Hard Sauce, '80 265; '82 14
Hard Sauce, Special, '86 318
Honey-Orange Sauce, '85 108
Honeyscotch Sundae Sauce, '82 167
Kahlúa Chocolate Sauce, '85 155
Lemon Dessert Sauce, '87 M165
Lemon Sauce, '84 258, 306;
    '85 77, 190
Lemon Sauce, Tart, '85 191
Mango Sauce, '83 120
Melba Sauce, '87 77
Mint Sauce, Party, '82 212
Orange Dessert Sauce, '87 58
Orange Sauce, Fresh, '85 209
Peach-Berry Sauce, '87 M165
Peach-Blueberry Pancake
    Sauce, '82 177
Peach Blueberry Sauce, '81 170
Peach-Praline Sauce, '85 161
Peach Sauce, '84 144
Peach Sauce, Creamy, '85 189
Peach Sauce, Fresh, '87 167
Peanut Butter Ice Cream
    Sauce, '84 30
Peanut Dessert Sauce, '86 M251
Pecan Sauce, '83 219
Piña Colada Topping,
    Chunky, '87 125
Pineapple Ice Cream Sauce, '81 M289
Pineapple Rum Sauce, '84 275
Praline Ice Cream Sauce, '85 189
Praline Ice Cream Sauce,
    Southern, '86 M227
Praline Sauce, '83 25; '84 143
Raspberry-Peach Topping, '87 126
Raspberry Sauce, '82 289; '83 108;
    '84 73, 213; '87 69, 117, 183
Raspberry Sauce, Crimson, '79 91;
    '85 30
Raspberry Sauce Dessert, '80 147
Raspberry Sauce Flambé, '84 142
Rum-Butter Sauce, '86 301
Rum-Fruit Sauce, '84 312
Rum-Raisin Sauce, '84 7
Rum Sauce, Brown Sugar-, '85 231

Rum Sauce, Hot, '79 86
Sherry Sauce, '84 109
Strawberry-Banana Topping, '87 125
Strawberry Sauce, '84 144;
    '87 93, 198
Strawberry Sauce, Fresh, '82 177
Strawberry Sauce, Peaches with,
    '85 8
Strawberry Sauce with Crunchy
    Topping, '81 170
Strawberry Sauce with
    Dumplings, '84 314
Taffy Dessert Sauce, '86 20
Watermelon Sauce, Melon Balls
    in, '79 177
Savarin, '79 171
Sopaipillas, '80 197
Sopaipillas, Pineapple, '83 179
Soufflé, Banana Daiquiri, '84 317
Soufflé, Brandy Alexander, '82 173;
    '83 M114
Soufflé, Chilled Orange, '84 317; '86 189
Soufflé, Chocolate-Mint, '81 16
Soufflé, Coconut, '85 212
Soufflé, Elegant Daiquiri, '80 69
Soufflé, Frozen Orange, '79 211
Soufflé, Frozen Vanilla, '79 230; '82 173
Soufflé, Grand Marnier, '79 281
Soufflé, Grasshopper, '81 248; '86 188
Soufflé, Kahlúa, '82 173
Soufflé, Lemon, '82 170
Soufflé, Lemon-Lime, Cold, '84 24
Soufflé, Light Chocolate, '83 278
Soufflé, Orange Dessert, '83 206
Soufflé, Pineapple Dessert, '80 153
Soufflé, Raspberry, '86 188
Soufflé, Raspberry-Topped, '85 317
Soufflé, Tart Lemon, '85 82
Strawberries, Almond Cream with
    Fresh, '87 93

Strawberries and Cream, '82 100
Strawberries, Deep-Fried, '84 109
Strawberries Jamaica, '85 161
Strawberries Juliet, '84 82
Strawberries Romanoff, '84 108
Strawberries, Ruby, '82 100
Strawberries Sabayon, '79 91
Strawberries with Brandied Orange
    Juice, '82 160
Strawberries with French Cream, '83 191
Strawberries with Strawberry
    Cream, '84 108
Strawberries with Walnuts,
    Stuffed, '85 122; '86 124
Strawberries Zabaglione, '81 95
Strawberry Cheese Delight, '79 50
Strawberry-Cream Cheese
    Dessert, '83 123
Strawberry Delight, '81 85
Strawberry Dessert, '83 123
Strawberry Dessert, Chilled, '84 164
Strawberry Dessert, Glazed, '84 33

Strawberry Frost, '81 279; '82 24
Strawberry-Lemon Dessert, '86 162
Strawberry Napoleons, '81 126
Strawberry Pizza, '79 94
Strawberry Shortcake Squares, '85 122
Strawberry Swirl, '84 108
Strawberry Yogurt Delight, '85 77
Sundae Dessert, Hot Fudge, '86 322
Sundaes, Cocoa-Kahlúa, '83 M58
Sundaes Flambé, Peach, '81 88
Sundaes, Hot Strawberry, '81 M5
Sundaes, Mauna Loa, '80 126
Sundaes, Quick Pear, '86 71
Trifle, Rum, '86 322
Trifle, Savannah, '80 121
Tropical Snow, '86 34
Vacherin Moka, '80 55
Vanilla Cream, '83 M115
Vanilla Sherry Dessert, Glorified, '81 85
Waffle, Whole Wheat Dessert, '79 92
White Christmas Dessert, '82 261
Wine Jelly, Rosy, '85 306
Yule Log, '79 281; '82 289
Doughnuts
Applesauce Doughnuts, '81 203
Banana Doughnuts, '86 137
Beignets, '84 56
Cake Doughnuts, Quick, '82 226
Chocolate-Covered Doughnuts, '84 55
Chocolate Doughnuts, '83 95
Cinnamon Puffs, '81 209
Dutch Doughnuts, '81 50
Fry Bread, '84 140
Glazed Doughnuts, '83 94
Jelly-Filled Doughnuts, '84 55
Orange Spiced Doughnuts, '79 136
Pineapple Drop Doughnuts, '83 95
Potato Doughnuts, Chocolate-
    Glazed, '85 6
Potato Doughnuts, Old-Fashioned, '84 56
Puffs, Doughnut, '86 85
Puffs, Wheat Quick Doughnut, '85 278
Spice Doughnuts, '84 56
Whole Wheat Doughnuts, '84 56
Dove
Enchiladas, Dove, '85 270
Gumbo, Dove and Sausage, '81 199
Roasted Doves, Pan-, '87 240
Dressings. *See* Stuffings and Dressings.
Duck and Duckling
Baked Duck, Sherried, '79 224
Blackberry Sauce, Ducklings with, '82 251
Breasts with Raspberry Sauce,
    Duck, '87 240
Casserole, Duck and Wild Rice, '79 224
Enchiladas with Red Pepper-Sour Cream,
    Smoked Duck, '87 121
Gumbo, Duck, Oyster, and
    Sausage, '79 226
Gumbo Ya Ya, '87 210
Holiday Duckling, '80 251
Marinated Duck Breasts,
    Charcoaled, '79 226
Orange Duck, Chafing Dish, '79 226
Orange Gravy, Duck with, '81 259
Pâté, Duck, '79 226
Pâté, Duck Liver, '79 227
Pecan Stuffing, Wild Duck with, '85 269
Prairie Wings Mallard, '83 252
Roast Ducklings with Cherry
    Sauce, '86 312
Roast Duckling with Orange
    Sauce, '81 125

Duck and Duckling *(continued)*

Roast Duck with Sweet Potato-Eggplant
  Gravy, '83 90
Roast Long Island Duckling, '84 87
Smoked Duck Breasts, '87 121
Wild Duck, Buffet, '86 268

Dumplings

Apple Dumplings, '82 273
Apple Dumplings, Old-Fashioned, '84 226
Beef Stew with Dumplings, '84 3
Blackberries and Dumplings, '86 196
Chicken and Dumplings, Country, '85 254
Chicken and Dumplings, Easy, '86 21
Chicken and Dumplings,
  Old-Fashioned, '79 55; '83 228
Chicken and Dumplings with
  Vegetables, '85 M56
Chicken Stew and Dumplings, '84 4
Cornmeal Dumplings, Turnip Greens
  with, '82 211
Drop Dumplings, Burgundy Stew
  with, '83 125
Old-Fashioned Dumplings, '81 191
Parsley Dumplings, Beef Stew
  with, '81 76; '82 13; '85 M246
Peach Dumplings, '80 143; '85 177
Peas and Dumplings, Green, '80 102
Potato Dumplings, Venison Stew
  with, '87 304
Shrimp with Dumplings, Stewed, '79 31
Strawberry Sauce with Dumplings, '84 314

E

Eggnog

Bread, Eggnog, '83 294
Breakfast Nog, Speedy, '82 47
Christmas Eggnog, '87 242
Coconut Nog, '83 275
Coffee Nog, Brandied, '86 329
Coffee Nog, Irish, '84 258
Cookies, Eggnog Christmas, '79 255
Creamy Eggnog, '80 259; '83 303; '85 300
Edenton Eggnog, '84 251
Eggnog, '83 318
Holiday Brew, '81 265
Holiday Eggnog Deluxe, '79 232
Irish Cream Nog, '82 312
Orange Spiced Nog, '82 48
Parfait, Eggnog Bavarian, '79 255
Pie, Eggnog, '80 254; '83 205; '86 317;
  '87 295
Pie, Eggnog Chiffon, '86 281
Pie, Fluffy Eggnog, '81 M269
Punch, Coffee-Eggnog, '86 281
Punch, Holiday Eggnog, '86 281
Salad, Eggnog Christmas, '86 281
Sparkling Eggnog, '79 232
Tarts, Creamy Eggnog, '79 255
Thick and Creamy Eggnog, '80 261

Eggplant

Almonds, Eggplant with, '79 179
Appetizer, Eggplant, '83 187
Bake, Eggplant, '80 82
Bake, Eggplant-Sausage, '85 221
Caponata, '87 166
Casserole, Easy Eggplant, '80 202
Casserole, Eggplant, '81 205; '84 217
Casserole, Eggplant and Noodle, '82 230
Casserole, Eggplant-and-Tomato, '83 187

Casserole, Eggplant-Sausage, '84 215
Casserole, Elegant Eggplant, '82 168
Casserole, Flavorful Eggplant, '79 92
Casserole, Moussaka, '79 179
Casserole, Potato-Eggplant, '87 166
Casserole, Super Eggplant, '80 202
Creole Eggplant, '82 107; '83 86
Creole, Eggplant, '86 110
Easy Eggplant, '87 M151
Fried Eggplant, '79 178; '83 187
Fried Eggplant, French-, '81 204
Fried Eggplant, Parmesan, '79 189
Fried Parmesan Eggplant, '87 166
Gravy, Roast Duck with Sweet
  Potato-Eggplant, '83 90
Grilled Eggplant, '80 202
Italian Eggplant, '84 216
Italian-Style Eggplant and
  Zucchini, '79 289; '80 26
Jackstraw Eggplant, '82 230
Julienne, Eggplant, '85 221
Lebanese Eggplant, '81 24
Main Dish, Sausage-Eggplant, '80 211
Medley, Eggplant-Shrimp, '79 188
Mexican Eggplant, '83 187
Mexicano, Eggplant à la, '82 229
Moussaka, '87 166
Parmesan, Eggplant, '82 230; '83 186;
  '84 215; '86 53
Parmigiana, Chicken-Eggplant, '82 212
Parmigiana, Eggplant, '81 19; '82 186
Patties, Eggplant, '83 186
Pizza, Eggplant, '85 221
Ratatouille, '84 105, 243
Ratatouille, Eggplant-Zucchini, '81 205
Ratatouille Niçoise, '81 22

Ratatouille, Quick-and-Easy, '80 212
Sandwiches, Baked Eggplant, '82 230
Sautéed Eggplant and Zucchini, '82 96
Soup, Eggplant Supper, '85 221
Spanish Eggplant, '79 21
Spread, Eggplant, '86 278
Squash, Eggplant and, '83 187
Stuffed Eggplant, '80 158
Stuffed Eggplant, Baked, '81 133
Stuffed Eggplant, Beefy, '81 204
Stuffed Eggplant, Cheesy, '79 188;
  '82 208
Stuffed Eggplant Creole, '82 230
Stuffed Eggplant, Ham-, '80 162
Stuffed Eggplant, Mushroom-, '83 136
Stuffed Eggplant, Ratatouille-, '83 187
Stuffed Eggplant, Ratatouille-Bran, '86 44
Stuffed Eggplant, Rolled, '80 63
Stuffed Eggplant, Sausage, '81 204
Stuffed Eggplant, Seafood, '79 187
Supper, Beef-and-Eggplant, '84 291

Supreme, Eggplant, '79 188; '86 170
Tophats, Eggplant, '79 188

Eggs

au Gratin, Broccoli-and-Eggs, '85 289
au Gratin, Potatoes and Eggs, '79 107
Bake, Breakfast, '85 45
Baked Egg Crisps, '83 57
Baked Eggs Florentine, '86 M12
Baked Eggs in Spinach Nests, '82 70
Bake, Egg and Rice, '83 119
Bake, Sausage Egg, '81 225
Bake, Smoked Sausage-Egg, '85 248
Bedeviled Eggs, '86 67
Benedict, Bacon-and-Tomato
  Eggs, '87 195
Benedict, Easy Eggs, '80 M268
Benedict, Eggs, '79 40, 254; '85 49
Benedict with Cheese Sauce,
  Eggs, '81 225
Brandied Cream Sauce, Eggs in, '82 70
Bread, Butter-Egg, '85 269
Bread, County Fair Egg, '87 68
Bread, Easter Egg, '84 94
Breakfast Eye-Openers, '82 231
Breakfast, Farmer's, '81 44
Brunch Eggs, '85 44
Bruncheon Eggs, '83 83
Brunch, Texas, '82 70
Bunwiches, '80 92
Casserole, Apple-Egg, '85 44
Casserole, Bacon and Egg, '81 225
Casserole, Breakfast Ham and
  Egg, '79 253
Casserole, Broccoli-and-Egg, '86 324
Casserole, Brunch Egg, '86 329
Casserole, Cheese-Egg-Zucchini, '84 114
Casserole, Cheesy Egg, '81 244; '86 15
Casserole, Cheesy Potato-Egg, '84 5
Casserole, Crab-Egg, '80 260
Casserole, Egg, '83 311
Casserole, Egg-and-Bacon, '85 248
Casserole, Egg-and-Cheese, '84 293
Casserole, Egg-Mushroom, '83 49
Casserole, Egg Soufflé, '83 55
Casserole, Sausage Breakfast, '81 270
Casserole, Sausage-Egg, '86 M12
Casserole, Spinach and Egg, '82 270
Casserole, Squash and Egg, '80 146
Casserole, Zucchini-Egg, '84 M113
Cottage Eggs, '85 44
Crabmeat and Eggs New Orleans, '82 45
Creamed Eggs à la Asparagus, '81 201
Creamed Eggs, Broccoli and, '83 84
Creamed Eggs in Patty Shells, '80 M267
Creamed Eggs in Toast Cups, '83 83
Creole Eggs, '82 42
Creole, Skillet Eggs, '85 143
Crêpes, Ham-and-Egg, '83 204
Crêpes with Mushroom Sauce,
  Ham-and-Egg, '82 46
Croquettes, Tuna-Egg, '80 275
Delight, Bacon-and-Egg, '85 143
Delight, Crab-and-Egg, '84 261
Delight, Mushroom-Egg, '83 14
Dip, Festive Egg, '79 285
Dressing, Egg, '86 79
Florentine, Eggs, '79 39; '83 56
Florentine-Style Eggs, '82 38
Foo Yong, Egg, '80 19; '86 232
Foo Yong Patties, '80 223
Foo Yong, Shrimp Egg, '83 22
Frittata, Broccoli-Cheese, '81 243
Frittata, Spinach, '81 53

Ham and Eggs, Creamed, '82 40
Ham and Eggs, Creamy, '87 286
Ham and Eggs on Toast with Cheese
    Sauce, '81 43
Ham and Eggs, Savory, '82 231
Hard-Cooked Eggs, '82 280
Hash Brown Skillet Breakfast, '82 5
Hominy, Bacon, Eggs, and, '85 143
Huevos Rancheros, '82 197
Medley, Cheddary Egg, '81 M176
Mexicana, Eggs, '82 146
Migas, '87 180
Mound, Frosted Egg, '79 33
Mushroom Eggs, Sherried, '83 49
Mushrooms and Eggs in Patty
    Shells, '85 143
Mushrooms and Eggs, Saucy, '79 138
Nests, Fluffy Egg, '79 128
Omelets
    Broccoli-Mushroom Omelet, '85 45
    Cheese Omelet, Zippy, '87 287
    Cheesy Picante Omelet, '86 95
    Chicken Liver Omelet, '82 44
    Fluffy Omelet, '84 56
    George's Omelets, '80 68
    Ham and Cheese Omelet, '79 262;
        '80 123
    Mexican Omelet, '79 128; '81 225
    Mushroom Omelet, Rolled, '82 70
    Mushroom Sauce, Puffy Omelets
        with, '85 40
    Olé Omelet, '87 M124
    Oyster Omelets, Smoked, '84 96
    Potato-Sprout Omelet, '79 128
    Primavera, Omelet, '87 71
    Rising Sun Omelet, '82 281; '83 42
    Sandwich, Omelet, '86 95
    Sausage Filling, Omelet with, '81 43

    Sausage Omelet, Puffy, '80 M268
    Shrimp-and-Cheddar Omelet, '84 57
    Sour Cream-Ham Omelet, '79 261
    Spanish Omelet, '81 201; '83 243;
        '84 101
    Spanish-Style Omelets, '83 188
    Spinach-Cheese Omelet, '83 119
    Sunrise Omelet, '83 289
    Swiss Oven Omelet, '80 189
    Tex-Mex Omelet con Carne, '81 209
    Vegetable Omelet, Beefy, '83 188
    Vegetable Omelet, Cheddar-, '83 205
    Vegetable Omelet, Cheesy, '85 49
    Vegetable Omelet, Fresh, '84 211
    Vegetable Omelet, Golden, '82 M123
    Vegetable Omelet, Puffy, '83 188
    Vegetarian Omelet, '84 114
    White Wine Omelet, '79 103

Yogurt-Avocado Omelet, '81 33
Zucchini Omelet, '81 99
Paint, Egg Yolk, '86 322
Peanut Butter Easter Eggs, '87 86
Pickled Eggs, Beet, '84 287
Pickled Eggs, Rosy, '86 68
Pickled Eggs, Spiced, '84 288
Pie, Egg-Stra Special Chicken, '86 264
Pie, Old-Fashioned Egg Custard, '82 261
Pizza, Breakfast, '85 44
Poached Eggs, Basic, '82 58
Poached Eggs, French-Style, '82 58
Puff, Egg-and-Cheese, '85 45
Rice, Egg Fried, '79 252; '80 19
Salad, Asparagus-and-Egg, '86 305
Salad, Deviled Egg, '83 124
Salad, Egg-Rice, '84 18; '86 169
Salad, Green Vegetable and Egg, '79 191
Salad, Ham-and-Egg Potato, '86 84
Salad, Ham 'n Egg, '81 36
Salad, Tossed Shrimp-Egg, '80 4
Salad, Tuna-Egg, '81 135
Sandwiches, Breakfast, '82 M123
Sandwiches, Confetti, '79 236
Sandwiches, Eggsclusive, '79 164; '80 130
Sandwiches, Eggs-Tra Special, '81 240;
    '83 69
Sandwiches, Open-Faced Cheesy
    Egg, '86 67
Sandwiches, Open-Face Egg, '83 292;
    '84 78; '86 160
Saucy Eggs, '83 84
Saucy Eggs on Toast, '81 209
Scotch Eggs, '79 261; '83 289
Scrambled
    Bacon-and-Eggs Scramble, '80 M267
    Buttermilk Scrambled Eggs, '79 72
    Casserole, Scrambled Egg, '80 51;
        '86 241
    Cottage Cheese Scrambled
        Eggs, '81 142
    Cottage-Scrambled Eggs, '80 49
    Country Eggs, '86 330
    Country-Style Scrambled Eggs, '79 22
    Cream Cheese Scrambled
        Eggs, '81 287
    Home-Style Scrambled Eggs, '84 66
    Mexican-Style Scrambled Eggs, '85 50
    Onion Scrambled Eggs,
        Creamy, '83 M203
    Shrimp and Crab Scrambled
        Eggs, '79 261
    Sonora, Eggs, '80 196
    Spanish Scrambled Eggs, '83 49;
        '84 60
    Special Scrambled Eggs, '81 103
    Supreme, Scrambled Eggs, '79 39
    Tostadas, Scrambled Egg, '86 95
    Wild Rice, Scrambled Eggs
        with, '80 42
Soufflés, Little Egg, '83 57
Soufflé, Three-Egg Cheese, '87 234
Soup, Egg Drop, '83 21; '86 16
Soup, Egg-Drop, '85 M12
Soup, Egg Flower, '81 307; '82 313;
    '83 65
Spread, Cottage-Egg Salad, '82 146
Spread, Egg Salad, '86 127
Spread, Egg, Sour Cream, and
    Caviar, '85 279
Spread, Ham-and-Egg, '79 59
Spread, Vegetable-Egg, '87 106
Strata, Cheese-Rice, '81 176

Strata, Sausage, '84 101
Strata, Tomato-Cheese, '81 209
Stuffed
    Creamed Eggs, '86 67
    Creamy Stuffed Eggs, '84 143
    Crunchy Stuffed Eggs, '86 67
    Deluxe, Eggs, '82 79
    Deviled Eggs, '86 176
    Deviled Eggs, Bacon, '86 136
    Deviled Eggs, Best, '80 159
    Deviled Eggs, Creamed, '82 79
    Deviled Eggs, Easy, '82 127
    Deviled Eggs, Nippy, '80 217
    Deviled Eggs, Pimiento-, '84 143
    Deviled Eggs, Saucy, '82 80
    Deviled Eggs Surprise, '79 83
    Deviled Eggs with Smoked
        Oysters, '84 161
    Deviled Eggs, Zesty, '84 205
    Devil's Island Eggs, '82 79
    Eggs, Stuffed, '80 155
    Mustard Eggs, Spicy, '84 143
    Pecan-Stuffed Eggs, '80 78
    Shrimp-Curried Eggs, Saucy, '84 143
    Tomato Slices, Stuffed
        Eggs-and-, '84 152
    Tuna-Stuffed Eggs, '83 83
Sunny-Side-Up Eggs, '79 38
Tacos, Breakfast, '80 43
Tomatoes, Bacon-and-Egg-Stuffed, '80 162
Tortillas, Chorizo and Egg, '81 193
Tortillas, Egg-and-Sausage, '83 246;
    '84 42
Tulsa Eggs, '87 95

Enchiladas
American Enchiladas, '81 170
Casserole, Enchilada, '87 287
Casserole, Firecracker Enchilada, '80 260
Casserole, Green Enchilada, '79 76
Casserole, Sour Cream Enchilada, '82 113
Cheese Enchiladas, '81 194; '85 154
Cheese Enchiladas, Saucy, '84 220
Chicken Enchiladas, '80 301; '86 296
Chicken Enchiladas, Easy, '82 89; '86 231
Chicken Enchiladas with Spicy Sauce,
    '84 76
Dove Enchiladas, '85 270
Duck Enchiladas with Red Pepper-Sour
    Cream, Smoked, '87 121
Green Chile-Sour Cream Enchiladas,
    '84 234
Hot and Saucy Enchiladas, '81 141; '82 6
New Mexican Flat Enchiladas, '85 244
Pie, Enchilada, '83 155
Sauce, Enchilada, '81 194
Sauce, Red Chile Enchilada, '85 245
Skillet Enchiladas, '82 89
Soup, Chicken Enchilada, '86 22

Enchiladas *(continued)*

Sour Cream Enchiladas, **'83** 200; **'87** 37
Sour Cream Enchiladas, Cheesy, **'79** 25
Spinach Enchiladas, **'83** 60; **'84** 14
Terrificas, Enchiladas, **'84** 32

Escargots

Provençal, Escargots, **'82** 238; **'83** 156

Escarole

Cooked Escarole, Easy, **'84** 85
Salad, Escarole-and-Bacon, **'84** 85

F

Fettuccine

Alfredo, Fettuccine, **'80** 236; **'86** 158
Chicken-Pecan Fettuccine, **'86** 52
Parsley, Fettuccine with, **'83** 115
Shrimp Élégante, **'83** 48
Spinach Fettuccine, Fresh, **'83** 60
Spinach Fettuccini, **'82** 179
Spinach Sauce, Fettuccine with, **'84** 329
Supreme, Fettuccine, **'83** 288; **'86** 333
Vegetable Fettuccine, **'83** 312

Figs

Cake, Easy Fig Coffee, **'80** 116
Cake, Fig, **'79** 32
Cake, Fig Preserve, **'79** 140; **'84** 316
Cobbler, Fig, **'79** 140
Cobbler, Super Fig, **'86** 206
Ice Cream, Fig, **'87** 139
Jam, Fig, **'86** 206
Muffins, Fig, **'86** 206
Pickled Figs, **'79** 140
Preserves, Fig, **'79** 140; **'82** 150
Sauce, Fig, **'79** 140
Snacks, Sliced Fig, **'86** 206

Fillings. *See* Frostings.

Fish. *See also* specific types and Seafood.

Amandine, Fillet of Fish, **'80** M54
Amandine, Fish, **'85** 179
Amandine, Orange Lake, **'80** 99
Asparagus Divan, Fish-, **'87** 128
Aspic, Fish 'n, **'84** 190
Baked Fillets, Creamy, **'84** 91
Baked Fillets in Lemon-Celery
  Sauce, **'84** 91
Baked Fish, Curried, **'87** 5
Baked Fish Fillets, Creamy, **'85** 217
Baked Fish Fillets, Crunchy, **'85** 217
Baked Fish, Southern, **'82** 73
Baked Fish with Barbecue Sauce, **'84** 92
Bake, Fast Fish, **'85** 218
Bake, Saucy Fish, **'79** 75
Beer-Batter Fish, **'85** 68
Bluefish Chowder, **'84** 282
Broiled Fish Fillets Piquante, **'84** 91
Broiled Herb Fish Fillets, **'79** 99
Cakes, Fish, **'85** 54

Captain's Spicy One, **'81** 125
Casserole, Green Chile-and-Fish, **'84** 32
Catfish Amandine, Mandarin, **'84** 183
Catfish, Barbecued, **'80** 157
Catfish, Crisp Fried, **'82** 242
Catfish, Crown Room's
  Shrimp-Stuffed, **'84** 182
Catfish Eldorado de Colorado, **'84** 183
Catfish, Fried, **'82** 135; **'83** 169
Catfish Fry, **'84** 184
Catfish, Golden Fried, **'80** 99
Catfish Kiev-Style, **'84** 184
Catfish Meunière, **'80** 57
Catfish, Middendorf's Broiled
  Manchac, **'84** 183
Catfish Parmesan, **'79** 184; **'86** 210
Catfish Pecan, **'85** 53
Catfish Sesame, **'81** 106
Catfish, Smoked, **'84** 47
Catfish, Soufflé-Stuffed, **'84** 183
Catfish, Southern Oven-Fried, **'87** 163
Catfish Stir, **'84** 184
Ceviche in Avocado Shells, **'81** 33
Ceviche (Marinated Raw Fish), **'80** 194;
  '82 220
Chart, Fat and Lean Fish, **'85** 180
Chowder, Basque Fish, **'86** 36
Chowder, Creamy Fish, **'79** 16
Chowder, Fish, **'79** 152; **'84** M38
Chowder, Tasty Fish, **'80** 188
Corned Fish, **'79** 32
Crawfish Étouffée, **'83** 91
Crawfish Salad, Dilled, **'83** 126
Crawfish Spaghetti, **'85** 104
Creole Fish, **'87** M79
Crust, Fish in a, **'84** 294
Delight, Fish, **'86** M212
Dip, Smoked Fish, **'84** 46
en Papillote, Fish with Snow
  Peas, **'86** 144
Fillets, Lemon-Coated, **'80** M53
Fillets, Parmesan, **'86** M112
Fillets, Spanish-Style, **'86** M112
Florentine, Fish, **'86** 35
Florentine in Parchment, Fish, **'87** 22
Flounder Ambassador, **'86** 234
Flounder au Fromage, Baked, **'86** 234
Flounder, Baked, **'79** 31
Flounder, Cheesy Broiled, **'84** 69
Flounder, Crab-Stuffed, **'80** 120; **'81** 176
Flounder, Creole-Style, **'85** 180
Flounder, Crispy Fried, **'84** 93
Flounder Dijon, **'85** 95
Flounder Fillets, Grilled, **'83** 213
Flounder Fillets in Shrimp Sauce, **'83** 227
Flounder Fillets, Stuffed, **'86** 234
Flounder-Grapefruit Broil, **'85** 53
Flounder in Wine Sauce, Fillet
  of, **'80** 179; **'81** 30
Flounder Nicole, **'85** 217
Flounder, Pesto Broiled, **'86** 150
Flounder Rolls, Vegetable-Stuffed, **'87** 6
Flounder Rolls with Citrus Sauce,
  Stuffed, **'85** 180
Flounder, Seasoned Fried, **'79** 214
Flounder Supreme, Baked, **'79** 75
Flounder Thermidor, **'85** 190
Flounder-Vegetable Medley, **'85** 217
Flounder with Hollandaise-Shrimp
  Sauce, **'86** 234
Fresh Fish, Preparing, **'82** 127
Fried Fish, **'79** 151
Fried Fish, Crispy, **'84** 92

Fried Fish Fillets, Oven-, **'79** 75
Fried Fish, Golden, **'82** 134
Gourmet Fish, **'86** 71
Greek Fish with Vegetable Sauce, **'82** 72
Grilled Fish with Heather Sauce, Catfish
  Inn's, **'84** 182
Grill Fish, How to Charcoal-, **'84** 48
Grouper, Creamy Baked, **'85** 292
Grouper, Grilled, **'86** 185
Grouper Macadamia, **'85** 127
Grouper Sauté, Shrimp-and-, **'87** 91
Grouper Spectacular, **'84** 163
Gumbo, Easy Fish, **'81** 6
Haddock, Baked, **'80** 179; **'81** 30
Haddock Italiano, **'81** M4
Halibut, Chinese-Style Fried, **'80** 179;
  '81 30
Halibut with Cider, **'79** 182
Halibut with Orange-Curry Sauce, **'87** 91
Halibut with Swiss Sauce, **'83** M195
Herb-Coated Fish, **'86** M112
Herbed Fish and Potato Bake, **'79** 287;
  '80 34
Heroes, Neptune, **'84** 281
Herring Dip, Yogurt, **'80** 232
Huachinango à la Veracruzana
  (Veracruz-Style Red Snapper), **'80** 193
Italian Fish, Easy, **'86** M112
Mackerel Creole, **'80** 126
Mackerel, Lemon-Baked, **'79** 182
Mackerel, Smoked Salmon or, **'84** 46
Marinated Beer-Battered Fish, **'86** 180
Monkfish, Greek-Style, **'87** M79
Monterey, Fish, **'84** 293
Mullet, Festive, **'79** 75
Mullet, Smoked, **'84** 47
Orange Roughy, Kiwi, **'87** 193
Papillote, Ocean, **'84** M287
Perch Fillets, Buttery Baked, **'81** 134
Poached Fish in Creamy Swiss
  Sauce, **'80** M53

Redfish Court Bouillon, **'83** 290; **'84** 93
Rolls, Vegetable-Filled Fish, **'86** M251
Rollups, Shrimp-Stuffed, **'82** 234
Salad, Smoked Fish-Potato, **'84** 233
Salad, Smoky Seafood, **'84** 46
Salmon Mousse, Irresistible, **'79** 284
Salmon or Mackerel, Smoked, **'84** 46
Salmon Steaks, Baked, **'85** 54
Sautéed Seafood Platter, **'83** 89
Scamp, Tangy Broiled, **'87** 5
Seviche Cocktail, **'83** 258
Shad Roe with Lemon-Butter Sauce,
  Baked, **'84** 252
Shark, Marinated, **'79** 151
Smoked Fish Log, **'85** 144
Snapper à l'Orange, Baked, **'85** 181
Snapper and Stuffing, Baked, **'82** 72
Snapper, Caribbean, **'87** 5
Snapper Chowder, Red, **'85** 217
Snapper, Company Red, **'82** 72
Snapper, Honey-Curried, **'85** 181
Snapper in Wine Sauce, Red, **'85** 138
Snapper Louisiane, Red, **'85** 217
Snapper, Poached, **'83** 101

Snapper, Poached Red, '85 127
Snapper Rolls, Cucumber-Stuffed
  Red, '83 176
Snapper Rome, Fillet of, '80 57
Snapper, Stuffed, '87 138
Snapper with Dill, '84 190
Snapper with Lime, Stuffed Red, '83 246
Snapper with Tarragon Stuffing,
  Baked, '82 136
Sole Divan, '87 21
Sole Fillets, Herbed, '82 21
Sole Fillets in Wine Sauce, '81 109
Sole in Papillote, '82 22
Sole Provençal, Fillet of, '85 78
Sole, Saucy, '82 M68
Sole Véronique, '85 181
Sole with Cucumber Sauce, '84 M286
Steaks, Soy Fish, '86 M112
Stew, Fish-and-Vegetable, '87 220
Surprise, Fish, '84 231
Sweet-and-Sour Fish, '80 M54
Swordfish, Foil-Baked, '87 5
Swordfish, Skewered, '86 256
Tomato Sauce, Fish in, '85 75
Trout Delmonico, '80 57
Trout Florentine, Cheesy, '85 53
Trout in Wine Sauce, '80 180; '81 31
Trout, Smoked, '84 47
Trout Spread, Smoked, '84 47
Trout, Sunshine, '84 M286
Trout with Ginger and Soy Sauce,
  Grilled, '85 228
Veracruz Fish with Shrimp, '86 130
Food Processor
  Appetizers
    Artichoke-Caviar Mold, '87 239
    Cheese Ring, Strawberry-, '86 14
    Dip, Blue Cheese, '80 285
    Dip, Cheese-Garlic, '80 192
    Dip, Herbal, '86 14
    Dip, Hot Cheesy Beef, '80 85
    Dip, Spinach, '86 159
    Dip, Yogurt Herring, '80 232
    Guacamole in Shells, '86 74
    Mousse, Salmon Dill, '81 21
    Mousse, Shrimp, '87 251
    Olive Quiche Appetizers, '86 159
    Pasta Bites, Pesto-Cheese, '87 251
    Pastry, Processor, '87 67
    Pâté, Chicken Liver, '81 235
    Pâté, Mock, '87 251
    Pâté with Cognac, '86 159
    Pâté with Dill Sauce, Shrimp, '85 39
    Pinwheels, Black-Eyed Pea, '85 300
    Salsa Cruda, '87 180
    Sandwiches, Dainty Cucumber,
      '81 119
    Shrimp Toast, '86 91
    Spread, Country Ham, '87 8
    Spread, Fiery Tomato-Cheese,
      '87 196
    Spread, Sherried Liver, '80 86
    Spread, Shrimp, '87 111
    Spread, Sombrero, '87 111
    Spread, Superb Crab, '81 235
    Spread, Tipsy Cheese, '80 150
  Beverages
    Coffee, Praline-Flavored, '87 69
    Lemonade, Strawberry, '80 160
    Milkshake, Banana, '85 47
  Breads
    Apple-Nut Bread, '85 281
    Baguettes, '85 70

Biscuits, Beaten, '86 54
    Biscuits, Easy Processor, '84 218
    Biscuits, Refrigerator Yeast, '85 48
    Cheese Bread, Crusty, '86 233
    Cream Cheese Loaves,
      Processor, '85 48
    Muffins, Blueberry-Cream
      Cheese, '86 14
    Muffins, Cinnamon-Pecan, '84 219
  Crêpes, Basic Processor, '87 289

Crêpes, Mushroom-Cheese, '87 289
  Desserts
    Apple Crisp, '84 122
    Cake, Fresh Coconut, '85 281
    Cake, Fresh Coconut-Carrot, '80 299
    Cheesecake with Orange-Pineapple
      Glaze, Lemon, '81 60
    Cheesecake, Yam, '81 224
    Cheese, Nutty Date Dessert, '87 299
    Coconut Puffs, '87 277
    Crêpes, Dessert, '87 290
    Crêpes, Strawberry Ice
      Cream, '87 290
    Crust, Pecan, '86 317
    Cupcakes, Mocha, '85 250
    Flan, Apple, '81 309
    Frosting, Cream Cheese, '80 299;
      '86 337; '87 58
    Frosting, Fluffy Chocolate, '86 336;
      '87 58
    Frosting, Snow Peak, '85 281
    Ice, Apricot Yogurt, '81 177
    Ice Cream, Mango, '86 216
    Ice Cream, Peach, '86 15
    Ice, Peach, '81 178
    Mousse, Elegant Amaretto-
      Chocolate, '86 337
    Pastry Shells, Cream Cheese, '86 13
    Phyllo Nests, Nutty, '87 277
    Pie Dough, Quick Food
      Processor, '84 219
    Pie, Pumpkin-Pecan, '85 233, 282
    Pies, Miniature Pecan, '86 13
    Sherbet, Instant Fruit, '85 158
    Sorbet, Cranberry Juice, '85 259
  Dressing, Cornbread-Sausage, '85 280
  Dressing, Pecan-Sage, '80 262
  Eggs and Omelets
    Scotch Eggs, '83 289
  Fruit Nuggets, Dried, '86 326
  Main Dishes
    Chicken Pie, Double-Crust, '87 111
    Chili, Zippy, '87 110
    Meatballs, Quick Processor, '87 111
    Oysters St. Jacques, '80 103
    Pizza, Pesto, '87 182
    Spareribs, Peach-Glazed, '86 14
    Steak, Herb-Marinated Flank, '85 275
    Turkey, Galantine of, '85 150
  Marmalade, Delicious Fruit, '81 285
  Pancakes, Pumpkin, '80 228

Pancakes, Strawberry, '84 219
  Pizza, Deep-Dish Mediterranean, '80 163
  Pizza Supreme, '81 214
  Relish, Cranberry, '85 258, 264; '86 283
  Relish, Cranberry-Nut, '86 275
  Relish, Cranberry-Pear, '85 232
  Relish, Easy Tomato, '80 126
  Salad Dressings
    French Dressing, Creamy, '81 60
    Pesto Salad Dressing, '86 150
    Poppy Seed Dressing, '86 305
    Russian-Style Salad Dressing, '86 305
  Salads
    Cranberry Salad, Jellied, '85 281
    Guacamole Salad, '87 181
    Relish Salad, '84 121
    Spinach-Mustard Twist, '86 209
    Tomato-Artichoke Aspic, '86 92
  Salsa, Hot Mexican, '85 136
  Salsa Picante, Homemade, '81 67
  Sauces and Gravies
    Berry Sauce, '87 290
    Dessert Sauce, Orange, '87 58
    Devonshire Sauce, Processor, '86 337;
      '87 58
    Green Sauce, Herbed, '86 244
    Orange Dessert Sauce, '86 337
    Peanut Hot Sauce, '86 305
    Pesto, Fresh, '86 150
    Pizza Sauce, '80 163
    Seafood Sauce, '86 304
    Tomato Sauce, Italian-Style, '87 182
    Tomato Sauce, Refrigerator, '85 188
  Soups and Stews
    Avocado Soup, Chilled, '81 34
    Bean Soup, '80 25
    Brunswick Stew, '80 264
    Brunswick Stew, Blakely, '87 4
    Cauliflower Soup, Creamy, '82 76
    Gazpacho, '80 266
    Melon Soup, Swirled, '87 162
    Mushroom Soup, Cream of,
      '85 93, 261
    Strawberry Soup Supreme, '81 M144
    Tomato Soup with Parmesan Cheese,
      Cream of, '86 161
  Spread, Benedictine Sandwich, '80 299
  Spread, Corned Beef, '87 196
  Terrine with Goat Cheese, Black
    Bean, '87 120
  Vegetables
    Asparagus with Basil Butter, '85 40
    Carrots, Honey-Glazed, '84 121
    Loaf, Pureed Vegetable-
      Cheese, '85 297
    Okra and Tomatoes, Fresh, '81 M165
    Peppers, Ham-and-Corn
      Stuffed, '81 87
    Potato-Apple Bake, Sweet, '86 282
    Potato Casserole, Processor, '86 159
    Potato Pancake, '85 20
    Ratatouille Niçoise, '81 22
    Squash Casserole, Jiffy, '81 M144
    Tomatoes, Spinach-Stuffed
      Baked, '86 14
  Waffles, Crunchy Walnut, '85 48
Frankfurters
  Appetizer Franks, Saucy, '84 M12
  Appetizers, Bourbon Frankfurter, '85 207
  Bacon-Wrapped Franks, '81 202
  Barbecued Frankfurters, '83 144; '84 M12
  Barbecued Frankfurters, Oven-, '83 11
  Barbecued Franks, '85 192

Frankfurters, *(continued)*

Barbecue, Tangy Frank, '79 63
Beans and Franks, '85 142
Beans and Franks, Hawaiian
  Baked, '80 136
Beans-and-Franks, Polynesian, '84 M11
Beany Hot Dogs, '82 190
Cabbage with Apples and Franks, '87 42
Casserole, Layered Frankfurter, '79 64
Chafing Dish Franks, '83 143
Chili-Cheese Dogs, '81 M176
Corn Dog Bites, '85 245
Corn Dogs, Favorite, '83 144
Corn Relish Dogs, '85 192
Crusty Franks, '80 166
Delicious, Hot Dogs, '81 202
Family-Style Franks, '79 54
Grilled Stuffed Franks, '82 163
Hash Browns, Franks and, '80 166
Hawaiian Franks, '81 202
Jubilee, Hot Dog, '81 113
Kraut and Franks, Beany, '79 64
Mexicali Hot Dogs, '82 131
Pickled Party Franks, '83 174
Potatoes, Cheesy Frank-Topped, '83 3
Potatoes, Frank-Filled, '84 M11
Sandwiches, Frankfurter, '84 M11
Skillet Dinner, Frankfurter, '80 166
Skillet, Frankfurter-Cabbage, '80 166
Skillet, Hot Dog and Spaghetti, '83 144
Sloppy Joe Dogs, '85 192
Soup, Split Pea and Frankfurter, '79 64
Spanish Frankfurters, '80 166
Spicy Frankfurters, '81 202
Stuffed Franks and Potatoes, '81 202
Tipsy Franks, '85 52

French Toast

Amandine, Baked Toast, '82 47
Baked French Toast, Oven-, '82 47
Cinnamon French Toast, '84 211
Cottage-Topped French Toast, '85 49
Easy French Toast, '82 M172
Macadamia French Toast, '86 96
Orange Butter, French Toast with, '81 42
Orange French Toast, '83 292; '84 78;
  '86 329
Orange Sauce, French Toast with, '82 47
Overnight French Toast Deluxe, '79 216
Slender French Toast, '86 103
Waffled French Toast, '82 47

Fritters

Apple Fritters, '81 105; '82 273; '85 14
Apple Holiday Fritters, '86 314
Banana Fritters, '79 213
Blueberry Fritters, '85 152
Broccoli Fritters, Cheesy, '79 53
Clam Fritters, '79 151; '86 71
Corn Fritters, '86 192
Corn Fritters, Golden, '80 165; '81 128
Corn Fritters, Skillet-Fried, '85 14
Ham Fritters, '82 39
Ham Fritters with Creamy Sauce,
  '81 105
Okra, Fritter-Fried, '86 218
Okra Fritters, '79 160
Orange Fritters, Puffy, '81 169
Oyster Fritters, '79 31
Pear Fritters, Ol' Timey, '86 51
Pecan Fritters, Chocolate-
  Covered, '79 205
Potato Fritters, Golden Sweet, '79 9
Zucchini Fritters, '81 163

Frog Legs

Crispy Frog Legs, '80 99

Frostings, Fillings, and Toppings

Almond-Butter Frosting, '86 107
Almond Cream Filling, '85 320
Almond Filling, '87 301
Almond Filling, Ground, '87 14
Almond Topping, '85 152; '86 200
Amaretto Filling, '87 241
Amaretto Frosting, '86 246
Apple-Date Filling, '83 301
Apple Filling, '85 5
Apple Filling, Dried, '85 242; '87 229
Apricot Filling, '83 84; '86 107
Apricot Frosting, '81 192
Apricot Glaze, '80 280; '82 8; '86 197
Apricot Glaze for Ham, '85 256
Apricot Glaze, Sweet, '82 304
Apricot-Kirsch Glaze, '87 14
Banana-Nut Frosting, '79 115
Beef Filling, '80 81
Berry Glaze, '83 225
Biscuit Topping, '86 157, 265
Blueberry Glaze, '83 143
Brandy Cream Frosting, '86 239
Brandy Glaze, Powdered Sugar-, '86 291
Broccoli Filling, '81 44
Brown Sugar Frosting, '79 13; '87 296
Brown Sugar Glaze, '83 312
Brown Sugar Meringue Frosting, '81 70
Brown Sugar Topping, '81 162
Buttercream Frosting, '85 322
Buttercream Icing, '83 73
Buttercream, Spiced, '84 226
Butter Frosting, '80 129
Butter Frosting, Browned, '86 248
Butter Frosting, Williamsburg, '81 120;
  '82 23
Buttermilk Frosting, '85 249
Buttermilk Glaze, '79 140; '81 70;
  '84 316
Butter Pecan Frosting, '80 229
Caramel Drizzle, '86 247
Caramel Frosting, '81 278, M289; '82 314;
  '83 43; '84 39, 263; '86 239; '87 265
Caramel Frosting, Creamy, '81 71
Caramel Frosting, Easy, '87 39
Caramel Frosting, Favorite, '83 106
Caramel Glaze, '85 320
Carob Frosting, '85 218
Catsup Topping, '81 170
Chantilly Cream, '83 91
Chantilly Crème, '80 280
Cheese Topping, '86 233
Cherry Filling, '83 302; '84 225
Cherry Frosting, '86 217
Cherry Glaze, '83 143
Chicken Divan Filling, '81 91
Chicken Filling, '81 200
Chicken Filling Luau, '79 81
Chicken-Olive Filling, '81 227
Chicken Salad Filling, '87 106
Chocolate-Almond Frosting, '83 241
Chocolate Buttercream, '84 156
Chocolate Candy Frosting, '81 238
Chocolate-Coffee Frosting, '84 36
Chocolate Filling, Rich, '79 68
Chocolate Frosting, '80 M171; '81 265;
  '82 262; '83 79, 99, M233, 253;
  '84 200; '85 323; '86 8, 93, 138,
  239, 314; '87 M97, 198, 199, 293
Chocolate Frosting, Creamy, '85 314;
  '86 316; '87 241

Chocolate Frosting, Fluffy, '86 336;
  '87 58
Chocolate Frosting, Rich, '84 304
Chocolate Frosting, Satiny, '85 126
Chocolate Fudge Frosting, '83 105
Chocolate Glaze, '81 119; '83 220;
  '84 10, 55, 253; '85 6; '86 315, 316
Chocolate Glaze, Creamy, '82 88
Chocolate-Honey Glaze, '82 306
Chocolate-Marshmallow Frosting, '83 245
Chocolate Nut Frosting, '80 140
Chocolate-Peanut Butter
  Frosting, '84 240; '87 222
Chocolate-Peanut Topping, '79 222
Chocolate Rum Frosting, '79 67
Chocolate Truffle Filling, '87 69
Cinnamon-Cream Frosting, '84 311
Cinnamon Frosting, Buttery, '81 M139
Cinnamon-Pecan Topping, '85 277
Citrus Glaze, '82 128
Cocoa Frosting, '86 60
Coconut Chocolate Frosting, '79 13
Coconut Cream Cheese Frosting, '86 60
Coconut Cream Filling, '84 200
Coconut Filling, '81 265
Coconut Frosting, '82 262
Coconut Frosting, Creamy, '80 287
Coconut Frosting, Nutty, '86 8
Coconut-Pecan Frosting, '81 296;
  '83 M233; '84 43, 322
Cola Frosting, '81 238
Cranberry Glaze, '84 306; '86 171
Cream Cheese Frosting, '79 45; '80 140,
  253, 299; '82 135, 244; '83 105, 215,
  M233; '84 201, 255, 315, 316; '85 118,
  121; '86 217; '87 58
Cream Cheese Frosting, Deluxe, '80 120
Cream Cheese Frosting, Fluffy, '80 245
Cream Cheese Frosting, Nutty, '85 117
Cream Cheese Glaze, '84 150
Cream Filling, '83 220; '84 37; '87 198
Cream, Luscious Pastry, '82 504
Cream, Mock Devonshire, '81 288
Cream Topping, Spicy, '85 177
Crème Chantilly, '87 9
Crème de Menthe Frosting, '86 245
Crème Pâtissière, '83 225
Crumb Topping, '83 183
Custard Filling, '82 52, 298; '85 281
Custard Filling, Creamy, '81 180
Custard Filling, Egg, '87 14
Date Cream Filling, '81 303
Date Filling, '80 15; '83 257; '86 314
Decorating Techniques, Cake, '83 72, 240
Decorator Frosting, '82 20, 307; '83 106;
  '87 86
Decorator Frosting, Creamy, '79 117
Divinity Frosting, '79 229
Drizzle Glaze, '87 94
Fluffy Filling, '81 192; '86 246
Fluffy Frosting, '79 246; '86 235
Fruit Filling, Crêpes with, '81 96
Fruit-Nut Filling, '80 289
Fruit Topping, '81 42; '87 225
Fruity Dessert Topping, '82 167
Fudge Frosting, '81 303; '87 296
Fudge Frosting, Quick, '81 278
Ginger Cream Topping, '84 312
Glaze, Dijon, '87 54
Glaze, Topping, '86 69
Heavenly Frosting, '80 140
Honey Chocolate Frosting, '79 83
Honey-Nut Glaze, '87 15

Honey Topping, '83 154
Honey-Walnut Filling, '80 21
Horseradish Glaze, Carrots with, '85 66
Kahlúa Glaze, '86 292
Lemon Buttercream Frosting, '83 301;
   '86 61
Lemon-Butter Cream Frosting, '85 117
Lemon-Cheese Filling, '79 68
Lemon Cream, '82 237
Lemon-Cream Cheese Frosting, '81 157
Lemon Cream Filling, '84 23; '87 14
Lemon Curd, '87 139
Lemon Filling, '81 172; '84 137; '85 191;
   '86 235; '87 293
Lemon Filling, Creamy, '80 70
Lemon Frosting, '85 191; '86 217
Lemon Frosting, Creamy, '79 93
Lemon Glaze, '79 285; '86 194; '87 41
Lemon-Orange Filling, '81 71
Lemon-Pineapple Topping, '86 60
Maple Frosting, '82 217; '85 322
Meringue, Cooked, '86 130
Meringue, Easy Cooked, '82 207; '83 158
Meringue Frosting, '86 336; '87 84
Mocha Butter Cream Frosting, '79 281
Mocha-Buttercream Frosting, '86 26
Mocha Cream Filling, '81 187; '84 305
Mocha Filling, '80 55; '82 262
Mocha Frosting, '83 301; '84 316; '87 224
Mocha Frosting, Creamy, '82 289; '84 311
Mushroom Filling, '81 89
Napoleon Cream, '84 138
Never Fail Frosting, '86 314
Nut-and-Fruit Filling, '84 263
Nutty Topping, '85 256; '86 16
Omelet Filling, Greek, '80 68
Omelet Filling, Spanish, '80 68
Orange Buttercream Frosting, '80 70
Orange Butter Frosting, '83 300

Orange-Cream Cheese Frosting, '81 70;
   '82 16
Orange Cream Frosting, '81 207; '82 14
Orange Filling, '79 229; '86 336; '87 84
Orange Frosting, '81 7; '86 61
Orange Frosting, Creamy, '83 24, 241
Orange Glaze, '79 2; '80 257; '81 34,
   107; '82 75, 206; '83 33, 114, 140, 267;
   '84 161; '86 298
Orange Glaze, Nutty, '80 45
Orange-Pineapple Glaze, '81 60
Orange Topping, Whipped, '80 254
Paint, Egg Yolk, '86 322
Papaya Topping, '86 181
Peanut Butter Frosting, '83 223; '84 153;
   '85 34
Peanut Butter-Fudge Frosting, '87 184
Peanut Butter Swirl Frosting, '86 109
Peanut Frosting, Creamy, '80 87
Pecan Frosting, '86 86
Peppermint Filling, '81 119
Pimiento Topping, '83 93
Pineapple Filling, '80 140; '83 179;
   '84 153

Pineapple Glaze, '83 143; '85 38
Pineapple Topping, '86 239
Powdered Sugar Glaze, '79 24; '82 92,
   283; '83 83, 295; '85 55
Praline Glaze, '82 196
Quick Pour Frosting, '85 119
Raspberry Topping, '85 317
Ricotta Filling, '80 58
Royal Icing, '80 278; '81 21; '83 73;
   '84 303; '85 323; '87 295
Rum Cream Topping, '80 255
Rum Glaze, Buttered, '83 220
Salt, Gourmet Seasoning, '82 297
Sea Foam Frosting, '81 211
Seasoning Blend, '82 296
Seven-Minute Double Boiler
   Frosting, '81 278
Seven-Minute Frosting, '80 289; '83 299,
   301; '87 296
Shrimp Salad Filling, '87 106
Snow Peak Frosting, '82 53; '85 281
Snowy Glaze, '82 295
Sour Cream Topping, '85 298; '86 120
Spinach-Mushroom Filling, '80 215
Spinach-Ricotta Filling, '81 53
Strawberry Glaze, '80 35; '83 142
Strawberry Topping, '86 32
Streusel, '85 326
Sugar Glaze, '86 161
Tips for Piping Icing, '84 302
Toffee Frosting, English, '85 125
Vanilla Cream, '81 248
Vanilla Frosting, '84 36; '85 236
Vanilla Glaze, '85 M89
Vanilla-Rum Frosting, '85 324
Vegetable Topping, '79 79
Whipped Cream Frosting, '83 229;
   '85 125; '87 263
Whipped Cream Topping, '87 264
Whipped Topping, Reduced-
   Calorie, '85 55
White Frosting, '83 268
White Frosting, Fluffy, '81 278
White Frosting, Luscious, '81 71
Fruit. *See also* specific types.
   Baked Fruit, Gingered, '81 232
   Baked Fruit Medley, '81 297
   Bake, Hot Fruit, '81 270
   Bake, Nutty Fruit, '83 127
   Balls, Fruit, '82 296; '84 299
   Bars, Fruit and Nut Granola, '81 49
   Beverage, Blender Fruit, '83 318
   Boats, Honeydew Fruit, '81 147
   Bowl, Sparkling Fresh Fruit, '80 146
   Braid, Fruit-and-Cheese, '86 214
   Brandied Fruit, Hot, '80 48
   Brandied Fruit Starter, '82 249
   Bread, Cranberry Fruit-Nut, '79 275
   Bread, Kahlúa Fruit-Nut, '79 235
   Cake, Fruit and Spice, '87 M97
   Cake, Fruited Pound, '81 265
   Cake, Fruity Ice Cream, '87 110
   Cake, Spicy Fruited Carrot, '85 117
   Cake, Stately Fruit-and-Nut, '84 226
   Canapés, Fruit-Topped, '85 80
   Canning and Preserving
      Apple Rings, Cinnamon, '85 107
      Berries (except Strawberries), '80 128
      Dehydration Chart, Fruit and
         Vegetable, '84 147
      Freezing Chart, Fruit, '85 187
      Juices, Fruit, '85 107
      Peaches, '80 128

Peaches and Pears, '85 106
   Peaches, Honey-Sweet, '85 107
Cascade, Fruit, '86 104
Cheesecake, Fruit-Glazed, '80 24
Cheese, Fruited Cream, '85 306
Chicken en Crème, Fruited, '83 264
Chicken, Fruit-Glazed, '80 211
Chicken with Almond Rice, Spiced
   Fruited, '81 195
Chicken with Almond Sauce, Spiced
   Fruited, '81 195
Chilled Fruit with Dressing, '85 222
Combo, Fresh Fruit, '86 178
Compote, Baked Fruit, '80 276; '84 314;
   '87 228
Compote, Baked Mustard Fruit, '85 47
Compote, Champagne Fruit, '81 309;
   '82 124
Compote, Chilled Fruit, '83 123
Compote, Fresh Fruit, '79 162; '82 197,
   272; '84 82
Compote, Fruit, '86 330
Compote, Hot Fruit, '81 203; '83 53;
   '86 324
Compote, Warm Praline Fruit, '85 260
Compote, Wine Fruit, '81 272
Conserve, Dried Fruit, '82 308
Cookies, Bourbon Fruit, '86 334
Cookies, Fruitcake, '79 291; '86 320
Cookies, Holiday Fruitcake, '81 301
Cookies, Rolled Fruit, '80 15
Cookies, Spicy Holiday Fruit, '83 298
Cooler, Four-Fruit, '86 101
Cooler, Fruited Wine, '86 176
Cream Freeze, Fruit, '82 144
Cream Puffs, Tutti-Frutti, '79 231
Crêpes, Tropical, '86 275
Crêpes, Tropical Fruit, '87 77
Cup, Appetizer Fruit, '86 131
Cup, Fruit, '81 141
Cups, Honeydew Fruit, '82 179
Cup, Snowball Citrus, '79 2
Cups, Royal Fruit, '81 146
Cup, Tipsy Fruit, '81 268
Cup, Vanilla Fruit, '80 183
Curried Fruit, Almond-, '83 261
Curried Fruit Bake, '87 241
Curried Fruit, Hot, '79 225; '81 264;
   '84 287
Custard over Fruit, Stirred, '84 83
Delight, Fruit, '86 131
Delight, Winter Fruit, '80 243
Dessert, Caribbean Fruit, '84 314
Dessert, Flaming Fruit, '83 302
Dessert, Rainbow Fruit, '85 108
Dip, Coconut-Honey Fruit, '84 171
Dip, Fresh Fruit, '80 265
Dip, Fruited Yogurt, '84 171
Dip, Heavenly Fruit, '81 160
Dip, Marshmallow Fruit, '84 171
Dressing, Avocado Fruit Salad, '82 93
Dressing, Baked Fruit, '87 253
Dressing, Fluffy Fruit, '79 69
Dressing for Fruit, Salad, '86 40
Dressing for Fruit Salad, '87 81
Dressing, Fresh Fruit, '87 134
Dressing, Fruit-and-Pecan, '84 252
Dressing, Fruited Cornbread, '80 262
Dressing, Fruit Salad, '79 69
Dressing, Lime-Honey Fruit Salad, '87 81
Dressing, Marmalade-Fruit, '84 171
Dressing, Tangy Coconut-Fruit, '84 171
Dressing, Whipped Cream Fruit, '79 270

Fruit *(continued)*

Drink, Three-Fruit, '79 38; '80 50;
  '87 199
Drink, Tropical Fruit, '85 43
Filling, Crêpes with Fruit, '81 96
Filling, Fruit-Nut, '80 289
Filling, Lemon Crêpes with Fruit, '82 46
Filling, Tutti-Frutti, '79 231
Float, Frosty Fruit, '87 159
Fresh Fruit, Mint Dip with, '87 146
Fresh Fruit with Cheese, Luscious,
  '79 153
Fresh Fruit with Lemon Sauce, '82 290
Fruitcakes
  Applesauce Fruitcake, '83 258
  Aronowitz Fruitcake, '86 285
  Bourbon Fruitcake, '85 315
  Brandy Fruitcake, '82 261
  Burgundy Fruitcake, '85 292
  Fondue, Fruitcake, '84 258
  Japanese Fruitcake, '83 268
  Kentucky Fruitcake, '86 266
  Layered Fruitcake, '87 265
  Lemon Fruitcake, '83 258
  Mom's Fruitcake, '85 321
  Old-South Fruitcake, '79 289
  Regal Fruitcake, '83 257
  Sherry-Nut Fruitcake, '84 266
  Spice Cake, Fruit and, '87 M97
  White Fruitcake, '80 280; '85 316
Garnishes, '82 280
Gingered Fruit, '83 151
Glazed Fruit, '85 83
Goose, Fruit- and Pecan-Stuffed,
  '83 268
Goose, Fruit Stuffed, '83 320
Granola, Fruity, '84 148
Ham Slice, Fruited, '83 M317
Hawaiian Fruit Dish, '82 112
Hot Fruit Delight, '83 281
Ice Cream, Tutti-Frutti, '86 129
Ice, Fruit, '86 176
Ice, Mixed Fruit, '81 178
Ice Tropical, '79 174
Juicy, Breakfast Fruit, '86 176
Kabobs, Fruit, '86 181
Kabobs with Coconut Dressing,
  Fruit, '87 251
Kabobs with Mint Marinade,
  Fruit, '82 157
Lemon Freeze, Fruity, '82 145
Marinated Fruit Bowl, '80 297
Marmalade, Delicious Fruit, '81 285
Medley, Chilled Fruit, '84 60
Medley, Chinese Fruit, '83 22
Medley, Fancy Fruit, '84 82
Medley, Fresh Fruit, '81 141
Medley, Frosty Fruit, '82 226
Medley, Fruit Cup, '85 47
Medley, Minted Fruit, '80 182
Medley of Fruit, Tropical, '86 53
Mélange Delight, Fruit, '81 302
Mélange, Melon, '84 139
Meringue Shells, Fruit-Filled, '86 151
Mixed Fruit, Unsweetened, '83 182
Muffins, Fruited Wheat, '79 93
Nuggets, Dried Fruit, '86 326
Picks, Fruit on, '80 159
Pie, Fruitcake, '80 237
Pie, Fruit-Topped Vanilla Cream, '84 49
Pie, Japanese Fruit, '80 238
Pies, Baked Fruit, '84 7

Pops, Fruit, '87 168
Pork Chops, Fruited, '87 194
Pork Chops, Fruited Stuffed, '86 197
Pork Chops, Fruit-Stuffed, '82 136
Pork Chops with Rice, Fruit-Glazed,
  '82 73
Pork Pilaf, Fruited, '82 246
Pork Tenderloins, Fruit-Stuffed, '87 270
Pudding Compote, Fresh Fruit, '86 151
Pudding, Fruited Rice, '86 95
Puff, Giant Fruit, '85 72
Punch, Fruit, '83 52
Punch, Golden Fruit, '80 299; '83 56
Punch, Holiday Fruit, '79 232
Punch, Hot Fruit, '83 33
Punch, Party Fruit, '82 137
Punch, Spirited Fruit, '81 100
Punch, Summertime Fruit, '80 160
Punch, Tropical Fruit, '81 51; '83 176
Refresher, Four-Fruit, '79 174
Refresher, Grape Juice-Fruit, '86 182
Rhapsody, Fruit, '80 158
Rice, Far East Fruited, '81 175
Rice Mix, Fruited Curry-, '86 326
Rice Pilaf, Fruit-and-Vegetable, '84 196

Salads
  Apricot Fruit Salad, '82 132
  Avocado Fruit Salad, '87 41
  Banana-Mixed Fruit Salad, '79 270
  Cabbage and Fruit Salad, '79 286
  Cantaloupe, Fruit-Filled, '83 120
  Carrot-and-Seed Salad, Fruity,
    '86 223
  Carrot-Fruit Toss, '82 235
  Chef Salad, Fruited, '85 222
  Chef's Fruit Salad, '86 35
  Cherry Fruit Salad, '87 236
  Chicken-Avocado Salad,
    Fruited, '82 101
  Chicken-Fruit Salad, '82 79
  Chicken Salad, Fruited, '84 25, 290
  Chicken Salad, Fruity, '83 157
  Chicken Salad in Avocados,
    Fruited, '87 41
  Chicken Salad with Fruit, '82 171
  Coconut Fruit Bowl, '83 111
  Coconut Salad, Chunky
    Fruit-and-, '84 24
  Coleslaw, Fruited, '83 209; '85 139
  Coleslaw, Three-Fruit, '86 250
  Colorful Fruit Salad, '82 113
  Cottage Cheese-and-Fruit
    Salad, '86 16
  Cottage-Fruit Split, '86 169
  Creamy Fruit Salad, '84 265
  Curried Fruit Salad, '85 107
  Date Dressing, Fruit Salad
    with, '87 57
  Dressed-Up Fruit, '82 5
  Easy Fruit Salad, '80 221

Fall Salad with Ginger
  Dressing, '82 194
Festive Fruit Salad, '80 16
Fresh Fruit Cup with Mint
  Dressing, '80 183
Fresh Fruit Salad, '82 165
Fresh Fruit Salad with Celery-Honey
  Dressing, '80 42
Frisky Fruit Salad, '85 46
Frozen Fruit Salad, '83 110
Frozen Fruit Salad, Dreamy, '79 126
Frozen Fruit Salad, Luscious, '81 204
Frozen Salad Christmas Wreath,
  '79 241
Fruit Salad, '83 209
Glazed Fruit Salad, '83 48; '84 290
Ham Salad, Fruited, '81 36, 146
Heavenly Salad, '81 252
Holiday Fruit Salad, '87 236
Honeydew Fruit Bowl, '84 186
Honey Dressing, Fruit Salad
  with, '87 129
Honey Fruit Salad, '80 276
Hurry-Up Fruit Salad, '87 236
Jicama-Fruit Salad, '86 83
Layered Fruit Salad, '84 290
Lemonade Fruit Salad, '84 24
Lettuce and Fruit Salad with Poppy
  Seed Dressing, '80 152
Main Dish Fruit Salad, '83 119
Marinated Fruit Deluxe, '81 146
Melon-Citrus Mingle, '79 177
Mixed Fruit Cup, '87 233
Nut Salad, Cheesy Fruit-'n'-, '87 56
Old-Fashioned Fruit Salad, '82 80
Persimmon Fruit Salad, '79 206
Pineapple Cream Dressing, Fruit Cups
  with, '83 81
Pineapple Dressing, Fruit Salad
  with, '85 207
Pineapple-Fruit Salad, Icy, '87 9
Platter, Fruit Salad, '83 261
Potato Salad, Fruity, '85 214
Quick-and-Easy Fruit Salad, '81 99
Raspberry Fruit Mounds, '79 35
Refreshing Fruit Salad, '85 92
Rum, Fruit Cup with, '83 55
Shrimp Salad, Fruited, '86 156
Sour Cream Fruit Salad, '80 138
Sparkling Fruit Salad, '82 266
Spiced Autumn Fruit Salad, '87 228
Springtime Fruit Salad, '81 96
Summer Fruit Salad, '82 164
Summer Salad, Favorite, '80 158
Sweet-and-Sour Fruit Salad, '80 13;
  '84 125
Tropical Fruit Salad with Fresh Mint
  Dressing, '84 126
Turkey-Fruit Salad, '79 56
Turkey Fruit Salad, '83 233; '84 244
Turkey Salad, Fruitful, '84 197
Watermelon Fruit Basket, '84 161
Winter Fruit Salad, '80 248; '82 23
Wreath, Della Robbia Fruit, '87 294
Yogurt Fruit Salad, '81 114
Sauce, Fruit, '81 177
Sauce, Hot Fruit Dessert, '87 299
Sauce, Quick Fruit, '82 212
Sauce, Rum-Fruit, '84 312
Shake, Frosty Fruit, '87 23
Shells, Fruited Meringue, '87 32
Sherbet, Freezer Fruit, '86 334
Sherbet, Frozen Fruit, '79 155

Sherbet, Fruit Punch, '86 129
Sherbet, Instant Fruit, '85 158
Sherried Fruit Casserole, '80 284
Sherried Fruit Flame, '85 313
Sherried Fruit Mélange, '80 158
Slush, Refreshing Fruit, '82 35
Slushy, Fruit, '80 146
Soup, Cold Fresh Fruit, '87 157
Soup Dessert, Fruit, '79 172
Soup, Dried Fruit, '79 23
Soup, Fruit, '87 98
Soup, Swedish Fruit, '82 313; '83 65
Soup, Yogurt Fruit, '86 176
Spareribs, Fruit-Stuffed, '79 14
Spiced Fruit, '79 23
Spiced Fruit Delight, '82 229
Spiced Fruit Dessert, '82 50
Spiced Fruit, Warm, '86 39
Spiced Winter Fruit, '83 262
Spread, Fruit, '85 135
Spread, Fruit and Cheese, '81 245
Spread, Nutty Fruit-and-Cheese, '87 246
Spread, Sugarless Fruit, '84 60
Squash, Fruited Acorn, '85 235
Squash, Fruit-Stuffed Acorn, '81 295
Strudel, Fruit Basket, '87 276
Syrup, Apricot Fruit, '82 10
Syrup, Fruit, '86 176

Tart, Fancy Fruit, '82 128
Tart, Fresh Fruit, '84 178
Tart, Open-Face Fruit, '84 207
Tart, Rainbow Fruit, '82 304
Tea, Christmas Fruit, '83 275
Tea, Hot Spiced Fruit, '87 242
Tequila, Fruit in, '82 223
Topping, Fruit, '81 42; '87 225
Topping, Fruity Dessert, '82 167
Turnovers, Fruit, '79 150
Twists, Fruit-Nut, '82 253
Wine, Fruit in White, '81 48
Wontons, Fruit-Filled, '85 287

G

Game. *See also* specific types.
Chili, Double-Meat, '80 12
Dove and Sausage Gumbo, '81 199
Dove Enchiladas, '85 270
Doves, Pan-Roasted, '87 240
Duck and Wild Rice Casserole, '79 224
Duck, Buffet Wild, '86 268
Duckling, Holiday, '80 251
Duckling, Roast Long Island, '84 87
Ducklings with Blackberry Sauce, '82 251

Ducklings with Cherry Sauce,
    Roast, '86 312
Duckling with Orange Sauce,
    Roast, '81 125
Duck, Oyster, and Sausage
    Gumbo, '79 226
Duck, Sherried Baked, '79 224
Duck with Orange Gravy, '81 259
Duck with Pecan Stuffing, Wild, '85 269
Duck with Sweet Potato-Eggplant Gravy,
    Roast, '83 90
Goose with Currant Sauce, Wild, '87 240
Mallard, Prairie Wings, '83 252
Pheasant Muscatel, '85 269
Quail Breasts, Southern, '85 270
Quail, Fried, '82 45
Quail, Magnificent, '82 214
Quail, Marinated, '80 221
Quail Superb, '81 303
Quail with Gravy, Georgia, '87 240
Quail with Mushrooms, '85 138
Quail with Mushrooms, Baked, '81 259
Quail with Onion Gravy, Fried, '82 214
Quail with Red Plum Sauce, '80 48
Rabbit, Hickory Barbecued, '82 216
Squab, Baked Stuffed, '82 260
Stew, Hunter's, '85 270
Venison and Tomatoes, '85 270
Venison Burgers, '87 304
Venison Chili, '82 216; '86 3; '87 304
Venison, Country-Fried, '81 233
Venison Kabobs, '82 215
Venison Roast, '82 226
Venison Roast with Red Wine
    Gravy, '85 270
Venison Sausage Balls, '80 42
Venison Sausage Stew, '87 238
Venison Soup, '82 216
Venison Steak, Country-Fried, '83 262
Venison Steaks, Country-Style, '82 215
Venison Steaks, Grilled, '82 215
Venison Stew, '86 294
Venison Stew with Potato
    Dumplings, '87 304
Venison-Vegetable Bake, '87 304
Garnishes
Broccoli Bouquet, '87 115
Butter Balls, '82 189
Butter Curls, '82 51, 189
Carrot Curls, '85 338
Carrot Flowers, '85 338
Celery Fans, '85 339
Chocolate Curls, '85 338
Chocolate Hearts and Shavings, '86 26
Citrus Cups, '85 339
Citrus Cups, Notched, '82 280
Cranberries, Frosted, '82 280; '85 339
Eggs, Hard-Cooked, '82 280
Grapes, Frosted, '82 51, '85 339
Green Onion Fans, '85 339
Guide, Garnishing, '82 138
Lemon or Orange Rose, '85 338
Lemon Roses, '82 280
Lemon Slices, Fluted, '82 51
Marinade, Dill, '87 115
Marinade, Garlic-and-Oregano, '87 115
Marinade, Sweet-and-Sour, '87 115
Mushrooms, Aztec, '82 51
Mushrooms, Fluted, '82 280; '85 338
Onion Mum, '85 339
Onion Rose, '87 114
Piped Garnishes, '82 280
Radish Rose, '85 339

Squash Buttercup, '87 114
Tomato Flower, Marinated Pasta
    in, '87 115
Tomato or Green Pepper Cups, '85 339
Tomato Rose, '82 51; '85 338
Vegetable and Fruit Garnishes, '82 280
Zucchini Fan, '87 114
Goose
Stuffed Goose, Fruit-, '83 320
Stuffed Goose, Fruit- and Pecan-, '83 268
Wild Goose with Currant Sauce, '87 240
Granola
Bars, Coconut Granola, '85 202
Bars, Fruit and Nut Granola, '81 49
Bars, Granola, '83 305
Bread, Honey-Granola, '86 56
Chocolate Morsels, Granola with, '86 69
Crisp, Granola Apple, '85 78
Crunchy Granola, '81 218; '84 144
Easy Granola, '81 49
Fruity Granola, '84 148
Granola, '79 190
Homemade Granola, '84 58
Mix, Granola Snack, '86 229
Orange Granola, Sunny, '84 212
Peanut Butter Granola, '82 296
Sunshine Granola, '79 37
Toasty Granola, '79 37
Whole Wheat Granola, '82 167
Grapefruit
Aspic, Grapefruit, '80 297; '82 112;
    '83 153
Biscuits, Grapefruit Juice, '83 10
Broiled Grapefruit, '85 7
Broiled Grapefruit, Sherried, '80 50
Broil, Flounder-Grapefruit, '85 53
Cup, Berry Grapefruit, '79 242
Delight, Winter Fruit, '80 243
Dressing, Grapefruit French, '80 101
Dressing, Grapefruit Salad, '84 262
Drink, Three-Fruit, '80 50
Ice, Pink Grapefruit, '85 304
Marmalade, Combination Citrus, '80 50
Marmalade, Grapefruit, '82 308
Refresher, Grapefruit-Orange, '82 174
Salad, Avocado-Grapefruit, '85 26
Salad, Congealed Grapefruit, '84 325;
    '85 279
Salad, Grapefruit, '83 124; '84 325
Salad, Grapefruit-Avocado, '83 316;
    '84 16
Salad, Grapefruit Combo, '80 50
Salad, Grapefruit Congealed, '83 190
Salad, Grapefruit-Cucumber, '80 100
Salad, Grapefruit Winter, '84 24
Supreme, Grapefruit, '80 50
Grapes
Carrots with Grapes, Glazed, '82 287
Chicken Véronique, '84 260; '85 302
Frosted Grapes, '82 51
Ham Véronique, '85 90
Ice, Grape, '83 162
Ice, Muscadine, '82 202
Jelly, Grape-Burgundy Freezer, '85 130
Jelly, Wild Muscadine, '79 32
Mold, Double Grape-Cantaloupe, '79 173
Pie, Grape, '85 212
Pie, Grape Juice, '79 123
Pie, Muscadine, '82 202
Punch, Sparkling Grape, '82 48
Refresher, Grape Juice-Fruit, '86 182
Salad, Marinated Chicken-Grape, '85 74
Salad Mold, Grape, '83 120

Grapes *(continued)*

Salad Véronique, Macaroni, '85 164
Salad with Grapes, Chicken, '86 117
Sauce, White Grape, '80 38
Scallops Véronique, '83 144
Slaw, Grape-Poppy Seed, '86 225
Sole Véronique, '85 181
Tart, Green Grape, '87 77
Tea, White Grape Juice, '87 57
Tuna Salad with Grapes, Curried, '87 201

Gravies. *See also* Sauces.

Cream Gravy, Country-Fried Steak
  with, '84 8
Cream Gravy, Fried Chicken
  with, '85 241
Currant Gravy, '83 276
Dill-Cream Gravy, Pork Chops with,
  '84 81
Fried Ripe Tomatoes with Gravy, '82 180
Giblet Gravy, '79 283
Ham with Gravy, Virginia, '86 15
Onion Gravy, Fried Quail with, '82 214
Orange Gravy, '81 259
Pea Gravy, Black-Eyed, '87 12
Red-Eye Gravy, Country Ham with,
  '79 37
Redeye Gravy, Country Ham with,
  '86 254
Sour Cream Gravy, Pot Roast with,
  '79 17
Sweet Potato-Eggplant Gravy, Roast Duck
  with, '83 90
Wine Gravy, Pot Roast in White, '81 299
Wine Gravy, Venison Roast with Red,
  '85 270

Greens. *See also* specific types.

Bake, Grits 'n Greens Dinner, '84 281
Chard, Buttered, '83 36
Chard with Tomatoes, Swiss, '83 36
Collard Greens, Seasoned, '82 211
Collards, '79 32
Collards, Southern-Style, '82 107
Escarole-and-Bacon Salad, '84 85
Escarole, Easy Cooked, '84 85
Kale, Scalloped, '86 224
Kale, Sweet-and-Sour, '80 298
Mustard Greens and Potatoes, '86 224
Turnip Greens and Ham Hock,
  Southern, '80 119
Turnip Greens, Old-Fashioned, '85 255
Turnip Greens, Saucy, '83 12
Turnip Greens with Cornmeal
  Dumplings, '82 211
Turnip Greens with Turnips, '84 230
Turnip Salad, '85 235

Grits

Bake, Grits 'n Greens Dinner, '84 281
Casserole, Cheesy Grits, '81 270
Casserole, Garlic Grits, '81 47
Casserole, Grits-Sausage, '84 75; '86 241
Cheese-and-Garlic Grits, Baked, '83 292;
  '84 78
Cheese Grits, '86 242
Cheese Grits, Baked, '80 49, 99; '83 311;
  '85 41
Cheese Grits, Garlic, '80 47; '81 197
Cheese Grits, Gruyère, '81 47
Cheese Grits, Jalapeño, '85 43
Cheese Grits, Quick, '83 M203
Cheese Grits, Sliced, '84 75
Country Grits and Sausage, '83 54
Fried Grits, '83 292; '84 78
Garlic-Cheese Grits, '86 180
Good Morning Grits, '87 156
Nassau Grits, '81 47
Orange Grits, '81 47
Patties, Grits, '83 52
Pie, Crustless Grits-and-Ham, '86 103
Sausage Grits, '86 92
Scrambled Grits, '80 48
Shrimp Stew and Grits, '80 118
Soufflé, Grits, '80 30
Soufflé, Mexican Grits, '79 55
Spoonbread, Grits, '79 38

Gumbos

Beef Gumbo, Ground, '87 283
Chicken and Oyster Gumbo, '81 198
Chicken Gumbo, '79 199
Chicken Gumbo, Easy, '83 156
Chicken Gumbo with Smoked
  Sausage, '81 199
Chicken-Ham-Seafood Gumbo, '81 6
Combo Gumbo, '81 198
Crab and Shrimp Gumbo, '81 200
Creole Gumbo, '86 228
Creole Gumbo, Quick, '82 87
Dove and Sausage Gumbo, '81 199
Duck, Oyster, and Sausage
  Gumbo, '79 226
Fish Gumbo, Easy, '81 6
Ham and Seafood Gumbo, '81 199
Okra Gumbo, '86 210
Okra Gumbo, Deep South, '79 48
Okra Gumbo Freezer Mix, '86 210
Seafood Gumbo, '79 198, 286; '80 34;
  '81 5; '83 90; '84 87, 92; '87 210
Seafood Gumbo, Champion, '86 293
Seafood Gumbo, Creole, '82 278
Seafood Gumbo with Whole Crabs, '85 2
Seafood-Okra Gumbo, Light, '86 155
Shrimp Gumbo, '81 199
Shrimp Gumbo, Quick, '86 71
Southern Gumbo, '82 242
Texas Ranch-Style Gumbo, '82 226
Turkey Gumbo, '82 268; '85 258
Ya Ya, Gumbo, '87 210

H

Ham. *See also* Pork.

Appetizers, Meat-and-Cheese, '87 7
Bake, Chicken, Ham, and Cheese,
  '87 217
Baked
    Apples, Baked Ham and, '82 M237
    Apricot Baked Ham, '84 160

Festive Baked Ham, '83 263
Glazed Ham, Molasses-, '84 24
Glazed Ham, Sunshine-, '84 252
Glazed Stuffed Ham, '84 321
Maple-Raisin Sauce, Baked Ham
  with, '83 215
Marinated Baked Ham, '86 94
Orange Sauce, Baked Ham
  with, '86 294
Pineapple-Baked Ham, '86 48
Plum Ham, '80 110
Royale, Ham, '84 260
Slice, Baked Ham, '83 12
Strata, Baked Ham, '83 283
Bake, Ham-Rice-Tomato, '87 78
Bake, Harvest Ham, '79 210
Bake, Layered Ham and Turkey, '79 252
Balls, Appetizer Ham, '82 39
Balls, Fried Ham-and-Cheese, '84 221
Balls, Ham, '84 91; '86 256
Balls with Spiced Cherry Sauce,
  Ham, '81 112; '82 12
Barbecued Ham Slices, '81 110
Beans with Ham, Baked, '80 136
Biscuits, Ham-Filled Angel, '80 159
Biscuits, Petite Ham and Cheese, '79 193
Bread, Ham-and-Cheese, '86 213
Cakes, Hawaiian Ham, '79 252
Casserole, Apple Ham, '79 213
Casserole, Breakfast Ham and
  Egg, '79 253
Casserole, Cheesy Ham-and-
  Potato, '84 326
Casserole, Golden Ham, '82 119
Casserole, Ham and Broccoli, '81 133
Casserole, Ham-and-Cheese, '87 78

Casserole, Ham and Lima, '79 192
Casserole, Ham and Noodle, '80 300
Casserole, Ham-and-Potato, '83 M87
Casserole, Ham-and-Rice, '84 75
Casserole, Macaroni-Ham, '81 M177;
  '83 283
Casserole, Quick Ham-Broccoli, '82 40
Casserole, Vegetable-and-Ham, '84 91
Cheese Chips, Ham-, '82 34
Cheese Toss, Ham and, '79 55
Cheesy Chicken-and-Ham Bundles,
  '84 261
Cheesy Ham-and-Turkey Specials, '84 14
Cheesy Ham Dinner, '84 90
Cheesy Ham Nuggets, '81 290
Cheesy Ham Towers, '82 M77
Chowder, Ham and Corn, '79 16
Chowder, Ham-and-Corn, '82 40
Chowder, Ham 'n Cheese, '79 199
Coleslaw, Ham, '84 195
Cordon Bleu, Chicken, '81 304; '82 83
Cordon Bleu, Company Chicken, '82 274

Cordon Bleu, Veal, '87 219
Country Ham
  Biscuits, Country Ham in
    Heart, '86 105
  Bread with Herb Butter, Country
    Ham, '86 255
  Brown Sugar Glaze, Smithfield Ham
    with, '86 253
  Cider-Baked Country Ham, '82 198
  Cider, Country Ham in Apple,
    '80 251
  Cornbread, Crab with Chile, '86 254
  Kentucky Hot Brown, '86 254
  Kentucky Jack, '86 254
  Loaves, Country Ham, '86 255
  Oysters and Ham, Edwards', '86 253

  Quiche, Country Ham, '87 287
  Red-Eye Gravy, Country Ham
    with, '79 37
  Redeye Gravy, Country Ham
    with, '86 254
  Roasted Country Ham,
    Edwards', '86 253
  Spread, Country Ham, '87 8
  Swirls, Veal-and-Smithfield
    Ham, '86 253
  Virginia Ham with Gravy, '86 15
  Wine, Country Ham in, '81 260
Creamed Ham and Chicken, '81 M74
Creamed Ham and Eggs, '82 40
Creamy Ham Medley, '84 90
Creamy Ham Towers, '79 138
Crêpes, Ham-and-Egg, '83 204
Crêpes with Mushroom Sauce,
  Ham-and-Egg, '82 46
Croquettes, Ham, '82 119
Cured Ham and Biscuits, '85 320
Curried Ham and Peaches, '82 60
Curried Ham Steak, '82 120
Curried Ham with Rice, '80 111
Delight, Ham-Asparagus, '86 48
Deviled Delight, '83 130
Deviled Ham Twists, '82 86
Dinner, Corn-and-Ham Skillet, '83 190
Dinner, Ham-Asparagus, '80 10
Dinner, Ham Skillet, '85 179
Eggplant, Ham-Stuffed, '80 162
Eggs, Creamy Ham and, '87 286
Eggs on Toast with Cheese Sauce, Ham
  and, '81 43
Eggs, Savory Ham and, '82 231
Fritters, Ham, '82 39
Fritters with Creamy Sauce, Ham, '81 105
Fruited Ham Slice, '83 M317
Glazed Ham, Cranberry, '81 274
Glazed Ham, Cranberry-Orange, '81 295
Glazed Ham, Honey-Orange, '83 320
Glazed Ham Slice, Honey-, '81 104
Glazed Ham, Sweet-Sour, '83 311

Grilled Ham, Golden, '79 90
Gumbo, Chicken-Ham-Seafood, '81 6
Gumbo, Combo, '81 198
Gumbo, Ham and Seafood, '81 199
Hideaways, Ham, '81 29
Hopping John with Ham, '81 7
Hot Rods, Ham, '86 136
Jambalaya, Creole, '87 210
Jambalaya de Covington, '87 211
Kabobs, Honey Ham, '80 156
Kabobs, Swiss-Ham, '81 124
Loaf, Cranberry-Ham, '82 M77
Loaf, Glazed Ham, '79 187
Loaf, Ham, '79 180; '80 272
Loaf, Hawaiian Ham, '79 71
Loaf, Pineapple Upside-Down
  Ham, '79 253
Loaf, Saucy Ham, '86 M328
Loaf, Spicy Ham, '80 110
Loaf, Supreme Ham, '79 242
Loaf, Upside-Down Ham, '82 40
Noodles, Ham and Swiss on, '87 108
Omelet, Ham and Cheese, '79 262;
  '80 123
Omelet, Sour Cream-Ham, '79 261
Pâté, Ham, '85 279
Patties, Ham, '81 99
Patties, Ham-Sprout, '85 51
Patties, Pineapple-Ham, '80 110
Peas and Ham, Southern, '85 138
Peas with Ham Hocks,
  Black-Eyed, '79 122
Peppers, Ham-and-Corn Stuffed, '81 87
Peppers, Ham-Stuffed Green, '80 65
Peppers with Rice and Ham,
  Stuffed, '82 131
Pie, Crustless Grits-and-Ham, '86 103
Pie, Golden Ham, '87 78
Pie with Cheese Crust, Ham, '80 286
Pie, Zucchini-Ham-Cheese, '80 272
Pilaf Mold, Ham, '86 222
Pineapple-Flavored Ham, '87 160
Pocket, Ham and Swiss in the, '83 31
Potatoes, Ham Stuffed, '79 210
Potatoes, Jalapeño-Ham
  Stuffed, '81 M161
Potatoes with Ham Bits, Creamy, '87 191
Praline Ham, '85 302
Prosciutto, Pizza with Artichoke
  and, '87 182
Puffs, Ham-and-Cheese, '86 277
Puffs, Ham-Filled Party, '84 116
Quiche, Cheesy Ham, '79 127
Quiche, Cheesy Jalapeño, '84 31
Quiche, Crustless Ham, '84 235
Quiche, Ham, '80 110
Quiche, Ham-and-Mushroom, '81 11
Quiche, Ham-and-Vegetable, '84 326
Quiche, Ham-Cheese, '79 26
Raisin Ham, '80 124
Raisin Sauce, Ham with, '82 M76
Rice, Savannah Red, '80 119
Rice Toss, Ham-, '82 40
Ring, Chili-Sauced Ham, '81 M122
Ring, Ham, '84 91
Roast, Peachy Ham, '86 118
Roll, Ham-and-Cheese, '79 234
Rolls, Ham, '79 153
Rolls, Ham-and-Broccoli, '86 212; '87 82
Rolls, Ham-and-Cheese, '82 3
Rolls, Ham-Asparagus, '79 41
Rolls, Hearty Salad, '81 206
Rolls, Rice-Stuffed Ham, '83 190

Roll-Ups, Ham and Spinach, '81 143
Rollups, Ham-and-Swiss, '85 113
Rollups, Spinach-and-Ham, '86 84
Salad Boats, '80 93
Salad, Congealed Ham, '81 36
Salad, Crunchy Baked Ham, '83 23
Salad, Fruitéd Ham, '81 36, 146
Salad, Ham-and-Egg Potato, '86 84
Salad, Ham and Macaroni, '79 220
Salad, Ham and Potato, '80 272
Salad, Ham 'n Egg, '81 36
Salad, Ham-Noodle, '85 249
Salad, Hawaiian Ham-Sweet
  Potato, '82 232
Salad, Hearty Ham, '82 40
Salad, Macaroni-Ham, '85 218
Salad, Mandarin Ham-and-Rice, '87 145
Salad, Spicy Italian Ham, '85 74
Sandwiches, Baked Ham, '81 29
Sandwiches, Creamy Blue
  Cheese-Ham, '87 279
Sandwiches, Denver Pita, '86 M12
Sandwiches, Ham-and-Cheese
  Pita, '87 202
Sandwiches, Hot Ham, '79 214
Sandwiches, Hot Ham-and-
  Cheese, '85 299
Sandwiches, Meal-in-One, '80 218
Sandwiches, Monte Cristo, '83 134
Sandwiches, Open-Faced, '79 214
Sandwiches, Open-Face Ham, '82 40;
  '85 8
Sandwiches, Tangy Ham-and-
  Swiss, '85 164
Sandwiches, Virginia Ham, '80 155

Sandwiches, Yummy, '81 229
Sandwich, Tangy Ham Salad, '80 272
Sandwich, Tex-Mex Ham-and-
  Cheese, '86 4
Sauce, Steak with Ham-and-
  Mushroom, '83 109
Skillet Ham-and-Vegetables, '84 90
Skillet, Ham-Noodle, '87 78
Skillet, Ham Spaghetti, '83 283
Smoked Ham, '86 92
Soup, Chicken, Ham, and Oyster, '79 198
Soup, Ham-and-Bean, '84 4
Soup, Hearty Ham, '82 4
Spread, Cold Ham, '82 248
Spread, Deviled Ham, '79 81
Spread, Ham, '86 126
Spread, Ham-and-Egg, '79 59
Spread, Ham and Pimiento, '80 285;
  '81 56
Spread, Ham Salad, '87 92
Spread, Hawaiian Ham, '87 106
Squash, Ham-Stuffed Acorn, '81 239;
  '83 66
Stew, Blakely Brunswick, '87 4

Ham (continued)

Stir-Fry, Easy Ham, '86 332
Stir-Fry, Ham and Zucchini, '79 47
Strata, Ham and Broccoli, '80 261
Stroganoff, Ham, '82 40
Stuffed Ham, '86 323
Superburgers, '79 89
Supper, Top-of-Stove, '86 332
Tart Milan, '87 70
Tart, Supreme Ham, '84 22
Tetrazzini, Ham, '82 M77; '84 241
Turnip Greens and Ham Hock,
  Southern, '80 119
Turnovers, Party Ham, '82 39
Véronique, Ham, '85 90
Waffles, Ham, '80 44
Zucchini, Ham and Cheese
  Stuffed, '79 157

Hearts of Palm

Salad, Different Vegetable, '82 143
Salad, Hearts of Palm, '81 252
Salad, Hearts-of-Palm, '87 138

Hominy

Bacon, Eggs, and Hominy, '85 143
Bake, Chili Hominy, '81 282; '82 58
Casserole, Cheesy Hominy, '83 170
Casserole, Chile-Hominy, '81 29
Casserole, Hominy-Chili, '86 255
Caviar, Texas, '86 218

Cheese Hominy, Hot, '84 77
Chiles and Cheese, Hominy with, '86 78
Gold Coast Hominy, '83 52
Jalapeño Hominy, '82 51
Mexican Hominy, '86 255
Skillet, Hominy-Sausage, '81 29
Soup, Southwest, '86 255

Honey

Ambrosia, Honey Bee, '83 267
Apple Quarters, Honey-Baked, '86 93
Apples, Honey-Baked, '83 234; '84 244
Bananas, Honey-Baked, '81 268
Bread, Applesauce-Honey Nut, '87 300
Bread, Honey-Granola, '86 56
Bread, Honey Oatmeal, '80 60
Bread, Honey Wheat, '85 18, 268
Bread, Whole Wheat Honey, '82 65;
  '83 106
Brownies, Heavenly Honey, '79 83
Buns, Honey Oatmeal, '83 154
Butter, Honey-Orange, '79 36; '85 19
Cake, Honey-Oatmeal, '87 222
Carrots, Honey-Glazed, '80 115; '84 121;
  '85 18
Carrots, Honey-Kissed, '84 122
Chicken, Honey, '82 55
Chicken, Honey-Curry, '87 36

Cornbread, Honey, '83 286; '84 17
Dip, Coconut-Honey Fruit, '84 171
Dip, Peanut Butter-Honey, '85 19
Dressing, Celery-Honey, '80 42
Dressing, Honey, '79 242; '83 146;
  '87 129
Dressing, Honey French, '87 81
Dressing, Honey-Lime, '83 139
Dressing, Lime-Honey Fruit Salad, '87 81
Dressing, Tomato-Honey French, '81 105
Filling, Honey-Walnut, '80 21
Frosting, Honey Chocolate, '79 83
Glaze, Chocolate-Honey, '82 306
Glaze, Honey-Nut, '87 15
Ham, Honey-Orange Glazed, '83 320
Ham Slice, Honey-Glazed, '81 104
Kabobs, Honey Ham, '80 156
Leeks, Honey-Glazed, '86 62
Loaves, Hint o' Honey, '81 104
Mousse, Honeyed Chocolate, '87 223
Muffins, Honey-Oatmeal, '84 229
Muffins, Honey-Wheat, '83 96
Muffins, Oatmeal-Honey, '83 95
Muffins, Peanut Butter-Honey, '82 56
Onions, Honey, '81 86
Peaches, Honey-Sweet, '85 107
Pears, Pineapple-Honey, '86 94
Pecans, Honeycomb, '84 300
Pecans, Sugar-and-Honey, '86 319
Preserves, Honeyed Peach, '85 130
Rice, Honey, '85 83
Rings, Honey Apple, '80 243
Rolls, Dilled Honey-Wheat, '83 254
Rolls, Honey Wheat, '83 278
Rolls, Super Honey, '80 115
Salad, Honey Fruit, '80 276
Sauce, Honey-Butter, '85 18
Sauce, Honey-Lemon Mustard, '84 275
Sauce, Honey-Lime, '82 85
Sauce, Honey-Mustard, '85 13
Sauce, Honey-Orange, '85 108
Sauce, Honeyscotch Sundae, '82 167
Snapper, Honey-Curried, '85 181
Spareribs, Honey-Glazed, '82 163
Spread, Honey, '81 229
Spread, Honey-Nut, '87 157
Swirl, Honey-Walnut, '80 21
Syrup, Maple-Honey-Cinnamon, '85 19
Tea, Honey, '81 105
Topping, Honey, '83 154
Twist, Honey, '79 80
Whip, Peaches with Honey-Lime, '85 108

Honeydew. *See* Melons.

Hors d'Oeuvres. *See* Appetizers.

Hot Dogs. *See* Frankfurters.

I

Ice Creams and Sherbets

Alaska, Apple Baked, '80 226
Alaska, Baked, '84 105; '85 295
Alaska, Brownie Baked, '80 66
Alaska, Mint Patty, '80 219
Alaskas, Banana Split, '87 10
Amaretto Freeze, '82 182
Ambrosia Cups, Sherbet, '82 159
Apricot Sherbet, '81 177
Apricot Yogurt Ice, '81 177
Avocado Ice, '83 179
Avocado Sherbet, '83 162

Balls, Almond Ice Cream, '86 315
Balls, Easy Ice Cream, '84 106
Banana-Orange Sherbet, '83 162
Bananas Foster, Elegant, '81 59
Banana Split Ice Cream, '80 176
Banana Split Pie, Layered, '83 189

Beverages

Almond Float, Nutmeg-, '84 106
Amaretto Breeze, '83 172
Apple Juice Shrub, Shenandoah,
  '79 282
Banana Flip, '83 303
Banana-Pineapple Milk Shake, '84 59
Banana Smoothie, '87 160
Brandy Cream, '84 312
Champagne Delight, '83 304
Chocolate-Mint Smoothie, '84 166
Coffee Floats, Maple-, '86 195
Coffee Punch, Creamy, '81 50
Coffee Refresher, Velvet, '79 149
Cranberry Float, Sparkling, '86 195
Cranberry-Orange Soda, '79 148
Cranberry Shake, '83 171
Fruit Float, Frosty, '87 159
Ginger Fizz, Ice Cream, '83 303
Golden Dream, '82 100
Kahlúa Velvet Frosty, '82 244
Lime Cooler, '87 160
Lime Fizz, '81 172
Lime-Pineapple Punch, '83 142
Mocha Punch, '84 166
Orange Milk Shake, '84 166
Orange Shake, Peachy, '81 156
Orange Sherbet Party Punch, '83 142
Peach Frosty, '81 156
Peanut Butter Milkshakes, '85 198
Peanut Butter Shake, '82 48
Pineapple Sherbet Float, '79 148
Punch, Double Sherbet, '79 232
Punch, Parsonage, '79 148
Raisin Shake, Amazin', '86 195
Rum Coffee Cream, Icy, '83 172
Shake, Pep, '79 38
Strawberry-Banana Float, '87 160
Strawberry Milkshake, Fresh, '82 113
Strawberry-Pineapple Shake, '84 166
Strawberry Punch, Creamy, '86 195
Strawberry Smoothie, '86 183
Strawberry Soda, Old-Fashioned,
  '79 149
Tahitian Flower, '87 159
Vanilla Frosty, French, '79 148
Whispers, '86 317

Blueberry-Kirsch Sorbet, '83 120
Bombe, Amber, '80 255
Bombe, Ice Cream, '82 305
Bourbon Ice Cream, '87 139
Brownie Dessert, Special-
  Occasion, '87 139
Buttermilk Sherbet, '84 184
Butter Pecan Ice Cream, '80 176;
  '86 129
Cake, Fruity Ice Cream, '87 110
Cake, Ice Cream, '86 321
Cake, Ice Cream Angel, '83 23
Cake, Praline Ice Cream, '80 84
Candy Crunch Ice Cream, '79 166
Cantaloupe Ice Cream, '79 177
Cantaloupe Sherbet, Frosty, '82 144
Caramel-Vanilla Helado (Caramel-Vanilla
  Ice Cream), '81 67
Cherry Ice Cream, '84 184
Cherry-Nut Ice Cream, '86 129

Chocolate Chunk-Peanut Butter Ice Cream, '85 297; '86 120
Chocolate Ice Cream, '80 176; '86 129
Cider Ice, '83 162
Coconut Ice Cream, Fresh, '79 166
Coffee Ice Cream Crunch, '82 182
Cranberry-Apple Ice, '82 290
Cranberry Ice, Tangy, '87 305
Cranberry Juice Sorbet, '85 259
Cranberry Sorbet, '82 251
Crêpes, Coffee Ice Cream, '84 85
Crêpes, Strawberry Ice Cream, '87 290
Delight, Ice Cream, '80 69
Dessert, Layered Ice Cream, '83 189; '84 94, 105; '86 163
Dessert, Layered Sherbet, '87 109
Fig Ice Cream, '87 139
Fried Ice Cream, Coconut, '85 141
Fried Ice Cream, French-, '85 141
Fried Ice Cream Puffs, '85 141
Fruit Ice, '86 176
Fruit Ice, Mixed, '81 178
Fruit Punch Sherbet, '86 129
Fruit Sherbet, Freezer, '86 334
Fruit Sherbet, Frozen, '79 155
Fruit Sherbet, Instant, '85 158
Grapefruit Ice, Pink, '85 304
Grape Ice, '83 162
Hawaiian Frappé, '81 178
Italian-Style Ice Cream, '79 245
Kiwi Ice, '84 315
Lemon Cream Sherbet, '79 114
Lemon Ice Cream, '79 142; '83 170
Lemon Ice Cream Tarts, '80 152
Lime Sherbet, '82 159
Lime Sherbet, Creamy, '84 165
Log, Ice Cream Yule, '83 253
Macaroon-Sherbet Frozen Dessert, '79 212
Making Ice Cream, About, '82 171
Mango Ice Cream, '86 216
Mango Sorbet, '86 196
Mexican Sherbet, '79 155
Muscadine Ice, '82 202
Orange-Pineapple Ice Cream, '86 117
Orange Sherbet, '79 155
Orange Sherbet Salad, '81 154

Parfaits, Chocolate-Crème de Menthe, '85 161
Parfaits, Coffee Crunch, '82 159
Parfait, Strawberry, '79 99
Parfait, Surprise Strawberry, '86 151
Peach Ice, '81 178
Peach Ice Cream, '81 184; '82 171; '83 159; '86 15
Peach Ice Cream, Creamy, '85 177
Peach Ice Cream, Deluxe, '80 176

Peach-Yogurt Ice, '84 83
Peanut Butter Ice Cream, '81 103
Peppermint Ice Cream, '80 176; '86 129
Pie, Absolutely Divine Ice Cream, '82 181
Pie, Caramel Ice Cream, '82 181
Pie, Carrot Ice Cream, '86 200
Pie, Chocolate-Ice Cream, '87 224
Pie, Chocolate-Mint Ice Cream, '81 144
Pie, Coffee Ice Cream, '79 231
Pie, Heavenly Ice Cream, '82 181
Pie, Kona Ice Cream, '83 189
Pie, Lemon Ice Cream, '80 70
Pie, Peanutty Ice Cream, '82 56
Pie, Peppermint Candy-Ice Cream, '87 260
Pie, Pumpkin Ice Cream, '81 272
Pie, Pumpkin-Ice Cream, '87 243
Pie with Rum-Fruit Sauce, Ice Cream, '84 312
Pineapple-Mint Ice Cream, '84 186
Pineapple Sherbet, '81 177; '84 83
Pineapple Sherbet, Creamy, '79 155
Pralines and Cream Ice Cream, '82 184; '83 159
Raspberry Ice Cream, '80 176
Raspberry Ice Cream, Fresh, '86 152
Raspberry Sherbet, '83 162
Roll, Chocolate-Frosted Ice Cream, '84 200
Roll, Strawberry Ice Cream, '84 105
Salad, Ice Cream, '79 126
Sandwiches, Chocolate Cookie Ice Cream, '87 147
Straw-Ba-Nut Ice Cream, '80 177
Strawberry-Champagne Sorbet, '83 162
Strawberry Ice, '84 175; '85 108
Strawberry Ice Cream, '80 177
Strawberry Ice Cream, Homemade, '84 184
Strawberry Ice Cream, Old-Fashioned, '79 94
Strawberry Ice Cream, Very, '81 155
Strawberry-Orange Ice, '86 196
Strawberry Sherbet, '82 112, 160
Sundae Dessert, Hot Fudge, '84 313
Sundaes, Cocoa-Kahlúa, '83 M58
Sundaes Flambé, Peach, '81 88
Sundaes, Hot Strawberry, '81 M5
Sundaes, Mauna Loa, '80 126
Sundaes, Quick Pear, '86 71
Sundaes, Spicy Apple Ice Cream, '86 M195
Toffee Ice Cream Dessert, '87 110
Treats, Crunchy Ice Cream, '86 300; '87 178
Tutti-Frutti Ice Cream, '86 129
Vanilla Ice Cream, '80 176; '86 129
Vanilla Ice Cream, Country, '82 143
Vanilla Ice Cream Spectacular, '82 166
Watermelon Sherbet, '79 155
Watermelon Sherbet, Light, '81 147
Wine Ice, '83 163

J

Jams and Jellies

Apple-Cranberry Conserve, '82 308
Apple Jelly, '82 149
Apple Marmalade, '79 120
Apple-Mint Jelly, '87 134

Apricot Jam, Golden, '80 31
Banana Jam, '82 296
Basil Jelly, '82 301
Blackberry Jam, '82 149
Blackberry Jam, Freezer, '84 M181
Blackberry Jelly, '82 149
Blueberry Conserve, '82 149
Blueberry Jam, '79 120; '85 130
Carrot-Citrus Marmalade, '81 148
Christmas Brunch Jam, '81 286
Citrus Marmalade, '80 101
Citrus Marmalade, Combination, '80 50
Citrus Marmalade, Mixed, '81 43
Crabapple Jelly, '79 120; '81 217
Cranberry Conserve, '79 243; '85 266

Cranberry-Wine Jelly, '81 290
Fig Jam, '86 206
Fig Preserves, '79 140; '82 150
Freezer Jelly, Christmas, '86 M288
Fruit Conserve, Dried, '82 308
Fruit Marmalade, Delicious, '81 285
Grape-Burgundy Freezer Jelly, '85 130
Grapefruit Marmalade, '82 308
Green Tomato Jam, '79 121
Mango-Pineapple Preserves, '79 137
Mint Jelly, '79 121; '82 301
Muscadine Jelly, Wild, '79 32
Orange Marmalade, '81 42
Orange-Pineapple Marmalade, '82 150
Peach-Banana Jam, Rosy, '80 142
Peach Conserve, '79 120
Peach Jam, Freezer, '83 182; '84 M182
Peach-Orange Marmalade, '82 150
Peach-Plum Freezer Jam, '85 130
Peach Preserves, '81 147
Peach Preserves, Honeyed, '85 130
Peach Preserves, Old-Fashioned, '82 150
Pear Jam, Paradise, '84 300
Pear Marmalade, '79 196
Pear Preserves, '82 195
Pepper Jelly, '79 121
Pepper Jelly, Unusual Green, '82 132
Pineapple Jam, '81 147
Plum Jelly, '82 150
Port Wine Jelly with Whipped Cream, '84 254
Raspberry Freezer Jam, '84 M181
Rose Geranium Jelly, '82 301
Rosemary Jelly, '82 301
Sage Jelly, '82 301
Strawberry Freezer Jam, '84 M182
Strawberry Jelly, '81 147
Strawberry-Pineapple Marmalade, '85 130
Strawberry Preserves, '79 120; '81 96
Strawberry Preserves Deluxe, '82 150
Strawberry Preserves, Freezer, '82 112
Thyme Jelly, '82 301
Watermelon Preserves, '79 120
Wine Jelly, Rosy, '85 306

Jicama
Fried Jicama, French-, **'81** 88
Parsleyed Jicama, **'81** 88
Salad, Jicama, **'87** 123
Salad, Jicama-Fruit, **'86** 83
Salad, Jicama-Orange, **'86** 83

K

Kabobs
Beef Kabobs, **'85** 110
Beef Kabobs Deluxe, **'82** 182
Beef Kabobs, Marinated, **'82** 105; **'85** 159
Beef Kabobs, Pineapple-, **'83** 212
Beef Kabobs, Saucy, **'83** 109
Beef Kabobs, Spirited, **'87** 142
Beef Kabobs, Teriyaki, **'80** 207
Beef Kabobs with Rice, Marinated, **'84** 32
Cantaloupe Wedges, Grilled, **'87** 162
Chicken-Avocado Kabobs, **'82** 9; **'83** 68
Chicken, Garlic-Grilled, **'87** 180
Chicken Kabobs, **'87** 141
Chicken Kabobs, Good-and-Easy, **'85** 87
Chicken Kabobs, Marinated, **'84** M144
Chicken Kabobs, Pineapple-, **'86** M328
Chicken Kabobs, Sesame, **'82** 165
Chicken Kabobs, Soy-, **'86** 156
Chicken Kabobs Supreme, **'81** 124
Chicken Livers en Brochette, **'84** 222
Fruit Kabobs, **'86** 181
Fruit Kabobs with Coconut Dressing, **'87** 251
Fruit Kabobs with Mint Marinade, **'82** 157
Ham Kabobs, Honey, **'80** 156
Ham Kabobs, Swiss-, **'81** 124
Hawaiian Kabobs, **'85** 157
Hot-and-Spicy Kabobs, **'87** 193

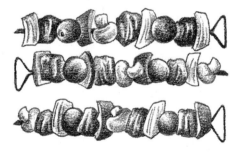

Lamb Kabobs, **'85** 159; **'86** 90
Lamb Kabobs, Savory, **'80** 184
Lamb Shish Kabobs, **'79** 142
Liver Kabobs, **'80** 185
Oysters Brochette, **'80** 56
Pork Kabobs, Spicy, **'82** 182
Rumaki Kabobs, **'82** 182
Salmon Kabobs, **'81** 182
Scallop-Bacon Kabobs, **'81** 111
Scallop Kabobs, Grilled, **'83** 101
Scallop Kabobs, Sea, **'82** 162
Scallops en Brochette with Vegetables, **'80** 163
Seafood Brochette, **'87** 96
Shish Kabobs, **'82** 182; **'85** M112
Shish Kabobs, Overnight, **'81** 124

Shish Kabobs Teriyaki, **'85** 37
Shrimp, Grilled Marinated, **'87** 173
Shrimp Kabobs, **'80** 150, 184
Shrimp Kabobs, Marinated, **'84** 276; **'85** 158
Shrimp, Marinated and Grilled, **'87** 141
Sirloin Kabobs, Marinated, **'82** 162
Steak-and-Shrimp Kabobs, **'80** 184
Steak Kabobs, **'82** 4
Steak Kabobs, Barbecued, **'79** 89
Steak Kabobs, Marinated, **'80** 184
Steak on a Stick, **'83** 109
Steak with Vegetables, Skewered, **'81** 124
Vegetable Kabobs, Fresh, **'81** 158
Vegetable Kabobs, Marinated, **'83** M195
Venison Kabobs, **'82** 215
Kiwifruit
Ice, Kiwi, **'84** 315
Jubilee, Kiwi, **'83** 120
Meringue Cups, Kiwi and Cream in, **'81** 279
Muffins, Kiwifruit, **'87** 255
Orange Roughy, Kiwi, **'87** 193
Parfait, Kiwi, **'86** 199; **'87** 55
Pizza, Kiwi-Berry, **'86** 198; **'87** 55
Salad, Spinach-Kiwifruit, **'87** 305

L

Lamb
Barbecued Lamb, **'79** 58
Burgoo, Five-Meat, **'87** 3
Casserole, Moussaka, **'79** 179
Chops, Barbecued Lamb, **'79** 89
Chops, Broiled Lamb, **'85** 22
Chops Dijonaise, Gourmet Lamb, **'82** 93
Chops, Dijon Lamb, **'84** 277
Chops, Orange Lamb, **'83** 35
Chops Teriyaki, Lamb, **'85** 109
Chops, Teriyaki Lamb, **'87** 60
Curried Lamb with Rice, **'82** 93
Curried Lamb with Rice Mold, **'85** 36
Curry with Rice, Lamb, **'80** 83; **'81** 10
Fillets of Lamb with Vegetables, **'85** 36
Hawaii, Lamb, **'81** 58
Kabobs, Lamb, **'85** 159; **'86** 90
Kabobs, Lamb Shish, **'79** 142
Kabobs, Overnight Shish, **'81** 124
Kabobs, Savory Lamb, **'80** 184
Kabobs, Shish, **'82** 182; **'85** M112
Kabobs Teriyaki, Shish, **'85** 37
Leg of Lamb, **'86** 90
Leg of Lamb, Glazed, **'86** 90
Leg of Lamb, Half of, **'86** 90
Leg of Lamb, Roast, **'87** 96
Leg of Lamb, Stuffed, **'82** 93; **'87** 248
Meatballs with Yogurt Sauce, Lamb, **'85** 132
Moussaka, **'87** 166
Pilaf, Hearty Lamb, **'83** 101
Pockets with Dilled Cucumber Topping, Lamb, **'87** 104
Rack of Lamb with Herb Mustard Glaze, **'81** 260
Roasted Rosemary Lamb, **'86** 89
Roast of Lamb, Crown, **'81** 58
Salad, Spinach-Lamb, **'85** 58
Shanks Milanaise, Lamb, **'82** 93
Steaks with Béarnaise Sauce, Lamb, **'85** 37

Stew-in-a-Loaf, Lamb, **'85** 37
Stew, Lamb, **'79** 293
Lasagna
Beefy Lasagna, **'80** 81
Cheesy Lasagna, **'82** 224
Chicken Lasagna, **'87** M302
Garden Lasagna, **'83** 119
Lasagna, **'82** 119; **'83** M6
Lean Lasagna, **'86** 37
Pizza, Lasagna, **'85** 285
Quick Lasagna, **'84** 220
Quick 'n Easy Lasagna, **'80** M10
Sausage Lasagna, **'83** 288
Sausage-Lasagna Rollups, **'80** 236
Sausage Pinwheels, Lasagna, **'79** 6
Simple Lasagna, **'81** 188
South-of-the-Border Lasagna, **'84** 31
Spinach Lasagna, **'79** 25; **'81** 243
Spinach Lasagna, Cheesy, **'80** 32; **'83** 204
Squash Lasagna, Spaghetti, **'84** 127
Tofu Lasagna, **'83** 312
Tuna Lasagna, **'83** 44; **'84** 123
Turkey Lasagna, **'83** 239
Two, Lasagna for, **'81** 91
Vegetable Lasagna, **'84** 201
Vegetable Lasagna, Cheesy, **'79** 84
Vegetable Lasagna, Colorful, **'87** 19
Vintage Lasagna, **'79** 194
Zesty Lasagna, **'87** M188
Zucchini Lasagna, **'85** 194

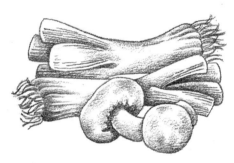

Leeks
Dilly Leek Combo, **'82** 26
Dip, Creamy Leek, **'86** 77
Glazed Leeks, **'82** 26
Glazed Leeks, Honey-, **'86** 62
Soup, Carrot-Leek, **'86** 34
Soup, Leek-and-Potato, **'84** 112
Soup, Leek-Vegetable, **'86** 304
Soup, Watercress-and-Leek, **'86** 161
Tarragon Leeks, **'84** 66
Lemon
Apples, Chilled Poached Lemon, **'86** 182
Beans, Lemony Green, **'85** 190
Beverages
Cooler, Lemon, **'82** 48
Cranberry Lemonade, Spiced, **'87** 292
Fresh Squeezed Lemonade, **'81** 172
Mist, Orange-Lemon, **'79** 288; **'80** 35
Punch, Lemon Balm, **'80** 42
Punch, Strawberry-Lemonade, **'85** 116
Sipper, Sunshine, **'86** 179
Slush, Pink Lemonade, **'80** 151
Strawberry Lemonade, **'80** 160
Syrup, Cherry-Lemonade, **'86** 214
Tea, Almond-Lemonade, **'86** 229
Tea Cubes, Lemonade with Frozen, **'85** 161
Tea, Lemon, **'82** 156
Tea, Lemon-Mint, **'85** 162

Bread, Blueberry-Lemon, '85 190
Bread, Lemon, '79 275; '87 256
Bread, Lemon-Nut, '79 24
Bread, Lemon-Pecan, '83 54
Broccoli Goldenrod, Lemon-, '84 M89
Brussels Sprouts with Celery,
  Lemony, '85 25
Butter, Asparagus in Lemon, '80 M123
Butter, Asparagus with Lemon, '87 M151
Butter, Shrimp in Lemon, '84 163
Canapés, Lemon-Cheese, '87 93
Carrots, Lemon, '82 300; '83 111
Carrots, Lemon-Glazed, '84 16
Cauliflower, Easy Lemon, '83 322
Cheese Patty, Lemon-Pepper, '84 117
Chicken, Baked Lemon, '85 190
Chicken Cutlets with Lemon, '85 8
Chicken, Grilled Yogurt-Lemon, '81 111
Chicken in Lemon and Wine, '83 281
Chicken, Lemon, '81 M138; '86 173
Chicken, Lemonade, '82 163
Chicken, Lemon-Fried, '79 77
Chicken, Lemon Fried, '82 275
Chicken, Lemon-Herb, '85 127
Chicken Nuggets, Lemon-, '86 337;
  '87 283
Chicken, Sweet-and-Sour Lemon, '84 93
Chicken, Sweet Lemon, '79 218
Chicken, Sweet Lemon-, '84 69
Cornish Hens, Lemon Roasted, '82 260
Cream, Strawberries 'n Lemon, '85 120
Crêpes with Fruit Filling, Lemon, '82 46
Cutlets, Lemon-Flavored, '79 105
Desserts
  Apples, Chilled Poached
    Lemon, '86 182
  Bars Deluxe, Lemon, '79 35
  Bars, Lemon Yogurt Wheat, '79 93
  Bars, Tangy Lemon, '86 217
  Cake, Easy Lemon, '83 24
  Cake, Glazed Lemon, '86 70
  Cake, Lemon Angel, '80 147
  Cake, Lemon-Coconut
    Cream, '81 179
  Cake, Lemon-Coconut Sheet, '85 117
  Cake, Lemon Gold, '83 301
  Cake, Lemon-Pineapple, '86 60, 239
  Cake, Lemon Pound, '82 88
  Cake, Lemon Pudding, '83 106
  Cake, Lemon-Sour Cream
    Pound, '87 38
  Cake, Lemon Tea, '82 169
  Cake, Lightly Lemon Coffee, '81 14
  Cake, Luscious Lemon Layer, '86 61
  Cake, Old-Fashioned Lemon
    Layer, '85 191
  Cake Roll, Elegant Lemon, '80 70
  Charlotte Russe, Fresh Lemon,
    '80 13
  Charlotte Russe, Lemon, '84 192
  Cheesecake, Lemon, '86 194
  Cheesecake with Orange-Pineapple
    Glaze, Lemon, '81 60
  Cookies, Lemonade, '79 51
  Cookies, Lemon Crinkle, '81 287
  Cookies, Lemony Cutout, '85 323
  Cookies, Sunshine Lemon, '86 69
  Cream Cheese Dessert, Lemon-,
    '84 95
  Cream Cheese Squares, Lemony,
    '82 159
  Cream, Frozen Lemon, '83 118
  Cream, Lemon, '82 237

Cream Puffs, Strawberry-Lemon,
  '87 75
Cupcakes, Lemon Moist, '82 112;
  '83 153
Cups, Baked Lemon, '87 128
Curd, Lemon, '87 139
Custard in Meringue Cups,
  Lemon, '80 295; '81 172
Dainties, Lemon Pecan, '80 208
Delight, Lemon, '82 227
Filling, Creamy Lemon, '80 70
Filling, Lemon, '81 172; '84 137;
  '85 191; '86 235; '87 293
Filling, Lemon-Cheese, '79 68
Filling, Lemon Cream, '84 23; '87 14
Filling, Lemon-Orange, '81 71
Frosting, Creamy Lemon, '79 93
Frosting, Lemon, '85 191; '86 217
Frosting, Lemon Buttercream,
  '83 301; '86 61
Frosting, Lemon-Butter Cream,
  '85 117
Frosting, Lemon-Cream
  Cheese, '81 157
Fruitcake, Lemon, '83 258
Glaze, Lemon, '79 285; '86 194;
  '87 41
Ice Cream, Lemon, '79 142; '83 170
Loaf, Lemon-Cream Tea, '84 50
Logs, Hazelnut-Lemon, '84 117
Melting Moments, '85 191
Meringue Cream Cups,
  Lemon, '84 23
Mousse, Strawberry-Lemon, '82 128
Parfaits, Strawberry-Lemon, '84 198
Pastry Shell, Lemon in, '84 137

Pears, Lemon Poached, '82 74
Pie, Angel, '79 123
Pie, Apple-Lemon Chess, '86 220
Pie, Buttermilk Lemon, '81 120;
  '82 23
Pie, Deluxe Lemon Meringue,
  '81 172
Pie, Frozen Lemon Cream, '82 86
Pie, Lemon Cheese, '81 136; '82 146
Pie, Lemon Chess, '79 32; '82 196
Pie, Lemon-Cottage Cheese, '79 44
Pie, Lemon Cottage Cheese, '81 143
Pie, Lemon Ice Cream, '80 70
Pie, Lemon Meringue, '85 M112;
  '86 130
Pie, Lemon-Orange, '85 172
Pie, Lemon-Sour Cream, '82 169
Pie, Lemon Sponge, '83 192
Pie, Lemon Twirl, '84 94
Pie, Slice of Lemon, '84 23
Pie, Tart Lemon-Apple, '80 100

Pie, Whipped Lemon, '79 124
Pudding, Layered Lemon, '82 128
Pudding, Lemon, '79 86; '81 99
Pudding, Lemon Fluff, '85 304
Roll, Snow-Capped Lemon, '79 68
Sauce, Lemon, '84 258, 306;
  '85 77, 190
Sauce, Tart Lemon, '85 191
Sherbet, Lemon Cream, '79 114
Soufflé, Cold Lemon-Lime, '84 24
Soufflé, Lemon, '82 170, 252
Soufflé, Tart Lemon, '85 82
Sponge Cups, Lemon, '83 10
Squares, Golden Carrot-
  Lemon, '80 40
Squares, Lemon, '81 197
Strawberry-Lemon Dessert, '86 162
Tarts, Dainty Lemon, '82 304
Tarts, Golden Lemon, '85 191
Tarts, Lemon, '82 156; '83 79
Tarts, Lemon-Cheese, '79 2
Tarts, Lemon Ice Cream, '80 152
Tarts, Lemon-Sour Cream, '81 304
Topping, Lemon-Pineapple, '86 60
Yogurt, Lemon-Chiffon
  Frozen, '85 54
Yummies, Lemon, '81 301
Zephers, Lemon, '81 172
Dressing, Green Salad with Lemony
  French, '85 67
Dressing, Lemon Cream, '82 170
Dressing, Lemon-Herb Salad, '82 67
Dressing, Lemon-Pepper, '87 55
Dressing, Lemon Salad, '79 8
Dressing, Tomato Slices with
  Lemon, '87 167
Fillets, Lemon-Coated, '80 53
Flounder Thermidor, '85 190
Freeze, Fruity Lemon, '82 145
Knots, Glazed Lemon, '86 290
Mackerel, Lemon-Baked, '79 182
Marmalade, Citrus, '80 101
Mayonnaise, Lemon-Cream, '85 264
Mold, Cheesy Lemon, '79 241
Mold, Lemon-Cucumber, '87 90
Muffins, Blueberry-Lemon, '79 7
Muffins, Fresh Lemon, '79 161
Pork Chops, Lemon-Herb, '84 81
Potatoes, Lemon and Nutmeg, '80 36
Potatoes, Lemon-Buttered New,
  '84 149
Potatoes, Lemon-Herb Stuffed,
  '83 173
Potatoes, Lemon-Steamed, '86 177
Potatoes, Lemony New, '82 158
Relish, Lemony Cranberry, '79 243
Ribs, Lemon Baked, '81 166
Ribs, Lemon Grilled, '81 154
Roses, Lemon, '82 280
Salad, Cauliflower-Lemon, '81 23
Salad, Lemonade Fruit, '84 24
Salad, Lemon-Cheese, '85 240
Salad, Lemon-Cranberry
  Congealed, '87 311
Salad, Lemon-Onion, '85 252
Salad, Lemon-Vegetable
  Congealed, '85 22
Salad, Lemony Apple-Bran, '86 223
Sauce and Pecans, Broccoli with Lemon,
  '86 71
Sauce, Asparagus with Lemon, '86 62
Sauce, Baked Fillets in
  Lemon-Celery, '84 91

Lemon *(continued)*

Sauce, Brussels Sprouts in Lemon, '82 269
Sauce, Honey-Lemon Mustard, '84 275
Sauce, Lemon, '82 290; '85 77, 190
Sauce, Lemon-Butter, '84 252
Sauce, Lemon Dessert, '87 M165
Sauce, Lemon Parsley, '81 106
Sauce, Lemony Cheese, '84 183
Sauce, New Potatoes with Lemon, '86 130
Sauce, Shrimp in Lemon Garlic, '83 67
Scones, Lemon-Raisin, '87 69
Shrimp, Lemon-Garlic Broiled, '82 29; '86 182
Slices, Fluted Lemon, '82 51
Spareribs, Lemony Sweet, '80 73
Spinach, Creamy Lemon, '82 302
Spinach with Feta, Lemon, '85 190
Spirals, French Lemon, '81 94
Sprouts, Lemon, '85 288
Steak with Brandy Sauce, Lemon-Butter, '85 78
Veal Piccata, Lemon, '86 118
Veal with Artichoke Hearts, Lemon, '87 219
Vermicelli, Lemon, '84 329
Vinegar, Lemon-Mint, '85 124
Vinegar, Raspberry-Lemon, '87 134
Vinegar, Spicy Oregano-Lemon, '85 124

Lime

Butter, Chicken with Lime, '84 68
Cooler, Lime, '87 160
Daiquiris, Freezer Lime, '79 141
Dressing, Honey-Lime, '83 139
Dressing, Lime, '79 2; '83 120
Dressing, Lime-Honey Fruit Salad, '87 81
Dressing, Lime-Parsley, '85 131
Dressing, Lime Sherbet, '80 221
Fizz, Lime, '81 172
Fuzz Buzz, '82 160
Loaf, Lime Layer, '85 96
Margaritas, Frosted, '84 115
Margaritas, Frosty, '83 172
Margaritas, Pitcher, '83 175
Marmalade, Citrus, '80 101
Mousse Freeze, Luscious Lime, '81 173
Parfaits, Lime, '80 153
Pie, Lime Chiffon, '86 130
Pie, Lime Fluff, '84 43
Punch, Foamy Lime, '82 264
Punch, Lime, '84 58
Punch, Lime-Pineapple, '83 142
Punch, Orange-Lime, '82 160
Refresher, Lime-Mint, '82 144
Rice, Lime-Flavored, '84 175
Salad, Emerald, '81 143
Salad, Frosted Lime-Cheese, '79 286
Salad, Pear-Lime, '84 152
Salad, Pineapple-Lime, '84 320
Salad, Snowy Emerald, '87 311
Sauce, Honey-Lime, '82 85
Sherbet, Creamy Lime, '84 165
Sherbet, Lime, '82 159
Snapper with Lime, Stuffed Red, '83 246
Sopa de Lima, '79 211
Soufflé, Cold Lemon-Lime, '84 24
Squares, Lime, '79 2
Whip, Peaches with Honey-Lime, '85 108

Linguine

Carbonara, Linguine, '87 108
Clam Sauce, Linguine in, '81 83
Clam Sauce, Linguine with, '84 124

Clam Sauce with Linguine, '84 9
Pasta Verde, '84 201
Salad, Pasta, '84 139
Seafood Linguine, '79 227
Seafood Sauce, Linguine with, '83 232
Tomato-Cream Sauce, Linguine with, '86 158
Whole Wheat Linguine, '84 177

Liver

Barbecued Liver, '85 219
Beef Liver Patties, '81 277
Calf's Liver with Vegetables, '85 219
Chicken Liver and Bacon Roll-Ups, '80 200; '81 57
Chicken Liver Omelet, '82 44
Chicken Liver Pâté, '79 153; '81 235; '83 108; '84 205
Chicken Livers and Potatoes, '82 218
Chicken Livers and Rice Dish, '82 218
Chicken Livers en Brochette, '84 222

Chicken Livers in Italian Sauce, '83 117
Chicken Livers in Orange Sauce, '82 218
Chicken Livers in Wine Sauce, '81 104
Chicken Livers, Party, '83 242
Chicken Livers Risotto, '82 218
Chicken Livers, Sautéed, '80 200; '81 57
Chicken Livers, Scrumptious, '84 230
Chicken Livers Stroganoff, '80 200; '81 57
Chicken Livers Supreme, '81 298
Chicken Livers with Marsala Wine Sauce, '81 76
Chicken Livers with Mushrooms, '81 133
Chicken Livers with Rice, '80 200; '81 58; '84 292
Chicken Liver Turnovers, '79 141
Creamy Liver and Noodle Dinner, '80 11
Creole Liver, '85 219; '86 108
Creole Sauce, Liver in, '87 33
Duck Liver Pâté, '79 227
French-Style Liver, '80 10
Gravy, Liver and, '80 10
Herbs, Liver with, '81 277
Italiano, Liver, '85 219
Kabobs, Liver, '80 185
Loaf, Skillet Liver, '80 11
Pâté, Country, '86 66
Pâté, Liver-Cheese, '85 276
Pâté with Cognac, '86 159
Rumaki, '80 M136
Rumaki Kabobs, '82 182
Saucy Liver, '81 277
Sauté, Liver, '81 277
Spanish-Style Liver, '80 11
Spread, Sherried Liver, '80 86
Stroganoff, Liver, '79 54
Sweet-and-Sour Liver, '81 277

Lobster

Beef Tenderloin, Lobster-Stuffed, '87 248
Clambake, Backyard, '81 92
Creamy Lobster, '79 181
How to Cook Lobster, '81 169
Orange Sauce, Lobster Tails with Spiced, '86 155
Salad, Lobster and Orange, '82 207

Taco with Yellow Tomato Salsa and Jicama Salad, Warm Lobster, '87 122
Thermidor, Lobster, '85 103

M

Macaroni

Beef and Macaroni, Ground, '85 218
Beef and Macaroni, Skillet, '82 130
Beef-Macaroni Combo, '79 194
Casserole, Chicken-Macaroni, '85 219
Casserole, Macaroni, '84 220; '87 154
Casserole, Macaroni and Chicken, '80 260
Casserole, Macaroni-Ham, '81 M177; '83 283
Casserole, Spinach-Beef-Macaroni, '83 313
Cheese, Baked Macaroni and, '82 199
Cheese Deluxe, Macaroni-and-, '79 84
Cheese Deluxe, Macaroni and, '80 236
Cheese, Macaroni and, '83 M7
Cheese Macaroni, Double, '82 224
Cheese Puff, Macaroni and, '79 5
Cheese, Tasty Macaroni and, '83 288
Cheese, Thick-and-Rich Macaroni and, '84 329
Cheese with Wine, Macaroni-and-, '86 78
Cheesy Macaroni-Mushroom Bake, '81 243
Dinner, Sausage Skillet, '83 29
Glorious Macaroni, '84 76
Oysters with Macaroni, Scalloped, '80 297
Peppers, Macaroni-and-Cheese-Stuffed, '80 65
Salad, Acini di Pepe, '83 163
Salad, Barbecue Macaroni, '82 276
Salad, Confetti Macaroni, '82 132; '85 297
Salad, Crunchy Macaroni, '82 24
Salad, Dilled Macaroni-Cheese, '86 208
Salad, Festive Macaroni-Shrimp, '85 165
Salad for Two, Macaroni, '81 31
Salad, Garden Macaroni, '84 290
Salad, Gourmet Macaroni, '81 253
Salad, Ham and Macaroni, '79 220
Salad, Hearty Macaroni, '84 90
Salad, Macaroni, '87 92
Salad, Macaroni-Chicken, '85 296; '86 302
Salad, Macaroni-Crabmeat, '81 153
Salad, Macaroni-Ham, '85 218
Salad, Macaroni-Salmon, '82 232
Salad, Macaroni Shell, '87 38
Salad, Macaroni-Shrimp, '85 121
Salad, Macaroni-Vegetable, '86 209
Salad, Olive Clubhouse, '81 114
Salad, Overnight Pasta, '82 276
Salad, Pineapple Macaroni, '79 220
Salad, Refreshing Macaroni, '80 177
Salad, Salmon-and-Macaroni, '81 114
Salad, Shrimp Macaroni, '79 220
Salad, Shrimp-Macaroni, '85 219
Salad, Spiral Macaroni, '82 276
Salad, Sweet-and-Sour Macaroni, '85 166
Salad, Taco Macaroni, '85 165
Salad, Tuna Macaroni, '83 44, 145
Salad, Tuna-Macaroni, '84 66
Salad, Turkey Macaroni, '83 282
Salad Véronique, Macaroni, '85 164
Salad, Whole Wheat Macaroni-Tuna, '84 193
Supper Supreme, Sunday, '79 76
Tomatoes, Tuna-Mac in, '87 188

Toss, Corkscrew Macaroni, '83 163
Treat, Tuna-Macaroni, '82 131

Mangoes
Cake, Mango, '83 150
Crêpes, Mango-Pineapple, '86 216
Frappé, Mango, '86 216
Ice Cream, Mango, '86 216
Orange Smoothie, Mango-, '86 216
Pan Dowdy, Mango, '83 150
Pie, Green Mango, '79 137
Preserves, Mango-Pineapple, '79 137
Salad, Fresh Mango, '84 126
Salad, Mango, '79 137
Salad with Mango, Chicken, '86 215
Sauce, Mango, '83 120
Sauce, Mango-Spiced Rum, '86 215
Sorbet, Mango, '86 196

Manicotti
Cheesy Manicotti, '83 216
Chicken Manicotti, Creamy, '85 60
Quick Manicotti, '79 6
Spinach Manicotti, '82 199
Stuffed Manicotti, '83 M6
Stuffed Manicotti, Saucy, '83 288
Zucchini Manicotti, '84 194

Marinades. *See* Sauces.

Marshmallows
Ambrosia, Carrot-Marshmallow, '80 5
Brownies, Chewy Marshmallow, '83 306
Brownies, Choco-Mallow, '87 198
Cake, No-Egg Chocolate
    Marshmallow, '87 97
Dip, Marshmallow Fruit, '84 171
Frosting, Chocolate-Marshmallow, '83 245
Parfaits, Mocha-Mallow, '80 219
Pudding, Banana-Mallow, '86 139

Mayonnaise
Anchovy Mayonnaise, '86 179
Cake, Chocolate Mayonnaise, '83 99
Dip, Artichokes with
    Herb-Mayonnaise, '84 67
Dressing, Mayonnaise, '86 11
Herbed Mayonnaise, '82 85, 192
Homemade Mayonnaise, '80 155
Homemade Mayonnaise, Easy, '84 12
Lemon-Cream Mayonnaise, '85 264
Muffins, Mayonnaise, '86 16
Parmesan Mayonnaise, '86 79
Russian Mayonnaise, '80 137
Sauce, Herb-Mayonnaise, '85 73
Tasty Mayonnaise, '82 192
Wine Mayonnaise, Hot, '81 83

Meatballs
Bacon Meatballs, Burgundy, '80 283
Bacon-Wrapped Meatballs, '79 81
Beef Balls Heidelberg, '83 164; '84 39
Brandied Meatballs, '83 78
Chafing Dish Meatballs, '81 260
Chestnut Meatballs, '79 110
Chinese Meatballs, '83 116; '87 194
Cocktail Meatballs, '79 63, 207
Creole, Meatball-Okra, '83 156
Creole, Meatballs, '82 233
Español, Meatballs, '82 110
Flavorful Meatballs, '84 206
Golden Nugget Meatballs, '82 233
Gravy, Meatballs in, '79 136
Ham Balls, '84 91; '86 256
Ham Balls, Appetizer, '82 39
Hawaiian Meatballs, '85 86
Hawaiian Meatballs, Tangy, '79 129
Lamb Meatballs with Yogurt
    Sauce, '85 132

Mock Meatballs, '81 243
Mushroom-Meatball Stroganoff, '85 85
Oven-Barbecued Meatballs, '82 233
Pizza Meatballs, '85 86
Polynesian Meatballs, '80 207
Processor Meatballs, Quick, '87 111
Red Delicious Meatballs, '85 85

Royal Meatballs, '87 268
Saucy Meatballs, '85 68
Saucy Party Meatballs, '80 149
Sauerbraten Meatballs, '85 85
Sauerkraut Meatballs, '86 257
Spaghetti-and-Herb Meatballs, '84 75
Spaghetti with Meatballs, '81 38
Spiced Meatballs, '79 284
Spicy Meatballs and Sausage, '79 163
Stew, Meatball, '79 198
Stroganoff, Meatball, '81 297
Swedish Meatballs, '80 80; '86 256
Sweet-and-Sour Meatballs, '82 233, 247;
    '86 240
Sweet-and-Sour Party Meatballs, '79 233
Tamale Meatballs, '80 194
Veal Meatballs, European, '85 30
Venison Sausage Balls, '80 42
Zesty Meatballs, '80 250

Meat Loaf. *See* Beef, Ground/Meat Loaf.

Melons
Balls, Minted Melon, '87 162
Blooming Melon, A, '83 171
Bowl with Cucumber-Mint Dressing,
    Melon Ball, '87 153
Cantaloupe Compote, '81 147
Cantaloupe Cooler Salad, '79 176
Cantaloupe Cream Delight, '82 179
Cantaloupe Cream, Frozen, '82 159
Cantaloupe Cream Pie, '79 177
Cantaloupe, Fruit-Filled, '83 120
Cantaloupe Ice Cream, '79 77
Cantaloupe Mold, Double-Grape, '79 173
Cantaloupe-Pecan Salad, '86 178
Cantaloupe Pie, '86 163
Cantaloupe Punch, '81 147
Cantaloupe Salad, '86 182
Cantaloupe Sherbet, Frosty, '82 144
Cantaloupe Soup, '83 120
Cantaloupe Soup, Chilled, '81 156
Cantaloupe Soup, Fresh, '84 190
Cantaloupe, Southern Plantation, '82 179
Cantaloupe Wedges, Grilled, '87 162
Citrus Mingle, Melon-, '79 177
Compote, Melon Ball, '85 157
Cooler, Melon, '81 146
Cooler, Melon Ball, '86 131
Filled Melon, Berry-, '86 93

Fruit Bowl, Sparkling Fresh, '80 146
Fruit Cup with Mint Dressing,
    Fresh, '80 183
Fruit Deluxe, Marinated, '81 146
Fruited Ham Salad, '81 146
Fruit Medley, Minted, '80 182
Honeydew-Berry Dessert, '83 120
Honeydew Fruit Boats, '81 147
Honeydew Fruit Bowl, '84 186
Honeydew Fruit Cups, '82 179
Honeydew Granita, '87 162
Honeydew Salad with Apricot Cream
    Dressing, '84 191
Julep, Melon-Mint, '86 196
Julep, Rainbow Melon, '80 183
Mélange, Melon, '84 139
Minted Melon Cocktail, '81 146
Mint Sauce, Melons in, '85 164
Salad, Avocado-Melon, '82 164
Salad, Congealed Melon Ball, '84 125
Salad, Summertime Melon, '82 101
Soup, Melon, '80 182
Soup, Swirled Melon, '87 162
Watermelon Frost, '86 196
Watermelon Fruit Basket, '84 161
Watermelon Preserves, '79 120
Watermelon Rind Pickles, '81 174
Watermelon Salad with Celery-Nut
    Dressing, '80 182
Watermelon Sauce, Melon Balls
    in, '79 177
Watermelon Sherbet, '79 155
Watermelon Sherbet, Light, '81 147
Watermelon Sparkle, '84 191
Wedges with Berry Sauce, Melon, '86 178

Meringues
Baked Pear Meringues, '85 232
Bars, Meringue-Chocolate Chip, '84 118
Basket, Summer Berry, '84 158
Cake, Brown Sugar Meringue, '81 70
Cake, Orange Meringue, '86 336; '87 84
Cakes, Spanish Wind, '84 157
Cooked Meringue, '86 130
Cooked Meringue, Easy, '82 207; '83 158
Cookies, Forget 'em, '83 256
Cookies, Meringue Kiss, '86 121
Cookies, Meringue Surprise, '86 320
Cups, Kiwi and Cream in Meringue,
    '81 279
Cups, Lemon Custard in Meringue,
    '80 295; '81 172
Cups, Lemon Meringue Cream, '84 23
Fingers, Chocolate-Almond
    Meringue, '84 158
Flowers, Meringue, '84 156
Frosting, Brown Sugar Meringue, '81 70
Frosting, Meringue, '86 336; '87 84
Meringue, '87 207
Peach Melba Meringues, '87 76
Pineapple, Meringue-Topped, '84 178
Piping Meringue, '84 156
Shell, Cinnamon Meringue, '82 263
Shells, Fruited Meringue, '87 32
Shells, Fruit-Filled Meringue, '86 151
Strawberry Meringues, '84 188
Torte, Toffee Meringue, '87 118
Vacherin Moka, '80 55

Microwave
Appetizers
    Bacon-Chestnut Wraps, '84 M216
    Canapés, Green Onion, '84 M216
    Cheese Log, Toasted
        Pecan, '86 M288

Cheese Sticks, Peppery, '81 M289
Crab-Zucchini Bites, '84 M216
Dip, Creamy Crab, '80 M135
Dip, Hot Artichoke
    Seafood, '85 M212
Franks, Saucy Appetizer, '84 M12
Mix, Spicy Party, '81 M138
Mushrooms, Shrimp-
    Stuffed, '80 M135
Mushrooms, Tipsy, '84 M216
Nachos, Make-Ahead, '80 M135
Nuts, Sherry-Orange, '86 M289
Pecans, Spicy, '81 M289
Popcorn, Caramel, '86 M212
Popcorn, Garlic, '83 M315
Potato Skins, Cheese, '84 M239
Rumaki, '80 M136
Spread, Hot Beef, '84 M216
Spread, Seafood, '86 M58
Apples, Rosy Cinnamon, '87 M37
Beverages
    Café Colombian Royal, '80 M290
    Chocolate, Creole Hot, '80 M290
    Chocolate, Flaming Brandied,
        '80 M290
    Chocolate Mix, Deluxe Hot,
        '80 M290
    Coffee, Mocha, '85 M329
    Tomato Cocktail, '83 M203
Blanching Chart, Microwave, '80 M181
Breads
    Caramel Ring, Easy, '85 M89
    Cheese-Herb Bread, '84 M144
    Coffee Cake, Cinnamon, '83 M203
    Coffee Cake, Orange, '85 M88
    Coffee Cake Ring, '85 M89
    Coffee Ring, Sugarplum, '83 M37
    Muffins, Apple-Bran, '85 M89
    Muffins, Cinnamon-Nut, '85 M88
    Muffins, Corn, '82 M282
    Rolls, Cherry-Almond, '84 M198
    Toast, Easy French, '82 M172
    Whole Wheat-Rye Bread, '83 M37
Croutons, '86 M288
Croutons, Microwave, '86 M227
Desserts
    Apple-Nut Crunch, '82 M238
    Apple Rings, Cinnamon, '82 M237
    Apples and Cream,
        Brandied, '82 M237
    Apples, Easy Baked, '82 M238
    Bananas Foster, '83 M114
    Bars, Blackberry Jam, '82 M185
    Bars, Chewy Peanut, '80 M172
    Bars, Date-Oat, '80 M172
    Bars, Peanut Butter-and-
        Fudge, '80 M172
    Bavarian Cream, '86 M165
    Brownies, Chocolate-Mint, '85 M294
    Brownies, Nutty Fudge, '80 M171
    Brownies, Quick, '87 M302
    Cake, Fruit and Spice, '87 M97
    Cake, German Chocolate, '83 M233
    Cake, No-Egg Chocolate
        Marshmallow, '87 M97
    Cake, Old-Fashioned Carrot,
        '83 M232
    Cake, Peanut Butter, '83 M233
    Charlotte Russe, '82 M142
    Cheesecake,
        Chocolate-Amaretto, '85 M294

Cheesecake, Pear-Berry, '82 M141
Cherries Jubilee, Quick, '82 M100
Cobbler, Apple-Pecan, '84 M198
Cookies, Doubly-Good
    Chocolate, '82 M185
Cookies, Nutty Oatmeal-Chocolate
    Chip, '82 M185
Cookies, Spice, '87 M278
Cookies, Wedding, '82 M185
Cream, Vanilla, '83 M115
Crème, Orange-Tapioca, '82 M283
Crust, Microwaved Graham
    Cracker, '82 M141
Cupcakes, Cinnamon-
    Chocolate, '81 M139
Custard, Chocolate-Topped
    Amaretto, '87 M37
Divinity, Peanut, '87 M278
Frosting, Buttery
    Cinnamon, '81 M139
Frosting, Caramel, '81 M289
Frosting, Chocolate, '80 M171;
    '83 M233; '87 M97
Frosting, Coconut-Pecan, '83 M233
Frosting, Cream Cheese, '83 M233
Fudge, Double-Good, '79 M263
Fudge, Double Good, '87 M278
Jam Squares, '81 M289
Kahlúa Delight, Make-
    Ahead, '84 M89
Kahlúa Velvet Dessert, '85 M294
Millionaires, '79 M262
Oranges, Wine-Poached, '84 M323
Pastry, Basic, '81 M268
Pastry, Basic Microwave, '82 M142;
    '85 M113
Pastry, Double-Crust, '82 M298
Peaches, Gingersnap, '85 M329
Peach Melba, '83 M114
Peanut Brittle, '79 M263
Peanut Butter Slice-and-
    Bakes, '82 M185
Pecan-Coconut Clusters, '86 M251
Pie, Caramel-Banana, '86 M165
Pie, Cranberry-Apple
    Holiday, '81 M269
Pie, Double Chocolate, '82 M282
Pie, Easy Cherry, '82 M299
Pie, Festive Pumpkin, '81 M269
Pie, Fluffy Eggnog, '81 M269
Pie, Glazed Strawberry, '82 M142
Pie, Lemon Meringue, '85 M112
Pie, Nutty Cranberry, '82 M298
Pie, Old-Fashioned Apple, '82 M299
Pie, Old-Fashioned Pecan, '81 M269
Pots de Crème, '84 M145
Pralines, '86 M288
Pralines, Southern, '79 M263
Pudding, Brown Sugar-Pecan,
    '86 M165
Pudding, Chocolate-
    Almond, '82 M142
Pudding, Mandarin-Almond,
    '85 M12
Soufflé, Brandy Alexander, '83 M114
Sundaes, Cocoa-Kahlúa, '83 M58
Sundaes, Hot Strawberry, '81 M5
Sundaes, Spicy Apple Ice
    Cream, '86 M195
Toffee, Nutty, '79 M263
Eggs and Omelets
    Baked Eggs Florentine, '86 M12
    Benedict, Easy Eggs, '80 M268

Creamed Eggs in Patty
    Shells, '80 M267
Medley, Cheddary Egg, '81 M176
Olé Omelet, '87 M124
Sausage Omelet, Puffy, '80 M268
Scramble, Bacon-and-Eggs, '80 M267
Scrambled Eggs, Creamy
    Onion, '83 M203
Vegetable Omelet, Golden, '82 M123
Grits, Quick Cheese, '83 M203
Jam, Freezer Blackberry, '84 M181
Jam, Freezer Peach, '84 M182
Jam, Raspberry Freezer, '84 M181
Jam, Strawberry Freezer, '84 M182
Jelly, Christmas Freezer, '86 M288
Macaroni and Cheese, '83 M7
Main Dishes
    Beans-and-Franks,
        Polynesian, '84 M11
    Beef Casserole, Easy, '86 M58
    Beef Casserole, Layered, '82 M203
    Beef with Pea Pods,
        Oriental, '86 M328
    Casserole, Mexi, '83 M87
    Chicken alla Romano, '83 M58
    Chicken and Cashews,
        Ginger, '85 M11
    Chicken and Dumplings with
        Vegetables, '85 M56
    Chicken and Spinach
        Rollups, '82 M68
    Chicken and Vegetables
        Vermouth, '87 M37

    Chicken-Asparagus Rolls, '86 M211
    Chicken, Crispy Parmesan, '80 M76
    Chicken, Crunchy Spiced, '85 M57
    Chicken Divan, '80 M10; '87 M218
    Chicken Divan Casserole, '82 M203
    Chicken in a Bag, '86 M57
    Chicken Kabobs,
        Pineapple-, '86 M328
    Chicken Lasagna, '87 M302
    Chicken, Lemon, '81 M138
    Chicken, Orange, '86 M140
    Chicken, Pineapple, '83 M194
    Chicken, Tangy Herbed, '87 M302
    Chicken Teriyaki, '80 M76
    Chicken Tetrazzini, '80 M75
    Chicken Tetrazzini, Cheesy, '83 M87
    Chicken Toss, Quick, '87 M124
    Chicken with Pecan-Rice
        Dressing, '85 M57
    Chicken with Wild Rice,
        Elegant, '80 M76
    Chicken, Zesty Barbecued, '80 M76
    Chili-Cheese Dogs, '81 M176
    Cornish Hens, Orange-Glazed
        Stuffed, '84 M89
    Crab Imperial, Pineapple-, '84 M286
    Crabmeat and Mushrooms on Toast
        Points, '82 M91
    Crêpes, Sherried Beef, '85 M29
    Dinner, Easy Steamed, '83 M314
    Filet Mignon Patties, Mock, '82 M68

Fillets, Lemon-Coated, '80 M53
Fillets, Parmesan, '86 M112
Fillets, Spanish-Style, '86 M112
Fish Amandine, Fillet of, '80 M54
Fish, Creole, '87 M79
Fish Delight, '86 M212
Fish, Easy Italian, '86 M112
Fish, Herb-Coated, '86 M112
Fish in Creamy Swiss Sauce,
  Poached, '80 M53
Fish Rolls, Vegetable-
  Filled, '86 M251
Fish Steaks, Soy, '86 M112
Fish, Sweet-and-Sour, '80 M54
Frankfurters, Barbecued, '84 M12
Haddock Italiano, '81 M4
Halibut with Swiss Sauce, '83 M195
Ham and Apples, Baked, '82 M237
Ham and Chicken, Creamed,
  '81 M74
Ham-Asparagus Dinner, '80 M10
Hamburger Patties, '82 M172
Ham Casserole, Macaroni-, '81 M177
Ham Loaf, Cranberry-, '82 M77
Ham Loaf, Saucy, '86 M328
Ham Ring, Chili-Sauced, '81 M122
Ham Slice, Fruited, '83 M317
Ham Tetrazzini, '82 M77
Ham Towers, Cheesy, '82 M77
Ham with Raisin Sauce, '82 M76
Kabobs, Marinated Chicken,
  '84 M144
Kabobs, Shish, '85 M112
Lasagna, '83 M6
Lasagna, Quick 'n Easy, '80 M10
Lasagna, Zesty, '87 M188
Manicotti, Stuffed, '83 M6
Meat Loaf, Cheesy Pizza, '81 M121
Meat Loaf, Oriental, '81 M122;
  '83 M194
Meat Loaf, Swedish, '81 M121
Meat Loaf, Vegetable, '85 M29
Monkfish, Greek-Style, '87 M79
Oysters on the Half Shell,
  Dressed, '87 M79
Papillote, Ocean, '84 M287
Pineapple Loaves,
  Individual, '81 M121
Pizza, Jiffy Jazzed-Up, '83 M314
Pork Casserole, Cheesy, '81 M74
Pork Chop, Saucy, '86 M140
Pork Chops, Pineapple, '87 M124
Potatoes, Frank-Filled, '84 M11
Pot Roast, Basic, '81 M208
Pot Roast with Vegetables, '81 M208
Quiche, Benedict, '80 M107
Quiche, Crab, '82 M122
Quiche Lorraine, '80 M108
Quiche, Spicy Sausage, '80 M108
Quiche, Spinach-Mushroom, '81 M74
Quiche, Vegetable, '87 M219
Salmon Patties, Open-Faced,
  '87 M218
Sausage and Rice Casserole,
  Oriental, '82 M123
Sausage Casserole, Easy, '87 M189
Sausage Dinner, Beefy, '80 M9
Sausage-Egg Casserole, '86 M12
Sausage Jambalaya Casserole,
  '82 M203
Shrimp, Garlic-Buttered, '86 M226
Shrimp in Cream Sauce, '84 M286
Shrimp, Quick Curried, '84 M198

Sloppy Joes, Pocket, '85 M328
Sole, Saucy, '82 M68
Sole with Cucumber Sauce,
  '84 M286
Spaghetti, Easy, '83 M317
Spaghetti Pie, '81 M32
Steak, Onion-Smothered, '87 M189
Taco Pies, Individual, '82 M282
Tacos, Jiffy, '83 M318
Tortilla Pie, '85 M211
Trout, Sunshine, '84 M286
Tuna Casserole, Easy, '82 M203
Veal and Carrots in Wine
  Sauce, '86 M139
Veal, Italian Style, '82 M68
Zucchini, Beef-Stuffed, '86 M139
Mustard, Coarse-and-Sweet, '86 M288
Noodles, Cheesy Parmesan, '83 M7

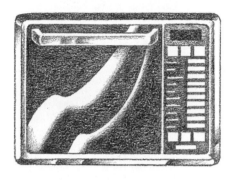

Pastry, Microwaved Quiche, '81 M74;
  '82 M122
Pastry, Quiche, '80 M107
Peaches with Rum, Ginger, '84 M323
Pears, Marmalade Breakfast, '83 M203
Pineapple, Scalloped, '84 M323
Relish, Cranberry-Orange, '81 M289
Relish, Spicy Apple, '84 M323
Rice, Almond, '85 M112
Rice, Basic Long-Grain, '83 M285
Rice, Basic Quick-Cooking, '83 M285
Rice, Chicken-Flavored, '84 M144
Rice, Curry-Spiced, '86 M226
Rice, Herbed, '83 M285
Rice, Oriental, '85 M12, 146
Rice, Parsleyed, '83 M58
Rice with Almonds, Curried,
  '83 M285
Salad Dressings
  Vinaigrette Dressing and
    Croutons, '86 M288
Salads
  Beef Salad, Tangy, '87 M218
  Fast-and-Easy Salad, '85 M328
  Potato Salad, Chunky, '81 M138
  Spinach Salad, Sweet-Sour,
    '85 M112
  Spinach Salad, Wilted, '81 M4
  Taco Salad Cups, '85 M29
  Tuna Salad, Cheese-Sauced,
    '87 M124
Sandwiches
  Breakfast Sandwiches, '82 M123
  Brown Bread-Cream Cheese
    Sandwiches, '87 M6
  Burgers, Pizza, '80 M201
  Crabmeat Sandwiches,
    Deluxe, '81 M74

Frankfurter Sandwiches, '84 M11
Grilled Cheese Sandwiches,
  '82 M172
Hot Brown Sandwiches, '80 M202
Pita Sandwiches, Denver, '86 M12
Pita Sandwiches, Hot, '87 M6
Pizza Sandwiches,
  Open-Face, '84 M198
Reuben Sandwiches, '80 M201
Tuna Sandwiches, Hot, '86 M194
Sauces and Gravies
  Amaretto-Strawberry Sauce,
    '87 M165
  Apple Dessert Sauce, '87 M165
  Béchamel Sauce, '84 M239
  Cheese Sauce, '79 M156; '82 M123
  Cherry Sauce, Elegant, '79 M156
  Chocolate Cherry Sauce, '87 M165
  Chocolate Mint Sauce, Quick,
    '86 M58
  Chocolate-Peanut Butter Sauce,
    '79 M156
  Chocolate-Praline Sauce, '85 M295
  Crab Marinara Sauce, Quick,
    '85 M151
  Cream Sauce, Sherried, '85 M152
  Curry Sauce, '79 M156; '84 M71
  Dill Sauce, '84 M70
  Dill Sauce, Creamy, '79 M156
  Garlic-Cheese Sauce, '84 M70
  Hollandaise Sauce, '80 M107, M268
  Lemon Dessert Sauce, '87 M165
  Mushroom Sauce, '84 M70
  Mustard Sauce, '84 M70
  Orange Sauce, '84 M286
  Parsley-Garlic Sauce, '84 M70
  Peach-Berry Sauce, '87 M165
  Peanut Dessert Sauce, '86 M251
  Pineapple Ice Cream Sauce,
    '81 M289
  Praline Ice Cream Sauce,
    Southern, '86 M227
  Sour Cream Sauce, '82 M68
  Swiss Sauce, '83 M195
  Taco Sauce, '82 M283
  Tomato Sauce, Herbed
    Fresh, '85 M151
  Tomato Sauce, Italian, '82 M68
  Vegetable-Cheese Sauce, '85 M152
  White Sauce, Basic, '79 M156
Soups and Stews
  Bacon-Beer Cheese Soup, '87 M7
  Beef Stew with Parsley
    Dumplings, '85 M246
  Broccoli Soup, '86 M194
  Broccoli Soup, Cream of, '80 M225
  Cauliflower Soup, Cream of, '87 M7
  Cheese Soup, Bacon-
    Topped, '80 M224
  Cheese Soup, Monterey
    Jack, '85 M211
  Chicken Soup, Quick, '86 M72
  Chili, Basic, '82 M11
  Chili, Beefy Sausage, '82 M11
  Chili, Cheese-Topped, '82 M11
  Chili, Chunky, '82 M11
  Chili with Rice, '82 M11
  Chowder, Corn, '84 M38
  Chowder, Fish, '84 M38
  Chowder, New England
    Clam, '86 M72
  Crab Soup, Creamy, '80 M224
  Egg-Drop Soup, '85 M12

Microwave, Soups and Stews *(continued)*

Mushroom Soup, '86 M73
Mushroom Soup, Curried, '84 M89
Onion Soup, French, '86 M212
Onion Soup, Shortcut
    French, '85 M328
Potato-Bacon Soup, '84 M38
Potato Soup, Cream of, '80 M224
Strawberry Soup Supreme, '81 M144
Tomato-Celery Soup, '83 M58
Tomato-Vegetable Soup, '81 M177
Vegetable Soup, Beefy, '84 M38
Vegetables
    Acorn Rings, Easy Glazed, '81 M231
    Asparagus in Lemon
        Butter, '80 M123
    Asparagus with Lemon
        Butter, '87 M151
    Beans Amandine, Green, '82 M20
    Beans, Bacon-Topped
        Green, '80 M123
    Beans, Green, '87 M151
    Beans, Herbed Green, '83 M147
    Beans, Marinated Italian, '86 M226
    Beans, Tangy Green, '85 M142
    Beets, Harvard, '83 M195

Broccoli au Gratin, '82 M20
Broccoli, Chinese, '85 M12
Broccoli Goldenrod,
    Lemon-, '84 M89
Broccoli, Marinated Fresh, '81 M139
Broccoli-Swiss Cheese
    Casserole, '85 M211
Carrots-and-Celery,
    Scalloped, '84 M112
Carrots, Orange-Glazed, '81 M165
Carrots, Spice-Glazed, '83 M58
Corn Fix-Up, Quick, '81 M4
Corn, Mexi-, '82 M21
Corn on the Cob,
    Microwaved, '80 M122
Corn on the Cob, Spicy, '87 M151
Corn, Seasoned Fresh, '83 M147
Corn, Southern-Style
    Creamed, '81 M165
Eggplant, Easy, '87 M151
Fresh Vegetables,
    Microwaving, '82 M138
Garden Harvest, '85 M142
Julienne Vegetables with
    Walnuts, '86 M251
Kabobs, Marinated
    Vegetable, '83 M195
Mixed Vegetables, '83 M195
Okra and Tomatoes, Fresh, '81 M165

Okra, Corn, and Peppers, '87 M151
Onion-Potato Bake, '83 M195
Onions and Peppers,
    Sautéed, '83 M148
Onions, Micro-Baked, '82 M32
Peas, Fresh Black-Eyed, '81 M165
Peas in a Potato Nest, '84 M239
Potato Casserole, Creamy, '84 M113
Potatoes, Cheesy
    Bacon-Stuffed, '81 M61
Potatoes, Herbed New, '83 M148
Potatoes, Jalapeño-Ham
    Stuffed, '81 M61
Potatoes, Micro-Baked, '81 M61
Potatoes, Quick Browned, '82 M172
Potatoes, Seasoned New, '87 M151
Potatoes, Shrimp-Sauced, '81 M61
Potatoes, Summertime, '86 M195
Potatoes with Béchamel Sauce,
    Stuffed, '84 M239
Potatoes with Chives, '81 M61
Potato Fans, Parmesan, '84 M240
Spinach Delight, '84 M144
Squash-and-Pepper Toss,
    Crisp, '87 M152
Squash, Apple-Stuffed
    Butternut, '81 M232
Squash Bake, Cheddar-, '84 M113
Squash Casserole, Jiffy, '81 M144
Squash, Cranberry-Filled
    Acorn, '81 M231
Squash Medley, Fresh, '81 M165
Squash Ring, Butternut, '81 M232
Squash, Sausage-Stuffed
    Acorn, '81 M231
Squash Toss, Simple, '85 M142
Stir-Fry, Vegetable, '82 M172
Tomatoes, Zippy Mustard, '86 M226
Zucchini Boats, '85 M143
Zucchini-Egg Casserole, '84 M113
Zucchini, Italian, '83 M147

Mincemeat
Apples, Baked Mincemeat-Filled, '80 276
Cake, Mincemeat Spice, '79 246
Cookies, Mincemeat, '79 51
Cookies, Mincemeat Drop, '79 246
Cookies, Mincemeat Sweetheart, '87 293
Cookies, Pear Mincemeat, '84 264
Homemade Mincemeat, '79 245
Peaches, Mincemeat, '85 178
Peaches with Mincemeat,
    Brandied, '81 47
Pear Mincemeat, '79 196; '84 264
Pie, Apple-Mincemeat, '85 316
Pie, Holiday Mincemeat, '80 282; '87 213
Pie, Mincemeat-Cheese, '80 253
Pie, Mincemeat Chiffon, '79 245
Pie, Mincemeat-Peach, '80 295; '81 188
Pie, Pear-Mince, '81 271
Pie, Pear Mincemeat, '84 264
Pudding, Steamed Mincemeat, '80 264
Salad, Holiday Mincemeat, '85 263

Mousses
Amaretto-Chocolate Mousse, '86 50
Amaretto-Chocolate Mousse,
    Elegant, '86 337
Amaretto Mousse, '86 188
Apricot Mousse, '82 72
Asparagus Mousse Salad, '86 252
Cake, Chocolate Mousse, '87 264
Caviar Mousse, '82 71; '85 86
Chocolate Mousse Baked Alaska, '85 195
Chocolate Mousse, Blender, '82 71

Chocolate Mousse, Blender-
    Quick, '80 269
Chocolate Mousse, Brandy-, '85 102
Chocolate Mousse, Creamy, '87 133
Chocolate Mousse, Honeyed, '87 223
Chocolate Mousse, Quick, '85 87
Chocolate-Orange Mousse, '81 16, 205
Chocolate Rum Mousse, '86 189
Coffee Mousse, '84 126
Coffee-Nut Mousse, '86 319
Crab Mousse, '79 117
Crème de Menthe Mousse, '80 109
Cucumber Mousse, '79 11
Horseradish Mousse, '84 126
Lime Mousse Freeze, Luscious, '81 173
Mustard Mousse, '84 127; '86 184
Orange Mousse, '86 69
Oyster Mousse, '81 245
Oyster Mousse, Smoked, '84 320
Peach Macaroon Mousse, '80 153
Peach Mousse, '85 54
Peppermint Candy Mousse, '82 71
Pie, Chocolate-Amaretto Mousse, '80 180;
    '81 30
Pie, Chocolate Mousse, '81 136
Pineapple Mousse, Elegant, '79 230
Quick-as-a-Wink Mousse, '84 311
Raspberry Mousse, '81 34
Roquefort Mousse, '82 71
Salmon Dill Mousse, '81 21
Salmon Mousse, Irresistible, '79 284
Sherried Mousse, '81 247
Shrimp Mousse, '79 57; '87 196, 251
Strawberry-Lemon Mousse, '82 128
Strawberry Mousse, '81 95
Strawberry Mousse, Fresh, '82 72
Tuna Mousse, '80 275

Muffins
Almond Muffins, Peachy-, '86 301
Apple-Bran Muffins, '85 M89
Apple Muffins, '83 96; '84 193; '87 23
Apple Muffins, Fresh, '84 264
Apple Muffins, Spiced, '79 60
Apple-Oat Muffins, Spicy, '86 45
Applesauce Muffins, '84 284
Applesauce Muffins, Bite-Size, '82 104
Banana Bran Muffins, '83 48
Banana Muffins, '80 88; '84 75
Banana-Oatmeal Muffins, '84 20

Banana-Oat Muffins, '87 188
Banana-Orange Muffins, '84 148
Banana Surprise Muffins, '82 105
Blueberry Buttermilk Muffins, '80 16
Blueberry-Cream Cheese Muffins, '86 14
Blueberry Ice Cream Muffins, '82 143
Blueberry-Lemon Muffins, '79 7
Blueberry Muffins, '80 143
Blueberry Muffins, Easy, '81 197
Blueberry Muffins, Golden, '79 235
Blueberry Muffins, Old-Fashioned,
    '86 161

Blueberry-Oatmeal Muffins, '87 24
Blueberry Streusel Muffins, '80 46
Bran-Buttermilk Muffins, '85 7
Bran Muffins, '84 53
Bran Muffins, Easy, '83 55
Bran Muffins, Ever-Ready, '81 106
Bran Muffins for Two, '84 211
Bran, Muffins Made of, '86 103
Bran Muffins, Quick, '86 85
Bran Muffins, Refrigerator, '79 6
Bran Muffins, Sour Cream-, '87 98
Bran Muffins, Spiced, '84 229
Breakfast Bites, '86 15
Carrot-and-Raisin Muffins, '87 24
Carrot-Date-Nut Muffins, '86 262
Carrot-Pineapple Muffins, '81 6
Cheese-and-Pepper Muffins, '84 139
Cheese Muffins, Marvelous, '83 96
Cherry Muffins, '82 105
Cinnamon-Nut Muffins, '85 M88
Cinnamon-Pecan Muffins, '84 219
Coconut-Molasses Muffins, '82 210
Coffee Cake Muffins, '79 7
Cornbread Muffins, Southern, '85 201
Cornmeal Muffins, '80 90
Corn Muffins, '82 M282; '84 16
Corn Muffins, Sage-, '83 207
Corn Muffins, Tomato, '81 137
Cranberry Muffins, '81 249
Cranberry-Pecan Muffins, '84 269
Date Muffins, '79 142
Date Muffins, Surprise, '79 216
Date-Nut Muffins, '84 75
Egg Muffins, One-, '83 9
English Muffins, '87 49
English Muffins, Raisin, '80 75
Fiber Muffins, High-, '85 250
Fig Muffins, '86 206
Gingerbread Muffins, '81 285
Gingerbread Muffins,
    Last-Minute, '82 105
Grain Muffins, Four-, '80 46
Honey-Oatmeal Muffins, '84 229
Honey-Wheat Muffins, '83 96
Jam Muffins, '79 7
Jelly-Filled Muffins, '80 16
Kiwifruit Muffins, '87 255
Lemon Muffins, Fresh, '79 161
Magic Muffins, '79 244
Mayonnaise Muffins, '83 57; '86 16
Merry Muffins, '82 253
Mix, Quick Bread, '81 90
Muffins, '81 90
Nut Crunch Muffins, Best Ever, '82 65;
    '83 106
Nut Muffins, Tasty, '79 208
Nutty Muffins, '86 141
Oatmeal Bran Muffins, '81 236
Oatmeal-Honey Muffins, '83 95
Oatmeal Muffins, '82 129, 210
Oatmeal Muffins, Best-Ever, '84 242
Orange Juice Muffins with Honey
    Spread, '81 229
Orange Muffins, '79 236; '81 107; '83 54
Orange Muffins, Streusel-Topped, '84 74
Orange-Oatmeal Muffins, '85 202
Orange-Pecan Muffins, '83 96
Peach Muffins, Special, '84 74
Peanut Butter-Honey Muffins, '82 56
Peanut Butter Muffins, '80 86; '87 158
Pecan Muffins, '80 16
Pecan Muffins, Country, '83 222
Pineapple Muffins, '81 14, 250

Plum Good Muffins, '83 96
Poppy Seed Muffins, '81 63
Potato Muffins, Sweet, '81 224; '85 6;
    '87 280
Prune Muffins, Miniature, '85 223
Pumpkin Muffins, '79 206, 275; '81 272
Pumpkin Muffins, Nutty, '86 291
Raisin Muffins, Breakfast, '84 59
Sausage-Cheese Muffins, '86 213
Sesame-Cheese Muffins, '86 16
Squash Muffins, Yellow, '81 163
Sunshine Muffins, '86 9
Tea Muffins, '82 105
Tropical Muffins, '84 299
Wheat Germ-Prune Muffins, '81 106
Wheat Muffins, Fruited, '79 93
Whole Wheat Raisin Muffins, '85 207
Yam Muffins, '79 7
Yeast Muffins, Quick, '84 69
Zucchini Muffins, '83 121; '86 146

Mushrooms

Asparagus and Mushrooms, '85 108
au Gratin, Mushrooms, '81 108
Aztec Mushrooms, '82 51
Bake, Cheesy Macaroni-
    Mushroom, '81 243
Baked Mushrooms, Creamy, '87 127
Balls, Cheese and Mushroom, '79 63
Beans with Mushrooms, Green, '82 21
Beef Tenderloin with Mushrooms, '87 115
Bisque, Brisk Mushroom, '81 190
Bundles, Chicken-Mushroom, '80 157
Canapés, Mushroom, '80 285
Casserole, Egg-Mushroom, '83 49
Casserole, Mushroom-Artichoke, '87 241
Casserole, Mushroom-Cheese, '83 216
Casserole, Mushroom-Potato, '84 5
Casserole, Sausage-Mushroom
    Breakfast, '86 95
Champignons au Vin, '79 47
Chicken and Mushrooms in Wine
    Sauce, '81 109
Chicken Livers with Mushrooms, '81 133
Chicken-Mushroom Dinner, '81 3
Chowder, Mushroom, '79 16
Consommé aux Champignons, '79 48
Crabmeat and Mushrooms on Toast
    Points, '82 M91
Creamed Mushrooms in Wild Rice
    Ring, '80 270
Creamed Mushrooms on Toast, '81 190
Crêpes, Cheese and Mushroom, '81 88
Crêpes, Coquilles St. Jacques, '83 13
Crêpes, Mushroom-Cheese, '87 289
Curried Mushrooms, '84 214
Dressing, Whole Wheat-
    Mushroom, '84 283
Drunk Mushrooms, '83 174
Egg Delight, Mushroom-, '83 14
Eggplant, Mushroom-Stuffed, '83 136
Filling in a Peel, Mushroom, '84 214
Filling, Mushroom, '81 89; '82 259;
    '83 51
Filling, Spinach-Mushroom, '80 215
Fluted Mushrooms, '82 280
Fresh Mushrooms, Savory, '85 268
Fried Mushrooms, French-, '82 78
Fried Mushrooms with Tartar Sauce,
    French-, '86 233
Heavenly Mushrooms, '87 281
Herbed Mushrooms, '84 214
Logs, Mushroom, '84 206
Marinated Herb Mushrooms, '86 327

Marinated Mushroom Caps, '83 128
Marinated Mushrooms, '80 82, 270;
    '81 69; '86 135
Marinated Mushrooms, Easy, '86 217
Marinated Mushrooms, Mexican, '81 66
Marinated Mushrooms, Special, '83 13
Muffin Stacks, Mushroom-Topped, '80 271
Noodles and Mushrooms, Cheesy, '79 84
Omelet, Broccoli-Mushroom, '85 45
Omelet, Rolled Mushroom, '82 70
Panuchos, Mushroom, '83 51
Patty Shells, Mushrooms and Eggs
    in, '85 143
Patty Shells, Mushrooms in, '80 283
Peas and Mushrooms, '83 141

Peas and Mushrooms, Buttered, '82 204
Peas with Mushrooms, Creamy, '84 196
Peas with Mushrooms, Green, '80 101
Pizza, Cheese-and-Mushroom, '83 226
Potatoes, Mushroom-Dill-Topped, '86 41
Potatoes, Mushroom Scalloped, '87 191
Pot Roast, Mushroom, '79 17
Quail with Mushrooms, '85 138
Quail with Mushrooms, Baked, '81 259
Quiche, Ham-and-Mushroom, '81 11
Quiche Lorraine, Mushroom-, '86 242
Quiche, Mushroom, '80 222; '81 244
Quiche, Spinach-Mushroom, '81 M74
Quiche, Zucchini-Mushroom, '79 127
Rollups, Mushroom, '85 318
Salad, Fabulous Mushroom, '81 190
Salad, Mushroom-and-Pepper, '86 68
Salad, Mushroom-Zucchini, '85 8
Salad, Spinach and Mushroom, '80 112
Salad with Fresh Mushrooms,
    Rice, '80 231
Sandwiches, Toasted Mushroom, '87 281
Sauce, Beef Tenderloin with
    Mushroom-Sherry, '87 306
Sauce, Broiled Tomatoes with
    Mushroom, '81 103
Sauce, Chicken Florentine with
    Mushroom, '87 250
Sauce, Mushroom, '81 90, 200; '82 46;
    '83 71, 205, 212; '84 M70; '85 40;
    '86 198; '87 36, 186, 284
Sauce, Mushroom-Cheese, '83 190; '86 48
Sauce, Mushroom-Dill, '80 271
Sauce, Mushroom-Wine, '84 84; '86 24
Sauce, Onion-Mushroom, '85 224; '86 84
Sauce, Steak with Ham-and-
    Mushroom, '83 109
Sauce, Steak with Mushroom, '83 212
Sauce Supreme on Vermicelli,
    Mushroom, '86 158
Saucy Mushrooms and Eggs, '79 138
Sautéed Mushrooms, '84 35
Sautéed Mushrooms, Easy, '81 131
Sautéed Mushroom Spectacular, '83 206
Scallops and Mushrooms, Creamy, '83 144
Seasoned Mushrooms, '83 291
Sherried Mushroom Eggs, '83 49

Mushrooms *(continued)*

Sherried Mushrooms, '83 13
Shrimp-Mushroom Italienne, Green Pasta
  with, '79 170
Soufflés, Mushroom, '87 282
Soup, Cream of Mushroom, '84 5;
  '85 93, 261
Soup, Creamy Avocado-Mushroom, '85 25
Soup, Creamy Mushroom, '79 243;
  '81 307
Soup, Curried Mushroom, '84 M89
Soup, Elegant Mushroom, '83 99
Soup, Fresh Mushroom, '81 109
Soup, Mushroom, '82 286; '86 M73
Soup, Mushroom-Onion, '80 25
Soup, Oyster-and-Mushroom, '87 39
Sour Cream-Dill Sauce, Mushrooms
  in, '84 215
Spaghetti with Mushrooms, Spicy, '85 2
Spinach with Mushrooms, '80 19
Spread, Hot Mushroom, '81 190
Squash, Mushroom-Stuffed
  Yellow, '84 154
Steak and Mushrooms, Flank, '87 61
Stems, Mushrooms with, '86 258
Stir-Fried Mushrooms with Bacon, '80 123
Stroganoff, Mushroom, '81 298
Stroganoff, Mushroom-Meatball, '85 85
Stuffed Mushroom Caps, Crab-, '84 160
Stuffed Mushroom Delight, '87 281
Stuffed Mushrooms, '79 212; '81 239;
  '83 13, 66, 126, 136
Stuffed Mushrooms, Black Olive-, '86 258
Stuffed Mushrooms, Cheese 'n' Bacon-,
  '86 258
Stuffed Mushrooms, Chicken-, '80 162
Stuffed Mushrooms, Crab-, '81 190
Stuffed Mushrooms, Crawfish-, '86 258
Stuffed Mushrooms, Elegant
  Cheese-, '81 57
Stuffed Mushrooms, Flavor-, '85 288
Stuffed Mushrooms Florentine, '82 270
Stuffed Mushrooms, Italian
  Sausage-, '83 127
Stuffed Mushrooms, Parmesan, '83 115
Stuffed Mushrooms, Pâté-, '85 118
Stuffed Mushrooms, Pecan-, '84 261
Stuffed Mushrooms, Pesto-, '86 150
Stuffed Mushrooms, Pistachio-, '86 141
Stuffed Mushrooms, Ricotta-, '85 20
Stuffed Mushrooms, Sausage-, '80 248
Stuffed Mushrooms, Seasoned, '84 206
Stuffed Mushrooms, Shrimp-, '80 M135
Stuffed Mushrooms, Spinach-, '86 81
Stuffed with Crab, Mushrooms, '82 249
Supreme, Mushrooms, '84 214
Tarts, Hot Sherried Mushroom, '83 78
Tipsy Mushrooms, '84 M216
Tomatoes, Mushroom-Stuffed, '86 218
Turnovers, Tiny Mushroom, '86 24
Vegetable Mushroom Caps, '81 246
Vermicelli with Mushrooms, '79 195
Wild Rice and Mushrooms, '83 278
Wine Sauce, Mushrooms with, '85 292

Mustard

Brussels Sprouts with Shallots and
  Mustard, '85 258
Coarse-and-Sweet Mustard, '86 M288
Compote, Baked Mustard Fruit, '85 47
Dressing, Mustard, '80 112
Flounder Dijon, '85 95
Herbed Mustard, '87 134

Homemade Mustard, '81 77
Homemade Mustard, Zesty, '82 55
Horseradish Mustard, Lower
  Sodium, '86 325
Hot German Mustard, '82 298
Hot Mustard, Chinese, '85 12
Hot Sweet Mustard, '85 12
Mousse, Mustard, '84 127; '86 184
Sauce, Creamy Mustard, '80 272;
  '86 257; '87 232
Sauce, Extra-Special Mustard, '79 82
Sauce, Honey-Lemon Mustard, '84 275
Sauce, Honey-Mustard, '85 13
Sauce, Light Mustard, '82 178
Sauce, Mild Mustard, '85 224; '86 84
Sauce, Mock Mustard-
  Hollandaise, '87 269
Sauce, Mustard, '80 222, 283; '83 21,
  321; '84 M70, 289; '85 148; '86 185;
  '87 22
Sauce, Mustard-Sour Cream, '81 68
Sauce, Sausage Sandwiches with
  Mustard, '84 250
Sauce, Stone Crab Mustard, '80 3
Sauce, Sweet Mustard, '85 12
Spread, Mustard, '86 105

N

Nectarines

Apple Juice, Nectarines in, '83 183
Butter, Nectarine, '79 175
Cocktail, Nectarine, '85 107
Royale, Nectarines, '85 132
Salad, Nectarine Chicken, '79 175

Noodles

Bake, Hamburger-Noodle, '81 140
Bake, Sausage-Noodle, '81 92
Bake, Sour Cream-Noodle, '79 55
Bake, Taco Beef-Noodle, '81 141
Beef and Noodles, Easy, '83 288
Caraway Buttered Noodles, '87 230
Casserole, Beef-and-Noodles, '84 72
Casserole, Chicken and Green
  Noodle, '80 32
Casserole, Eggplant and Noodle, '82 230
Casserole, Ham and Noodle, '80 300
Casserole, Sausage and Noodle, '82 123
Cheesy Noodles and Mushrooms, '79 84
Chili with Noodles, '81 282; '82 57
Crispy Noodles, Chow Mein over, '85 286
Dinner, Beefy Noodle, '81 179
Dinner, Creamy Liver and Noodle, '80 11
Green Noodles, '80 211
Ham and Swiss on Noodles, '87 108
Italian Sauce with Noodles, '84 250
Orange Noodles, '84 177
Parmesan Noodles, '83 118
Parmesan Noodles, Cheesy, '83 M7
Parslied Noodles, '85 31
Rice Noodles, Shredded Beef over, '85 74
Ring, Noodle, '85 285
Salad, Ham-Noodle, '85 249
Scallops and Pasta, Fresh, '83 164
Skillet, Ham-Noodle, '87 78
Soup, Chicken Noodle, '80 264
Spinach Noodles, Chicken and, '82 19
Spinach with Noodles, Creamed, '84 29
Stew with Noodles, Hungarian, '80 263
Veal Sauce, Noodles with, '80 236
White Noodles, '80 211

O

Oatmeal

Bars, Apricot-Oatmeal, '86 216
Bars, Chocolate-Topped Oatmeal, '86 110
Bars, Date-Oat, '80 M172
Bars, Layered Oatmeal-Date, '85 10
Bars, Oatmeal-Caramel, '85 247
Bars, Yummy Fudge, '87 158
Bread, Blueberry-Oatmeal, '83 139
Bread, Caraway-Raisin Oat, '86 44
Bread, Honey Oatmeal, '80 60
Bread, Oatmeal, '81 236, 300
Bread, Oatmeal Raisin, '81 14
Bread, Oatmeal-Raisin, '83 59
Bread, Oat-Molasses, '82 139
Bread, Round Oatmeal, '84 20
Bread, Whole Wheat-Oatmeal, '87 85
Breakfast Oatmeal, Swiss Style, '81 49
Brownies, Oatmeal, '87 199
Buns, Honey Oatmeal, '83 154
Cake, Dutch Oatmeal, '83 95
Cake, Golden Apple-Oatmeal, '86 301
Cake, Honey-Oatmeal, '87 222
Cake, Oatmeal-Coconut Coffee, '83 312
Cookies, Apple-Nut, '80 228
Cookies, Apple-Oatmeal, '85 215
Cookies, Banana Oatmeal, '79 217
Cookies, Chocolate Chip-Oatmeal, '84 119
Cookies, Chocolate-Oatmeal, '80 105
Cookies, Cinnamon Oatmeal, '84 72
Cookies, Crunchy Oatmeal, '85 202
Cookies, Date-Filled Oatmeal, '86 314
Cookies, Easy Oatmeal, '80 105
Cookies, Frosted Oatmeal-Raisin, '79 290
Cookies, Giant Oatmeal-Spice, '80 105
Cookies, Lace, '86 8

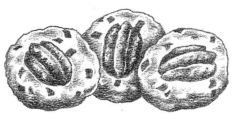

Cookies, Nutty Oatmeal, '81 130
Cookies, Nutty Oatmeal-Chocolate
  Chip, '82 M185
Cookies, Oatmeal-Coconut, '80 218
Cookies, Oatmeal-Date, '82 109
Cookies, Oatmeal-Date Sandwich, '83 257
Cookies, Oatmeal-Peanut Butter, '85 171
Cookies, Oatmeal-Raisin, '87 221
Cookies, Old-Fashioned Oatmeal, '80 106;
  '85 250
Cookies, Orange-Glazed Oatmeal, '80 60
Cookies, Peanut Butter-Oatmeal, '81 218;
  '84 72
Cookies, Peanutty Oatmeal, '80 106;
  '83 95
Cookies, Slice-and-Bake Oatmeal, '80 105
Cookies, Special Oatmeal, '81 236
Cookies, Spicy Oatmeal, '81 197
Cookies, Take-Along Breakfast, '84 59
Crackers, Oatmeal-Wheat Germ, '84 236
Crispies, Oat, '83 96
Crispies, Oatmeal Nut, '80 208
Granola Bars, '83 305
Granola, Crunchy, '81 218; '84 144

Granola, Easy, **'81** 49
Granola, Fruity, **'84** 148
Granola, Homemade, **'84** 58
Granola, Sunny Orange, **'84** 212
Krispies, Oatmeal, **'85** 115
Loaf, Banana-Oat Tea, **'87** 256
Loaf, Pumpkin-Oatmeal, **'81** 49
Mix, Rolled Oats, **'84** 72
Muffins, Banana-Oat, **'87** 188
Muffins, Banana-Oatmeal, **'84** 20
Muffins, Best-Ever Oatmeal, **'84** 242
Muffins, Blueberry-Oatmeal, **'87** 24
Muffins, Honey-Oatmeal, **'84** 229
Muffins, Oatmeal, **'82** 129, 210
Muffins, Oatmeal Bran, **'81** 236
Muffins, Oatmeal-Honey, **'83** 95
Muffins, Orange-Oatmeal, **'85** 202
Muffins, Spicy Apple-Oat, **'86** 45
Pancakes, Oatmeal, **'80** 44
Piecrust, Crisp Cereal, **'83** 100
Piecrust, Oatmeal, **'79** 79
Waffles, Oatmeal-Nut, **'83** 96

Okra
Bake, Okra-Tomato, **'80** 298; **'81** 26
Casserole, Okra, **'79** 160
Cheese, Okra with, **'80** 185
Chowder, Quick Okra, **'80** 185
Corn, and Peppers, Okra, **'87** M151
Cream, Okra and Corn in, **'79** 160
Creole, Meatball-Okra, **'83** 156
Creole Okra, **'81** 182
Creole, Okra-Corn, **'83** 157
Fingers, Okra, **'85** 196
Fresh Okra and Tomatoes, **'87** 89
Fried Okra, **'79** 122; **'86** 211; **'87** 89
Fried Okra, Crispy, **'86** 169
Fried Okra, French-, **'82** 126
Fried Okra, Fritter-, **'86** 218
Fried Okra, Old-Time, **'80** 185
Fritters, Okra, **'79** 160
Fry, Okra-Potato, **'81** 159
Gumbo, Deep South Okra, **'79** 48
Gumbo Freezer Mix, Okra, **'86** 210
Gumbo, Light Seafood-Okra, **'86** 155
Gumbo, Okra, **'86** 210
How to Can Okra, **'80** 127
Medley, Okra-Corn-Tomato, **'81** 159
Pickles, Okra, **'81** 173
Pilaf, Okra, **'80** 185; **'82** 126
Plantation Okra, **'82** 126
Puffs, Okra, **'83** 157
Sautéed Corn and Okra, **'84** 158
Soup, Charleston Okra, **'87** 156
Soup, Sausage and Okra, **'80** 209
Stewed Okra, Southern, **'82** 134
Stew, Old-Fashioned Okra, **'84** 158
Surprise, Okra, **'79** 160; **'84** 158
Tomato Combo, Okra-, **'83** 157
Tomatoes and Okra, **'86** 170; **'87** 164
Tomatoes, Fresh Okra and, **'81** M165
Tomatoes, Okra and, **'80** 185; **'81** 139
Tomatoes, Okra and Green, **'79** 160
Tomatoes with Okra, **'85** 106
Olives
Antipasto, Easy, **'85** 114
Appetizers, Cheesy Olive, **'85** 113
Appetizers, Cheesy-Olive, **'87** 246
Ball, Blue Cheese-Olive, **'82** 248
Ball, Olive Cheese, **'80** 258
Black Olives, Shrimp Spaghetti
 with, **'85** 13
Black Olive-Stuffed Mushrooms, **'86** 258
Casserole, Turkey-Olive, **'87** 268
Chalupas, Chicken-Olive, **'81** 227
Chicken-and-Rice Valencia, **'85** 113
Filling, Chicken-Olive, **'81** 227
Ham-and-Swiss Rollups, **'85** 113
Potatoes, Olive, **'80** 114
Salad, Mexican Olive, **'85** 84
Salad, Olive Clubhouse, **'81** 114
Salad, Olive-Potato, **'85** 114
Spread, Antipasto, **'81** 25
Spread, Cheese-Olive, **'79** 82
Spread, Cream Cheese-Olive, **'82** 35
Spread, Creamy Olive, **'81** 290
Spread, Tomatoes with Olive, **'85** 114
Toss, Cauliflower-Olive, **'85** 198; **'86** 147
Toss, Tomato-Olive Pasta, **'86** 209
Omelets
Broccoli-Mushroom Omelet, **'85** 45
Cheese Omelet, Zippy, **'87** 287
Cheesy Picante Omelet, **'86** 95
Chicken Liver Omelet, **'82** 44
Filling, Greek Omelet, **'80** 68
Filling, Spanish Omelet, **'80** 68
Fluffy Omelet, **'84** 56
George's Omelets, **'80** 68
Ham and Cheese Omelet, **'79** 262;
 '80 123
Mexican Omelet, **'79** 128; **'81** 225
Mushroom Omelet, Rolled, **'82** 70
Mushroom Sauce, Puffy Omelets
 with, **'85** 40
Omelet, Olé, **'87** M124
Oyster Omelets, Smoked, **'84** 96
Potato-Sprout Omelet, **'79** 128
Primavera, Omelet, **'87** 71
Rising Sun Omelet, **'82** 281; **'83** 42
Sandwich, Omelet, **'86** 95
Sausage Filling, Omelet with, **'81** 43
Sausage Omelet, Puffy, **'80** M268
Shrimp-and-Cheddar Omelet, **'84** 57
Sour Cream-Ham Omelet, **'79** 261
Spanish Omelet, **'81** 201; **'83** 243; **'84** 101
Spanish-Style Omelets, **'83** 188
Spinach-Cheese Omelet, **'83** 119
Sunrise Omelet, **'83** 289
Swiss Oven Omelet, **'80** 189
Tex-Mex Omelet con Carne, **'81** 209
Vegetable Omelet, Beefy, **'83** 188
Vegetable Omelet, Cheddar-, **'83** 205
Vegetable Omelet, Cheesy, **'85** 49
Vegetable Omelet, Fresh, **'84** 211
Vegetable Omelet, Golden, **'82** M123
Vegetable Omelet, Puffy, **'83** 188
Vegetarian Omelet, **'84** 114
Wine Omelet, White, **'79** 103
Yogurt-Avocado Omelet, **'81** 33
Zucchini Omelet, **'81** 99

Onions
Bake, Cheese Onion, **'82** 32
Baked Onions, Micro-, **'82** M32
Baked Onions, Spicy, **'84** 65
Bake, Onion-Potato, **'83** M195
Beans and Scallions, Fresh Lima, **'82** 133
Bean Sauce, Pork-and-Onions with, **'85** 76
Beef and Onions, Smothered, **'85** 293
Beef Burgundy with Pearl
 Onions, **'81** 108
Bread, Easy Onion, **'81** 162
Bread, Easy Onion-Dill, **'85** 5
Bread, Onion-Cheese, **'79** 180; **'81** 8
Bread, Onion-Cheese Supper, **'83** 112
Bread, Onion-Parmesan, **'84** 284
Bread, Toasted Onion-Herb, **'83** 266
Buns, Cheesy Onion, **'85** 5
Butter, Onion, **'86** 253

Carrots with Bacon and Onion,
 Glazed, **'87** 200
Casserole, Cheesy Onion, **'79** 101
Cheese Onions, Sherried, **'82** 32
Cornbread, Onion-Topped, **'84** 153
Creole Onions, **'82** 32
Deluxe, Broccoli-Onion, **'81** 75
Dip, Cheesy Onion, **'83** 145
Dip, Chunky Onion, **'84** 257
Dip, Cream Cheese-Onion, **'79** 236
Dressing, Green Pepper-Onion
 Salad, **'84** 12
Dressing, Onion-French, **'84** 283
Eggs, Creamy Onion
 Scrambled, **'83** M203
Fried
 Crisp Fried Onion Rings, **'84** 65
 Crispy Fried Onion Rings, **'80** 108
 Crispy Onion Rings, **'86** 110
 Deluxe Fried Onion Rings, **'80** 108
 Easy Onion Rings, **'80** 108
 Favorite Fried Onion Rings, **'81** 86
 French-Fried Onion Rings
  Supreme, **'80** 109
 Green Onions, Fried, **'81** 106
 Rings, Fried Onion, **'83** 85; **'85** 69
Glazed Carrots and Onions, **'83** 25;
 '87 128
Glazed Onions, **'84** 104
Glazed Pearl Onions, **'85** 258
Gourmet Onions, **'81** 86
Gravy, Fried Quail with Onion, **'82** 214
Green Onion Canapés, **'84** M216
Green Onion Quiche, Cheesy, **'83** 194;
 '84 42
Green Onion Relish, **'84** 65
Green Onion Teasers, **'82** 42
Grilled Squash and Onion, **'79** 150
Herbed Carrots and Onions, **'87** 31
Herbed Onions, **'84** 149

Onions *(continued)*

Honey Onions, '81 86
Hush Puppies, Onion, '85 14
Italian Dressing, Tomato, Onion, and
Cucumber in, '81 83
Loaves, Onion Twist, '84 300
Peas with Onions, Buttered, '80 242
Pickled Refrigerator Onion Rings, '84 265
Pie, Onion, '82 191
Quiche, Onion, '83 121
Relish, Pepper-Onion, '84 180
Rice, Seasoned Onion, '82 166
Rolls, Poppy Seed Onion, '81 63
Salad Bowl, Spinach-and-Onion, '81 157
Salad, Lemon-Onion, '85 252
Salad, Tomato-Cucumber-Onion, '81 239
Salad, Vidalia-Tomato, '84 65
Sandwiches on Salt-Rising Bread,
Vidalia, '79 145
Sauce, Brussels Sprouts in
Onion, '81 308
Sauce, Onion, '82 72; '87 248
Sauce, Onion Cream, '87 232
Sauce, Onion-Mushroom, '85 224; '86 84
Sauce, Onion-Parsley, '85 148
Sauce, Pepper-Onion, '84 125
Sautéed Onions and Peppers, '83 M148
Selecting and Storing Onions, '84 65
Shells, Cheese and Limas in
Onion, '81 86
Soufflé, Onion, '79 247
Soup
Cheese Onion Soup, Double-, '85 227
Cheese Soup, Onion-, '87 81
Classic Onion Soup, '84 65
Double Cheese-Topped Onion
Soup, '79 49
Easy Onion Soup, '85 226
French Onion-Beef Soup, '87 54
French Onion Soup, '79 49; '80 188;
'83 126; '85 226; '86 M212

French Onion Soup,
Shortcut, '85 M328
French Onion Soup, Toasty, '81 306
Green Onion Soup, '84 112
Green Onion Soup, Creamed, '83 82
Mushroom-Onion Soup, '80 25
Oven-Browned Onion Soup, '79 49
Rich Onion Soup, '85 226
Superb Onion Soup, '81 86
Vichyssoise, '86 181
Sour Cream, Cucumber and Onion
in, '81 69
Spread, Braunschweiger-Onion, '79 82
Squares, Creamy Onion, '79 48
Squares, Sausage-Onion, '83 112
Steak, Onion-Smothered, '87 M189
Stew, Beef-and-Onion, '87 18
Stuffed Baked Onions, '82 32

Stuffed Onions and Wine, '85 268
Stuffed Onions, Baked, '83 135
Stuffed Onions, Broccoli-, '84 154
Stuffed with Peas, Onions, '84 68
Sweet-Hot Onions, '85 139
Turnips and Onions, '83 242
Veal and Onions, Herbed, '79 108
Oranges
Appetizer, Orange-Berry, '85 81
Apples, Orange-Glazed, '82 51
Asparagus with Orange Butter
Sauce, '85 43
Asparagus with Orange Sauce, '83 46
Bake, Butternut-Orange, '86 295
Baked Oranges, '79 247
Bake, Sweet Potato-Orange, '83 226
Beets, Orange-Ginger, '80 137
Beets, Orange-Glazed, '81 167;
'85 289; '86 187
Beverages
Blush, Orange, '80 51
Breakfast Eye-Opener, '87 199
Citrus Cooler, '82 160
Cocktail, Orange-Champagne, '79 39
Cocktail, Tomato-Orange
Juice, '83 169
Coffee, Viennese Orange, '84 54
Flip, Orange-Banana, '82 48
Flips, Orange Blossom, '80 51
Frosty, Orange, '86 101
Frosty Sours, '81 156
Liqueur, Orange, '81 287
Magnolia Blossoms, '87 72
Magnolias, '82 196
Mist, Orange-Lemon, '79 288; '80 35
Nog, Orange Spiced, '82 48
Pick-Me-Up, Orange, '80 232
Punch, Citrus Party, '83 141
Punch, Orange Blossom, '83 142
Punch, Orange-Lime, '82 160
Punch, Orange-Mint, '82 121
Punch, Orange Sherbet Party, '83 142
Punch, Orange Soda, '87 214
Punch, Pineapple-Orange, '85 236
Punch, Refreshing Orange, '81 39
Refresher, Grapefruit-Orange, '82 174
Sangría, '81 67
Sangría, Easy Citrus, '80 218
Sangría, Orange, '81 237
Shake, Orange Milk, '84 166
Shake, Peachy Orange, '81 156
Shake, Tropical, '87 200
Slush, Banana-Orange, '80 48;
'81 155
Slush, Orange, '82 49
Slush, Strawberry-Orange, '83 172
Smoothie, Mango-Orange, '86 216
Smoothie, Tropical, '81 50
Soda, Cranberry-Orange, '79 148
Breads
Anise-Orange Bread, '83 295
Baba au Orange, '86 138
Blueberry-Orange Bread, '87 140
Breakfast Ring, Orange, '81 229
Coffee Cake, Cranberry-
Orange, '82 283
Coffee Cake, Orange, '85 M88
Coffee Cake, Orange Marmalade
Swirl, '87 107
Coffee Cake, Orange-Pecan, '86 86
Coffee Ring, Caramel-Orange, '80 45
Cranberry Bread, Orange-, '85 266
Cranberry-Orange Bread, '87 244

Cream Cheese Bread, Orange-,
'82 210
Muffins, Banana-Orange, '84 148
Muffins, Orange, '79 236; '81 107;
'83 54
Muffins, Orange-Oatmeal, '85 202
Muffins, Orange-Pecan, '83 96
Muffins, Streusel-Topped
Orange, '84 74

Muffins with Honey Spread, Orange
Juice, '81 229
Nut Bread, Blueberry-
Orange, '84 141
Nut Bread, Cranberry-
Orange, '80 288
Nut Bread, Orange-, '82 75
Nut Loaf, Orange, '80 226
Pecan Bread, Glazed
Orange-, '81 250
Pecan Bread, Orange-, '79 148
Pecan Loaves, Orange-, '79 215
Puffs, Upside-Down Orange, '83 57
Pumpkin Bread, Orange-, '87 300
Rolls, Frosted Hot Orange, '80 257
Rolls, Luscious Orange, '86 298
Rolls, Orange, '80 22; '82 17
Rolls, Orange Butter, '82 206; '83 33
Rye Bread, Swedish Orange-, '85 111
Tea Bread, Orange, '79 234
Toast, Orange French, '83 292;
'84 78; '86 329
Toast, Orange Praline, '79 36
Toast Topper, Orange, '79 36
Toast with Orange Sauce,
French, '82 47
Whole Wheat Orange Bread, '85 5
Broccoli, Easy Orange, '85 267
Broccoli with Orange Sauce, '80 243
Broiled Orange Halves, '85 288
Brussels Sprouts, Orange, '84 34
Butter, Honey-Orange, '79 36; '85 19
Butter, Orange, '81 8, 42
Butter, Orange-Pecan, '84 75
Candied Orange Peel, '81 286
Carrots in Orange Sauce, '82 107
Carrots, Orange-Glazed, '79 12; '81 M165
Carrots, Orange-Raisin, '80 24
Catfish Amandine, Mandarin, '84 183
Celery in Orange Sauce, '79 70
Chicken á l'Orange, '84 277
Chicken á l'Orange, Stir-Fry, '83 82
Chicken Breasts with Orange
Sauce, '79 77
Chicken Breasts with Parslied Rice,
Orange, '87 242
Chicken, Crispy Mandarin, '86 119
Chicken in Orange-Almond
Sauce, '79 219; '80 13
Chicken in Orange Sauce, '83 8

Chicken Livers in Orange Sauce, '82 218
Chicken, Orange, '83 278; '86 M140
Chicken, Orange-Avocado, '80 38
Chicken Stir-Fry, Kyoto Orange-, '87 96
Chicken Stir-Fry, Orange-, '84 68
Chutney, Cranberry-Orange, '79 292
Chutney, Orange-Cranberry, '86 266
Cornish Hens, Orange-Glazed, '83 267
Cornish Hens, Orange-Glazed
   Grilled, '86 250
Cornish Hens, Orange-Glazed
   Stuffed, '84 M89
Cornish Hens with Cranberry-Orange
   Sauce, '86 119
Cornish Hens with Orange Glaze, '79 244
Crêpes, Chocolate-Orange, '85 263
Desserts
   Alaska, Orange, '83 177
   Baked Apples, Orange-Pecan, '85 45
   Baked Apples with Orange
      Sauce, '84 314
   Baked Bananas with Orange
      Sauce, '79 115
   Baked Orange Elegance, '80 13
   Bars, Pineapple-Orange, '82 129
   Baskets, Orange, '81 308
   Cake, Fresh Orange, '83 300
   Cake, Mandarin Orange, '83 24
   Cake, Mandarin-Rum, '84 150
   Cake, Orange, '86 61
   Cake, Orange-Cranberry, '85 314
   Cake, Orange Liqueur, '87 84
   Cake, Orange Marmalade, '85 53
   Cake, Orange Meringue, '86 336;
      '87 84
   Cake, Orange Nut, '80 70
   Cake, Orange-Nut Butter, '80 254
   Cake, Orange-Pecan Crunch, '83 10
   Cake, Orange Pound, '87 84, 221
   Cake, Orange Rum, '79 2
   Cake, Orange-Slice, '81 264
   Cake Squares, Apple-Orange, '84 150
   Cake Squares, Orange, '81 34
   Cake Squares, Orange-
      Pumpkin, '83 242
   Cake, Williamsburg Orange, '81 120;
      '82 23
   Cheesecake, Orange, '81 84; '85 38
   Chocolate-Orange Roll, '87 21
   Cookies, Carrot-Orange, '83 149
   Cookies, Frosted Orange, '83 114
   Cookies, Orange-Chocolate, '83 113
   Cookies, Orange-Glazed Oatmeal,
      '80 60
   Cookies, Orange Refrigerator,
      '86 230
   Cream Dessert, Orange, '80 254;
      '84 165
   Cream, Orange, '81 12
   Cream, Orange Chantilly, '84 156
   Cream, Orange-Coconut, '84 24
   Crème, Orange-Tapioca, '82 M283
   Crêpes, Amaretto-and-
      Orange, '86 260
   Crêpes, Orange Dream, '82 183
   Crispies, Orange, '84 205
   Crisp, Orange-Apple, '80 295
   Delight, Pumpkin-Orange, '86 321
   Dip, Creamy Orange, '84 117
   Filling, Lemon-Orange, '81 71
   Filling, Orange, '79 229; '86 336;
      '87 84
   Fingers, Orange, '87 57.

Flambé, Dessert Orange, '85 313
Flan, Orange, '84 95
Frosted Oranges, '83 270
Frosting, Creamy Orange, '83 24, 241
Frosting, Orange, '81 7; '86 61
Frosting, Orange Butter, '83 300
Frosting, Orange Buttercream, '80 70
Frosting, Orange Cream, '81 207;
   '82 14
Frosting, Orange-Cream
   Cheese, '81 70; '82 16
Fruit Dessert Orange, '84 314
Glazed Oranges and
   Pineapple, '86 318
Ice Cream, Orange-Pineapple, '86 117
Ice, Strawberry-Orange, '86 196
Ice, Tart Cranberry-Orange, '86 317
Juice, Strawberries with Brandied
   Orange, '82 160
Molded Dessert, Orange, '83 302
Mousse, Chocolate-Orange,
   '81 16, 205
Mousse, Orange, '86 69
Parfaits, Chilled Orange, '80 219
Peanut Brittle, Orange, '80 302
Pears Flambé, Orange-
   Poached, '85 313
Pears in Orange Sauce,
   Poached, '82 19
Pears, Orange Poached, '80 218
Pie, Lemon-Orange, '85 172
Pie, Orange Ambrosia, '80 237
Pie, Orange Chiffon, '87 260
Pie, Orange Meringue, '81 12, 309
Pie, Orange-Pecan, '79 282; '83 222
Poached Oranges, Wine-, '84 M323
Pops, Orange-Banana, '82 129
Pudding, Mandarin-Almond, '85 M12
Pudding, Orange, '81 85; '82 111;
   '83 153
Rice Cream with Mandarin
   Oranges, '85 317
Sherbet Ambrosia Cups, '82 159
Sherbet, Banana-Orange, '83 162
Sherbet, Orange, '79 155
Shortcake, Fresh Orange, '80 100
Soufflé, Chilled Orange, '84 317;
   '86 189
Soufflé, Frozen Orange, '79 211
Soufflé, Grand Marnier, '79 281
Soufflé, Orange Dessert, '83 206
Special, Orange Blossom, '79 48
Squares, Orange-Crunch, '86 136
Tapioca Fluff, Orange, '87 31
Tarts, Frozen Orange, '80 154
Topping, Whipped Orange, '80 254
Dip, Creamy Orange, '87 247
Dip, Orange Sour Cream, '79 208
Dip, Spicy Orange, '85 230
Doughnuts, Orange Spiced, '79 136
Dressing, Marmalade-Fruit, '84 171
Dressing, Orange, '81 141
Dressing, Orange Blossom, '82 266
Dressing, Orange-Coconut, '80 158
Dressing, Orange-Poppy Seed, '87 187
Dressing, Orange-Yogurt, '85 304
Duck, Chafing Dish Orange, '79 226
Fritters, Puffy Orange, '81 169
Granola, Sunny Orange, '84 212
Gravy, Orange, '81 259
Grits, Orange, '81 47
Halibut with Orange-Curry Sauce, '87 91
Ham, Cranberry-Orange Glazed, '81 295

Lamb Chops, Orange, '83 35
Lobster Tails with Spiced Orange
   Sauce, '86 155
Marmalade, Orange, '81 42
Marmalade, Orange-Pineapple, '82 150
Marmalade, Peach-Orange, '82 150
Noodles, Orange, '84 177
Nuts, Sherry-Orange, '86 M289
Pancakes, Orange-Yogurt, '87 225
Pears, Marmalade Breakfast, '83 M203
Pears, Orange-Glazed, '79 247
Pecans, Orange, '84 299; '87 292
Popcorn, Orange, '86 230
Porc à l'Orange, '80 242
Pork Chops, Orange, '84 81
Pork Chops, Orange-Cranberry, '86 335;
   '87 84
Pork Chops, Orange-Glazed, '81 234;
   '82 25; '83 39
Potatoes, Coconut-Orange Sweet, '84 252
Potatoes in Orange Cups, Sweet, '82 272
Potatoes, Orange-Glazed Sweet, '81 223;
   '83 280
Potatoes, Orange Sweet, '86 279
Potato-Stuffed Orange Cups,
   Sweet, '81 223
Prunes, Orange-Spiced, '85 224
Relish, Cranberry-Orange, '81 M289
Rice, Orange, '79 43; '81 175; '82 200
Roast, Orange Marinated Chuck, '85 179

Salads
   Ambrosia Supreme, Orange, '79 37
   Aspic, Orange-and-Carrot, '86 199
   Carrot Salad, Orange-, '80 89;
      '84 325
   Carrot-Tangerine Salad, '83 316;
      '84 16
   Cauliflower Salad, Orange-, '82 266
   Cherry-Orange Salad, '79 74; '82 56
   Chicken-and-Orange Salad,
      Curried, '87 144
   Chicken Salad, Persian, '81 12
   Congealed Salad, Pineapple-
      Orange, '83 218
   Cottage Cheese Salad,
      Orange-, '79 44
   Creamy Orange Salad, '84 124
   Cups, Citrus Salad in Orange, '85 47
   Cups, Orange, '86 92
   Cups, Orange Salad, '85 40
   Frosted Orange Salad, '81 154;
      '83 123
   Ham-and-Rice Salad,
      Mandarin, '87 145
   Jeweled Orange Salad, '83 210
   Jicama-Orange Salad, '86 83

Oranges, Salads *(continued)*

Lobster and Orange Salad, **'82** 207
Mandarin Chicken, Carousel, **'79** 88
Mandarin Orange and Pineapple
   Salad, **'82** 266
Mandarin Orange Salad, **'81** 252;
   '84 161
Mandarin Salad Molds, **'85** 54
Mandarin Spinach Salad, **'85** 163
Pear Salad, Orange-, **'84** 164
Quick Orange Salad, **'87** 80
Romaine Salad, Orange-, **'84** 325;
   '87 239
Sesame-Citrus Green Salad, **'86** 33
Sherbet Salad, Orange, **'81** 154
Shrimp-and-Orange Rice Salad,
   Zesty, **'87** 155
Shrimp Salad, Orange-, **'84** 197
Slaw, Cabbage-Orange, **'79** 135
Spinach-and-Orange Salad, **'86** 15
Spinach Salad, Orange-, **'83** 316;
   '84 16
Sunshine Delight, **'86** 117
Surprise Salad, Orange, **'79** 12
Walnut Salad, Orange, **'80** 246
Sauces and Glazes
Chocolate-Orange Sauce, **'86** 165
Coconut-Orange Sauce, **'85** 189
Dessert Sauce, Orange, **'86** 337;
   '87 58
Fresh Orange Sauce, **'85** 209
Honey-Orange Sauce, **'85** 108
Liqueur Sauce, Orange, **'86** 142
Mandarin Sauce, **'84** 60
Nutty Orange Glaze, **'80** 45
Orange Glaze, **'79** 2; **'80** 257; **'81** 34,
   107; **'82** 75, 206; **'83** 33, 114, 140,
   267; **'84** 161; **'86** 298
Orange Sauce, **'82** 47; **'83** 10, 277;
   '84 M286; **'86** 294
Pineapple Glaze, Orange-, **'81** 60
Pineapple-Orange Sauce, **'84** 14
Syrup, Orange, **'80** 228
Scampi, Orange, **'85** 303
Shake, Strawberry-Orange
   Breakfast, **'87** 186
Slices, Spicy Orange, **'81** 12
Snapper à l'Orange, Baked, **'85** 181
Soup, Carrot-Orange, **'79** 172
Spareribs, Orange-Glazed, **'84** 296
Spareribs with Orange Barbecue
   Sauce, **'83** 11
Spread, Orange Cheese, **'87** 292
Squash à l'Orange, **'85** 230
Turkey-Orange Skillet, Oriental, **'86** 284
Oysters
Bacon, Oysters in, **'83** 211
Baked Oysters, Bacon-, **'86** 132
Baked Oysters over Toast Points, **'84** 214
Bake, Oyster-and-Corn, **'83** 34; **'84** 44
Barbecued Oysters, **'82** 247
Bienville, Oysters, **'79** 182
Bisque, Oyster, **'83** 252
Brochette, Oysters, **'80** 56
Buccaneer, Oysters, **'87** 40
Casino on Cornbread, Oysters, **'79** 34
Casino, Oysters à la, **'80** 296
Casserole, Oyster, **'79** 228
Casserole, Oyster-and-Spinach, **'83** 34;
   '84 44
Casserole, Oyster-and-Wild Rice,
   '83 34; **'84** 44

Casserole, Wild Rice-Oyster, **'86** 256
Chowder, Oyster, **'83** 229
Chowder, Oyster-Corn, **'83** 211
Creamy Oysters and Crabmeat, **'83** 211
Crêpes, Virginia, **'79** 264
Dip, Smoked Oyster, **'79** 233
Dressed Oysters on the Half
   Shell, **'87** M79
Dressing, Oyster, **'79** 250
Dressing, Oyster Bread, **'82** 251
Fresh Oysters, Preparing, **'82** 127
Fried Oyster Bubbles, **'80** 296
Fried Oysters, **'85** 104
Fried Oysters, Delicious, **'83** 212
Fried Raw Oysters, **'81** 135; **'82** 14
Fritters, Oyster, **'79** 31
Fry, Hangtown, **'80** 297
Gino, Oysters à la, **'81** 126

Gumbo, Chicken and Oyster, **'81** 198
Gumbo, Duck, Oyster, and
   Sausage, **'79** 226
Gumbo, Seafood, **'83** 90; **'87** 210
Ham, Edwards' Oysters and, **'86** 253
Johnny Reb, Oysters, **'82** 42
Landmark, Oyster, **'84** 88
Loaves, Spinach-Oyster, **'84** 213
Mornay, Seafood, **'83** 67
Mousse, Oyster, **'81** 245
Mousse, Smoked Oyster, **'84** 320
Nachos, Texas Oyster, **'87** 39
Omelets, Smoked Oyster, **'84** 96
Patty Shells, Oysters in, **'83** 212; **'85** 257
Pie, Creole Oyster, **'84** 214
Pie, Turkey-and-Oyster, **'82** 267
Poor Boys, Oyster-and-Bacon, **'87** 40
Rockefeller, Southern Oysters, **'80** 212
Sandwich, Oyster Submarine, **'80** 92
Sautéed Oysters, **'86** 132
Sautéed Seafood Platter, **'83** 89
Scalloped Oysters, **'79** 225; **'84** 213;
   '86 132
Scalloped Oysters with Macaroni, **'80** 297
Shrimp Sauce, Oysters in, **'87** 40
Smoked Oysters, Deviled Eggs
   with, **'84** 161
Smoky Oysters Supreme, **'87** 60
Soup, Chicken, Ham, and Oyster, **'79** 198
Soup, Oyster, **'79** 228; **'83** 211
Soup, Oyster-and-Mushroom, **'87** 39
Soup, Oyster-Cheese, **'84** 213
Stew, Company Oyster, **'80** 297
Stew, Golden Oyster, **'86** 132
Stew, Holiday Oyster, **'85** 264
Stew, Oyster, **'80** 221
St. Jacques, Oysters, **'80** 103
Stuffing, Roast Turkey with
   Oyster, **'80** 251

P

Pancakes
Apple Pancakes with Cider Sauce,
   Spicy, **'87** 224
Applesauce Pancakes, **'79** 114
Apricot Delight, **'81** 42
Blueberry Buttermilk Pancakes, **'79** 114
Blueberry Pancakes, **'85** 152
Blueberry Pancakes, Sour Cream, **'81** 164
Buttermilk Griddle Cakes, **'81** 120; **'82** 22
Buttermilk Pancakes, **'83** 243; **'84** 101
Cornmeal Batter Cakes, **'87** 16
Cottage Cheese Pancakes, **'79** 115
Filled Pancake, Apple-, **'86** 96
Fluffy Pancakes, **'86** 137
Fruit Topping, Pancakes with, **'81** 42
Gingerbread Pancakes, **'84** 242
Island Pancakes, **'87** 225
Oatmeal Pancakes, **'80** 44
Orange-Yogurt Pancakes, **'87** 225
Pancakes, **'81** 90
Potato Pancake, **'85** 20
Potato Pancakes, **'79** 115
Potato Pancakes, Moist, **'80** 36
Potato Pancakes, Sweet, **'87** 280
Pumpkin Pancakes, **'80** 228
Quick Bread Mix, **'81** 90
Rice Pancakes, **'85** 147
Sauce, Peach-Blueberry Pancake, **'82** 177
Sausage Rollups, Pancake-, **'83** 246;
   '84 42
Sour Cream Pancakes, **'79** 213
Sour Cream Pancakes, Fluffy, **'79** 209
Strawberry Pancakes, **'84** 219
Supper Pancake, **'86** 242
Wheat Germ-Banana Pancakes, **'79** 114
Wheat Germ Pancakes, **'86** 242
Wheat Pancakes, Shredded, **'84** 59
Wheat Quick Pancakes, **'85** 278
Whole Wheat Pancakes, **'83** 18
Parsnips
Candied Parsnips, **'86** 224
Soufflé, Golden Parsnip, **'83** 266
Pastas. *See also* specific types.
Antipasto, Pasta, **'85** 286
Artichoke Hearts, Pasta with, **'86** 209
Bean-Salami Pasta Toss, Kidney, **'85** 165
Bites, Pesto-Cheese Pasta, **'87** 251
Broccoli and Sausage, Pasta with, **'87** 109
Broccoli Pasta, **'84** 176
Cannelloni, **'85** 60
Chicken-and-Broccoli Pasta, **'87** 286
Clam Sauce, Pasta with, **'84** 291
Crab Bake, Quick, **'87** 192
Dressing, Pasta Salad, **'86** 121
Frittata, Pasta, **'85** 286
Garden Pasta, **'82** 199
Green Pasta with Shrimp-Mushroom
   Italienne, **'79** 170
Mexican Luncheon, **'87** 192
Minestrone, **'82** 4
Oregano Pasta, **'84** 176
Pepperoni Pasta, **'83** 105
Pie, Spinach-Pasta, **'85** 286
Pimiento Pasta, **'84** 176
Primavera, Almost Pasta, **'86** 38
Primavera, Pasta, **'85** 86
Primavera, Tomato-Pasta, **'86** 209
Ravioli, Homemade, **'87** 230
Ravioli Pasta, Homemade, **'87** 231

Rotelle, Chicken and Tomato
  with, '87 108
Rotelle, Shrimp, '85 165
Rotini Romano, '87 193
Salad, Acini di Pepe, '83 163
Salad, Crabmeat-Shrimp Pasta, '86 208
Salad, Crunchy Pasta, '85 166
Salad, Crunchy Rotelle, '86 209
Salad, Garden Pasta, '86 188
Salad, Italian, '87 145
Salad, Main-Dish Pasta, '82 199
Salad, Overnight Pasta, '82 276
Salad, Pasta, '84 139; '86 120; '87 36
Salad, Pasta-and-Shrimp, '83 163
Salad, Pasta-Bean, '86 169
Salad, Pistachio-Pasta, '86 141
Salad, Salmon-Pasta, '87 9
Salad, Seashell, '86 209
Salad, Tarragon Pasta-Chicken, '87 155
Salad, Vermicelli Vinaigrette, '82 189
Salad, Ziti-Cheddar, '85 165
Salmon Carbonara, '83 43
Sauerkraut Salad, Crunchy, '87 9
Sausage and Mixed Vegetables, Pasta
  with, '84 249
Scallops and Pasta, Fresh, '83 164
Seafood Delight, '86 208
Seashell-Provolone Casserole, '80 189
Seashells Florentine, Jumbo, '79 6
Shells, Cheesy Beef-Stuffed, '83 217
Shells, Salmon Salad, '85 286
Shells, Spinach-Stuffed, '85 60; '87 20
Shrimp Elégante, '83 48
Shrimp Marinara, '84 233
Snappy Pasta, '83 164
Spinach-Mustard Twist, '86 209
Straw and Hay Pasta, '80 211
Tetrazzini, Chicken, '79 268
Tetrazzini, Ham, '82 M77
Tomato-Olive Pasta Toss, '86 209
Tortellini Salad, Chicken, '87 288
Toss, Pasta-Basil, '87 33
Vegetable Sauce, Pasta with, '83 163
Vegetables, Pasta and Garden, '87 192
Verde, Pasta, '84 201
Vermicelli, Anchovy-Garlic Sauce
  over, '86 158
Vermicelli and Sprouts with Red Clam
  Sauce, '86 143
Vermicelli, Lemon, '84 329
Vermicelli, Mushroom Sauce Supreme
  on, '86 158
Vermicelli, Scallop-Vegetable, '87 143
Vermicelli, Shrimp and Feta Cheese
  on, '87 108
Vermicelli with Clam Sauce, '85 295
Vermicelli with Mushrooms, '79 195
Vermicelli with Tomato Sauce, '83 164

Peaches
Ambrosia, Peach, '83 53
Baked Peaches and Sausage, '82 50
Baked Peaches, Spicy, '86 39
Baked Peaches with Ginger,
  Oven-, '82 170
Brandied Peaches with Mincemeat, '81 47
Brandy Peaches, '85 275
Bread, Georgia Peach, '79 161
Bread, Peach, '82 170
Butter, Peach, '82 308
Cake, Fresh Peach, '85 178
Cake, Peaches and Cream, '80 142
Cake, Peach Upside-Down, '87 8
Cake, Peachy Picnic, '79 178

Champagne, Peaches, '79 146
Charlotte, Peach, '79 68
Chicken Breasts, Peach-Stuffed, '79 177
Chicken Peach Dinner, '79 77
Chutney, Peach, '84 179
Cobbler, Fresh Peach, '82 139
Cobbler, Grenadine-Peach, '85 178
Cobbler, Lattice-Topped Peach, '79 154
Cobbler, No-Dough Blueberry-
  Peach, '86 177
Cobbler, Old-Fashioned Peach, '82 170
Cobbler, Peach, '83 175; '84 178
Cobbler, Peach-Caramel, '86 300; '87 178
Cobbler, Peachy Blueberry, '80 143
Cobbler, Quick Peach, '79 215; '81 142
Cobbler, Spicy Peach, '85 178
Cobbler Supreme, Peach, '81 184
Compote, Berry-Peach, '82 133
Conserve, Peach, '79 120
Cooler, Peach, '85 198; '86 6
Crabapple Peaches, Broiled Pork Chops
  with, '81 83
Cream, Bavarian Peach, '82 171
Cream, Peach Almond, '82 108
Cream, Peaches 'n' Almond, '86 229
Cream, Peachy-Apricot, '86 163
Crêpes, Fresh Peach, '84 186
Crêpes, Peach, '82 184
Crisp, Peach, '83 113

Crumble, Easy Peach, '83 116
Curried Ham and Peaches, '82 60
Custard Dessert, Fresh Peach, '86 162
Dessert, Peachy Melt-Away, '87 298
Dessert, Quick Peach, '85 178
Dip, Creole Peach, '80 142
Dumplings, Peach, '80 143; '85 177
Flambé, Banana-Peach, '85 316
Flambé, Peach Sundaes, '81 88
Flip, Peach, '79 217
Foster, Peaches, '86 240
Freeze, Creamy Peach, '82 144
Frost, Peach, '84 164
Frosty, Peach, '81 156; '83 318
Fuzz Buzz, '82 160
Ginger Peaches with Rum, '84 M323
Gingersnap Peaches, '85 M329
Ham Roast, Peachy, '86 118
Honey-Lime Whip, Peaches with, '85 108
Honey-Sweet Peaches, '85 107
Ice Cream, Creamy Peach, '85 177
Ice Cream, Deluxe Peach, '80 176
Ice Cream, Peach, '81 184; '82 171;
  '83 159; '86 15
Ice, Peach, '81 178

Ice, Peach-Yogurt, '84 83
Jam, Freezer Peach, '83 182; '84 M182
Jam, Peach-Plum Freezer, '85 130
Jam, Rosy Peach-Banana, '80 142
Marmalade, Peach-Orange, '82 150
Melba, Peach, '81 83; '83 M114
Meringues, Peach Melba, '87 76
Mincemeat Peaches, '85 178
Mold, Peachy Berry Cream, '83 130
Mousse, Peach, '85 54
Mousse, Peach Macaroon, '80 153
Muffins, Peachy-Almond, '86 301
Muffins, Special Peach, '84 74
Nest, Peaches in a Garden, '87 154
Parfait, Peach, '82 166
Pears, Peaches and, '85 106
Pickled Peaches, Perfect, '85 178
Pickles, Peach, '85 177
Pie, Fresh Peach, '82 170
Pie, Luscious Peach, '81 136
Pie, Mincemeat-Peach, '80 295; '81 188
Pie, Peach-Cranberry, '83 249
Pie, Peaches-and-Cream, '81 184
Pie, Rhubarb-Peach, '86 140
Pies, Delicious Fried, '83 84
Pies, Easy Peach Fried, '85 178
Pies, Fried Peach, '81 272
Pies, Little Peach, '86 303
Pork Steaks, Peachy, '79 166
Potatoes and Peaches, Sweet, '86 11
Preserves, Cream Cheese and
  Peach, '84 264
Preserves, Honeyed Peach, '85 130
Preserves, Old-Fashioned Peach, '82 150
Preserves, Peach, '81 147
Puffs, Peach Sweet Potato, '87 280
Refresher, Peach, '86 103
Relish, Peach, '85 136
Ring, Spicy Peach-Cranberry, '85 264
Salad, Frosted Peach, '82 145
Salad, Frozen Peach, '82 54
Salad, Georgia Peach, '80 142
Salad, Peaches-and-Cream, '83 108
Salad, Peach Party, '84 290
Salad, Peach Pinwheel, '79 11
Salad, Pickled Peach, '80 104; '85 264
Salad Supreme, Easy Peach, '79 177
Sauce, Creamy Fresh Peach, '79 177
Sauce, Creamy Peach, '85 189
Sauce, Fresh Peach, '87 167
Sauce, Peach, '84 144
Sauce, Peach-Berry, '87 M165
Sauce, Peach-Blueberry, '81 170
Sauce, Peach-Blueberry Pancake, '82 177
Sauce, Peach-Praline, '85 161
Shake, Peachy Orange, '81 156
Shake, Pep, '79 38
Slaw, Party Peach, '86 250
Soup, Peach, '83 120, 180
Soup, Peach-Plum, '87 157
Spareribs, Peach-Glazed, '86 14
Spiced Peach Dessert, '83 9
Spiced Peaches, Brandy, '80 142
Spiced Peaches, Ginger, '86 15
Spiced Peaches with Nutty
  Dumplings, '87 164
Split, Peach, '85 277
Spread, Peachy-Raisin, '86 326
Strawberry Sauce, Peaches with, '85 8
Stuffed Peaches, Macaroon-, '79 178
Stuffed Peach Halves, '86 196
Topping, Raspberry-Peach, '87 126
Wine Sauce, Peaches in, '79 184

Peanut Butter

Balls, Chocolate-Peanut Butter, '80 87
Balls, No-Cook Candy, '85 14
Balls, Peanut Butter-Chocolate, '80 269
Bars, Peanut Butter, '84 243
Bars, Peanut Butter-and-Fudge, '80 M172
Bars, Peanut Butter 'n' Jelly, '83 305
Bread, Peanut Butter, '86 171
Brownies, Chocolate Chip-Peanut Butter, '84 73
Brownies, Peanut Butter, '87 199
Cake, Chocolate-Peanut Butter, '84 240
Cake, Fudgy Peanut Butter, '85 91
Cake, Peanut Butter, '79 51; '83 M233
Cake, Peanut Butter-and-Jelly, '85 34
Cake, Peanut Butter-Banana, '80 87
Cake, Peanut Butter Swirl, '86 109
Cheese Ball, Peanut Butter-, '86 136
Chicken, Peanut Butter-Marmalade, '81 282; '82 30
Cones, Chocolate-Peanut Butter, '85 14
Cookies, Chocolate-Peanut Butter, '85 90
Cookies, Choco Surprise, '80 60
Cookies, Double Chip, '81 301
Cookies, Double Peanut Butter, '80 209
Cookies, Freezer Peanut Butter-Chocolate Chip, '86 230
Cookies, Miracle, '83 149
Cookies, Monster, '84 36
Cookies, Oatmeal-Peanut Butter, '85 171
Cookies, Peanut Butter, '82 56; '87 58
Cookies, Peanut Butter-Chocolate Kiss, '86 49
Cookies, Peanut Butter-Cinnamon, '84 30
Cookies, Peanut Butter-Coconut, '83 113
Cookies, Peanut Butter-Oatmeal, '81 218; '84 72
Cookies, Quick Peanut Butter, '86 109
Cooler, Peanut Butter, '84 115
Creams, Peanut Butter, '79 273
Crisps, Peanut Butter, '79 50
Cupcakes, Chocolate Surprise, '85 91
Cups, Chocolate-Peanut Butter, '85 14
Dip, Peanut Butter, '86 135
Dip, Peanut Butter-Honey, '85 19
Eggs, Peanut Butter Easter, '87 86
Fingers, Peanut Butter, '79 256

Frosting, Chocolate-Peanut Butter, '84 240; '87 222
Frosting, Creamy Peanut, '80 87
Frosting, Peanut Butter, '83 223; '84 153; '85 34
Frosting, Peanut Butter-Fudge, '87 184
Frosting, Peanut Butter Swirl, '86 109
Frosts, Peanut Butter, '84 153
Fudge, Chocolate-Peanut Butter, '87 257

Fudge, Double-Good, '79 M263
Fudge, Double Peanut, '85 91
Fudge, Peanut Butter, '80 302
Granola, Peanut Butter, '82 296
Ice Cream, Chocolate Chunk-Peanut Butter, '85 297; '86 120
Ice Cream, Peanut Butter, '81 103
Logs, No-Bake Peanut Butter, '84 211
Milkshakes, Peanut Butter, '85 198
Muffins, Peanut Butter, '80 86; '87 158
Muffins, Peanut Butter-Honey, '82 56
Parfaits, Crunchy Peanut Butter, '79 176; '80 6
Pie, Chocolate-Peanut Butter, '85 91
Pie, Chocolate-Peanut Butter Swirl, '87 262
Pie, Peanut Butter, '85 275; '86 109
Pie, Peanut Butter Cream, '79 50
Pie, Peanut Butter Meringue, '84 30
Pie, Tin Roof, '85 91
Pudding, Peanut Butter, '85 95
Sandwich, Peanut Butter Breakfast, '82 55
Sauce, Chocolate-Peanut Butter, '79 91, M156
Sauce, Peanut Butter Barbecue, '81 233
Sauce, Peanut Butter Ice Cream, '84 30
Shake, Peanut Butter, '82 48
Slice-and-Bakes, Peanut Butter, '82 M185
Snaps, Peanut Butter, '81 237
Soup, Cream of Peanut Butter, '84 29
Soup, Creamy Peanut, '79 50
Squares, Chocolate Chip-Peanut Butter, '84 118
Squares, Peanut Butter, '83 116
Squares, Peanut Butter-Chocolate Candy, '82 56
Temptations, Peanut Butter, '84 29
Tiger Butter, '86 48
Yummies, Peanut Butter, '83 223

Peanuts

Apples, Peanutty Stuffed, '85 25
Balls, Peanut-Date, '81 92
Bananas, Nutty, '79 251
Bars, Chewy Peanut, '80 M172
Bars, Fruit and Nut Granola, '81 49
Bread, Peanut, '87 184
Brittle, Golden Peanut, '83 223
Brittle, Never-Fail Peanut, '79 273
Brittle, Orange Peanut, '80 302
Brittle, Peanut, '79 M263; '80 87; '84 298
Brittle with Crushed Peanuts, '87 184
Cake, Chocolate-Caramel-Nut, '83 23
Cake, Chocolate-Peanut Cluster, '87 184
Cake, Super Peanutty Layer, '83 222
Candied Popcorn and Peanuts, '82 295
Chicken with Peanuts, Oriental, '82 236
Chili Nuts, Hot, '81 254
Clusters, Chocolate-Peanut, '81 16
Clusters, Nut, '81 254
Clusters, Peanut, '87 184
Clusters, Peanutty, '83 143
Cookies, Chocolate-Peanut, '83 223
Cookies, Peanutty Oatmeal, '80 106; '83 95
Cookies, Salted Peanut, '87 92
Crust, Peanut-Graham Cracker, '79 50
Dessert, Peanut-Chocolate, '80 86
Divinity, Peanut, '85 233; '87 M278
Dressing, Roast Turkey with Peanut, '79 283
Frosting, Creamy Peanut, '80 87
Fudge, Double Peanut, '85 91
Pie, Caramel-Peanut, '86 259

Pie, Peanut Raisin, '79 85
Pie, Peanutty Ice Cream, '82 56
Puff Nibbles, '84 191
Salad, Green Bean-Peanut, '86 117
Salad, Nutty Cabbage, '87 42
Salad, Nutty Green, '87 168
Salad, Peanut-Apple, '80 5
Sauce, Peanut Dessert, '86 M251
Sauce, Peanut Hot, '86 305
Sauce, Pork Chops with Peanut, '83 29
Slaw, Banana-Nut, '86 250
Slaw, Peanut, '85 139
Slaw, Peanutty-Pear, '86 250
Snack, Toasted Cereal, '85 215
Soup, Chilled Peanut, '79 130
Soup, Creamy Peanut, '79 50
Soup, Peanut, '87 184
Spicy Nuts, '82 161
Squares, Caramel-Peanut, '85 247
Sugared Peanuts, '82 249

Pears

Belle Helene, Pears, '86 164
Bread, Pear, '80 218
Breakfast Pears, Marmalade, '83 M203
Breakfast Treat, Pear, '87 72
Butter, Pear, '85 130
Butter, Spiced Pear, '80 218
Cake, Pear Preserve, '85 52
Cake, Upside-Down Sunburst, '87 9
Cake with Caramel Drizzle, Pear, '86 247
Casserole, Pear-Sweet Potato, '86 280
Cheesecake, Pear-Berry, '82 141
Cheesecake, Pear-Glazed, '79 67
Cobbler, Best Ever Pear, '82 194
Coconut Pears, Spicy, '83 207
Cookies, Pear Mincemeat, '84 264
Cream, Pears in Orange, '84 245
Crisp, Cranberry-Pear, '83 207
Crumble, Pear, '85 221
Delight, Pineapple-Pear, '82 54
Dressing, Pear, '83 146
Filled Pears, Cheese-, '81 268
Flaming Pears, '84 313
Fritters, Ol' Timey Pear, '86 51
Glazed Pears, Orange-, '79 247
Jam, Paradise Pear, '84 300
Marmalade, Pear, '79 196
Meringues, Baked Pear, '85 232
Mincemeat, Pear, '79 196; '84 264
Peaches and Pears, '85 106
Pickles, Mustard Pear, '79 196
Pie, Apple-Pear, '83 249
Pie, Deep-Dish Pear, '80 219
Pie, Double-Crust Pear, '82 194
Pie, French Pear, '87 213
Pie, Pear Crumble, '83 207

Pie, Pear-Mince, '81 271
Pie, Pear Mincemeat, '84 264
Pie, Pear Streusel, '83 234; '84 244
Pie, Tennessee Pear, '85 230
Pineapple-Honey Pears, '86 94
Poached in Red Wine, Pears, '83 302
Poached Pears Flambé, Orange-, '85 313
Poached Pears in Orange Sauce, '82 19
Poached Pears in Wine, '82 194
Poached Pears, Lemon, '82 74
Poached Pears, Orange, '80 218
Poached Pears with Berry Sauce,
    Wine-, '86 144
Poached Pears with Raspberry
    Sauce, '84 213; '87 69
Preserves, Pear, '82 195
Relish, Cranberry-Pear, '85 232
Relish, Pear, '79 196
Ruby Pears, '81 288
Salad, Blue Cheese-Pear-Apple, '81 224
Salad, Crunchy Pear, '83 234; '84 244
Salad, Festive Fruit, '80 16
Salad, Festive Pear-and-Spinach, '85 131
Salad, Orange-Pear, '84 164
Salad, Pear-and-Celery, '87 56
Salad, Pear-Lime, '84 152
Salad, Royal Pear, '84 265
Slaw, Peanutty-Pear, '86 250
Stuffed Pears, Almond-, '83 207
Stuffed with Cheese, Pears, '82 290
Sugared Pears, Maple-, '81 232
Sundaes, Quick Pear, '86 71
Tart, Pear, '82 304
Wild Rice, Cranberry-Pear, '83 279
Wine, Pears in Red, '82 254
Peas
Baked Peas, Chinese-Style, '86 305
Black-Eyed
    Casserole, Reunion Pea, '87 11
    Caviar, Texas, '86 218
    Creole Black-Eyed Peas, '86 252
    Creole Black-Eyes and Rice, '85 6
    Delight, Tomato-Pea, '84 196
    Dinner, Black-Eyed Pea Skillet, '86 6
    Dip, Black-Eyed Pea, '81 8
    Flips, Pea, '80 7
    Fresh Black-Eyed Peas, '81 M165
    Gravy, Black-Eyed Pea, '87 12
    Ham Hocks, Black-Eyed Peas
        with, '79 122

Hearty Black-Eyed Peas, '85 7
Hopping Good Peas, '80 7
Hopping John, '80 7
Hopping John, Skillet, '79 10
Hopping John with Ham, '81 7
Jambalaya, Good Luck, '87 11
Marinated Black-Eyed Peas, '82 156
Mexican Black-Eyed Peas, '84 327
Mexicano, Black-Eyed Peas, '79 10
Pickled Black-Eyed Peas, '79 10
Pinwheels, Black-Eyed Pea, '85 300;
    '86 18

Rice, Black-Eyed Peas with, '83 12
Salad, Black-Eyed Pea, '80 112;
    '86 225
Salad, Hot Bacon and
    Black-Eyed, '85 7
Salad, Mexi-Pea, '81 7
Salad, Overnight Black-Eyed
    Pea, '81 280
Salad, Plentiful P's, '87 12
Sausage, Black-Eyed Peas with, '86 7
Seasoned Black-Eyed Peas, '85 138
Soup, Beefy Black-Eyed, '85 6
Southern-Style Black-Eyed
    Peas, '82 107
South-of-the-Border Black-Eyed
    Peas, '86 7
Spaghetti, Black-Eyed Pea, '81 7
Special, Black-Eyed Pea, '86 7
Spicy Black-Eyed Peas,
    Hot-and-, '84 9
Spicy Hot Black-Eyed Peas, '81 8
Spread, Black-Eyed Pea, '86 77
Sweet-and-Sour Black-Eyed
    Peas, '85 290
Vinaigrette, Black-Eyed Pea, '86 7
Casserole, Curry Pea, '87 154
English
    Baked Tuna and Peas in Wine
        Sauce, '83 196
    Braised Rice and Peas, '79 101
    Broil, Tomato-English Pea, '83 192
    Buttered Peas and
        Mushrooms, '82 204
    Buttered Peas with Onions, '80 242
    Casserole, Asparagus-and-English
        Pea, '86 324
    Casserole, Asparagus and
        Peas, '80 152
    Casserole, Cauliflower-Pea, '85 260
    Casserole, Cheesy English
        Pea, '83 216
    Casserole, English
        Pea-Pimiento, '83 207
    Casserole, Quick Fresh English
        Pea, '84 145
    Casserole Supreme, Pea, '82 281;
        '83 32
    Cauliflower and Peas with Curried
        Almonds, '79 221; '80 82
    Cauliflower, Peas and, '82 288
    Celery, Deluxe Peas and, '81 267
    Continental, Peas, '84 254
    Country-Style Peas, '80 101
    Country Style, Peas, '81 101
    Creamed Peas and New
        Potatoes, '79 102
    Creole Peas, Quick, '84 123
    Deluxe English Peas, '84 68
    Deviled Peas in Toast Cups, '86 280
    Dumplings, Green Peas and, '80 102
    Glazed English Peas, '83 111
    Italian Peas, '81 83
    Lettuce Peas, French, '86 62
    Medley, English Pea, '85 236
    Medley, Spring Pea, '83 141
    Minted Peas, '83 141; '87 56
    Mushrooms, Creamy Peas
        with, '84 196
    Mushrooms, Green Peas
        with, '80 101
    Mushrooms, Peas and, '83 141
    Onions Stuffed with Peas, '84 68
    Party Peas, '79 102

Pignoli, Peas, '83 190
Potato Nest, Peas in a, '84 M239
Rice, Holiday Peas and, '86 328
Rice with Green Peas, '87 45
Salad, Cauliflower-Pea, '87 231
Salad, Cheddar-Pea, '84 82
Salad, Chicken-Pea, '83 218
Salad, Creamy Pea, '80 111
Salad, English Pea, '81 280
Salad, English Pea-and-Apple, '87 24
Salad, Marinated English Pea, '82 54
Salad, Marinated Pea, '81 204
Salad, Peas-and-Asparagus, '83 141
Salad, Rice-Pea, '85 163
Salad, Savory Cauliflower and
    Pea, '81 280
Salad, Special Pea, '83 239
Sauce, Green Pea, '83 22
Scallions, Peas and, '80 101
Sherry, Peas with, '80 102
Soup, Chilled Pea, '84 181
Soup Élégante, Pea, '79 53
Soup, Fresh Pea, '86 181
Soup, Peppery Pea, '82 271
Ham, Southern Peas and, '85 138
Medley, Peas-and-Corn, '85 138
Salad, Three Pea, '84 290

Snow
    Appetizers, Sugar Snap Pea, '86 115
    Beef and Snow Peas,
        Oriental, '79 105
    Beef with Pea Pods,
        Oriental, '86 M328
    Chicken with Snow Peas, '83 137
    Chinese Peas, Easy, '83 206
    Crunchy Snow Peas and Dip, '86 62
    Dip, Sugar Peas with, '86 170
    en Papillote, Fish with Snow
        Peas, '86 144
    Medley, Cauliflower-Snow
        Pea, '87 305
    Piquant, Snow Peas, '79 21
    Salad, Sugar Snap Pea, '86 115
    Sesame Snow Peas and Red
        Pepper, '84 175
    Shrimp Combo, Snow Pea-, '79 57
    Shrimp with Snow Peas, '85 75
    Skillet Snow Peas with
        Celery, '84 123
    Stir-Fried Peas and Peppers, '87 51
    Stir-Fry, Beef and Pea, '82 98
    Stir-Fry Beef and Pea Pods, '80 19
    Stir-Fry, Beef and Snow Pea, '82 98
    Stir-Fry Beef and Snow Peas, '83 22
    Stir-Fry, Potato-Snow Pea, '86 173
    Stuffed Snow Peas, '84 80
    Stuffed Snow Peas, Crab-, '85 288
    Tomatoes, Snow Peas and, '83 111
    Vegetable Medley, Spring, '86 115
Soup, Country-Style Pea, '86 267
Soup, Split Pea and Frankfurter, '79 64

Pecans

Apples, Orange-Pecan Baked, **'85** 45
Ball, Deviled Pecan, **'80** 258
Ball, Party Pecan Cheese, **'81** 235
Ball, Pecan Cheese, **'83** 127
Balls, Date-Nut, **'85** 10
Ball, Tuna-Pecan, **'87** 94
Barbecued Pecans, **'83** 222
Bars, Pecan, **'82** 209
Bites, Cheesy Pecan, **'82** 248
Bread, Apple-Nut, **'85** 281
Bread, Applesauce Nut, **'81** 305
Bread, Banana-Nut, **'86** 8, 70
Bread, Banana-Nut-Raisin, **'81** 59
Bread, Cheddar-Nut, **'85** 41
Bread, Cherry Nut, **'81** 306; **'82** 36
Bread, Chocolate Date-Nut, **'81** 284
Bread, Glazed Orange-Pecan, **'81** 250
Bread, Kahlúa Fruit-Nut, **'79** 235
Bread, Lemon-Pecan, **'83** 54
Bread, Maraschino Cherry Nut, **'79** 234
Bread, Orange-Nut, **'82** 75
Bread, Orange-Pecan, **'79** 148
Bread, Persimmon Date-Nut, **'82** 218
Bread, Pineapple-Nut, **'79** 215
Bread, Pineapple-Pecan Loaf, **'87** 256
Bread, Prune-Nut, **'87** 255
Bread, Pumpkin-Nut, **'83** 294
Bread, Pumpkin-Pecan, **'87** 221
Bread, Quick Cherry-Nut, **'85** 55
Bread, Strawberry-Nut, **'79** 24
Bread, Wine-Date Nut, **'82** 253
Brittle, Chocolate, **'83** 315
Broccoli with Lemon Sauce and
  Pecans, **'86** 71
Brownies, Chocolate-Pecan, **'81** 64
Brownies, Nutty Blonde, **'81** 64
Brownies, Nutty Cocoa, **'81** 64
Brownies, Nutty Fudge, **'80** M171
Buns, Nutty, **'86** 290
Butter, Orange-Pecan, **'84** 75
Cake, Apple-Pecan Coffee, **'84** 242
Cake, Bourbon-Pecan, **'84** 25
Cake, Butter Pecan, **'80** 229
Cake, Cinnamon-Pecan Coffee, **'87** 69
Cake, Date Nut, **'79** 176; **'80** 5
Cake, Kentucky Pecan, **'84** 263
Cake, Orange Nut, **'80** 70
Cake, Orange-Nut Butter, **'80** 254
Cake, Orange-Pecan Coffee, **'86** 86
Cake, Orange-Pecan Crunch, **'83** 10
Cake, Pecan-Topped Coffee, **'81** 41
Cake, Pineapple-Pecan
  Upside-Down, **'84** 25
Cake, Praline Pound, **'82** 88
Cake, Rich Chocolate-Nut, **'86** 8
Cake with Praline Glaze, Pecan,
  '82 196
Candied Nuts, **'81** 261
Candy, Chocolate-Nut Log, **'86** 335
Carrots and Celery with Pecans,
  '84 254
Catfish Pecan, **'85** 53
Cheesecake, Butter Pecan, **'86** 61
Cheesecake, Pecan, **'85** 38
Chews, Chocolate-Nut, **'81** 92
Chicken, Nutty Oven-Fried, **'85** 160
Chicken, Oven-Fried Pecan, **'84** 288
Chicken, Sweet-and-Sour, **'79** 106
Clusters, Pecan, **'81** 266
Clusters, Pecan-Coconut, **'86** M251
Clusters, Roasted Pecan, **'85** 233
Cobbler, Apple-Pecan, **'84** M198

Cookies, Butter Pecan, **'82** 139
Cookies, Butter Pecan
  Shortbread, **'80** 282
Cookies, Butterscotch-Pecan, **'84** 36
Cookies, Cherry Pecan, **'82** 136
Cookies, Easy Pecan, **'80** 208
Cookies, Nutty Oatmeal, **'81** 130
Cookies, Nutty Oatmeal-Chocolate
  Chip, **'82** 185
Cookies, Pecan-Butter, **'83** 113
Cookies, Pecan Crescent, **'85** 324
Crispies, Oatmeal Nut, **'80** 208
Crispies, Pecan-Cheese, **'87** 168
Crisps, Sugar Pecan, **'86** 230
Crunch, Apple-Nut, **'82** M238
Crust, Pecan, **'86** 317
Crust, Spiced Nut, **'87** 295
Cupcakes, Apple-Nut, **'82** 279
Dainties, Lemon Pecan, **'80** 208
Dessert, Maple Nut, **'81** 84
Dressing, Chicken with
  Pecan-Rice, **'85** M57
Dressing, Fruit-and-Pecan, **'84** 252
Dressing, Pecan-Sage, **'80** 262
Dressing, Watermelon Salad with
  Celery-Nut, **'80** 182
Dumplings, Spiced Peaches with
  Nutty, **'87** 164
Eggs, Pecan-Stuffed, **'80** 78
Fettuccine, Chicken-Pecan, **'86** 52
Filling, Fruit-Nut, **'80** 289
Fritters, Chocolate-Covered
  Pecan, **'79** 205
Frosting, Banana-Nut, **'79** 115
Frosting, Butter Pecan, **'80** 229
Frosting, Chocolate Nut, **'80** 140
Frosting, Coconut-Pecan, **'81** 296;
  '83 M233; **'84** 43, 322
Frosting, Nutty Coconut, **'86** 8
Frosting, Nutty Cream Cheese, **'85** 117
Frosting, Pecan, **'86** 86
Fudge, Cherry Nut, **'83** 315
Fudge, Creamy Pecan, **'84** 321
Fudge, Nutty White, **'81** 253
Fudge, Quick Nut, **'83** 316
Glazed Pecans, **'81** 254; **'82** 136
Glaze, Honey-Nut, **'87** 15
Goose, Fruit- and Pecan-Stuffed, **'83** 268
Honeycomb Pecans, **'84** 300
Hot Pepper Pecans, **'85** 4
Ice Cream, Butter Pecan, **'80** 176;
  '86 129
Ice Cream, Cherry-Nut, **'86** 129

Loaves, Orange-Pecan, **'79** 215
Log, Chicken-Pecan, **'81** 290
Log, Toasted Pecan Cheese, **'86** M288
Maple-Nut Coffee Twist, **'86** 290
Muffins, Cinnamon-Nut, **'85** M88
Muffins, Cinnamon-Pecan, **'84** 219
Muffins, Country Pecan, **'83** 222
Muffins, Cranberry-Pecan, **'84** 269
Muffins, Nutty Pumpkin, **'86** 291
Muffins, Orange-Pecan, **'83** 96
Muffins, Pecan, **'80** 16
Mushrooms, Pecan-Stuffed, **'84** 261
Nuggets, Cherry Nut, **'81** 286
Orange Nuts, Sherry-, **'85** M289
Orange Pecans, **'84** 299; **'87** 292
Pepper Pecans, **'87** 137
Pie, Bourbon-Pecan, **'85** 90
Pie, Bourbon-Pecan Pumpkin, **'87** 264
Pie, Caramel-Pecan Apple, **'85** 247
Pie, Chocolate Pecan, **'80** 237; **'83** 12
Pie, Choco-Pecan, **'82** 86
Pie, Coconut Pecan, **'81** 161
Pie, Coconut-Pecan Chess, **'81** 248
Pie, Coffee Pecan, **'82** 74
Pie, Custard Pecan, **'87** 184
Pie, Date-Pecan, **'80** 15
Pie, Golden Pecan, **'81** 266
Pie, Grandmother's Pecan, **'86** 269
Pie, Holiday Pecan, **'81** 296
Pie, Layered Pecan, **'83** 305
Pie, Maple-Pecan, **'81** 266
Pie, Molasses-Pecan, **'86** 259
Pie, Nutty Cranberry, **'82** 298
Pie, Nutty Pumpkin, **'82** 67
Pie, Old-Fashioned Pecan, **'81** M269
Pie, Orange-Pecan, **'79** 282; **'83** 222
Pie, Pecan, **'79** 251; **'80** 57; **'85** 255
Pie, Pumpkin-Pecan, **'85** 233, 282
Pie, Raisin-Pecan, **'87** 213
Pies, Individual Pecan, **'85** 295
Pies, Miniature Pecan, **'79** 205; **'86** 13
Pie, Spicy Pecan, **'84** 240
Pies, Tiny Pecan, **'79** 225
Pie, Sweet Potato-Pecan, **'83** 90
Pie, Texas Pecan, **'83** 159
Popovers, Giant Pecan, **'83** 208
Praline Cheesecake, **'83** 270
Praline Clusters, Dark, **'86** 313
Praline Delights, Spicy, **'84** 299
Praline Fruit Compote, Warm, **'85** 260
Praline Glaze, **'82** 196
Praline Ham, **'85** 302
Praline Ice Cream Cake, **'80** 84
Praline Ice Cream Sauce, **'85** 189
Praline Ice Cream Sauce,
  Southern, **'86** M227
Praline Pie, Chocolate-, **'86** 259
Praline Pound Cake, **'82** 88
Pralines, **'79** 272; **'86** M288
Pralines and Cream Ice Cream, **'82** 184;
  '83 159
Praline Sauce, **'83** 25; **'84** 143
Praline Sauce, Bourbon, **'81** 170
Praline Sauce, Chocolate-, **'85** M295
Praline Sauce, Peach-, **'85** 161
Pralines, Butterscotch, **'81** 253
Pralines, Creamy, **'80** 198
Pralines, Dark, **'83** 52
Pralines, Maple-Pecan, **'83** 222
Pralines, New Orleans-Style, **'86** 335
Pralines, Original Pecan, **'81** 11
Pralines, Plantation Coffee, **'86** 241
Pralines, Southern, **'79** M263

Ice Cream, Straw-Ba-Nut, **'80** 177
Loaf, Date-Nut, **'85** 10
Loaf, Orange Nut, **'80** 226
Loaf, Tasty Apricot-Nut, **'82** 10

Pralines, Texas-Size, '79 186
Praline Toast, Orange, '79 36
Pudding, Brown Sugar-Pecan, '86 M165
Pudding, with Hot Rum Sauce,
  Apple-Nut, '79 86
Rice, Nutted, '85 269
Rice, Pecan, '85 53
Roll, Banana-Nut, '85 112
Roll, Date Nut, '79 249
Rolls, Buttered Rum-Nut, '86 291
Rolls, Caramel-Nut, '86 312
Rolls, Pecan, '79 285; '81 62
Roulade, Pecan, '87 183
Salad, Apple-Nut, '80 226
Salad, Beet-Nut, '79 74
Salad, Cantaloupe-Pecan, '86 178
Salad, Creamy Carrot-Nut, '86 331
Salted Pecans, Southern, '80 285
Sauce, Butterscotch-Pecan, '82 212
Sauce, Date-Nut Sundae, '82 167
Sauce, Éclairs with Pecan, '83 219
Sauce, Pecan, '83 219
Spiced Pecans, '79 296; '80 31; '81 286
Spicy Curried Nuts, '82 250
Spicy Pecans, '81 M289
Spread, Honey-Nut, '87 157
Squares, Butter Pecan Pie, '81 262
Squares, Easy Pecan, '79 292; '81 230
Squares, Pecan, '79 205
Squares, Twice-Baked Pecan, '79 291
Squash with Molasses and Pecans,
  Acorn, '85 205
Stuffing, Pecan, '79 292; '80 32
Stuffing, Wild Duck with Pecan, '85 269
Sugar-and-Honey Pecans, '86 319

Sugar and Spice Pecans, '82 297
Sugar-and-Spice Pecans, '86 121
Sugared Pecans, '82 167
Sugar Pecans, Brown, '81 266
Sugarplums, Pecan Shortbread, '83 298
Syrup, Chunky Pecan, '85 278
Syrup, Maple-Nut, '80 228
Tarts, Apple-Pecan, '80 282
Tarts, Easy Pecan, '84 313
Tarts, Pecan, '81 266
Tarts, Special Pecan, '87 224
Tassies, Teatime, '84 321
Toasted Chili Pecans, '85 154
Toasted Pecans, '84 321; '86 229
Toffee, Nutty, '79 M263
Topping, Cinnamon-Pecan, '85 277
Topping, Nutty, '85 256
Torte, Carob-Pecan, '85 218
Torte, Heavenly Pecan, '81 266
Torte, Mocha-Pecan, '86 26
Wafers, Pecan-Cheese, '81 119
Waffles, Pecan, '87 225
Waffles, Pumpkin-Nut, '86 96

Waffles, Southern Chicken-Pecan, '82 231
Zucchini with Pecans, '87 31
Peppermint
Bavarian, Peppermint, '80 153
Dessert, Peppermint Wafer, '79 176;
  '80 7
Filling, Peppermint, '81 119
Flip, Hot Peppermint, '86 329
Ice Cream, Peppermint, '80 176; '86 129
Mints, Party, '79 273; '81 119
Mousse, Peppermint Candy, '82 71
Patties, Peppermint, '86 278
Pie, Peppermint Candy-Ice
  Cream, '87 260
Soufflé, Chocolate Mint, '81 16
Squares, Chocolate-Peppermint, '81 119
Twists, Mint, '86 106
Wreaths, Melt-Away Peppermint, '85 324
Peppers
Chicken Scaloppine with Peppers, '85 78
Chile
  Casserole, Chile-Cheese, '82 90
  Casserole, Chiles Rellenos, '79 84;
    '84 31, 234
  Casserole, Chili-Rice, '79 54
  Casserole, Green
    Chile-and-Fish, '84 32
  Casserole, Mexican Rice, '83 31
  Chimichangas (Fried
    Burritos), '81 196; '85 244
  con Queso, Chile, '80 194
  con Queso Supreme, Chile, '80 265
  Cream, Ancho Chile, '87 121
  Dip, Cheese-and-Chile, '83 31
  Dip, Hot Chile, '82 248
  Dip, Hot Chile-Beef, '83 218
  Egg Rolls, Chiles Rellenos, '86 296
  Enchiladas, Green Chile-Sour
    Cream, '84 234
  Enchiladas, New Mexican
    Flat, '85 245
  Pie, Green Chile-Cheese, '84 234
  Powder, Red Chile, '85 245
  Quiche, Chile Pepper, '82 224
  Quiche, Green Chile, '83 31
  Quiche, Shrimp, '83 50
  Rellenos, Chiles (Stuffed
    Chiles), '82 220; '83 150
  Rice and Green Chiles, '83 152
  Rice, Chili-Cheesy, '79 43
  Sauce, Ancho Chile, '87 122
  Sauce, Green Chile, '82 220
  Sauce, Red Chile, '85 245
  Sauce, Red Chile Enchilada, '85 245
  Squash, Chile, '84 77
  Squash, Mexican, '83 31
  Squash with Green Chiles,
    Stuffed, '83 148
  Tamales, Hot, '83 51
  Tamales, Sweet, '83 52
Green
  Beef and Green Peppers, '79 104
  Beefed-Up Peppers, '82 186
  Bread, Pepper, '85 156
  Casserole, Peppered Pork
    Chop, '82 25
  Chicken Peppers, Devilish, '80 65
  Cups, Potato Salad in Pepper, '79 78
  Deluxe, Peppers, '81 159
  Dressing, Green Pepper-Onion
    Salad, '84 12
  Fried Pepper Strips, '82 208
  Jelly, Pepper, '79 121

Jelly, Unusual Green Pepper, '82 132
Mexican Green Peppers, '80 65
Muffins, Cheese-and-Pepper, '84 139
Pizza Peppers, '83 135
Potato Salad 'n' Peppers, '83 135
Ratatouille, '85 92
Relish, Pepper, '83 183
Relish, Pepper-Onion, '84 180
Salad, Ruby-and-Emerald, '85 79
Sauce, Pepper-Onion, '84 125
Sausage and Peppers, Italian, '84 9
Sautéed Onions and Peppers,
  '83 M148
Sauté, Tomato-Pepper, '84 142
Stacks, Pepper-Cheese, '87 80
Steak and Rice, Pepper, '81 17
Steak, Pepper, '81 273; '85 57
Steak, Pepper-Beef, '85 21
Stir-Fry Steak, Pepper, '81 240
Stuffed Green Peppers, Beefy, '81 86
Stuffed Green Peppers, Ham-, '80 65
Stuffed Pepper Medley, '82 131
Stuffed Peppers, '81 239; '83 66;
  '84 202
Stuffed Peppers, Beef-, '84 154;
  '85 146
Stuffed Peppers, Corn-, '84 104
Stuffed Peppers, Curried
  Chicken-, '87 19
Stuffed Peppers for Two, '80 84
Stuffed Peppers, Ham-and-
  Corn, '81 87
Stuffed Peppers, Macaroni-and-
  Cheese-, '80 65
Stuffed Peppers, Rice-, '80 65
Stuffed Peppers, Shrimp-, '80 162;
  '86 131, 197
Stuffed Peppers, Spinach-, '82 180
Stuffed Peppers with Rice and
  Ham, '82 131
Stuffed with Beef, Peppers, '84 72
Taco Peppers, '81 86
Veal and Peppers, Spaghetti
  with, '81 201; '82 14
Jalapeño
  Bread, Jalapeño Pepper, '83 121
  Casserole, Jalapeño Corn, '83 256
  Casserole, Jalapeño Rice, '81 66
  Celery, Jalapeño Stuffed, '79 70
  Cheese, Shrimp with Herbed
    Jalapeño, '87 112
  Cheesy, Jalapeño Peppers, '80 195
  Cornbread, Beefy Jalapeño, '82 142
  Cornbread, Cheddar-Jalapeño, '85 3
  Cornbread, Jalapeño, '85 200
  Grits, Jalapeño Cheese, '85 43
  Hominy, Jalapeño, '82 51
  Loaf, Jalapeño-Cheese, '84 76
  Potatoes, Jalapeño, '84 39
  Potatoes, Jalapeño-Ham
    Stuffed, '81 M61
  Quiche, Cheesy Jalapeño, '84 31
  Quiche, Jalapeño-Corn, '85 122
  Quiche Squares, Cheesy Hot,
    '79 124
  Rice, Jalapeño, '79 43
  Rice, Jalapeño Hot, '80 126
  Salsa Picante, '84 108
  Salsa Picante, Homemade, '81 67
  Sauce, Jalapeño, '80 193
  Sauce, San Antonio Hot, '84 291
  Spread, Jalapeño-Cheese, '82 248
  Squares, Jalapeño Cheese, '80 195

Peppers *(continued)*

Okra, Corn, and Peppers, **'87** M151
Red Pepper Salad, Broccoli and, **'83** 224
Red Pepper, Sesame Snow Peas
  and, **'84** 175
Red Peppers, Potatoes with Sweet,
  '87 192
Roasted Peppers, Marinated, **'87** 90
Salad, Mushroom-and-Pepper, **'86** 68
Stir-Fried Peas and Peppers, **'87** 51
Strips, Green Beans and Pepper, **'86** 170
Toss, Crisp Squash-and-Pepper, **'87** M152

Persimmons

Bread, Persimmon, **'80** 228
Bread, Persimmon Date-Nut, **'82** 218
Cake, Persimmon, **'79** 205
Cookies, Persimmon-Raisin, **'85** 232
Pie, Persimmon, **'79** 206
Pudding, Persimmon, **'79** 206
Salad, Persimmon Fruit, **'79** 206

Pheasants

Muscatel, Pheasant, **'85** 269
Port Wine Sauce, Pheasants with, **'84** 252

Pickles and Relishes

Antipasto Relish, **'86** 327
Apple Relish, Spicy, **'84** M323
Asparagus, Pickled, **'83** 46
Avocado Relish, **'87** 120
Beet Pickles, **'81** 210
Beet Relish, **'84** 179
Beet Relish, Colorful, **'85** 136
Beets, Easy Pickled, **'80** 137
Beets, Pickled, **'81** 216
Black Bean-Tomatillo Relish, **'87** 121
Broccoli, Pickled, **'81** 308
Cabbage Relish, **'83** 260
Chow Chow, **'82** 196
Chowchow, **'87** 150
Chutney
    Commander's Chutney, **'87** 245
    Cranberry-Amaretto Chutney with
      Cream Cheese, **'87** 244
    Cranberry Chutney, **'80** 243;
      '83 260; **'84** 265
    Cranberry-Orange Chutney, **'79** 292
    Orange-Cranberry Chutney, **'86** 266
    Pâté, Chutney-Cheese, **'84** 152
    Peach Chutney, **'84** 179
    Plum Chutney, **'84** 179
    Rhubarb Chutney, **'87** 245
    Roll, Chutney, **'83** 259
    Rosy Chutney, **'80** 120
    Tomato-Apple Chutney, **'84** 180

Corn Relish, **'81** 129, 175; **'83** 189;
  '84 107; **'85** 136; **'87** 120, 245
Corn Relish, Easy, **'83** 260
Corn Relish, Virginia, **'79** 283
Cran-Apple Relish, **'84** 300
Cranberry Conserve, **'79** 243
Cranberry-Nut Relish, **'86** 275
Cranberry-Orange Relish, **'81** M289
Cranberry-Pear Relish, **'85** 232
Cranberry Relish, **'81** 275; **'83** 144;
  '85 258; **'86** 283; **'87** 245
Cranberry Relish, Lemony, **'79** 243
Cranberry Relish, Old-Fashioned, **'82** 297
Cucumber Chips, **'85** 176
Cucumber Pickles, Sour, **'85** 176
Cucumber Relish, **'85** 176
Cucumber Sandwich Pickles, **'81** 174
Dill Pickles, **'81** 174
Dill Pickles, Fried, **'84** 206
Dills, Lazy Wife, **'87** 149
Eggs, Beet Pickled, **'84** 287
Eggs, Spiced Pickled, **'84** 288
Figs, Pickled, **'79** 140
Garden Relish, **'83** 259
Garden Relish, End-of-the-, **'80** 179
Icicle Pickles, Sweet, **'85** 176
India Relish, **'84** 179
Mixed Pickles, **'81** 174
Okra Pickles, **'81** 173
Onion Relish, Green, **'84** 65
Onion Rings, Pickled
  Refrigerator, **'84** 265
Orange Slices, Spicy, **'81** 12
Peaches, Perfect Pickled, **'85** 178
Peach Pickles, **'85** 177
Peach Relish, **'85** 136
Pear Pickles, Mustard, **'79** 196
Pear Relish, **'79** 196
Pepper-Onion Relish, **'84** 180
Pepper Relish, **'83** 183
Pineapple, Pickled, **'79** 24
Problem Chart, Pickle, **'85** 176
Salad, Relish, **'84** 121
Salsa, **'80** 196
Salsa Cruda, **'87** 180
Salsa, Fresh Summer, **'87** 89
Salsa, Hot Mexican, **'85** 136
Salsa Picante, **'84** 108
Salsa Picante, Homemade, **'81** 67
Salsa, Tomato, **'87** 120
Salsa, Yellow Tomato, **'87** 122
Sauerkraut Relish, **'85** 136
Squash Pickles, **'81** 174; **'87** 150
Sweet Pickles, Quick, **'87** 149
Tomato Pickles, Green, **'87** 134
Tomato Relish, **'85** 188
Tomato Relish, Easy, **'80** 126
Vegetable Relish, Eight-, **'84** 179
Watermelon Rind Pickles, **'81** 174;
  '84 106
Zucchini, Dilled Fresh, **'81** 174
Zucchini Relish, **'87** 200

Pies and Pastries

Almond Combs, **'84** 136
Almond Pie, Toasted, **'86** 163
Ambrosia Pie, **'79** 284
Angel Pie, **'79** 123; **'80** 238
Apple
    Autumn Apple Pie, **'79** 205
    Brandy-Apple Pie, **'86** 301
    Brandy Raisin-Apple Pie, **'83** 192
    Cake, Apple Pie, **'82** 226
    Chess Pie, Apple-Lemon, **'86** 220

Cider Pie, Apple, **'84** 227
Cranberry-Apple Holiday
  Pie, **'81** M269
Cranberry-Apple Pie, **'79** 264
Cream Cheese Pie, Apple-, **'81** 247
Danish, Deep-Dish Apple, **'86** 161
Dumplings, Old-Fashioned
  Apple, **'84** 226
Dutch Apple Pie, **'81** 105; **'82** 273
Easy-Crust Apple Pie, **'87** 11
Flan, Apple, **'81** 309
Foldovers, Apple, **'84** 136
Fresh Apple Pie, **'84** 178
Fried Apple Pies, **'81** 217; **'86** 302
Fried Apple Turnovers, **'81** 161
Grandmother's Apple Pie, **'87** 212
Grated Apple Pie, **'83** 304
Holiday Apple Pie, **'87** 260
Lemon-Apple Pie, Tart, **'80** 100
Mincemeat Pie, Apple-, **'85** 316
Old-Fashioned Apple Pie, **'82** M299
Pear Pie, Apple-, **'83** 249
Red Apple Pie, **'79** 282
Roll, Apple, **'82** 178
Strudel, Apple, **'85** 259
Turnovers, Delicious Apple, **'86** 25
Turnovers, Puffy Apple, **'87** 276
Apricot Fried Pies, **'86** 269
Apricot Pastries, **'83** 297
Apricot Pie, Yogurt-, **'85** 132
Apricot Pinwheels, **'87** 276
Banana Cream Pie, **'84** 48; **'87** 207
Bavarian Cream Pie, **'79** 281
Blackberry-Apple Pie, **'87** 130
Blackberry Cream Pie, **'81** 132
Blackberry Pie, **'84** 141; **'86** 152
Blackberry Roll, **'82** 178
Blueberry Cream Pie, **'84** 142
Blueberry Cream Pie, Fresh, **'80** 144
Blueberry Kuchen, **'80** 143
Blueberry Pie, Fresh, **'83** 183; **'85** 152
Blueberry-Sour Cream Pie, **'83** 183
Boston Cream Pie, **'83** 220
Bourbon Pie, Kentucky, **'84** 87
Boysenberry Pie, **'82** 133
Brownie Pie, Crustless, **'82** 33
Buttermilk Lemon Pie, **'81** 120; **'82** 23
Buttermilk Pie, **'82** 53; **'83** 158
Buttermilk Pie, Old-Fashioned, **'79** 72
Butterscotch Cream Pie, **'84** 48; **'87** 207
Butterscotch Meringue Pie, **'83** 158
Cannoli, **'80** 58
Cantaloupe Cream Pie, **'79** 177
Cantaloupe Pie, **'86** 163
Caramel-Banana Pie, **'86** M165
Caramel Banana Pie, Luscious, **'79** 115
Caramel-Peanut Pie, **'86** 259
Caramel Pie, Burnt, **'82** 53
Carrot Custard Pie, **'79** 45
Caviar Pie, **'79** 154
Cheese
    Camembert Bars, **'86** 58
    Cottage Cheese Pie, **'82** 85
    Cream Puffs with Chicken Salad,
      Cheesy, **'86** 260
    Date-Filled Cheese Pastries, **'83** 259
    Lemon Cheese Pie, **'81** 136; **'82** 146
    Lemon-Cottage Cheese Pie, **'79** 44
    Lemon Cottage Cheese Pie, **'81** 143
    Make-Ahead Cheesecake Pie,
      '81 233
    Mincement-Cheese Pie, **'80** 253
    Phyllo-Cheese Triangles, **'87** 246

Puffs, Mexican Cheese, '87 8
Yogurt-Cheese Pie, '82 121
Cherry Pie, Easy, '82 299
Cherry Pie, Prize-Winning, '82 57
Cherry Pie, Red, '83 192
Cherry Pie, Scrumptious, '83 250
Chess Pie, Brown Sugar, '86 220
Chess Pie, Old-Fashioned, '86 220
Chicken Puffs, Appetizer, '85 72

Chocolate
Almond Pie, Creamy
Chocolate-, '85 102
Amandine, Chocolate Pie, '83 300
Amaretto Mousse Pie,
Chocolate-, '80 180; '81 30
Berry Pie, Heavenly
Chocolate-, '85 102
Black Bottom Pie, '82 53
Chess Pie, Chocolate, '81 161;
'86 220
Chip Pie, Chocolate, '85 114
Cream Cheese Pie, Chocolate-, '80 69
Cream Pie, Chocolate, '83 192;
'84 49; '87 208
Creamy Chocolate Pie, '85 298;
'86 119
Double Chocolate Pie, '82 M282
Easy Chocolate Pie, '83 158
French Silk Pie, '80 247
Frozen Chocolate Pie, '80 154
Fudge Pie, '87 168
Fudge Pie, Sweetheart, '86 316
Heavenly Chocolate Pie, '87 260
Ice Cream Pie, Chocolate-, '87 224
Meringue Pie, Chocolate, '80 238;
'82 206; '83 158
Meringue Pie, Chocolate-
Filled, '86 121
Mocha Crunch Pie,
Chocolate-, '81 136
Mousse Pie, Chocolate, '81 136
Mud Pie, Tipsy, '80 255
Peanut Butter Pie, Chocolate-, '85 91
Peanut Butter Swirl Pie,
Chocolate-, '87 262
Praline Pie, Chocolate-, '86 259
Whipped Cream Pie,
Chocolate, '79 124
Cobblers
Apple Cobbler, Easy, '83 174
Apple Cobbler for Two, '85 261
Apple Crisp, '84 122
Apple-Pecan Cobbler, '84 M198
Apple Walnut Cobbler, '79 154
Apple-Walnut Cobbler, '81 248

Apricot Cobble Up, '82 138
Berry-Cherry Cobbler, '83 270
Berry Crisp, '83 130
Blackberry-Almond Cobbler, '81 132
Blackberry Cobbler, '82 139; '83 175
Blackberry Cobbler,
Deep-Dish, '80 186
Blackberry Cobbler, Deluxe, '81 132
Blackberry Cobbler,
New-Fashioned, '87 164
Blackberry Cobbler, Southern,
'81 132
Blueberry Buckle, '85 30
Blueberry Cobbler, '83 175
Blueberry Cobbler, Easy, '83 183
Blueberry Cobbler, Fresh, '80 144
Blueberry Cobbler, Peachy, '80 143
Blueberry Crisp, '84 177
Blueberry Crunch, Fresh, '82 143
Blueberry, Huckle-Buckle, '86 151
Blueberry-Peach Cobbler,
No-Dough, '86 177
Blueberry Pinwheel Cobbler, '87 140
Boysenberry Cobbler, '82 133
Cherry Cobbler, '82 91, 139
Cherry Cobbler, Fresh, '84 178
Cherry Slump, '83 139
Cranberry-and-Apple Cobbler,
'84 306
Cranberry Cobbler, '81 275
Cranberry Cobbler, Easy, '86 260
Cranberry Cobbler Roll, '80 288;
'81 248
Cranberry-Pear Crisp, '83 207
Fig Cobbler, '79 140
Fig Cobbler, Super, '86 206
Grenadine-Peach Cobbler, '85 178
Peach-Caramel Cobbler, '86 300;
'87 178
Peach Cobbler, '83 175; '84 178
Peach Cobbler, Fresh, '82 139
Peach Cobbler, Lattice-
Topped, '79 154
Peach Cobbler,
Old-Fashioned, '82 170
Peach Cobbler, Quick, '79 215;
'81 142
Peach Cobbler, Spicy, '85 178
Peach Cobbler Supreme, '81 184
Peach Crisp, '83 113
Peach Crumble, Easy, '83 116
Pear Cobbler, Best Ever, '82 194
Pear Crumble, '85 221
Pineapple-Apple Betty, '85 46
Strawberry-Rhubarb Cobbler,
Rosy, '79 154
Coconut-Caramel Pies, '87 260
Coconut Chess Pie, '86 220
Coconut Cloud, '80 70
Coconut Cream Pie, '80 238; '81 136;
'82 85; '84 49; '87 207
Coconut Cream Pie, Fresh, '80 289
Coconut Custard Pie, '82 33
Coconut Pie, Blender, '84 236
Coconut Pie, Magic, '79 53
Coconut Pie, Mock, '86 200
Coconut Pie, Quick, '83 115
Coconut-Pineapple Pie, '84 256
Coconut Puffs, '87 277
Cracker Pie, '79 113
Cranberry-Cherry Pie, Tart, '87 299
Cranberry Freezer Pie, Festive, '84 306
Cranberry Pie, Frosty, '79 249

Cranberry Pie, Nutty, '82 M298
Cranberry Pie, Walnut-, '87 259
Cranberry-Raisin Pie, '80 283; '85 316
Cran-Raspberry Pie, '87 244
Cream Horns, '84 137
Cream Pie, Texas, '81 181
Cream Puffs, Captivating, '81 180
Cream Puffs, Java, '81 187
Cream Puffs, Strawberry, '81 95
Cream Puffs, Strawberry-Lemon, '87 75
Cream Puffs, Tutti-Frutti, '79 231
Custard Pie, Old-Fashioned Egg, '82 261
Custard Pie, Perfect, '82 92
Daiquiri Pie, '79 68
Danish Pastry Puffs, '85 311
Dream Pie, '80 90
Éclairs with Pecan Sauce, '83 219
Eggnog Chiffon Pie, '86 281
Eggnog Pie, '80 254; '83 205; '86 317;
'87 295
Eggnog Pie, Fluffy, '81 M269
Fig Snacks, Sliced, '86 206

Fried Pies, Delicious, '83 84
Fruitcake Pie, '80 237
Fruit Pie, Dried, '83 249
Fruit Pie, Japanese, '80 238
Fruit Pies, Baked, '84 7
Fruit Puff, Giant, '85 72
Grape Juice Pie, '79 123
Grape Pie, '85 212
Grasshopper Freeze, Creamy, '81 180
Grasshopper Pie, '83 145
Heavenly Pie, '83 158
Ice Cream Delight, '80 69
Ice Cream Pie, Absolutely Divine,
'82 181
Ice Cream Pie, Caramel, '82 181
Ice Cream Pie, Carrot, '86 200
Ice Cream Pie, Chocolate-Mint, '81 144
Ice Cream Pie, Coffee, '79 231
Ice Cream Pie, Heavenly, '82 181
Ice Cream Pie, Kona, '83 189
Ice Cream Pie, Lemon, '80 70
Ice Cream Pie, Peanutty, '82 56
Ice Cream Pie, Peppermint
Candy-, '87 260
Ice Cream Pie, Pumpkin, '81 272
Ice Cream Pie with Rum-Fruit
Sauce, '84 312
Kahlúa Pie, '83 191
Lemon Chess Pie, '79 32; '82 196
Lemon Cream Pie, Frozen, '82 86
Lemon in Pastry Shell, '84 137
Lemon Meringue Pie, '85 M112; '86 130
Lemon Meringue Pie, Deluxe, '81 172
Lemon-Orange Pie, '85 172

Pies and Pastries (continued)

Lemon Pie, Buttermilk, '81 120; '82 23
Lemon Pie, Slice of, '84 23
Lemon Pie, Whipped, '79 124
Lemon-Sour Cream Pie, '82 169
Lemon Sponge Pie, '83 192
Lemon Twirl Pie, '84 94
Lime Chiffon Pie, '86 130
Lime Fluff Pie, '84 43
Macadamia Pie, '80 238
Main Dish
    Artichoke Pie, '79 25
    Beef Pies, Carry-Along, '80 224;
       '81 56
    Breakfast Pie, '86 242
    Broccoli-Beef Pie, '83 196
    Burrito Pie, Mexican, '87 287
    Cheese-Beef Pie, '85 33
    Cheese Pie, Mexican, '82 9; '83 69
    Chicken Breasts Wellington, '84 22
    Chicken, Company Creamed, '82 84
    Chicken in Pastry, '86 122

    Chicken in Phyllo, '87 286
    Chicken Liver Turnovers, '79 141
    Chicken Pie, '81 281; '82 31
    Chicken Pie, Biscuit-Topped,
      '86 157, 264
    Chicken Pie, Cheesy Mexican,
      '82 142
    Chicken Pie, Double-Crust, '87 111
    Chicken Pie, Egg-Stra Special,
      '86 264
    Chicken Pot Pie, '81 210; '82 114;
      '84 21
    Chicken Pot Pie, Easy, '83 156
    Chicken Pot Pie, Thick 'n'
      Crusty, '87 267
    Chicken Pot Pie with Cheese
      Crust, '86 264
    Chicken Salad in Cream Puff
      Bowl, '86 232
    Chicken-Vegetable Pot Pie, '81 281;
      '82 30
    Chile-Cheese Pie, Green, '84 234
    Chili-Tamale Pie, '82 9; '83 68
    Cornbread-Sausage-Apple Pie, '87 171
    Corn Burger Pie, '83 156
    Country Pie, '83 155
    Enchilada Pie, '83 155
    Fish in a Crust, '84 294
    Grits-and-Ham Pie, Crustless, '86 103
    Hamburger Pie, '81 92; '84 13
    Ham Pie, Golden, '87 78
    Ham Pie with Cheese Crust, '80 286
    Ham Tart, Supreme, '84 22
    Ham Towers, Cheesy, '82 77
    Meat-and-Potato Pie, '84 23

Meat Pie, Mexicali, '81 194
Meat Pie, Old-Fashioned, '82 110
Meat Pie, Reuben, '80 189
Meat Pies, Cornish, '84 23
Meat Pies, Natchitoches, '84 21
Meat Turnovers, '86 326
Oyster Pie, Creole, '84 214
Pancake, Supper, '86 242
Pea Flips, '80 7
Pineapple-Chicken Salad Pie, '80 138
Salmon-Spinach Turnovers, '83 44
Sausage Log, Phyllo, '84 294
Sausage Pizza Pie, Link-, '85 33
Seafood Pie, Hot, '80 32
Shepherd Pie, '83 116
Shrimp Puffs, Luncheon, '85 72
Sombrero Pie, '81 140
Spaghetti Pie, '81 32
Spanakópita, '86 58
Spinach-Pasta Pie, '85 286
Taco Pie, Crescent, '80 80
Taco Pies, Individual, '82 M282
Tortilla Pie, '85 M211
Tortilla Pie, Montezuma, '83 199
Tuna Pie with Cheese Roll
    Crust, '80 286
Tuna-Rice Pie, '84 123
Turkey-and-Dressing Pie, '84 326
Turkey-and-Oyster Pie, '82 267
Turkey Pie, '80 285
Turkey Pie, Crumb-Crust
    Curried, '86 265
Turkey Pie, Golden, '79 253
Turkey Pie, Lattice-Topped, '81 277;
    '82 7
Turkey Pie, Potato-Topped, '86 265
Turkey Pot Pie, '86 265
Vegetable-Beef Pies, '80 286
Zucchini-Ham-Cheese Pie, '80 272
Mango Pie, Green, '79 137
Mexican Fiesta Confection, '82 223
Mincemeat Chiffon Pie, '79 245
Mincemeat-Peach Pie, '80 295; '81 188
Mincemeat Pie, Holiday, '80 282; '83 250;
    '87 213
Mincemeat Pie, Pear, '84 264
Mocha Meringue Pie, '80 242
Molasses Pie, '86 20
Muscadine Pie, '82 202
Napoleons, '84 138
Napoleons, Strawberry, '81 126
Nesselrode Pie, Fluffy, '87 261
Orange Ambrosia Pie, '80 237
Orange Blossom Special, '79 48
Orange Chiffon Pie, '87 260
Orange Meringue Pie, '81 12, 309
Orange Shortcake, Fresh, '80 100
Palmiers, '81 277
Papaya Pie, '86 53
Pastries and Crusts
    Almond Pastry, '85 177
    Basic Microwave Pastry, '82 M142;
      '85 M113
    Basic Pastry, '79 282; '81 M268;
      '82 114; '84 48
    Butter Pastry, Golden, '84 22
    Cereal Piecrust, Crisp, '82 209;
      '83 100
    Cheddar Cheese Pastry, '80 219;
      '82 194
    Cheddar Pastry, '86 206
    Cheese Crust, '80 286; '86 264
    Cheese Rolls, '80 286

Chocolate-Coconut Crust, '87 261
Chocolate-Coconut Pie Shell, '82 210;
    '83 100
Chocolate Crumb Crust, '87 261
Chocolate Crust, '87 264
Chocolate Cups, '80 207
Chocolate Pastry Shell, '87 262
Cinnamon Meringue Shell, '82 263
Cornmeal Pastry, '81 140
Cream Cheese Pastries, '80 250
Cream Cheese Pastry, '82 39
Cream Cheese Pastry Shells, '86 13
Cream Cheese Pastry Shells,
    Miniature, '87 190
Cream Cheese Patty Shells, '81 266;
    '82 249
Cream Cheese Shells, '79 2
Decorating Pie Crusts, '83 248
Deluxe Piecrust, '79 79
Double-Crust Pastry, '81 105; '82 85,
    M298; '83 248; '85 191; '87 299
Double-Crust Pastry, Flaky, '82 57
Flaky Pastry, '80 224; '81 56, 210;
    '83 156
German Pastries, '86 78
Graham Cracker Crust, '79 45;
    '86 32; '87 139, 243
Graham Cracker Crust,
    Microwaved, '82 M141
Graham Cracker Crust,
    Peanut-, '79 50
Heart Tart Pastry, '87 14
Italian Sweet Crust, Plum Pie
    with, '79 162
Make-Ahead Pastry, '82 209; '83 100
Mocha Pastry Shell, '81 136
Never Fail Pastry, '79 79
Nut Crust, Spiced, '87 295
Oatmeal Piecrust, '79 79
Pastry, '82 85, 139, 259; '83 84, 91,
    175; '84 21, 23; '86 24, 25, 242,
    259, 303, 326; '87 212, 267
Pâté Pastry, '86 65
Pecan Crust, '86 317
Perfect Pastry Mix, '81 142
Perfect Pastry Shell, '81 142
Perfect Piecrust, Making, '82 234
Pizza Crust, '80 233; '83 226; '86 77
Pizza Crust, Crispy, '87 181
Processor Pastry, '87 67
Processor Pie Dough, Quick
    Food, '84 219
Puff Pastry, Basic, '84 135
Puff Pastry, Cream, '85 72
Puff Pastry, Quick, '84 207
Quiche Pastry, '80 M107
Quiche Pastry, Microwaved, '81 M74;
    '82 M122
Rice-Cheese Shell, '82 49
Rice Crust, Crispy, '84 43
Seasoned Pastry, '79 253
Sesame Pastry Shell, '82 67
Shell, Pastry, '84 31, 127; '87 262
Shells, Pastry, '83 93
Shortcake Pastry, '80 100
Spice Crust, '82 298
Tart Crust, '84 178
Tart Shell, '87 77
Tart Shells, '82 304; '83 279; '85 300;
    '86 18, 105
Tart Shells, Cheese Pastry, '85 216
Tart Shells, Tea, '85 120
Timbale Shells, '82 108

Triple-Crust Pastry, '80 186
Whole Wheat Crust, '82 298
Whole Wheat Pastry, '81 229
Peach-Cranberry Pie, '83 249
Peach Cream Pie, Dried, '84 146
Peaches-and-Cream Pie, '81 184
Peach Fried Pies, Easy, '85 178
Peach Pie, Fresh, '82 170
Peach Pie, Luscious, '81 136
Peach Pies, Fried, '81 272
Peach Pies, Little, '86 303
Peanut Butter Cream Pie, '79 50
Peanut Butter Meringue Pie, '84 30
Peanut Butter Pie, '85 275; '86 109
Peanut-Raisin Pie, '79 85
Pear Crumble Pie, '83 207
Pear-Mince Pie, '81 271
Pear Pie, Deep-Dish, '80 219
Pear Pie, Double-Crust, '82 194
Pear Pie, French, '87 213
Pear Pie, Tennessee, '85 230
Pear Streusel Pie, '83 234; '84 244
Pecan
Bourbon Pecan Pie, '85 90
Butter Pecan Pie Squares, '81 262
Caramel-Pecan Apple Pie, '85 247
Chocolate Pecan Pie, '80 237; '83 12
Choco-Pecan Pie, '82 86
Coconut-Pecan Chess Pie, '81 248
Coconut Pecan Pie, '81 161
Coffee Pecan Pie, '82 74
Custard Pecan Pie, '87 184
Date-Pecan Pie, '80 15
Golden Pecan Pie, '81 266
Grandmother's Pecan Pie, '86 269
Holiday Pecan Pie, '81 296
Individual Pecan Pies, '85 295
Layered Pecan Pie, '83 305
Maple-Pecan Pie, '81 266
Miniature Pecan Pies, '79 205; '86 13
Molasses-Pecan Pie, '86 259
Old-Fashioned Pecan Pie, '81 M269
Orange-Pecan Pie, '79 282; '83 222
Pecan Pie, '79 251; '80 57; '85 255
Pumpkin-Pecan Pie, '85 233, 282
Raisin-Pecan Pie, '87 213
Spicy Pecan Pie, '84 240
Sweet Potato-Pecan Pie, '83 90
Texas Pecan Pie, '83 159
Tiny Pecan Pies, '79 225
Persimmon Pie, '79 206
Phyllo Cheesecakes, Little, '87 275
Phyllo Nests, Nutty, '87 277
Pineapple Phyllo Bundles, '87 277
Pineapple Pie, '80 237
Pineapple Pie, Double-Crust, '82 85
Pistachio Pie, '80 56
Plum Cream Pie, Easy, '86 174
Plum Kuchen, '79 161
Plum Pie with Italian Sweet
Crust, '79 162
Preserve-Filled Foldovers, '80 7
Profiteroles, '84 208
Pumpkin Chiffon Pie, '84 312
Pumpkin Empanadas, '82 223
Pumpkin-Ice Cream Pie, '87 243
Pumpkin Pie, Autumn, '87 213
Pumpkin Pie, Bourbon-Pecan, '87 264
Pumpkin Pie, Festive, '81 M269
Pumpkin Pie, Fluffy, '80 283
Pumpkin Pie in Spiced Nut Crust, '87 295
Pumpkin Pie, Nutty, '82 67
Pumpkin Pie, Rich, '86 292

Pumpkin Pie, Sour Cream-, '84 263
Pumpkin Pies, Spicy, '84 322
Pumpkin Pie Supreme, '82 217
Pumpkin Pie, Traditional, '85 256
Pumpkin Praline Pie, '80 244
Raisin Pie, '83 220
Raisin Pie, Spiced, '84 148
Raspberry-Nut Strudel, '83 304
Rhubarb-Peach Pie, '86 140
Rhubarb-Raisin Pie, '79 112
Rugelach, '85 276
Rum Bisque Pie, '79 123
Rum Cream Pie, '85 212
Sour Cream Pie, '86 260
Sour Cream Pie, Tropical, '79 176; '80 6
Strawberry-Banana Glazed Pie, '81 181
Strawberry-Glaze Pie, '81 141
Strawberry Pie, Chilled, '82 112
Strawberry Pie, Glazed, '82 M142
Strawberry Yogurt Pie, '80 232
Strawberry-Yogurt Pie, '85 122; '86 124
Strudel, Fruit Basket, '87 276

Tarts
Almond Tea Tarts, '85 120
Apple Cream Tart, '84 207
Apple-Pecan Tarts, '80 282
Apple Tart, Deluxe, '84 227
Apricot Tarts, '79 282
Blue Cheese Appetizer
Tarts, '85 300; '86 18
Bouilli, Tarte à la, '83 92
Caramel Tarts, '82 43
Cheese Tart, Herb-, '87 98
Cherry and Blackberry Tart, '83 225
Cherry Tarts, Cheery, '80 238
Chicken Salad Tarts, '84 257
Cranberry-Cream Cheese
Tarts, '80 154
Cranberry Holiday Tarts, '83 279
Cranberry-Nut Tart, '84 305
Cranberry Tartlets, Fresh, '87 244
Cream Cheese Tarts, '84 74
Eggnog Tarts, Creamy, '79 255
French Silk Tarts, '79 236
Fruit Tart, Fancy, '82 128
Fruit Tart, Fresh, '84 178
Fruit Tart, Open-Face, '84 207
Fruit Tart, Rainbow, '82 304
Grape Tart, Green, '87 77
Grasshopper Tarts, '80 220
Heart Tarts, '87 14
Kentucky Derby Tarts, '79 102
Lemon-Cheese Tarts, '79 2
Lemon Ice Cream Tarts, '80 152
Lemon-Sour Cream Tarts, '81 304
Lemon Tarts, '82 156; '83 79
Lemon Tarts, Dainty, '82 304
Lemon Tarts, Golden, '85 191

Little Bits, '79 196
Milan, Tart, '87 70
Orange Tarts, Frozen, '80 154
Pear Tart, '82 304
Pecan Tarts, '81 266
Pecan Tarts, Easy, '84 313
Pecan Tarts, Special, '87 224
Pommes, La Tarte aux, '80 125
Prune Tarts, Brandied, '85 223
Puddin' Pies, President Tyler's, '80 43
Pumpkin Tarts, No-Bake, '86 291
Seafood Tartlets, '87 247
Shrimp Tart, '87 70
Spinach Tarts, '82 249
Strawberry Tart, '84 138
Strawberry Tarts, '80 70
Teatime Tassies, '84 321
Tin Roof Pie, '85 91
Transparent Pie, '80 238
Turnovers, Fried Apricot, '86 24
Turnovers, Fruit, '79 150
Turnovers, Party Ham, '82 39
Vanilla Cream Pie, Fruit-Topped, '84 49
Vegetable
Bean Pie, Pinto, '80 40
Broccoli-Cheese Pie, '84 235
Carrot Pie, '83 117
Cauliflower-Carrot Pie, '82 191
Corn Pie, Quick and Cheesy, '82 191
Florentine Crêpe Pie, '79 34
Mushrooms in Patty Shells, '80 283
Mushroom Tarts, Hot
Sherried, '83 78
Mushroom Turnovers, Tiny, '86 24
Onion Pie, '82 191
Spinach Pie, '82 191
Spinach Pie, Greek, '85 59
Squash Chiffon Pie,
Butternut, '83 296; '84 285
Squash Pie, Butternut, '80 40;
'87 212
Squash Pie, Spaghetti, '80 186
Squash Pie, Spicy, '85 9
Squash Pie, Spicy Butternut, '80 296
Sweet Potato Cream Pie,
Southern, '87 260
Sweet Potato Meringue Pie, '81 126;
'83 225
Sweet Potato Pie, '79 207; '85 255,
275; '86 269
Sweet Potato Pie, No-Crust, '84 236
Sweet Potato Pie,
Old-Fashioned, '79 9
Sweet Potato Pone Pie, '80 288
Tomato Pie, Green, '79 195
Vegetable Turnovers, '86 24
Yam Pie, Louisiana, '81 223
Zucchini Pie, Cheesy, '82 191
Zucchini Pie, Italian-Style, '83 43

Pimiento
Ball, Pimiento Cheese, '80 258
Bread, Pimiento-Cheese, '85 223
Casserole, English Pea-Pimiento, '83 207
Cheese, Chunky Pimiento, '86 295
Cheese, Creamy Pimiento, '86 296
Cheeses, Pimiento and Three, '86 296
Cheese, West Texas Pimiento, '84 9
Eggs, Pimiento-Deviled, '84 143
Pasta, Pimiento, '84 176
Popovers, Pimiento, '79 138
Sandwiches, Pimiento Cheese, '82 278
Sauce, Cauliflower with Pimiento, '87 232
Spread, Garlic Pimiento Cheese, '79 58

Pimiento (continued)

Spread, Ham and Pimiento, '80 285; '81 56
Spread, Low-Calorie Pimiento Cheese, '85 215
Spread, Pimiento Cheese, '82 35; '83 93; '86 127
Topping, Pimiento, '83 93

Pineapple

Appetizer, Shrimp-Pineapple, '85 80
Bacon-Wrapped Pineapple Chunks, '84 25
Baked Pineapple, '83 261; '84 287
Baked Pineapple with Natillas Sauce, '83 179
Bake, Pineapple, '79 251
Bake, Pineapple-Cheese, '79 106
Ball, Pineapple Cheese, '81 160
Ball, Pineapple-Cheese, '84 26
Bars, Pineapple-Orange, '82 129
Basket, Summer Berry, '84 158
Beans and Franks, Hawaiian Baked, '80 136
Beans, Hawaiian-Style Baked, '86 210
Beefburgers Hawaiian, '86 137
Beets with Pineapple, '79 249; '82 204
Betty, Pineapple-Apple, '85 46
Boat Aloha, Pineapple, '80 102
Boats Ahoy, Pineapple, '80 148
Bread, Carrot-Pineapple, '82 210
Bread, Pineapple, '83 139
Bread, Pineapple-Apricot, '84 7
Bread, Pineapple-Carrot, '79 106
Bread, Pineapple-Nut, '79 215
Bread, Pineapple-Pecan Loaf, '87 256
Buns, Easy Pineapple, '85 14
Burgers, Pineapple, '82 169
Cake, Cajun, '87 138
Cake, Coconut-Pineapple Layer, '80 140
Cake, Heavenly Pineapple, '83 303
Cake, Lemon-Pineapple, '86 60, 239
Cake, Pineapple-Pecan Upside-Down, '84 25
Cake, Pineapple Pound, '79 148
Cake, Pineapple Upside-Down, '80 102
Cake Roll, Coconut-Pineapple, '84 304
Cake, Skillet Pineapple Upside-Down, '85 242
Cake, Stacked Pineapple Upside-Down, '86 239
Carrots, Pineapple, '83 198
Cheesecake, Pineapple, '81 32
Cheesecake, Ultimate Pineapple, '85 38
Chicken and Pineapple, '81 281; '82 30
Chicken Bake, Pineapple, '82 120
Chicken, Hawaiian Sesame, '81 106
Chicken, Oriental Pineapple, '84 288
Chicken, Piña Colada, '86 21
Chicken, Pineapple, '83 M194; '85 3
Chicken with Pineapple, Oriental, '86 42
Chops, Pineapple-Curry Glazed, '82 106
Cookies, Pineapple, '79 216
Crab Imperial, Pineapple-, '84 M286
Crêpes, Mango-Pineapple, '86 216
Delight, Pineapple-Almond, '85 96
Delight, Pineapple-Pear, '82 54
Dessert Chimichangas, Pineapple, '86 4
Dip, Cheesy Pineapple, '80 249
Dip, Pineapple-Ginger, '86 104
Doughnuts, Pineapple Drop, '83 95
Dressing, Fruit Salad with Pineapple, '85 207
Dressing, Pineapple Cream, '83 81

Dressing, Pineapple-Poppy Seed, '85 55
Drink, Coconut-Pineapple, '83 172
Filling, Pineapple, '80 140; '83 179; '84 153
Float, Pineapple Sherbet, '79 148
Franks, Hawaiian, '81 202
Frappé, Hawaiian, '81 178
Fresh Pineapple Boats, '83 153
Fresh Pineapple Delight, '79 111
Fried Pineapple, '81 232
Glazed Oranges and Pineapple, '86 318
Glaze, Orange-Pineapple, '81 60
Glaze, Pineapple, '83 143; '84 26; '85 38
Ham, Pineapple-Baked, '86 48
Ham, Pineapple-Flavored, '87 160
Hawaiian Dream Boats, '86 151
Ice Cream, Orange-Pineapple, '86 117
Ice Cream, Pineapple-Mint, '84 186
Jam, Pineapple, '81 147
Kabobs, Pineapple-Beef, '83 212
Kabobs, Pineapple-Chicken, '86 M328
Loaf, Hawaiian, '80 225
Loaf, Pineapple Upside-Down Ham, '79 253
Loaves, Individual Pineapple, '81 M121
Marmalade, Orange-Pineapple, '82 150
Marmalade, Strawberry-Pineapple, '85 130
Meatballs, Chinese, '87 194
Meatballs, Polynesian, '80 207
Meringue-Topped Pineapple, '84 178
Milkshake, Pineapple, '87 199
Mold, Minted Pineapple, '85 240

Mousse, Elegant Pineapple, '79 230
Muffins, Carrot-Pineapple, '81 6
Muffins, Pineapple, '81 14, 250
Muffins, Sunshine, '86 9
Nog, Speedy Breakfast, '82 47
Parfait, Pineapple, '84 83
Patties, Pineapple-Ham, '80 110
Pears, Pineapple-Honey, '86 94
Phyllo Bundles, Pineapple, '87 277
Pickled Pineapple, '79 24
Pie, Coconut-Pineapple, '84 256
Pie, Double-Crust Pineapple, '82 85
Pie, Pineapple, '80 237
Pie, Pineapple-Chicken Salad, '80 138
Pineapple Topping, Cherry-, '87 126
Pork and Pineapple, Polynesian, '83 102
Pork Chops, Hawaiian, '86 212
Pork Chops, Pineapple, '87 M124
Pork, Pineapple, '82 60
Pork, Pineapple Sweet-and-Sour, '82 120
Pork Roast, Pineapple, '79 41
Pot Roast, Hawaiian, '81 298
Pot Roast, Polynesian, '80 59

Preserves, Mango-Pineapple, '79 137
Pudding, Pineapple, '80 102
Punch, False-Kick, '82 121
Punch, Hot Pineapple, '82 264
Punch, Lime-Pineapple, '83 142
Punch, Pineapple, '79 174; '80 128
Punch, Pineapple-Orange, '85 236
Punch, Spiced Pineapple, '83 33
Rice with Pineapple, Curried, '79 142
Rolls, Cranberry-Pineapple, '86 275
Salad, Cucumber-Pineapple, '84 124
Salad Dressing, Pineapple, '81 36
Salad, Heavenly Frosted, '79 286
Salad, Icy Pineapple-Fruit, '87 9
Salad, Mandarin Orange and Pineapple, '82 266
Salad, Pineapple-Buttermilk, '82 80
Salad, Pineapple-Celery, '85 95
Salad, Pineapple-Cucumber Congealed, '83 118
Salad, Pineapple Daiquiri, '84 232
Salad, Pineapple-Lime, '84 320
Salad, Pineapple Macaroni, '79 220
Salad, Pineapple-Nut Chicken, '83 80
Salad, Pineapple-Orange Congealed, '83 218
Sauce, Banana-Pineapple, '83 48
Sauce, Jezebel, '81 29; '82 55
Sauce, Pineapple, '84 236
Sauce, Pineapple-Curry, '79 252
Sauce, Pineapple Ice Cream, '81 M289
Sauce, Pineapple-Orange, '84 14
Sauce, Pineapple-Rum, '84 275
Sauce, Raisin-Pineapple, '82 177
Sauce, Sweet-and-Sour Pineapple, '85 66
Scalloped Pineapple, '79 106; '82 254; '84 M323
Shake, Banana-Pineapple Milk, '84 59
Shake, Pineapple-Banana, '85 215
Shake, Strawberry-Pineapple, '84 166
Sherbet, Creamy Pineapple, '79 155
Sherbet, Pineapple, '81 177; '84 83
Skewered Pineapple and Strawberries, '84 251
Slaw, Apple-Pineapple, '79 241
Slaw, Colorful Pineapple, '86 250
Slicing Pineapples, Instructions for, '82 94
Sopaipillas, Pineapple, '83 179
Soufflé, Pineapple Dessert, '80 153
Spiced Pineapple, '80 102
Spread, Hawaiian Cheese, '87 158
Spread, Pineapple-Cheese, '86 126
Spread, Pineapple-Cream Cheese, '82 35
Spread, Pineapple Sandwich, '84 166
Spritz, Pineapple, '86 94
Squash, Pineapple-Stuffed Acorn, '84 255
Sundaes, Mauna Loa, '80 126
Topping, Lemon-Pineapple, '86 60
Topping, Pineapple, '86 239
Tropical Snow, '86 34
Wassail, Pineapple-Apricot, '83 275

Pizza

Artichoke and Prosciutto, Pizza with, '87 182
Beef-and-Sausage Pizza, Double Cheesy, '86 77
Bread, Pizza Batter, '85 56
Breakfast Pizza, '85 44
Burger, Pizza, '87 185
Burgers, Easy Pizza, '82 190
Burger Snacks, Pizza-, '84 30
Burgers, Pizza, '80 M201; '81 73
Calzone, '85 94

Casserole, Quick Pizza, '83 266
Cheese-and-Mushroom Pizza, '83 226
Clam Pizza, Baby, '87 182
Cocktail Pizzas, '79 110
Crust, Crispy Pizza, '87 181
Crust, Pizza, '80 233; '83 226; '85 243;
  '86 77
Crust, Thick, '81 214
Crust, Thin, '81 214
Cups, Pizza, '81 215
Deep-Dish Mediterranean Pizza, '80 163
Deep-Dish Pizza Luncheon Pie, '80 286
Deep-Dish Vegetarian Pizza, '85 243
Eggplant Pizza, '85 221
French Bread, Pizza on, '82 131
Gruyère-Chicken Pizza, '87 182
Hamburger Pizza, Quick, '85 243
Homemade Pizza, Best Ever, '80 233
Italian-Style Pizza, Original, '87 182
Jazzed-Up Pizza, Jiffy, '83 M314
Kiwi-Berry Pizza, '86 198; '87 55
Lasagna Pizza, '85 285
Meatballs, Pizza, '85 86
Meat Loaf, Cheesy Pizza, '81 121
Pan Pizza, Quick, '86 160
Party Pizzettes, '80 192
Pepperoni Pizza, Thick 'n' Crusty, '85 244
Peppers, Pizza, '83 135
Pesto Pizza, '87 182
Popcorn, Pizza-Flavored, '85 236
Quiche, Pizza, '86 53
Salad Pizza, '87 182
Sandwiches, Open-Face Pizza, '82 3;
  '83 85; '84 M198; '85 22
Sandwich, Giant Pizza, '80 93
Sauce, Pizza, '84 33; '85 285

Sausage-Pepperoni Pizza, Spicy, '83 226
Sausage Pizza Pie, Link-, '85 33
Slices, Pizza, '84 269
Snacks, Pizza Party, '86 262
Snacks, Tasty Little Pizza, '79 248
Speedy Pizza, '81 214
Squares, Pizza, '87 168
Strawberry Pizza, '79 94
Supreme, Pizza, '81 214
Tostada Pizza, '81 16; '82 13
Turnovers, Little Pizza, '85 327
Two-Way Pizza, '79 93
Whole Wheat Pizza, '84 33

Plums
Bread, Sugar Plum, '80 256
Chutney, Plum, '84 179
Crunch, Layered Plum, '86 174
Ham, Plum, '80 110
Jam, Peach-Plum Freezer, '85 130

Jelly, Plum, '82 150
Kuchen, Plum, '79 161
Muffins, Plum Good, '83 96
Pie, Easy Plum Cream, '86 174
Pie with Italian Sweet Crust,
  Plum, '79 162
Pudding, Flamed Plum, '84 276
Pudding-Gelatin Mold, Plum, '86 300;
  '87 178
Pudding, Light Plum, '86 318
Pudding, Old-Fashioned Plum, '80 264
Pudding, Plum, '79 281
Sauce, Chinese Plum, '82 237
Sauce, Gingered Plum, '87 175
Sauce, Plum, '80 249; '82 40
Sauce, Quail with Red Plum, '80 48
Sauce, Spicy Plum, '86 11
Slush, Plum, '84 139
Soup, Chilled Purple Plum, '79 162
Soup, Peach-Plum, '87 157
Soup, '85 107

Popcorn
Bacon-Cheese Popcorn, '86 74
Cake, Popcorn-Gumdrop, '87 262
Candied Popcorn and Peanuts,
  '82 295
Caramel Corn, Baked, '81 218
Caramel Corn Candy, '84 243
Caramel Popcorn, '79 219; '86 M212
Caramel Popcorn, Crispy, '85 247
Cinnamon-Popcorn Crunch, '86 136
Garlic Popcorn, '83 M315
Harvest Popcorn, '84 300
Mix, Curried Popcorn, '86 326
Nutty Popcorn, '85 208
Orange Popcorn, '86 230
Oriental Popcorn, '86 74
Pizza-Flavored Popcorn, '85 236
Pretzel Popcorn, '84 30
Scramble, Popcorn, '87 185
Sesame-Cheese Popcorn, '79 220
Spiced Popcorn Snack, '87 8

Pork. *See also* Bacon, Ham, Sausage.
Backbones, Smoked
  Country-Style, '82 162
Bake, Pork Spaghetti, '81 11
Barbecue
  Chops, Barbecued Pork, '81 10
  Chops, Marinated Barbecued
    Pork, '79 90
  Chops, Oven-Barbecued
    Pork, '81 234; '82 26; '83 40
  Pork, Barbecued, '80 72
  Ribs, Apple Barbecued, '80 111
  Ribs, Barbecued, '80 111; '85 159
  Ribs, Country-Style Barbecued,
    '79 42
  Ribs, Herbed Barbecued, '86 185
  Ribs, Smoky Barbecued, '80 111
  Ribs, Tangy Barbecued, '83 160
  Roast, Barbecued Pork, '82 11
  Roast, Barbecue Pork, '82 97;
    '83 104
  Roast, Berry Barbecued Pork,
    '80 288
  Shoulder, Barbecued Pork, '81 111;
    '82 11
  Spareribs, Barbecued, '81 112;
    '82 12; '86 232
  Spareribs, Barbecued
    Country-Style, '80 73
  Spareribs, Easy Barbecued, '82 97;
    '83 104

  Spareribs, Saucy Barbecued, '79 14
  Spareribs, Southern Barbecued,
    '79 90
  Spareribs, Spicy Barbecued, '84 93
  Spareribs, Tangy Barbecued, '82 106
  Spareribs with Orange Barbecue
    Sauce, '83 11
  Spicy Barbecued Pork, '84 296
Bean Sauce, Pork-and-Onions with, '85 76
Brunch Eggs, '85 44
Burgers, Hearty Sauced Pork, '84 125
Burgoo, Five-Meat, '87 3
Burgoo, Harry Young's, '87 3
Burritos, '80 196
Burritos, Meat-and-Bean, '81 194
Calabaza Guisada con Puerco (Pumpkin
  Cooked with Pork), '80 193
Casserole, Cheesy Pork, '81 M74
Casserole, Pork, '83 116
Chalupa, Bean, '80 223
Chalupas, Pork, '83 160
Chili, Double-Meat, '79 269; '80 12
Chops. *See also* Pork/Barbecue.
  Apple-Kraut Pork Chops, '84 50
  Apple Pork Chops, Spicy, '87 230
  Apricot-Sauced Pork Chops, '85 22
  Arlo, Pork, '87 229
  Baked Pork Chops and Apples,
    '81 10
  Bake, Fiesta Pork, '79 265
  Braised Pork Chops, Bourbon-,
    '85 89
  Broiled Pork Chops with Crabapple
    Peaches, '81 83
  Casserole, Peppered Pork
    Chop, '81 235; '82 25; '83 39
  Cheesy Pork Chops, '83 102
  Chili Chops, '87 10
  Cider-Sauced Pork Chops, '86 213;
    '87 81
  Company Pork Chops, '85 109
  Costillas Rellenos (Stuffed Pork
    Chops), '82 219
  Country Pride Pork Chops, '79 159
  Cranberry Pork Chops, '80 288
  Creamy Gravy, Pork Chops
    and, '81 207
  Creole Pork Chops, '83 102
  Dill-Cream Gravy, Pork Chops
    with, '84 81
  Dinner, Pork Chop, '80 84; '81 180
  Fiesta, Pork Chops, '86 118
  Fruited Pork Chops, '87 194
  Glazed Apple Pork Chops, '86 300
  Glazed Chops, Pineapple-
    Curry, '82 106
  Glazed Pork Chops, '86 185
  Glazed Pork Chops, Apple-, '84 212;
    '87 35
  Glazed Pork Chops with Rice,
    Fruit-, '82 73
  Glazed Pork Steaks, '83 178
  Gourmet Pork Chops, '79 180
  Grilled Pork Chops, Hawaiian,
    '85 159
  Grilled Pork Chops, Marinated,
    '81 110
  Hawaiian Pork Chops, '86 212;
    '87 82
  Italiano, Pork Chops, '80 72
  Italian, Pork Chops, '79 47
  Jardinière, Pork Chops, '81 112;
    '82 12

Pork, Chops *(continued)*

Lemon-Herb Pork Chops, **'84** 81
Meal for Two, Pork Chop, **'81** 273
Orange-Cranberry Pork
Chops, **'86** 335; **'87** 84
Orange-Glazed Pork Chops,
'84 234
Orange Pork Chops, **'84** 81
Oriental Pork Chops, **'84** 81
Peanut Sauce, Pork Chops
with, **'83** 29
Pineapple Pork Chops, **'87** M124
Pleasing Pork Chops, **'79** 125
Polynesian Pork and
Pineapple, **'83** 102
Rice, Pork Chops and
Spanish, **'83** 103; **'85** 293
Risotti, Pork Chops, **'81** 234; **'82** 26
Saucy Company Pork Chops, **'83** 102
Saucy Pork Chop, **'86** M140
Savory Pork Chops, **'87** 194
Scallop, Pork Chops and
Potato, **'82** 114
Sherry, Chops in, **'79** 125
Skillet Dinner, Pork Chop, **'79** 125
Skillet Pork Chops, Easy, **'79** 255
Sour Cream Sauce, Pork Chops
with, **'83** 102
Special, Pork Chop, **'79** 81
Stuffed Baked Pork Chops, **'79** 222;
'80 64
Stuffed Chops, Barbecued, **'87** 229
Stuffed Pork Chops, **'84** 195; **'86** 89

Stuffed Pork Chops, Apple-, **'79** 125
Stuffed Pork Chops, Apple-Crumb,
'81 234; **'82** 26; **'83** 39
Stuffed Pork Chops, Apricot-,
'86 76
Stuffed Pork Chops, Braised, **'87** 249
Stuffed Pork Chops, Cheese-, **'84** 81
Stuffed Pork Chops, Easy, **'81** 10
Stuffed Pork Chops, Fruit-, **'82** 136
Stuffed Pork Chops, Fruited, **'86** 197
Stuffed Pork Chops, Rice-, **'83** 102
Stuffed with Prunes, Pork
Chops, **'84** 7
Sweet-and-Sour Pork Chops, **'83** 160
Vegetable Pork Chops,
Skillet, **'85** 179
Chow Mein, Pork, **'80** 208
Combo, Vegetable-Pork, **'85** 113
Curry, Hurry, **'79** 103
Egg Rolls, **'86** 81
Eggrolls, Shrimp and Pork,
'82 240; **'83** 18

Eggs, Tulsa, **'87** 95
Hominy, Mexican, **'86** 255
Hot-and-Spicy Pork, **'81** 228
Kabobs, Spicy Pork, **'82** 182
Loin Stuffed with Wild Rice, Pork, **'84** 35
Meatballs in Gravy, **'79** 136
Meatballs, Sauerkraut, **'86** 257
Meatballs, Tangy Hawaiian, **'79** 129
Meat Loaf
Glazed Ham Loaf, **'79** 187
Ham Loaf, **'79** 180
Italian Meat Loaf, **'79** 187
Mozzarella-Layered Meat
Loaf, **'79** 71
Pineapple Upside-Down Ham
Loaf, **'79** 253
Savory Meat Loaf, **'87** 216
Skillet Liver Loaf, **'80** 11
Stuffed Meat Loaf, **'79** 187
Supreme Ham Loaf, **'79** 242
Swedish Meat Loaf, **'81** 121
Triple Meat Loaf, **'79** 186
Oriental, Pork, **'81** 212
Paella, Chicken-Pork-Shrimp, **'82** 245
Pâté, Country, **'86** 66
Pâté en Croûte, **'86** 65
Pâté with Spinach and Cream,
Pork, **'83** 224
Pies, Natchitoches Meat, **'84** 21
Pie, Sombrero, **'81** 140
Pilaf, Fruited Pork, **'82** 246
Pineapple Pork, **'82** 60
Polynesian Pork, **'85** 78
Ribs. *See also* Pork/Barbecue.
Baked Ribs, Easy, **'86** 20
Baked Ribs, Lemon, **'81** 166
Chinese Spareribs, **'81** 10
Glazed Spareribs, Honey-, **'82** 163
Glazed Spareribs, Orange-, **'84** 296
Glazed Spareribs, Peach-, **'86** 14
Grilled Ribs, Lemon, **'81** 154
Lemony Sweet Spareribs, **'80** 73
Oven Ribs, Smoky, **'81** 166
Plantation Ribs, **'84** 217
Saucy Oven Spareribs, **'80** 207
Saucy-Sweet Ribs, **'81** 166
Smoky Ribs, **'84** 172
Stuffed Spareribs, Fruit-, **'79** 14
Sweet-and-Sour Spareribs, **'83** 21
Risotto, Pork, **'82** 60
Roasts
à l'Orange, Porc, **'80** 242
Arista of Pork, **'81** 260
Braised Pork, Brown Sugar, **'84** 36
Crown Roast of Pork, Royal, **'80** 252
Crown Roast of Pork,
Stuffed, **'86** 323
Glazed Pork Loin, **'87** 229
Indonesian Pork Roast, **'81** 227
Loin of Pork, Roast, **'84** 276
Mandarin Pork Roast, **'83** 47
Marinated Pork Roast, **'80** 71;
'84 260
Pineapple Pork Roast, **'79** 41
Pineapple Sweet-and-Sour
Pork, **'82** 120
Rio Grande Pork Roast, **'84** 35, 296
Smoked Pork Shoulder, **'82** 225
Stuffed Crown Pork Flambé, **'83** 263
Stuffed Pork Loin Roast,
Prune-, **'80** 29
Stuffed Pork Roast, **'81** 111;
'82 12; **'85** 229

Stuffed Pork Shoulder, **'81** 11
Tomato Sauce, Pork Roast
with, **'87** 249
Zesty Pork Roast, **'85** 179
Salad, Pork-'n'-Bean, **'87** 83
Sausage, Pork, **'81** 55
Sloppy Joes, Pork, **'86** 294
Soup, Homemade, **'79** 198
Steaks, Herbed Pork, **'80** 72
Steaks, Peachy Pork, **'79** 166
Stew, Bama Brunswick, **'87** 4
Stew, Brunswick, **'80** 264
Stew, Sonny Frye's Brunswick, **'87** 4
Stir-Fried Pork, **'87** 51
Stir-Fried Pork in Garlic Sauce, **'84** 141
St. Tammany, Pork, **'82** 260
Swedish Porkburgers, **'79** 42
Sweet-and-Pungent Pork, **'86** 118
Sweet-and-Sour Pork, **'79** 42; **'80** 72, 227;
'81 26, 104, 111; **'82** 12; **'84** 218;
'85 34, 194; **'86** 241
Tamales, **'80** 195
Tamales, Hot, **'83** 51
Tempting Twosome, **'81** 240
Tenderloin
Apple-Ginger Pork Tenderloin, **'86** 75
Blue Cheese, Pork Tenderloin
with, **'86** 76
Curried Pork Tenderloin, **'86** 76
Danish Pork Tenderloin, **'82** 186
Marinated Pork Tenderloin, **'84** 175
Medallions with Chutney Sauce,
Pork, **'87** 35
Picatta, Pork Tenderloin, **'86** 76
Platter, Tenderloin, **'79** 42
Roast Pork Tenderloin, **'84** 35
Sandwiches, Beef and Pork
Tenderloin, **'80** 175
Stuffed Pork Tenderloins,
Fruit-, **'87** 270
Sunrise Pork Tenderloin, **'79** 103
Towers, Pork Tenderloin, **'86** 75
Terrine, Jeweled Pork, **'84** 130
Wontons, Crispy Fried, **'83** 21

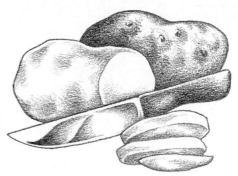

Potatoes
au Gratin, Potatoes and Eggs, **'79** 107
au Gratin, Potatoes-and-Zucchini, **'84** 5
Bake, Chive-Potato, **'82** 229
Bake, Creamy Potato, **'82** 201
Baked. *See also* Potatoes/Stuffed.
Avocado-Topped Potatoes, **'83** 3
Beef and Chicken-Topped Potatoes,
Creamed, **'83** 210
Broccoli-and-Almond-Topped
Potatoes, **'83** 3
Broccoli-Topped Baked
Potatoes, **'86** 17
Cheese Potato Skins, **'84** M239

Cheese Sauce, Baked Potatoes
  with, '83 239
Cheesy Frank-Topped Potatoes, '83 3
Cheesy Potato Skins, '82 78
Chili-Topped Potatoes, '83 3
Crabmeat-Topped Potatoes, '83 3
Frank-Filled Potatoes, '84 M11
Garden Potato Cups, '83 76
Garden-Topped Potatoes, '83 4
Mexican-Topped Potatoes, '83 3
Micro-Baked Potatoes, '81 M61
Million Dollar Potatoes, '83 210
Mushroom-Dill-Topped
  Potatoes, '86 41
Mushroom Filling in a Peel, '84 214
Oven-Baked Potatoes, Easy, '82 202
Salmon-Topped Potatoes, '84 124
Skins, Baked Potato, '86 81
Sweet-and-Sour-Topped
  Potatoes, '83 4
Taco-Baked Potatoes, '84 119
Bake, Herbed Fish and Potato, '79 287;
  '80 34
Bake, Onion-Potato, '83 M195
Bake, Potato, '83 209
Bake, Potato-Broccoli-Cheese, '80 114
Bake, Potato-Tomato, '86 17
Baskets, Potato, '86 193
Basque-Style Potatoes, '79 46
Beans and Potatoes, Down-Home, '85 254
Beets, Potato-Stuffed, '83 234
Bisque, Spinach-Potato, '86 66
Bread, Old-Fashioned Potato, '86 57
Bread, Potato, '85 56
Breakfast, Farmer's, '81 44
Breakfast Potatoes, Mexican, '81 209
Browned Potatoes, Quick, '82 M172
Candy, Potato, '79 273
Caraway Potatoes, '85 85
Caraway Potatoes, Cheesy, '86 17
Casserole, Cheesy Ham-and-
  Potato, '84 326
Casserole, Cheesy Potato, '80 244; '83 53
Casserole, Cheesy Potato-Egg, '84 5
Casserole, Creamy Potato, '84 M113
Casserole, Easy Potato, '80 114
Casserole, Fluffy Potato, '80 268
Casserole, Ham-and-Potato, '83 M87
Casserole, Hash Brown Potato, '81 40
Casserole, Irish Potato, '81 263
Casserole, Italian, '80 81
Casserole, Mashed Potato, '85 296
Casserole, Mushroom-Potato, '84 5
Casserole, Potato, '87 190
Casserole, Potato Breakfast, '80 52
Casserole, Potato-Cheese, '79 101
Casserole, Potato-Eggplant, '87 166
Casserole, Processor Potato, '86 159
Casserole, Saucy Potato, '81 276
Casserole, Saucy Potato-Tomato, '79 46
Casserole, Sausage-Potato, '86 217
Caviar Potatoes, '84 80
Caviar Potatoes, Appetizer, '86 223
Cheese Potatoes, Double-, '86 6
Cheese Potatoes, Two-, '80 114
Cheesy Potatoes, '82 211
Chicken Livers and Potatoes, '82 218
Chili, Savory Potato, '83 284
Chips, Homemade Potato, '82 25
Chive Potatoes, Cheesy, '79 46
Chives, Potatoes with, '81 M61
Creamed Potatoes, '83 25
Cream-Wine Sauce, Potatoes in, '86 18

Creamy Potatoes with Ham Bits, '87 191
Creole Potatoes, '87 138
Croquettes, Parmesan Potato, '84 210
Croquettes, Potato, '87 116
Deviled Potatoes, Hot, '84 296; '85 196
Doughnuts, Chocolate-Glazed
  Potato, '85 6
Doughnuts, Old-Fashioned Potato, '84 56
Duchesse, Potatoes, '84 210
Dumplings, Venison Stew with
  Potato, '87 304
Fans, Parmesan Potato, '84 M240
Feta Cheese, Potatoes with, '84 295;
  '85 196
Fluffy Potatoes, '84 296; '85 196
French Fries, Herb, '82 211
Fried Potatoes, Almond-, '82 25
Fried Potatoes, Herb-, '82 25
Fried Potatoes, Oven-, '82 25
Fried Potatoes, Southern-, '82 25
Fried Potato Patties, '82 25
Fry, Okra-Potato, '81 159
Garlic Potatoes, '84 296; '85 196
Gourmet, Potatoes, '80 114
Greens and Potatoes, Mustard, '86 224
Grilled Herb Potatoes, '84 172
Gruyère Potatoes, '83 193
Hash Brown Cheese Bake, '82 50
Hash Brown Potatoes, '81 48
Hash Browns, Company, '79 268; '80 14
Hash Browns, Franks and, '80 166
Hash Brown Skillet Breakfast, '82 5
Herb Butter, Potatoes with, '81 276
Jalapeño Potatoes, '84 39
Latkes, '84 318
Lemon and Nutmeg Potatoes, '80 36
Lightbread, Potato, '80 225
Loaves, Potato, '86 162
Lorraine, Potatoes, '87 190
Mashed Potatoes, Jazzy, '87 192
Missy Potatoes, '85 259
Mustard Potatoes, '79 32
Nest, Peas in a Potato, '84 M239
Nests with Savory Shavings,
  Potato, '84 209
New Potatoes, Browned, '86 244
New Potatoes, Cheesy, '85 156
New Potatoes, Creamed Peas
  and, '79 102
New Potatoes, Green Beans with, '87 164
New Potatoes, Herbed, '81 102
New Potatoes, Lemon-Buttered, '84 149
New Potatoes, Lemony, '82 158
New Potatoes, Parsley, '79 122
New Potatoes, Seasoned, '87 M151
New Potatoes with Lemon Sauce, '86 130
New Potatoes with Parsley-Chive
  Sauce, '84 212
Olive Potatoes, '80 114
Omelet, Potato-Sprout, '79 128
Oven Potatoes, Crispy, '82 96
Pancake, Potato, '85 20
Pancakes, Moist Potato, '80 36
Pancakes, Potato, '79 115
Parmesan Potatoes, '82 270
Parslied Potatoes, '86 18
Peppers, Potatoes with Sweet
  Red, '87 192
Pie, Meat-and-Potato, '84 23
Pie, Potato-Topped Turkey, '86 265
Potage, Subtle Potato, '80 78
Puffs, Potato, '80 36
Quiche, Crustless Potato, '83 49

Rolls, Feathery Light Potato, '81 305;
  '82 36
Rolls, Homemade Potato, '82 252
Rolls, Potato, '81 300
Rolls, Potato Yeast, '87 53
Rolls, Refrigerated Potato, '83 254
Rolls, Refrigerator Potato, '87 15
Rolls, Southern Potato, '86 299
Rolls, Super Potato, '85 145
Rolls, Supreme Potato, '82 130
Rosemary, Potatoes Anna with, '84 209
Roses, Potato, '81 246
Salads
  Any Day Potato Salad, '81 154
  Bacon-Topped Potato Salad, '85 59
  Bean Salad, Potato-, '82 301
  Broccoli-Potato Salad, Hot, '85 23
  Chunky Potato Salad, '81 M138
  Confetti Potato Salad, '80 5
  Corned Beef-Potato Salad, '85 213
  Corned Beef Salad, Potato-, '81 36
  Cottage Cheese-Potato Salad,
    '79 147, 285
  Creamy Potato Salad, '80 178
  Deluxe Potato Salad, '80 155
  Dill Potato Salad, '85 213
  Dill Potato Salad, Hot, '79 78
  Dutch Potato Salad, Hot, '87 176
  Fish-Potato Salad, Smoked, '84 233
  Fruity Potato Salad, '85 214
  Garden Patch Potato Salad, '84 82
  German Potato Salad, '82 134, 239;
    '84 18
  German Potato Salad, Hot, '79 78
  German-Style Potato Salad, '83 23
  Grecian Potato Salad, '82 55

  Green Bean-Potato Salad, '83 80
  Ham-and-Egg Potato Salad, '86 84
  Ham and Potato Salad, '80 272
  Herbed Potato Salad, '87 171
  Hot Dutch Potato Salad, '86 297
  Hot Potato Salad, '79 78; '81 276;
    '86 10
  Hot Potato Salad Supreme, '79 78
  Layered Creamy Potato Salad,
    '81 23
  Mustard Potato Salad, '86 302
  New Potato Salad, '84 120, 139
  New Potato Salad, Asparagus-and-,
    '86 69
  Olive-Potato Salad, '85 114
  Parmesan Potato Salad, Hot, '79 78
  Parslied Potato Salad, '85 240
  Pepper Cups, Potato Salad in, '79 78
  Peppers, Potato Salad 'n', '83 135
  Pickle-Potato Salad, Sweet, '85 213
  Pole Bean-Potato Salad, Hot, '79 74
  Salmon-Potato Salad, '87 285
  Saucy Potato Salad, '87 123
  Savory Potato Salad, '80 30

Potatoes, Salads *(continued)*

Sour Cream Potato Salad, '79 104; '80 79
Sour Cream-Potato Salad, '84 149
Spring Salad, Mediterranean, '80 148
Sweet and Sour Potato Salad, '80 152
Tuna-Potato Salad, '84 289
Saucy Potatoes for Company, '82 202
Scalloped Potatoes, '82 300; '83 211
Scalloped Potatoes and Turnips, '85 235
Scalloped Potatoes, Cheesy, '83 82
Scalloped Potatoes, Mushroom, '87 191
Scalloped Potatoes, Party, '87 191
Scalloped Potatoes, Skillet, '79 46
Scalloped Potatoes, Wayside, '79 283
Scalloped Potatoes with Pimiento, '81 75
Scallop, Pork Chops and Potato, '82 114
Seasoned Potatoes, '87 253
Shavings, Savory, '84 209
Shoestring Potato Tuna Bake, '82 211
Shrimp-Sauced Potatoes, '81 M61
Skillet Potatoes, Peppy, '86 110
Skins, Baked Potato, '86 81
Skins, Cheesy Potato, '82 78
Slims, Potato, '81 276
Snow-Capped Potatoes, '84 255
Soufflé Potatoes, '84 295; '85 196
Soup, Asparagus-Potato, '85 23
Soup, Celery-and-Potato, '84 279
Soup, Chilled Cucumber-Potato, '85 93
Soup, Cream of Potato, '80 M224; '82 21
Soup, Creamy Potato, '81 19, 98; '84 112
Soup, Golden Cream of Potato, '86 302
Soup, Holiday Potato, '79 236
Soup, Leek-and-Potato, '84 112
Soup, Potato, '82 278; '83 292
Soup, Potato-Bacon, '84 M38
Soup, Sausage-Potato, '80 25
Soup, Special Potato, '82 3
Soup, Three-Potato, '86 16
Sour Cream Potatoes, '84 39
Special Potatoes, '83 169
Steak 'n Potatoes, Skillet, '81 18
Steamed Potatoes, Lemon-, '86 177
Stir-Fry, Potato-Snow Pea, '86 173
Stuffed
Bacon-Stuffed Potatoes, '86 193
Bacon-Stuffed Potatoes, Cheesy, '81 M61
Bacon-Topped Blue Cheese Potatoes, '79 46
Baked Potatoes, Stuffed, '83 322
Baked Stuffed Potatoes, '84 38
Béchamel Sauce, Stuffed Potatoes with, '84 M239
Blue Cheese Stuffed Potatoes, '81 276
Cheese Sauce, Stuffed Potatoes with, '87 192
Chicken-Cheese Stuffed Potatoes, '86 55
Chive-Stuffed Baked Potatoes, '79 52
Chive-Stuffed Potatoes, Creamy, '80 268
Crab-Stuffed Potatoes, Cheesy, '86 17
Creamy Stuffed Baked Potatoes, '86 55
Creamy Stuffed Potatoes, '79 211
Fluffy Stuffed Potatoes, '86 223
Franks and Potatoes, Stuffed, '81 202
Ham Stuffed Potatoes, '79 210
Herb Stuffed Potatoes, '79 211

Jalapeño-Ham Stuffed Potatoes, '81 M61
Lemon-Herb Stuffed Potatoes, '83 173
Patchwork Potatoes, '86 54
Roquefort, Potatoes, '79 211
Savory Stuffed Potatoes, '81 101
Shrimp Boats, '79 57
Shrimp-Stuffed Potatoes, Creamy, '80 36
South-of-the-Border Stuffed Potatoes, '86 54
Tuna Stuffed Potatoes, '79 210
Twice-Baked Potatoes, '83 227
Vegetable-Topped Stuffed Potatoes, '85 235
Summertime Potatoes, '86 M195
Turnips and Potatoes, '79 254
Turnips, Southern, '87 190
Vichyssoise, '86 181
Vinaigrette, Potato-Broccoli, '85 84
Wedges, Beer-Batter Potato, '83 211
Yeast, Potato, '87 53
Potatoes, Sweet
Apple Shells, Sweet Potatoes in, '85 206
Apricot Sweet Potatoes, '82 228
Bake, Southern Sweet Potato, '85 229
Bake, Sweet Potato, '80 287
Bake, Sweet Potato-Apple, '83 25; '86 282
Bake, Sweet Potato-Apricot, '85 206
Bake, Sweet Potato-Orange, '83 226
Balls, Sweet Potato, '86 312
Biscuits, Sweet Potato, '80 287; '84 140
Boats, Sweet Potato, '80 287
Bourbon Sweet Potatoes, '86 324; '87 280
Broiled Sweet Potatoes, Coconut-, '84 231
Cake, Sweet Potato, '79 207
Cake, Sweet Potato Loaf, '81 224
Cake, Sweet Potato Pound, '83 85
Cake, Sweet Potato Surprise, '80 287
Candied Sweet Potatoes, '79 9, 251; '86 111
Casserole, Pear-Sweet Potato, '86 280
Casserole, Sweet Potato, '79 289; '80 26; '85 256
Casserole, Sweet Potato-Banana, '86 276
Casserole, Sweet Potatoes-and-Berries, '84 231
Casserole, Sweet Potato-Rum, '84 231
Cheesecake, Sweet Potato, '80 287
Cheesecake, Yam, '81 224
Coconut-Orange Sweet Potatoes, '84 252
Croquettes, Sweet Potato, '81 223
Cups, Sunshine Sweet Potato, '82 195
Delight, Sweet Potato, '86 335; '87 83
Festive Sweet Potatoes, '80 244
Fried Sweet Potatoes, '83 226
Fried Sweet Potatoes, French-, '81 223
Fritters, Golden Sweet Potato, '79 9
Glazed Sweet Potatoes, '85 206
Glazed Sweet Potatoes, Apple-, '82 303
Glazed Sweet Potatoes, Apricot-, '81 295
Glazed Sweet Potatoes, Orange-, '81 223; '83 280
Glazed Sweet Potatoes, Tropical, '83 226
Gravy, Roast Duck with Sweet Potato-Eggplant, '83 90
Mashed Sweet Potatoes, '85 25
Muffins, Sweet Potato, '81 224; '85 6; '87 280
Muffins, Yam, '79 7
Orange Cups, Sweet Potatoes in, '82 272

Orange Cups, Sweet Potato-Stuffed, '81 223
Orange Sweet Potatoes, '86 279
Pancakes, Sweet Potato, '87 280
Peaches, Sweet Potatoes and, '86 11
Pie, Louisiana Yam, '81 223
Pie, No-Crust Sweet Potato, '84 236
Pie, Old-Fashioned Sweet Potato, '79 9
Pie, Southern Sweet Potato Cream, '87 260
Pie, Sweet Potato, '79 207; '85 255, 275; '86 269
Pie, Sweet Potato Meringue, '81 126; '83 225
Pie, Sweet Potato-Pecan, '83 90
Pie, Sweet Potato Pone, '80 288
Pudding, Sweet Potato, '79 244; '80 228; '86 52
Puffs, Peach Sweet Potato, '87 280
Puffs, Sweet Potato, '87 253
Puff, Sweet Potato, '85 235
Raspberry Sweet Potatoes, '87 280
Roll, Sweet Potato Log, '82 227
Salad, Fresh Sweet Potato, '86 226
Salad, Hawaiian Ham-Sweet Potato, '82 232
Sherry and Walnuts, Sweet Potatoes with, '86 286
Soufflé, Sweet Potato, '82 286; '86 121
Stuffed Baked Sweet Potatoes, '79 207; '84 231
Stuffed Sweet Potatoes, '86 224
Stuffed Sweet Potatoes, Bacon-, '86 224
Stuffed Sweet Potatoes, Coconut-, '82 204
Stuffed Sweet Potatoes, Fluffy, '79 9
Stuffed with Apples, Sweet Potatoes, '82 228
Surprise, Holiday Sweet Potato, '84 254
Surprise, Sweet Potato, '81 267
Yam Rolls, Golden, '86 299
Yams, Cornwallis, '79 276
Pralines
Bananas, Praline, '84 313
Butterscotch Pralines, '81 253
Cake, Praline, '81 162
Cake, Praline Ice Cream, '80 84
Cake, Praline Pound, '82 88
Cheesecake, Praline, '83 270
Clusters, Dark Praline, '86 313
Coffee, Praline-Flavored, '87 69
Coffee Pralines, Plantation, '86 241
Compote, Warm Praline Fruit, '85 260
Creamy Pralines, '80 198
Dark Pralines, '83 52
Delights, Spicy Praline, '84 299
Glaze, Praline, '82 196
Ham, Praline, '85 302
Ice Cream, Pralines and Cream, '82 184; '83 159
Maple-Pecan Pralines, '83 222
New Orleans-Style Pralines, '86 335
Pecan Pralines, Original, '81 11
Pie, Chocolate-Praline, '86 259
Pie, Pumpkin Praline, '80 244
Pralines, '79 272; '86 M288
Sauce, Bourbon Praline, '81 170
Sauce, Chocolate-Praline, '85 M295
Sauce, Peach-Praline, '85 161
Sauce, Praline, '83 25; '84 143
Sauce, Praline Ice Cream, '85 189
Sauce, Southern Praline Ice Cream, '86 M227
Southern Pralines, '79 M263

Texas-Size Pralines, '79 186
Toast, Orange Praline, '79 36
Torte, Chocolate Praline, '84 165
Pretzels
Brownies, Saucepan Pretzel, '85 171
Chocolate-Covered Pretzels, '82 295
Dressing, Pretzel, '86 280
Herb Pretzels with Lower Sodium
    Horseradish Mustard, '86 325
Homemade Pretzels, '84 159
Popcorn, Pretzel, '84 30
Soft Pretzels, '83 18
Soft Pretzels, Chewy, '87 159
Prunes
Bavarian, Prune, '86 223
Bread, Prune-Nut, '87 255
Cake and Sauce, Prune, '85 118
Cake, Prune, '85 223
Cake, Spicy Prune, '79 136
Muffins, Miniature Prune, '85 223
Muffins, Wheat Germ-Prune, '81 106
Pork Chops Stuffed with Prunes, '84 7
Pork Loin Roast, Prune-Stuffed, '80 29
Raspberry Prunes, '82 124
Spiced Prunes, Orange-, '85 224
Stuffed Prunes, '85 47
Tarts, Brandied Prune, '85 223

Puddings. *See also* Custards.
Apple-Nut Pudding with Hot Rum
    Sauce, '79 86
Applesauce-Graham Cracker
    Pudding, '81 34
Banana-Mallow Pudding, '86 139
Banana Pudding, '82 53; '84 94; '85 255
Banana Pudding, Basic, '81 59
Banana Pudding, Delicious, '80 9
Banana Pudding, Surprise, '86 7
Biscuit Pudding, '79 86
Bread Pudding, Amish, '80 8
Bread Pudding, Apricot, '85 24
Bread Pudding, Cheesy, '83 68
Bread Pudding, Chocolate, '80 8
Bread Pudding, French, '85 231
Bread Pudding, Old-Fashioned, '83 213
Bread Pudding with Whiskey
    Sauce, '80 58
Brownie Pudding, '79 265; '80 295
Brown Sugar-Pecan Pudding, '86 M165
Cake, Carrot Pudding, '83 24
Cake, Lemon Pudding, '83 106
Cake Pudding, Chocolate, '81 99
Cake Pudding, Wine, '79 230
Cheese Pudding, Baked, '86 78
Chocolate-Almond Pudding, '82 M142
Chocolate Pudding, Creamy, '83 106
Chocolate-Rum Dessert, '81 247
Christmas Pudding, '79 230
Christmas Pudding, Flaming, '85 312

Corn-Cheese Pudding, '80 244
Corn Pudding, '79 276; '81 128; '86 192
Corn Pudding, Baked, '83 314
Corn Pudding, Creamy, '81 267
Corn Pudding, Easy, '83 280
Corn Pudding, Fresh, '80 157, 165
Cranberry Pudding, '84 306
Fruit Pudding Compote, Fresh, '86 151
Fudge Pudding, Hot, '81 208
Hansel Pudding, '80 9
Lemon Fluff Pudding, '85 304
Lemon Pudding, '79 86; '81 99
Lemon Pudding, Layered, '82 128
Mandarin-Almond Pudding, '85 M12
Orange Pudding, '81 85; '82 111;
    '83 153
Orange-Tapioca Crème, '82 M283
Peanut Butter Pudding, '85 95
Persimmon Pudding, '79 206
Pineapple Pudding, '80 102
Plum Pudding, '79 281
Plum Pudding, Flamed, '84 276
Plum Pudding-Gelatin Mold, '86 300;
    '87 178
Plum Pudding, Light, '86 318
Plum Pudding, Old-Fashioned, '80 264
Potato Pudding, Sweet, '79 244;
    '80 228; '86 52
Pumpkin Pudding, Baked, '80 244
Raisin-Pumpkin Pudding, '84 315
Raisin-Rice Pudding, '87 46
Rice Pudding, Amaretto, '86 334
Rice Pudding, Brown, '85 77
Rice Pudding, Creamy, '81 51, 205
Rice Pudding, Fruited, '81 205; '86 95
Rice Pudding, Fudgy, '81 205
Rice Pudding, Old-Fashioned, '85 147
Rice Pudding, Velvety, '81 205
Rum Pudding with Raspberry
    Sauce, '82 288
Snowflake Pudding, '85 30
Snow White Pudding, '85 77
Squash Pudding, '82 277; '83 15
Steamed Date Pudding, '79 86
Steamed Holiday Pudding, '84 275
Steamed Mincemeat Pudding, '80 264
Tipsy Pudding, Parson's, '80 156
Vanilla Pudding, Creamy, '83 227
Woodford Pudding, '79 86
Yorkshire Pudding, '80 252
Pumpkin
Baked Pumpkin, '82 217
Bars, Pumpkin, '80 40
Bars, Pumpkin Nut, '82 217
Bisque, Spicy Pumpkin, '86 67
Bread, Moist Pumpkin, '80 245
Bread, Orange-Pumpkin, '87 300
Bread, Pumpkin, '81 8
Bread, Pumpkin-Coconut, '87 255
Bread, Pumpkin-Nut, '83 294
Bread, Pumpkin-Pecan, '87 221
Bread with Cream Cheese and Preserves,
    Pumpkin, '84 264
Cake Bars, Pumpkin, '80 245
Cake, Pumpkin, '81 272
Cake, Pumpkin Date, '79 251
Cake, Pumpkin Kahlúa, '86 292
Cake, Pumpkin Layer, '80 245
Cake Squares, Orange-Pumpkin, '83 242
Calabaza Guisada con Puerco (Pumpkin
    Cooked with Pork), '80 193
Cheesecake, Pumpkin, '80 254; '85 280
Chiffon, Pumpkin, '82 216; '86 283

Cookies, Frosted Pumpkin-
    Walnut, '82 217
Cookies, Jack-O'-Lantern, '87 214
Cookies, Pumpkin Drop, '79 206
Cupcakes, Pumpkin, '85 121
Delight, Pumpkin-Orange, '86 321
Empanadas, Pumpkin, '82 223
Flan, Pumpkin, '82 217
Loaf, Harvest Pumpkin, '85 232
Loaf, Pumpkin-Oatmeal, '81 49
Mold, Pumpkin, '82 311
Muffins, Nutty Pumpkin, '86 291
Muffins, Pumpkin, '79 206, 275; '81 272
Pancakes, Pumpkin, '80 228
Pie, Autumn Pumpkin, '87 213
Pie, Bourbon-Pecan Pumpkin, '87 264
Pie, Festive Pumpkin, '81 M269
Pie, Fluffy Pumpkin, '80 283
Pie in Spiced Nut Crust,
    Pumpkin, '87 295
Pie, Nutty Pumpkin, '82 67
Pie, Pumpkin Chiffon, '84 312
Pie, Pumpkin Ice Cream, '81 272
Pie, Pumpkin-Ice Cream, '87 243
Pie, Pumpkin-Pecan, '85 233, 282
Pie, Pumpkin Praline, '80 244
Pie, Rich Pumpkin, '86 292
Pie, Sour Cream-Pumpkin, '84 263
Pies, Spicy Pumpkin, '84 322
Pie Supreme, Pumpkin, '82 217
Pie, Traditional Pumpkin, '85 256
Pudding, Baked Pumpkin, '80 244
Pudding, Raisin-Pumpkin, '84 315
Roll, Pumpkin, '79 206
Rolls, Pumpkin, '87 254
Soup, Pumpkin, '79 48
Soup, Pumpkin-Tomato, '86 291
Tarts, No-Bake Pumpkin, '86 291
Waffles, Pumpkin-Nut, '86 96

Q

Quail
Baked Quail with Mushrooms, '81 259
Breasts, Southern Quail, '85 270
Currant Jelly Sauce, Quail with, '86 94
Fried Quail, '82 45
Fried Quail with Onion Gravy, '82 214
Gravy, Georgia Quail with, '87 240
Magnificent, Quail, '82 214
Marinated Quail, '80 221
Mushrooms, Quail with, '85 138
Orange Sauce in Potato Baskets, Quail
    with, '86 193
Plum Sauce, Quail with Red, '80 48
Superb, Quail, '81 303
Quiches
Bacon-Cheese Quiches, Miniature, '83 93
Bacon Quiche, '85 60
Benedict Quiche, '80 M107
Blue Cheese Quiche, '84 52
Broccoli Quiche, Easy, '82 34
Broccoli Quiche, Italian, '85 45
Broccoli-Rice Quiche, '81 228
Cauliflower Quiche, '83 86
Cheese Pie, Mexican, '83 69
Cheese Quiches, Miniature, '80 150
Cheese-Vegetable Quiche, '81 228
Chile Pepper Quiche, '82 224
Chile Quiche, Green, '83 31
Clam Quiche, '83 215

Quiches *(continued)*

Crab Quiche, '82 M122, 243
Crab Quiche, Almond-Topped, '79 127
Crab Quiche, Quick, '84 96
Crab Quiche, Sherried, '83 180
Crab Quiche, Simple, '85 207
Eggless Quiche, '87 220
Ham-and-Mushroom Quiche, '81 11
Ham-and-Vegetable Quiche, '84 326
Ham-Cheese Quiche, '79 26
Ham Quiche, '80 110
Ham Quiche, Cheesy, '79 127
Ham Quiche, Country, '87 287
Ham Quiche, Crustless, '84 235
Jalapeño-Corn Quiche, '85 122
Jalapeño Quiche, Cheesy, '84 31
Lorraine, Classic Quiche, '81 131
Lorraine, Mushroom-Quiche, '86 242
Lorraine, Peppery Quiche, '81 228
Lorraine, Perfect Quiche, '79 127
Lorraine, Quiche, '79 40; '80 M108
Mushroom Quiche, '80 222; '81 244
Noël, Quiche, '82 310
Olive Quiche Appetizers, '86 159
Onion Quiche, '83 121
Onion Quiche, Cheesy Green, '83 194;
   '84 42
Pastry, Microwaved Quiche, '81 M74;
   '82 M123
Pastry, Quiche, '80 M107
Pizza Quiche, '86 53
Potato Quiche, Crustless, '83 49
Salmon Quiche, '82 87; '87 38
Sausage-Apple Quiche, Crustless, '87 70
Sausage-Cheddar Quiche, '79 26
Sausage Quiche, Easy, '79 261
Sausage Quiche, Italian, '81 200
Sausage Quiche, Spicy, '80 M108
Shrimp Miniquiches, '87 146
Shrimp Quiche, '83 50
Spinach-Mushroom Quiche, '81 M74
Spinach Quiche, '81 44; '85 49
Spinach Quiche, Cheesy, '81 228
Spinach Quiche, Crustless, '84 235
Spinach Quiche, Greek, '86 10
Spinach Quichelets, '87 67
Spinach Quiches, Individual, '86 38
Spinach Quiches, Miniature, '82 38
Springtime Quiche, '83 122
Squares, Cheesy Hot Quiche, '79 124
Squares, Quiche, '84 222

Swiss-Zucchini Quiche, '82 49
Tarragon Cocktail Quiches, '84 127
Tasty Quiche, '82 264
Vegetable Quiche, '87 M219

Zucchini Frittata, '86 103
Zucchini-Mushroom Quiche, '79 127
Zucchini Pie, Italian-Style, '83 43
Zucchini Quiche, Cheesy, '83 312
Zucchini-Sausage Quiche, '83 122

R

Raisins
Bread, Banana-Nut-Raisin, '81 59
Bread, Butternut-Raisin, '79 25
Bread, Caraway-Raisin Oat, '86 44
Bread, Cinnamon Raisin, '80 22
Bread, Curried Chicken Salad on
   Raisin, '85 96
Bread, Homemade Raisin, '87 300
Bread, Oatmeal Raisin, '81 14
Bread, Oatmeal-Raisin, '83 59
Bread, Raisin-Cranberry, '81 305; '82 36
Bread, Salt-Free Raisin Batter, '86 33
Buns, Rum-Raisin, '80 22
Butter, Raisin, '81 272
Cake, Spicy Raisin Layer, '79 230
Candy, Mixed Raisin, '84 111
Carrots, Orange-Raisin, '80 24
Cookies, Alltime Favorite Raisin, '80 24
Cookies, Frosted Oatmeal-Raisin, '79 290
Cookies, Nugget, '79 291
Cookies, Oatmeal-Raisin, '87 221
Cookies, Persimmon-Raisin, '85 232
Gingersnaps, Raisin, '85 324
Gravy, Currant, '83 276
Ham, Raisin, '80 124
Mix, Raisin-Nut Party, '83 60
Muffins, Breakfast Raisin, '84 59
Muffins, Carrot-and-Raisin, '87 24
Muffins, Raisin English, '80 75
Muffins, Whole Wheat Raisin, '85 207
Pie, Brandy Raisin-Apple, '83 192
Pie, Cranberry-Raisin, '80 283; '85 316
Pie, Peanut-Raisin, '79 85
Pie, Raisin, '83 220
Pie, Raisin-Pecan, '87 213
Pie, Rhubarb-Raisin, '79 112
Pie, Spiced Raisin, '84 148
Pudding, Raisin-Pumpkin, '84 315
Pudding, Raisin-Rice, '87 46
Pull-Aparts, Raisin Cinnamon, '82 205;
   '83 32
Rice with Curry, Raisin, '85 83
Rolls, Raisin Cinnamon, '81 107
Rollups, Sweet Raisin, '86 290
Salad, Carrot-Raisin, '83 117; '84 174;
   '87 10
Salad, Curried Apple-Raisin, '80 24
Sauce, Ham with Raisin, '82 M76
Sauce, Raisin, '83 59, 215; '84 91, 275;
   '87 127
Sauce, Raisin-Pineapple, '82 177
Sauce, Rum-Raisin, '84 7
Scones, Currant, '84 69
Scones, Lemon-Raisin, '87 69
Shake, Amazin' Raisin, '86 195
Spread, Peachy-Raisin, '86 326
Teacakes, Currant, '80 88
Raspberries
Appetizer, Orange-Berry, '85 81
Bars, Raspberry, '82 209; '84 212
Cake, Raspberry Coffee, '83 112
Chocolate Cups, Miniature, '87 132
Cobbler, Berry-Cherry, '83 270

Compote, Berry, '81 275
Compote, Berry-Peach, '82 133
Crêpes, Raspberry, '87 126
Crêpes Suzette, Raspberry, '84 84
Custard with Raspberries,
   Amaretto, '86 152
Dessert, Frozen Raspberry, '84 192
Dessert, Raspberry-Jellyroll, '85 95
Dessert, Raspberry Sauce, '80 147
Dream, Raspberry, '83 108
Dressing, Raspberry, '87 153
Ice Cream, Fresh Raspberry, '86 152
Ice Cream, Raspberry, '80 176
Jam, Raspberry Freezer, '84 M181
Kir, Raspberry, '86 183
Mold, Raspberry Holiday, '84 253
Mounds, Raspberry Fruit, '79 35
Mousse, Raspberry, '81 34
Pie, Cran-Raspberry, '87 244
Potatoes, Raspberry Sweet, '87 280
Prunes, Raspberry, '82 124
Punch, Raspberry-Rosé, '87 242
Punch, Raspberry Sparkle, '84 57
Salad, Frozen Raspberry, '79 287; '80 35
Salad, Raspberry, '86 286
Salad, Raspberry Ribbon, '87 236
Sauce, Crimson Raspberry, '79 91; '85 30
Sauce, Duck Breasts with
   Raspberry, '87 240
Sauce Flambé, Raspberry, '84 142
Sauce, Melba, '87 77
Sauce, Peach-Berry, '87 M165
Sauce, Poached Pears with
   Raspberry, '87 69
Sauce, Raspberry, '82 289; '83 108;
   '84 73, 213; '87 69, 117, 183
Sherbet, Raspberry, '83 162
Soufflé, Raspberry, '86 188
Soufflé, Raspberry-Topped, '85 317
Soup, Chilled Raspberry, '81 130
Strudel, Raspberry-Nut, '83 304
Topping, Raspberry, '85 317
Topping, Raspberry-Peach, '87 126
Vinegar, Raspberry-Lemon, '87 134
Relishes. *See* Pickles and Relishes.
Rhubarb
Bavarian, Rhubarb-Strawberry, '86 140
Chutney, Rhubarb, '87 245
Cobbler, Rosy Strawberry-
   Rhubarb, '79 154
Pie, Rhubarb-Peach, '86 140
Pie, Rhubarb-Raisin, '79 112
Salad, Rhubarb Congealed, '86 140
Squares, Rosy Rhubarb, '79 111
Whip, Rhubarb, '79 112
Rice
Almond Rice, '81 195; '85 M112
Apple-Cinnamon Rice, '86 249
au Gratin, Rice, '83 129
au Gratin Supreme, Rice, '86 78
Bacon-Chive Rice, '83 129
Bake, Egg and Rice, '83 119
Bake, Ham-Rice-Tomato, '87 78
Balls, Rice, '81 51
Basic Long-Grain Rice, '83 M285
Basic Molding Rice, '86 221
Basic Quick-Cooking Rice, '83 M285
Basic Rice, '79 64
Beans and Rice, Black, '80 222
Beans and Rice, Cajun Red, '83 26
Beans and Rice, Creole, '80 223
Beans and Rice, Red, '80 58; '83 89;
   '84 37; '87 45

Beans and Rice, South Texas, '85 252
Beans, and Rice, Texas Sausage, '84 296
Beef and Rice, Spiced, '84 285
Beef and Rice, Spicy, '83 231
Beef Rollups with Rice, Royal, '79 105
Beef Tips on Rice, '85 87
Black-Eyed Peas with Rice, '83 12
Black-Eyes and Rice, Creole, '85 6
Boudin, Old-Fashioned, '85 250
Braised Rice and Peas, '79 101
Broccoli with Rice, Holiday, '87 252
Brown Rice, '82 275
Brown Rice, Calico, '86 33
Brown Rice, Cornish Hens with, '82 275
Brown Rice Parmesan, '84 196
Brown Rice, Roast Chicken and, '83 268
Brown Rice, Spanish, '84 196
Brussels Sprouts and Rice, '79 288;
  '80 26
Calico Rice, '85 83
Casserole, Broccoli-Rice, '81 101
Casserole, Brown Rice, '87 118
Casserole, Chicken and Rice, '80 260
Casserole, Chicken-Rice, '86 52
Casserole, Chili-Rice, '79 54
Casserole, Colorful Rice, '82 199
Casserole, Ham-and-Rice, '84 75
Casserole, Jalapeño Rice, '81 66
Casserole, Mexican Rice, '83 31
Casserole, Oriental Sausage and
  Rice, '82 M123
Casserole, Rice, '87 45
Casserole, Rice-and-Chicken, '87 154
Casserole, Sausage-Rice, '82 50; '83 75
Casserole, Shrimp and Rice, '79 228
Casserole, Spanish Rice, '79 192
Chantilly, Rice, '86 82
Chicken-and-Rice Valencia, '85 113
Chicken-Flavored Rice, '84 M144
Chicken Livers and Rice Dish, '82 218
Chicken Livers with Rice, '80 200;
  '81 58; '84 292
Chicken, Rice-Stuffed, '81 4
Chicken with Rice, Sherry, '81 97
Chiles, Rice and Green, '83 152
Chili-Cheesy Rice, '79 43
Chili with Rice, '82 11
Consommé Rice, '80 246
Cornish Hens, Rice-Stuffed, '82 302
Cream with Mandarin Oranges,
  Rice, '85 317
Cumin Rice, '85 83
Curried Rice and Shrimp, '83 231
Curried Rice, Quick, '86 81
Curried Rice with Almonds, '83 M285
Curried Rice with Pineapple, '79 142
Curry-Spiced Rice, '86 M226
Dirty Rice, '86 142
Dressing, Chicken and Rice, '79 288
Dressing, Chicken with
  Pecan-Rice, '85 M57
Dressing, Mexican Rice, '87 253
Dressing, Roast Turkey with
  Rice, '82 286
Fiesta Rice, '84 76
French Rice, '83 24
Fried Rice, '83 129; '84 197
Fried Rice, Bacon, '80 115
Fried Rice, Easy, '84 76
Fried Rice, Egg, '79 252; '80 19
Fried Rice for Two, '81 31
Fried Rice Special, '80 56
Fried Rice, Turkey, '83 282

Fried Rice with Sausage, '83 12
Fruited Rice, Far East, '81 175
Ginger Rice, Fluffy, '83 102
Glorified Rice, '83 129
Golden Rice, '79 270
Green Rice Bake, '79 43
Green Rice, Celebrity, '81 207
Ham-Rice Toss, '82 40
Ham Rolls, Rice-Stuffed, '83 190
Ham with Rice, Curried, '80 111
Herbed Rice, '83 M285
Honey Rice, '85 83
Hopping John, Skillet, '79 10
Indian Rice, '79 64
Jalapeño Hot Rice, '80 126
Jalapeño Rice, '79 43
Lamb Curry with Rice, '80 83; '81 10
Lentil-and-Rice Supper, '84 202
Lime-Flavored Rice, '84 175
Lyonnaise, Rice, '83 151
Meatballs Paprikash with Rice, '85 31
Medley, Rice, '79 270
Mélange, Rice, '87 240
Mexican Rice, '83 85; '85 147

Mix, Crunchy Rice, '85 327
Mix, Fruited Curry-Rice, '86 326
Mold, Chile-Rice, '86 221
Mold, Curried Rice, '85 36
Mold, Saffron Rice, '86 221
Noodles, Shredded Beef over Rice,
  '85 74
Nutted Rice, '85 269
Orange Rice, '79 43; '81 175; '82 200
Oriental Rice, '85 M12, 146
Oven Rice, '83 89
Paella, Chicken-Pork-Shrimp, '82 245
Paella, Garden, '82 245
Paella, Seafood, '82 245
Paella, Spanish, '85 26
Paella Valenciana, '82 246
Pancakes, Rice, '85 147
Parsleyed Rice, '83 M58
Parsley Rice, '84 197; '85 95
Parslied Rice, '87 167, 243
Peas and Rice, Holiday, '86 328
Peas, Rice with Green, '87 45
Pecan Rice, '85 53
Peppered Rice, '82 4
Peppers, Beef-Stuffed, '85 146
Peppers, Rice-Stuffed, '80 65
Pepper Steak and Rice, '81 17
Peppers with Rice and Ham,
  Stuffed, '82 131
Pie, Tuna-Rice, '84 123
Pilaf, Browned Rice, '87 305
Pilaf, Chicken, '82 246
Pilaf, Fruit-and-Vegetable Rice, '84 196

Pilaf, Fruited Pork, '82 246
Pilaf Mold, Ham, '86 222
Pilaf, Near-Eastern, '82 246
Pilaf, Okra, '80 185; '82 126
Pilaf, Rice, '86 82; '87 229
Pilaf, Savory, '83 93
Pilaf, Shrimp, '82 246
Pilaf, Turkey-Rice, '86 284
Pilaf, Turkish, '79 184
Pork Chops, Rice-Stuffed, '83 102
Pudding, Amaretto Rice, '86 334
Pudding, Brown Rice, '85 77
Pudding, Creamy Rice, '81 51, 205
Pudding, Fruited Rice, '81 205; '86 95
Pudding, Fudgy Rice, '81 205
Pudding, Old-Fashioned Rice, '85 147
Pudding, Raisin-Rice, '87 46
Pudding, Velvety Rice, '81 205
Quiche, Broccoli-Rice, '81 228
Raisin Rice with Curry, '85 83
Red Rice, Savannah, '80 119
Ring, Oregano Rice, '86 222
Ring, Rice-Carrot, '79 246
Ring, Shrimp Creole in a Rice, '86 222
Ring with Beets, Rice, '79 225
Risotto alla Milanese, '85 228
Rolls, Crunchy Cabbage-Rice, '85 32
Saffron Rice, '79 43
Salads
  Artichoke Hearts, Rice Salad
    with, '80 232
  Artichoke-Rice Salad, '80 178;
    '81 41; '85 81
  Bacon, Rice Salad with, '79 52
  Bean-and-Rice Salad,
    Marinated, '87 152
  Bean Salad, Rice-and-, '85 22
  Brown Rice-and-Vegetable
    Salad, '84 202
  Chicken-and-Rice Salad, Hot, '83 22
  Chicken-Rice Salad, '81 203
  Chicken-Rice Salad, Nutty, '83 157
  Colorful Rice Salad, '81 253
  Confetti Rice Salad, '80 232
  Crunchy Rice Salad, '82 302;
    '85 147, 220
  Curried Rice Salad, '80 84
  Egg-Rice Salad, '84 18; '86 169
  Gazpacho-Rice Salad,
    Molded, '86 221
  Ham-and-Rice Salad,
    Mandarin, '87 145
  Hearty Rice Salad, '82 233
  Mushrooms, Rice Salad with
    Fresh, '80 231
  Paella Salad, '86 207
  Pea Salad, Rice-, '85 163
  Red Rice Salad, Charleston, '79 146
  Rice Salad, '79 74; '81 51
  Salmon-Rice Salad, '84 289
  Shrimp-and-Orange Rice Salad,
    Zesty, '87 155
  Shrimp and Rice Salad, '80 231;
    '82 207
  Shrimp-Rice Salad, Baked, '83 22
  Shrimp-Rice Salad, Tangy, '84 66
  Shrimp Salad, Rice-, '79 270
  Shrimp Salad, Rice-and-, '83 82
  Tuna-Rice Salad, '87 202
  Vegetable-Rice Salad, '80 148;
    '83 198; '85 87
  Vegetable Salad, Rice-and-, '86 42
  Zesty Rice Salad, '81 23

Rice (continued)

Sausage and Rice, Italian, '86 53
Seasoned Onion Rice, '82 166
Seasoned Rice, '79 244; '83 212
Shell, Rice-Cheese, '82 49
Shrimp and Sausage Rice, '79 64
Soufflé, Rice-Cheese, '79 270
Soup, Tomato-and-Rice, '85 24
Spanish Rice, '81 51; '83 209
Spanish Rice, Pork Chops and, '83 103;
  '85 293
Spanish-Style Rice, '83 152
Spicy Rice, '83 215; '85 256
Spinach Rice, '85 146
Squares, Creamed Chicken over Confetti
  Rice, '81 282; '82 31
Stew, Lentil-Rice, '82 232
Strata, Cheese-Rice, '81 176
Vegetables, Rice with, '79 64; '85 83
Waldorf Rice, '84 281
Wild Rice
  Almond Wild Rice, '86 50
  Belvedere, Wild Rice, '86 82
  Casserole, Chicken-Wild
    Rice, '84 241; '85 65
  Casserole, Duck and Wild
    Rice, '79 224
  Casserole, Oyster-and-Wild
    Rice, '83 34; '84 44
  Casserole, Sausage and Wild
    Rice, '83 196
  Casserole, Sausage-Wild Rice, '84 250
  Casserole, Veal and Wild
    Rice, '79 180
  Casserole, Wild Rice, '82 199
  Casserole, Wild Rice-Oyster, '86 256
  Chicken and Wild Rice, '79 248
  Chicken, Wild Rice-Stuffed, '79 219
  Chicken-Wild Rice Supreme, '79 77
  Chicken with Wild Rice,
    Elegant, '80 M76
  Cranberry-Pear Wild Rice, '83 279
  Creole, Wild Rice-and-Shrimp,
    '84 292
  Eggs with Wild Rice,
    Scrambled, '80 42
  Mushrooms, Wild Rice and, '83 278
  Popped Wild Rice, '85 65
  Pork Loin Stuffed with Wild
    Rice, '84 35
  Ring, Creamed Mushrooms in Wild
    Rice, '80 270
  Ring, Wild Rice, '83 253
  Salad, Crab and Wild Rice, '79 116
  Salad, Crab-Wild Rice, '86 207
  Salad, Wild Rice, '85 65
  Salad, Wild Rice-Chicken, '83 146
  Sausage and Wild Rice, '85 65
  Sausage, Wild Rice and, '86 268
  Stuffing, Cornish Hens with Wild
    Rice, '79 222; '80 64; '82 136
Yellow Rice, Black Beans with, '82 2
Yellow Rice with Water Chestnuts, '85 24
Rolls and Buns. See also Breads.
Apple Pinwheel, Quick, '85 42
Blueberry Buns, Deluxe, '81 164
Blueberry Pinwheels, '82 205
Bran Rolls, '85 145
Bran Yeast Rolls, '87 116
Butter-and-Herb Rolls, '86 306
Buttered Rum-Nut Rolls, '86 291
Butterhorns, '84 267

Buttermilk Rolls, Quick, '83 155
Caramel Breakfast Rolls, '79 193
Caramel-Nut Rolls, '86 312
Caraway Puffs, '82 174
Cheese Buns, Hurry-Up, '81 300
Cheese Crescents, '82 18
Cherry-Almond Rolls, '84 M198
Chocolate-Cinnamon Buns, '85 5
Chocolate Sticky Buns, '81 300; '82 124
Cinnamon Crisps, '81 113
Cinnamon Rolls, '79 80
Cinnamon Rolls, Easy, '85 290
Cinnamon Rolls, Glazed, '86 312
Cinnamon Rolls, Old-Fashioned, '86 298
Cinnamon Rolls, Spiral, '82 205; '83 32
Cinnamon Sticky Buns, '83 244
Cinnamon Twists, '83 53
Cloverleaf Refrigerator Rolls, '80 256
Cloverleaf Rolls, '82 18
Cloverleaf Rolls, Light, '83 290
Cornmeal Rolls, '79 60
Cornmeal Yeast Rolls, '86 177
Cottage Cheese Rolls, '81 78
Cranberry-Pineapple Rolls, '86 275
Cream Cheese Pinches, '87 85
Crescent Rolls, '84 267
Crescent Rolls, Butter-Rich, '81 211
Crescent Rolls, Buttery, '83 180
Crescent Rolls, Deep South, '82 309;
  '83 16
Crescent Rolls, Easy, '79 60
Crescent Rolls, French-Style, '82 288
Crescents, Festive, '80 281
Croissants, '83 54

Cross Buns, Hot, '81 77
Dinner Rolls, '79 251
Dinner Rolls, Fancy, '86 299
Dinner Rolls, How to Shape, '83 323
Dinner Rolls, Italian, '83 254
Dinner Rolls, Italiano, '85 32
Dinner Rolls, Refrigerator, '81 78
Dough, Basic Roll, '82 17
Dough, Sweet Roll, '79 80
Fantan Rolls, French, '80 276
Finger Rolls, '83 254
Garlic Rolls, Easy, '86 234
Hard Rolls, '86 85, 306
Holiday Sparkle Rolls, '83 296
Honey Oatmeal Buns, '83 154
Honey Rolls, Super, '80 115
Honey Wheat Rolls, '83 278
Honey-Wheat Rolls, Dilled, '83 254
Icebox Rolls, '80 242
Jam Kolaches, '85 290
Jam Teasers, '81 8
Lemon Knots, Glazed, '86 290
Lemon Spirals, French, '81 94

Moravian Feast Buns, '83 295
Nutty Buns, '86 290
Onion Buns, Cheesy, '85 5
Onion Rolls, Poppy Seed, '81 63
Orange Butter Rolls, '82 206; '83 33
Orange Rolls, '80 22; '82 17
Orange Rolls, Frosted Hot, '80 257
Orange Rolls, Luscious, '86 298
Overnight Rolls, '86 233
Parker House Refrigerator Rolls,
  '82 310; '83 17
Parkerhouse Rolls, Super, '81 78
Parmesan Rolls, '79 181
Pecan Rolls, '81 62
Pepperoni Rolls, Ground-, '83 244
Pineapple Buns, Easy, '85 14
Potato Rolls, '81 300
Potato Rolls, Feathery Light, '81 305;
  '82 36
Potato Rolls, Homemade, '82 252
Potato Rolls, Refrigerated, '83 254
Potato Rolls, Refrigerator, '87 15
Potato Rolls, Southern, '86 299
Potato Rolls, Super, '85 145
Potato Rolls, Supreme, '82 130
Potato Yeast Rolls, '87 53
Pull-Apart Buns, Easy, '83 100
Pumpkin Rolls, '87 254
Raisin Cinnamon Pull-Aparts, '82 205;
  '83 32
Raisin Cinnamon Rolls, '81 107
Raisin Rollups, Sweet, '86 290
Refrigerator Rolls, '82 287
Refrigerator Rolls, Buttermilk,
  '81 120; '82 22
Refrigerator Rolls, Low-Sodium,
  '82 67
Refrigerator Rolls, Party, '79 248
Refrigerator Rolls, Three-Day, '86 306
Romano Sesame Rolls, '87 144
Rounds, Individual Bread, '83 159
Rum Buns, '81 299
Rum-Raisin Buns, '80 22
Rum Rolls, Easy, '79 287; '80 35
Saffron Rolls, '83 296
Sesame Buns, '82 17
Snack Buns, '87 279
Sour Cream Rolls, '80 71
Sour Cream Yeast Rolls, '85 259
Sourdough Hot Rolls, '82 201
Spoon Rolls, '87 15
Sticky Buns, '80 23
Sweet Rolls, Mexican, '81 285
Sweet Rolls, Yummy, '80 281
Twists, Austrian, '80 45
Wheat Bread and Rolls, Hearty
  Whole, '79 92
Wheat Buns, Whole, '86 236
Wheat Feather Rolls, Shredded, '82 309;
  '83 16
Wheat Rolls, Easy Whole, '86 286;
  '87 74
Wheat Rolls, Light, '87 254
Wheat Rolls, Petite Whole, '85 146
Wheat Rolls, Whole, '79 275
Yam Rolls, Golden, '86 299
Yeast Rolls, Buttermilk, '79 59
Yeast Rolls, Easy, '81 78; '86 16
Yeast Rolls, Low-Sodium, '84 228
Yeast Rolls, Quick, '84 267
Yeast Rolls, Refrigerator, '81 296, 307;
  '82 309; '83 17, 118
Yeast Rolls, Speedy, '82 309; '83 17

Rutabagas
au Gratin, Rutabaga, '79 254
Bacon, Rutabaga with, '83 243
Boiled Rutabagas, '86 224
Buttered Rutabagas, '81 274
Creamy Rutabaga, '79 254
Mashed Rutabagas, '86 295
Simple Rutabaga, '83 243
Steamed Rutabagas, '81 274

S

Salad Dressings
Almond Salad Dressing, '81 37
Apple Dressing, '83 181
Artichoke Dressing, '84 126
Avocado Dressing, '80 15
Avocado Fruit Salad Dressing, '82 93
Bacon Dressing, Hot, '84 12
Barbecue Salad Dressing, '80 74
Blender Dressing, '80 78
Blue Cheese Dressing, '79 69; '82 166;
'86 233
Blue Cheese Dressing, Apple Salad
with, '87 103
Blue Cheese Dressing, Creamy, '81 150
Blue Cheese Dressing, Special, '80 30
Blue Cheese Dressing, Tangy, '87 81
Blue Cheese Dressing, Zesty, '79 104
Blue Cheese Salad Dressing, '82 94
Blue Cheese Salad Dressing,
Creamy, '86 123
Buttermilk Dressing,
Down-Home, '84 114
Buttermilk Salad Dressing, '79 69
Caesar Salad Dressing, '82 94
Celery-Honey Dressing, '80 42
Celery Seed Dressing, '82 265
Celery Seed Salad Dressing, '82 94
Citrus Dressing, '85 92

Coconut Dressing, '87 251
Coconut-Fruit Dressing, Tangy, '84 171
Creamy Dressing, '79 159; '83 81; '85 26
Creamy Salad Dressing, '83 181
Cucumber Dressing, '80 74
Cucumber-Mint Dressing, '87 153
Cucumber Salad Dressing, Creamy, '82 79
Curried Dressing, '84 115
Curry Dressing, '80 242; '82 78
Dairy Land Salad Dressing, '86 85
Date Dressing, '87 57
Delightful Salad Dressing, '83 181
Dilly Dressing, '80 74
Egg Dressing, '86 79
French Dressing, Creamy, '81 60
French Dressing, Grapefruit, '80 101

French Dressing, Green Salad with
Lemony, '85 67
French Dressing, Honey, '87 81
French Dressing, Miracle, '82 79
French Dressing, Onion-, '84 283
French Dressing, Piquant, '87 202
French Dressing, Spicy, '81 150; '86 123
French Dressing, Sweet, '82 94
French Dressing, Tangy, '84 12
French Dressing, Tomato-Honey, '81 105
Fruit Dressing, Fluffy, '79 69
Fruit Dressing, Fresh, '87 134
Fruit Dressing, Marmalade-, '84 171
Fruit Dressing, Sweet-and-Sour, '84 125
Fruit Dressing, Whipped Cream, '79 270
Fruit Salad Dressing, '79 69
Fruit Salad Dressing, Creamy, '82 94
Fruit, Salad Dressing for, '86 40
Fruit Salad, Dressing for, '87 81
Fruit Salad Dressing, Red, '83 231
Garden Dew Dressing, '86 50
Garden Dressing, Spring, '85 157
Garlic Dressing, '79 269; '80 14
Garlic-Herb Salad Dressing,
Creamy, '84 66
Garlic Salad Dressing, '86 123
Ginger Dressing, '82 194
Ginger-Yogurt Dressing, '81 302
Grapefruit Salad Dressing, '84 262
Greek Goddess Dressing, '81 150
Herb Dressing, '80 122
Herb-Mayonnaise Sauce, '85 73
Herb Salad Dressing, '86 40
Honey Dressing, '79 242; '83 146; '87 129
Honey-Lime Dressing, '83 139
Horseradish Dressing, '87 152
Italian-American Salad Dressing,
Creamy, '79 69
Italian Dressing, '79 52; '85 261
Italian Dressing, Special, '79 190
Italian Dressing, Tomato, Onion, and
Cucumber in, '81 83
Italian Salad Dressing, '80 82; '84 12
Lemon Cream Dressing, '82 170
Lemon-Herb Salad Dressing, '82 67
Lemon-Pepper Dressing, '87 55
Lemon Salad Dressing, '79 8
Lime Dressing, '79 2; '83 120
Lime-Honey Fruit Salad Dressing, '87 81
Lime-Parsley Dressing, '85 131
Lime Sherbet Dressing, '80 221
Mayonnaise Dressing, '86 11
Mayonnaise Dressing, Herbed-, '86 119
Mayonnaise, Easy Homemade, '84 12
Mayonnaise, Homemade, '80 155
Mayonnaise, Hot Wine, '81 83
Mayonnaise, Parmesan, '86 79
Mayonnaise, Russian, '80 137
Mint Dressing, '80 183
Mint Dressing, Fresh, '84 126
Mustard Dressing, '80 112
Olive Oil Dressing, '84 266
Orange Blossom Dressing, '82 266
Orange-Coconut Dressing, '80 158
Orange Dressing, '81 141
Orange-Poppy Seed Dressing, '87 187
Orange-Yogurt Dressing, '85 304
Oregano Dressing, '86 141
Oregano-Vinaigrette Dressing, '79 113
Paprika Dressing, '86 191
Parmesan Dressing, '86 192
Pasta Salad Dressing, '86 121
Pear Dressing, '83 146

Pepper Dressing, '80 174
Pepper-Onion Salad Dressing,
Green, '84 12
Peppery Salad Dressing, '79 69
Pesto Salad Dressing, '86 150
Pimiento Dressing, Lettuce Wedges
with, '84 212
Pineapple Cream Dressing, '83 81
Pineapple Dressing, Fruit Salad
with, '85 207
Pineapple-Poppy Seed Dressing, '85 55
Pineapple Salad Dressing, '81 36
Poppy Seed Dressing, '80 152; '81 63,
252; '83 153, 316; '84 16; '86 123, 305
Poppy Seed Dressing, Blender, '79 176
Raspberry Dressing, '87 153
Rémoulade Dressing, '86 123
Romano Dressing, '80 174
Roquefort Dressing, '79 85; '80 74
Roquefort Dressing, Creamy, '84 12
Rosemary Dressing, '81 131
Rum Dressing, '80 139
Russian Dressing, '80 4
Russian Dressing, Spinach Salad
with, '79 144
Russian Sour Cream Dressing, '79 55
Russian-Style Dressing, '83 181
Russian-Style Salad Dressing, '86 305
Sesame Seed Dressing, '87 81
Sherry Dressing, Cherry Salad
with, '79 165
Sour Cream Dressing, '82 164; '86 331
Sour Cream Sauce, '87 233
Soy Dressing, '86 191
Soy-Sesame Dressing, '87 153
Spicy Dressing, '80 55
Spinach Salad Dressing, '83 181
Stay Trim Dressing, '86 40
Strawberry Dressing, Creamy, '84 161
Sweet-and-Sour Dressing, '80 247; '84 70,
161; '85 163; '87 305
Sweet-Sour Dressing, '80 246
Tangy Dressing, '83 9
Tangy Red Dressing, '86 191
Tangy Salad Dressing, '80 146; '84 115
Thousand Island Dressing, '80 74;
'81 104; '83 135; '86 123
Thousand Island Dressing, Special, '82 79
Tomato-Cream Cheese Dressing, Garden
Salad with, '79 173
Tomato Salad Dressing, Fresh, '83 193
Tossed Salad Dressing, '84 115
Touchdown Salad Dressing, '81 197
Vinaigrette Dressing, '79 171; '87 138
Vinaigrette Dressing and
Croutons, '86 M288
Whipped Cream Salad Dressing, '82 145
Wine Dressing, Creamy, '85 20
Yogurt Dressing, '85 59, 215
Yogurt Dressing, Sweet-Hot, '86 40
Yogurt-Honey Poppy Seed
Dressing, '83 177
Yogurt Salad Dressing, '79 69
Salads
Acini di Pepe Salad, '83 163
Alfalfa-Celery Salad, Overnight, '82 97
Ambrosia
Anytime Ambrosia, '86 182
Baked Ambrosia, '83 303
Bowl, Ambrosia, '80 138; '84 313
Brunch Ambrosia, '83 57
Carrot-Ambrosia Salad, '81 252
Carrot-Marshmallow Ambrosia, '80 5

Salads, Ambrosia *(continued)*

Chicken Salad Ambrosia, '85 216
Citrus Ambrosia, '82 287
Fruit Ambrosia, Mixed, '83 10
Honey Bee Ambrosia, '83 267
Mold, Ambrosia, '79 241
Mold, Ambrosia Cream
   Cheese, '79 249
Old-Fashioned Ambrosia, '80 5
Orange Ambrosia Supreme, '79 37
Peach Ambrosia, '83 53
Salad, Ambrosia, '83 231
Sherried Ambrosia, '84 324; '86 317
Tropical Ambrosia, '79 74
Antipasto, Easy, '85 114
Antipasto, Pasta, '85 286
Antipasto Salad, '84 66
Apple-Bran Salad, Lemony, '86 223
Apple-Carrot Salad, '85 22
Apple-Cream Salad, Frozen, '82 80
Apple-Nut Salad, '80 226
Apple-Raisin Salad, Curried, '80 24
Apple Salad, '87 233
Apple Salad, Cheesy, '86 301
Apple Salad, Crunchy, '80 138
Apple Salad, Double, '84 227
Apple Salad, Fresh, '81 207
Apple Salad, Spicy, '85 215
Apple Salad, Summer, '80 149
Apple Salad, Swiss-, '84 81
Apple Salad with Blue Cheese
   Dressing, '87 103
Apple Snow Salad, '81 224
Apple Wedges with Poppyseed
   Dressing, '86 131
Apricot Salad, Frosted, '80 248
Artichoke-Rice Salad, '80 178; '81 41;
   '85 81
Artichoke Salad, '86 333
Artichoke Salad, Marinated, '83 241
Artichoke-Tomato Salad, '82 239
Asparagus-and-Egg Salad, '86 305
Asparagus-Artichoke Salad, '85 162
Asparagus-Horseradish Salad, '87 80
Asparagus, Marinated, '83 46; '86 92
Asparagus Salad Cups, '83 47
Asparagus Salad, Marinated, '79 20
Asparagus Vinaigrette, '80 77
Asparagus Vinaigrette, Light, '82 50
Asparagus with Tarragon
   Marinade, '83 47

Asparagus with Yogurt Dressing, '79 66
Aspic
   Apple Aspic, Sunshine, '81 73
   Basic Aspic for Garnishing, '84 189
   Coating, White Aspic, '85 151
   Fish Aspic, '84 190
   Fish 'n Aspic, '84 190
Grapefruit Aspic, '80 297; '82 112;
   '83 153
Madeira Aspic, '86 65
Orange-and-Carrot Aspic, '86 199
Shrimp-Coleslaw Aspic, '79 88
Shrimp-Cucumber Aspic, '83 108
Sunshine Aspic, '80 103
Tomato-Artichoke Aspic, '84 320;
   '86 92
Tomato Aspic, Bloody Mary-, '81 77
Tomato Aspic, Chicken in, '84 190
Tomato Aspic, Chili Sauce, '85 252
Tomato Aspic, Herbed, '81 73
Tomato Aspic, Light, '85 83
Tomato Aspic, Ranch, '83 218
Tomato Aspic, Spicy, '81 40
Tomato Aspic, Tangy, '83 124
Tomato Aspic with Shrimp, '79 241
Tomato-Crab Aspic, '85 287
Two, Aspic for, '83 209
Vegetable Aspic, Cheesy, '81 73
Vegetable Aspic with Horseradish
   Dressing, Crisp, '87 152
Avocado Acapulco, '83 2
Avocado and Zucchini Salad,
   Creamy, '79 208
Avocado Garbanzo Salad, '81 33
Avocado-Grapefruit Salad, '85 26
Avocado-Melon Salad, '82 164
Avocado Salad, '81 195; '82 9; '83 69
Avocado Salad, Citrus-, '82 265
Avocado Salad, Spanish, '87 41
Avocados, Salmon-Stuffed, '86 74
Avocados, Shrimp-Filled, '83 2
Avocado with Crabmeat, '86 119
Bacon and Black-Eyed Salad, Hot, '85 7
Banana Salad, '87 80
Banana Salad, Frozen, '82 80, 132
Bananas, Nutty, '79 251
Bean
   Chilled Bean Salad, '80 178
   Cucumber-Bean Salad, '83 81
   Five-Bean Salad, Hot, '81 149
   Four-Bean Salad, '79 20; '84 82
   Full o' Beans Salad, '81 38
   Garbanzo Salad, '82 2
   Garbanzo Salad, Avocado-, '81 33
   Green Bean-and-Tomato
      Salad, '86 180
   Green Bean-Peanut Salad, '86 117
   Green Bean-Potato Salad, '83 80
   Green Bean Salad, '87 90
   Green Bean Salad, Cold, '84 106
   Green Bean Salad, Crispy, '82 239
   Green Bean Salad, Hot, '86 298;
      '87 176
   Green Bean Salad, Lettuce and,
      '80 79
   Green Bean Salad, Paprika-, '86 191
   Green Bean Salad, Pickled, '82 239
   Green Bean Salad, Speedy, '84 283
   Green Beans, Marinated, '83 145
   Green Beans Vinaigrette, '83 25
   Hacienda Salad, '81 67
   Kidney Bean-Salami Pasta
      Toss, '85 165
   Lima Beans, Chilly, '81 206
   Lima Bean-Tomato Salad, '85 137
   Marinated Bean-and-Rice
      Salad, '87 152
   Marinated Bean Salad, '85 137, 296
   Marinated Bean Salad,
      Crunchy, '84 197
   Marinated Corn-Bean Salad, '87 9
Mexican Salad, '81 113
Mexican-Style Salad, '83 240
Mexican Tossed Salad, '81 280
Mixed Bean Salad, '83 217
Niçoise, Salad, '86 35
Overnight Fiesta Salad, '83 80
Pasta-Bean Salad, '86 169
Pinto Salad, '86 169
Pole Bean-Potato Salad, Hot, '79 74
Pork-'n'-Bean Salad, '87 83
Potato-Bean Salad, '82 301
Rice-and-Bean Salad, '85 22
Sandwiches, Bean Salad, '81 243
Saucy Bean Salad, '84 18
Six-Bean Salad, Colorful, '87 82
Southwest Salad, '81 113
Sprout Salad, Bean, '82 113
Sweet-and-Sour Bean Salad, '85 198;
   '86 147
Sweet-and-Sour Beans with
   Sprouts, '86 32
Beef-and-Broccoli Salad, '87 187
Beef-Cauliflower Salad, Corned, '83 16
Beef-Potato Salad, Corned, '85 213
Beef Salad, Potato-Corned, '81 36
Beef Salad, Roast, '80 223; '81 56
Beef Salad, Tangy, '87 M218
Beef Salad, Vegetable-Corned, '80 148
Beef Salad, Zesty, '79 56
Beet Salad, Marinated, '83 216
Beets and Cauliflower, Chilled, '80 137

Berry Grapefruit Cup, '79 242
Blue Cheese-Pear-Apple Salad, '81 224
Boats, Salad, '80 93
Broccoli and Cauliflower Salad, '81 280
Broccoli and Cauliflower Salad,
   Creamy, '81 23
Broccoli and Cauliflower Toss,
   Crunchy, '83 25
Broccoli and Red Pepper Salad, '83 224
Broccoli-Corn Salad, '87 24
Broccoli, Marinated, '81 40
Broccoli Medley, '81 206
Broccoli Salad, '82 24; '85 249
Broccoli Salad, Creamy, '79 143
Broccoli Salad, Crunchy, '83 39
Broccoli Salad, Curried, '86 225
Broccoli Salad, Fresh, '82 34; '87 103
Broccoli Salad, Marinated, '83 240
Broccoli Salad Supreme, '83 260
Brussels Sprouts Salad, '87 233
Cabbage and Fruit Salad, '79 286
Cabbage Salad, '87 120, 233
Cabbage Salad, Chinese, '81 271
Cabbage Salad, Garden, '81 210
Cabbage Salad, Nutty, '87 42
Cabbage Salad, Overnight, '79 83

Cabbage Salad, Tangy, '82 55
Cabbage, Sweet-Sour Red, '79 5
Cantaloupe Cooler Salad, '79 176
Cantaloupe-Pecan Salad, '86 178
Cantaloupe Salad, '86 182
Carrot-and-Seed Salad, Fruity, '86 223
Carrot-and-Zucchini Salad, '83 240
Carrot-Fruit Toss, '82 235
Carrot-Raisin Salad, '83 117; '84 174;
  '87 10
Carrot Ring, Festive, '82 16
Carrot Salad, Favorite, '80 33
Carrot Salad, Shredded, '80 178
Carrot Salad, Simple, '82 101; '84 152
Carrot Salad, Sunshine, '82 132
Carrots, Creamy Marinated, '87 200
Carrot-Tangerine Salad, '83 316; '84 16
Cauliflower and Pea Salad,
  Savory, '81 280
Cauliflower-Broccoli Salad, '79 20
Cauliflower-Broccoli Toss, '82 54
Cauliflower-Brussels Sprouts
  Salad, '83 240
Cauliflower-Olive Toss, '85 198; '86 147
Cauliflower Salad, '79 221; '80 83;
  '81 225; '84 291; '85 240, 279
Cauliflower Salad, Creamy, '82 102
Cauliflower Salad, Crunchy, '80 4; '82 75
Cauliflower Salad, Layered, '83 240
Cauliflower Salad, Marinated, '82 303;
  '84 232
Cauliflower Salad, Sweet-and-Sour, '81 2
Cauliflower-Vegetable Salad, '85 158
Celery-and-Cauliflower Salad, '83 39
Celery Salad, '79 70
Cheese-Banana Splits, Cottage, '87 56
Cheesy Italian Salad, '84 33
Chef Salad, Mexican, '85 84
Chef's Garden Salad, '83 146
Chef's Salad, '86 186
Chef's Salad Bowl, '84 66
Chef's Salad, Combination, '86 47
Chef's Salad, Vinaigrette, '81 9
Cherry-Orange Salad, '79 74; '82 56
Cherry Salad, Delicious Frozen, '81 252
Cherry Salad, Fresh, '83 120
Cherry Salad, Frozen, '79 126
Cherry Salad with Honey-Lime
  Dressing, '83 139
Cherry Salad with Sherry
  Dressing, '79 165
Chicken
    Almond Salad, Chicken-, '81 133
    Aloha Chicken Salad, '80 297
    Amandine, Chicken Salad, '81 37
    Ambrosia, Chicken Salad, '85 216
    Artichokes, Chicken Salad
      with, '86 186
    Avocado-Chicken Salad, '87 107
    Avocado Salad, Chicken-, '80 139
    Avocado Salad, Fruited
      Chicken, '82 101
    Avocado Salad Platter,
      Chicken-, '83 2
    Avocado Salad, Tossed
      Chicken-, '80 4
    Avocados, Chicken Salad in, '85 216
    Baked Chicken Salad, '86 297;
      '87 176
    BLT Chicken Salad, '87 144
    Celery Salad, Chicken-, '81 187
    Chicken Salad, '86 232, 261
    Chop Suey Salad, '81 37

Chutney-Chicken Salad, '87 74
Chutney Salad, Chicken, '82 108
Coleslaw, Chicken, '84 2
Cream Puff Bowl, Chicken Salad
  in, '86 232
Crunchy Chicken Salad, '86 157, 207
Curried Chicken-and-Orange
  Salad, '87 144
Curried Chicken Salad, '79 219;
  '84 66; '85 96; '86 131
Curried Chicken Salad on Raisin
  Bread, '85 96
Curried Chicken Salad with
  Asparagus, '81 36
Fancy Chicken Salad, '79 55
Filling, Chicken Salad, '87 106
Fruit, Chicken Salad with, '82 171
Fruited Chicken Salad, '84 25, 290
Fruited Chicken Salad in
  Avocados, '87 41
Fruit Salad, Chicken-, '82 79
Fruity Chicken Salad, '83 157
Grapes, Chicken Salad with, '86 117
Green Salad with Chicken,
  Mixed, '80 54
Hot Chicken Salad, '81 201; '83 196
Hot Chicken Salad, Country
  Club-Style, '86 10
Hot Chicken Salad, Crunchy, '80 138
Hot Chicken Salad Pinwheel, '80 139
Macadamia Chicken Salad, '80 138

Macaroni-Chicken Salad, '85 296;
  '86 302
Mandarin Chicken, Carousel, '79 88
Mango, Chicken Salad with, '86 215
Marinated Chicken-Grape
  Salad, '85 74
Mexican Chicken Salad, '85 84
Nectarine Chicken Salad, '79 175
Old-Fashioned Chicken Salad, '83 79
Oriental Chicken Salad, '85 216
Pasta-Chicken Salad,
  Tarragon, '87 155
Pea Salad, Chicken-, '83 218
Persian Chicken Salad, '81 12
Pineapple-Chicken Salad Pie, '80 138
Pineapple-Nut Chicken Salad, '83 80
Poulet Rémoulade, '87 144
Rice Salad, Chicken-, '81 203
Rice Salad, Hot Chicken-and-, '83 22
Rice Salad, Nutty Chicken-, '83 157
Sandwiches, Chicken-Salad
  Finger, '85 119
Special Chicken Salad, '85 82;
  '87 183
Spinach Tossed Salad,
  Chicken-and-, '83 157
Stack-Up Salad, Chicken, '83 80

Summer Chicken Salad, '83 145
Super Chicken Salad, '82 174
Supreme, Chicken Salad, '79 107, 152
Tahitian Chicken Salad, '84 120
Tarts, Chicken Salad, '84 257
Tortellini Salad, Chicken, '87 288
Tropical Chicken Boats for
  Two, '82 186
Tropical Chicken Salad, '85 216
Twist, Chicken Salad with a, '84 221
Wild Rice-Chicken Salad, '83 146
Chili Salad, Spicy, '86 71
Citrus Salad, '87 103
Citrus Salad Bowl, '86 335; '87 83
Citrus Salad in Orange Cups, '85 47
Citrus Salad, Southern-Style, '84 262
Citrus Vinaigrette Salad, '86 192
Committee, Salad by, '87 288
Congealed
    Apple Cider Salad, '83 123
    Apple Cider Salad Mold, '85 54
    Apple Crunch Salad, '84 232; '86 331
    Apple Salad, Congealed, '85 252
    Apricot Fruit Salad, '82 132
    Apricot Nectar Salad, '83 218;
      '87 236
    Apricot Salad, '81 251; '83 123
    Apricot Salad, Creamy, '85 263
    Asheville Salad, '86 199
    Asparagus-Cucumber Mold, '85 252
    Asparagus Mold, '80 104
    Asparagus Mousse Salad, '86 252
    Asparagus Salad, Congealed, '83 260
    Asparagus Salad, Tart, '81 203
    Avocado Crunch Salad,
      Congealed, '85 26
    Avocado Salad, Congealed, '84 266
    Avocado Salads, Congealed, '87 42
    Bean Salad, Molded Green, '85 252
    Beef Salad, Corned, '80 104
    Beef Salad, Molded Corned, '82 86
    Beet-Nut Salad, '79 74
    Beet Salad Mold, '82 267
    Beet Salad, Pickled, '83 234
    Beet Salad, Tangy, '86 199
    Berry Salad, Layered, '79 173
    Broccoli Salad, Congealed, '84 124
    Cantaloupe, Southern
      Plantation, '82 179
    Carrot-Nut Salad, Creamy, '86 331
    Carrot Salad, '82 137
    Cauliflower-Lemon Salad, '81 23
    Cheese Molds, Snowcap, '79 242
    Cherry-Apple Salad, '86 31
    Cherry Cola Salad, '80 104
    Cherry-Salad, Best, '82 302
    Cherry Salad, Festive, '84 265
    Cherry Salad, Port Wine-, '86 11
    Cherry-Wine Salad, Elegant, '82 56
    Chicken-Cucumber Mold, '80 175
    Chicken Jewel Ring Salad, '83 282
    Chicken-Pea Salad, '83 218
    Chicken Salad Mold, '83 80; '84 163
    Christmas Snow Salad, '82 266
    Citrus Mold, Sparkling, '86 331
    Citrus Salad Mold, Golden, '85 303
    Crabmeat-and-Asparagus, Congealed
      Salad with, '84 86
    Cranberry Mold, '79 250
    Cranberry Salad, Festive, '81 264, 296
    Cranberry Salad, Holiday, '82 266, 288
    Cranberry Salad, Jellied, '83 279;
      '85 281

Salads, Congealed *(continued)*

Cranberry Salad, Layered, '84 322; '86 325
Cranberry Salad Ring, '80 247
Crème de Menthe Salad, '82 122
Creole Salad, '79 147
Cucumber Mold, Creamy, '84 164
Cucumber-Pineapple Salad, '84 124
Cucumber Salad, Creamy, '86 147
Cucumber Salad Mold, '82 111; '83 81, 253
Eggnog Christmas Salad, '86 281
Egg Salad, Deviled, '83 124
Emerald Salad, '81 143
Emerald Salad, Snowy, '87 311
Fall Salad with Ginger Dressing, '82 194
Frosted Salad, Heavenly, '79 286
Fruit Salad, Cherry, '87 236
Fruit Salad, Sparkling, '82 266
Fruit Salad, Spiced Autumn, '87 228
Garden-Patch Salad Molds, '86 283
Garden Salad, Molded, '86 199
Gazpacho Salad Mold, '87 311
Gazpacho Salad, Molded, '79 159
Grape-Cantaloupe Mold, Double, '79 173
Grapefruit Congealed Salad, '83 190
Grapefruit Salad, '83 124; '84 325
Grapefruit Salad, Congealed, '84 325; '85 279
Grape Salad Mold, '83 120
Green Spring Salad, '83 124
Ham Salad, Congealed, '81 36
Holiday Jewel Salad, '81 252
Horseradish Salad, '85 66
Layered Congealed Salad, '81 143
Layered Holiday Salad, '81 252
Layer Mold, Three-, '82 54
Lemon-Cheese Salad, '85 240
Lemon-Cranberry Congealed Salad, '87 311
Lemon-Cucumber Mold, '87 90
Lemon Mold, Cheesy, '79 241
Lemon-Onion Salad, '85 252
Lemon-Vegetable Congealed Salad, '85 22
Lime-Cheese Salad, Frosted, '79 286
Lime Sherbet Salad, '80 104
Mandarin Salad Molds, '85 54
Melon Ball Salad, Congealed, '84 125
Mincemeat Salad, Holiday, '85 263
Molds, Perfection, '81 153
Orange-Pear Salad, '84 164
Orange Salad, Creamy, '84 124
Orange Salad, Frosted, '81 154; '83 123
Orange Salad, Jeweled, '83 210
Orange Sherbet Salad, '81 154
Orange Surprise Salad, '79 12
Peach-Cranberry Ring, Spicy, '85 264
Peaches-and-Cream Salad, '83 108
Peach Frost, '84 164
Peach Party Salad, '84 290
Peach Salad, Pickled, '80 104; '85 264
Peachy Berry Cream Mold, '83 130
Pear-Lime Salad, '84 152
Pear Salad, Royal, '84 265
Pimiento Salad, Sunshine, '84 124
Pineapple-Buttermilk Salad, '82 80

Pineapple-Cucumber Congealed Salad, '83 118
Pineapple Daiquiri Salad, '84 232
Pineapple-Lime Salad, '84 320
Pineapple Mold, Minted, '85 240
Pineapple-Orange Congealed Salad, '83 218
Pineapple-Pear Delight, '82 54
Raspberry Fruit Mounds, '79 35
Raspberry Holiday Mold, '84 253

Raspberry Ribbon Salad, '87 236
Raspberry Salad, '86 286
Rhubarb Congealed Salad, '86 140
Roquefort Salad, Creamy, '79 73
Ruby-and-Emerald Salad, '85 79
Salmon Salad, Chilly, '80 104
Sangría Salad, '86 331
Shrimp Salad, '84 221
Strawberry Salad, Hidden Treasure, '79 11
Strawberry-Wine Salad Mold, '83 261
Sunshine Delight, '86 117
Tomato Mold, Tangy, '79 74
Tomato Ring, Tangy, '84 164
Tomato Salad, Frozen, '84 52
Tomato-Vegetable Ring, '81 302
Tuna-Cheese Mold, Creamy, '81 135
Tuna Ring, Creamy, '80 275
Tuna Salad, Congealed, '84 163
Tuna Salad, Creamy, '82 87, 208
Tuna Salad, Luncheon, '81 135
Vegetable Congealed Salad, Cheesy-, '86 199
Vegetable Relish Salad, '82 267
Vegetable Salad, Congealed, '79 276
Vegetable Salad, Congealed Fresh, '82 240
Waldorf Salad, Congealed, '82 80
Waldorf Salad, Molded, '84 326
Cornbread Salad, '87 172
Corn Salad, '80 247; '81 139; '85 236
Corn Salad, Chilled, '79 20
Corn Salad, Shoepeg, '81 23
Corn Salad, Tasty, '84 289
Cottage Cheese Salad, Different, '85 328; '86 22
Cottage Cheese Salad in Tomatoes, '86 208
Cottage Cheese Salad, Out-of-This-World, '79 44
Cottage-Tomato Salad, '85 163
Crab and Wild Rice Salad, '79 116

Crab-Avocado Salad, '81 114
Crabmeat Luncheon Salad, '82 207
Crabmeat-Shrimp Pasta Salad, '86 208
Crab Mousse, '79 117
Crab Salad, Delightful, '87 145
Crab-Wild Rice Salad, '86 207
Cranberry-Cheese Ribbon Salad, '79 241
Cranberry Christmas Salad, '79 243
Cranberry Oriental, '79 126
Cranberry Salad, Tart, '79 286
Cranberry-Whipped Cream Salad, '83 261
Crawfish Salad, Dilled, '83 126
Cucumber-Almond Salad, '86 147
Cucumber and Tomato Salad, Dilled, '81 153
Cucumber Cooler, Simple, '86 147
Cucumber Mousse, '79 11
Cucumber Salad, Dilled, '82 229
Cucumber Salad, Marinated, '82 111
Cucumbers and Artichokes, Marinated, '82 111
Cucumbers, Cool, '84 152
Cucumbers in Sour Cream, '79 52; '80 178
Cucumber-Vinaigrette Oriental, '85 198; '86 147
Cucumber-Yogurt Salad, '87 33
Curry Salad, Hot Indian, '83 23
Dude Ranch Salad, '80 15
Egg-Rice Salad, '84 18; '86 169
Egg Salad, Green Vegetable and, '79 191
Egg Salad Spread, Cottage-, '82 146
Escarole-and-Bacon Salad, '84 85
Extravaganza, Salad, '87 233
Fast-and-Easy Salad, '85 M328
Fruit. *See also* Salads/Congealed.
Ambrosia, Mixed Fruit, '83 10
Avocado Fruit Salad, '87 41
Chef Salad, Fruited, '85 222
Chef's Fruit Salad, '86 35
Chilled Fruit with Dressing, '85 222
Coconut Fruit Bowl, '83 111
Coconut Salad, Chunky Fruit-and-, '84 24
Colorful Fruit Salad, '82 113
Cottage Cheese-and-Fruit Salad, '86 16
Cottage-Fruit Split, '86 169
Creamy Fruit Salad, '84 265
Cups, Royal Fruit, '81 146
Cups with Pineapple Cream Dressing, Fruit, '83 81
Curried Fruit Salad, '85 107
Date Dressing, Fruit Salad with, '87 57
Delight, Fruit, '86 131
Dressed-Up Fruit, '82 5
Easy Fruit Salad, '80 221
Festive Fruit Salad, '80 16
Fresh Fruit Bowl, Sparkling, '80 146
Fresh Fruit Cup with Mint Dressing, '80 183
Fresh Fruit Salad, '82 165
Fresh Fruit Salad with Celery-Honey Dressing, '80 42
Fresh Fruit Salad with Poppy-Seed Dressing, '80 137
Fresh Fruit with Lemon Sauce, '82 290
Frisky Fruit Salad, '85 46
Frozen Fruit Salad, '83 110
Frozen Fruit Salad, Dreamy, '79 126
Frozen Fruit Salad, Luscious, '81 204

Frozen Salad, Christmas Wreath,
  '79 241
Glazed Fruit Salad, '83 48; '84 290
Hawaiian Fruit Dish, '82 112
Heavenly Salad, '81 252
Holiday Fruit Salad, '87 236
Honeydew Fruit Boats, '81 147
Honeydew Fruit Bowl, '84 186
Honey Dressing, Fruit Salad
  with, '87 129
Honey Fruit Salad, '80 276
Hurry-Up Fruit Salad, '87 236
Jicama-Fruit Salad, '86 83
Layered Fruit Salad, '84 290
Lemonade Fruit Salad, '84 24
Lemon Freeze, Fruity, '82 145
Lettuce and Fruit Salad with Poppy
  Seed Dressing, '80 152
Main Dish Fruit Salad, '83 119
Marinated Fruit Bowl, '80 297
Marinated Fruit Deluxe, '81 146
Medley, Chilled Fruit, '84 60
Medley, Fruit Cup, '85 47
Mélange Delight, Fruit, '81 302
Melon Balls in Watermelon
  Sauce, '79 177
Melon-Citrus Mingle, '79 177
Melon Cocktail, Minted, '81 146
Melon Cooler, '81 146

Melon Mélange, '84 139
Melon Salad, Summertime, '82 101
Minted Fruit Medley, '80 182
Mixed Fruit Cup, '87 233
Mixed Fruit Salad, Banana-, '79 270
Nut Salad, Cheesy Fruit-'n'-, '87 56
Old-Fashioned Fruit Salad, '82 80
Persimmon Fruit Salad, '79 206
Picks, Fruit on, '80 159
Pineapple Dressing, Fruit Salad
  with, '85 207
Pineapple-Fruit Salad, Icy, '87 9
Platter, Fruit Salad, '83 261
Quick-and-Easy Fruit Salad, '81 99
Refreshing Fruit Salad, '85 92
Rhapsody, Fruit, '80 158
Ring, Fruit Cup with, '81 11
Salad, Fruit, '83 209
Sherried Fruit Mélange, '80 158
Shrimp Salad, Fruited, '86 156
Sour Cream Fruit Salad, '80 138
Springtime Fruit Salad, '81 96
Summer Fruit Salad, '82 164
Summer Salad, Favorite, '80 158
Sunny Salad, '80 138
Sweet-and-Sour Fruit Salad, '80 13;
  '84 125
Tropical Fruit Salad with Fresh Mint
  Dressing, '84 126
Vanilla Fruit Cup, '80 183
Watermelon Fruit Basket, '84 161
Wine, Fruit in White, '81 48

Winter Fruit Delight, '80 243
Winter Fruit Salad, '80 248; '82 23
Wreath, Della Robbia Fruit, '87 294
Yogurt Fruit Salad, '81 114
Grapefruit-Avocado Salad, '83 316; '84 16
Grapefruit Combo Salad, '80 50
Grapefruit-Cucumber Salad, '80 100
Grapefruit Winter Salad, '84 24
Greek Salad, '87 103
Green. See also Salads/Spinach.
  Bibb Salad, Tossed, '87 128
  Caesar Salad, '80 112; '86 80
  Caesar Salad, Easy, '87 116
  Caesar Salad, Flippo, '87 61
  California Green Salad, '81 84
  Chef's Salad. See Salads/Chef.
  Citrus Green Salad, '85 304
  Citrus Salad, Southern-Style, '84 262
  Combination Salad Bowl, '85 132
  Combo Salad Bowl, '81 9
  Company's Coming Salad, '79 113
  Cranberry-Topped Green
    Salad, '87 311
  Crimson Greens, '87 153
  Fenron Salad, '79 85
  Garden Salad, '85 92
  Garden Salad Centerpiece, '83 171
  Garden Salad, Herbed, '85 328;
    '86 22
  Garden Salad, Summer, '87 153
  Garden Salad Toss, '81 9
  Garden Salad with Rosemary
    Dressing, Fresh, '81 131
  Grecian Green Salad, '84 266
  Grecian Tossed Salad, '79 174
  Hill Country Salad, '81 9
  Lemony French Dressing, Green
    Salad with, '85 67
  Lettuce, Cheesy Stuffed, '79 175
  Lettuce, Confetti-Stuffed, '87 24
  Lettuce, Delicate Garden, '87 62
  Lettuce, Garden-Stuffed, '83 135
  Lettuce Salad, French, '84 187
  Lettuce Salad, Wilted, '82 302
  Lettuce Salad, Wilted
    Bacon-and-, '85 69
  Lettuce Wedges with Pimiento
    Dressing, '84 212
  Lettuce, Wilted, '86 269
  Mixed Green Salad, Wilted, '85 69
  Mixed Green Salad with
    Chicken, '80 54
  Mixed Greens Salad, '87 62
  Nutty Green Salad, '87 168
  Oriental, Green Salad, '85 92
  Romaine Salad, Tangy, '80 155
  Salmagundi Salad, '83 146
  Savory Green Salad, '81 74
  Sensational Salad, '84 320
  Sesame-Citrus Green Salad, '86 33
  Simply Good Salad, '85 131
  Soy Dressing, Green Salad
    with, '86 191
  Spinach-Kiwifruit Salad, '87 305
  Spring Salad, '87 62
  Spring Salad, Mediterranean,
    '80 148
  Spring Salad Wedges, '87 62
  Summer Salad, Crisp, '85 92
  Summertime Salad, '79 143; '84 195
  Tangy Wilted Salad, '85 69
  Tossed Mixed Green Salad, '84 126
  Tossed Salad, Blue Cheese, '84 195
  Tossed Salad, Boston, '84 85
  Tossed Salad, Radish-Dressed,
    '79 104
Guacamole Salad, '80 14; '87 181
Guacamole-Tomato Salad, '81 302
Ham and Cheese Toss, '79 55
Ham and Macaroni Salad, '79 220
Ham-and-Rice Salad, Mandarin, '87 145
Ham 'n Egg Salad, '81 36
Ham-Noodle Salad, '85 249
Ham-Rice Toss, '82 40
Ham Salad, Crunchy Baked, '83 23
Ham Salad, Fruited, '81 36, 146
Ham Salad, Hearty, '82 40
Ham Salad Sandwich, Tangy, '80 272
Ham Salad, Spicy Italian, '85 74
Ham Salad Spread, '87 92
Ham-Sweet Potato Salad,
  Hawaiian, '82 232
Hearts of Palm Salad, '81 252
Hearts-of-Palm Salad, '87 138
Herb Salad, '87 90
Honeydew Salad with Apricot Cream
  Dressing, '84 191
Ice Cream Salad, '79 126
Italian Salad, '87 145
Jicama-Orange Salad, '86 83
Jicama Salad, '87 123

Layered Salad, '86 35, 79
Layered Salad, Cheesy, '81 37
Layered Salad Deluxe, '81 153
Layered Salad, Hearty, '86 79
Layered Salad, Majestic, '86 79
Layered Salad, Make-Ahead, '81 296
Layered Salad, Overnight, '81 188
Lobster and Orange Salad, '82 207
Macaroni-Cheese Salad, Dilled, '86 208
Macaroni-Crabmeat Salad, '81 153
Macaroni-Ham Salad, '85 218
Macaroni Salad, '87 92
Macaroni Salad, Barbecue, '81 170
Macaroni Salad, Confetti, '82 132;
  '85 297
Macaroni Salad, Crunchy, '82 24
Macaroni Salad for Two, '81 31
Macaroni Salad, Garden, '84 290
Macaroni Salad, Gourmet, '81 253
Macaroni Salad, Hearty, '84 90
Macaroni Salad, Pineapple, '79 220
Macaroni Salad, Refreshing, '80 177
Macaroni Salad, Spiral, '82 276
Macaroni Salad, Sweet-and-Sour, '85 166
Macaroni Salad, Taco, '85 165
Macaroni Salad Véronique, '85 164
Macaroni-Salmon Salad, '82 232
Macaroni Shell Salad, '87 38

Salads (continued)

Macaroni-Shrimp Salad, '85 121
Macaroni-Shrimp Salad, Festive, '85 165
Macaroni Toss, Corkscrew, '83 163
Macaroni-Tuna Salad, Whole
    Wheat, '84 193
Macaroni-Vegetable Salad, '86 209
Madras Salad, '86 82
Main-Dish Salad, '86 191
Mandarin, Salad, '84 231
Mandarin Spinach Salad, '85 163
Mango Salad, '79 137
Mango Salad, Fresh, '84 126
Marinated Salad, '83 170
Meal-in-One Salad, '86 43
Melon Balls, Minted, '87 162
Mexican Salad in a Shell, '86 4
Mexican Salad Supper, '82 9; '83 68
Middle Eastern Salad, '87 107
Minestrone Salad, '79 220
Mushroom-and-Pepper Salad, '86 68
Mushroom Salad, Fabulous, '81 190
Mushroom-Zucchini Salad, '85 8
Olive Clubhouse Salad, '81 114
Olive Salad, Mexican, '85 84
Orange and Pineapple Salad,
    Mandarin, '82 266
Orange-Carrot Salad, '80 89; '84 325
Orange-Cauliflower Salad, '82 266
Orange-Cottage Cheese Salad, '79 44
Orange Cups, '86 92
Orange-Romaine Salad, '84 325; '87 239
Orange Salad Cups, '85 40

Orange Salad, Mandarin, '81 252; '84 161
Orange Salad, Quick, '87 80
Orange-Shrimp Salad, '84 197
Orange-Spinach Salad, '83 316; '84 16
Orange Walnut Salad, '80 246
Oriental Salad Bowl, '87 153
Paella Salad, '86 207
Party Freeze Salad, '82 145
Pasta-and-Shrimp Salad, '83 163
Pasta Salad, '84 139; '86 120; '87 36
Pasta Salad, Crunchy, '85 166
Pasta Salad, Garden, '86 188
Pasta Salad, Main-Dish, '82 199
Pasta Salad, Overnight, '82 276
Pasta, Snappy, '83 164
Pea-and-Apple Salad, English, '87 24
Peaches in a Garden Nest, '87 154
Peach Pinwheel Salad, '79 11
Peach Salad, Frosted, '82 145
Peach Salad, Frozen, '82 54
Peach Salad, Georgia, '80 142
Peach Salad Supreme, Easy, '79 177

Peanut-Apple Salad, '80 5
Pear-and-Celery Salad, '87 56
Pear-and-Spinach Salad, Festive, '85 131
Pear Salad, Crunchy, '83 234; '84 244
Pea Salad, Black-Eyed, '80 112; '86 225
Pea Salad, Cheddar-, '84 82
Pea Salad, Creamy, '80 111
Pea Salad, English, '81 280
Pea Salad, Marinated, '81 204
Pea Salad, Marinated English, '82 54
Pea Salad, Mexi-, '81 7
Pea Salad, Overnight Black-Eyed, '81 280
Pea Salad, Special, '83 239
Pea Salad, Sugar Snap, '86 115
Pea Salad, Three, '84 290
Peas-and-Asparagus Salad, '83 141
Peas, Marinated Black-Eyed, '82 156
Pea Vinaigrette, Black-Eyed, '86 7
Pepper-Cheese Stacks, '87 80
Pepperoni-and-Broccoli Salad, '83 216
Pineapple Boat Aloha, '80 102
Pineapple Boats Ahoy, '80 148
Pineapple Boats, Fresh, '83 153
Pineapple-Celery Salad, '85 95
Pistachio-Pasta Salad, '86 141
Pita Salad Sandwiches, '83 134
Pizza, Salad, '87 182
Plentiful P's Salad, '87 12
Potato
    Any Day Potato Salad, '81 154
    Asparagus-and-New Potato
        Salad, '86 69
    Bacon-Topped Potato Salad, '85 59
    Bean Salad, Potato-, '82 301
    Broccoli-Potato Salad, Hot, '85 23
    Chunky Potato Salad, '81 M138
    Confetti Potato Salad, '80 5
    Corned Beef-Potato Salad, '85 213
    Corned Beef Salad, Potato-, '81 36
    Cottage Cheese-Potato Salad,
        '79 147, 285
    Creamy Potato Salad, '80 178
    Deluxe Potato Salad, '80 155
    Dill Potato Salad, '85 213
    Dill Potato Salad, Hot, '79 78
    Dutch Potato Salad, Hot, '87 176
    Fish-Potato Salad, Smoked, '84 233
    Fruity Potato Salad, '85 214
    Garden Patch Potato Salad, '84 82
    German Potato Salad, '82 134, 239;
        '84 18
    German Potato Salad, Hot, '79 78
    German-Style Potato Salad, '83 23
    Grecian Potato Salad, '82 55
    Green Bean-Potato Salad, '83 80
    Ham-and-Egg Potato Salad, '86 84
    Ham and Potato Salad, '80 272
    Herbed Potato Salad, '87 171
    Hot Dutch Potato Salad, '86 297
    Hot Potato Salad, '79 78; '81 276;
        '86 10
    Hot Potato Salad Supreme, '79 78
    Layered Creamy Potato Salad, '81 23
    Mustard Potato Salad, '86 302
    New Potato Salad, '84 120, 139
    Olive-Potato Salad, '85 114
    Parmesan Potato Salad, Hot, '79 78
    Parslied Potato Salad, '85 240
    Pepper Cups, Potato Salad in, '79 78
    Peppers, Potato Salad 'n', '83 135
    Pickle-Potato Salad, Sweet, '85 213
    Pole Bean-Potato Salad, Hot, '79 74
    Salmon-Potato Salad, '87 285

Saucy Potato Salad, '87 123
Savory Potato Salad, '80 30
Sour Cream Potato Salad, '79 104;
    '80 79
Sour Cream-Potato Salad, '84 149
Spring Salad, Mediterranean, '80 148
Sweet and Sour Potato Salad, '80 152
Sweet Potato Salad, Fresh, '86 226
Tuna-Potato Salad, '84 289
Raspberry Salad, Frozen, '79 287; '80 35
Relish Salad, '84 121

Rice-and-Shrimp Salad, '83 82
Rice-and-Vegetable Salad, Brown, '84 202
Rice-Carrot Ring, '79 246
Rice-Pea Salad, '85 163
Rice Salad, '79 74; '81 51
Rice Salad, Charleston Red, '79 146
Rice Salad, Colorful, '81 253
Rice Salad, Confetti, '80 232
Rice Salad, Crunchy, '82 302
Rice Salad, Curried, '80 84; '85 147, 220
Rice Salad, Hearty, '82 233
Rice Salad, Molded Gazpacho-, '86 221
Rice Salad, Vegetable-, '80 148; '83 198;
    '85 87
Rice Salad, Wild, '85 65
Rice Salad with Artichoke Hearts, '80 232
Rice Salad with Bacon, '79 52
Rice Salad with Fresh
    Mushrooms, '80 231
Rice Salad, Zesty, '81 23
Rice-Shrimp Salad, '79 270
Rolls, Hearty Salad, '81 206
Rolls, Picnic Salad, '79 127
Rotelle Salad, Crunchy, '86 209
Salmon-and-Macaroni Salad, '81 114
Salmon-Pasta Salad, '87 9
Salmon-Rice Salad, '84 289
Salmon Salad, Crunchy, '81 148
Salmon Salad Shells, '85 286
Salmon Salad, Summertime, '82 207
Salmon-Spinach Salad, '87 145
Sauerkraut Salad, '80 178
Sauerkraut Salad, Crunchy, '87 9
Seafood Salad, Baked, '86 10
Seafood Salad, Hot, '79 117; '80 164
Seafood Salad, Polynesian, '79 57
Seafood Salad, Smoky, '84 46
Seashell Salad, '86 209
Shrimp and Avocado Salad, '80 266
Shrimp-and-Orange Rice Salad,
    Zesty, '87 155
Shrimp and Rice Salad, '80 231; '82 207
Shrimp Bowl, Mediterranean, '80 174
Shrimp-Egg Salad, Tossed, '80 4
Shrimp-Endive Salad, '85 73
Shrimp Macaroni Salad, '79 220
Shrimp-Macaroni Salad, '85 219
Shrimp Mousse, '79 57
Shrimp-Rice Salad, Baked, '83 22
Shrimp-Rice Salad, Tangy, '84 66
Shrimp Rotelle, '85 165

Shrimp Salad, '81 94; '86 186
Shrimp Salad, Avocado Stuffed
  with, '82 207
Shrimp Salad, Creamy, '79 56
Shrimp Salad Filling, '87 106
Shrimp Salad in Pastry, '86 105
Shrimp Salad, Marinated, '85 82
Shrimp Salad on the Half Shell, '86 73
Shrimp Salads, Individual, '83 146
Shrimp Salad, Super, '81 37
Shrimp Salad, Vegetable-, '79 190
Slaws
    Apple-Pineapple Slaw, '79 241
    Apple Slaw, Fresh, '81 63
    Bacon Coleslaw, '83 58
    Banana-Nut Slaw, '86 250
    Bean Slaw, Red, '79 247
    Cabbage-and-Apple Slaw, Red, '87 31
    Cabbage-Orange Slaw, '79 135
    Cabbage Slaw, Fresh, '85 139
    Chicken Coleslaw, '84 2
    Chili Coleslaw, '80 178
    Coleslaw, '79 152; '82 135
    Corn and Cabbage Slaw, '79 135
    Cottage Coleslaw, '80 64
    Country-Style Coleslaw, '83 59
    Creamy Coleslaw, '83 170
    Crunchy Coleslaw, '86 295
    Curried Coleslaw, '85 139
    Freezer Slaw, '81 279; '82 24;
      '83 154
    Frozen Coleslaw, '82 102
    Fruit Coleslaw, Three-, '86 250
    Fruited Coleslaw, '83 209; '85 139
    Grape-Poppy Seed Slaw, '86 225
    Grapes and Almonds, Coleslaw
      with, '83 59
    Guacamole Mexican
      Coleslaw, '82 302
    Ham Coleslaw, '84 195
    Hot-and-Creamy Dutch Slaw, '87 127
    Hot-and-Sour Chinese Slaw, '85 139
    Kentucky Coleslaw, '81 216
    Layered Coleslaw, '86 180
    Make-Ahead Coleslaw, '81 155
    Marinated Coleslaw, '79 135
    Mexicali Coleslaw, '84 18
    Old-Fashioned Coleslaw, '80 120;
      '82 225
    Old-Fashioned Slaw, '84 149
    Overnight Cabbage Slaw, '81 88;
      '82 7
    Overnight Coleslaw, '79 135
    Overnight Slaw, '79 5
    Peach Slaw, Party, '86 250
    Peanut Slaw, '85 139
    Pear Slaw, Peanutty-, '86 250
    Pineapple Slaw, Colorful, '86 250
    Polka Dot Slaw, '83 59
    Seafood Slaw, '79 56
    Sour Cream Slaw, '87 10
    Swedish Slaw, '79 135
    Sweet and Crunchy Slaw, '79 104
    Sweet-and-Sour Slaw, '81 237
    Sweet Cabbage Slaw, '79 76
    Tangy Coleslaw, '83 59
    Tomatoes, Coleslaw with, '80 34
    Vegetable Slaw, '81 280
    Zesty Slaw, '82 127
Spaghetti Salad, '82 277; '84 205
Spinach and Bacon Salad, '81 143
Spinach and Mushroom Salad, '80 112
Spinach-and-Onion Salad Bowl, '81 157

Spinach-and-Orange Salad, '86 15
Spinach-Beet Salad, '83 227
Spinach-Blue Cheese Salad, '82 166
Spinach-Lamb Salad, '85 58
Spinach-Lettuce Salad, Layered, '84 266
Spinach, Pickled, '81 69
Spinach Salad, '82 102; '86 302; '87 62
Spinach Salad, Combination, '85 327;
  '86 22
Spinach Salad, Creamy, '83 60
Spinach Salad, Crunchy, '80 147; '81 225
Spinach Salad, Curry, '80 242
Spinach Salad Delight, Fresh, '80 146
Spinach Salad, Festive, '80 247
Spinach Salad, French, '79 8
Spinach Salad, Fresh, '82 73; '83 240;
  '84 15, 77; '86 130

Spinach Salad, Green, '79 142
Spinach Salad, Layered, '80 5
Spinach Salad, Oriental, '82 23
Spinach Salad, Southern, '80 55
Spinach Salad, Special, '80 78
Spinach Salad, Springtime, '81 114
Spinach Salad, Supreme, '79 243
Spinach Salad, Sweet-Sour, '85 M112
Spinach Salad, Wilted, '81 M4
Spinach Salad with Creamy Dressing,
  Crisp, '83 81
Spinach Salad with Hot Bacon
  Dressing, '82 211
Spinach Salad with Orange
  Dressing, '87 187
Spinach Salad with Russian
  Dressing, '79 144
Spinach Salad, Zesty, '79 88
Spinach-Sprout Salad, Fresh, '82 281;
  '83 42
Spinach with Feta, Lemon, '85 190
Spinach with Spicy Dressing,
  Fresh, '80 55
Sprout Salad, Spanish, '85 327; '86 22
Steak Salad Cups, Pepper, '86 206
Strawberry Yogurt Salad, '80 232
Tabbouleh, '85 148
Taco Salad, '79 56; '83 145; '84 221;
  '85 84
Taco Salad Cups, '85 M29
Taco Salad, Meatless, '81 204
Taco Salad, Spicy, '87 287
Tomato-Avocado Salad, '86 74
Tomato-Basil Vinaigrette, '87 89
Tomato-Cucumber-Onion Salad, '81 239
Tomato-Cucumber Salad, '86 218
Tomatoes, Avocado-Stuffed, '82 101
Tomatoes, Cold Stuffed, '80 100
Tomatoes, Herbed, '83 173
Tomatoes, Marinated, '85 156, 163
Tomatoes, Marinated Salsa, '82 164
Tomatoes, Oregano, '83 145
Tomatoes Vinaigrette, '84 106
Tomato-Feta Salad, '81 246

Tomato Petal Salad, '79 88
Tomato Refresher, '81 94
Tomato Relish Salad, '83 111
Tomato Salad, Artichoke-Stuffed, '82 101
Tomato Salad, Cherry, '87 156
Tomato Salad, Crab-Stuffed, '80 148
Tomato Salad, Oriental-Stuffed, '82 101
Tomato Salad, Vidalia-, '84 65
Tomato Slices, Marinated, '83 193
Tomato Slices with Lemon
  Dressing, '87 167
Tomato Treat, Summer, '79 143
Tossed Salad with Parmesan
  Dressing, '86 192
Tropical Salad, '85 91
Tuna
    Cannellini Bean Salad,
      Tuna-and-, '86 143
    Cheese-Sauced Tuna Salad, '87 M124
    Chef Salad, Tuna, '82 78
    Company Tuna Salad, '87 201
    Confetti Salad, '80 4
    Crunchy Tuna Salad, '87 201
    Curried Tuna Salad, '86 208
    Curried Tuna Salad with
      Grapes, '87 201
    Egg Salad, Tuna-, '81 135
    Favorite Tuna Salad, '82 208
    Flavorful Tuna Salad, '81 37
    Greens and Tuna Salad,
      Fresh, '80 55
    Layered Tuna Salad, '84 221
    Macaroni Salad, Tuna, '83 44
    Macaroni Salad, Tuna-, '83 145;
      '84 66
    Potato Salad, Tuna-, '84 289
    Rice Salad, Tuna-, '87 202
    Rolls, Hot Tuna Salad, '84 281
    Swiss Tuna Salad, '86 186
    Taco Salad, Tuna-, '87 145
    Tomatoes, Tuna-Mac in, '87 188
    Whole Wheat Macaroni-Tuna
      Salad, '84 193
Turkey-Carrot Salad, '86 283
Turkey-Fruit Salad, '79 56
Turkey Fruit Salad, '83 233; '84 244
Turkey Macaroni Salad, '83 282
Turkey Salad Bake, '79 253
Turkey Salad, Fruitful, '84 197
Turkey Salad, Holiday, '84 320
Turkey Salad, Hot, '86 10, 297; '87 176
Turkey Salad, Layered, '86 332
Turkey Salad Pita Sandwiches, '87 202
Turkey Salad, Polynesian, '87 285
Turkey Salad with Hot Bacon
  Dressing, '87 285
Turkey Salad with Sautéed
  Walnuts, '86 117
Turkey-Zucchini Salad, '85 74
Turnip Salad, '85 235
Vegetable. See also Salads/Congealed.
    Antipasto, Vegetable, '85 263
    Boats, Salad, '80 93
    Calico Salad, '82 35
    Cauliflower-Pea Salad, '87 231
    Chinese Salad, '80 4
    Composée, Salad, '79 171
    Creamy Vegetable Salad, '79 47
    Creole Salad, '79 147
    Crunchy Vegetable Salad, '79 11;
      '80 217; '83 216
    Different Vegetable Salad, '82 143
    Easy Vegetable Salad, '83 316; '84 16

Salads, Vegetable *(continued)*

Garden Medley Salad, '80 122
Garden Salad, '87 62
Garden Salad Bowl, '82 239
Garden Salad with Tomato-Cream
    Cheese Dressing, '79 173
Greek Salad, Garden, '86 173
Green-and-White Vegetable
    Salad, '79 286
Green Vegetable Salad,
    Overnight, '80 5
Italian Vegetable Salad, '81 253;
    '82 19
Luncheon Salad, '84 232
Marinade, Fresh Vegetable, '83 209
Marinade, Garden, '81 23
Marinade, Medley, '79 20
Marinade, Tossed Vegetable, '84 266
Marinated Combo Salad, '82 267
Marinated Garden
    Vegetables, '87 252
Marinated Salad,
    Eight-Vegetable, '80 218
Marinated Summer Salad, '81 153
Marinated Vegetable-Bacon
    Bowl, '79 191
Marinated Vegetable Patch
    Salad, '84 232
Marinated Vegetables, '79 146;
    '81 239; '85 67
Marinated Vegetable Salad, '79 106,
    143; '81 280; '82 163; '83 260;
    '84 13; '87 243
Marinated Vegetable Salad,
    Crispy, '84 193
Marinated Vegetable Salad,
    Fresh, '86 173
Marinated Vegetables,
    Sweet-and-Sour, '83 266
Marinated Vegetables, Zesty, '82 272
Marinate, Fresh Vegetable, '80 33;
    '81 230
Meal-in-One Salad, '82 232
Mexican Salad, '81 36, 113
Mixed Vegetable Salad, '80 115;
    '81 302; '82 239; '83 317; '84 16;
    '86 136
Next-Day Vegetable Salad, '83 81
Oriental Salad, Make-Ahead, '82 163
Oriental Vegetable Salad, '84 290
Party Vegetable Salad, '86 79
Rainbow Vegetable Salad, '83 111
Refrigerated Vegetable Salad, '84 120
Rice-and-Vegetable Salad, '86 42
Rolls, Vegetable Salad, '82 278
Senator's Salad, '79 191
Seven-Layer Vegetable Salad, '79 88
Swedish Vegetable Salad, '82 23
Sweet-and-Sour Vegetable
    Salad, '81 25
Tangy Vegetable Toss, '79 144
Tarragon-Vegetable Salad, '85 288
Variety Salad, '79 113
Vinaigrette Salad, Vegetable-
    Chicken, '86 135
Vinaigrette, Vegetables, '82 225, 290
Walnuts, Vegetable Salad
    with, '86 118
Winter Vegetable Salad, '86 42
Vermicelli Vinaigrette Salad, '82 189
Waldorf Salad, Creamy, '87 311
Waldorf Salad, Deluxe, '83 81
Waldorf Salad, Frozen, '79 126; '82 145
Waldorf Salad, Old-Fashioned, '81 295
Waldorf Salad, Overnight, '81 309
Watercress Salad, '79 144
Watercress-Tomato Salad, '85 132
Watermelon Salad with Celery-Nut
    Dressing, '80 182
Watermelon Sparkle, '84 191
Yogurt-Cucumber Salad, '82 122
Ziti-Cheddar Salad, '85 165
Zucchini Chef's Salad, '83 143
Zucchini, Marinated, '80 33
Zucchini Salad, '82 104; '87 103
Zucchini Salad, Marinated, '82 164

Salmon

Avocados, Salmon-Stuffed, '86 74
Ball, Salmon, '80 149; '86 262
Ball, Smoky Salmon Cheese, '82 247
Barbecued Salmon, '81 181
Carbonara, Salmon, '83 43
Casserole, Salmon, '81 22
Chilled Salmon with Dill Sauce, '84 285
Croquettes, Baked Salmon, '81 22
Florentine, Salmon, '83 43
Kabobs, Salmon, '81 182
Loaf, Easy Salmon, '80 4
Loaf with Cucumber-Dill Sauce,
    Salmon, '86 5
Log, Salmon, '81 22
Mousse, Irresistible Salmon, '79 284
Mousse, Salmon, '83 79
Mousse, Salmon Dill, '81 21
Patties, Open-Faced Salmon, '87 M218
Poached Salmon, '83 35
Potatoes, Salmon-Topped, '84 124
Quiche, Salmon, '82 87; '87 38
Roll, Salmon Party, '83 127
Salad, Chilly Salmon, '80 104
Salad, Crunchy Salmon, '81 148
Salad, Macaroni-Salmon, '82 232
Salad, Salmon-and-Macaroni, '81 114
Salad, Salmon-Pasta, '87 9
Salad, Salmon-Potato, '87 285
Salad, Salmon-Rice, '84 289
Salad, Salmon-Spinach, '87 145

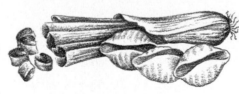

Salad Shells, Salmon, '85 286
Salad, Summertime Salmon, '82 207
Scalloped Salmon, '81 273
Soufflé, Fresh Salmon, '81 182
Spread, Salmon, '81 149
Spread, Salmon-and-Horseradish,
    '87 146
Spread, Smoked Salmon, '84 324
Steaks, Baked Salmon, '85 54
Steaks, Glazed Salmon, '86 256
Steaks, Marinated Salmon, '87 6
Steaks, Oven-Fried Salmon, '81 181
Steaks with Dill Sauce, Salmon,
    '85 164
Steaks with Tarragon Butter,
    Salmon, '87 155
Terrine, Layered Salmon-and-
    Spinach, '84 132
Turnovers, Salmon-Spinach, '83 44

Sandwiches

Alfalfa Pocket Bread Sandwiches, '82 282;
    '83 41
Apple-Cinnamon Breakfast
    Sandwiches, '85 298
Apple Sandwiches, '79 164; '80 130
Asparagus Grill Sandwiches, '79 164;
    '80 130
Asparagus Spear Sandwiches, '84 165
Avocado, Bacon, and Cheese
    Sandwiches, '87 279
Avocado-Crabmeat Sandwiches, '83 2
Bacon, Cheese, and Tomato
    Sandwiches, '84 14
Bacon-Cheese Sandwiches,
    Grilled, '83 242
Bacon Sandwiches, Open-Faced
    Cheesy, '80 78
Basket of Sandwiches, Bread, '86 126
Bean Salad Sandwiches, '81 243
Beef and Pork Tenderloin
    Sandwiches, '80 175
Beef-Eater Sandwiches, '86 72
Beef Pocket Sandwich, Saucy, '80 92
Beef Salad Pocket Sandwiches, '83 267
Beef Sandwiches, Barbecued, '81 25;
    '82 31; '83 34
Beef Sandwiches, Grilled Corned, '87 54
Beef Slice, French, '79 125
BLT's, Cheesy, '85 92
Breakfast Sandwiches, '80 52; '82 M123
Brown Bread-Cream Cheese
    Sandwiches, '87 M6
Bunwiches, '80 92
Calzone, '85 94
Cheeseburger Biscuits, '79 194
Cheese-Ham Sandwiches, Creamy
    Blue, '87 279
Cheese Sandwiches, Grilled, '82 M172
Cheese Sandwiches, Hot French, '82 3
Chef's Salad, '86 186
Chicken-Almond Pocket
    Sandwiches, '81 240; '83 69
Chicken-and-Cheese Sandwiches,
    Toasted, '85 242
Chicken Club Sandwiches, '86 160
Chicken in a Sandwich,
    Marinated, '86 185
Chicken-Salad Finger Sandwiches, '85 119
Chicken Salad on Raisin Bread,
    Curried, '85 96
Chicken Salad with Artichokes, '86 186
Chicken Sandwich, Crispy, '81 114
Chicken Sandwiches, Baked, '79 164;
    '80 130; '84 165
Chicken Sandwiches, Cheesy, '82 190
Chicken Sandwiches, Hot, '83 291
Chicken Sandwiches, Marinated, '86 M45
Chicken Sandwiches, Puffed, '82 35
Chicken Spread, Tasty, '84 193
Chick-Wiches, Saucy, '81 25; '82 31;
    '83 34
Club Sandwiches, Tangy, '80 93
Club Sandwich, South Seas, '84 282
Confetti Sandwiches, '79 236
Corned Beef and Cheese
    Sandwich, '79 214
Corned Beef Sandwiches, '83 291; '85 242
Corned Beef Sandwiches,
    Barbecued, '83 130
Crab-and-Cheese Sandwiches,
    Hot, '87 279
Crabmeat Sandwiches, '84 285

Crabmeat Sandwiches, Deluxe, '81 M74
Crab Sandwiches, Open-Faced, '87 106
Crab Sandwiches, Puffy, '83 291
Crab Tomato Sandwiches,
  Open-Face, '81 29
Cucumber Pinwheel Sandwiches, '85 120
Cucumber Sandwiches, Dainty, '81 119
Deviled Delight, '83 130
Eggplant Sandwiches, Baked, '82 230
Egg Sandwiches, Open-Face, '83 292;
  '84 78; '86 160
Egg Sandwiches, Open-Faced
  Cheesy, '86 67
Eggsclusive Sandwiches, '79 164; '80 130
Eggs-Tra Special Sandwiches, '81 240;
  '83 69
English Muffin Delight, '82 45
Frankfurter Sandwiches, '84 M11
Garden Sandwiches, Open-Faced, '87 105
Garden, The, '83 134
Grilled Sandwiches, Tasty, '84 30
Grinder Sandwich, '85 299
Guacamole Sandwiches, '82 9; '83 68
Guacamole Subs, '84 293
Ham-and-Cheese Pita Sandwiches, '87 202
Ham-and-Cheese Rolls, '82 3
Ham-and-Cheese Sandwiches,
  Hot, '85 299
Ham-and-Cheese Sandwich,
  Tex-Mex, '86 4
Ham and Swiss in the Pocket, '83 31

Ham-and-Swiss Sandwiches,
  Tangy, '85 164
Ham-and-Turkey Specials, Cheesy, '84 14
Ham Hideaways, '81 29
Ham Hot Rods, '86 136
Ham Loaves, Country, '86 255
Ham Salad Sandwich, Tangy, '80 272
Ham Sandwiches, Baked, '81 29
Ham Sandwiches, Hot, '79 214
Ham Sandwiches, Open-Face, '82 40;
  '85 8
Ham Sandwiches, Virginia, '80 155
Heroes, Neptune, '84 281
Hot Brown Sandwiches, '80 M202
Lamb Pockets with Dilled Cucumber
  Topping, '87 104
Loaf, Big Wheel, '84 281
Meal-in-One Sandwiches, '80 218
Monte Cristo Sandwiches, '83 134
Muffaletta-Style Po-Boys, '83 230
Muffin Stacks, Mushroom-Topped, '80 271
Mushroom Sandwiches, Toasted, '87 281
Omelet Sandwich, '86 95
Open-Faced Sandwiches, '79 214
Open-Face Sandwiches, '84 13
Oyster-and-Bacon Poor Boys, '87 40
Oyster Submarine Sandwich, '80 92

Peanut Butter-and-Jelly Sandwiches,
  Christmas Tree, '85 319
Peanut Butter Breakfast Sandwich, '82 55
Pimiento Cheese Sandwiches, '82 278
Pita Salad Sandwiches, '83 134
Pita Sandwiches, '84 139
Pita Sandwiches, Bavarian, '83 31
Pita Sandwiches, Denver, '86 M12
Pita Sandwiches, Dried Beef, '86 160
Pita Sandwiches, Hot, '83 217; '87 M6
Pita Sandwiches, Vegetarian, '84 193
Pitas, Curried Beef, '85 220
Pitas, Taco, '83 31
Pizza Sandwiches, Open-Face, '82 3;
  '83 85; '84 M198; '85 22
Pizza Sandwich, Giant, '80 93
Pocket Sandwiches, Hearty, '80 93
Pockets, Oriental Stuffed, '79 14
Rarebit, Uptown Welsh, '87 279
Reuben Sandwiches, '80 M201
Reuben Sandwiches, Broiled, '81 240;
  '83 69
Reuben Sandwiches, Crispy, '85 299
Reuben Sandwiches, Grilled, '81 206
Salad Boats, '80 93
Salad Rolls, Hearty, '81 206
Salami Sandwiches, Open-Faced, '87 279
Sausage and Pepper Loaves,
  Italian, '83 11
Sausage Sandwiches with Mustard
  Sauce, '84 250
Sausage Sandwich, Italian, '80 92
Sausage Sloppy Joes, Italian, '86 160
Shrimp-Cheese Sandwiches, '85 242
Shrimp Destin, '82 29
Shrimp Salad, '86 186
Sloppy Joe Pocket Sandwiches, '81 200
Snack Buns, '87 279
Spinach-Oyster Loaves, '84 213
Spinach Sandwiches, Fresh, '85 59
Spinach-Walnut Pitas, '87 202
Sprout Sandwiches, Polynesian, '85 51
Stacking Sandwiches, '86 127
Steaks, Greek Pocket, '81 262
Steak Stroganoff Sandwiches, '85 110
Submarine Sandwiches, Superb, '84 250
Tea Sandwiches, Gingered, '84 116
Tempting Twosome, '81 240; '83 69
Tofu-Veggie Sandwiches,
  Open-Face, '86 5
Tuna Burgers, Zippy, '81 135
Tuna Cheesies, '82 191
Tuna Club Sandwiches, '83 134
Tuna-in-a-Pita Pocket, '87 202
Tuna Salad Rolls, Hot, '84 281
Tuna Salad, Swiss, '86 186
Tuna Sandwiches, French
  Toasted, '80 275
Tuna Sandwiches, Hot, '85 299; '86 M194
Turkey-Cheese Puffs, '87 301
Turkey-Mozzarella Rounds, '82 3
Turkey Open-Facers, '82 190
Turkey Salad Pita Sandwiches, '87 202
Vegetable Garden Heroes, '84 14
Vegetable Pockets, '85 215
Vegetable Puff Sandwich, '85 51
Vegetable Salad Rolls, '82 278
Vegetarian Melt, Open-Faced, '87 106
Vidalia Sandwiches on Salt-Rising
  Bread, '79 145
Wake-Up Sandwiches, '84 58
Wreath, Festive Sandwich, '86 333
Yummy Sandwiches, '81 229

Sauces. *See also* Desserts/Sauces.
Anchovy-Garlic Sauce over
  Vermicelli, '86 158
Apple-Horseradish Sauce, '82 229
Apricot Sauce, '87 172
Apricot-Sauced Pork Chops, '85 22
Avocado Sauce, '80 198; '83 200
Barbecue
  Beer Barbecue Sauce, '84 173
  Bourbon Barbecue Sauce, '85 90
  Dressed-Up Barbecue Sauce, '84 173
  Easy Barbecue Sauce, '79 90; '82 178
  Mustard Barbecue Sauce, '84 173
  Oven Barbecue Sauce, '82 233
  Paprika Barbecue Sauce, '79 90
  Peanut Butter Barbecue
    Sauce, '81 233
  Piquant Barbecue Sauce, '79 159
  Sauce, Barbecue, '84 172; '86 153
  Savory Barbecue Sauce, '86 153
  Special Barbecue Sauce, '82 177
  Tomato Barbecue Sauce,
    Fresh, '84 172

Basil Sauce, Asparagus with, '86 33
Bean Sauce, Pork-and-Onions with,
  '85 76
Béarnaise Sauce, '83 138; '85 37; '86 193
Béarnaise Sauce, Blender, '81 90
Béarnaise Sauce, Classic, '86 244
Béarnaise Sauce, Quick, '82 84
Béchamel Sauce, '80 190; '83 277;
  '84 M239; '87 286
Blueberry Sauce, '80 144; '86 248
Bordelaise Sauce, '83 138, 262
Bouillon Sauce, '80 8
Brandy-Butter Sauce, '79 230
Brandy Sauce, Carrots in, '83 86
Brandy Sauce, Lemony-Butter Steak
  with, '85 78
Buttermilk Sauce, '84 6
Butter Sauce, '86 268
Butter Sauce, Vegetable, '86 174
Catsup Sauce, '81 228
Catsup Topping, '81 170
Champagne Sauce, Chicken Breasts
  with, '86 49
Cheese
  Brussels Sprouts with Cheese
    Sauce, '79 246
  Cottage Cheese Sauce, '87 232
  Cream Sauce, Cheesy, '82 79
  Easy Cheese Sauce, '79 22
  Garlic-Cheese Sauce, '84 M70
  Lemony Cheese Sauce, '84 183
  Monterey Jack Sauce, '84 293
  Mornay Sauce, '80 120; '81 90;
    '83 138; '84 295
  Mushroom-Cheese Sauce, '83 190;
    '86 48
  Parmesan Cheese Sauce, '79 165;
    '80 162; '85 143

Sauces, Cheese *(continued)*

    Rich Cheese Sauce, '81 89
    Sauce, Cheese, '79 M156; '81 43, 44,
      225; '82 M123; '83 49, 138, 188;
      '84 57; '85 92; '86 241
    Swiss Cheese Sauce, '79 35; '87 289
    Swiss Sauce, '83 M195
    Swiss Sauce, Creamy, '80 M53
    Topper, Vegetable-Cheese
      Potato, '86 6
    Turnips in Cheese Sauce, '84 229
    Vegetable-Cheese Sauce, '85 M152
Cherry Sauce, '83 276; '84 91
Cherry Sauce, Elegant, '79 M156
Cherry Sauce, Roast Ducklings
  with, '86 312
Cherry Sauce, Royal, '85 224; '86 83
Cherry Sauce, Spicy, '83 244
Chervil Sauce, '83 128
Chicken Sauce, Creamy, '81 91
Chile Cream, Ancho, '87 121
Chile Sauce, Ancho, '87 122
Chile Sauce, Green, '82 220
Chili Meat Sauce, '83 4
Chili Sauce, '81 175
Chili Sauce, Chunky, '85 188
Chili Sauce, Red, '85 245
Chili Sauce, Spicy, '87 127
Chive Sauce, Steamed Broccoli with
  Tangy, '83 101
Cider Sauce, '87 224
Cilantro Cream, '87 121
Citrus Sauce, Stuffed Flounder Rolls
  with, '85 180
Clam Sauce, Vermicelli and Sprouts with
  Red, '86 143
Cocktail Sauce, '87 128
Cocktail Sauce, Boiled Shrimp
  with, '79 151
Cocktail Sauce, French Fried Zucchini
  with, '86 146
Cocktail Sauce, Spicy, '83 258

Cranberry-Apricot Sauce, Fresh, '87 243
Cranberry Juice Sauce, '85 224; '86 83
Cranberry Sauce, Cornish Hens
  with, '79 180
Cranberry Sauce, Fresh, '79 283; '84 275
Cranberry Sauce, Tart, '83 261
Cranberry Wine Sauce, '83 276
Cream Sauce, '85 291
Cream Sauce, Brandied, '82 70
Cream Sauce, Sherried, '84 210;
  '85 M152
Cream Sauce, Shrimp in, '84 M286
Cream Sauce, Spicy, '82 45
Cream-Wine Sauce, Potatoes in, '86 18
Creamy Sauce, '79 41

Creolaise Sauce, '83 91, 262
Cucumber-Dill Sauce, '86 5
Cucumber Sauce, '82 111; '84 M286
Currant Jelly Sauce, Quail with, '86 94
Currant Sauce, '87 240
Curry Sauce, '79 M156; '83 138; '84 M71
Devonshire Cream, Mock, '81 288
Devonshire Sauce, Processor, '87 58
Dill Sauce, '84 M70, 107; '85 39
Dill Sauce, Chilled Salmon with, '84 285
Dill Sauce, Creamy, '79 M156
Dill Sauce, Salmon Steaks with, '85 164
Egg Foo Yong Sauce, '86 232
Enchilada Sauce, '81 194
Enchilada Sauce, Red Chile, '85 245
Foo Yong Sauce, '80 223
French Sauce, Broccoli with, '81 295
Fruit Sauce, '81 177
Garlic Sauce, Stir-Fried Pork in, '84 141
Grape Sauce, White, '80 38
Green Sauce, Herbed, '86 244
Ham-and-Mushroom Sauce, Steak
  with, '83 109
Heather Sauce, '84 182
Herb Butter Sauce, Corn with, '79 150
Herb-Mayonnaise Sauce, '85 73
Herb Sauce, Green, '83 36
Hollandaise Sauce, '80 M107, M268;
  '81 90; '83 137; '85 295; '86 94;
  '87 195
Hollandaise Sauce, Blender, '79 39;
  '82 84, 234
Hollandaise Sauce, Broccoli
  with, '79 244, 276
Hollandaise Sauce, Broccoli with
  Mock, '82 272
Hollandaise Sauce, Mock, '85 49
Hollandaise-Shrimp Sauce, Flounder
  with, '86 234
Hollandaise, Tangy, '85 148
Honey-Butter Sauce, '85 18
Honey-Lemon Mustard Sauce, '84 275
Honey-Lime Sauce, '82 85
Honey-Mustard Sauce, '85 13
Horseradish Sauce, '84 190; '85 224;
  '86 83; '87 127
Horseradish Sauce and Curried Bananas,
  Fillets with, '85 230
Horseradish Sauce, Broccoli with, '81 2;
  '83 206; '84 33
Horseradish Sour Cream, '86 244
Hot Sauce, '79 185; '83 74
Hot Sauce, San Antonio, '84 291
Italian Sauce, '80 63
Italian Sauce, Quick, '82 230
Italian-Style Sauce, '83 250
Jalapeño Sauce, '80 193
Jezebel Sauce, '81 29; '82 55
Lemon-Butter Sauce, '84 252
Lemon-Celery Sauce, Baked Fillets
  in, '84 91
Lemon Garlic Sauce, Shrimp in, '83 67
Lemon Parsley Sauce, '81 106
Lemon Sauce, '82 290
Lemon Sauce, Asparagus with, '86 62
Lemon Sauce, Chicken Scaloppine
  with, '86 156
Mandarin-Almond Cream Sauce, '84 183
Mandarin Sauce, '84 60
Marinade, '86 153
Marinade, Sweet-and-Sour, '86 113
Marinade, Tangy Beef, '86 113
Marinade, Tangy Light, '82 178

Marinade, Teriyaki, '86 114
Marinara Sauce, '82 178
Meat Sauce, Italian, '83 193
Meunière Sauce, '80 57
Mexican Sauce, '80 198
Microwaving Sauces, '84 M70
Mint Sauce, '84 107
Mushroom-Dill Sauce, '80 271

Mushroom Sauce, '81 90, 200; '82 46;
  '83 71, 205, 212; '84 M70; '86 198;
  '87 36, 186, 284
Mushroom Sauce Supreme on
  Vermicelli, '86 158
Mushroom-Wine Sauce, '84 84; '86 24
Mustard-Hollandaise Sauce,
  Mock, '87 269
Mustard Sauce, '80 222, 283; '83 21, 321;
  '84 M70; '86 185; '87 22
Mustard Sauce, Creamy, '80 272; '86 257;
  '87 232
Mustard Sauce, Extra-Special, '79 82
Mustard Sauce, Hamburger Steaks
  with, '84 230
Mustard Sauce, Light, '82 178
Mustard Sauce, Mild, '85 224; '86 84
Mustard Sauce, Sausage Sandwiches
  with, '84 250
Mustard Sauce, Scallops with, '84 163
Mustard Sauce, Smoked Sausages
  with, '81 56
Mustard Sauce, Sweet, '85 12
Mustard-Sour Cream Sauce, '81 68
Mustard-Vinaigrette Sauce, '84 174
Natillas Sauce, '83 179
Olive-Butter Sauce, Broccoli with, '83 118
Onion Cream Sauce, '87 232
Onion-Mushroom Sauce, '85 224; '86 84
Onion-Parsley Sauce, '85 148
Onion Sauce, '82 72; '87 248
Onion Sauce, Brussels Sprouts in, '81 308
Orange-Almond Sauce, Chicken
  in, '79 219; '80 13
Orange Butter Sauce, Asparagus
  with, '85 43
Orange Liqueur Sauce, '86 142
Orange Sauce, '82 47; '83 10, 277;
  '84 M286
Orange Sauce, Asparagus with, '83 46
Orange Sauce, Brussels Sprouts in, '86 55
Orange Sauce, Celery in, '79 70
Orange Sauce, Chicken Breasts
  with, '79 77
Orange Sauce, Lobster Tails with
  Spiced, '86 155
Parsley-Chive Sauce, '84 212
Parsley-Garlic Sauce, '83 138; '84 M70
Parsley Sauce, '82 248; '86 108
Peach-Blueberry Pancake Sauce, '82 177
Peach-Blueberry Sauce, '81 170
Peach Sauce, Creamy Fresh, '79 177
Peanut Hot Sauce, '86 305
Pea Sauce, Green, '83 22
Pepper-Onion Sauce, '84 125

Pesto, '80 242
Pesto, Fresh, '86 150
Pesto, Garlic, '84 108
Pesto, Tomatoes, '86 150
Pico de Gallo, '79 185; '86 19
Pineapple-Curry Sauce, '79 252
Pineapple Sauce, '84 236
Pizza Sauce, '84 33; '85 285
Plum Sauce, '80 249; '82 40
Plum Sauce, Chinese, '82 237
Plum Sauce, Gingered, '87 175
Plum Sauce, Red, '80 49
Plum Sauce, Spicy, '86 11
Port Wine Sauce, '84 252
Raisin-Pineapple Sauce, '82 177
Raisin Sauce, '83 59, 215; '84 91, 275;
    '87 127
Raisin Sauce, Ham with, '82 M76
Rémoulade Sauce, '80 58; '81 89; '82 178
Rum Sauce, Mango-Spiced, '86 215
Salsa, '87 217
Salsa, Chunky, '86 130
Savory Sauce, '84 196
Seafood
    Clam Sauce, Linguine with, '84 124
    Clam Sauce, Pasta with, '84 291
    Clam Sauce, Vermicelli with, '85 295
    Clam Sauce with Linguine, '84 9
    Crab and Shrimp Sauce
        Piquante, '83 92
    Crab Marinara Sauce,
        Quick, '85 M151
    Delight, Seafood Sauce, '82 91
    Linguine with Seafood Sauce, '83 232
    Sauce, Seafood, '79 3; '82 84; '83 36;
        '86 304
    Shrimp Sauce, Broccoli and
        Cauliflower with, '84 248
    Shrimp Sauce, Flounder Fillets
        in, '83 227
    Stone Crab Mustard Sauce, '80 3
    Stone Crab Sauce, Tangy, '80 3
Sesame Sauce, Vegetables with, '83 112
Sherry Sauce, '87 96
Shrimp-and-Almond Sauce, '87 282
Shrimp Sauce, '87 138, 232
Sour Cream-Dill Sauce, Mushrooms
    in, '84 215
Sour Cream, Mock, '83 71, 205
Sour Cream Sauce, '82 68; '84 132;
    '87 233
Sour Cream Sauce, Broccoli with, '87 127
Soy Sauce, Grilled Trout with Ginger
    and, '85 228
Spaghetti Sauce, Beer, '85 13
Spaghetti Sauce, Herbed, '85 13
Spaghetti Sauce, Thick, '84 118
Spaghetti Sauce, Turkey, '85 13
Spicy Sauce, '84 77
Spinach Sauce, Fettuccine with, '84 329
Strawberry-Banana Sauce, '81 41
Sunshine Sauce, '87 96
Sweet-and-Sour Sauce, '80 20; '85 12, 34;
    '86 240
Taco Sauce, '82 M283
Tarragon Sauce, '83 56; '84 190; '87 229
Tarragon-Tomato Sauce, '84 131
Tartar Sauce, '79 184; '81 134; '82 135;
    '86 233
Tartar Sauce, Bold-and-Spicy, '86 180
Tartar Sauce, Creamy, '80 164
Tartar Sauce, Quick, '87 128
Tempura Sauce, Basic, '81 68

Tomato-Cream Sauce, Linguine
    with, '86 158
Tomato Sauce, '85 193, 244; '87 249
Tomato Sauce, Fish in, '85 75
Tomato Sauce for Spaghetti,
    Italian, '81 134
Tomato Sauce, Fresh, '83 224; '87 171
Tomato Sauce, Herbed, '86 277
Tomato Sauce, Herbed Fresh, '85 M151
Tomato Sauce, Italian, '82 M68
Tomato Sauce, Italian-Style, '87 182
Tomato Sauce, Refrigerator, '85 188
Tomato Sauce, Seasoned, '83 150
Tomato Sauce, Spicy, '84 294
Tomato Sauce, Vermicelli with, '83 164
Tomato Sauce with Green Chiles, '81 196
Vegetable Sauce, Greek Fish with, '82 72
Vegetable Sauce, Pasta with, '83 163
Velouté Sauce, '84 22
Walnut Sauce, Spaghetti with Parsley
    and, '80 30
Whiskey Sauce, '80 58
White Sauce, '82 269; '83 138, 245;
    '87 166

White Sauce, Asparagus, '80 147
White Sauce, Basic, '79 M156; '81 89
White Sauce, Low-Calorie,
    Medium, '87 26
White Sauce, Thick, '82 42
Wine Sauce, Beef Cubes in, '79 264
Wine Sauce, Broccoli with, '84 187
Wine Sauce, Chicken in, '80 8
Wine Sauce, Marsala, '81 77
Wine Sauce, Mushrooms with, '85 292
Wine Sauce, Red Snapper in, '85 138
Wine Sauce, Skillet Steak in Red, '85 21
Wine Sauce, Veal and Carrots
    in, '86 M139
Wine Sauce, White, '84 132
Yogurt-Horseradish Sauce, '85 66
Yogurt Sauce, Lamb Meatballs
    with, '85 132
Zippy Sauce, '86 44
Zucchini Sauce, Spaghetti with, '81 38
Sauerkraut
    Beany Kraut and Franks, '79 64
    Bratwurst and Sauerkraut, '84 250
    Homemade Sauerkraut, '81 216
    Meatballs, Sauerkraut, '86 257
    Relish, Sauerkraut, '85 136
    Salad, Crunchy Saukerkraut, '87 9
    Salad, Sauerkraut, '80 178
    Sausage and Kraut, '83 11
Sausage
    Appetizers, Party Rye, '86 262
    Baked Peaches and Sausage, '82 50
    Baked Zucchini and Sausages, '80 300
    Bake, Eggplant-Sausage, '85 221
    Bake, Sausage Egg, '81 225
    Bake, Sausage-Noodle, '81 92
    Bake, Smoked Sausage-Egg, '85 248
    Balls in Cheese Pastry, Sausage, '80 248
    Balls, Venison Sausage, '80 42
    Barbecued Sausage, '86 153

Beans, and Rice, Texas Sausage, '84 296
Biscuit Bites, Sausage, '84 95
Biscuits, Cheesy Sausage, '80 78
Biscuits, Southern Sausage and, '82 43
Biscuits with Sausage, Angel
    Heart, '87 156
Boudin, Old-Fashioned, '85 250
Bratwurst and Sauerkraut, '84 250
Bratwurst Dinner, Krause's Cafe, '87 238
Breakfast Dish, Sausage-Apricot, '82 10
Burgers, Sausage, '83 212
Burritos, Breakfast, '84 57
Cabbage, Italian Stuffed, '84 294
Cabbage Rolls, Hot-and-Spicy, '84 249
Cabbage, Sausage-Sauced, '81 271
Cabbage, Stuffed, '84 282
Calzone, '85 94
Casserole, Brunch, '82 124
Casserole, Cheesy Sausage, '82 124
Casserole, Country Sausage, '79 192
Casserole, Crunchy Sausage, '81 288
Casserole, Easy Sausage, '87 M189
Casserole, Eggplant-Sausage, '84 215
Casserole, Grits-Sausage, '84 75; '86 241
Casserole, Ground Beef and
    Sausage, '80 260
Casserole, Hawaiian Sausage, '85 42
Casserole, Oriental Sausage and
    Rice, '82 M123
Casserole, Sausage, '81 112; '82 12
Casserole, Sausage and Broccoli, '80 33
Casserole, Sausage and Noodle, '82 123
Casserole, Sausage and Wild
    Rice, '83 196
Casserole, Sausage Breakfast, '81 270
Casserole, Sausage-Egg, '86 M12
Casserole, Sausage Jambalaya, '82 M203
Casserole, Sausage-Mushroom
    Breakfast, '86 95
Casserole, Sausage-Potato, '86 217
Casserole, Sausage-Rice, '82 50; '83 75
Casserole, Sausage-Wild Rice, '84 250
Casserole, Spanish Rice, '79 192
Casserole, Swiss Sausage, '80 209
Chicken Rolls Élégante, '80 210
Chile con Queso Supreme, '80 265
Chili, Beefy Sausage, '82 11
Chili, Company, '82 311
Chili con Carne, Beef and
    Sausage, '83 284
Chili con Queso Dip, '86 81
Chili, Sausage-Beef, '86 232
Chili, Texas-Style, '82 311; '83 30
Chorizo and Egg Tortillas, '81 193
Chorizo (Spicy Spanish Sausage), '81 193
Chorizo Substitute, '87 238
Chowder, Sausage-Bean, '83 20
Cocktail Sausages, Saucy, '87 173
Crêpes, Cheesy Sausage, '82 240; '83 71
Crêpes, Sausage-Filled, '79 39
Dinner, Beefy Sausage, '80 M9
Dinner, Sausage-Vegetable, '84 250
Dip, Braunschweiger-and-Beer, '85 69
Dressing, Cajun, '82 307
Dressing, Cornbread-and-Sausage, '83 213
Dressing, Cornbread-Sausage, '82 307;
    '85 280
Dressing, Sausage, '86 280
Dressing, Turkey with
    Sausage-Cornbread, '83 287
Eggplant Parmesan, '86 53
Eggplant, Sausage Stuffed, '81 204
Eggs, Scotch, '79 261; '83 289

Sausage *(continued)*

Filling, Omelet with Sausage, '81 43
Grits and Sausage, Country, '83 54
Grits, Sausage, '86 92
Gumbo, Dove and Sausage, '81 199
Gumbo, Duck, Oyster, and
  Sausage, '79 226
Gumbo Ya Ya, '87 210
Homemade Sausage, Spicy, '84 320
Hominy-Sausage Skillet, '81 29
Italian Meat Sauce, '83 193
Italian Sauce with Noodles, '84 250
Italian Sausage and Pepper Loaves, '83 11

Italian Sausage and Peppers, '84 9
Italian Sausage and Rice, '86 53
Italian Sausage Quiche, '81 200
Italian Sausage Sandwich, '80 92
Italian Sausage Sloppy Joes, '86 160
Italian Sausage Soup, '84 235
Italian Sausage-Stuffed
  Mushrooms, '83 127
Italian Sausage-Zucchini Soup, '84 4
Jambalaya, Creole, '81 51
Jambalaya de Covington, '87 211
Jambalaya, Northshore, '87 45
Jambalaya, Oven, '84 44
Jambalaya, Sausage, '80 210; '84 249
Kielbasa and Cabbage, '85 67
Kielbasa, Cabbage, '87 42
Kraut, Sausage and, '83 11
Lasagna Rollups, Sausage-, '80 236
Lasagna, Sausage, '83 288
Lasagna Sausage Pinwheels, '79 6
Loaf, Hawaiian Ham, '79 71
Loaf, Skillet Liver, '80 11
Log, Phyllo Sausage, '84 294
Log, Stuffed Beef, '79 71
Main Dish, Sausage-Eggplant, '80 211
Manicotti, Saucy Stuffed, '83 288
Meatballs and Sausage, Spicy, '79 163
Meatballs, Chestnut, '79 110
Meatballs, Sweet-and-Sour, '82 247
Meat Loaf, Mozzarella-Layered, '79 71
Mexican Luncheon, '87 192
Muffins, Sausage-Cheese, '86 213
Mushrooms, Sausage-Stuffed, '80 248
Omelet, Puffy Sausage, '80 M268
Onions, Baked Stuffed, '83 135
Pasta with Broccoli and Sausage, '87 109
Pasta with Sausage and Mixed
  Vegetables, '84 249
Patties, Apples on Sausage, '82 120
Peas Mexicano, Black-Eyed, '79 10

Peas with Sausage, Black-Eyed, '86 7
Pepperoni-and-Broccoli Salad, '83 216
Pepperoni and Cheese Loaf, '82 32
Pepperoni Biscuits, '84 95
Pepperoni Pasta, '83 105
Pepperoni Rolls, Ground-, '83 244
Pepperoni-Squash Toss, '84 127
Pie, Breakfast, '86 242
Pie, Cornbread-Sausage-Apple, '87 171
Pinwheels, Sausage, '80 209
Pizza, Breakfast, '85 44
Pizza, Double Cheesy
  Beef-and-Sausage, '86 77
Pizza Luncheon Pie, Deep-Dish, '80 286
Pizza Peppers, '83 135
Pizza Pie, Link-Sausage, '85 33
Pizza Sandwich, Giant, '80 93
Pizza Snacks, Tasty Little, '79 248
Pizza, Speedy, '81 214
Pizza, Spicy Sausage-Pepperoni, '83 226
Pizza, Thick 'n' Crusty Pepperoni,
  '85 244
Polish Sausage, Cabbage with, '83 104
Pork Sausage, '81 55
Pork Sausage Ring, '80 49
Potatoes, Mexican-Topped, '83 3
Quiche, Crustless Sausage-Apple, '87 70
Quiche, Easy Sausage, '79 261
Quiche, Pizza, '86 53
Quiche, Sausage-Cheddar, '79 26
Quiche, Spicy Sausage, '80 M108
Quiche, Zucchini-Sausage, '83 122
Rice, Shrimp and Sausage, '79 64
Rice with Sausage, Fried, '83 12
Rolls with Sweet-and-Sour Sauce,
  Sausage, '83 74
Rollups, Pancake-Sausage, '83 246; '84 42
Salami-Corn Casserole, '80 209
Salami Sandwiches, Open-Faced, '87 279
Sandwiches, Breakfast, '80 52
Sandwiches with Mustard Sauce,
  Sausage, '84 250
Skillet Dinner, Sausage, '83 29
Skillet Express, Sausage, '83 117
Skillet, Mexican-Style, '83 12
Skillet Supper, Sausage, '85 293
Smoked Sausage, '86 154
Smoked Sausage, Chicken Gumbo
  with, '81 199
Smoked Sausage, Jambalaya, '79 42
Smoked Sausage Stew, '82 231
Smoked Sausages with Mustard
  Sauce, '81 56
Soup, Sausage and Okra, '80 209
Soup, Sausage-Bean, '85 88
Soup, Sausage-Potato, '80 25
Soup, Spicy Sausage-Bean, '83 229
Spaghetti Dinner, Sausage, '79 194
Spaghetti, Italian, '81 38
Spaghetti, Italian Zucchini, '85 2
Spaghetti, Real Italian, '81 233
Spaghetti, Sausage, '83 160
Spicy Sausage, Dieters', '85 49
Squares, Chile-Sausage, '86 297
Squares, Sausage-Onion, '83 112
Squash, Harvest, '80 214
Squash, Sausage-Stuffed, '81 183
Squash, Sausage Stuffed Acorn, '81 231;
  '83 296; '84 285
Squash, Sausage-Stuffed Turban, '80 214
Squash with Sausage, Acorn, '85 9
Stew, Venison Sausage, '87 238
Stir-Fry, Sausage, '82 236

Stir-Fry Sausage and Vegetables, '86 213;
  '87 82
Strata, Sausage, '83 243; '84 101
Supper, Sausage-Bean, '86 52
Surprise, Sausage, '83 245; '84 42
Tacos, Breakfast, '80 43
Taquitos, Breakfast, '87 237
Tomatoes, Sausage-Stuffed, '80 47
Tortillas, Egg-and-Sausage, '83 246;
  '84 42
Vegetables and Sausage, Spicy, '80 82
Venison-Vegetable Bake, '87 304
Waffles, Sausage, '83 50
Wild Rice and Sausage, '86 268
Wild Rice, Sausage and, '85 65
Zucchini and Sausage, Sautéed, '83 289

Scallops
Appetizer, Scallop, '86 155
Appetizers, Flaky Scallop, '86 327
Artichokes Stuffed with Shrimp and
  Scallops, '84 174
Broiled Scallops with Tartar
  Sauce, '80 164
Broth with Black Beans and Cilantro,
  Southwestern Scallop, '87 123
Casserole, Scallop, '79 228
Ceviche (Marinated Raw Fish), '82 220
Cheese Scallops, Chip and, '80 301
Coquilles Saint Cyrano, '86 90
Creamy Scallops and Mushrooms, '83 144
Crêpes, Coquilles St. Jacques, '83 13
Fresh Scallops and Pasta, '83 164
Grilled Scallops, Marinated, '84 171
Kabobs, Grilled Scallop, '83 101
Kabobs, Scallop-Bacon, '81 111
Kabobs, Sea Scallop, '82 162
Mornay, Scallops, '80 164
Mustard Sauce, Scallops with, '84 163
Provençal, Scallops, '85 66
Salad, Hot Seafood, '80 164
Sautéed Scallops with Cranberry
  Relish, '83 144
Sauté, Shrimp-and-Scallop, '85 103
Savannah, Scallops, '79 145
Sherried Scallops, '83 281
Supreme, Seafood, '82 284
Tostada, Grilled Scallops, '87 120
Vegetables, Bay Scallops with, '84 233
Vegetables, Scallops en Brochette
  with, '80 163
Vermicelli, Scallop-Vegetable, '87 143
Véronique, Scallops, '83 144
Seafood. *See also* specific types and Fish.
Bisque, Seafood, '86 66
Boil, Low Country Seafood, '80 119
Bouillabaisse, Florida, '79 158
Brochette, Seafood, '87 96
Broiled Shellfish, Quick, '79 228
Casserole, Seafood, '87 109
Chowder, Seafood, '85 9
Chowder, Southern Seafood, '83 20

Delight, Seafood, **'86** 208
Dip, Hot Artichoke-Seafood, **'80** 241
Dip, Hot Artichoke Seafood, **'85** M212
Dip, Hot Cheesy Seafood, **'84** 221
Dip, Seafood, **'79** 3
Eggplant, Seafood Stuffed, **'79** 187
Gumbo, Champion Seafood, **'86** 293
Gumbo, Chicken-Ham-Seafood, **'81** 6
Gumbo, Creole, **'86** 228
Gumbo, Creole Seafood, **'82** 278
Gumbo, Ham and Seafood, **'81** 199
Gumbo, Light Seafood-Okra, **'86** 155
Gumbo, Quick Creole, **'82** 87
Gumbo, Seafood, **'79** 198, 286; **'80** 34;
  '81 5; **'83** 90; **'84** 87, 92; **'87** 210
Imperials, Individual Seafood, **'84** 162
Jambalaya, Three-Seafood, **'82** 126
Linguine, Seafood, **'79** 227
Mayonnaise, Seafood with Dill, **'86** 234
Mold, Chilled Seafood, **'86** 70
Mornay, Seafood, **'83** 67
Paella, Seafood, **'82** 245
Papillote, Ocean, **'84** M287
Pie, Hot Seafood, **'80** 32
Salad, Baked Seafood, **'86** 10
Salad, Hot Seafood, **'79** 117; **'80** 164
Salad, Paella, **'86** 207

Salad, Polynesian Seafood, **'79** 57
Salad, Seaside, **'86** 183
Salad, Smoky Seafood, **'84** 46
Sauce Delight, Seafood, **'82** 91
Sauce, Linguine with Seafood, **'83** 232
Sauce, Seafood, **'79** 3; **'82** 48; **'86** 304
Sautéed Seafood Platter, **'83** 89
Scallops, Bacon-Wrapped, **'87** 94
Slaw, Seafood, **'79** 56
Spread, Seafood, **'86** M58; **'87** 146
Spread, Seafood Sandwich, **'82** 87
Stew, Seafood, **'84** 280
Supreme, Seafood, **'82** 284
Tartlets, Seafood, **'87** 247
Tempura, Basic, **'81** 68
Tempura, Cornmeal, **'81** 68
Seasonings
  Blend, Seasoning, **'82** 296
  Salt, Gourmet Seasoning, **'82** 297
Sherbets. *See* Ice Creams and Sherbets.
Shrimp
  Appetizer, Shrimp-Pineapple, **'85** 80
  Ariosto, Shrimp and Chicken, **'79** 31
  Artichokes, Shrimp-Stuffed, **'84** 67; **'87** 55
  Artichokes Stuffed with Shrimp and
    Scallops, **'84** 174
  Aspic, Shrimp-Coleslaw, **'79** 88
  Aspic, Shrimp-Cucumber, **'83** 108

Aspic with Shrimp, Tomato, **'79** 241
au Gratin, Shrimp, **'85** 79
Avocados, Shrimp-Filled, **'83** 2
Baked Shrimp, **'87** 35
Ball, Shrimp-Cheese, **'85** 208
Barbecued Shrimp, **'82** 74; **'84** 93
Barbecued Shrimp, Cajun, **'87** 95
Bisque, Shrimp-Cucumber, **'79** 172
Bisque, Shrimp-Vegetable, **'82** 313; **'83** 66
Bisque, Tomato-Shrimp, **'86** 66
Boats, Shrimp, **'79** 57
Boiled Shrimp, **'79** 3
Boiled Shrimp, Ray Kidd's, **'84** 87
Boiled Shrimp, Special, **'83** 36
Boiled Shrimp, Spicy, **'83** 320; **'84** 289
Boiled Shrimp with Cocktail
  Sauce, **'79** 151
Boil, Low Country Seafood, **'80** 119
Broiled Shrimp, Beer-, **'87** 142
Broiled Shrimp, Garlic-, **'83** 193
Broiled Shrimp, Lemon-Garlic, **'82** 29;
  '86 182
Broiled Shrimp Supreme, **'79** 3
Canapés, Shrimp, **'84** 116
Cashew Shrimp Supreme, **'83** 29
Casserole, Chayotes and Shrimp, **'80** 230
Casserole, Crab-and-Shrimp, **'84** 71
Casserole, Shrimp, **'85** 240
Casserole, Shrimp and Rice, **'79** 228
Catfish, Crown Room's
  Shrimp-Stuffed, **'84** 182
Cheese Ball, Curried Shrimp, **'86** 135
Cheese, Shrimp with Herbed
  Jalapeño, **'87** 112
Chowder, Shrimp and Corn, **'79** 199
Chow Mein, Shrimp, **'82** 30
Cocktail, Shrimp, **'87** 173
Coconut-Beer Shrimp, **'85** 230
Combo, Snow Pea-Shrimp, **'79** 57
Cream Sauce, Shrimp in, **'84** M286
Creole in a Rice Ring, Shrimp, **'86** 222
Creole, Shrimp, **'86** 256; **'87** 18
Creole, Special Shrimp, **'87** 172
Creole, Spicy Shrimp, **'79** 181
Creole, Wild Rice-and-Shrimp, **'84** 292
Curried Rice and Shrimp, **'83** 231
Curried Shrimp, **'84** 110
Curried Shrimp, Quick, **'84** M198
Curried Shrimp, West Indian, **'79** 227
Curry, Charleston-Style Shrimp, **'84** 109
Curry, Shrimp Malai, **'84** 110
Curry, Sour Cream and Shrimp, **'81** 10
Curry, Sour Cream Shrimp, **'80** 83
de Jonghe, Shrimp, **'79** 228
Delight, English Muffin, **'82** 45
Delight, Shrimp, **'79** 192
Destin, Shrimp, **'82** 29
Dijonnaise, Shrimp, **'87** 91
Dilled Sauced Shrimp, **'86** 88
Dip, Hot Cheesy Seafood, **'84** 221
Dip, Hot Shrimp, **'87** 190
Dippers, Shrimp, **'84** 324
Dip, Quick Shrimp, **'79** 153
Dip, Shrimp, **'86** 84
Dip, Zesty Shrimp, **'80** 150
Egg Foo Yong, **'80** 19; **'86** 232
Egg Foo Yong, Shrimp, **'83** 22
Egg Rolls, **'86** 81
Eggrolls, Shrimp and Pork, **'82** 240;
  '83 18
Eggs, Saucy Shrimp-Curried, **'84** 143
Eggs, Shrimp and Crab
  Scrambled, **'79** 261

Élégante, Shrimp, **'83** 48
en Papillote, Shrimp with
  Asparagus, **'86** 145
Étouffée, Shrimp, **'79** 4
Filling, Shrimp Salad, **'87** 106
Fish with Shrimp, Veracruz, **'86** 130
Fondue, Shrimp, **'86** 244
French Shrimp, **'80** 85
Fresh Shrimp, Preparing, **'82** 127
Fried Shrimp, French-, **'79** 4
Fried Shrimp, Golden, **'82** 29
Fried Shrimp, Puffy, **'79** 4
Fried Shrimp with Apricot Sauce, **'87** 172
Garlic-Buttered Shrimp, **'86** M226
Garlic Shrimp, **'79** 268; **'80** 14
Grilled Shrimp, **'85** 103
Gumbo, Crab and Shrimp, **'81** 200
Gumbo, Quick Shrimp, **'86** 71
Gumbo, Seafood, **'87** 210

Gumbo, Shrimp, **'81** 199
Jambalaya, Creole, **'81** 51; **'87** 210
Jambalaya, Good Luck, **'87** 11
Jambalaya, Oven, **'84** 44
Jambalaya, Sausage, **'80** 210
Kabobs, Marinated Shrimp, **'84** 276;
  '85 158
Kabobs, Shrimp, **'80** 150, 184
Kabobs, Steak-and-Shrimp, **'80** 184
Lemon Butter, Shrimp in, **'84** 163
Lemon Garlic Sauce, Shrimp in, **'83** 67
Manale, Shrimp, **'86** 268
Marinara, Shrimp, **'84** 233
Marinated and Grilled Shrimp, **'87** 141
Marinated Shrimp, Grilled, **'87** 173
Marinated Shrimp, Icy, **'84** 215
Marinated Shrimp, Zesty, **'87** 173
Mediterranean Shrimp Bowl, **'80** 174
Medley, Eggplant-Shrimp, **'79** 188
Melba, Shrimp, **'84** 86
Miniquiches, Shrimp, **'87** 146
Mold, Shrimp, **'87** 94
Mornay, Seafood, **'83** 67
Mousse, Shrimp, **'79** 57; **'87** 196, 251
Mushrooms, Shrimp-Stuffed, **'80** M135
Omelet, Shrimp-and-Cheddar, **'84** 57
Paella, Chicken-Pork-Shrimp, **'82** 245
Paella, Spanish, **'85** 26
Paella Valenciana, **'82** 246
Pasta with Shrimp-Mushroom Italienne,
  Green, **'79** 170
Pâté with Dill Sauce, Shrimp, **'85** 39
Peas, Shrimp with Snow, **'85** 75
Peppers, Shrimp-Stuffed, **'80** 162;
  '86 131, 197
Pickled Shrimp, **'79** 3

Shrimp *(continued)*

Pickled Shrimp, New Orleans, '79 145
Pickle, Shrimp-in-a-, '86 326
Pie, Hot Seafood, '80 32
Pilaf, Shrimp, '82 246
Polynesian Shrimp, '79 3
Potatoes, Creamy Shrimp-Stuffed, '80 36
Potatoes, Shrimp-Sauced, '81 M61
Puffs, Gouda-Shrimp, '79 234
Puff, Shrimp-Crab, '79 57
Puffs, Luncheon Shrimp, '85 72
Quiche, Shrimp, '83 50
Rémoulade, Shrimp, '83 173
Rice, Shrimp and Sausage, '79 64
Rock Shrimp Conga, '80 2
Rock Shrimp Tails, Batter-Fried, '80 2
Rock Shrimp Tails, Broiled, '80 3
Rock Shrimp Tails, Sweet-and-Sour, '80 3
Rollups, Shrimp-Stuffed, '82 234
Rotelle, Shrimp, '85 165
Sailor Shrimp for Two, '82 276
Salad, Avocado Stuffed with Shrimp, '82 207
Salad, Baked Shrimp-Rice, '83 22
Salad, Crabmeat-Shrimp Pasta, '86 208
Salad, Creamy Shrimp, '79 56
Salad, Festive Macaroni-Shrimp, '85 165
Salad, Fruited Shrimp, '86 156
Salad in Pastry, Shrimp, '86 105
Salad, Macaroni-Shrimp, '85 121
Salad, Marinated Shrimp, '85 82
Salad on the Half Shell, Shrimp, '86 73
Salad, Orange-Shrimp, '84 197
Salad, Pasta-and-Shrimp, '83 163
Salad, Rice-and-Shrimp, '83 82
Salad, Rice-Shrimp, '79 270
Salad, Shrimp, '81 94; '84 221; '86 186
Salad, Shrimp and Avocado, '80 266
Salad, Shrimp and Rice, '80 231; '82 207
Salad, Shrimp-Endive, '85 73
Salad, Shrimp Macaroni, '79 220
Salad, Shrimp-Macaroni, '85 219
Salad, Shrimp-Walnut, '86 182
Salads, Individual Shrimp, '83 146
Salad, Super Shrimp, '81 37
Salad, Tangy Shrimp-Rice, '84 66
Salad, Tossed Shrimp-Egg, '80 4
Salad, Vegetable-Shrimp, '79 190
Salad, Zesty Shrimp-and-Orange Rice, '87 155
Sandwiches, Shrimp-Cheese, '85 242
Sauce, Broccoli and Cauliflower with Shrimp, '84 248
Sauce, Flounder Fillets in Shrimp, '83 227
Sauce, Flounder with Hollandaise-Shrimp, '86 234
Sauce, Oysters in Shrimp, '87 40
Sauce Piquante, Crab and Shrimp, '83 92
Sauce, Shrimp, '87 138, 232
Sauce, Shrimp-and-Almond, '87 282
Sautéed Seafood Platter, '83 89
Sautéed Shrimp, '79 3
Sauté, Shrimp-and-Grouper, '87 91
Sauté, Shrimp-and-Scallop, '85 103
Scampi, Easy, '84 291
Scampi, Orange, '85 303
Scampi, Shrimp, '84 230
Shells, Creamy Shrimp, '79 4
Sirloin Supreme, Shrimp and, '81 131
Skillet, Quick Shrimp, '87 50
Soup, Shrimp-and-Corn, '84 88
Soup, Shrimp-Mushroom, '85 87

Spaghetti with Black Olives, Shrimp, '85 13
Spread, Chunky Shrimp, '85 300; '86 18
Spread, Curried Shrimp, '87 158
Spread, Shrimp, '81 306; '85 135; '87 111
Spread, Shrimp-Cucumber, '79 81
Spread, Tempting Shrimp, '79 57
Squash, Shrimp-Stuffed Yellow, '84 194
Stew and Grits, Shrimp, '80 118
Stewed Shrimp with Dumplings, '79 31
Stew, Shrimp, '83 4
Stir-Fry Shrimp and Vegetables, '87 91
Stroganoff, Oven-Baked Shrimp, '81 297
Stroganoff, Shrimp, '79 81
Stuffed Shrimp Bundles, Crab-, '81 176
Stuffed Shrimp, Crab-, '84 259
Stuffed Shrimp, Parmesan-, '85 103
Supreme, Seafood, '82 284
Sweet-and-Sour Shrimp, '83 278
Sweet-and-Sour Shrimp and Chicken, '87 267
Szechuan Shrimp, '86 173
Tart, Shrimp, '87 70
Toast, Shrimp, '86 91
Tree, Shrimp, '83 320; '84 288; '85 318
Vegetables, Shrimp and, '82 6
Vermicelli, Shrimp and Feta Cheese on, '87 108

Soufflés

Asparagus Soufflé, '79 66; '83 265
Banana Daiquiri Soufflé, '84 317
Brandy Alexander Soufflé, '82 173; '83 M114
Broccoli Soufflé, '81 24
Broccoli Soufflé, Golden, '84 283
Butternut Soufflé, '83 266
Carrot Soufflé, '79 73; '83 265
Cauliflower Soufflé, '82 76
Cheese Soufflé, '79 72, 261
Cheese Soufflé for Two, '81 226

Cheese Soufflé, Three-Egg, '87 234
Chicken-Chestnut Soufflé, '79 107
Chocolate Mint Soufflé, '81 16
Chocolate Soufflé, '84 317
Chocolate Soufflé, Light, '83 278
Coconut Soufflé, '79 73; '85 212
Crab Soufflé Spread, '85 4
Cranberry-Topped Holiday Soufflé, '84 306
Cups, Hot Soufflé, '85 284
Daiquiri Soufflé, Elegant, '80 69
Egg Soufflé Casserole, '83 55
Egg Soufflés, Little, '83 57
Frozen Soufflés, Individual, '80 52

Grand Marnier Soufflé, '79 281
Grasshopper Soufflé, '81 248; '86 188
Grits Soufflé, '80 30
Grits Soufflé, Mexican, '79 55
Individual Soufflés, '80 190
Kahlúa Soufflé, '82 173
Lemon-Lime Soufflé, Cold, '84 24
Lemon Soufflé, '82 170, 252
Lemon Soufflé, Tart, '85 82
Mushroom Soufflés, '87 282
Onion Soufflé, '79 247
Orange Dessert Soufflé, '83 206
Orange Soufflé, Chilled, '84 317; '86 189
Orange Soufflé, Frozen, '79 211
Parsnip Soufflé, Golden, '83 266
Pineapple Dessert Soufflé, '80 153
Potatoes, Soufflé, '84 295; '85 196
Potato Soufflé, Sweet, '82 286; '86 121
Raspberry Soufflé, '86 188
Raspberry-Topped Soufflé, '85 317
Rice-Cheese Soufflé, '79 270
Salmon Soufflé, Fresh, '81 182
Sour Cream Soufflé, '80 43
Spinach Soufflé, '79 73; '81 304; '84 78; '85 248; '86 108
Spinach Soufflé, Cheesy, '81 53
Spinach Soufflé Deluxe, '79 8
Spinach Soufflé Roll, '80 215
Squash Soufflé, Cheesy, '82 146
Turkey Soufflé, '80 271
Turnip Soufflé, '79 254
Vanilla Soufflé, Frozen, '79 230; '82 173
Zucchini-and-Corn Soufflé, '83 265
Zucchini Soufflé, '79 157

Soups. *See also* Chili, Chowders, Gumbos, Stews.

Almond Soup, '79 48
Artichoke Soup, Cream of, '82 232
Asparagus Soup, '84 67
Asparagus Soup, Cream of, '84 111
Avocado-Banana-Yogurt Soup, '80 78
Avocado-Mushroom Soup, Creamy, '85 25
Avocado Soup, Chilled, '81 34; '87 37
Avocado Soup, Creamy, '79 107
Avocado Soup, Sherried, '84 181
Bacon-Beer Cheese Soup, '87 M7
Bean and Bacon Soup, '83 26
Bean-and-Barley Soup, Hearty, '86 304
Bean Pot, White, '86 194
Bean Soup, '80 25
Bean Soup, Capitol Hill, '80 222
Bean Soup, Chunky Navy, '83 291
Bean Soup, Cream of Green, '84 111
Bean Soup, Drunken, '87 283
Bean Soup, Ham-and-, '84 4
Bean Soup, Leafy, '86 223
Bean Soup, Navy, '84 280
Bean Soup, Sausage-, '85 88
Bean Soup, Savory Navy, '87 282
Bean Soup, Spicy Sausage-, '83 229
Bean Soup, White, '83 229
Beer-Cheese Soup, '84 246
Bisque, Brisk Mushroom, '81 190
Bisque, Clam, '86 228
Bisque, Crab-and-Corn, '87 137
Bisque, Oyster, '83 252
Bisque, Seafood, '86 66
Bisque, Shrimp-Cucumber, '79 172
Bisque, Shrimp-Vegetable, '82 313; '83 66
Bisque, Spicy Pumpkin, '86 67
Bisque, Spinach-Potato, '86 66
Bisque, Squash, '84 280
Bisque, Tomato-Shrimp, '86 66

Bisque, Tuna, '79 76
Black-Eyed Soup, Beefy, '85 6
Borscht, Ruby Red, '83 176
Bouillabaisse, Florida, '79 158
Bouillon, Redfish Court, '83 290; '84 93
Bouillon, Tomato, '83 8
Broccoli Soup, '86 161, M194; '87 288
Broccoli Soup, Cheesy-, '86 258
Broccoli Soup, Creamed, '85 24
Broccoli Soup, Cream of, '79 130;
    '80 188, M225; '82 314; '83 66; '86 259
Broccoli Soup, Creamy, '81 75; '82 13;
    '83 99
Broccoli Soup, Easy, '81 307
Broccoli Soup, Hot, '81 235; '83 44
Broccoli Soup, Mock Cream of, '85 288
Broccoli-Swiss Soup, '86 6
Broth, Savory Vegetable, '81 230
Cabbage Soup, '83 291; '85 88
Cantaloupe Soup, '83 120
Cantaloupe Soup, Chilled, '81 156
Cantaloupe Soup, Fresh, '84 190
Carrot-Leek Soup, '86 34
Carrot-Orange Soup, '79 172
Carrot Soup, '80 88
Carrot Soup, Cheesy, '81 262
Carrot Soup, Cream of, '81 307
Carrot Soup, Curried, '82 157
Carrot Soup, Savory, '84 107
Cauliflower and Caraway Soup, '82 264
Cauliflower and Watercress Soup, Cream
    of, '83 126

Cauliflower Soup, Cream of, '87 M7
Cauliflower Soup, Creamy, '82 76
Cauliflower Soup, Fresh, '84 279
Celery Soup, Burnet-, '84 107
Celery Soup, Cream of, '79 71
Celery Soup, Light Cream-of-, '82 279
Cheese Soup, Bacon-Topped, '80 M224
Cheese Soup, Cream of, '83 99
Cheese Soup, Hearty, '84 4
Cheese Soup, Monterey Jack, '81 112;
    '85 M211
Cheese Velvet Soup, '80 74
Cheesy Anytime Soup, '81 307; '82 314;
    '83 66
Chicken Enchilada Soup, '86 22
Chicken, Ham, and Oyster Soup, '79 198
Chicken Noodle Soup, '80 264
Chicken Soup, '81 98
Chicken Soup, Cream of, '85 243
Chicken Soup, Curried, '86 34
Chicken Soup, Homemade, '82 34
Chicken Soup, Mexican, '84 234

Chicken Soup, Quick, '86 M72
Chill-Chaser Soup, '87 282
Clam Florentine Soup, '85 23
Consommé aux Champignons, '79 48
Corned Beef Soup, '83 16
Corn Soup, '80 56; '85 243; '87 156
Corn Soup, Favorite, '85 155
Corn Soup, Grilled, '87 121
Crabmeat Soup, '84 123
Crab Soup, Creamy, '80 M224
Crab Soup, Elegant, '80 188
Crab Soup, Quick, '84 279
Crab Soup, Steamboat's Cream
    of, '81 127
Crab Soup with Marigold, She-, '79 32
Cucumber Soup, Chilled, '79 144
Cucumber Soup, Cold, '79 130; '81 130
Cucumber Soup, Cold Minted, '86 34
Cucumber Soup, Cream of, '81 98
Cucumber Soup, Creamy, '80 171
Cucumber-Yogurt Soup, '82 157; '83 205
Curried Soup, '81 130
Dill Soup, Cold, '84 107
Egg Drop Soup, '83 21; '86 16
Egg-Drop Soup, '85 M12
Egg Flower Soup, '81 307; '82 313;
    '83 65
Eggplant Supper Soup, '85 221
Fire Water, '80 188
French Market Soup, '85 277
Fruit Soup, '87 98
Fruit Soup, Cold Fresh, '87 157
Fruit Soup Dessert, '79 172
Fruit Soup, Dried, '79 23
Fruit Soup, Swedish, '82 313; '83 65
Garden Soup, '85 241
Gazpacho, '79 172; '80 266; '81 98;
    '82 73; '84 112; '85 164
Gazpacho, Blender, '85 93
Gazpacho, Chilled, '84 138
Gazpacho, Cool, '83 140
Gazpacho, Saucy, '82 157
Gazpacho, Spring, '81 112
Gazpacho, Summer, '84 181
Hamburger Soup, '80 263
Ham Soup, Hearty, '82 4
Harvest Soup, '79 101
Homemade Soup, '79 198
Hot-and-Sour Soup, '83 68
Jambalaya, '84 282
Jambalaya, Creole, '81 51; '87 210
Jambalaya de Covington, '87 211
Jambalaya, Good Luck, '87 11
Jambalaya, Oven, '84 44
Jambalaya, Sausage, '80 210; '84 249
Jambalaya, Smoked Sausage, '79 42
Jambalaya, Three-Seafood, '82 126
Jambalaya, Tuna, '82 11
Lemon Soup, '85 94
Lentil Soup, '83 292; '86 304
Lentil Soup, Beefy, '87 282
Melon Soup, '80 182
Melon Soup, Swirled, '87 162
Minestrone, '82 4
Minestrone Soup, '84 202; '86 144
Mix, French Market Soup, '85 277
Mushroom-Onion Soup, '80 25
Mushroom Soup, '82 286; '86 M73
Mushroom Soup, Cream of, '84 5;
    '85 93, 261
Mushroom Soup, Creamy, '79 243;
    '81 307
Mushroom Soup, Curried, '84 M89

Mushroom Soup, Elegant, '83 99
Mushroom Soup, Fresh, '81 109
Mushroom Soup, Shrimp-, '85 87
Okra Soup, Charleston, '87 156
Onion-Beef Soup, French, '87 54
Onion-Cheese Soup, '87 81
Onion Soup, Classic, '84 65
Onion Soup, Creamed Green, '83 82
Onion Soup, Double-Cheese, '85 227
Onion Soup, Double
    Cheese-Topped, '79 49
Onion Soup, Easy, '85 226
Onion Soup, French, '79 49; '80 188;
    '83 126; '85 226; '86 M212
Onion Soup, Green, '84 112
Onion Soup, Oven-Browned, '79 49
Onion Soup, Rich, '85 226
Onion Soup, Shortcut French, '85 M328
Onion Soup, Superb, '81 86

Onion Soup, Toasty French, '81 306
Oyster-and-Mushroom Soup, '87 39
Oyster-Cheese Soup, '84 213
Oyster Soup, '79 228; '83 211
Peach-Plum Soup, '87 157
Peach Soup, '83 120, 180
Peanut Butter Soup, Cream of, '84 29
Peanut Soup, '87 184
Peanut Soup, Chilled, '79 130
Peanut Soup, Creamy, '79 50
Pea Soup, Chilled, '84 181
Pea Soup, Country-Style, '86 267
Pea Soup Élégante, '79 53
Pea Soup, Fresh, '86 181
Pea Soup, Peppery, '82 271
Plum Soup, '85 107
Plum Soup, Chilled Purple, '79 162
Potato-Bacon Soup, '84 M38
Potato Potage, Subtle, '80 78
Potato Soup, '82 278; '83 292
Potato Soup, Asparagus-, '83 25
Potato Soup, Celery-and-, '84 279
Potato Soup, Chilled Cucumber-, '85 93
Potato Soup, Cream of, '80 M224; '82 21
Potato Soup, Creamy, '81 19, 98; '84 112
Potato Soup, Golden Cream of, '86 302
Potato Soup, Holiday, '79 236
Potato Soup, Leek-and-, '84 112
Potato Soup, Sausage-, '80 25
Potato Soup, Special, '82 3
Potato Soup, Three-, '86 16
Pot-of-Gold Soup, '86 259
Pumpkin Soup, '79 48
Pumpkin-Tomato Soup, '86 291
Raspberry Soup, Chilled, '81 130
Sausage and Okra Soup, '80 209

Soups *(continued)*

Sausage Soup, Italian, **'84** 235
Sausage-Zucchini Soup, Italian, **'84** 4
Scallop Broth with Black Beans and
   Cilantro, Southwestern, **'87** 123
Shrimp-and-Corn Soup, **'84** 88
Sopa de Lima, **'79** 211
Southwest Soup, **'86** 255
Spinach Soup, Cream of, **'82** 38
Spinach Soup, Hot Cream of, **'84** 29
Spinach Soup, Oriental, **'83** 151
Split Pea and Frankfurter Soup, **'79** 64
Squash Soup, Cold Cream of, **'81** 130

Squash Soup, Cream of, **'81** 246
Squash Soup, Perky, **'85** 20
Squash Soup, Summer, **'83** 99; **'84** 193;
   '85 136
Strawberry-Banana Soup, **'86** 181
Strawberry Soup, Cold, **'82** 157
Strawberry Soup Supreme, **'81** M144
Tomato-and-Rice Soup, **'85** 24
Tomato-Celery Soup, **'83** M58
Tomato Cream Soup, Refreshing, **'79** 172
Tomato Juice Soup, Hot, **'86** 302
Tomato Potage, **'79** 250
Tomato Soup, **'81** 236; **'83** 44
Tomato Soup, Appetizer, **'86** 258
Tomato Soup, Chilled, **'82** 155
Tomato Soup, Creamy, **'83** 267; **'86** 258
Tomato Soup, Easy, **'84** 14
Tomato Soup, Fresh, **'83** 140
Tomato Soup, Iced, **'79** 170
Tomato Soup, Sour Cream-Topped,
   '80 246
Tomato Soup, Summer, **'79** 130
Tomato Soup with Parmesan Cheese,
   Cream of, **'86** 161
Tomato-Vegetable Soup, **'81** M177; **'86** 9
Turkey Carcass Soup, **'86** 284
Turkey Soup, Curried, **'86** 332
Turkey-Vegetable Soup, **'84** 4
Turnip Soup, Creamy, **'84** 279
Turtle Soup au Sherry, **'80** 56
Vegetable-Bean Soup, **'83** 317
Vegetable-Beef Soup, Hearty, **'84** 102
Vegetable-Burger Soup, **'82** 6
Vegetable-Cheese Soup, Creamy, **'81** 244
Vegetable Cheese Soup, Creamy, **'83** 230
Vegetable Soup, **'80** 128; **'84** 148;
   '85 106; **'86** 187; **'87** 83, 123
Vegetable Soup, Beefy, **'79** 113; **'84** M38
Vegetable Soup, Cheesy, **'80** 73
Vegetable Soup, Clear, **'79** 130
Vegetable Soup, Cold Garden, **'84** 197
Vegetable Soup, Garden, **'83** 140;
   '86 160
Vegetable Soup, Hearty, **'80** 26
Vegetable Soup, Leek-, **'86** 304
Vegetable Soup, Light, **'84** 280
Vegetable Soup, Marvelous, **'82** 3
Vegetable Soup Mix, **'84** 148

Vegetable Soup, Old-Fashioned, **'86** 304
Vegetable Soup, Quick, **'79** 190;
   '85 24, 32
Vegetable Soup, Quick Beefy, **'80** 25
Vegetable Soup, Spicy, **'79** 198
Venison Soup, **'82** 216
Vichyssoise, **'86** 181
Vichyssoise, Velvety Roquefort, **'83** 223
Watercress-and-Leek Soup, **'86** 161
Watercress Soup, **'79** 82
Yogurt Fruit Soup, **'86** 176
Zucchini Soup, **'82** 104; **'84** 181; **'86** 181
Zucchini Soup, Chilled, **'87** 90
Zucchini Soup, Cold, **'85** 265
Zucchini Soup, Cream of, **'83** 99
Zucchini Soup, Creamy, **'83** 140

Spaghetti

Bacon Spaghetti, **'86** 213; **'87** 82
Carbonara, Salmon, **'83** 43
Carbonara, Spaghetti, **'85** 34; **'87** 167
Carbonara, Spaghetti alla, **'81** 38
Casserole, Asparagus-Spaghetti, **'80** 77
Casserole, Chicken-Spaghetti, **'84** 15
Casserole, Spaghetti, **'84** 241
Casserole, Spaghetti and Beef, **'79** 129
Cheese Spaghetti, Three-, **'83** 105
Chicken Spaghetti, **'83** 105; **'87** 221
Chili-Spaghetti, Herbed, **'84** 222
Crawfish Spaghetti, **'85** 104
Easy Spaghetti, **'83** M317; **'84** 72
Etcetera, Spaghetti, **'83** 105
Ham Spaghetti Skillet, **'83** 283
Herbal Dressing, Spaghetti with,
   '86 158
Hot Dog and Spaghetti Skillet, **'83** 144
Italian Spaghetti, **'81** 38
Italian Spaghetti, Real, **'81** 233
Meatballs, Spaghetti-and-Herb, **'84** 75
Meatballs, Spaghetti with, **'81** 38
Meaty Spaghetti, **'82** 19
Mushrooms, Spicy Spaghetti with, **'85** 2
Parmesan Noodles, Cheesy, **'83** M7
Parsley and Walnut Sauce, Spaghetti
   with, **'80** 30
Parsley, Spaghetti with, **'80** 236
Pea Spaghetti, Black-Eyed, **'81** 7
Pepperoni Pasta, **'83** 105
Pie, Spaghetti, **'81** M32
Pizzazz, Spaghetti with, **'80** 85
Pork Spaghetti Bake, **'81** 11
Pot Roast with Spaghetti, **'80** 59
Salad, Spaghetti, **'82** 277; **'84** 205
Sauce, Beer Spaghetti, **'85** 13
Sauce for Spaghetti, Italian
   Tomato, **'81** 134
Sauce, Herbed Spaghetti, **'85** 13
Sauce, Pasta with Vegetable, **'83** 163
Sauce, Spaghetti with Zucchini, **'81** 38
Sauce, Thick Spaghetti, **'84** 118
Sauce, Turkey Spaghetti, **'85** 13
Sausage Spaghetti, **'83** 160
Sausage Spaghetti Dinner, **'79** 194
Shrimp Spaghetti with Black
   Olives, **'85** 13
Tetrazzini, Chicken, **'79** 268; **'80** 75;
   '83 288
Tetrazzini, Ham, **'82** 77; **'84** 241
Tetrazzini, Herbed Turkey, **'86** 47
Thick-and-Spicy Spaghetti, **'83** 287
Veal and Peppers, Spaghetti
   with, **'81** 201; **'82** 14
Veal Spaghetti, **'84** 276
Vegetables, Spaghetti with, **'85** 67

Vegetables with Spaghetti, Fresh, **'86** 257
Vegetables with Spaghetti,
   Sautéed, **'81** 89
Zucchini Spaghetti, **'83** 160
Zucchini Spaghetti, Italian, **'85** 2

Spice

Balls, Decorative Ribbon-Spice, **'84** 325

Spinach

Baked Spinach, Gourmet, **'82** 180
Bisque, Spinach-Potato, **'86** 66
Bread, Spinach, **'83** 121; **'87** 144
Cannelloni, **'85** 60
Casserole, Cheesy Spinach, **'81** 263
Casserole, Cottage Cheese-and-
   Spinach, **'84** 77
Casserole, Creamy Crab and
   Spinach, **'80** 3
Casserole, Creamy Spinach, **'86** 111
Casserole, Oyster-and-Spinach, **'83** 34;
   '84 44
Casserole, Spinach, **'79** 265
Casserole, Spinach and Artichoke, **'81** 103
Casserole, Spinach and Beef, **'79** 192
Casserole, Spinach-and-Celery, **'84** 294
Casserole, Spinach and Egg, **'82** 270
Casserole, Spinach-Beef-Macaroni, **'83** 313
Casserole, Spinach-Cheese, **'83** 216
Casserole, Spinach-Parmesan, **'82** 281;
   '83 32
Casserole, Turkey-Spinach, **'84** 71
Cheesy Topped Spinach, **'84** 85
Chicken Rolls, Spinach-Stuffed, **'86** 248
Chinese Spinach, **'79** 179; **'82** 39
Chinese Spinach Sauté, **'83** 208
Creamed Spinach, **'81** 54; **'86** 110
Creamed Spinach with Noodles, **'84** 29
Creamy Spinach, **'85** 289
Crêpes, Spinach-Ricotta, **'81** 52
Cups, Cottage Cheese-Spinach, **'87** 190
Delight, Spinach, **'84** M144

Dip, Cheesy Spinach, **'82** 59
Dip, Hot Spinach, **'80** 249
Dip in Cabbage, Spinach, **'82** 155
Dip, Spinach, **'80** 86; **'86** 159;
   '87 25, 214
Dressing, Spinach Salad, **'83** 181
Enchiladas, Spinach, **'83** 60; **'84** 14
Fettuccine, Fresh Spinach, **'83** 60
Fettuccini, Spinach, **'82** 179
Filling, Spinach, **'79** 34
Filling, Spinach-Mushroom, **'80** 215
Filling, Spinach-Ricotta, **'81** 53
Florentine, Baked Eggs, **'86** M12
Florentine, Cheesy Trout, **'85** 53
Florentine Crêpe Pie, **'79** 34
Florentine, Crêpes, **'80** 190
Florentine, Eggs, **'79** 39; **'83** 56
Florentine, Fish, **'86** 35
Florentine in Parchment, Fish, **'87** 22
Florentine, Jumbo Seashells, **'79** 6
Florentine, Salmon, **'83** 43
Florentine, Stuffed Mushrooms, **'82** 270

Florentine-Style Eggs, '82 38
Florentine with Mushroom Sauce,
  Chicken, '87 250
Frittata, Spinach, '81 53
Garden, The, '83 134
Lasagna, Cheesy Spinach, '80 32; '83 204
Lasagna, Spinach, '79 25; '81 243
Lemon Spinach, Creamy, '82 302
Loaves, Spinach-Oyster, '84 213
Madeleine in Chafing Dish,
  Spinach, '85 319
Manicotti, Spinach, '82 199
Mushrooms, Spinach-Stuffed, '86 81
Mushrooms, Spinach with, '80 19
Nests, Baked Eggs in Spinach, '82 70
Noodles, Chicken and Spinach, '82 19
Omelet, Spinach-Cheese, '83 119
Parmesan Spinach, Savory, '85 68
Pasta Bites, Pesto-Cheese, '87 251
Pasta Verde, '84 201
Pasta with Shrimp-Mushroom Italienne,
  Green, '79 170
Pâté with Spinach and Cream,
  Pork, '83 224
Peppers, Spinach-Stuffed, '82 180
Phyllo Triangles, Spinach-Filled, '84 52
Pie, Greek Spinach, '85 59
Pie, Spinach, '82 191
Pie, Spinach-Pasta, '85 286
Pitas, Spinach-Walnut, '87 202
Puffs, Cheese-and-Spinach, '87 246
Puff, Spinach-Cheese, '84 96
Quiche, Cheesy Spinach, '81 228
Quiche, Crustless Spinach, '84 235
Quiche, Greek Spinach, '86 10
Quichelets, Spinach, '87 67
Quiches, Miniature Spinach, '82 38
Quiches, Individual Spinach, '86 38
Quiche, Spinach, '81 44; '85 49
Quiche, Spinach-Mushroom, '81 M74
Rice Bake, Green, '79 43
Rice, Spinach, '85 146
Ring au Fromage, Spinach, '79 8
Rollups, Chicken and Spinach, '80 90;
  '82 M68
Roll-Ups, Ham and Spinach, '81 143
Rollups, Spinach-and-Ham, '86 84
Salads
    Bacon Dressing, Spinach Salad with
      Hot, '82 211
    Bacon Salad, Spinach and, '81 143
    Beet Salad, Spinach-, '83 227
    Blue Cheese Salad, Spinach-, '82 166
    Chicken-and-Spinach Tossed
      Salad, '83 157
    Combination Spinach Salad, '85 327;
      '86 22
    Creamy Spinach Salad, '83 60
    Crisp Spinach Salad with Creamy
      Dressing, '83 81
    Crunchy Spinach Salad, '80 147;
      '81 225
    Curry Spinach Salad, '80 242
    Festive Spinach Salad, '80 247
    French Spinach Salad, '79 8
    Fresh Spinach Salad, '82 73; '83 240;
      '84 15, 77; '86 130
    Fresh Spinach Salad Delight, '80 146
    Fresh Spinach with Spicy
      Dressing, '80 55
    Garden Salad Toss, '81 9
    Green Spinach Salad, '79 142
    Kiwifruit Salad, Spinach-, '87 305

Lamb Salad, Spinach-, '85 58
Layered Salad, Make-Ahead, '81 206
Layered Spinach-Lettuce
  Salad, '84 266
Layered Spinach Salad, '80 5
Lemon Spinach with Feta, '85 190
Mandarin Spinach Salad, '85 163
Mushroom Salad, Spinach
  and, '80 112

Onion Salad Bowl,
  Spinach-and-, '81 157
Orange Dressing, Spinach Salad
  with, '87 187
Orange Salad, Spinach-and-, '86 15
Orange-Spinach Salad, '83 316;
  '84 16
Oriental Spinach Salad, '82 23
Pickled Spinach, '81 69
Russian Dressing, Spinach Salad
  with, '79 144
Salmon-Spinach Salad, '87 145
Southern Spinach Salad, '80 55
Special Spinach Salad, '80 78
Spinach Salad, '82 102; '86 302;
  '87 62
Springtime Spinach Salad, '81 114
Sprout Salad, Fresh
  Spinach-, '82 281; '83 42
Supreme, Spinach Salad, '79 243
Sweet-Sour Spinach Salad, '85 M112
Twist, Spinach-Mustard, '86 209
Vinaigrette Spinach, '79 8
Wilted Spinach Salad, '81 M4
Zesty Spinach Salad, '79 88
Sandwiches, Fresh Spinach, '85 59
Sauce, Fettuccine with Spinach, '84 329
Sauce, Herbed Green, '86 244
Scalloped Spinach with Cheese, '79 8
Shells, Spinach-Stuffed, '85 60; '87 20
Soufflé, Cheesy Spinach, '81 53
Soufflé Deluxe, Spinach, '79 8
Soufflé Roll, Spinach, '80 215
Soufflé, Spinach, '79 73; '81 304; '84 78;
  '85 248; '86 108
Soup, Cream of Spinach, '82 38
Soup, Hot Cream of Spinach, '81 39
Soup, Oriental Spinach, '83 151
Spanakópita, '86 58
Spread, Savory Spinach, '82 180
Squash, Spinach-Stuffed, '82 4
Stir-Fry Spinach, '81 182
Supreme, Layered Spinach, '82 38
Supreme, Spinach, '84 77
Surprise, Spinach, '82 42
Tart Milan, '87 70
Tarts, Spinach, '82 249
Terrine, Layered Salmon-and-
  Spinach, '84 132
Timbales, Spinach, '84 29
Tomatoes, Spinach-Stuffed Baked, '86 14
Triangles, Phyllo-Spinach, '87 53

Turnovers, Salmon-Spinach, '83 44
Wontons, Spinach, '83 74
Zucchini Boats with Spinach, '82 252
Spreads. *See also* Appetizers/Spreads.
Almond Cheese Spread, '87 292
Aloha Spread, '83 93
Antipasto Spread, '81 25
Apricot Brie Spread, '86 275
Apricot-Cream Cheese Spread, '87 158
Artichoke-Crab Spread, Hot, '85 81
Artichoke Hearts with Caviar, '79 142
Artichoke Spread, Hot, '79 110
Beef Spread, Hot, '83 50
Braunschweiger-Onion Spread, '79 82
Bread Spread, Party, '82 161
Caraway Spread, '85 276
Cheese-Horseradish Spread, '84 222
Cheese-Olive Spread, '79 82
Cheese-Olive Spread, Cream, '82 35
Cheese Spread, '86 135
Cheese Spread, Apricot-Cream, '82 161
Cheese Spread, Bacon-, '83 241
Cheese Spread, Beer, '81 69
Cheese Spread, Beer-, '85 69
Cheese Spread, Caviar-Cream, '84 256
Cheese Spread, Chile-, '86 297
Cheese Spread, Confetti, '84 256
Cheese Spread, Cottage, '87 107
Cheese Spread, Creamy Sweet, '79 264
Cheese Spread, Cucumber and
  Cream, '82 140
Cheese Spread, Deviled Cream, '81 235
Cheese Spread, Fruit and, '81 245
Cheese Spread, Garlic Pimiento, '79 58
Cheese Spread, German, '79 82
Cheese Spread, Hawaiian, '87 158
Cheese Spread, Herb-Cream, '83 24
Cheese Spread, Herbed, '87 247
Cheese Spread, Jalapeño-, '82 248
Cheese Spread, Low-Calorie
  Pimiento, '85 215
Cheese Spread, Pimiento, '82 35; '83 93;
  '86 127
Cheese Spread, Pineapple-Cream, '82 35
Cheese Spread, Tipsy, '80 150
Cheese Spread, Tomato-, '81 157
Cheese Spread, Zesty, '82 140
Cheese Spread, Zippy, '85 4
Cheesy Beer Spread, '87 196
Chicken Spread, Festive, '87 158
Chicken Spread, Low-Fat, '82 290
Chicken Spread, Tasty, '84 193
Chocolate Cheese Spread, '87 292
Corned Beef Spread, '87 196
Crabmeat Spread, '79 81
Crabmeat Spread, Layered, '83 127
Crab Soufflé Spread, '85 4
Crab Spread, Baked, '80 86
Crab Spread, Superb, '81 255
Cucumber Spread, '79 295; '80 31
Date Spread, Breakfast, '84 7
Date-Walnut Spread, '87 292
Deviled Delight, '83 130
Edam-Sherry Spread, '84 257
Eggplant Spread, '86 278
Egg Salad Spread, '86 127
Egg Salad Spread, Cottage-, '82 146
Egg, Sour Cream, and Caviar
  Spread, '85 279
Fruit-and-Cheese Spread, Nutty, '87 246
Fruit Spread, '85 135
Fruit Spread, Sugarless, '84 60
Garden Spread, '86 135

Spreads (continued)

Garlic Spread, '85 111
Gruyère-Apple Spread, '81 160
Ham-and-Egg Spread, '79 59
Ham and Pimiento Spread, '80 285;
'81 56
Ham Spread, '86 126
Ham Spread, Cold, '82 248
Ham Spread, Country, '87 8
Ham Spread, Deviled, '79 81
Ham Spread, Hawaiian, '87 106
Honey-Nut Spread, '87 157
Honey Spread, '81 229
Italian Spread, '85 135
Liver Spread, Sherried, '80 86
Mushroom Spread, Hot, '81 190
Mustard Spread, '86 105
Olive Spread, Creamy, '81 290
Olive Spread, Tomatoes with, '85 114
Orange Cheese Spread, '87 292
Orange Toast Topper, '79 36
Pineapple-Cheese Spread, '86 126
Pineapple Sandwich Spread, '84 166
Radish Spread, Fresh, '84 166
Raisin Spread, Peachy-, '86 326
Salad Dressing Spread, '82 140
Salmon-and-Horseradish Spread, '87 146
Salmon Spread, '81 149
Salmon Spread, Smoked, '84 324
Sandwich Spread, Benedictine, '80 299
Sandwich Spread, Chunky, '82 140
Sandwich Spread, Home-Style, '80 179
Seafood Sandwich Spread, '82 87
Seafood Spread, '86 M58; '87 146
Shrimp-Cucumber Spread, '81 306; '85 135; '87 111
Shrimp Spread, '81 306; '85 135; '87 111
Shrimp Spread, Chunky, '85 300
Shrimp Spread, Curried, '87 158
Shrimp Spread, Tempting, '79 57
Sombrero Spread, '87 111
Spinach Spread, Savory, '82 180
Strawberry Spread, Light, '85 55
Sweet 'n' Sour Spread, '86 184
Tomato-Cheese Spread, Fiery, '87 196
Trout Spread, Smoked, '84 47
Tuna Spread, '83 174
Turkey Party Spread, '83 282
Vegetable-Egg Spread, '87 106
Vegetable Party Spread, '84 166
Vegetable Sandwich Spread, '83 174;
'85 135

Sprouts

Beans with Sprouts,
Sweet-and-Sour, '86 32
Beef and Bean Sprouts, '82 281; '83 42
Meat Loaf, Sprout, '85 51
Omelet, Potato-Sprout, '79 128
Omelet, Rising Sun, '82 281
Patties, Ham-Sprout, '85 51
Salad, Bean Sprout, '82 113
Salad, Fresh Spinach-Sprout, '82 281;
'83 42
Salad, Spanish Sprout, '85 327; '86 22
Sandwiches, Alfalfa Pocket
Bread, '82 282; '83 41
Sandwiches, Polynesian Sprout, '85 51

Squash. *See also* Zucchini.

Acorn
Bake, Acorn Squash, '83 280
Baked Acorn Squash, '81 24
Bake, Squash, '82 107
Bread, Squash, '79 210

Custard-Filled Acorn Squash, '86 334
Delight, Acorn Squash, '81 267
Deluxe Acorn Squash, '80 215
Filled Acorn Squash,
Cranberry-, '81 M231
Fruited Acorn Squash, '85 235

Molasses and Pecans, Acorn Squash
with, '85 205
Nutmeg, Acorn Squash with, '85 267
Rings, Easy Glazed Acorn, '81 M231
Rings, Glazed Acorn, '80 214
Sausage, Acorn Squash with, '85 9
Sherried Acorn Squash, '85 9
Stuffed Acorn Squash, '82 277;
'83 15
Stuffed Acorn Squash,
Apple-, '83 296; '84 285
Stuffed Acorn Squash, Fruit-, '81 295
Stuffed Acorn Squash,
Ham-, '81 239; '83 66
Stuffed Acorn Squash,
Pineapple-, '84 255
Stuffed Acorn Squash, Sausage-,
'81 M231; '83 296; '84 285
Stuffed Baked Squash, '85 206
Stuffed Squash, Apple-, '85 206
Stuffed Squash, Maple-
Flavored, '85 205
Butternut
Bake, Butternut-Orange, '86 295
Baked Butternut Squash, '85 205
Bake, Squash and Apple, '79 210
Bisque, Squash, '84 280
Bread, Butternut-Raisin, '79 25
Bread, Squash, '79 210
Casserole, Butternut, '83 280
Casserole, Butternut Squash, '79 210
Casserole, Squash and Apple, '79 209
Casserole, Sweet Butternut, '83 256
Harvest Squash, '80 214
Pie, Butternut Squash, '80 40;
'87 212
Pie, Butternut Squash
Chiffon, '83 296; '84 285
Pie, Spicy Butternut Squash, '80 296
Pie, Spicy Squash, '85 9
Pudding, Squash, '82 277; '83 15
Puff, Butternut Squash, '85 205
Ring, Butternut Squash, '81 M232
Sauté, Savory Butternut, '85 205
Skillet Butternut and Bacon, '85 9
Soufflé, Butternut, '83 266
Stuffed Butternut Squash,
Apple-, '81 232
Sunshine Squash, '85 205
Whipped Squash, Tasty, '82 277;
'83 15
Casserole, Squash, '87 163
Casserole, Two-Squash, '79 101
Chile Squash, '84 77
Dressing, Turkey with Squash, '87 248
Hubbard Squash, Tart, '80 214

Medley, Carrot-Lima-Squash, '80 123
Medley, Fresh Squash, '81 M165
Medley, Sautéed Vegetable, '83 101
Medley, Squash, '81 139; '84 128
Pattypan Squash, Stuffed, '82 103;
'85 136
Pattypan-Zucchini Skillet, '82 103
Pickles, Squash, '87 150
Pie, Mock Coconut, '86 200
Puff, Golden Squash, '82 288
Sauté, Squash, '82 67
Scallop, Green-and-Gold, '81 159
Skillet Squash, '82 195
Spaghetti Squash Lasagna, '84 127
Spaghetti Squash Pie, '80 186
Spaghetti Squash, Sautéed Vegetables
with, '84 128
Stir-Fried Squash Medley, '80 123
Stir-Fry, Squash, '80 184
Stir-Fry, Two-Squash, '86 174
Tomatoes, Squash-Stuffed, '82 102
Tomato Squash, '86 111
Toss, Pepperoni-Squash, '84 127
Turban Squash, Glazed, '81 24
Turban Squash, Sausage-Stuffed, '80 214
Yellow
à l'Orange, Squash, '85 230
Bacon-Flavored Squash, '82 158
Bake, Cheddar-Squash,
'84 M113, 128
Bake, Cheesy Squash, '80 183
Beans, and Tomatoes,
Squash, '83 148
Bread, Spicy Squash, '83 121
Bread, Yellow Squash, '84 140
Buttered Summer Squash, '81 84
Cake, Squash, '86 200
Casserole, Baked Squash, '83 149
Casserole, Blender Squash, '81 212
Casserole, Cheesy Squash, '79 123;
'82 M21
Casserole, Company Squash, '81 183
Casserole, Crunchy Squash, '84 293
Casserole, Fresh Squash, '82 204
Casserole, Jiffy Squash, '81 M144
Casserole, Squash and Egg, '80 146
Casserole, Squash-Carrot, '81 157
Casserole, Summer Squash,
'81 102, 184
Casserole, Yellow Squash, '79 179;
'85 135
Casserole, Zippy Squash, '80 183
Country Club Squash, '79 158
Croquettes, Squash, '79 157; '83 148
Dressing, Squash, '83 315; '86 280
Fiesta Squash, '82 102
Fried Yellow Squash, '86 211
Grilled Squash and Onion, '79 150
Grilled Vegetables, '84 172
Marinated Cucumbers and
Squash, '86 146
Medley, Summer Garden, '84 158
Mexican Squash, '82 103
Muffins, Yellow Squash, '81 163
Pats, Squash, '80 298; '81 25
Patties, Squash, '79 158
Patties, Summer Squash, '81 184
Pickles, Squash, '81 174
Plantation Squash, '79 225
Posh Squash, '81 159
Puffs, Yellow Squash, '82 103
Puppies, Squash, '83 170
Rings, Asparagus in Squash, '87 68

Skillet Summer Squash, '82 96
Soufflé, Cheesy Squash, '82 146
Soup, Cold Cream of Squash, '81 130
Soup, Cream of Squash, '81 246
Soup, Perky Squash, '85 20
Soup, Summer Squash, '83 99;
   '85 136
Stir-Fried Squash Medley, '80 123
Stuffed Squash, Beef-, '83 134
Stuffed Squash Boats,
   Parmesan-, '79 156
Stuffed Squash, Cheesy, '82 134
Stuffed Squash, Sausage-, '81 183
Stuffed Squash, Spinach-, '82 4
Stuffed Squash, Vegetable-, '84 104
Stuffed Squash with Green
   Chiles, '83 148
Stuffed Yellow Squash, Garden-,
   '84 106
Stuffed Yellow Squash, Italian,
   '86 111
Stuffed Yellow Squash,
   Mushroom-, '84 154
Stuffed Yellow Squash, Shrimp-,
   '84 194
Stuffed Yellow Squash with Cheese
   Sauce, '80 162
Summer Squash, '80 127; '85 105
Toss, Crisp Squash-and-
   Pepper, '87 M152
Toss, Simple Squash, '85 M142
Vegetable-Herb Trio, '83 172

Stews. *See also* Chili, Gumbos, Stews.
Bean Pot, White, '86 194
Beef-and-Onion Stew, '87 18
Beef and Vegetable Stew,
   Sweet-and-Sour, '85 87
Beef Stew, '86 51
Beef Stew, Company, '83 85
Beef Stew, Oven, '79 222; '80 64
Beef Stew, Quick, '86 302
Beef Stew, Spicy, '86 228
Beef Stew with Dumplings, '84 3
Beef Stew with Parsley
   Dumplings, '81 76; '82 13; '85 M246
Brown Stew, '85 239
Brunswick Stew, '80 264
Brunswick Stew, Aunt Willette's, '85 320
Brunswick Stew, Bama, '87 4
Brunswick Stew, Blakely, '87 4
Brunswick Stew, Sonny Frye's, '87 4
Burgoo, Five-Meat, '87 3
Burgoo, Harry Young's, '87 3
Burgoo, Old-Fashioned, '87 3
Burgundy Stew with Drop
   Dumplings, '83 125
Chicken Stew and Dumplings, '84 4
Chicken Stew, Brunswick, '87 4
Fish-and-Vegetable Stew, '87 220
Fisherman's Stew, '81 98

Hamburger Oven Stew, '84 4
Hungarian Stew with Noodles, '80 263
Hunter's Stew, '85 270
Lamb Stew, '79 293
Lamb Stew-in-a-Loaf, '85 37
Lentil-Rice Stew, '82 232
Meatball Stew, '79 198
Mexican Stew, '82 231
Mexican Stew Olé, '86 296
Okra Stew, Old-Fashioned, '84 158
Oyster Stew, '80 221
Oyster Stew, Company, '80 297
Oyster Stew, Golden, '86 132
Oyster Stew, Holiday, '85 264
Sausage Stew, Smoked, '82 231
Seafood Stew, '84 280
Shrimp Creole, Spicy, '79 181
Shrimp Creole, Wild Rice-and-, '84 292
Shrimp Stew, '83 4
Shrimp Stew and Grits, '80 118
Turkey Stew, Hearty, '79 252
Vegetable Stew, Mixed, '84 13
Venison Sausage Stew, '87 238
Venison Stew, '86 294
Venison Stew with Potato
   Dumplings, '87 304
White Wine Stew, '82 228
Strawberries
Bars, Strawberry, '81 301
Bavarian, Rhubarb-Strawberry, '86 140
Beets, Strawberry-Glazed, '83 234
Brandied Orange Juice, Strawberries
   with, '82 160
Bread, Strawberry, '81 250; '83 140;
   '84 49
Bread, Strawberry Jam, '79 216
Bread, Strawberry-Nut, '79 24
Butter, Strawberry, '79 36; '81 286
Cake Roll, Strawberries 'n Cream
   Sponge, '81 95
Cake Roll, Strawberry, '79 49; '83 129;
   '84 305; '85 172
Cake, Strawberry Coffee, '85 46
Cake, Strawberry Cream, '86 61
Cake, Strawberry Crunch, '79 288;
   '80 35
Cake, Strawberry Delight, '85 30
Cake, Strawberry Meringue, '86 240
Cake with Strawberries and Chocolate
   Glaze, White, '87 76
Cheesecake, Almost Strawberry, '86 32
Cheesecake, Pear-Berry, '82 M141
Cherry-Berry on a Cloud, '79 94
Christmas Strawberries, '87 293
Cobbler, Rosy Strawberry-
   Rhubarb, '79 154
Combo, Strawberry-Chocolate, '85 96
Cooler, Strawberry, '83 56; '84 51
Cooler, Strawberry-Mint, '84 57
Cream Puffs, Strawberry, '81 95
Cream Puffs, Strawberry-Lemon, '87 75
Cream, Strawberries and, '82 100
Cream, Strawberries 'n Lemon, '85 120
Cream, Strawberries with
   Chocolate, '85 81
Cream, Strawberries with French, '83 191
Cream, Strawberries with
   Strawberry, '84 108
Cream with Fresh Strawberries,
   Almond, '87 93
Crêpes, Nutritious Brunch, '80 44
Crêpes, Strawberry Dessert, '83 122
Crêpes, Strawberry Ice Cream, '87 290

Crêpes with Fruit Filling, '81 96
Daiquiri, Strawberry, '81 156
Delight, Frozen Strawberry, '82 112, 174
Delight, Strawberry, '81 85
Delight, Strawberry Cheese, '79 50
Delight, Strawberry Yogurt, '85 77
Dessert, Chilled Strawberry, '84 164
Dessert, Glazed Strawberry, '84 33
Dessert, Honeydew-Berry, '83 120
Dessert, Strawberry, '83 123
Dessert, Strawberry-Cream
   Cheese, '83 123
Dessert, Strawberry-Lemon, '86 162
Dressing, Creamy Strawberry, '84 161
Float, Strawberry-Banana, '87 160
Fried Strawberries, Deep-, '84 109
Frost, Banana-Strawberry, '87 199
Frost, Strawberry, '81 279; '82 24;
   '83 154
Glaze, Strawberry, '80 35; '83 142
Ice Cream, Homemade
   Strawberry, '84 184
Ice Cream, Old-Fashioned
   Strawberry, '79 94
Ice Cream Roll, Strawberry, '84 105
Ice Cream, Straw-Ba-Nut, '80 177
Ice Cream, Strawberry, '80 177
Ice Cream Torte, Chocolate-
   Strawberry, '79 7
Ice Cream, Very Strawberry, '81 155
Ice, Strawberry, '84 175; '85 108
Ice, Strawberry-Orange, '86 196
Jamaica, Strawberries, '85 161
Jam, Strawberry Freezer, '84 M182
Jellyroll, Easy, '82 176
Jelly, Strawberry, '81 147
Juliet, Strawberries, '84 82
Lemonade, Strawberry, '80 160
Marmalade, Strawberry-Pineapple, '85 130
Melon, Berry-Filled, '86 93
Meringues, Strawberry, '84 188
Milkshake, Fresh Strawberry, '82 113
Mousse, Fresh Strawberry, '82 72
Mousse, Strawberry, '81 95
Mousse, Strawberry-Lemon, '82 128
Napoleons, Strawberry, '81 126
Pancakes, Strawberry, '84 219
Parfait, Crunchy Strawberry-
   Yogurt, '79 124
Parfaits, Frosty Strawberry, '85 213
Parfaits, Strawberry-Lemon, '84 198
Parfait, Strawberry, '79 99
Parfait, Surprise Strawberry, '86 151
Pie, Chilled Strawberry, '82 112
Pie, Glazed Strawberry, '82 M142
Pie, Heavenly Chocolate-Berry, '85 102
Pie, Strawberry-Banana Glazed, '81 181
Pie, Strawberry-Glaze, '81 141
Pie, Strawberry Yogurt, '80 232
Pie, Strawberry-Yogurt, '85 122; '86 124
Pizza, Kiwi-Berry, '86 198; '87 55
Pizza, Strawberry, '79 94
Popsicles, Smoothie Strawberry, '82 112
Preserves Deluxe, Strawberry, '82 150
Preserves, Freezer Strawberry, '82 112
Preserves, Strawberry, '79 120; '81 96
Puff, Strawberry, '82 5
Punch, Creamy Strawberry, '86 195
Punch, Strawberry-Lemonade, '85 116
Ring, Strawberry-Cheese, '86 14
Roll, Heavenly Strawberry, '82 176
Roll, Strawberry, '82 120
Romanoff, Strawberries, '84 108

Strawberries *(continued)*

Ruby Strawberries, '82 100
Sabayon, Strawberries, '79 94
Salad, Hidden Treasure
   Strawberry, '79 11
Salad Mold, Strawberry-Wine, '83 261
Salad, Strawberry Yogurt, '80 232
Sangría, Teaberry, '87 147
Sauce, Amaretto-Strawberry, '87 M165
Sauce, Berry, '87 290
Sauce, Fresh Strawberry, '82 177
Sauce, Melon Wedges with Berry,
   '86 178
Sauce, Peaches with Strawberry, '85 8
Sauce, Strawberry, '84 144; '87 93, 198
Sauce, Strawberry-Banana, '81 41
Sauce with Crunchy Topping,
   Strawberry, '81 170
Sauce with Dumplings,
   Strawberry, '84 314
Shake, Strawberry-Orange
   Breakfast, '87 186
Shake, Strawberry-Pineapple, '84 166
Shake, Strawberry-Yogurt, '87 199

Sherbet, Strawberry, '82 112, 160
Shortcake Squares, Strawberry, '86 124
Shortcake, Strawberry, '81 96; '83 122
Skewered Pineapple and
   Strawberries, '84 251
Slurp, Strawberry, '81 96
Slush, Strawberry-Orange, '83 172
Smoothie, Strawberry, '86 183
Smoothie, Strawberry-Banana, '81 59
Smoothie, Tropical, '81 50
Soda, Old-Fashioned Strawberry, '79 149
Soda, Strawberry, '84 115
Sorbet, Strawberry-Champagne, '83 162
Soup, Cold Strawberry, '82 157
Soup, Strawberry-Banana, '86 181
Soup Supreme, Strawberry, '81 M144
Spread, Light Strawberry, '85 55
Squares, Strawberry Shortcake, '85 122
Stuffed Strawberries with
   Walnuts, '85 122; '86 124
Sundaes, Hot Strawberry, '81 M5
Supreme, Banana-Berry, '81 205
Swirl, Strawberry, '84 108
Tarts, Strawberry, '80 70
Tart, Strawberry, '84 138
Topping, Strawberry, '86 32
Topping, Strawberry-Banana, '87 125
Zabaglione, Strawberries, '81 95

Stroganoff

Beef Burgundy Stroganoff, '85 31
Beef Stroganoff, '79 163; '81 179
Beef Stroganoff, Ground, '84 71
Beef Stroganoff, Light, '86 36
Chicken Livers Stroganoff, '80 200; '81 57
Chicken Livers Supreme, '81 298
Crab Stroganoff, '79 116
Hamburger Stroganoff, '82 108, 110

Hamburger Stroganoff, Easy, '79 208
Ham Stroganoff, '82 40
Liver Stroganoff, '79 54
Meatballs, European Veal, '85 30
Meatballs Paprikash with Rice, '85 31
Meatball Stroganoff, '81 297
Mushroom-Meatball Stroganoff, '85 85
Mushroom Stroganoff, '81 298
Quickie Stroganoff, '81 200
Shrimp Stroganoff, '79 81
Shrimp Stroganoff, Oven-Baked, '81 297
Sirloin Stroganoff, '81 297
Steak Stroganoff Sandwiches, '85 110
Steak Stroganoff with Parslied
   Noodles, '85 31
Tofu, Stroganoff, '84 202
Veal Stroganoff, '79 108

Stuffings and Dressings

Apple-Crumb Stuffing, '81 234; '82 26;
   '83 39
Cajun Dressing, '82 307
Chicken and Dressing, Baked, '79 296
Cornbread-and-Sausage Dressing, '83 213
Cornbread-Biscuit Dressing, '79 296
Cornbread Dressing, '86 286
Cornbread Dressing, Fruited, '80 262
Cornbread Dressing,
   Herb-Seasoned, '83 315
Cornbread Dressing, Kentucky, '86 281
Cornbread Dressing,
   Old-Fashioned, '84 321
Cornbread Dressing, Sage-, '84 283
Cornbread Dressing, Texas, '82 243
Cornbread Dressing, Turkey with
   Sausage-, '83 287
Cornbread-Sage Dressing, '80 262
Cornbread-Sausage Dressing, '82 307;
   '85 280
Corn Dressing Balls, Zesty, '82 307
Crabmeat Stuffing, Chicken Breasts
   with, '85 302
Fruit-and-Pecan Dressing, '84 252
Fruit Dressing, Baked, '87 253
Low-Sodium Stuffing, '82 66
Oyster Bread Dressing, '82 251
Oyster Dressing, '79 250
Oyster Stuffing, Roast Turkey
   with, '80 251
Peanut Dressing, Roast Turkey
   with, '79 283
Pecan-Rice Dressing, Chicken
   with, '85 M57
Pecan-Sage Dressing, '80 262
Pecan Stuffing, '79 292; '80 32
Pecan Stuffing, Wild Duck with, '85 269
Pretzel Dressing, '86 280
Rice Dressing, Chicken and, '79 288
Rice Dressing, Mexican, '87 253
Rice Dressing, Roast Turkey
   with, '82 286
Sausage Dressing, '86 280
Seasoned Dressing, Stuffed Turkey Breast
   with, '83 320; '84 128
Squash Dressing, '83 315; '86 280
Squash Dressing, Turkey with, '87 248
Turkey and Dressing, Easy, '79 296
Turkey-and-Dressing Pie, '84 326
Turkey Dressing, '85 298
Whole Wheat-Mushroom
   Dressing, '84 283
Wild Rice Stuffing, Cornish Hens
   with, '79 222; '80 64; '82 136
Zucchini Dressing, '86 282

Sweet-and-Sour

Beans and Carrots, Sweet-and-Sour
   Green, '83 6
Beans, Sweet-and-Sour, '87 197
Beans, Sweet-and-Sour Green, '79 184;
   '81 158; '82 90
Beans with Sprouts,
   Sweet-and-Sour, '86 32
Beets, Sweet-and-Sour, '81 167; '82 22
Cabbage, Sweet-and-Sour, '86 295;
   '87 189
Cabbage, Sweet-Sour Red, '79 5
Carrots, Sweet-and-Sour, '82 137
Chicken, Sweet-and-Sour, '79 106;
   '86 217, 240
Chicken, Sweet-and-Sour Lemon, '84 93
Dressing, Sweet-and-Sour, '80 247;
   '84 70, 161; '85 163; '87 305
Dressing, Sweet-and-Sour Fruit, '84 125
Dressing, Sweet-Sour, '80 246
Fish, Sweet-and-Sour, '80 M54
Ham, Sweet-Sour Glazed, '83 311
Kale, Sweet-and-Sour, '80 298
Liver, Sweet-and-Sour, '81 277
Marinade, Sweet-and-Sour, '86 113;
   '87 115
Meatballs, Sweet-and-Sour, '82 233, 247;
   '86 240
Meatballs, Sweet-and-Sour Party, '79 233

Peas, Sweet-and-Sour Black-Eyed, '85 290
Pork Chops, Sweet-and-Sour, '83 160
Pork, Pineapple Sweet-and-Sour, '82 120
Pork, Sweet-and-Sour, '79 42; '80 72,
   227; '81 26, 104, 111; '82 12; '84 218;
   '85 34, 194; '86 241
Potatoes, Sweet-and-Sour-Topped, '83 4
Pot Roast, Sweet-and-Sour, '83 8
Riblets, Sweet-and-Sour, '85 276
Salad, Sweet-and-Sour Bean, '85 198;
   '86 147
Salad, Sweet-and-Sour Cauliflower, '81 2
Salad, Sweet-and-Sour Fruit, '80 13;
   '84 125
Salad, Sweet-and-Sour Macaroni, '85 166
Salad, Sweet and Sour Potato, '80 152
Salad, Sweet-and-Sour Vegetable, '81 25
Salad, Sweet-Sour Spinach, '85 M112
Sauce, Sausage Rolls with
   Sweet-and-Sour, '83 74
Sauce, Sweet-and-Sour, '80 20;
   '85 12, 34; '86 240
Sauce, Sweet-and-Sour Pineapple, '85 66
Shrimp and Chicken,
   Sweet-and-Sour, '87 267
Shrimp, Sweet-and-Sour, '83 278
Shrimp Tails, Sweet-and-Sour Rock, '80 3
Slaw, Sweet-and-Sour, '81 237
Spareribs, Sweet-and-Sour, '83 21
Spread, Sweet 'n' Sour, '86 184
Steaks, Sweet-and-Sour
   Marinated, '83 110
Stew, Sweet-and-Sour Beef and
   Vegetable, '85 87

Turkey, Sweet-and-Sour, '79 252
Turnips, Sweet-and-Sour, '81 274
Vegetables, Sweet-and-Sour
Marinated, '83 266

Swiss Chard
Buttered Chard, '83 36
Tomatoes, Swiss Chard with, '83 36

Syrups
Almond Syrup, '82 47
Anise Sugar Syrup, '86 248
Apple Syrup, Spiced, '79 114
Apricot Fruit Syrup, '82 10
Caramel Syrup, '82 43
Cherry-Lemonade Syrup, '86 214
Citrus Syrup, Sweet, '86 270
Fruit Syrup, '86 176
Kirsch Syrup, '80 280
Maple-Honey-Cinnamon Syrup, '85 19
Maple-Nut Syrup, '80 228
Maple Syrup, '81 120; '82 23
Maple Syrup, Homemade, '79 114
Orange Syrup, '80 228
Pecan Syrup, Chunky, '85 278

T

Tacos
al Carbón, Tacos, '86 19
al Carbon, Tailgate Tacos, '79 185
Appetizer, Layered Taco, '84 206
Bake, Taco Beef-Noodle, '81 141
Basic Tacos, '83 199
Breakfast Tacos, '80 43
Casserole, Taco, '80 33
Corn Chip Tacos, '81 67
Jiffy Tacos, '83 M318
Lobster Taco with Yellow Tomato Salsa
and Jicama Salad, Warm, '87 122
Navajo Tacos, '84 246
Peppers, Taco, '81 86
Pie, Crescent Taco, '80 80
Pies, Individual Taco, '82 M282
Pitas, Taco, '83 31
Salad Cups, Taco, '85 M29
Salad, Meatless Taco, '81 204
Salad, Spicy Taco, '87 287
Salad, Taco, '79 56; '83 145; '85 84
Salad, Taco Macaroni, '85 165
Salad, Tuna-Taco, '87 145
Sauce, Taco, '82 M283
Tacos, '80 196

Tamales
Bake, Cornbread Tamale, '79 163
Hot Tamales, '83 51
Meatballs, Tamale, '80 194
Miniature Tamales, '85 154
Pie, Chili-Tamale, '82 9; '83 68
Sweet Tamales, '83 52
Tamales, '80 195

Tea
Almond-Lemonade Tea, '86 229
Almond Tea, '85 43; '86 329
Apple-Cinnamon Tea, Hot, '87 57
Brew, Quilter's, '85 43
Citrus Tea, Hot, '83 275
Citrus Tea, Iced, '85 162
Cubes, Frozen Tea, '85 161
Fruit Tea, Christmas, '83 275
Fruit Tea, Hot Spiced, '87 242
Ginger Tea, '81 100
Grape Juice Tea, White, '87 57

Grape Tea, Spiced, '79 174
Hawaiian Tea, '87 57
Honey Tea, '81 105
Iced Tea, Bubbly, '81 168
Johnny Appleseed Tea, '85 23
Lemon-Mint Tea, '85 162
Lemon Tea, '82 156
Minted Tea, '86 101
Mint Tea, '87 107
Mint Tea, Frosted, '84 161
Mint Tea, Iced, '83 170
Mix, Friendship Tea, '83 283
Mix, Spiced Tea, '86 32
Punch, Apple-Tea, '85 82
Punch, Bourbon-Tea, '87 57
Punch, Citrus-Tea, '85 116
Punch, Spiked Tea, '86 101
Sangría, Teaberry, '87 147
Spiced Tea Cooler, '83 55
Spiced Tea, Hot, '83 244
Summer Tea, '85 162
Summertime Tea, '81 167
Sun Tea, Southern, '81 168
Yaupon Tea, '79 31

Tempura
Basic Tempura, '81 68
Chicken Tempura Delight, '85 66
Cornmeal Tempura, '81 68
Sauce, Basic Tempura, '81 68
Sauce, Mustard-Sour Cream, '81 68
Vegetable Tempura, '79 112

Terrines
Black Bean Terrine with Goat
Cheese, '87 120
Chicken Terrine Ring, '84 132
Chicken-Vegetable Terrine, '84 131
Pork Terrine, Jeweled, '84 130
Salmon-and-Spinach Terrine,
Layered, '84 132
Vegetable-Chicken Terrine, '83 224

Timbales
Cheesy Mexicali Appetizer, '82 108
Chicken Chutney Salad, '82 108
Hamburger Stroganoff, '82 108
Peach Almond Cream, '82 108
Shells, Timbale, '82 108
Spinach Timbales, '84 29

Tofu
Dip, Tofu, '86 109
Lasagna, Tofu, '83 312
Sandwiches, Open-Face
Tofu-Veggie, '86 5
Stroganoff Tofu, '84 202

Tomatoes
Aspic, Bloody Mary-Tomato, '81 77
Aspic, Chicken in Tomato, '84 190
Aspic, Chili Sauce Tomato, '85 252
Aspic, Herbed Tomato, '81 73
Aspic, Light Tomato, '85 83
Aspic, Ranch Tomato, '83 218
Aspic, Spicy Tomato, '81 40
Aspic, Tangy Tomato, '83 124
Aspic, Tomato-Artichoke, '84 320; '86 92
Aspic, Tomato-Crab, '85 287
Aspic with Shrimp, Tomato, '79 241
au Gratin, Zucchini and Tomato, '82 208
Bake, Chicken-Tomato, '83 35
Baked Cheddar Tomatoes, '85 43
Baked Tangy Tomatoes, '81 168
Baked Tomatoes, '83 53; '87 197
Baked Tomatoes, Spinach-Stuffed, '86 14
Baked Tomatoes with Corn, '80 161
Baked Tomato Halves, Zippy, '81 182

Bake, Ham-Rice-Tomato, '87 78
Bake, Okra-Tomato, '80 298; '81 26
Bake, Potato-Tomato, '86 17
Bake, Tomato-and-Artichoke
Heart, '85 81
Bake, Zucchini and Tomato, '82 158
Beans and Tomatoes, Basil, '83 172
Beans with Tomatoes, Green, '85 137
Beef Saltillo (Beef with
Tomatillos), '82 219
Biscuits, Tomato, '86 72
Bisque, Tomato-Shrimp, '86 66
Bites, Tomato, '84 80
Bouillon, Tomato, '83 8
Bowl, Tomato, '81 69
Broiled Tomatoes, '80 152
Broiled Tomatoes, Quick, '79 153
Broiled Tomatoes, Romano, '80 42
Broiled Tomatoes with Dill
Sauce, '80 161
Broiled Tomatoes with Mushroom
Sauce, '81 103
Broil, Tomato-English Pea, '83 192
Buffet Tomatoes, '82 180
Butter, Tomato, '86 128
Cabbage and Tomatoes, '83 104
Cabbage and Tomatoes, Tasty, '86 72
Cacciatore, Chicken, '86 42
Canning Tomatoes, '80 128; '85 106
Casserole, Corn and Tomato, '81 127
Casserole, Corn-and-Tomato, '84 145
Casserole, Eggplant-and-Tomato, '83 187
Casserole, Saucy Potato-Tomato, '79 46
Catsup, Spicy Tomato, '83 182
Cheese Herbed-Topped Tomatoes, '86 108
Cheese-Topped Tomatoes, '81 160
Cheesy Puff-Top Tomatoes, '86 187
Cherry Tomatoes, Cheesy, '83 135
Cherry Tomatoes, Crab-Stuffed, '82 289
Cherry Tomatoes, Green Beans
with, '86 177
Cherry Tomatoes, Herbed, '82 128
Cherry Tomatoes in Brown Butter
Sauce, '81 168
Cherry Tomatoes, Stuffed, '84 160
Cherry Tomatoes with Rum, '83 192
Chicken, Tomato-Baked, '81 281; '82 30
Chowder, Tomato-Clam, '84 251
Chutney, Tomato-Apple, '84 180
Cocktail, Tomato, '83 M203
Cocktail, Tomato-Clam, '87 252
Cocktail, Tomato Juice, '79 212; '83 230
Cocktail, Tomato-Orange Juice, '83 169
Cocktail, Zesty Tomato Juice, '83 289
Coleslaw with Tomatoes, '80 34

Creole-Style Tomatoes-and-Corn, '84 142
Cucumber on Tomatoes, Dilled, '84 142
Cups, Turkey-Tomato, '84 119

Tomatoes *(continued)*

Delights, Tomato, '81 140
Delight, Tomato-Pea, '84 196
Dressing, Fresh Tomato Salad, '83 193
Dressing, Garden Salad with
    Tomato-Cream Cheese, '79 173
Dressing, Tomato-Honey French, '81 105
Eggs Benedict, Bacon-and-
    Tomato, '87 195
Fire-and-Ice Tomatoes, '87 92
Fried Red Tomatoes, '81 102
Fried Ripe Tomatoes, '81 168
Fried Ripe Tomatoes with Gravy, '82 180
Fried Tomatoes with Bacon,
    Saucy, '81 210
Fried Tomatoes with Gravy, '86 211
Green Tomatoes, Fried, '79 123; '80 178;
    '81 210; '85 214
Green Tomatoes, Herb-Baked, '85 214
Green Tomatoes, Italian-Sauced, '85 214
Green Tomatoes, Okra and, '79 160
Green Tomatoes, Oven-Fried, '82 107
Green Tomato Jam, '79 121
Green Tomato Pie, '79 195
Grilled Tomatoes, '85 158
Grilled Tomatoes, Cheesy, '79 150
Herbed Tomatoes, '81 102; '82 49;
    '83 173
Italian Dressing, Tomato, Onion, and
    Cucumber in, '81 83
Juice, Homemade Tomato, '81 50
Juice, Spicy Tomato, '85 189
Lemon Dressing, Tomato Slices
    with, '87 167
Lima and Tomato Combo, Hot, '83 219
Marinated Salsa Tomatoes, '82 164
Marinated Tomatoes, '85 156, 163
Marinated Tomato Slices, '82 134;
    '83 193
Medley, Okra-Corn-Tomato, '81 159
Medley, Tomato, '81 159
Mold, Tangy Tomato, '79 74
Muffins, Tomato Corn, '81 137
Mustard, Green Beans and Tomatoes
    with, '87 83
Mustard Tomatoes, Zippy, '86 M226
Okra and Tomatoes, '80 185; '81 139
Okra and Tomatoes, Fresh, '81 M165;
    '87 89
Okra-Tomato Combo, '83 157
Okra, Tomatoes and, '86 170; '87 164
Okra, Tomatoes with, '85 106
Olive Spread, Tomatoes with, '85 114
Oregano Tomatoes, '83 145
Parmesan Tomatoes, '80 161
Pasta Toss, Tomato-Olive, '86 209
Peas and Tomatoes, Snow, '83 111
Pesto, Tomatoes, '86 150
Pickles, Green Tomato, '87 134
Potage, Tomato, '79 250
Primavera, Tomato-Pasta, '86 209
Provençal, Tomatoes, '82 181
Puffs, Tomato Cheese, '81 48
Puree, Seasoned Tomato, '83 182
Ratatouille, '84 105, 243; '85 92
Ratatouille-Bran Stuffed Eggplant,
    '86 44
Ratatouille, Eggplant-Zucchini, '81 205
Ratatouille, Niçoise, '81 22
Ratatouille, Quick-and-Easy, '80 212
Ratatouille-Stuffed Eggplant, '83 187
Refresher, Tomato, '81 94; '83 318

Relish, Black Bean-Tomatillo, '87 121
Relish, Easy Tomato, '80 126
Relish, End-of-the-Garden, '80 179
Relish, Tomato, '85 188
Ring, Tangy Tomato, '84 164
Ring, Tomato-Vegetable, '81 302
Rose, Tomato, '82 51; '85 338
Rotelle, Chicken and Tomato
    with, '87 108
Salad, Artichoke-Stuffed Tomato, '82 101
Salad, Artichoke-Tomato, '82 239
Salad, Cherry Tomato, '87 156
Salad, Cottage-Tomato, '85 163
Salad, Crab-Stuffed Tomato, '80 148
Salad, Dilled Cucumber and
    Tomato, '81 153
Salad, Frozen Tomato, '84 52
Salad, Guacamole-Tomato, '81 302
Salad in Tomatoes, Cottage
    Cheese, '86 208
Salad, Lima Bean-Tomato, '85 137
Salad, Marinated, '83 170
Salad, Oriental-Stuffed Tomato, '82 101
Salad, Ruby-and-Emerald, '85 79
Salad, Tomato-Avocado, '86 74
Salad, Tomato-Cucumber, '86 218
Salad, Tomato-Cucumber-Onion, '81 239
Salad, Tomato-Feta, '81 246
Salad, Tomato Petal, '79 88
Salad, Tomato Relish, '83 111
Salad, Vidalia-Tomato, '84 65
Salad, Watercress-Tomato, '85 132
Salsa, Chunky, '86 130
Salsa, Tomato, '87 120
Salsa, Yellow Tomato, '87 122
Sandwiches, Bacon, Cheese, and
    Tomato, '84 14
Sandwiches, Open-Face Crab
    Tomato, '81 29
Sauce, Asparagus with Tomato, '83 46
Sauce, Chunky Chili, '85 188
Sauce, Fish in Tomato, '85 75
Sauce for Spaghetti, Italian
    Tomato, '81 134
Sauce, Fresh Tomato, '83 224; '87 171
Sauce, Hamburgers with Tomato, '81 73

Sauce, Herbed Fresh Tomato, '85 M151
Sauce, Italian-Style Tomato, '87 182
Sauce, Italian Tomato, '82 M68
Sauce, Linguine with Tomato-
    Cream, '86 158
Sauce, Quick Crab Marinara, '85 M151
Sauce, Refrigerator Tomato, '85 188
Sauce, Seasoned Tomato, '83 150
Sauce, Spicy Tomato, '84 294
Sauce, Tarragon-Tomato, '84 131
Sauce, Tomato, '85 193, 244; '87 249
Sauce, Turkey Patties in
    Vegetable-Tomato, '87 18
Sauce, Vermicelli with Tomato, '83 164
Sauce with Green Chiles,
    Tomato, '81 196
Sauté, Tomato-Pepper, '84 142
Scalloped Tomatoes, '84 142

Scalloped Tomato Slices, '81 168
Sesame Tomatoes, '84 142
Skillet, Cabbage-and-Tomato, '86 110
Skillet Tomatoes, '81 108
Soup, Appetizer Tomato, '86 258
Soup, Chilled Tomato, '82 155
Soup, Creamy Tomato, '83 267; '86 258
Soup, Easy Tomato, '84 14
Soup, Fresh Tomato, '83 140
Soup, Hot Tomato Juice, '86 302
Soup, Iced Tomato, '79 170
Soup, Pumpkin-Tomato, '86 291
Soup, Refreshing Tomato Cream, '79 172
Soup, Sour Cream-Topped
    Tomato, '80 246
Soup, Summer Tomato, '79 130
Soup, Tomato, '81 236; '83 44
Soup, Tomato-and-Rice, '85 24
Soup, Tomato-Celery, '83 M58
Soup, Tomato-Vegetable, '81 M177;
    '86 9
Soup with Parmesan Cheese, Cream of
    Tomato, '86 161
Spicy Tomato Sipper, '86 229
Spread, Fiery Tomato-Cheese, '87 196
Spread, Home-Style Sandwich, '80 179
Spread, Tomato-Cheese, '81 157
Squash, Beans, and Tomatoes, '83 148
Squash, Tomato, '86 111
Stack-Ups, Jiffy Tomato, '80 161
Stewed Tomatoes, '83 182
Stir-Fry, Tomato-Zucchini, '80 158
Stir-Fry, Zucchini-and-Tomato, '85 108
Strata, Tomato-Cheese, '81 209
Stuffed Eggs-and-Tomato Slices, '84 152
Stuffed Tomatoes, '83 252
Stuffed Tomatoes, Avocado-, '82 101
Stuffed Tomatoes, Bacon-and-
    Egg-, '80 162
Stuffed Tomatoes, Bean-, '84 34
Stuffed Tomatoes, Broccoli-, '83 136
Stuffed Tomatoes, Cheesy, '80 161
Stuffed Tomatoes, Cold, '80 100
Stuffed Tomatoes, Corn-, '82 270
Stuffed Tomatoes, Easy, '82 264
Stuffed Tomatoes, Maque Chou, '87 89
Stuffed Tomatoes, Mushroom-, '86 218
Stuffed Tomatoes, Sausage-, '80 47
Stuffed Tomatoes, Squash-, '82 102
Swiss Chard with Tomatoes, '83 36
Treat, Summer Tomato, '79 143
Tuna-Mac in Tomatoes, '87 188
Venison and Tomatoes, '85 270
Vinaigrette, Tomato-Basil, '87 89
Vinaigrette, Tomatoes, '84 106
Tortillas. *See also* Burritos, Enchiladas,
    Tacos.
Appetizers, Tex-Mex Tortilla, '86 297
Bake, Cheesy Beef-and-Bean, '82 89
Bake, Chicken Tortilla, '82 89
Buñuelos, '80 199
Buñuelos, King-Size, '86 5
Casserole, Chicken Tortilla, '81 166
Casserole, El Dorado, '81 140
Casserole, Mexican Chicken, '82 143
Chalupas, Bean, '83 313
Chalupas, Chicken, '79 185
Chalupas, Chicken-Olive, '81 227
Chalupas, Texas Turkey, '80 196
Cheesy Tortillas, '81 62
Chicken Acapulco, '84 32
Chicken-Tortilla Stack, Cheesy, '86 3
Chilaquiles, '82 220

Chilaquiles con Pollo, '81 66
Chimichangas, '86 114
Chimichangas, Pineapple Dessert, '86 4
Chorizo and Egg Tortillas, '81 193
Dippers, Rolled Tortilla, '86 4
Egg-and-Sausage Tortillas, '83 246; '84 42
Eggs Sonora, '80 196
Fajitas, '84 233
Fajitas, Favorite, '86 114
Flautas, '83 199
Flour Tortillas, '81 303
Flour Tortillas, Never-Fail, '80 198

Picadillo, '84 118
Pie, Mexican Cheese, '82 9; '83 69
Pie, Montezuma Tortilla, '83 199
Pie, Tortilla, '85 M211
Salad in a Shell, Mexican, '86 4
Sandwiches, Guacamole, '82 9; '83 68
Sandwich, Tex-Mex Ham-and-
   Cheese, '86 4
Tostada Compuestas, '81 194
Tostadas, Crispy, '83 2
Tostadas, Super, '83 199

Tuna
Baked Tuna and Peas in Wine
   Sauce, '83 196
Bake, Shoestring Potato Tuna, '82 211
Ball, Tuna-Pecan, '87 94
Barbecued Tuna, '80 275
Bisque, Tuna, '79 76
Boats, Cucumber Tuna, '83 136
Burgers, Zippy Tuna, '81 135
Casserole, Biscuit-Topped Tuna, '79 113
Casserole, Easy Tuna, '82 M203
Casserole, Nippy Tuna, '84 241
Casserole, Tangy Tuna-Broccoli, '83 75
Casserole, Tuna, '82 119
Casserole, Tuna Vegetable, '81 135
Cheesies, Tuna, '82 191
Croquettes, Tuna-Egg, '80 275
Croquettes with Parsley
   Sauce, Tuna, '86 108
Dip, Low-Cal Tuna, '87 25
Dip, Tuna-Curry, '84 31
Eggs, Tuna-Stuffed, '83 83
Jambalaya, Tuna, '83 44
Lasagna, Tuna, '83 44; '84 123
Macaroni Treat, Tuna-, '82 131
Mold, Creamy Tuna-Cheese, '81 135
Mound, Tuna, '80 276
Mousse, Tuna, '80 275
Pie, Tuna-Rice, '84 123
Pie with Cheese Roll Crust,
   Tuna, '80 286
Pita Pocket, Tuna-in-a-, '87 202
Potatoes, Tuna-Stuffed, '79 210
Ring, Creamy Tuna, '80 275
Salad, Cheese-Sauced Tuna, '87 M124

Salad, Company Tuna, '87 201
Salad, Confetti, '80 4
Salad, Congealed Tuna, '84 163
Salad, Creamy Tuna, '82 87, 208
Salad, Crunchy Tuna, '87 201
Salad, Curried Tuna, '86 208
Salad, Favorite Tuna, '82 208
Salad, Flavorful Tuna, '81 37
Salad, Fresh Greens and Tuna, '80 55
Salad, Layered Tuna, '84 221
Salad, Luncheon Tuna, '81 135
Salad, Meal-in-One, '82 232
Salad Rolls, Hot Tuna, '84 281
Salad, Swiss Tuna, '86 186
Salad, Tuna-and-Cannellini Bean, '86 143
Salad, Tuna Chef, '82 78
Salad, Tuna-Egg, '81 135
Salad, Tuna Macaroni, '83 44, 145
Salad, Tuna-Macaroni, '84 66
Salad, Tuna-Potato, '84 289
Salad, Tuna-Rice, '87 202
Salad, Tuna-Taco, '87 145
Salad, Whole Wheat
   Macaroni-Tuna, '84 193
Salad with Grapes, Curried Tuna, '87 201
Sandwiches, French Toasted
   Tuna, '80 275
Sandwiches, Hot Tuna, '85 299; '86 M194
Sandwiches, Tuna Club, '83 134
Spread, Tuna, '83 174
Tomatoes, Tuna-Mac in, '87 188

Turkey
Baked Turkey, Cider, '83 263
Bake, Layered Ham and Turkey, '79 252
Braised Turkey Breast, '84 260
Breast, Herb Butter-Basted
   Turkey, '86 285
Buffet Turkey, '80 29
Casserole, Golden Turkey, '80 271
Casserole, Turkey, '84 327
Casserole, Turkey-and-Broccoli, '86 332
Casserole, Turkey-Asparagus, '86 284
Casserole, Turkey-Olive, '87 268
Casserole, Turkey-Spinach, '84 71
Casserole, Turkey-Swiss, '86 283
Chalupas, Texas Turkey, '80 196
Chili Topping, '84 246
Chowder, Turkey, '85 10
Chowder, Turkey-Corn, '81 98
Creamed Turkey, Southern, '80 272
Crêpes, Elegant Turkey, '83 282
Cups, Turkey-Tomato, '84 119
Divan, Turkey, '82 268
Dressing, Easy Turkey and, '79 296
Dressing, Turkey, '85 298
Fast-and-Savory Turkey, '87 306
Galantine of Turkey, '85 150
Gumbo, Turkey, '82 268; '85 258
Ham and Turkey Specials, Cheesy, '84 14
Indian Turkey, '85 302
Jambalaya de Covington, '87 211
Lasagna, Lean, '86 37
Lasagna, Turkey, '83 239
Loaf, Cranberry-Glazed Turkey, '86 171
Loaf, Ground Turkey, '86 171
Open-Facers, Turkey, '82 190
Oriental Turkey, '82 268
Parmesan, Turkey, '82 268
Parmigiana, Turkey, '87 193
Patties in Vegetable-Tomato Sauce,
   Turkey, '87 18
Patties, Stuffed Ground Turkey, '86 171
Pie, Crumb-Crust Curried Turkey, '86 265

Pie, Golden Turkey, '79 253
Pie, Lattice-Topped Turkey, '81 277;
   '82 7
Pie, Potato-Topped Turkey, '86 265
Pie, Turkey, '80 285
Pie, Turkey-and-Dressing, '84 326
Pie, Turkey-and-Oyster, '82 267
Pie, Turkey Pot, '86 265
Pilaf, Turkey-Rice, '86 284
Puffs, Turkey-Cheese, '87 301
Rice, Turkey Fried, '83 282
Roast Turkey, '79 250; '80 262; '86 47
Roast Turkey Breast with Special
   Gravy, '86 282
Roast Turkey, How to, '83 286
Roast Turkey with Oyster
   Stuffing, '80 251
Roast Turkey with Peanut
   Dressing, '79 283
Roast Turkey with Rice Dressing, '82 286
Rollups, Turkey, '86 198
Rounds, Turkey-Mozzarella, '82 3
Salad Bake, Turkey, '79 253
Salad, Fruitful Turkey, '84 197
Salad, Holiday Turkey, '84 320
Salad, Hot Turkey, '86 10, 297; '87 176
Salad, Layered Turkey, '86 332
Salad, Meal-in-One, '86 43
Salad Pita Sandwiches, Turkey, '87 202
Salad, Polynesian Turkey, '87 285
Salad, Turkey-Carrot, '86 283
Salad, Turkey-Fruit, '79 56
Salad, Turkey Fruit, '83 233; '84 244
Salad, Turkey Macaroni, '83 282
Salad, Turkey-Zucchini, '85 74
Salad with Hot Bacon Dressing,
   Turkey, '87 285

Salad with Sautéed Walnuts,
   Turkey, '86 117
Sandwiches, Hot Brown, '80 M202
Sandwiches, Meal-in-One, '80 218
Sandwiches, Monte Cristo, '83 134
Sandwiches, Open-Faced, '79 214
Sauce, Turkey Spaghetti, '85 13
Sausage-Cornbread Dressing, Turkey
   with, '83 287
Schnitzel, Turkey, '84 230
Skillet, Oriental Turkey-Orange, '86 284
Smoked Turkey, '79 293; '84 160;
   '85 258
Soufflé, Turkey, '80 271
Soup, Curried Turkey, '86 332
Soup, Turkey Carcass, '86 284
Soup, Turkey-Vegetable, '84 4
Spread, Turkey Party, '83 282
Squash Dressing, Turkey with, '87 248
Stew, Hearty Turkey, '79 252
Stuffed Turkey Breast, '87 270
Stuffed Turkey Breast with Seasoned
   Dressing, '83 320; '84 128
Sweet-and-Sour Turkey, '79 252
Tetrazzini, Herbed Turkey, '86 47

Turnips

au Gratin, Turnip, '79 289
au Gratin, Turnips, '84 229
Boiled Turnips, '83 242
Casserole, Baked Turnip, '82 274
Casserole, Turnip, '83 242; '84 229
Cheese Sauce, Turnips in, '84 229
Cooked Turnips, Creamy, '86 224
Fried Turnips, Shoestring, '81 274
Gingered Turnips, '82 274
Glazed Turnips, '81 274
Greens and Ham Hock, Southern
  Turnip, '80 119
Greens, Old-Fashioned Turnip, '85 255
Greens with Turnips, Turnip, '84 230
Hash Brown Turnips, '79 254
Julienne, Turnips and Carrots, '86 295
Onions, Turnips and, '83 242
Parsleyed Turnips and Carrots, '79 253

Party Turnips, '84 230
Potatoes, Turnips and, '79 254
Saucy Turnips, '85 289
Scalloped Potatoes and Turnips, '85 235
Scalloped Turnips, '79 254
Soufflé, Turnip, '79 254
Soup, Creamy Turnip, '84 279
Southern Turnips, '87 190
Supreme, Turnip, '79 254
Sweet-and-Sour Turnips, '81 274

Turtle

Fried Cooter (Soft-Shell Turtle), '80 99
Soup au Sherry, Turtle, '80 56

V

Vanilla

Cake, Vanilla Chiffon, '79 266
Cookies, Vanilla Slice-and-Bake, '85 171
Cream, Vanilla, '81 248; '83 M115
Crescents, Vanilla, '82 307
Cupcakes, Golden Vanilla, '85 121
Custard, Baked Vanilla, '82 129
Dessert, Glorified Vanilla Sherry, '81 85
Extract, Home-Brewed Vanilla, '83 228
Extract, Homemade Vanilla, '83 228
Frosting, Vanilla, '84 36; '85 236
Frosting, Vanilla-Rum, '85 324
Frosty, French Vanilla, '79 148
Fruit Cup, Vanilla, '80 183
Glaze, Vanilla, '85 M89
Helado, Caramel-Vanilla (Caramel-Vanilla
  Ice Cream), '81 67

Ice Cream, Country Vanilla, '82 143
Ice Cream Spectacular, Vanilla, '82 166
Ice Cream, Vanilla, '80 176; '86 129
Pie, Fruit-Topped Vanilla Cream, '84 49
Pudding, Creamy Vanilla, '83 227
Soufflé, Frozen Vanilla, '79 230; '82 173

Veal

Amelio, Veal, '86 142
au Madeira, Veal, '81 131
Birds, Veal, '84 260
Burgoo, Five-Meat, '87 3
Casserole, Veal and Wild Rice, '79 180
Casserole, Veal Cutlet, '79 109
Chops, Apple Veal, '87 220
Chops Mediterranean, Veal, '79 108
Company Veal and Carrots, '85 22
Cordon Bleu, Veal, '87 219
Delight, Veal, '79 109
Herbed Veal and Onions, '79 108
Herbed Veal with Wine, '86 193
Italian Style, Veal, '82 M68
Lemon Veal Piccata, '86 118
Lemon Veal with Artichoke
  Hearts, '87 219
Meatballs, European Veal, '85 30
Meat Loaf, Italian, '79 187
Meat Loaf, Savory, '87 216
Meat Loaf, Triple, '79 186
New Orleans Veal with Crabmeat, '86 94
Parmigiana, Veal, '81 227
Peppercorns, Veal with Green, '87 220
Picante, Veal, '87 31
Picatta with Capers, Veal, '87 142
Roast, Best Baked Veal, '87 219
Sauce, Noodles with Veal, '80 236
Savory Veal, '83 281
Scallopini à la Marsala, Veal, '79 109
Scallopini Marsala, Veal, '85 295
Scallopini, Veal, '83 8, 125
Scaloppine of Veal al Sorriso, '79 85
Schnitzel, Swiss, '80 189
Skillet Veal, '83 200
Spaghetti, Veal, '84 276
Spaghetti with Veal and Peppers, '81 201;
  '82 14
Steak, Veal, '82 276
Stroganoff, Veal, '79 108
Supreme, Veal, '85 109
Swirls, Veal-and-Smithfield Ham, '86 253
Wine Sauce, Veal and Carrots in,
  '81 31; '86 M139

Vegetables. *See also* specific types and
  Canning.

Antipasto, Vegetable, '85 263
Appetizer, Tarragon Vegetable, '83 277
Aspic, Cheesy Vegetable, '81 73
Beef and Vegetables in a Noodle
  Ring, '85 285
Beef and Vegetables, Savory, '79 163
Beef with Chinese Vegetables, '81 211
Blanching Chart, Microwave, '80 M181
Bread, Breakaway Vegetable, '82 74
Burgers, Beef-and-Vegetable, '84 125
Burritos, Vegetable, '80 197
Burritos with Avocado Sauce,
  Vegetable, '83 200
Buttermilk Sauce, Vegetables with, '84 6
Casserole, Beef and Vegetable Chow
  Mein, '83 313
Casserole, Beefy Vegetable, '79 248
Casserole, Cheesy Vegetable, '81 103
Casserole, Fresh Vegetable, '82 225
Casserole, Garden, '82 168

Casserole, Mixed Vegetable, '83 208, 256;
  '86 327
Casserole, Mixed-Vegetable, '87 154
Casserole, Tuna Vegetable, '81 135
Casserole, Vegetable-and-Ham, '84 91
Chicken and Dumplings with
  Vegetables, '85 M56
Chicken and Vegetables, Almond, '86 21
Chicken and Vegetables, Chinese, '81 212
Chicken and Vegetables, Roast, '81 3
Chicken and Vegetables, Walnut, '85 194
Chili, Vegetarian, '84 280, 327
Cocktail, Fresh Vegetable, '82 165
Creamed Spring Vegetables, '87 127
Crêpes, Chicken-Vegetable, '83 70
Crêpes, Vegetable-Filled Bran, '86 44
Croutons, Vegetable-Flavored, '84 148
Dip, Creamy Vegetable, '83 180
Dip, Cucumber-Cheese Vegetable, '83 128
Dip, Fresh Vegetable, '80 249
Dip, Starburst Vegetable, '82 248
Dip, Tangy Vegetable, '87 196
Dip, Vegetable, '79 52; '82 161
Dip, Vegetable Garden, '85 215
Dip, Zippy Vegetable, '84 256
Egg Rolls, Vegetarian, '86 148
en Papillote, Chicken and
  Vegetables, '86 145
Fettuccine, Vegetable, '83 312
Fish Rolls, Vegetable-Filled, '86 M251
Flounder Rolls, Vegetable-Stuffed, '87 6
Flounder-Vegetable Medley, '85 217
Freezing Chart, Vegetable, '85 185
Fresh Vegetable Party Tray, '82 122
Fresh Vegetable Potpourri, '79 208
Fresh Vegetables, Parsley-Dill Dip
  with, '85 79
Garden Combo, '86 172
Garden Harvest, '85 M142
Garden Surprise, '83 112
Garnishes, '82 280; '85 338, 339

Grilled Vegetables, '84 172
Ham-and-Vegetables, Skillet, '84 90
Herbed-Smoked Vegetables, '85 145
Heroes, Vegetable Garden, '84 14
Juice Delight, Vegetable, '84 58
Julienne Vegetables with
  Walnuts, '86 M251
Kabobs, Fresh Vegetable, '81 158
Kabobs, Marinated Vegetable, '83 M195
Kabobs, Vegetable, '87 116
Lamb with Vegetables, Fillets of, '85 36
Lasagna, Cheesy Vegetable, '79 84
Lasagna, Colorful Vegetable, '87 19
Lasagna, Garden, '83 119
Lasagna, Vegetable, '84 201
Liver with Vegetables, Calf's, '85 219
Loaf, Beef-Vegetable, '79 164
Loaf, Pureed Vegetable-Cheese, '85 297
Marinade, Fresh Vegetable, '83 209

Marinated Vegetable Medley, **'85** 319
Marinated Vegetables, **'79** 146; **'81** 239;
  '85 67; **'86** 286
Marinated Vegetables, Sweet-and-
  Sour, **'83** 266
Marinated Vegetables, Zesty, **'82** 272
Marinated Vegetable Toss, **'82** 113
Meat Loaf, Vegetable, **'85** M29
Medley, Baked Vegetable, **'81** 75
Medley Bake, Vegetable, **'81** 268
Medley, Chinese Vegetable, **'84** 33
Medley, Crunchy Vegetable, **'84** 254
Medley, Fresh Vegetable, **'85** 155
Medley, Green Vegetable, **'79** 287; **'80** 34
Medley, Mixed Vegetable, **'82** 126
Medley, Sautéed Vegetable, **'83** 101
Medley, Skillet Vegetable, **'81** 134
Medley, Spring Vegetable, **'86** 115
Medley, Summer Garden, **'84** 158
Medley, Summer Vegetable, **'83** 208
Medley, Vegetable, **'79** 102; **'83** 112;
  '86 327
Microwaving Fresh Vegetables, **'82** M138
Minestrone, **'82** 4
Mixed Vegetables, **'83** M195
Mixed Vegetables, Pasta with Sausage
  and, **'84** 249
Mushroom Caps, Vegetable, **'81** 246
Omelet, Beefy Vegetable, **'83** 188
Omelet, Cheddar-Vegetable, **'83** 205
Omelet, Cheesy Vegetable, **'85** 49
Omelet, Fresh Vegetable, **'84** 211
Omelet, Golden Vegetable, **'82** 123
Omelet Primavera, **'87** 71
Omelet, Puffy Vegetable, **'83** 188
Omelet, Vegetarian, **'84** 114
Open-Faced Vegetarian Melt, **'87** 106
Oriental Vegetables, **'84** 26; **'85** 108
Oriental Vegetables, Beef with, **'84** 140
Paella, Garden, **'82** 245
Paella, Spanish, **'85** 26
Pasta and Garden Vegetables, **'87** 192
Pasta, Garden, **'82** 199
Pasta Primavera, **'85** 86
Pasta Primavera, Almost, **'86** 38
Pâté, Vegetable-Chicken, **'86** 66
Pie, Chicken-Vegetable Pot, **'81** 281;
  '82 30
Pies, Vegetable-Beef, **'80** 286
Pizza, Deep-Dish Vegetarian, **'85** 243
Pockets, Vegetable, **'85** 215
Pork Chops, Skillet Vegetable, **'85** 179
Pork Combo, Vegetable-, **'85** 113
Potatoes, Vegetable-Topped
  Stuffed, **'85** 235
Pot Roast Medley, Vegetable-, **'83** 319
Pot Roast with Vegetables, **'80** 59;
  '81 M208
Quiche, Cheese-Vegetable, **'81** 228
Quiche, Ham-and-Vegetable, **'84** 326
Quiche, Vegetable, **'87** M219
Ratatouille, **'84** 105, 243; **'85** 92
Ratatouille-Bran Stuffed Eggplant, **'86** 44
Ratatouille, Eggplant-Zucchini, **'81** 205
Ratatouille Niçoise, **'81** 22
Ratatouille, Quick-and-Easy, **'80** 212
Ratatouille Supreme, **'86** 172
Relish, Eight-Vegetable, **'84** 179
Relish, Garden, **'83** 259
Relish Tree, Christmas, **'84** 257
Rice Pilaf, Fruit-and-Vegetable, **'84** 196
Rice with Vegetables, **'79** 64; **'85** 83
Ring, Tomato-Vegetable, **'81** 302

Salads
  Aspic with Horseradish Dressing,
    Crisp Vegetable, **'87** 152
  Boats, Salad, **'80** 93
  Calico Salad, **'82** 35
  Cauliflower-Vegetable Salad, **'85** 158
  Chinese Salad, **'80** 4
  Composée, Salad, **'79** 171
  Congealed Fresh Vegetable
    Salad, **'82** 240
  Congealed Salad,
    Cheesy-Vegetable, **'86** 199
  Congealed Vegetable Salad, **'79** 276
  Corned Beef Salad,
    Vegetable-, **'80** 148
  Creamy Vegetable Salad, **'79** 47
  Creole Salad, **'79** 147
  Crunchy Vegetable Salad, **'79** 11;
    '80 217; **'83** 216
  Different Vegetable Salad, **'82** 143
  Easy Vegetable Salad, **'83** 316; **'84** 16
  Garden Medley Salad, **'80** 122
  Garden Salad, **'87** 62
  Garden Salad Bowl, **'82** 239
  Greek Salad, Garden, **'86** 173
  Green-and-White Vegetable
    Salad, **'79** 286
  Green Vegetable and Egg
    Salad, **'79** 191

  Green Vegetable Salad,
    Overnight, **'80** 5
  Italian Vegetable Salad, **'81** 253;
    '82 19
  Lemon-Vegetable Congealed
    Salad, **'85** 22
  Luncheon Salad, **'84** 232
  Macaroni-Vegetable Salad, **'86** 209
  Marinade, Garden, **'81** 23
  Marinade, Medley, **'79** 20
  Marinade, Tossed Vegetable, **'84** 266
  Marinated Combo Salad, **'82** 267
  Marinated Garden
    Vegetables, **'87** 252
  Marinated Salad,
    Eight-Vegetable, **'80** 218
  Marinated Summer Salad, **'81** 153
  Marinated Vegetable-Bacon
    Bowl, **'79** 191
  Marinated Vegetable Patch
    Salad, **'84** 232
  Marinated Vegetable Salad, **'79** 106,
    143; **'81** 280; **'82** 163; **'83** 260;
    '84 13; **'87** 243
  Marinated Vegetable Salad,
    Crispy, **'84** 193
  Marinated Vegetable Salad,
    Fresh, **'86** 173

  Marinate, Fresh Vegetable, **'80** 33;
    '81 230
  Meal-in-One Salad, **'82** 232
  Mexican Salad, **'81** 113
  Mixed Vegetable Salad, **'80** 115;
    '81 302; **'82** 239; **'83** 317; **'84** 16;
    '86 136
  Next-Day Vegetable Salad, **'83** 81
  Oriental Salad, Make-Ahead, **'82** 163
  Oriental Vegetable Salad, **'84** 290
  Rainbow Vegetable Salad, **'83** 111
  Refrigerated Vegetable Salad, **'84** 120
  Relish Salad, Vegetable, **'82** 267
  Rice-and-Vegetable Salad, **'86** 42
  Rice-and-Vegetable Salad,
    Brown, **'84** 202
  Rice Salad, Vegetable-, **'80** 148;
    '83 198; **'85** 87
  Rolls, Vegetable Salad, **'82** 278
  Senator's Salad, **'79** 191
  Seven-Layer Vegetable Salad, **'79** 88
  Shrimp Salad, Vegetable-, **'79** 190
  Slaw, Vegetable, **'81** 280
  Summertime Salad, **'79** 143
  Swedish Vegetable Salad, **'82** 23
  Sweet-and-Sour Vegetable
    Salad, **'81** 25
  Tangy Vegetable Toss, **'79** 144
  Tarragon-Vegetable Salad, **'85** 288
  Variety Salad, **'79** 113
  Vinaigrette Salad,
    Vegetable-Chicken, **'86** 135
  Vinaigrette, Vegetables, **'82** 225, 290
  Walnuts, Vegetable Salad
    with, **'86** 118
  Winter Vegetable Salad, **'86** 42
Sandwiches, Open-Face
  Tofu-Veggie, **'86** 5
Sandwiches, Vegetarian Pita, **'84** 193
Sandwich, Vegetable Puff, **'85** 51
Sauce, Greek Fish with Vegetable, **'82** 72
Sauce, Pasta with Vegetable, **'83** 163
Sauce, Turkey Patties in
  Vegetable-Tomato, **'87** 18
Sauce, Vegetable Butter, **'86** 174
Sauce, Vegetable-Cheese, **'85** M152
Sausage Vegetable Dinner, **'84** 250
Sautéed Vegetables with Spaghetti, **'81** 89
Sautéed Vegetables with Spaghetti
  Squash, **'84** 128
Sauté, Garden, **'87** 90
Sautéing Fresh Vegetables, **'82** 138
Scalloped Mixed Vegetables, **'83** 5
Scallops en Brochette with
  Vegetables, **'80** 163
Scallops with Vegetables, Bay, **'84** 233
Sesame Sauce, Vegetables with, **'83** 112
Shrimp and Vegetables, **'82** 6
Skillet, Vegetable-Beef, **'86** 172
Soups
  Bean Soup, Vegetable-, **'83** 317
  Beef Soup, Hearty
    Vegetable-, **'84** 102
  Beefy Vegetable Soup, **'79** 113;
    '84 M38
  Beefy Vegetable Soup, Quick, **'80** 25
  Burger Soup, Vegetable-, **'82** 6
  Cheese Soup, Creamy
    Vegetable-, **'81** 244
  Cheese Soup, Creamy
    Vegetable, **'83** 230
  Cheesy Vegetable Chowder, **'80** 25;
    '83 20

Vegetables, Soups *(continued)*

    Cheesy Vegetable Soup, '80 73
    Clear Vegetable Soup, '79 130
    Garden Soup, '85 241
    Garden Vegetable Soup, '83 140;
      '86 160
    Garden Vegetable Soup,
      Cold, '84 197
    Gazpacho, '84 112; '85 164
    Gazpacho, Chilled, '84 138
    Gazpacho, Cool, '83 140
    Gazpacho, Spring, '81 112
    Gazpacho, Summer, '84 181
    Harvest Chowder, '83 317
    Harvest Soup, '79 101
    Hearty Vegetable Soup, '80 26
    Homemade Soup, '79 198
    Leek-Vegetable Soup, '86 304
    Light Vegetable Soup, '84 280
    Marvelous Vegetable Soup, '82 3
    Mix, Vegetable Soup, '84 148
    Old-Fashioned Vegetable
      Soup, '86 304
    Quick Vegetable Soup, '79 190;
      '85 24, 32
    Savory Vegetable Broth, '81 230
    Shrimp-Vegetable Bisque, '82 313;
      '83 66
    Spicy Vegetable Soup, '79 198
    Tomato-Vegetable Soup, '81 177;
      '86 9
    Turkey-Vegetable Soup, '84 4
    Vegetable Soup, '80 128; '84 148;
      '85 106; '86 187; '87 83, 123
Spaghetti, Fresh Vegetables with, '86 257
Spaghetti with Vegetables, '85 67
Spicy Vegetables and Sausage, '80 82
Spread, Garden, '86 135
Spread, Vegetable-Egg, '87 106
Spread, Vegetable Party, '84 166
Spread, Vegetable Sandwich, '83 174;
    '85 135
Squash, Vegetable-Stuffed, '84 104
Steak with Vegetables, Skewered, '81 124
Steak with Vegetables, Swiss, '81 273

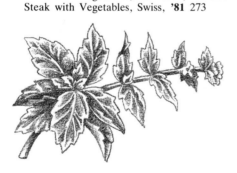

Steamed and Minted Garden
    Toss, '83 173
Steamed Dinner, Easy, '83 M314
Steamed Vegetable Medley, '86 50
Steamed Vegetables with Mustard
    Sauce, '83 208
Steaming Fresh Vegetables, '82 138, 183
Stew, Fish-and-Vegetable, '87 220
Stew, Mixed Vegetable, '84 13
Stew, Sweet-and-Sour Beef and
    Vegetable, '85 87
Stir-Fried Vegetables, '79 217; '83 193
Stir-Fried Vegetables with Curry, '87 51

Stir-Fry, Almond-Vegetable, '86 222
Stir-Fry, Beef-and-Vegetable, '81 211;
    '87 22
Stir-Fry Beef-and-Vegetables, '84 141
Stir-Fry, Chicken and Vegetable, '82 237
Stir-Fry Chicken and Vegetables, '86 249
Stir-Fry Chicken-and-Vegetables, '86 68
Stir-Fry, Chicken-Vegetable, '83 151;
    '84 13, 141
Stir-Frying Fresh Vegetables, '82 138
Stir-Fry, Mixed Vegetable, '79 268;
    '80 14
Stir-Fry Sausage and Vegetables, '86 213;
    '87 82
Stir-Fry Shrimp and Vegetables, '87 91
Stir-Fry, Steak-and-Vegetable, '84 8
Stir-Fry, Three-Vegetable, '86 174
Stir-Fry, Vegetable, '79 214; '82 M172,
    208; '84 104
Stir-Fry, Vegetable Medley, '85 109
Stir-Fry Vegetables with Chicken,
    '84 195
Succotash, '85 106
Succotash, Easy, '80 165
Succotash, Summer, '86 170
Supper, Vegetarian, '86 222
Tempura, Basic, '81 68
Tempura, Cornmeal, '81 68
Tempura, Vegetable, '79 112
Terrine, Chicken-Vegetable, '84 131
Terrine, Vegetable-Chicken, '83 224
Topper, Vegetable-Cheese Potato, '86 6
Topping, Vegetable, '79 79
Torte, Layered Vegetable, '84 52
Trio, Vegetable-Herb, '83 172
Turnovers, Vegetable, '86 24
Venison-Vegetable Bake, '87 304
Vermicelli, Scallop-Vegetable, '87 143
Vermouth, Chicken and
    Vegetables, '87 M37
Wine-Soaked Vegetables, Baked Chicken
    with, '84 277

Venison
    Bake, Venison-Vegetable, '87 304
    Balls, Venison Sausage, '80 42
    Burgers, Venison, '87 304
    Chili, Double-Meat, '79 269; '80 12
    Chili, Venison, '82 216; '86 3; '87 304
    Fried Venison, Country-, '81 233
    Kabobs, Venison, '82 215
    Roast, Venison, '82 226
    Roast with Red Wine Gravy,
      Venison, '85 270
    Soup, Venison, '82 216
    Steak, Country-Fried Venison, '83 262
    Steaks, Country-Style Venison, '82 215
    Steaks, Grilled Venison, '82 215
    Stew, Venison, '86 294
    Stew, Venison Sausage, '87 238
    Stew with Potato Dumplings,
      Venison, '87 304
    Tomatoes, Venison and, '85 270

Vinegars
    Dill-and-Chive Vinegar, '84 300
    Garlic-Basil Vinegar, '85 124
    Herb Vinegar, Five-, '85 124
    Herb Vinegar, Homemade, '79 100
    Herb Vinegar, Mixed, '84 107
    Lemon-Mint Vinegar, '85 124
    Oregano-Lemon Vinegar, Spicy, '85 124
    Raspberry-Lemon Vinegar, '87 134
    Tarragon-Dill Vinegar, '85 124
    Tarragon Vinegar, '84 107

W

Waffles
    Banana-Ginger Waffles, '86 96
    Chicken-Pecan Waffles, Southern,
      '82 231
    Cornbread Waffles, '79 265
    Cornmeal Waffles, '85 201
    Crunchy Brunch Waffles, '81 41
    French Toast, Waffled, '82 47
    French Waffles, '86 138
    Ham Waffles, '80 44
    Oatmeal-Nut Waffles, '83 96
    Pecan Waffles, '87 225
    Pumpkin-Nut Waffles, '86 96
    Quick Bread Mix, '81 90
    Quick Mix Waffles, '86 9

    Refrigerator Waffles, Best Ever, '87 225
    Sausage Waffles, '83 50
    Sorghum-Ginger Waffles, '85 239
    Southern Waffles, '87 225
    Waffles, '81 90
    Walnut Waffles, Crunchy, '85 48
    Whole Wheat Dessert Waffle, '79 92
    Whole Wheat Waffles, '84 228

Walnuts
    Bonbons, Coconut-Black Walnut, '82 307
    Bread, Apple-Nut, '79 12
    Bread, Applesauce-Honey Nut, '87 300
    Bread, Apricot-Nut, '79 24
    Bread, Cherry Nut, '81 306; '82 36
    Bread, Chocolate Date-Nut, '81 284
    Bread, Cinnamon-Nut Bubble, '80 22
    Bread, Cranberry-Orange Nut, '80 288
    Bread, Date-Nut, '85 306
    Bread, Fresh Apple-Nut, '87 256
    Bread, Wine-Date Nut, '82 253
    Brie, Walnut-Fried, '86 244
    Brownies, Walnut-Cream Cheese, '84 240
    Burgers, Nutty, '87 185
    Cake, Apple-Nut, '87 76
    Cake, Black Walnut, '80 253; '84 316
    Cake, Cranberry-Nut Coffee, '81 250
    Cake, Orange Nut, '80 70
    Cake, Orange-Nut Butter, '80 254
    Cake, Sour Cream-Walnut Coffee,
      '79 209
    Candied Nuts, '81 261
    Carrots with Walnuts, Julienne, '84 188
    Cheese, Nutty Date Dessert, '87 299
    Chicken and Vegetables, Walnut,
      '85 194
    Chicken Breasts, Walnut-Stuffed, '85 293
    Chicken, Deep-Fried Walnut, '87 175
    Chicken, Walnut, '85 126

Chocolate-Nut Chews, '81 92
Cobbler, Apple-Walnut, '79 154; '81 248
Cookies, Apple-Nut, '80 228
Cookies, Frosted
    Pumpkin-Walnut, '82 217
Cookies, Nutty Oatmeal, '81 130
Cookies, Walnut, '81 301
Cupcakes, Apple-Nut, '82 279
Cups, Chocolate-Walnut, '85 213
Filling, Honey-Walnut, '80 21
Fried Walnuts, Chinese, '81 254
Frosting, Nutty Coconut, '86 8
Fudge, Nutty White, '81 253
Honey-Walnut Swirl, '80 21
Loaf, Apricot-Nut, '81 8
Loaf, Blue Ribbon Date-Walnut, '80 15

Meatballs, Mock, '81 243
Mousse, Coffee-Nut, '86 319
Muffins, Carrot-Date-Nut, '86 262
Muffins, Nutty Pumpkin, '86 291
Pie, Walnut-Cranberry, '87 259
Pitas, Spinach-Walnut, '87 202
Salad, Orange Walnut, '80 246
Salad, Shrimp-Walnut, '86 182
Salad with Walnuts, Vegetable, '86 118
Sauce, Spaghetti with Parsley and
    Walnut, '80 30
Sautéed Walnuts, Turkey Salad
    with, '86 117
Sherry-Orange Nuts, '86 M289
Spread, Date-Walnut, '87 292
Spread, Nutty Fruit-and-Cheese, '87 246
Strawberries with Walnuts,
    Stuffed, '85 122; '86 124
Sweet Potatoes with Sherry and
    Walnuts, '86 286
Syrup, Maple-Nut, '80 228
Topping, Nutty, '86 16
Twists, Fruit-Nut, '82 253
Vegetables with Walnuts,
    Julienne, '86 M251
Waffles, Crunchy Walnut, '85 48
Zucchini with Walnuts, '84 213
Watermelon. *See* Melons.
Wheat Germ
    Biscuits, Wheat Germ, '86 261
    Bread, Banana Wheat, '81 14
    Crackers, Oatmeal-Wheat Germ,
        '84 236
    Crisps, Sesame Wheat, '81 106
    Muffins, Wheat Germ-Prune, '81 106
    Pancakes, Wheat Germ, '86 242
    Pancakes, Wheat Germ-Banana, '79 114
    Squares, Spicy Wheat Germ, '80 44
Wild Rice. *See* Rice/Wild Rice.

Wok Cooking
    Asparagus and Mushrooms, '85 108
    Asparagus, Stir-Fried, '87 52
    Bean Medley, Green, '85 108
    Beans, Stir-Fried Green, '85 148
    Beef and Broccoli, Stir-Fry, '79 47
    Beef and Pea Pods, Stir-Fry, '80 19
    Beef and Snow Peas, Oriental, '79 105
    Beef and Snow Peas, Stir-Fry, '83 22
    Beef and Snow Pea Stir-Fry, '82 98
    Beef-and-Vegetables, Stir-Fry, '84 141
    Beef-and-Vegetable Stir-Fry, '81 211;
        '87 22
    Beef, Chinese-Style, '87 50
    Beef, Mongolian, '85 2, 75
    Beef, Oriental, '85 20
    Beef over Rice Noodles, Shredded, '85 74
    Beef Stew, '86 51
    Beef, Stir-Fried, '84 26
    Beef Stir-Fry, Chinese, '83 151
    Beef with Chinese Vegetables, '81 211
    Beef with Oriental Vegetables, '84 140
    Bok Choy-Broccoli Stir-Fry, '84 2
    Broccoli and Beef, Stir-Fry, '83 110
    Broccoli, Jade-Green, '80 12
    Broccoli, Stir-Fried, '83 227
    Broccoli, Stir-Fry, '80 19
    Broccoli with Sesame, '80 13
    Broccoli with Sesame Seeds, '82 34
    Brussels Sprouts Stir-Fry, '81 308
    Cabbage, Stir-Fried, '81 75, 271; '85 109
    Catfish Stir, '84 184
    Cheese Wontons with Hot Sauce, '83 74
    Chicken à l'Orange, Stir-Fry, '83 82
    Chicken and Vegetables, Almond, '86 21
    Chicken and Vegetables, Chinese, '81 212
    Chicken-and-Vegetables, Stir-Fry, '86 68
    Chicken and Vegetable Stir-Fry, '82 237
    Chicken and Vegetables, Walnut, '85 194
    Chicken, Braised Bourbon, '86 51
    Chicken-Broccoli Stir-Fry, '82 33
    Chicken, Cashew, '79 255; '83 21
    Chicken Curry, Stir-Fried, '87 51
    Chicken-in-a-Garden, '80 18
    Chicken in Soy and Wine, '84 26
    Chicken, Lemon, '86 173
    Chicken, Princess, '86 122
    Chicken Stir-Fry, Kyoto Orange-, '87 96
    Chicken Stir-Fry, Orange-, '84 68
    Chicken, Stir-Fry Vegetables with, '84 195
    Chicken, Sweet-and-Sour, '86 240
    Chicken, Szechwan, '83 85
    Chicken Tempura Delight, '85 66
    Chicken-Vegetable Stir-Fry, '83 151;
        '84 13, 141
    Chicken, Walnut, '85 126
    Chicken with Cashews, '79 207
    Chicken with Cashews, Szechwan, '81 212
    Chicken with Peanuts, Oriental, '82 236
    Chicken with Pineapple, Oriental, '86 42
    Chicken with Plum Sauce, '82 236
    Chicken, Zesty Stir-Fried, '83 82
    Chicken-Zucchini Stir-Fry, '84 50
    Chinese-Style Dinner, '84 26
    Egg Rolls, '86 81
    Eggrolls, Shrimp and Pork, '82 240;
        '83 18
    Egg Rolls, Vegetarian, '86 148
    Ham and Zucchini Stir-Fry, '79 47
    Ham Stir-Fry, Easy, '86 332
    Meatballs, Sweet-and-Sour, '86 240
    Mushrooms with Bacon,
        Stir-Fried, '80 123
    Pear Fritters, Ol' Timey, '86 51
    Peas and Peppers, Stir-Fried, '87 51
    Pork-and-Onions with Bean Sauce,
        '85 76
    Pork, Hot-and-Spicy, '81 228
    Pork in Garlic Sauce, Stir-Fried, '84 141
    Pork Oriental, '81 212
    Pork, Stir-Fried, '87 51
    Pork, Sweet-and-Sour, '79 42; '80 227;
        '81 26; '85 34, 194
    Pork Tenderloin, Curried, '86 76
    Potato Pudding, Sweet, '86 52
    Potato-Snow Pea Stir-Fry, '86 173
    Rice, Easy Fried, '84 76
    Rice, Egg Fried, '80 19
    Rice Special, Fried, '80 56
    Rice with Sausage, Fried, '83 12
    Sausage Rolls with Sweet-and-Sour
        Sauce, '83 74
    Sausage Stir-Fry, '82 236
    Shrimp and Sirloin Supreme, '81 131
    Shrimp and Vegetables, Stir-Fry, '87 91
    Shrimp Skillet, Quick, '87 50
    Shrimp, Szechuan, '86 173
    Shrimp with Snow Peas, '85 75

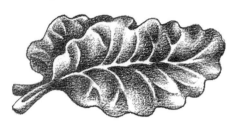

    Spinach, Chinese, '79 179
    Spinach, Stir-Fry, '81 182
    Spinach with Mushrooms, '80 19
    Spinach Wontons, '83 74
    Squash Medley, '84 128
    Squash Medley, Stir-Fried, '80 123
    Squash Stir-Fry, '80 184
    Squash Stir-Fry, Two-, '86 174
    Steak, Chinese Pepper, '82 236
    Steak, Fast-and-Easy Stir-Fried, '87 50
    Steak, Pepper Stir-Fry, '81 240
    Sugar Flips, '83 74
    Teriyaki Stir-Fry, '83 110
    Tomato-Zucchini Stir-Fry, '80 158
    Vegetable Medley, Chinese, '84 33
    Vegetable Medley Stir-Fry, '85 109
    Vegetables, Oriental, '84 26; '85 108
    Vegetables, Stir-Fried, '79 217; '83 193
    Vegetable Stir-Fry, '82 208; '84 104
    Vegetable Stir-Fry, Mixed, '79 268; '80 14
    Vegetable Stir-Fry, Three-, '86 174
    Vegetables with Curry, Stir-Fried, '87 51
    Wontons, Tex-Mex, '87 196
    Zucchini-and-Tomato Stir-Fry, '85 108
    Zucchini, Italian-Style, '80 123
    Zucchini Pesto, '84 194
Wontons
    Cheese Wontons with Hot Sauce, '83 74
    Fried Wontons, Crispy, '83 21
    Fruit-Filled Wontons, '85 287
    Nibbles, Wonton, '85 287
    Preparation Techniques, '83 74
    Sausage Rolls with Sweet-and-Sour
        Sauce, '83 74
    Spinach Wontons, '83 74
    Sugar Flips, '83 74
    Tex-Mex Wontons, '87 196

Y

Yogurt
Bars, Lemon Yogurt Wheat, '79 93
Cake, Yogurt Pound, '84 10
Chicken, Grilled Yogurt-Lemon, '81 111
Dip, Curry, '85 132
Dip, Fruited Yogurt, '84 171
Dip, Yogurt Herring, '80 232
Dressing, Asparagus with Yogurt, '79 66
Dressing, Ginger-Yogurt, '81 302
Dressing, Orange-Yogurt, '85 304
Dressing, Sweet-Hot Yogurt, '86 40
Dressing, Yogurt, '85 59, 215
Dressing, Yogurt-Honey Poppy
  Seed, '83 177
Dressing, Yogurt Salad, '79 69
Frozen Yogurt, Lemon-Chiffon, '85 54
Ice, Apricot Yogurt, '81 177
Ice, Peach-Yogurt, '84 83
Nectarines Royale, '85 132
Omelet, Yogurt-Avocado, '81 33
Pancakes, Orange-Yogurt, '87 225
Parfait, Crunchy Strawberry-
  Yogurt, '79 124
Pie, Strawberry Yogurt, '80 232
Pie, Strawberry-Yogurt, '85 122; '86 124
Pie, Yogurt-Apricot, '85 132
Pie, Yogurt-Cheese, '82 121
Salad, Crème de Menthe, '82 122
Salad, Cucumber-Yogurt, '87 33
Salad, Strawberry Yogurt, '80 232
Salad, Yogurt-Cucumber, '82 122
Salad, Yogurt Fruit, '81 114
Sauce, Lamb Meatballs with
  Yogurt, '85 132
Sauce, Yogurt-Horseradish, '85 66
Shake, Strawberry-Yogurt, '87 199
Soup, Avocado-Banana-Yogurt, '80 78

Soup, Cucumber-Yogurt, '82 157;
  '83 205
Soup, Yogurt Fruit, '86 176
Strawberry Yogurt Delight, '85 77

Z

Zucchini
au Gratin, Potatoes-and-Zucchini, '84 5
au Gratin, Zucchini and Tomato,
  '82 208
Bake, Corn-Zucchini, '79 178
Baked Zucchini, '83 209
Baked Zucchini and Sausages, '80 300
Baked Zucchini Fans, '87 243
Bake, Squash, '82 107
Bake, Zucchini and Tomato, '82 158
Bake, Zucchini-Beef, '86 146
Bars, Zucchini, '85 77
Beans with Zucchini, Green, '84 128
Bites, Crab-Zucchini, '84 M216
Boats with Spinach, Zucchini, '82 252
Boats, Zucchini, '85 M143
Bread, Banana-Zucchini, '85 326
Bread, Spiced Zucchini, '85 161; '86 162
Bread, Spicy Zucchini, '81 305; '82 36
Bread, Zucchini, '85 111; '86 93
Bread, Zucchini-Apple, '87 255
Bread, Zucchini-Carrot, '83 190
Broiled Zucchini, Quick-and-Easy, '86 169
Buttered Zucchini and Carrots, '83 252
Cake, Chocolate-Zucchini, '85 156
Cake, Zucchini, '79 24
Calabaza Guisada con Puerco (Pumpkin
  Cooked with Pork), '80 193
Calabaza Mexicana (Mexican
  Squash), '81 196
Carrots and Zucchini, '84 262
Casserole, Carrot and Zucchini, '83 256
Casserole, Cheese-Egg-Zucchini, '84 114
Casserole, Cheesy Zucchini, '82 168;
  '84 145
Casserole, Italian Zucchini, '85 59
Casserole, Zucchini, '79 157; '87 154
Casserole, Zucchini-Egg, '84 M113
Casserole, Zucchini-Jack, '85 296
Combo, Zucchini-Corn, '86 218
Corn and Zucchini, '83 190
Corn, Zucchini and, '86 177
Crêpes, Zucchini, '79 157
Delight, Zucchini-Basil, '85 267
Dilled Fresh Zucchini, '81 174
Dilled Zucchini and Corn, '83 173
Dressing, Zucchini, '86 282
Easy Zucchini, '87 167
Eggplant and Squash, '83 187
Eggplant and Zucchini,
  Italian-Style, '79 289; '80 26
Eggplant and Zucchini, Sautéed, '82 96
Fried Zucchini, Oven-, '86 211
Fried Zucchini Strips, '81 184
Fried Zucchini with Cocktail Sauce,
  French, '86 146
Fries, Zucchini French, '82 78
Frittata, Zucchini, '86 103
Fritters, Zucchini, '81 163
Fry, Zucchini, '81 102
Herbed Zucchini, '84 104
Hors d'Oeuvres, Zucchini, '80 151
Italiano, Zucchini, '81 183
Italian Squash, '79 158
Italian-Style Zucchini, '80 123
Italian Zucchini, '83 M147
Lasagna, Garden, '83 119
Lasagna, Zucchini, '85 194
Manicotti, Zucchini, '84 194
Marinated Zucchini, '80 33
Medley, Zucchini-and-Corn, '80 298;
  '81 25
Mexican Squash, '83 31
Mexican Style, Zucchini, '80 184
Muffins, Zucchini, '83 121; '86 146
Omelet, Zucchini, '81 99
Parmesan, Zucchini, '81 108; '82 103
Parmesan Zucchini, '81 234
Pecans, Zucchini with, '87 31
Pesto, Zucchini, '84 194
Pie, Cheesy Zucchini, '82 103
Pie, Italian-Style Zucchini, '83 43
Pie, Zucchini-Ham-Cheese, '80 272
Pollo con Calabacita (Mexican Chicken
  with Zucchini), '82 219
Provençal, Zucchini, '86 146
Quiche, Cheesy Zucchini, '83 312
Quiche, Swiss-Zucchini, '82 49
Quiche, Zucchini-Mushroom, '79 127
Quiche, Zucchini-Sausage, '83 122
Ratatouille, '84 105, 243; '85 92
Ratatouille, Eggplant-Zucchini, '81 205
Ratatouille Niçoise, '81 22
Ratatouille, Quick-and-Easy, '80 212
Ratatouille-Stuffed Eggplant, '83 187
Relish, Zucchini, '87 200
Salad, Carrot-and-Zucchini, '83 240
Salad, Creamy Avocado and
  Zucchini, '79 208
Salad, Marinated Zucchini, '82 164
Salad, Mushroom-Zucchini, '85 8
Salad, Turkey-Zucchini, '85 74
Salad, Zucchini, '82 104; '87 103
Salad, Zucchini Chef's, '83 143
Sauce, Spaghetti with Zucchini, '81 38
Sautéed Zucchini, '83 86
Sautéed Zucchini and Sausage, '83 289

Sauté, Zucchini, '81 183; '84 35
Scallop, Green-and-Gold, '81 159
Scramble, Zucchini-Basil, '87 34
Skillet, Pattypan-Zucchini, '82 103
Skillet, Squash, '82 195
Skillet, Zippy Zucchini, '82 158
Soufflé, Zucchini, '79 157
Soufflé, Zucchini-and-Corn, '83 265
Soup, Chilled Zucchini, '87 90
Soup, Cold Zucchini, '85 265
Soup, Cream of Zucchini, '83 99
Soup, Creamy Zucchini, '83 140
Soup, Italian Sausage-Zucchini, '84 4
Soup, Summer Squash, '84 193
Soup, Zucchini, '82 104; '84 181;
  '86 181
South-of-the-Border Zucchini, '85 135
Spaghetti, Italian Zucchini, '85 2
Spaghetti, Zucchini, '83 160
Squares, Zucchini, '82 103
Stir-Fried Squash Medley, '80 123
Stir-Fry, Chicken-Zucchini, '84 50
Stir-Fry, Ham and Zucchini, '79 47
Stir-Fry, Squash, '80 184
Stir-Fry, Tomato-Zucchini, '80 158
Stir-Fry, Two-Squash, '86 174
Stir-Fry, Zucchini-and-Tomato, '85 108
Stuffed Zucchini, '86 54, 187
Stuffed Zucchini, Beef-, '86 M139
Stuffed Zucchini, Ham and
  Cheese, '79 157
Stuffed Zucchini, Italian, '84 119
Stuffed Zucchini Main Dish, '79 215
Stuffed Zucchini, Savory, '80 161
Stuffed Zucchini, Supreme, '83 136
Walnuts, Zucchini with, '84 213

Favorite Recipes

Record your favorite recipes below for quick and handy reference.

Appetizers	Source/Page	Remarks

Beverages	Source/Page	Remarks

Breads	Source/Page	Remarks

Desserts	Source/Page	Remarks

Eggs and Cheese   **Source/Page**   **Remarks**

Main Dishes   **Source/Page**   **Remarks**

Salads	Source/Page	Remarks

Soups and Stews	Source/Page	Remarks

Vegetables and Side Dishes	Source/Page	Remarks